Perspectives on Digital Transformation in Contemporary Business

Mohammed Albakri
University of Salford, UK

IGI Global
Scientific Publishing
Publishing Tomorrow's Research Today

Published in the United States of America by
    IGI Global Scientific Publishing
    701 E. Chocolate Avenue
    Hershey PA, USA 17033
    Tel: 717-533-8845
    Fax: 717-533-8661
    E-mail: cust@igi-global.com
    Web site: https://www.igi-global.com

Library of Congress Cataloging-in-Publication Data

    CIP PENDING

ISBN13: 9798369359662
Isbn13Softcover: 9798369359679
EISBN13: 9798369359686

Vice President of Editorial: Melissa Wagner
Managing Editor of Acquisitions: Mikaela Felty
Managing Editor of Book Development: Jocelynn Hessler
Production Manager: Mike Brehm
Cover Design: Phillip Shickler

British Cataloguing in Publication Data
A Cataloguing in Publication record for this book is available from the British Library.

Table of Contents

Detailed Table of Contents

Chapter 1
Mohammed Albakri, University of Salford, UK

This chapter explores digital transformation (DT) in UK businesses, highlighting its significance for economic growth. Defined as integrating digital technologies into all business areas, DT drives profound operational, cultural, and customer engagement changes. Despite the UK's leadership in digital innovation, a digital divide persists between large enterprises and SMEs, and between urban and rural regions, due to limited resources, digital skills, and infrastructure. Key sectors driving DT include healthcare and financial services, while barriers encompass financial constraints, outdated IT systems, cybersecurity concerns, skill shortages, and organizational resistance. Bridging this divide requires targeted support, policies, and technologies like AI, cloud computing, IoT, and 5G. The chapter also discusses emerging technologies and offers recommendations for inclusive growth, emphasizing the need for public-private partnerships to sustain the UK's digital leadership.

Chapter 2

Mohammed Albakri, University of Salford, UK
Muktar Bello, University of Salford, UK
Safiya Al Rashdi, Innovation Oases Company, Oman

The Gulf Cooperation Council (GCC) has undergone significant digital transformation driven by strategies like Saudi Arabia's Vision 2030 and the UAE's National Innovation Strategy. This shift has advanced sectors such as energy, finance, healthcare, and transportation, making the GCC a hub for technological innovation and smart city development. However, the increasing reliance on digital technologies has heightened cybersecurity risks, including data breaches, ransomware, phishing, and advanced persistent threats (APTs). These threats pose significant risks to critical infrastructure and societal stability, exacerbated by regional conflicts and state-sponsored cyber activities. This chapter explores cybersecurity challenges and strategies within the GCC, emphasizing the need for robust measures. Key strategies include adopting comprehensive frameworks, enhancing governance, fostering regional collaboration, and investing in education and training. Addressing these challenges can enhance the GCC's cybersecurity resilience and ensure long-term digital protection.

Chapter 3

Mark Schofield, Research and Training Centre, Manchester, UK

In the modern age, the demand for seamless digital services extends into government sectors, including healthcare. NHS England exemplifies significant digital transformation in this domain. Understanding governmental digital evolution in healthcare is crucial for stakeholders on similar paths. This chapter dissects common trends in government digital transformation and lessons from NHS England's efforts. By exploring digital dynamics within government, with a focus on healthcare, it elucidates methodologies, challenges, and potential pathways for sustainable digital evolution. It offers insights for stakeholders, emphasizing user-centric design, iterative approaches, and transparent governance. Additionally, it highlights the complexities and unique challenges in healthcare digitization, providing valuable lessons for stakeholders.

Digital transformation in Montenegro is an evolving process that aims to use digital technologies to boost economic growth, improve governance, enhance public services and foster innovation. The main objective of this chapter is to analyze the impact of public administration reform as a determinant of Montenegro's economic development on the achieved economic and social results, which are determined by the achieved level of various key economic parameters, such as: GDP, FDI, import and export of goods and services. In this context, special emphasis was placed on the analysis of two indicators: EGDI (E-Government Development Index) and EPI (E-Participation Index). The methodological concept and the analysis of the first part are based on official data from the World Bank and Monstat, while the second part is based on the UN eGovernment Survey, an official report of the United Nations (UN E-Government Knowledgebase). The period covered by the survey is from 2012 to 2023. The results show that public administration reform is an important factor for Montenegro's economic development.

This chapter addresses challenges that leaders face when leveraging the advantages of data analytics (DA) and business intelligence (BI) especially in the context of digital transformation. It also discusses the increasing significance of data analytics and business intelligence in driving digital transformation and their influence on business leadership. Further, it closely examines the integration challenges that leaders face when leveraging digital technology to promote organizational change and data governance. In pursuit of the research objective, this chapter is organized as follows: Section 1 presents the introduction. Section 2 offers an extensive review of the literature encompassing digital transformation, DA BI, and organizational leadership. The subsequent section elucidates the different opportunities and challenges that leaders encounter with the integration of digital technology. Furthermore, digital technology, tools, and platforms are discussed, with implications and, at last, conclusion.

Chapter 6
Wong Sing Yun, Universiti Malaysia Sabah, Malaysia
Saizal Pinjaman, Universiti Malaysia Sabah, Malaysia
Debbra Toria Nipo, Universiti Malaysia Sabah, Malaysia
Shaierah Gulabdin, Universiti Malaysia Sabah, Malaysia

The emergence of digital technology has help business to grow, thrive, innovate and resolve obstacles in sustaining their operation development. The Malaysian Government has been proactive in implementing various initiatives to embrace digital transformation across different sectors. To extend the knowledge within the literature, this book chapter intends to identify the factors that contribute to the digital transformation in Malaysia. While digital transformation may seems to be the answer to a more sustainable development growth, however there are still challenge remains. Besides that, this book literature will also examine the government policies that has been implemented by the Malaysia Government in support of the digital transformation. The knowledge finding from this book chapter will help to ensure that the benefits of the digital transformation can be delivered to all sectors and help policy makers to devise new policies that can assists all businesses to transform their operation digitally.

Chapter 7
Afeefa Fatima, Babu Banarasi Das University, Lucknow, India
Rinki Verma, Babu Banarasi Das University, Lucknow, India
Shreyanshu Singh, Babu Banarasi Das University, Lucknow, India
Manoj Kumar, Shri Ramswaroop Memorial University, Barabanki, India
Karnika Srivastava, Techno Group of Institutions, Lucknow, India

The rapid emergence of the fourth industrial revolution (4-IR) and technological progress is driving significant digitalization and the adoption of automated, efficient technologies capable of complex tasks with minimal physical interaction. These advancements are accelerating economic growth and transforming sectors, including higher education (Ho et al., 2020). The COVID-19 pandemic revolutionized teaching pedagogy in higher education, prompting universities to shift from traditional methods to modern tech-based approaches. This study investigates the continuance intention of students and academic institutions towards integrating online learning technologies as a permanent shift. It examines factors influencing students' willingness to continue using these technologies post-COVID-19. A quantitative approach explores the relationship between online learning platforms and students' continuance intention in Indian colleges and universities, focusing on remote/rural students selected through convenience sampling. Advanced statistical tools SPSS and AMOS analyze the data.

Chapter 8

Digital transformation in governance enhances public participation, collaboration, empowerment, and accountability, improving quality of life. This study explores strategies like innovation ecosystems, crowdsourcing, and open government data (OGD), including the role of Chief Innovation Officers (CInOs). Examples include the Ministry of Manpower's Open Data Innovation System for public engagement, Manor Labs' crowdsourcing in Texas, and Kenya's OGD portal for transparency. CInOs, pivotal since 2008, align government with societal needs, fostering digital innovation and engagement. This paper advocates for the integration of CInOs at the highest levels of governance to bridge the gap between government policies and societal aspirations, fostering a culture of continuous digital innovation and engagement. These digital transformation-driven strategies enable governments to establish an efficient 'innovation ecosystem,' improving public services and promoting a collaborative, digitally innovative society.

Chapter 9

In an era featured by technological disruption and the pervasive integration of artificial intelligence (AI) into business processes, organizations come across strategic challenges in assessing their readiness for AI-based digital transformation. This study emphasizes on the necessary elements needed to analyse an organization's current state in preparation for AI-driven digital transformation. Drawing from a comprehensive literature review and practical insights derived from industrial system engineering experience, this study focuses on the relevance of process performance measurement and Key Performance Indicators (KPIs) in increasing organizational performance within the context of AI adoption. By establishing and monitoring relevant KPIs for process performance, organizations can quantifiably assess operational efficiency, identify areas for improvement, and track the effect of AI implementation on business processes.

Chapter 10

Zeeshan Syed, University of Salford, UK
Oluwaseun Okegbola, University of Salford, UK
Cynthia Abiemwense Akiotu, University of Salford, UK

This chapter explores the transformative potential of Artificial Intelligence (AI) and Machine Learning (ML) in enhancing regulatory compliance within financial institutions. Following the 2008 financial crisis, increased regulation has driven the need for advanced solutions. AI and ML, integrated into Regulatory Technology (RegTech), offer significant benefits, including improved efficiency, reduced compliance costs, and enhanced risk management. This paper examines the application of RegTech tools in processing large datasets, identifying patterns, and predicting regulatory challenges. It also addresses the challenges associated with AI and ML, such as overfitting, decision-making opacity, and legal implications. Ultimately, AI and ML are critical to the future of regulatory compliance, offering financial institutions a path to more efficient adherence to complex regulations.

Chapter 11

Suaad Jassem, College of Banking and Financial Studies, Oman
Karima Toumi Sayari, Al Zahra College for Women, Oman
Fadi Abdelfattah, Modern College of Business and Science, Oman

This chapter explores blockchain technology, a revolutionary distributed ledger system transforming the financial sector by enabling secure, transparent, decentralized transaction recording and management. Focusing on the accounting and finance industries, the chapter examines how blockchain technology is being adopted to enhance operations and service automation. It highlights blockchain's significant benefits, such as increased transparency, faster transaction processing, cost reduction, improved accuracy, and enhanced security. The chapter comprehensively discusses blockchain's diverse applications in accounting, banking, and finance, including its role in cross-border payments, stock exchanges, identity verification, and the standardization of bookkeeping, accounting, and auditing practices. Additionally, it critically analyzes the potential risks associated with blockchain adoption, like regulatory challenges and security vulnerabilities, underlining the importance for businesses to weigh both risks and benefits in the rapidly digitalizing financial landscape.

    Vishal Jain, Sharda University, India
    Archan Mitra, Presidency University, India

This study explores the key drivers and obstacles of innovation in achieving
sustainable development goals (SDGs) within emerging economies. Utilizing a
multi-case study approach, this research identifies and analyzes the critical factors
that either promote or hinder innovation aimed at sustainability. Key drivers, such
as governmental policies, financial incentives, and technological advancements,
are assessed alongside obstacles like regulatory barriers, resource constraints, and
socio-economic disparities. The findings highlight the complex interplay between
these factors and provide actionable insights for policymakers and stakeholders
to enhance innovation efforts. By offering a comparative analysis across different
emerging markets, this study contributes to a deeper understanding of how innovation
can be leveraged to achieve SDGs. This work aims to inform future strategies and
policies to foster innovation-driven sustainability in emerging economies.

    Damla Cevik Aka, Kirklareli University, Turkey

This study aims to examine the effects of the use of blockchain technology in
production on the motivation to switch to a circular economy (CE). Additionally,
the study aims to assess the significance of blockchain technology's impacts on
businesses, with a focus on CE initiatives. In this context, thirty-five managers
from seven companies in Turkey's automotive subindustry were interviewed, and
the criteria were evaluated by seven expert groups. Considering the presence of
different groups and high uncertainty, the Q-Rung Orthopair fuzzy set was used. The
study findings reveal that the primary factors driving circular economy motivation
are "waste management," "information sharing and enhanced cooperation among
supply chain stakeholders," and "operating costs," in that order. The article explores
blockchain as a promising technology to facilitate the circular economy process.
This study is expected to enrich the circular economy literature and be a road map
for automotive supplier industry manufacturers in developing countries.

    Mohammad Badruddoza Talukder, International University of Business
      Agriculture and Technology, Bangladesh
    Mushfika Hoque, Daffodil Institute of IT, Bangladesh

This chapter investigates the transformative impact of technological improvements on traditional travel agencies, a topic that is becoming increasingly important in the fast-changing travel industry. Through the previous related literature, this study aims to shed light on how travel firms are adjusting to the changing demands and tastes of travellers in the digital era by studying the integration of artificial intelligence, virtual and augmented reality, and data-driven personalisation. So, the paper aims to identify travel agencies' challenges and opportunities by analysing digital transformation's impact on old business models. In addition, it investigates the shifting behaviour of travellers, who are increasingly looking for ease and personalised experiences through internet platforms. Finally, this chapter emphasises the significance of travel agencies embracing digital innovation, streamlining operations, and developing immersive travel experiences to maintain their competitive edge in a constantly moving market.

    Kamalendu Pal, University of London, UK

Global trade and supply chains have experienced significant disruptions in recent years, revealing their vulnerabilities. Events like the coronavirus pandemic (COVID-19), the Ever-Given blockage in the Suez Canal, and the Russian invasion of Ukraine have highlighted these challenges. Concurrently, digitalization is transforming supply chain management, notably through the increasing use of the Internet of Things (IoT) to develop decision-support systems that analyze operational data and provide crucial insights for stakeholders. This chapter presents a knowledge-based framework for designing and implementing these operational support services using advanced web services. It emphasizes the importance of semantic interoperability through ontologies and similarity assessment techniques. The practical application of these concepts is not just theoretical but achievable, aiming to engage business stakeholders and build their confidence in digitally transforming supply chain operations. Finally, the chapter offers a compelling business case that illustrates the benefits of employing ontologies and algorithmic concept similarity assessment in operational service design.

This chapter examines how digital technologies; Artificial Intelligence, blockchain technology, digital marketing, and digital entrepreneurship have revolutionized innovation and growth of contemporary businesses. This study focuses on the practical aspect of business operations, customer relations, and security issues that benefit from applications of AI solutions like dynamic pricing, optimal route selection, and fraud detection, among others. The capabilities of blockchain technology is examined to bring transparency and security in the business transaction by having the ability to develop, implement and regulate smart contracts. The efficiency of various online marketing techniques such as advertising and content marketing is evaluated to grab the attention of the targeted customer base and increase their loyalty. Furthermore, it highlights the areas of digital entrepreneurship, examples of how technology assists individuals in creating new business models and practical applications of these technologies in industries as illustrated by Uber and Airbnb are discussed in detail.

Foreword

The digital transformation of industries is reshaping the business landscape, offering new opportunities for growth, innovation, and resilience. As we enter an era where advanced technologies such as artificial intelligence, blockchain, and data analytics are central to every aspect of commerce, it is crucial to understand and harness their potential to drive competitive advantage and organisational success.

Perspectives on Digital Transformation in Contemporary Business provides an insightful and timely exploration of the myriad ways in which digital technologies are transforming industries, reimagining business strategies, and fostering sustainable growth. This book is an essential read for anyone interested in understanding the transformative power of digital technologies, offering a comprehensive overview of current trends, strategic challenges, and opportunities in the business world.

The editor, Dr. Mohammed Albakri, have brought together an impressive collection of scholars and industry experts whose contributions provide a rich, multifaceted perspective on digital transformation. Their collective expertise spans various sectors, including healthcare, education, and finance, making this book a valuable resource for a broad audience. The diversity of insights presented here allows readers to appreciate the breadth of digital transformation, from sector-specific challenges to overarching themes in organisational resilience and economic development.

As someone who has closely followed the evolution of digital technologies over recent decades, I am particularly impressed by the depth and breadth of the topics covered in this book. From discussions on bridging the digital transformation divide in UK business communities to the role of blockchain in enhancing financial transparency, each chapter offers both practical insights and theoretical frameworks that are innovative and grounded in real-world applications.

One of the standout features of this book is its emphasis on the strategic adoption of digital technologies to create long-term value. The exploration of digital adoption strategies, cybersecurity challenges, and the regulatory considerations of technology integration are crucial for understanding how organisations can successfully navigate the complexities of digital transformation. Equally significant is the focus on inclusion, ensuring that the benefits of digital transformation are accessible across all sectors of society.

The emphasis on creating competitive advantage through digital technologies is another critical theme that resonates throughout the book. By highlighting how innovations can enhance organisational performance, drive informed decision-making, and foster a culture of resilience, the authors provide a roadmap for businesses seeking to thrive in the digital age.

In addition to its academic rigour, Perspectives on Digital Transformation in Contemporary Business is highly practical. The case studies and examples presented offer valuable lessons for industry practitioners and policymakers, illustrating how digital transformation can be effectively implemented across various sectors. These real-world applications demonstrate that digital transformation is not a distant goal but a present reality, offering tangible benefits to those willing to adapt.

As you delve into the pages of this book, I encourage you to think about the broader implications of digital transformation. Consider how these technologies can be leveraged not only to improve efficiency and productivity but also to create meaningful and impactful change within organisations and society as a whole.

In conclusion, Perspectives on Digital Transformation in Contemporary Business is a seminal work that sheds light on the transformative potential of digital technologies in reshaping industries. It is a must-read for academics, business leaders, industry professionals, and anyone interested in the future of business in the digital age.

I extend my heartfelt congratulations to the editors and contributors for their outstanding work. May this book inspire and guide readers on their journey towards achieving excellence through digital transformation.

Aniekan Essien

University of Bristol, UK

Preface

In an era characterised by unprecedented digital transformation, businesses and economies across the globe are undergoing rapid and significant changes. *Perspectives on Digital Transformation in Contemporary Business* explores how the integration of advanced digital technologies is reshaping industries, redefining business strategies, and enabling new avenues for growth and competitiveness.

This book emerges from the recognition that digital transformation is not merely a technological shift but a fundamental reimagining of how businesses operate. Over the past decade, advancements in artificial intelligence, blockchain, data analytics, and the Internet of Things have disrupted traditional business models, offering both challenges and opportunities. These innovations have redefined customer experiences, streamlined processes, and opened doors for creative approaches to value creation.

Our exploration begins by providing insights into the role of digital transformation in various sectors, including healthcare, education, and national security. The chapters in this book present a detailed analysis of the benefits, challenges, and strategic implications of digital adoption, supported by real-world examples and case studies. Esteemed experts from diverse fields contribute their insights into the adoption of digital technologies, examining how these changes impact economic development and organisational resilience.

For instance, the discussion on bridging the digital transformation divide in UK business communities highlights the disparities that exist in digital access and the measures necessary to promote an inclusive approach to innovation. Similarly, the chapters on blockchain's transformative role in the financial sector and on supply chain management illustrate how these technologies are disrupting conventional practices to foster transparency, efficiency, and resilience.

One of the core themes of this book is the critical role of strategic digital adoption in achieving sustainable business growth. Whether it is enhancing organisational performance through process optimisation or leveraging data analytics for informed decision-making, the focus remains on how digital transformation can be effectively harnessed to create long-term value and drive competitive advantage.

Additionally, this book addresses the inherent challenges associated with digital transformation, including cybersecurity fears, regulatory considerations, and the complexities of technology integration. By exploring these issues, we emphasise the importance of a strategic and resilient approach to managing the risks that accompany digital innovation.

Perspectives on Digital Transformation in Contemporary Business is intended for academics, industry practitioners, and business leaders who are navigating the complex landscape of digital change. It aims to provide a comprehensive understanding of the opportunities and challenges of digital transformation while offering actionable insights to guide successful implementation.

We are grateful to the contributing authors for their expertise and commitment, which have been instrumental in making this book possible. Their research and experiences underscore the transformative potential of digital technologies across industries, and we hope that this work serves as an inspiration and a guide for those seeking to capitalise on the opportunities brought by digital transformation.

As you explore the different facets of digital transformation presented in this book, we hope you gain valuable insights into how businesses can adapt, thrive, and lead in the digital age. The journey towards a digitally integrated future is both challenging and exciting, and this book aims to illuminate the path forward.

ORGANIZATION OF THE BOOK

Chapter 1: Bridging the Digital Transformation Divide Paradox in UK Business Communities

In this chapter, the author delves into the digital transformation (DT) landscape within UK businesses, shedding light on its pivotal role in driving economic growth. DT, defined as the integration of digital technologies into all facets of business, has brought significant changes in operations, culture, and customer engagement. Despite the UK's strong position in digital innovation, a digital divide remains between large enterprises and SMEs, as well as between urban and rural areas, primarily due to disparities in resources, digital skills, and infrastructure. Sectors like healthcare and financial services are at the forefront of DT, but barriers such as financial constraints, outdated IT systems, cybersecurity concerns, and organizational resistance hinder progress. The chapter highlights the importance of targeted support, policies, and the adoption of advanced technologies like AI, cloud computing, IoT, and 5G to bridge this divide. It concludes by emphasizing the necessity of public-private partnerships to ensure inclusive growth and maintain the UK's digital leadership.

Chapter 2: Digital Transformation and Cybersecurity Fears on National Security in GCC

This chapter explores the rapid digital transformation in the Gulf Cooperation Council (GCC) states, driven by strategic visions like Saudi Arabia's Vision 2030 and the UAE's National Innovation Strategy. While sectors such as energy, healthcare, and finance are being transformed into innovation hubs, the increasing digitalization exposes these nations to heightened cybersecurity risks, including data breaches, ransomware, and state-sponsored cyberattacks. The authors discuss how such threats jeopardize critical infrastructure and regional stability. The chapter provides an in-depth analysis of cybersecurity challenges and highlights strategies for mitigating these risks, such as adopting comprehensive cybersecurity frameworks, enhancing governance, fostering regional cooperation, and investing in education and training. By addressing these cybersecurity concerns, the GCC can ensure resilience and long-term protection against the growing threats accompanying digital transformation.

Chapter 3: Digital Transformation in UK Contemporary Healthcare: Lessons from NHS England

Chapter 3 examines the digital transformation within the UK healthcare sector, focusing on NHS England as a key case study. This chapter analyzes the broader governmental trend of digital transformation, emphasizing healthcare's unique challenges and opportunities in adapting to the digital age. The author discusses how NHS England has embraced digital strategies to improve patient care, operational efficiency, and stakeholder engagement. The chapter offers insights into the lessons learned from NHS England's digital journey, highlighting the importance of user-centric design, iterative processes, and transparent governance in the successful implementation of digital technologies. By exploring these dynamics, the chapter provides valuable guidance for other stakeholders in healthcare systems embarking on similar digital transformation paths.

Chapter 4: Digital Transformation as a Factor in The Economic Development of Montenegro

This chapter provides a detailed analysis of digital transformation's role in Montenegro's economic development. This chapter explores how the integration of digital technologies has driven economic growth, improved governance, and enhanced public services. By examining key indicators such as GDP, foreign direct investment (FDI), and trade metrics, the authors assess the impact of digitalization on the country's economic performance. Particular attention is given to Montenegro's progress in e-government, measured by the E-Government Development Index (EGDI) and the E-Participation Index (EPI). The chapter underscores the importance of public administration reform as a driving force behind Montenegro's digital transformation and its contribution to economic and social advancement.

Chapter 5: Leveraging Data Analytics and Business Intelligence for Seamless Digital Transformation

In this chapter, the authors explore the growing importance of data analytics (DA) and business intelligence (BI) in driving digital transformation across industries. The chapter discusses how these tools empower business leaders to make informed decisions, improve operational efficiency, and foster innovation. It highlights the challenges organizations face in integrating DA and BI into their digital strategies, including issues related to data governance and technology adoption. The authors also delve into the role of leadership in navigating these challenges and leveraging digital technologies for organizational change. The chapter concludes with insights into the opportunities and implications of DA and BI for seamless digital transformation.

Chapter 6: Digital Transformation in Reshaping Industries

Chapter 6 explores the impact of digital transformation on various industries in Malaysia. This chapter investigates the factors driving digital adoption in sectors such as manufacturing, services, and government, with a focus on policies implemented by the Malaysian government to support this shift. The authors emphasize the benefits of digital transformation, including innovation, operational efficiency, and sustainable growth, while also addressing the challenges faced by businesses in the process. The chapter provides policy recommendations to ensure that digital transformation delivers broad benefits across sectors and helps businesses overcome the obstacles that remain in their digital journeys.

Chapter 7: Digital Transformation and Continuance Intention of Online Learning Platforms among Students in Higher Education Institutions in Remote India

Chapter 7 investigates the factors influencing the continued use of online learning platforms among students in rural higher education institutions in India. This chapter explores how the COVID-19 pandemic accelerated the shift to digital education, pushing universities to adopt new technologies. Using a quantitative approach, the authors examine the relationship between students' intentions to continue using these platforms post-pandemic and the various factors that contribute to this decision, such as convenience, accessibility, and perceived value. The study offers insights into how digital transformation in education can be sustained, particularly for students in remote areas, and provides recommendations for improving the online learning experience in the long term.

Chapter 8: Digital Transformation for Better Innovation Governance

This chapter delves into how digital transformation enhances public governance by fostering participation, collaboration, empowerment, and accountability. It presents strategies like innovation ecosystems, crowdsourcing, and open government data (OGD) initiatives, with a special emphasis on the role of Chief Innovation Officers (CInOs). The case studies of the Ministry of Manpower, Manor Labs, and Kenya's OGD portal illustrate how digital tools bridge the gap between government policies and societal aspirations, ultimately promoting a culture of digital innovation.

Chapter 9: Enhancing Organizational Performance through Process Performance Measurement and KPIs in AI-Based Digital Transformation

This chapter emphasizes the critical role of process performance measurement and Key Performance Indicators (KPIs) in improving organizational performance during AI-based digital transformation. By assessing operational efficiency and tracking AI's impact, businesses can optimize their performance and identify areas for improvement. The study is grounded in both literature and industrial practices.

Chapter 10: Utilising Artificial Intelligence and Machine Learning for Regulatory Compliance in Financial Institutions

This chapter explores the use of AI and ML in enhancing regulatory compliance in financial institutions. RegTech tools powered by AI/ML can process vast datasets, predict regulatory issues, and reduce compliance costs. However, challenges such as overfitting and decision-making opacity are also addressed, emphasizing the role of AI in shaping the future of compliance.

Chapter 11: Blockchain's Transformative Role in the Financial Sector

This chapter explores blockchain's transformative impact on the financial sector, focusing on its application in accounting, finance, and banking. Benefits like transparency, faster processing, and cost reduction are analyzed, along with blockchain's role in identity verification and cross-border payments. The risks of blockchain adoption, including regulatory and security challenges, are also discussed.

Chapter 12: Navigating the Digital Frontier: Strategic Integration of Blockchain Technology in Enhancing Digital Entrepreneurship and Ethical Business Practices

This study explores how blockchain technology contributes to digital entrepreneurship and ethical business practices in emerging economies. It identifies key drivers such as governmental policies and technological advancements, along with obstacles like resource constraints. Through multi-case studies, it provides insights into fostering innovation for achieving sustainable development goals (SDGs).

Chapter 13: Impacts of Blockchain on Circular Economy Motivation via the Q-Rung Orthopair Fuzzy Set

This chapter examines how blockchain technology impacts businesses in switching to a circular economy, focusing on the automotive industry in Turkey. Using the Q-Rung Orthopair fuzzy set for evaluation, the study reveals that blockchain enhances waste management, information sharing, and supply chain cooperation. It offers a road map for industries in developing countries to embrace blockchain for circular economy initiatives.

Chapter 14: Navigating the Digital Horizon: Transforming Travel Agencies in the Digital Era

This chapter addresses the impact of digital transformation on travel agencies. It discusses the integration of AI, virtual/augmented reality, and personalized data-driven experiences. The chapter highlights the challenges and opportunities for traditional travel agencies in adapting to evolving customer preferences and digital innovation, offering strategies to maintain competitiveness in the market.

Chapter 15: Leveraging Internet of Things Applications With Service-Oriented Computing for Supply Chain Operations

This chapter focuses on using IoT and service-oriented computing to optimize supply chain operations. It discusses semantic interoperability, ontologies, and similarity assessment methods for designing knowledge-based decision support systems. A business case is provided to demonstrate the practical applications and benefits of IoT in improving operational services and supply chain efficiency.

Chapter 16: Empowering Digital Business Innovation: AI, Blockchain, Marketing, and Entrepreneurship for Dynamic Growth

This chapter examines the role of AI, blockchain, digital marketing, and digital entrepreneurship in driving business innovation and growth. It evaluates AI solutions for business operations, blockchain's role in securing transactions, and various online marketing techniques to engage customers. Case studies such as Uber and Airbnb are analyzed to demonstrate how digital technologies support the creation of new business models and enhance customer experiences.

Mohammed Albakri
Salford Business School, University of Salford, UK

Chapter 1
Bridging the Digital Transformation Divide Paradox in UK Business Communities

Mohammed Albakri
https://orcid.org/0000-0001-5854-8245
University of Salford, UK

ABSTRACT

This chapter explores digital transformation (DT) in UK businesses, highlighting its significance for economic growth. Defined as integrating digital technologies into all business areas, DT drives profound operational, cultural, and customer engagement changes. Despite the UK's leadership in digital innovation, a digital divide persists between large enterprises and SMEs, and between urban and rural regions, due to limited resources, digital skills, and infrastructure. Key sectors driving DT include healthcare and financial services, while barriers encompass financial constraints, outdated IT systems, cybersecurity concerns, skill shortages, and organizational resistance. Bridging this divide requires targeted support, policies, and technologies like AI, cloud computing, IoT, and 5G. The chapter also discusses emerging technologies and offers recommendations for inclusive growth, emphasizing the need for public-private partnerships to sustain the UK's digital leadership.

DOI: 10.4018/979-8-3693-5966-2.ch001

1. INTRODUCTION

Digital transformation (DT) has become a pivotal force reshaping the business landscape across the globe, and the United Kingdom is no exception. Defined as the integration of digital technologies into all areas of business, resulting in fundamental changes to how businesses operate and deliver value to customers, digital transformation encompasses organisational, cultural, and operational changes (Hinings et al., 2018).

The UK has been at the forefront of digital innovation with numerous government initiatives and policies aimed at fostering a digital economy. The UK Digital Strategy underscores the importance of digital technology in driving productivity and economic growth (UK Government, 2024). Recent data from the UK Business Data Survey 2024 reveals that 99% of businesses with at least 10 employees handled digitised data of any type in 2024, highlighting the pervasiveness of digital technologies in the business landscape (UK Business Data Survey, 2024). However, despite these efforts, there exists a significant digital divide within UK business communities. This divide is characterised by disparities in digital adoption between large enterprises and small to medium-sized enterprises (SMEs) as well as regional imbalances (Good Things Foundation, 2024). The UK Business Data Survey 2024 found that while 99% of large businesses handled digitised data, only 77% of all UK businesses did so, indicating a gap in digital adoption among smaller businesses (UK Business Data Survey, 2024).

This disparity suggests that despite the overall high adoption rates, smaller businesses are significantly lagging. The reasons for this gap can be attributed to limited financial resources, lack of access to digital skills, and inadequate infrastructure, especially in rural areas. The overarching narrative of digital transformation success in the UK thus masks underlying inequalities that need to be addressed for a truly inclusive digital economy.

Digital transformation is crucial for businesses to remain competitive in an increasingly digital world. It enables enhanced customer experiences, streamlined operations, and the development of new business models. The COVID-19 pandemic has accelerated the need for digital transformation as businesses have had to adapt rapidly to remote working, online services, and digital customer interactions (Kraus et al., 2020; Kuckertz et al., 2020; Nagel, 2020). Recent data underscores the economic potential of digital transformation. According to a study commissioned by Amazon Web Services, digital technology could grow the UK economy by over £413 billion by 2030, equivalent to approximately 19% of the entire UK economy (Amazon Web Services, 2024). This highlights the significant role that digital transformation can play in driving economic growth and improving living standards (Cosa, 2024).

While the potential economic benefits of digital transformation are substantial, the uneven pace of adoption risks exacerbating existing inequalities. For SMEs, the challenges include not just financial barriers but also a lack of strategic direction and digital literacy. Without targeted support, these businesses may be unable to realise the full benefits of digital transformation, thereby widening the economic divide.

Despite the recognised importance of digital transformation, many UK businesses face challenges in implementation. The UK Innovation Survey 2023 reported that only 36% of UK businesses were innovation active in 2020-2022, a decrease from 45% in 2018-2020. This suggests that while the potential for digital transformation is significant, many businesses are struggling to innovate and adapt to the digital landscape (Xledger, 2022). Furthermore, a report by Deloitte highlights that 74% of business leaders consider digital transformation to be the single most important investment for driving enterprise value. However, the same report notes that organisations often struggle to make the necessary investments in infrastructure, data applications, cyber, and workforce capabilities to adapt to the future (TechUK, 2022).

The decline in innovation activity signals underlying issues such as risk aversion, lack of access to capital, and insufficient government support for innovation among smaller enterprises. Furthermore, while large organisations may prioritise digital transformation, they often encounter significant hurdles in execution, including integrating new technologies with legacy systems and managing change within the workforce.

The UK digital transformation market is experiencing rapid growth. According to Grand View Research, the market size was valued at USD 35.11 billion in 2022 and is expected to grow at a compound annual growth rate (CAGR) of 27.7% from 2023 to 2030 (Grand View Research, 2023). This growth is driven by increasing adoption of advanced technologies such as cloud computing, big data, IoT, and analytics. The COVID-19 pandemic has accelerated digital transformation efforts, with UK government departments implementing policies in weeks rather than months or years. Cloud technology adoption has surged as businesses adapt to remote work, while initiatives like the Government Digital Service (GDS) have created centralised information hubs to assist vulnerable individuals (Grand View Research, 2023). The market's expansion is further supported by investments in cloud infrastructure from major providers like Microsoft Azure, Google Cloud, and Amazon Web Services (AWS). Additionally, the UK government's Digital Development Strategy 2024-2030 underscores the importance of digital technology in driving productivity and economic growth (UK Government, 2024).

The rapid market growth and technology adoption highlight the dynamic nature of digital transformation in the UK. However, this also brings to light the risk of digital exclusion for businesses that cannot keep pace with these advancements. Without comprehensive policies that address the specific needs of lagging sectors and regions, the benefits of digital transformation will remain unevenly distributed, potentially stalling overall economic progress.

Figure 1. Conceptual Model of Digital Transformation Divide in UK Business Communities

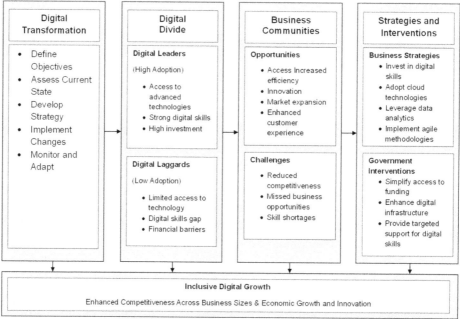

2. THE DIGITAL TRANSFORMATION LANDSCAPE IN THE UK

Digital transformation is a comprehensive process that integrates digital technology into all aspects of a business, fundamentally altering how organisations operate and deliver value to customers. This transformation involves a significant shift in organisational culture, requiring businesses to continually challenge the status quo, experiment, and embrace failure as a learning opportunity (Hinings et al., 2018; Kane et al., 2015; McCarthy et al., 2023). It is not merely about adopting new technologies but also about rethinking business models, processes, and strategies to leverage digital advancements effectively.

2.1 Current State of Digital Transformation

The United Kingdom has emerged as a frontrunner in digital transformation with a rapidly evolving landscape that spans various sectors of the economy. Recent data from the UK Business Data Survey 2024 reveals that 99% of businesses with at least 10 employees handled digitised data of any type in 2024, underscoring the pervasiveness of digital technologies in the business ecosystem (UK Business Data Survey, 2024). This widespread adoption reflects a significant shift towards digital-first strategies across industries. However, the digital transformation journey is not uniform across all business segments. While large enterprises have shown robust adoption rates, there exists a notable disparity when it comes to small and medium-sized enterprises (SMEs). The same survey found that only 86% of micro businesses and 73% of sole traders engaged with digitised data, highlighting a digital divide that persists within the UK business community (UK Business Data Survey, 2024; Good Things Foundation, 2024).

The data highlights a critical issue: the pervasiveness of digital technologies among larger businesses is not mirrored in smaller enterprises. This digital divide is a significant barrier to achieving a truly inclusive digital economy. Smaller businesses face unique challenges, including limited financial resources, inadequate digital skills, and lack of access to advanced digital infrastructure. These barriers must be addressed through targeted policies and support mechanisms to ensure that all businesses can benefit from digital transformation.

Table 1. Comparison of Digital Adoption Between SMEs and Large Enterprises

Metric	SMEs (0-249 employees)	Large Enterprises (250+ employees)
Percentage using digitised data	86% (Micro) 73% (Sole traders)	99%
Financial resources for IT	Limited	Extensive
Dedicated IT personnel	Often lacking	Well-staffed IT departments
Access to high-speed internet	Lower in rural areas	Higher in urban areas
Adoption of advanced technologies	Slower adoption of AI, IoT, and blockchain	Faster adoption

2.2 Key Sectors Leading Digital Transformation

Several sectors have emerged as pioneers in digital transformation:

Healthcare: The NHS has embarked on an ambitious digital transformation journey with the UK government pledging £3.4 billion to modernise IT systems across the healthcare sector. This includes initiatives such as implementing electronic patient records across all NHS Trusts by March 2026 and integrating AI into medical imaging technologies (NHS England, 2024; GOV.UK, 2024). These efforts aim to enhance patient care, improve operational efficiency, and reduce costs (NHS England, 2024). While the healthcare sector's digital transformation initiatives are promising, they also reveal the disparity in digital readiness between sectors with substantial public funding and those without. The successful implementation in healthcare underscores the need for similar investments in other critical sectors like education and local government services.

Financial Services: The fintech revolution continues to reshape the banking and insurance sectors, with the UK maintaining its position as a global fintech hub. Innovations in areas such as open banking, blockchain, and AI-driven financial services are driving significant changes in how financial products are delivered and consumed (Kraus et al., 2022). The adoption of these technologies is enhancing customer experiences, improving security, and enabling new business models (Kraus et al., 2022). The rapid digital advancements in financial services highlight the sector's agility and innovation capacity. However, this also underscores the widening gap between tech-savvy sectors and more traditional industries struggling with digital adoption. Policymakers must consider these disparities to foster a more balanced economic landscape.

Public Services: The UK government's commitment to digital transformation is evident in its 'Digital Development Strategy 2024 to 2030,' which aims to catalyse digital transformation across the economy, government, and society. This includes ambitious goals such as supporting at least 20 partner countries to reduce their digital divides by an average of 50% by 2030 (UK Government, 2024). The strategy focuses on enhancing digital public infrastructure, promoting digital inclusion, and fostering innovation (ICTworks, 2024). While the government's strategy is comprehensive, its implementation is uneven, particularly in rural and underfunded areas. There is a risk that such broad strategies may not address specific local needs, leading to persistent regional digital divides.

2.3 Government Initiatives and Policies

The UK government has been proactive in fostering a conducive environment for digital transformation through various initiatives and policies.

UK Digital Strategy: The UK Digital Strategy, first introduced in 2017 and updated in 2022, sets out a comprehensive vision for the country's digital future. Key elements of this strategy include enhancing digital infrastructure and connectivity, developing digital skills and talent, fostering innovation and research in emerging technologies, ensuring a secure and ethical digital environment, and promoting the UK as a global leader in digital technologies (UK Government, 2022). Despite its forward-looking goals, the strategy's success hinges on its implementation. The gap between policy and practice can often result in uneven benefits, with larger, urban businesses reaping more advantages than their smaller, rural counterparts. Effective implementation will require sustained investment, localised support programs, and ongoing assessments to ensure equitable progress.

Digital Development Strategy 2024 to 2030: This strategy focuses on four interconnected objectives: digital transformation, digital inclusion, digital responsibility, and digital sustainability. The strategy aims to support partner countries in developing their digital public infrastructure (DPI) and creating regulatory frameworks for responsible AI use. By fostering international collaboration, the UK seeks to leverage its expertise in digital innovation to support global development (PwC, 2023; NHS England, 2024). While international collaboration is vital, the primary focus should remain on bridging the domestic digital divide. The strategy should ensure that local businesses and underserved communities are not overlooked in the drive for global leadership.

NHS Digital Transformation: The government's commitment to modernising the NHS through digital means is evident in its recent budget allocation. The £3.4 billion funding aims to update fragmented IT systems, improve data utilisation, and transform patient access and services. Specific initiatives include scaling up AI use in healthcare settings, equipping NHS staff with modern computing technology, upgrading over 100 MRI scanners with AI capabilities, and implementing electronic patient records across all NHS Trusts (Pinsent Masons, 2024). These efforts are expected to significantly enhance the quality of healthcare delivery and operational efficiency. This investment is a testament to the potential of digital transformation in public services. However, the focus on healthcare should not overshadow the need for similar investments in other public sectors facing digital lag, such as local councils and education.

2.4 Market Trends and Drivers

The UK digital transformation market is experiencing robust growth driven by several key trends and technologies.

Market Size and Growth Projections: According to Grand View Research (2023), the UK digital transformation market was valued at USD 35.11 billion in 2022 and is expected to grow at a compound annual growth rate (CAGR) of 27.7% from 2023 to 2030. This growth is underpinned by increasing adoption of advanced technologies across various sectors, reflecting the dynamic and rapidly evolving nature of the digital landscape. These growth projections, while promising, risk creating a false sense of uniform progress. The focus on high growth rates can obscure the slower adoption among SMEs and in rural areas, where the digital divide remains a significant barrier. Policymakers and business leaders must address these disparities to ensure inclusive growth.

Key Technologies Driving Transformation:

Artificial Intelligence and Machine Learning: AI and ML are revolutionising business processes, decision-making, and customer interactions. In the UK, 80% of global business leaders believe that generative AI will increase efficiencies in their operations (Deloitte, 2023). These technologies are being integrated into various applications, from predictive analytics to personalised marketing, driving significant improvements in efficiency and innovation (Bouncken et al., 2021). The integration of AI and ML, while beneficial, also raises concerns about data privacy, ethical considerations, and the potential for job displacement. The regulatory framework must evolve to address these issues, ensuring that the benefits of AI and ML are equitably distributed and do not exacerbate existing inequalities.

Cloud Computing: The shift towards cloud-based solutions continues to accelerate, with businesses increasingly adopting multi-cloud and hybrid cloud strategies to enhance flexibility and security (Consultancy.uk, 2024). Cloud computing enables organisations to scale their operations, reduce costs, and improve collaboration, making it a critical component of digital transformation. While cloud computing offers significant advantages, smaller businesses often struggle with the cost of transition and the complexity of managing cloud environments. Support mechanisms, such as subsidies and training programs, are essential to help these businesses overcome the initial hurdles and fully leverage cloud technologies.

Internet of Things (IoT): IoT technologies are being leveraged to optimise supply chain management, enhance healthcare delivery through wearable devices, and improve operational efficiencies across industries (Consultancy.uk, 2024). The integration of IoT devices provides real-time data and insights, enabling businesses to make informed decisions and streamline operations (Kraus et al., 2022). The adoption of IoT is not without challenges, particularly related to data security and privacy. Smaller businesses may also lack the technical expertise to implement IoT solutions effectively. Addressing these challenges requires comprehensive support and regulatory frameworks to ensure safe and effective IoT deployment.

5G and Advanced Connectivity: The rollout of 5G networks is enabling faster, more reliable connectivity, paving the way for innovations in areas such as autonomous vehicles, smart cities, and industrial automation (UK Government, 2022). 5G technology is expected to drive significant advancements in connectivity, supporting the development of new applications and services. The benefits of 5G will not be realised uniformly across the UK. Rural and underserved urban areas may continue to lag, creating a digital divide within the country. Targeted infrastructure investments and policies are needed to ensure that the benefits of 5G are accessible to all regions and communities.

Blockchain: While still in its early stages of adoption, blockchain technology is showing promise in areas such as supply chain management, financial services, and digital identity verification (Kraus et al., 2022). Blockchain provides a secure and transparent way to record transactions, reducing fraud and improving trust in digital transactions. Blockchain technology, despite its potential, faces significant barriers to widespread adoption, including regulatory uncertainty and high implementation costs. Efforts must be made to create a supportive regulatory environment and provide financial incentives for businesses to explore blockchain applications.

In conclusion, the digital transformation landscape in the UK is characterised by rapid technological advancements, proactive government policies, and a growing market for digital solutions. However, challenges remain, particularly in bridging the digital divide between large enterprises and SMEs and ensuring that the benefits of digital transformation are realised across all sectors of the economy. As the UK continues to position itself as a global leader in digital innovation, addressing these challenges will be crucial for sustaining long-term growth and competitiveness in the digital age.

3. CHALLENGES IN DIGITAL TRANSFORMATION

Digital transformation, while offering numerous benefits, presents a range of challenges that businesses in the UK must navigate. These challenges span financial, technological, cultural, and organisational domains, each requiring strategic approaches to overcome.

3.1 Financial Barriers

Initial Costs and Investment Challenges: One of the primary financial barriers to digital transformation is the significant initial investment required. This includes costs associated with upgrading legacy systems, purchasing new technologies, and training staff. According to the National CIO Review, many organisations are overwhelmed by the investment needed to establish an ecosystem of partners and navigate the complexity of connecting a mix of cloud services and other technologies (National CIO Review, 2023). The high upfront costs can deter smaller businesses from pursuing digital transformation initiatives. Financial support mechanisms, such as grants and low-interest loans, are essential to mitigate these barriers and encourage broader participation in digital transformation efforts.

Funding and Financial Support Mechanisms: Securing funding for digital transformation projects can be challenging, particularly for SMEs. Government grants and incentives, such as the UK Government's Digital Development Strategy 2024-2030, aim to alleviate some of these financial burdens by providing support for digital initiatives (UK Government, 2024). However, the availability and accessibility of these funds can vary, and businesses must navigate complex application processes to secure financial support (TechUK, 2022). While government incentives are beneficial, the complexity of the application process and the limited awareness among SMEs can hinder their effectiveness. Simplifying access to funding and increasing awareness through targeted outreach programs are critical steps to enhance the impact of these financial support mechanisms.

3.2 Technological Barriers

Legacy IT Systems and Infrastructure Issues: Outdated IT infrastructure is a significant barrier to digital transformation. Many organisations rely on legacy systems that are not compatible with modern digital solutions, leading to technical debt and difficulties in transitioning to new technologies. The UK Parliament's report on digital transformation in government highlights that legacy systems are a key source of inefficiency and a major constraint to improving and modernising services (UK Government, 2023). Overcoming legacy IT issues requires substantial investment in infrastructure upgrades and a strategic approach to phasing out outdated systems. This transition can be particularly challenging for SMEs with limited IT budgets, necessitating targeted support and incentives to facilitate the modernisation process.

Cybersecurity and Data Privacy Concerns: Ensuring data protection and compliance with privacy regulations is critical during digital transformation. The integration of new technologies often involves moving business data to the cloud and centralising it for easier access, which can increase vulnerabilities to cyber threats.

According to the World Economic Forum's Global Risks Report, cybersecurity measures are increasingly being rendered obsolete by the growing sophistication of cybercriminals, making data protection a significant challenge (Bouncken et al., 2021). The increasing threat of cyberattacks highlights the need for robust cybersecurity measures and regulatory frameworks. Businesses must invest in advanced security solutions and foster a culture of cybersecurity awareness to protect their digital assets effectively.

3.3 Skills and Talent Shortages

Digital Skills Gap and Workforce Readiness: The shortage of skilled professionals with the expertise required to drive digital transformation efforts is a major barrier. A report by Gigged.AI reveals that 72% of UK businesses are currently engaged in digital transformation projects, but 57% claim that the tech talent shortage has substantially increased compared to the previous year. This skills gap affects all sectors, with a particular impact on industries such as financial services, technology, and telecommunications (Digital Skills Global, 2018). Addressing the digital skills gap requires a multifaceted approach, including educational reforms, targeted training programs, and collaboration between industry and academia. Businesses must also invest in upskilling their existing workforce to bridge the skills gap and ensure that they can fully leverage digital technologies.

Training and Education Initiatives: Addressing the digital skills gap requires comprehensive training and education initiatives. Companies must invest in upskilling their existing workforce and fostering a culture of continuous learning. Initiatives such as the UK Government's Digital Skills Partnership aim to bridge the skills gap by providing training programs and resources to develop digital competencies across the workforce (FutureDotNow, 2024). While training initiatives are essential, their success depends on their accessibility and relevance to the needs of businesses. Tailoring training programs to specific industry requirements and ensuring that they are accessible to all employees, regardless of their location or role, is crucial for closing the skills gap effectively.

3.4 Cultural and Organisational Barriers

Resistance to Change within Organisations: Organisational resistance to change is a significant barrier to digital transformation. Employees accustomed to traditional ways of working may resist adopting new technologies and processes, making it difficult to retire legacy applications and embrace digital solutions. According to a survey by Jabil, employee pushback is one of the largest barriers to digital transformation, with organisational culture universally recognised as a critical factor (Jabil, 2023). Overcoming resistance to change requires strong leadership and effective change management strategies. Leaders must communicate the benefits of digital transformation clearly and involve employees in the process to foster buy-in and reduce resistance.

Leadership and Management Challenges: Effective leadership is crucial for successful digital transformation. Leaders must communicate the benefits and reasons behind the transformation, address employee concerns, and ensure a smooth transition. Establishing a center of excellence (COE) can facilitate knowledge dissemination and support organisational alignment (Forbes, 2021). However, inadequate vision or leadership can impede progress, as highlighted by the Boston Consulting Group, which found that only 30% of digital transformation initiatives meet their intended objectives (Meléndez, 2021). Leadership challenges underscore the importance of developing strong digital leadership capabilities. Investing in leadership training and creating a culture of innovation and agility are essential to navigating the complexities of digital transformation successfully.

Overcoming the challenges of digital transformation requires a holistic approach that addresses financial, technological, cultural, and organisational barriers. By strategically planning and implementing effective change management, businesses can navigate these challenges and position themselves for long-term success in the digital age.

4. THE DIGITAL DIVIDE IN UK BUSINESS COMMUNITIES

The digital divide within UK business communities represents a complex and multifaceted challenge that extends beyond mere access to technology. This section explores the nuanced landscape of digital exclusion among UK businesses, examining its definition, scope, socioeconomic factors, and illustrative case studies.

4.1 Definition and Scope of the Digital Divide

The digital divide in UK business communities refers to the gap between organisations that have full access to digital technologies and the skills to use them effectively and those that do not. This divide is not simply binary but exists on a spectrum encompassing various dimensions of digital capability and adoption (Lythreatis et al., 2022).

Table 2. Socioeconomic Factors Influencing the Digital Divide

Factor	Impact on Digital Divide
Business Size and Resources	SMEs face greater challenges due to limited financial resources and lack of IT personnel (Politico, 2024)
Geographic Location	Rural areas have less access to high-speed internet and digital infrastructure (Ofcom, 2023)
Industry Sector	Traditional industries like manufacturing and agriculture lag in digital adoption (Tech Nation, 2023)
Socioeconomic Status	Businesses led by individuals from disadvantaged backgrounds are less likely to invest in digital tools (ONS, 2019)

Addressing the digital divide requires a comprehensive understanding of these socioeconomic factors. Policymakers must tailor interventions to address the unique challenges faced by different segments of the business community. This includes providing targeted financial support, enhancing digital infrastructure in rural areas, and offering specialised training programs to bridge the skills gap.

4.2 Dimensions of the Digital Divide

Access Divide: This refers to the physical access to digital infrastructure and devices. While basic internet access is widespread in the UK, there are still significant disparities in the quality and speed of connections, particularly in rural areas (Ofcom, 2023; ONS, 2019). Bridging the access divide requires significant investment in digital infrastructure, particularly in underserved rural areas. Policies should focus on expanding high-speed internet access and ensuring that all businesses, regardless of location, have the necessary digital tools to compete in the digital economy.

Skills Divide: This dimension focuses on the digital literacy and competencies required to effectively utilise digital technologies. A report by the UK Department for Digital Culture, Media & Sport (2021) found that 52% of the UK workforce lack essential digital skills for work (FutureDotNow, 2024). The skills divide highlights the need for comprehensive and accessible digital literacy programs. Businesses and educational institutions must collaborate to develop training programs that equip the workforce with the skills required to thrive in a digital economy.

Usage Divide: This relates to the extent and sophistication of digital technology use within businesses. While some organisations leverage advanced technologies like AI and big data analytics, others struggle with basic digital operations (Lloyds Bank, 2023). Addressing the usage divide involves not only providing access to advanced technologies but also supporting businesses in their effective utilisation. This requires ongoing support, training, and resources to help businesses integrate digital technologies into their operations.

Outcome Divide: This dimension examines the tangible benefits derived from digital technology use, such as increased productivity, innovation, and market reach (Ueno et al., 2023). The outcome divide underscores the importance of measuring the impact of digital transformation initiatives. Policymakers and business leaders must track and assess the outcomes of digital investments to ensure that the benefits are realised across all sectors and regions.

4.3 Case Studies

Case Study 1: Digital Transformation Success in a Rural SME: "Farm to Fork Digital," a small agricultural business in Cornwall, successfully bridged the digital divide by leveraging government grants and partnering with a local tech startup. They implemented IoT sensors for crop monitoring and an e-commerce platform for direct sales, resulting in a 40% increase in revenue within two years (Digital Catapult, 2023). This case study illustrates the potential for digital transformation to drive growth and innovation in traditional sectors. It also highlights the importance of targeted support and partnerships in overcoming digital barriers.

Case Study 2: Challenges Faced by Traditional Retailers: A study of independent bookshops in Northern England revealed that 60% struggled to compete with online retailers due to limited digital skills and resources. However, a community-led digital literacy program helped 30% of these businesses establish an online presence, leading to an average 25% increase in sales (Booksellers Association, 2023). The challenges faced by traditional retailers underscore the need for community-driven initiatives and support programs to enhance digital literacy and adoption. Localised efforts can play a crucial role in bridging the digital divide.

Case Study 3: Sector-Specific Digital Divide: The UK's construction industry exemplifies sector-specific digital challenges. While large construction firms are adopting Building Information Modelling (BIM) and other advanced technologies, 67% of small construction businesses report difficulties in implementing basic digital tools due to cost and skills barriers (Construction Industry Training Board, 2023). Sector-specific digital divides highlight the need for tailored strategies that address the unique challenges of different industries. Policymakers must consider the specific needs of each sector to develop effective interventions.

The digital divide in UK business communities is a multifaceted issue that goes beyond simple access to technology. It encompasses complex interactions between business size, geographic location, industry sector, and socioeconomic factors. Addressing this divide requires targeted interventions that consider these nuanced aspects, as illustrated by the diverse experiences highlighted in the case studies. As the UK strives to maintain its position as a leading digital economy, bridging this divide is crucial for ensuring inclusive growth and competitiveness across all sectors and regions. Future policies and initiatives must focus not only on improving infrastructure but also on enhancing digital skills, fostering innovation, and providing tailored support to businesses at risk of digital exclusion.

5. STRATEGIES FOR BRIDGING THE DIGITAL TRANSFORMATION DIVIDE

Bridging the digital transformation divide in UK business communities requires a multifaceted approach involving government policies, business strategies, and technological solutions. This section uses the **Dynamic Capabilities Framework** to explore innovative strategies for addressing barriers and achieving inclusive digital growth. By focusing on the core components of **sensing opportunities and threats**, **seizing opportunities**, and **transforming and reconfiguring resources**, the framework provides a structured approach to adapt to the challenges of digital transformation through effective use of policies, strategies, and solutions (Teece et al., 1997).

5.1 Sensing Opportunities and Threats

Government and policy interventions play a critical role in sensing opportunities to foster digital inclusion and address barriers. The UK government has set ambitious targets in the "Transforming for a Digital Future" roadmap (UK Government, 2022), aiming to address the needs of SMEs and rural businesses. By recognising the specific requirements of these communities, the government can implement targeted support for digital infrastructure and skills development, ensuring that businesses are prepared for the challenges of digital transformation.

5.2 Seizing Opportunities

Businesses must seize opportunities by adopting best practices and aligning their digital strategies with business objectives. A well-defined digital strategy involves assessing current capabilities, identifying areas for improvement, and setting measurable goals (Pareto UK, 2023). Continuous investment in digital skills, fostering a learning culture, and embracing agile methodologies are crucial for SMEs to effectively seize the opportunities presented by digital transformation. This flexibility allows SMEs to overcome challenges associated with limited resources and compete with larger enterprises.

5.3 Transforming and Reconfiguring Resources

The deployment of technology solutions, such as **AI**, **cloud computing**, and **IoT**, represents a transformation of business capabilities to enhance efficiency and competitiveness. AI and ML can automate processes and improve decision-making, while cloud computing provides scalable infrastructure to reduce costs and facilitate collaboration. The use of IoT in traditional industries, like manufacturing, helps modernise operations and improve productivity. However, transforming these opportunities into tangible benefits requires businesses to reconfigure their resources, such as investing in training programs and ensuring responsible data management practices (TechUK, 2023; Kraus et al., 2022).

Case studies, such as the NHS's digital transformation initiative, demonstrate the importance of investing in advanced technologies to enhance operational efficiency and outcomes (Pinsent Masons, 2024). These examples show that while the benefits of digital transformation can be significant, comprehensive support and tailored strategies are necessary for successfully implementing changes across different sectors and regions.

By employing the **Dynamic Capabilities Framework**, the strategies outlined in this section aim to enable businesses to adapt to the evolving digital landscape effectively. The framework underscores the importance of sensing opportunities, seizing them through strategic actions, and transforming existing capabilities to address barriers, thereby ensuring that the digital transformation divide is effectively bridged. This collaborative effort involving government policies, business strategies, and technology solutions will help the UK maintain its leadership in digital innovation while promoting inclusive growth.

6. CONCLUSION: FUTURE OUTLOOK AND RECOMMENDATIONS

As digital transformation continues to reshape the UK business landscape, it is imperative to look ahead and identify emerging trends, technologies, and strategies that will drive future growth. This section explores the future outlook for digital transformation in the UK, providing policy and business recommendations to ensure sustained digital growth and competitiveness.

6.1 Emerging Trends and Technologies

Generative AI and Machine Learning: Generative AI and machine learning are set to revolutionise various sectors by automating complex tasks, enhancing decision-making, and providing personalised customer experiences. According to Deloitte, 80% of global business leaders believe that generative AI will increase efficiencies in their business operations (Deloitte, 2023). In the UK, the adoption of AI technologies is expected to accelerate, driving innovation in areas such as healthcare, finance, and manufacturing. The widespread adoption of generative AI must be managed carefully to address ethical concerns, data privacy issues, and the potential for job displacement. A balanced approach that includes regulatory oversight and workforce reskilling is essential to mitigate these risks.

Quantum Computing: Quantum computing represents a significant leap forward in computational power, enabling the solving of complex problems that are currently intractable for classical computers. The UK government has invested heavily in quantum research, positioning the country as a leader in this emerging field. Quantum computing is expected to have profound implications for cryptography, materials science, and optimisation problems (UK Government, 2022). While quantum computing holds great promise, its practical applications are still in their infancy. Continued investment in research and development is necessary to realise its full potential, along with efforts to ensure that the benefits are widely shared across different sectors and regions.

5G and Advanced Connectivity: The rollout of 5G networks will provide faster, more reliable connectivity, enabling innovations in areas such as autonomous vehicles, smart cities, and industrial automation. The UK government has prioritised the expansion of 5G infrastructure, aiming to ensure that the majority of the population has access to this transformative technology by 2025 (Ofcom, 2023). Ensuring equitable access to 5G technology is crucial. Policymakers must address the digital divide by prioritising investments in rural and underserved areas to ensure that all communities can benefit from the advancements in connectivity.

Internet of Things (IoT): IoT technologies will continue to play a crucial role in optimising operations, improving asset management, and providing real-time insights. The integration of IoT devices in sectors such as agriculture, manufacturing, and logistics will drive efficiency and innovation, helping businesses to remain competitive in a digital-first world (Kraus et al., 2022). The successful deployment of IoT requires addressing significant challenges, including data privacy, security concerns, and the need for robust infrastructure. Businesses must also ensure that they have the technical expertise to manage and utilise IoT effectively.

6.2 Policy and Business Recommendations

Long-Term Strategies for Sustained Digital Growth: To ensure sustained digital growth, the UK government and businesses must adopt long-term strategies that address the challenges and opportunities of digital transformation. Long-term strategies should focus on enhancing digital infrastructure, fostering digital skills, supporting SMEs, and promoting research and innovation. Policymakers must prioritise inclusivity and ensure that all regions and sectors can benefit from digital transformation.

Enhancing Digital Infrastructure: Investing in digital infrastructure is critical for supporting future growth. The government should continue to expand fiber networks and 5G coverage, ensuring that all regions have access to high-speed internet. This will enable businesses to leverage advanced technologies and remain competitive on a global scale (STL Tech, 2023). Infrastructure investments must be coupled with targeted support for businesses in underserved areas to ensure that they can fully leverage new technologies. This includes providing financial incentives and technical assistance to facilitate the transition.

Fostering Digital Skills and Talent: Addressing the digital skills gap is essential for maintaining the UK's competitive edge. The government should expand initiatives such as the Digital Skills Partnership, providing targeted training programs to develop digital competencies across the workforce. Businesses should also invest in upskilling their employees, fostering a culture of continuous learning (FutureDotNow, 2024). Effective skill development programs must be accessible to all segments of the workforce, including those in rural and disadvantaged areas. Collaboration between government, industry, and educational institutions is essential to ensure the relevance and impact of training initiatives.

Supporting SMEs in Digital Transformation: SMEs are the backbone of the UK economy, and their successful digital transformation is crucial for overall economic growth. The government should provide financial support and incentives for SMEs to adopt digital technologies, such as grants, tax credits, and low-interest loans. Additionally, creating a supportive ecosystem through public-private partnerships can help SMEs navigate the complexities of digital transformation (UK Government, 2022). Support for SMEs must be tailored to address their specific challenges, including limited financial resources and lack of digital expertise. Simplifying access to funding and providing targeted advisory services can significantly enhance the effectiveness of support programs.

Promoting Innovation and Research: Investing in research and development is key to driving innovation and maintaining the UK's position as a global leader in digital technologies. The government should increase funding for research in emerging technologies such as AI, quantum computing, and IoT. Encouraging collaboration between academia, industry, and government can accelerate the development and deployment of cutting-edge technologies (TechUK, 2023). Innovation policies must be inclusive and ensure that all regions and sectors can participate in and benefit from research and development initiatives. This includes providing support for regional innovation hubs and fostering cross-sector collaboration.

6.3 Conclusion

The future of digital transformation in the UK is bright, with emerging technologies offering unprecedented opportunities for growth and innovation. By adopting long-term strategies that enhance digital infrastructure, foster digital skills, support SMEs, and promote research and innovation, the UK can ensure sustained digital growth and maintain its position as a global leader in the digital economy. As the UK continues to navigate the complexities of digital transformation, collaboration between government, businesses, and academia will be essential. By working together, stakeholders can create an inclusive digital ecosystem that drives economic growth, improves living standards, and enhances the UK's competitiveness on the global stage.

REFERENCES

Bouncken, R. B., Kraus, S., & Roig-Tierno, N. (2021). Digital transformation in entrepreneurial ecosystems: A co-evolutionary perspective. *Technological Forecasting and Social Change*, 168, 120785. DOI: 10.1016/j.techfore.2021.120785

British Business Bank. (2022). *Going digital - The challenges facing European SMEs*. British Business Bank.

Construction Industry Training Board (2023) *Digital skills for the UK construction sector*. Kings Lynn: CITB.

Cosa, M. (2024). Business digital transformation: Strategy adaptation, communication, and future agenda. *Journal of Strategy and Management*, 17(2), 244–259. DOI: 10.1108/JSMA-09-2023-0233

Deloitte. (2023) *Digital transformation: The future of work*. Available at: https://www2.deloitte.com (Accessed: 30 September 2024).

Digital Catapult. (2023). *Rural digital innovation: Case studies from the UK*. Digital Catapult.

Digital Skills Global. (2018) *Digital skills gap is a risk to companies*. Available at: https://digitalskillsglobal.com (Accessed: 14 September 2024).

Enterprisers Project. (2023) *7 digital transformation barriers to overcome*. Available at: https://enterprisersproject.com (Accessed: 30 September 2024).

Federation of Small Businesses. (2023). *The digital readiness of UK small businesses*. FSB.

Forbes (2021) *Five barriers to digital transformation and how to overcome them*. Available at: https://www.forbes.com (Accessed: 22 September 2024).

FutureDotNow. (2024) *The essential digital skills gap*. Available at: https://futuredotnow.uk (Accessed: 15 September 2024).

Gigged.AI. (2024) *Digital transformation in crisis*. Available at: https://gigged.ai (Accessed: 30 September 2024).

Good Things Foundation. (2024). *Digital exclusion and UK business leadership*. Good Things Foundation.

GOV.UK. (2024) *A plan for digital health and social care*. Available at: https://www.gov.uk/government/publications/a-plan-for-digital-health-and-social-care/a-plan-for-digital-health-and-social-care (Accessed: 30 September 2024).

Grand View Research. (2023) *U.K. digital transformation market size share & trends analysis report by solution, by service, by deployment, by enterprise size, by end-use, and segment forecasts, 2023 - 2030*. Available at: https://www.grandviewresearch.com (Accessed: 18 September 2024).

Hinings, B., Gegenhuber, T., & Greenwood, R. (2018). Digital innovation and transformation: An institutional perspective. *Information and Organization*, 28(1), 52–61. DOI: 10.1016/j.infoandorg.2018.02.004

ICTworks. (2024) *Introducing FCDO's new digital development strategy*. Available at: https://www.ictworks.org (Accessed: 30 September 2024).

Jabil (2023) *Biggest barriers to digital transformation - Top 5*. Available at: https://jabil.com (Accessed: 17 September 2024).

Kraus, S., Clauss, T., Breier, M., Gast, J., Zardini, A., & Tiberius, V. (2020). The economics of COVID-19: Initial empirical evidence on how family firms in five European countries cope with the corona crisis. *International Journal of Entrepreneurial Behaviour & Research*, 26(5), 1067–1092. DOI: 10.1108/IJEBR-04-2020-0214

Kraus, S., Durst, S., Ferreira, J. J., Veiga, P., Kailer, N., & Weinmann, A. (2022). Digital transformation in business and management research: An overview of the current status quo. *Journal of Business Research*, 123, 1–15.

Kuckertz, A., Brändle, L., Gaudig, A., Hinderer, S., Reyes, C. A. M., Prochotta, A., & Berger, E. S. (2020). Startups in times of crisis–A rapid response to the COVID-19 pandemic. *Journal of Business Venturing Insights*, 13, e00169. DOI: 10.1016/j.jbvi.2020.e00169

Lloyds Bank. (2023). *UK business digital index 2023*. Lloyds Banking Group.

Lythreatis, S., Singh, S. K., & El-Kassar, A. N. (2022). The digital divide: A review and future research agenda. *Technological Forecasting and Social Change*, 174, 121173. DOI: 10.1016/j.techfore.2021.121359

Meléndez, C. M. (2021) 'Five barriers to digital transformation and how to overcome them', *Forbes*. Available at: https://www.forbes.com (Accessed: 25 September 2024).

Nagel, L. (2020). The influence of the COVID-19 pandemic on the digital transformation of work. *The International Journal of Sociology and Social Policy*, 40(9/10), 861–875. DOI: 10.1108/IJSSP-07-2020-0323

National, C. I. O. Review (2023) *How to overcome cost-barriers to digital transformation*. Available at: https://nationalcioreview.com (Accessed: 30 September 2024).

NHS England. (2024a) *Digital transformation*. Available at: https://www.england .nhs.uk/digitaltechnology (Accessed: 30 September 2024).

NHS England. (2024b) *Inclusive digital healthcare: A framework for NHS action on digital inclusion*. Available at: https://www.england.nhs.uk/long-read/inclusive -digital-healthcare-a-framework-for-nhs-action-on-digital-inclusion (Accessed: 21 September 2024).

Ofcom (2023) *Connected nations 2023*. London: Ofcom.

Office for National Statistics. (2019) *Exploring the UK's digital divide*. Available at: https://www.ons.gov.uk (Accessed: 23 September 2024).

Optimising, I. T. (2023) *The ultimate guide to digital transformation services*. Available at: https://www.optimisingit.co.uk (Accessed: 30 September 2024).

Pareto, U. K. (2023) *How to prepare your business for digital transformation*. Available at: https://pareto.co.uk (Accessed: 28 September 2024).

Pinsent Masons. (2024) *NHS to receive £3.4bn funding for digital transformation*. Available at: https://www.pinsentmasons.com (Accessed: 30 September 2024).

Politico (2024) *Boosting SME digital skills is key for UK economic growth*. Available at: https://www.politico.eu (Accessed: 30 September 2024).

PwC. (2023) *The responsible AI framework - Accelerating innovation through responsible AI*. Available at: https://www.pwc.co.uk/services/risk/insights/accelerating -innovation-through-responsible-ai/responsible-ai-framework.html (Accessed: 30 September 2024).

Tech, S. T. L. (2023) *UK's digital divide: Bridged!* Available at: https://stl.tech (Accessed: 12 September 2024).

Tech, U. K. (2022) *Tackling the digital divide and empowering the future workforce*. Available at: https://www.techuk.org (Accessed: 30 September 2024).

Tech, U. K. (2023) *How the emerging technologies can bring disruptive change across UK public sectors*. Available at: https://www.techuk.org (Accessed: 15 September 2024).

Tech Nation. (2023). *The future of UK tech*. Tech Nation.

TechResort. (2024) *Digital inclusion and the general election*. Available at: https:// www.techresort.org (Accessed: 13 September 2024).

Teece, D. J., Pisano, G., & Shuen, A. (1997). Dynamic capabilities and strategic management. *Strategic Management Journal*, 18(7), 509–533. DOI: 10.1002/ (SICI)1097-0266(199708)18:7<509::AID-SMJ882>3.0.CO;2-Z

Ueno, A., Dennis, C., & Dafoulas, G. A. (2023). Digital exclusion and relative digital deprivation: Exploring factors and moderators of internet non-use in the UK. *Technological Forecasting and Social Change*, 197, 122935. DOI: 10.1016/j. techfore.2023.122935

UK Government. (2022) *Transforming for a digital future: 2022 to 2025 roadmap for digital and data*. Available at: https://www.gov.uk/government/publications/uks -digital-strategy/uk-digital-strategy (Accessed: 22 September 2024).

UK Government. (2024) *Digital development strategy 2024 to 2030*. Available at: https://assets.publishing.service.gov.uk/media/6613e7f7c4c84d4b31346a68/FCDO -Digital-Development-Strategy-2024-2030.pdf (Accessed: 30 September 2024).

Xledger (2022) *Why is the UK lagging behind when it comes to digital transformation?* Available at: https://xledger.com (Accessed: 26 September 2024).

ADDITIONAL READING

Ali, M. (2021). *Remote Work and Sustainable Changes for the Future of Global Business*. IGI Global. https://www.igi-global.com/book/remote-work-sustainable -changes-future/264375

Ali, M. (2022). *Future Role of Sustainable Innovative Technologies in Crisis Management*. IGI Global. https://www.igi-global.com/book/future-role-sustainable -innovative-technologies/281281

Ali, M. (2023). *Shifting Paradigms in the Rapidly Developing Global Digital Ecosystem: A GCC Perspective*. In Digital Entrepreneurship and Co-Creating Value Through Digital Encounters (pp. 145-166). IGI Global. https://www.igi-global.com/chapter/ shifting-paradigms-in-the-rapidly-developing-global-digital-ecosystem/323525

Ali, M. (2023). T*axonomy of Industry 4.0 Technologies in Digital Entrepreneurship and Co-Creating Value*. In *Digital Entrepreneurship and Co-Creating Value Through Digital Encounters* (pp. 24–55). IGI Global., https://www.igi-global.com/ chapter/taxonomy-of-industry-40-technologies-in-digital-entrepreneurship-and-co -creating-value/323520 DOI: 10.4018/978-1-6684-7416-7.ch002

Ali, M., & Wood-Harper, T. (2021). *Fostering Communication and Learning with Underutilized Technologies in Higher Education*. IGI Global. https://www.igi-global.com/book/fostering-communication-learning-underutilized-technologies/244593

Ali, M., Wood-Harper, T., & Kutar, M. (2023). Multi-Perspectives of Contemporary Digital Transformation Models of Complex Innovation Management. In *Digital Entrepreneurship and Co-Creating Value Through Digital Encounters* (pp. 79–96). IGI Global., https://www.igi-global.com/chapter/multi-perspectives-of-contemporary-digital-transformation-models-of-complex-innovation-management/323522 DOI: 10.4018/978-1-6684-7416-7.ch004

Ali, M. B. (2021). Internet of Things (IoT) to Foster Communication and Information Sharing: A Case of UK Higher Education. In Ali, M. B., & Wood-Harper, T. (Eds.), *Fostering Communication and Learning With Underutilized Technologies in Higher Education* (pp. 1–20). IGI Global., https://www.igi-global.com/chapter/internet-of-things-iot-to-foster-communication-and-information-sharing/262718/ DOI: 10.4018/978-1-7998-4846-2.ch001

Ali, M. B., & Wood-Harper, T. (2022). Artificial Intelligence (AI) as a Decision-Making Tool to Control Crisis Situations. In *Future Role of Sustainable Innovative Technologies in Crisis Management*. IGI Global., https://www.igi-global.com/chapter/artificial-intelligence-ai-as-a-decision-making-tool-to-control-crisis-situations/298931 DOI: 10.4018/978-1-7998-9815-3.ch006

Ali, M. B., Wood-Harper, T., & Ramlogan, R. (2020). A Framework Strategy to Overcome Trust Issues on Cloud Computing Adoption in Higher Education. In Modern Principles, Practices, and Algorithms for Cloud Security (pp. 162-183). IGI Global. https://www.igi-global.com/chapter/a-framework-strategy-to-overcome-trust-issues-on-cloud-computing-adoption-in-higher-education/238907/

Chapter 2
Digital Transformation and Cybersecurity Fears on National Security in GCC

Mohammed Albakri
https://orcid.org/0000-0001-5854-8245
University of Salford, UK

Muktar Bello
University of Salford, UK

Safiya Al Rashdi
Innovation Oases Company, Oman

ABSTRACT

The Gulf Cooperation Council (GCC) has undergone significant digital transformation driven by strategies like Saudi Arabia's Vision 2030 and the UAE's National Innovation Strategy. This shift has advanced sectors such as energy, finance, healthcare, and transportation, making the GCC a hub for technological innovation and smart city development. However, the increasing reliance on digital technologies has heightened cybersecurity risks, including data breaches, ransomware, phishing, and advanced persistent threats (APTs). These threats pose significant risks to critical infrastructure and societal stability, exacerbated by regional conflicts and state-sponsored cyber activities. This chapter explores cybersecurity challenges and strategies within the GCC, emphasizing the need for robust measures. Key strategies include adopting comprehensive frameworks, enhancing governance, fostering regional collaboration, and investing in education and training. Addressing these

DOI: 10.4018/979-8-3693-5966-2.ch002

challenges can enhance the GCC's cybersecurity resilience and ensure long-term digital protection.

INTRODUCTION

The Gulf Cooperation Council (GCC) region, comprising Bahrain, Kuwait, Oman, Qatar, Saudi Arabia, and the United Arab Emirates (UAE), has undergone significant digital transformation over the past few decades. Historically, the region's economy was heavily reliant on oil and gas exports. However, recognising the need for economic diversification and technological advancement, GCC countries have embarked on ambitious national strategies to modernise their digital infrastructure and embrace new technologies. Initiatives such as Saudi Arabia's Vision 2030 and the UAE's National Innovation Strategy exemplify this shift towards a knowledge-based economy driven by digital innovation (Deloitte, 2020). As a result, the GCC has witnessed rapid advancements in sectors such as energy, finance, healthcare, and transportation, making it a hub for technological innovation and smart city development (Alghawi et al., 2024).

Figure 1. Internet Penetration in MENA Region

Mobile internet user penetration in the Middle East and Africa in 2022, by country

The GCC faces significant cyber vulnerability due to its high internet penetration rates, with Bahrain and UAE having nearly universal mobile internet access (98% and 96%, respectively) (Statista, 2024a). This widespread connectivity, coupled with the prevalent use of mobile devices, expands the potential attack surface for cyber threats. The forecasted increase in global cybersecurity market revenue to 271.91 billion USD by 2029 highlights the escalating threat landscape (Statista, 2024b). The GCC's strategic economic sectors, such as finance and oil, are attractive targets for cyber-attacks, underscoring the need for robust cybersecurity measures to protect sensitive data and ensure economic stability.

Figure 2. Cybersecurity Market

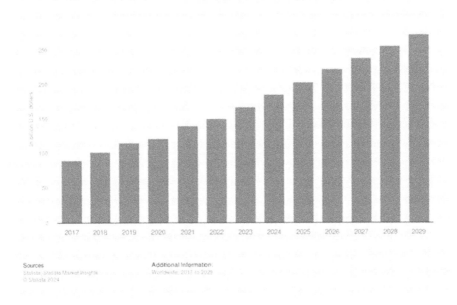

Revenue in the cybersecurity market Worldwide from 2017 to 2029 (in billion U.S. dollars)

With the increasing reliance on digital technologies, the importance of cyberse-curity in national security has become paramount. The GCC region faces a diverse array of cyber threats, including data breaches, ransomware, phishing, and advanced persistent threats (APTs), which pose significant risks to its critical infrastructure and societal stability (IBM Security, 2023; FireEye, 2023). The geopolitical landscape of the GCC, marked by regional conflicts and rivalries, further exacerbates these threats, as state-sponsored cyber activities and global cybersecurity trends impact the region's security dynamics (Chatham House, 2020). Ensuring robust cybersecurity measures is essential for protecting critical infrastructure, maintaining economic stability, and safeguarding public trust in digital systems and e-government services (Javaid et al., 2023). As such, cybersecurity has emerged as a critical component of national security strategies in the GCC, necessitating a comprehensive and proactive approach to address the evolving cyber threat landscape.

Figure 3. Cyber Issues in GCC

This chapter aims to provide a comprehensive understanding of cybersecurity challenges and strategies within the context of the GCC. It will explore the evolution of cybersecurity in the region, highlighting its historical context and current state. The chapter will discuss the growing significance of cybersecurity in ensuring national security amid rising cyber threats and the unique vulnerabilities faced by critical sectors such as energy, finance, healthcare, and transportation. Additionally, the chapter will outline potential strategies to mitigate cybersecurity fears, including the adoption of comprehensive frameworks, enhancement of cybersecurity governance, regional collaboration, and investment in education and training. By examining these aspects, the chapter seeks to offer valuable insights into the multifaceted nature of cybersecurity in the GCC and the measures required to protect its digital infrastructure and ensure long-term resilience and to meet each country's DT Visions (see Table 1).

Table 1. Summary of GCC Countries' Digital Transformation Initiatives

Country	Year Launched	Initiative Name	Description
Saudi Arabia	2016	Vision 2030	Aims to diversify the economy and modernise infrastructure, including digital transformation
United Arab Emirates	2021	UAE Digital Government Strategy 2025	Focuses on enhancing digital services, promoting cross-sectoral collaboration, and leveraging emerging technologies
Qatar	2014	Qatar National Vision 2030	Aims to transform Qatar into an advanced society capable of sustaining its development and providing a high standard of living
Oman	2017	Oman Vision 2040	Focuses on economic diversification and digital transformation to improve public services and infrastructure
Kuwait	2018	New Kuwait Vision 2035	Aims to transform Kuwait into a regional financial and commercial hub through digital transformation and economic diversification
Bahrain	2019	Bahrain Economic Vision 2030	Focuses on enhancing the quality of life through digital transformation and economic diversification

Figure 4. Stages of DT

THE SIX STAGES OF DIGITAL TRANSFORMATION

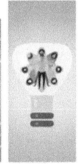

BUSINESS AS USUAL: Organizations operate with a familiar legacy perspective of customers, processes, metrics, business models, and technology, believing that it remains the solution to digital relevance

PRESENT AND ACTIVE: Pockets of experimentation are driving digital literacy and creativity, albeit disparately, throughout the organization while aiming to improve and amplify specific touch points and processes.

FORMALIZED: Experimentation becomes intentional while executing at more promising and capable levels. Initiatives become bolder and, as a result, change agents seek executive support for new resources and technology

STRATEGIC: Individual groups recognize the strength in collaboration as their research, work, and shared insights contribute to new strategic roadmaps that plan for digital transformation ownership, efforts, and investments.

CONVERGED: A dedicated digital transformation team forms to guide strategy and operations based on business and customer-centric goals. The new infrastructure of the organization takes shape as roles, expertise, models, processes, and systems to support transformation are solidified.

INNOVATIVE AND ADAPTIVE: Digital transformation becomes a way of business as executives and strategists recognize that change is constant. A new ecosystem is established to identify and act upon technology and market trends in pilot and, eventually, at scale.

ALTIMETER

The GCC region's rapid digital transformation, driven by national strategies like Saudi Arabia's Vision 2030 and the UAE's National Innovation Strategy, underscores the need for robust cybersecurity measures to protect national security. The multifaceted nature of DT in the GCC involves various levels of analysis: **Individual Level**: Emphasises the human side of DT, including the adoption and utilisation of digital technologies by individuals. This level is crucial in ensuring that the workforce is equipped with the necessary skills and knowledge to navigate the digital landscape (Nadkarni & Prügl, 2021). **Organisational Level**: Focuses on strategising and coordinating internal and external transformation efforts within organisations. This involves realigning operations, processes, and business models to integrate new technologies effectively (Bughin et al., 2019). **Ecosystem Level**: Involves harnessing digital technologies for governance and co-producing value propositions within broader ecosystems. This level highlights the interconnectedness of various stakeholders and the need for collaborative efforts in the digital transformation process (Grajek, 2020). **Geopolitical Level**: Considers the regulatory environments and geopolitical factors that influence DT processes. The geopolitical landscape in the GCC, marked by regional conflicts and international tensions, further complicates the cybersecurity challenges associated with digital transformation (Bughin et al., 2019).

Figure 5. DT Progression

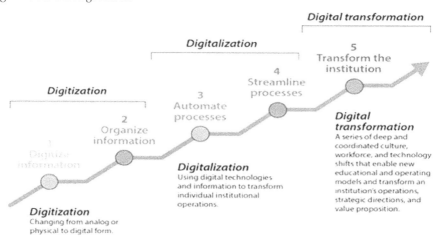

Successful digital transformation requires navigating several challenges, including stakeholder engagement, operational realignment, and cybersecurity concerns. Engaging all stakeholders in the DT process is crucial for aligning goals and ensuring smooth implementation. Organisations must realign their operations to integrate new technologies effectively, which often involves significant cultural shifts. The rapid pace of digital transformation in the GCC has exposed the region to sophisticated cyber threats, necessitating a proactive approach to cybersecurity (Nadkarni & Prügl, 2021).

Digital transformation in the GCC has profound implications for national security. Cyberattacks can disrupt essential services and compromise sensitive information, leading to significant economic losses. Ensuring robust cybersecurity measures is crucial for maintaining public trust in digital systems and government services. The geopolitical landscape in the GCC, marked by regional conflicts and international tensions, further complicates the cybersecurity challenges associated with digital transformation (Bughin et al., 2019).

Table 2. Summary of Key DT Definitions

Source	Definition
Vial, 2019	Integration of digital technology into all areas of a business, fundamentally changing how you operate and deliver value to customers.
Bughin et al., 2019	Fundamental rewiring of how an organisation operates, with the goal of continuously deploying technology at scale to create value.
Grajek, 2020	Series of deep and coordinated culture, workforce, and technology shifts that enable new educational and operating models, transforming an institution's operations, strategic directions, and value proposition.
Nadkarni & Prügl, 2021	Actor-driven organisational transformation triggered by the adoption of technology-driven digital disruptions.

Cybersecurity Definitions

Cybersecurity is a broad and multi-disciplinary field that involves the application of technologies, processes, and controls to protect systems, networks, programs, devices, and data from cyber threats. Definitions of cybersecurity vary across different sources, reflecting its complex and evolving nature. **Protecting Information Systems**: According to the National Institute of Standards and Technology (NIST), cybersecurity involves measures and controls that ensure the confidentiality, integrity, and availability of information processed and stored by a computer. This definition highlights the prevention of damage, protection, and restoration of electronic systems to ensure their security (NIST, 2021). **Application of Technologies and Controls**: IT Governance defines cybersecurity as the application of technologies, processes, and controls to protect systems, networks, programs, devices, and data from cyber-attacks. This definition emphasises the practical aspects of cybersecurity, focusing on the implementation of specific measures to reduce risks and protect against unauthorised exploitation (IT Governance, 2023). **Comprehensive Protection**: The Cybersecurity and Infrastructure Security Agency (CISA) describes cybersecurity as the practice of protecting networks, devices, and data from unauthorised access or criminal use and ensuring the confidentiality, integrity, and availability of information. This definition underscores the comprehensive nature of cybersecurity, encompassing various elements such as networks, devices, and data (CISA, 2023). **Multidisciplinary Approach**: Craigen, Diakun-Thibault, and Purse (2014) define cybersecurity as the body of technologies, processes, and practices designed to protect networks, devices, programs, and data from attack, damage, or unauthorised access. This definition highlights the multidisciplinary nature of cybersecurity, involving a combination of technical, physical, and personnel-focused measures (Craigen et al., 2014).

Figure 6. Cybersecurity Threat Landscape in Arab and GCC Regions

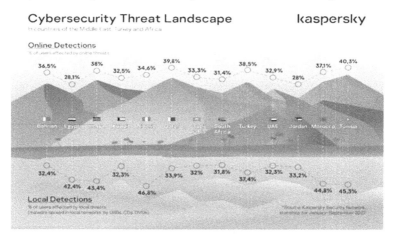

The rapid digital transformation in the GCC region, driven by initiatives like Saudi Arabia's Vision 2030 and the UAE's National Innovation Strategy, necessitates robust cybersecurity measures to protect national security. The multifaceted nature of cybersecurity in the GCC involves various levels of analysis: **Individual Level**: Emphasises the role of individuals in maintaining cybersecurity by adopting best practices and being aware of potential threats. This level is crucial in ensuring that users are equipped with the knowledge and skills to protect their digital environments (Craigen et al., 2014). **Organisational Level**: Focuses on the implementation of comprehensive cybersecurity strategies within organisations. This involves deploying technologies, processes, and controls to safeguard systems and data from cyber threats (IT Governance, 2023). **Ecosystem Level**: Involves the protection of interconnected systems and networks within broader ecosystems. This level highlights the need for collaborative efforts among various stakeholders to enhance cybersecurity across the digital landscape (CISA, 2023). **Geopolitical Level**: Considers the regulatory environments and geopolitical factors that influence cybersecurity practices. The geopolitical landscape in the GCC, marked by regional conflicts and international tensions, further complicates the cybersecurity challenges associated with digital transformation (NIST, 2021).

Successful cybersecurity requires navigating several challenges, including the implementation of effective policies, raising awareness among users, and addressing the evolving nature of cyber threats. Engaging all stakeholders in the cybersecurity process is crucial for aligning goals and ensuring robust protection. Organisations must adopt a proactive approach to cybersecurity, involving regular risk assessments and updates to security measures (Craigen et al., 2014).

Cybersecurity has profound implications for national security in the GCC. Cyberattacks can disrupt essential services, compromise sensitive information, and lead to significant economic losses. Ensuring robust cybersecurity measures is crucial for maintaining public trust in digital systems and government services. The geopolitical landscape in the GCC, marked by regional conflicts and international tensions, further complicates the cybersecurity challenges associated with digital transformation (NIST, 2021).

Table 3. Summary of Key Cybersecurity Definitions

Source	Definition
NIST, 2021	Measures and controls that ensure confidentiality, integrity, and availability of information processed and stored by a computer.
IT Governance, 2023	Application of technologies, processes, and controls to protect systems, networks, programs, devices, and data from cyber-attacks.
CISA, 2023	Practice of protecting networks, devices, and data from unauthorised access or criminal use and ensuring confidentiality, integrity, and availability of information.
Craigen et al., 2014	Body of technologies, processes, and practices designed to protect networks, devices, programs, and data from attack, damage, or unauthorised access.

National Security Definitions

National security is a multifaceted concept that has evolved significantly over time. While traditionally focused on military defence, modern definitions encompass a broader range of issues affecting a nation's stability and well-being. **Traditional Military-Centric Definition**: Walter Lippmann defined national security in 1943 as "A nation has security when it does not have to sacrifice its legitimate interests to avoid war, and is able, if challenged, to maintain them by war" (Lippmann, 1943). This definition emphasises the ability to defend national interests through military means if necessary. **Comprehensive Approach**: Harold Brown, U.S. Secretary of Defense (1977-1981), offered a more expansive definition: "National security is the ability to preserve the nation's physical integrity and territory; to maintain its economic relations with the rest of the world on reasonable terms; to preserve its nature, institution, and governance from disruption from outside; and to control its borders" (Brown, 1983). This definition encompasses territorial, economic, and institutional aspects of security. **Human Security Perspective**: The United Nations promotes a broader concept of human security, which includes "economic security, food security, health security, environmental security, personal security, community security, and political security" (United Nations, 1994). This approach shifts the focus from state-centric security to the security of individuals and communities. **Holistic Approach**: The Chinese government emphasises a holistic approach to national security, encompassing political, economic, military, social, and cultural dimensions (China's National Security Strategy, 2015). This definition reflects the interconnected nature of various security aspects. **Multidimensional Definition**: Prabhakaran Paleri lists multiple elements of national security, including military, economic, resource, border, demographic, disaster, energy, geostrategic, informational, food, health, ethnic, environmental, cyber, and genomic security (Paleri, 2008). This comprehensive definition highlights the diverse factors that contribute to national security.

The concept of national security has expanded to address new challenges and threats. Modern definitions include economic security, cybersecurity, environmental security, and energy security as crucial components of national security (Holmes, 2015). The rise of non-state actors, transnational crime, and global pandemics has broadened the scope of national security concerns (Makinda, 2006). Cybersecurity and the protection of critical digital infrastructure have become integral to national security strategies (CISA, 2023). The interconnectedness of global economies has made economic security a key aspect of national security (Heritage Foundation, 2015).

There is an ongoing debate about balancing individual rights with national security measures (Williams, 2008). Different nations may prioritise various aspects of national security based on their geopolitical situations and perceived threats (UN Chronicle, 2020). The dynamic nature of global threats requires constant reassessment and adaptation of national security strategies (Holmes, 2015).

Table 4. Summary Table of Key Definitions

Source	Definition
Lippmann (1943)	A nation has security when it does not have to sacrifice its legitimate interests to avoid war, and is able, if challenged, to maintain them by war.
Brown (1983)	The ability to preserve the nation's physical integrity and territory; to maintain its economic relations with the rest of the world on reasonable terms; to preserve its nature, institution, and governance from disruption from outside; and to control its borders.
United Nations (1994)	Economic security, food security, health security, environmental security, personal security, community security, and political security.
Paleri (2008)	Multiple elements including military, economic, resource, border, demographic, disaster, energy, geostrategic, informational, food, health, ethnic, environmental, cyber, and genomic security.

The Digital Transformation Landscape in the GCC

The Gulf Cooperation Council (GCC) countries are at the forefront of digital transformation, driven by ambitious national strategies aimed at economic diversification and technological innovation. This transformation is characterised by comprehensive initiatives across various sectors and significant technological advancements that are reshaping the region's infrastructure and services.

Key Digital Initiatives

Smart cities and digital government projects are central to the GCC's digital transformation efforts. These initiatives focus on integrating advanced technologies to enhance urban living and governance. For instance, the UAE's Smart Dubai initiative and Saudi Arabia's NEOM project exemplify the region's commitment to creating technologically advanced urban environments (Albakri, 2023). These smart city projects aim to improve quality of life, enhance sustainability, and optimise resource management through the integration of Internet of Things (IoT) technologies and data analytics (Economist Intelligence Unit, 2020). Sector-specific transformations are also pivotal in the GCC's digital landscape. In healthcare, digital solutions are being implemented to improve patient care and operational efficiency. The energy sector is leveraging Industry 4.0 technologies to optimise operations and enhance sustainability. Financial services are undergoing significant digital transformation, with banks adopting innovative technologies to improve customer experience and streamline operations (Albakri, 2023). These sector-specific initiatives are not only enhancing service delivery but also contributing to the overall economic diversification goals of GCC countries (Deloitte, 2020).

Technological Advancements

Technological advancements are central to the GCC's digital transformation efforts, profoundly impacting infrastructure and services. The adoption of cloud computing, artificial intelligence (AI), the Internet of Things (IoT), and blockchain is reshaping various sectors. AI and machine learning technologies are being utilised to develop smart city solutions, optimise energy consumption, and improve public services (McKinsey, 2023). For example, AI-powered traffic management systems are being implemented in cities like Dubai to reduce congestion and improve urban mobility (Economist Intelligence Unit, 2020). The impact of these technological advancements extends to urban planning and infrastructure development. GCC countries are increasingly adopting digital twin technologies to create virtual replicas of physical assets, enabling better management and optimisation of urban infrastructure (Alghawi et al., 2024). This approach allows for more efficient resource allocation and predictive maintenance, ultimately leading to more sustainable and resilient urban environments. However, the digital transformation journey in the GCC is not without challenges. One significant hurdle is the need for a skilled workforce capable of implementing and managing these advanced technologies. GCC countries are investing heavily in education and training programs to bridge the digital skills gap and ensure a sustainable digital transformation (Albakri, 2023). Additionally, cybersecurity concerns have become increasingly prominent as the region becomes more digitally connected, necessitating robust security measures and policies (Deloitte, 2020).

Cybersecurity in GCC

This section discusses the underlying issues of cybersecurity in GCC from the models to the challenges involved in the cyber infrastructure in GCC (see Figure 7). The Iceberg Model provides a comprehensive understanding of the multifaceted nature of digital transformation and cybersecurity fears in the GCC. By addressing the deeper systemic structures and mental models, the region can develop more effective strategies to enhance cybersecurity resilience and support its digital transformation goals. Following the issues, discussed in this section, the proceeding section thereafter discusses potential strategies to mitigate cybersecurity fears.

Figure 7. Iceberg Model of tangible and intangible issues pertaining to digital transformation and cybersecurity in the GCC

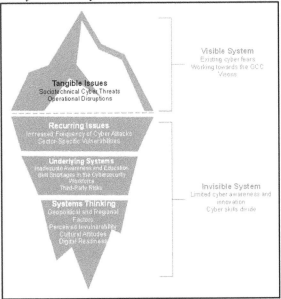

Cybersecurity Models

The GCC countries have developed robust national cybersecurity frameworks to safeguard their critical infrastructure and digital assets. One notable example is the Saudi Arabian Monetary Authority (SAMA) Cybersecurity Framework, which is specifically designed for financial institutions. This framework is based on international cybersecurity standards such as NIST, ISO, and PCI, and it aims to ensure that cybersecurity risks are effectively managed across all member organisations. The SAMA Cybersecurity Framework provides comprehensive guidelines for implementing, maintaining, and improving cybersecurity controls, covering aspects such as confidentiality, integrity, and availability of information assets (SAMA, 2021). This framework exemplifies the GCC's commitment to aligning with global best practices to enhance cybersecurity resilience (Bassant & Shires, 2022).

Figure 8. NIST Cybersecurity Framework

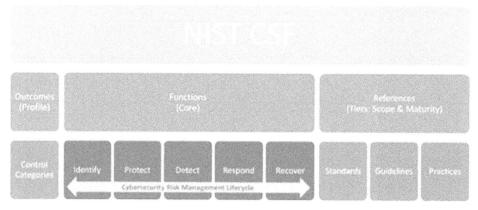

Implementation of the Dubai Cyber Security Strategy

Dubai has implemented a multi-phased cybersecurity strategy to protect its digital infrastructure and enhance its resilience against cyber threats. The first phase of the Dubai Cyber Security Strategy, launched in 2017, focused on creating a cyber-smart nation, fostering innovation, and ensuring cybersecurity and resilience. The second phase, announced in 2023, builds on these foundations and introduces new pillars such as a cyber-secure society, an incubator for innovation, a resilient cyber city, and active cyber collaboration. This strategy aims to position Dubai as a global leader in cybersecurity by adopting advanced technical solutions and fostering public-private partnerships (Dark Reading, 2023; Gulf Business, 2023). The strategy's comprehensive approach has been instrumental in enhancing Dubai's cybersecurity posture and fostering a culture of cybersecurity awareness (Shires & Hakmeh, 2020).

Cybersecurity Agencies and Organisations

Dedicated cybersecurity organisations and Computer Emergency Response Teams (CERTs) play a crucial role in the GCC's cybersecurity landscape. These entities are responsible for coordinating responses to cyber incidents, conducting threat assessments, and providing guidance on best practices. For example, the UAE's National Electronic Security Authority (NESA) and Saudi Arabia's National Cybersecurity Authority (NCA) are pivotal in shaping national cybersecurity policies and strategies. These agencies work closely with CERTs to enhance the region's cyber resilience and respond effectively to cyber threats (Chatham House, 2020). The establishment of these organisations underscores the GCC's proactive approach to cybersecurity and its commitment to building robust defensive capabilities (Bassant & Shires, 2022).

Regulatory and Compliance Standards

Adhering to international standards and best practices is essential for maintaining robust cybersecurity in the GCC. Key regulations and compliance requirements include the implementation of ISO 27001 standards and the adoption of the NIST Cybersecurity Framework. These standards help organisations establish a systematic approach to managing sensitive information and ensure compliance with legal and regulatory requirements. For instance, the UAE's Information Assurance Standards (IAS) are based on ISO 27001 and NIST frameworks, providing a comprehensive set of guidelines for securing information systems (Chatham House, 2020; Cloud Networks, 2023). Compliance with these standards is crucial for mitigating risks and enhancing the overall cybersecurity posture of organisations in the GCC (Shires & Hakmeh, 2020).

Public-Private Partnerships

Public-private partnerships are vital for enhancing cybersecurity in the GCC. Collaboration between government entities and private sector organisations facilitates the sharing of expertise, resources, and threat intelligence. Successful case studies include the partnership between Dubai's Electronic Security Centre and various private sector firms to implement the Dubai Cyber Security Strategy. These partnerships have led to significant advancements in cybersecurity capabilities and have fostered a collaborative approach to addressing cyber threats (Ipsos, 2021). Such collaborations are essential for building a resilient cybersecurity ecosystem and ensuring the protection of critical infrastructure (Shires & Hakmeh, 2020).

Cyber Threat Intelligence and Sharing

The implementation of Cyber Threat Intelligence (CTI) principles is particularly prominent in Saudi Arabia, where the National Cybersecurity Authority (NCA) has established frameworks for sharing threat intelligence among critical infrastructure sectors. This approach enhances situational awareness and enables proactive measures to mitigate cyber threats. The benefits of threat intelligence sharing among GCC countries include improved detection and response capabilities, reduced duplication of efforts, and a more coordinated approach to cybersecurity (Chatham House, 2020). Effective CTI practices are crucial for enhancing the region's ability to anticipate and respond to emerging cyber threats (Bassant & Shires, 2022).

RISING CYBER THREATS IN THE GCC

Types of Cyber Threats

The GCC region faces a diverse array of cyber threats, both technical and sociotechnical, that pose significant risks to its digital infrastructure and societal stability. Technical threats such as data breaches, ransomware, phishing, and advanced persistent threats (APTs) are prevalent in the GCC. Data breaches have become increasingly costly, with the average cost of a data breach in the GCC reaching $8.07 million in 2023, significantly higher than the global average of $4.45 million (IBM Security, 2023). Ransomware attacks have also surged, targeting critical sectors such as healthcare and finance. For instance, some organisations in the UAE and Saudi Arabia have paid up to $1.4 million in ransom to recover their data (Palo Alto Networks, 2023). Phishing attacks are another major concern, with over 755 phishing incidents recorded against GCC targets in a recent study period (Kaspersky, 2023). APTs, often state-sponsored, are increasingly targeting critical infrastructure and government entities, aiming to disrupt operations and steal sensitive information (FireEye, 2023). Sociotechnical impacts of cyber threats in the GCC are profound, affecting both individuals and society at large. Disruptions to essential services and critical infrastructure can have cascading effects on economic stability and public safety. For example, ransomware attacks on healthcare providers during the COVID-19 pandemic not only caused financial losses but also jeopardised patient care and public health (World Health Organisation, 2021). Additionally, the erosion of public trust in digital systems and e-government services due to frequent cyber incidents can undermine the region's digital transformation efforts (Alghawi et al., 2024). Notable cyber incidents in the GCC highlight the severity of these threats. The 2012 Shamoon attack on Saudi Aramco, which wiped out data on over 30,000 computers, remains one of the most devastating cyberattacks in the region's history (Bronk & Tikk-Ringas, 2013). The 2017 hack of the Qatar News Agency, allegedly orchestrated by UAE-based actors, triggered a major diplomatic crisis and showcased the geopolitical dimensions of cyber threats in the GCC (BBC News, 2017). More recently, ransomware attacks on financial institutions and healthcare providers have underscored the persistent and evolving nature of cyber threats in the region (Palo Alto Networks, 2023).

Geopolitical and Regional Factors

Geopolitical and regional factors significantly influence the cybersecurity landscape in the GCC. Regional conflicts and rivalries, particularly between Iran and GCC states, drive increased state-sponsored cyber activities. Iran-linked APT groups have been implicated in numerous cyberattacks targeting the energy and aviation sectors in Saudi Arabia and the UAE, reflecting the strategic importance of these industries (FireEye, 2023). The rapid digitalization and smart city initiatives in the GCC have expanded the attack surface, making the region an attractive target for cyber adversaries (Alghawi et al., 2024). Global cybersecurity trends, such as the rise of ransomware-as-a-service, also impact the GCC. These trends facilitate the proliferation of sophisticated cyber tools and techniques, enabling even less skilled attackers to launch impactful cyberattacks (Palo Alto Networks, 2023). Major events like the 2022 FIFA World Cup in Qatar have further heightened the region's exposure to cyber threats, as high-profile events attract cybercriminals seeking to exploit vulnerabilities for financial gain or political motives (Kaspersky, 2023). Case studies of significant cyber-attacks illustrate the complex interplay of regional and global factors. The alleged UAE-based hack of the Qatar News Agency in 2017, which involved the dissemination of false information, exemplifies how cyber operations can be used to exacerbate geopolitical tensions (BBC News, 2017). Similarly, Iran-linked APT groups have conducted cyber espionage campaigns against critical infrastructure in Saudi Arabia and the UAE, aiming to gather intelligence and disrupt operations (FireEye, 2023). The ransomware attacks on healthcare providers in the UAE and Saudi Arabia during the COVID-19 pandemic highlight the opportunistic nature of cybercriminals who exploit crises to maximise their impact (World Health Organisation, 2021).

CYBERSECURITY CHALLENGES IN THE GCC

Awareness and Education Deficits

The current state of cybersecurity literacy in the GCC is marked by significant gaps, despite the region's rapid digital transformation and increasing cyber threats. A detailed study by Chatham House (2020) highlights that while GCC states have made strides in developing national cybersecurity strategies and frameworks, there remains a lack of detailed guidance for individuals and organisations on implementing these strategies effectively. This gap in cybersecurity awareness and education is further exacerbated by the limited availability of publicly accessible information on the services provided by national cybersecurity organisations. Consequently, these organisations struggle to promote effective IT security practices and create a culture of cyber hygiene. To address these deficits, various initiatives have been launched to improve cybersecurity awareness and education in the GCC. For instance, the UAE has introduced the Information Assurance Standards (IAS), which are based on international standards such as ISO 27001 and the NIST Cybersecurity

Framework, to provide comprehensive guidelines for securing information systems (Cloud Networks, 2023). Additionally, universities across the GCC are increasingly offering undergraduate and graduate programs in cybersecurity, with significant enrolment by female students, indicating a growing interest in the field (Chatham House, 2020). These educational initiatives aim to build a knowledgeable workforce capable of addressing the region's cybersecurity challenges.

Skill Shortages and Workforce Development

The GCC region faces a critical shortage of cybersecurity professionals, which poses a significant challenge to its efforts to enhance digital security. A report by Ipsos (2022) reveals that the cybersecurity talent gap in the GCC is widening, with a notable lack of skilled professionals to meet the growing demand for cybersecurity expertise. This shortage is particularly pronounced in critical sectors such as telecommunications, banking, and oil and gas, where the complexity of cyber threats necessitates advanced technical skills and expertise. To bridge this talent gap, several training programs and educational initiatives have been implemented. For example, Saudi Arabia's National Cybersecurity Authority (NCA) has launched various capacity-building programs aimed at developing local cybersecurity talent (Ipsos, 2022). These programs include hands-on training initiatives, certification courses, and partnerships with international cybersecurity organisations to provide advanced training and accreditation. Additionally, the UAE has established cybersecurity centres of excellence in collaboration with leading universities to promote research and development in cybersecurity (Chatham House, 2020). These efforts are crucial for nurturing a skilled cybersecurity workforce capable of protecting the region's critical infrastructure and digital assets.

Figure 9. Skills Divide in GCC Contributing on Cyber Fears

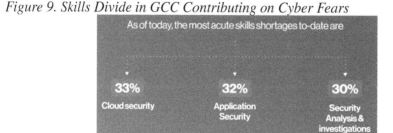

Third-Party Risks

The reliance on external vendors and partners introduces significant third-party cybersecurity risks in the GCC. A compromised third-party vendor can unknowingly introduce vulnerabilities into an organisation's digital ecosystem, creating potential entry points for cyber attackers. This risk is particularly acute in the context of smart cities, where interconnected systems and devices rely heavily on third-party technologies and services (A.T. Kearney, 2023). The complexity of these ecosystems makes it challenging to monitor and manage third-party risks effectively. To mitigate these risks, GCC countries have adopted various strategies. For instance, the Saudi Arabian Monetary Authority (SAMA) Cybersecurity Framework includes specific requirements for managing third-party cybersecurity risks, such as conducting regular security assessments and audits of external vendors (SAMA, 2021). Additionally, the Central Bank of the UAE has established a networking and cybersecurity operations centre to monitor and manage cyber risks associated with third-party service providers (The National, 2022). These measures are designed to enhance the overall security posture of organisations by ensuring that third-party vendors adhere to stringent cybersecurity standards and practices.

NATIONAL AND REGIONAL CYBERSECURITY STRATEGIES

National Cybersecurity Strategies

The GCC countries have developed comprehensive national cybersecurity strategies to address the rapidly evolving cyber threat landscape. These strategies are aligned with international standards and tailored to the specific needs of each country. For instance, Saudi Arabia's National Cybersecurity Authority (NCA) has launched a National Cybersecurity Strategy aimed at enhancing cyber resilience, fostering technical capabilities, and promoting awareness and education (National Cybersecurity Authority, 2023). The strategy includes initiatives such as the HA-SEEN portal, which provides cybersecurity services and supports communication mechanisms for national beneficiaries (Microminder, 2023). Similarly, the UAE's National Cybersecurity Strategy focuses on creating a secure and resilient cyberspace by developing cyber capabilities and encouraging global cooperation. This strategy includes the implementation of the Information Assurance Standards (IAS), which are based on international standards such as ISO 27001 and the NIST Cybersecurity Framework (Cloud Networks, 2023). The UAE has also established a national cybersecurity agency to oversee the implementation of these standards and ensure compliance across various sectors. Oman, Bahrain, Kuwait, and Qatar have also developed their own national cybersecurity strategies, each focusing on enhancing their cybersecurity posture through the adoption of international standards, the establishment of dedicated cybersecurity agencies, and the implementation of robust regulatory frameworks (Chatham House, 2020). These strategies are designed to protect critical infrastructure, safeguard personal information, and promote a culture of cybersecurity awareness and hygiene.

Regional Cybersecurity Collaboration

Regional collaboration is a key component of the GCC's approach to cybersecurity. The GCC countries have recognised the importance of working together to share threat intelligence, best practices, and resources to combat cyber threats effectively. Initiatives such as joint cybersecurity exercises and the establishment of regional cybersecurity agencies have been instrumental in enhancing the collective cybersecurity posture of the region (Chatham House, 2020). One notable example of regional collaboration is the GCC Cybersecurity Alliance, which facilitates information sharing and cooperation among member states. This alliance aims to create a unified defence against cyber threats by leveraging the collective expertise and resources of the GCC countries. The alliance also promotes the development of common cybersecurity standards and practices to ensure a consistent and robust defence across the region (Cybil Portal, 2021). In addition to regional collaboration, the GCC countries have also engaged in international partnerships to enhance their cybersecurity capabilities. For instance, Saudi Arabia has established bilateral partnerships with other countries' cybersecurity authorities for threat intelligence exchange and best practices. The country also actively participates in international forums and conventions to contribute to global cybersecurity discussions and initiatives (Microminder, 2023).

Implementation of Cybersecurity Strategies

The implementation of national and regional cybersecurity strategies in the GCC involves several key components. First, the adoption of comprehensive cybersecurity frameworks such as the NIST Cybersecurity Framework (CSF) 2.0 provides a structured approach to managing cybersecurity risks. These frameworks offer a common language and set of standards for organisations to better understand, assess, prioritise, and communicate their cybersecurity efforts (NIST, 2024). Second, enhancing cybersecurity governance is crucial for integrating cybersecurity as a key component of enterprise risk management. This involves recognising cybersecurity alongside financial and reputational risks and ensuring that cybersecurity considerations are embedded in the organisation's overall risk management strategy (NCSC, 2023).

Third, investing in cybersecurity education and training is essential for addressing skill shortages and building a knowledgeable workforce. The GCC countries have established specialised cybersecurity academies, promoted certifications, and provided scholarships to attract and retain cybersecurity professionals (Ipsos, 2022). These educational initiatives aim to develop a strong cybersecurity workforce capable of combating sophisticated threats. Fourth, implementing multi-layered security measures is necessary to protect against a wide range of cyber threats. This involves deploying various security controls, such as firewalls, intrusion detection systems, and endpoint protection, to create a robust defence-in-depth strategy (Imperva, 2023). Regular vulnerability assessments and the development of incident response plans are also critical for ensuring systems are resilient against emerging threats (CISA, 2023). Finally, promoting cyber hygiene practices and leveraging emerging technologies securely are essential for maintaining a strong cybersecurity posture. Encouraging the adoption of basic cybersecurity practices and addressing the security implications of adopting AI, IoT, and cloud computing are crucial for protecting against new vulnerabilities (Chatham House, 2020).

PROTECTING CRITICAL INFRASTRUCTURE

Sector-Specific Vulnerabilities

The protection of critical infrastructure in the GCC is paramount, given the region's reliance on sectors such as energy, finance, healthcare, and transportation. Each of these sectors faces unique cybersecurity threats that require tailored mitigation strategies. In the energy sector, for example, the integration of Industrial Control Systems (ICS) with IT networks has introduced significant vulnerabilities. Cyberattacks targeting these systems can disrupt operations, as seen in the 2012 Shamoon attack on Saudi Aramco, which significantly impacted the company's operations (Bronk & Tikk-Ringas, 2013). To mitigate such threats, energy companies are increasingly adopting advanced threat detection systems and implementing robust incident response plans (Energy Sector Cybersecurity Framework, 2023). The finance sector in the GCC is also a prime target for cybercriminals due to the high value of transactions and sensitive financial data. Ransomware and phishing attacks are particularly prevalent, with financial institutions in the UAE and Saudi Arabia frequently targeted. To counter these threats, banks are investing in multi-factor authentication (MFA), regular security audits, and employee training programs to recognise and respond to phishing attempts (FTI Consulting, 2023). Additionally, regulatory frameworks such as the Saudi Arabian Monetary Authority (SAMA) Cybersecurity Framework mandate stringent cybersecurity measures for financial institutions, enhancing their resilience against cyber threats (SAMA, 2021). Health-care is another critical sector vulnerable to cyberattacks, particularly ransomware. The interconnected nature of healthcare systems, including electronic health records and medical devices, creates numerous entry points for attackers. A comprehensive review by Javaid et al. (2023) highlights the need for healthcare organisations to implement robust cybersecurity measures, such as network segmentation, regular software updates, and staff training, to protect patient data and ensure the continuity of care. The transportation sector, with its reliance on interconnected systems for logistics and operations, also faces significant cybersecurity risks. Cyberattacks on transportation infrastructure can lead to severe disruptions, affecting both economic activities and public safety. Implementing advanced monitoring systems and conducting regular vulnerability assessments are crucial strategies to mitigate these risks (Chatham House, 2020).

Case Studies

Several case studies illustrate successful protection measures and lessons learned from past incidents in the GCC. The 2017 cyberattack on Qatar's Ministry of Transport and Communications serves as a notable example. The ministry had implemented a comprehensive cybersecurity strategy that included real-time threat monitoring, incident response protocols, and regular security drills. These measures enabled the ministry to quickly detect and contain the attack, minimising its impact on critical transportation systems (Chatham House, 2020). Another successful case is the cybersecurity framework adopted by the Dubai Electricity and Water Authority (DEWA). DEWA's cybersecurity strategy includes the deployment of advanced threat intelligence platforms, continuous network monitoring, and a robust incident response plan. This proactive approach has significantly enhanced DEWA's ability to detect and respond to cyber threats, ensuring the security of its critical infrastructure (A.T. Kearney, 2023). The lessons learned from these case studies emphasise the importance of a proactive cybersecurity posture, continuous monitoring, and regular training and drills to enhance resilience against cyber threats. In contrast, the 2012 Shamoon attack on Saudi Aramco underscores the devastating impact of insufficient cybersecurity measures. The attack, which wiped out data on over 30,000 computers, highlighted the need for robust backup systems, comprehensive incident response plans, and regular security assessments. Following the attack, Saudi Aramco invested heavily in enhancing its cybersecurity infrastructure, including the implementation of advanced threat detection systems and the establishment of a dedicated cybersecurity operations centre (Bronk & Tikk-Ringas, 2013).

Potential Strategies to Mitigate Cybersecurity Fears

Based on the above discussions, potential strategies to mitigate cybersecurity fears in GCC have been proposed:

Tangible Issues

Sociotechnical Cyber Threats: To mitigate sociotechnical cyber threats, the GCC must invest in comprehensive cybersecurity training and awareness programs. Research indicates that human error is a significant factor in cyber breaches, with over 90% of data breaches linked to phishing and social engineering attacks (Verizon, 2023). Implementing regular cybersecurity drills and simulations can prepare organisations for real-world scenarios, while fostering a culture of security awareness among employees (IBM Security, 2023). Collaboration between technical teams and end-users can create a more integrated approach to identifying and responding to threats, leveraging frameworks like the NIST Cybersecurity Framework for structured guidance (NIST, 2024).

Operational Disruptions: Operational disruptions can be mitigated by adopting robust incident response plans and continuity strategies. The National Institute of Standards and Technology (NIST) highlights the importance of developing and regularly updating incident response protocols to quickly address and recover from cyber incidents (NIST, 2021). Implementing redundant systems and backup processes ensures that critical operations can continue even during a cyber attack, as demonstrated by the successful containment of the 2017 WannaCry ransomware attack by organisations with robust continuity plans (Europol, 2018). Regular testing of these plans through simulations and drills can help identify and address any weaknesses (CISA, 2023).

Intangible Issues

Recurring Issues

Increased Frequency of Cyber Attacks: To combat the increasing frequency of cyber-attacks, the GCC should invest in advanced threat detection and response technologies. The use of artificial intelligence and machine learning can enhance the ability to detect and mitigate threats in real time, as noted by McKinsey & Company (2023). Establishing a regional cyber threat intelligence sharing platform can help organisations stay informed about the latest threats and best practices, similar to the EU's approach with ENISA (European Union Agency for Cybersecurity, 2022).

Continuous monitoring and regular updates to security protocols are essential to stay ahead of evolving cyber threats (FireEye, 2023).

Sector-Specific Vulnerabilities: Addressing sector-specific vulnerabilities requires tailored cybersecurity frameworks for different industries. For instance, the energy sector might focus on securing industrial control systems, while the financial sector prioritises data encryption and transaction security. The Saudi Arabian Monetary Authority (SAMA) Cybersecurity Framework mandates stringent cybersecurity measures for financial institutions, enhancing their resilience against cyber threats (SAMA, 2021). Regulatory bodies should develop industry-specific guidelines and standards, ensuring compliance and promoting best practices, as seen in the healthcare sector's adoption of the Health Insurance Portability and Accountability Act (HIPAA) in the United States (HHS, 2023).

Underlying Systems

Inadequate Awareness and Education: To overcome inadequate awareness and education, GCC countries should implement widespread cybersecurity literacy programs. According to a report by Chatham House (2020), integrating cybersecurity education into school curricula and professional development courses ensures a broad understanding of cybersecurity principles. Public awareness campaigns can inform the general population about the importance of cybersecurity, similar to initiatives in Estonia, which has one of the highest levels of cybersecurity awareness globally (World Bank, 2020). Encouraging certification and continuous learning for cybersecurity professionals can keep them updated with the latest trends and threats (ISC2, 2023).

Skill Shortages in the Cybersecurity Workforce: Addressing skill shortages involves investing in education and training programs to develop local talent. The GCC countries should establish cybersecurity academies and partnerships with international institutions to provide high-quality training, following the model of Singapore's Cybersecurity Agency (CSA, 2021). Offering scholarships and incentives for students pursuing careers in cybersecurity can attract more individuals to the field (Ipsos, 2022). Promoting diversity within the cybersecurity workforce can also tap into a broader talent pool and bring varied perspectives to problem-solving (WiCyS, 2023).

Third-Party Risks: Mitigating third-party risks requires stringent vendor management practices. Organisations should conduct thorough security assessments of third-party vendors and require them to comply with established cybersecurity standards. Regular audits and continuous monitoring of third-party activities can help identify potential vulnerabilities (Gartner, 2023). Establishing clear contracts that define security responsibilities and expectations can ensure that vendors maintain robust cybersecurity practices, as exemplified by the guidelines set forth by the UK's National Cyber Security Centre (NCSC, 2023).

Systems Thinking

Geopolitical and Regional Factors: Geopolitical and regional factors necessitate a collaborative approach to cybersecurity. GCC countries should engage in regional cooperation to share threat intelligence, best practices, and resources, similar to the European Union's approach with ENISA (European Union Agency for Cybersecurity, 2022). Establishing a GCC-wide cybersecurity framework can provide a unified defense against state-sponsored and regional cyber threats (Chatham House, 2020). Diplomatic efforts should also focus on building international partnerships to enhance cybersecurity resilience and response capabilities (MITRE, 2023).

Perceived Invulnerability: To address the perception of invulnerability, it is crucial to foster a culture of cybersecurity vigilance. Regular risk assessments and transparent communication about potential threats and vulnerabilities are essential (NIST, 2021). Leadership should emphasise the importance of cybersecurity at all levels of the organisation, demonstrating a commitment to proactive security measures. Encouraging a mindset that views cybersecurity as a shared responsibility can help mitigate complacency (IBM Security, 2023).

Cultural Attitudes: Changing cultural attitudes towards cybersecurity involves promoting a proactive and security-conscious mindset. Continuous education and awareness programs that highlight the importance of cybersecurity in everyday activities are essential (Chatham House, 2020). Encouraging the reporting of suspicious activities and fostering an environment where employees feel comfortable discussing security concerns can enhance overall security posture (Verizon, 2023). Celebrating cybersecurity successes and recognising the contributions of individuals can also reinforce positive attitudes towards security (NIST, 2021).

Digital Readiness: Enhancing digital readiness requires a strategic approach to technology adoption and integration. GCC countries should invest in modernising their digital infrastructure and ensuring that security is a fundamental component of all digital initiatives (McKinsey & Company, 2023). Providing training and resources to help organisations and individuals adapt to new technologies securely can reduce the risk of vulnerabilities. Regular assessments of digital maturity and readiness can help identify areas for improvement and guide strategic investments in technology and security (Chatham House, 2020).

CONCLUSION

This chapter has explored the multifaceted landscape of cybersecurity in the GCC, highlighting the region's rapid digital transformation and the concurrent rise in cyber threats. The historical context underscores the shift from an oil-dependent economy to a knowledge-based one driven by technological innovation, as seen in initiatives like Saudi Arabia's Vision 2030 and the UAE's National Innovation Strategy (Deloitte, 2020). The importance of cybersecurity in national security has been emphasised, given the diverse array of cyber threats, including data breaches, ransomware, phishing, and advanced persistent threats (APTs) that pose significant risks to critical infrastructure and societal stability (IBM Security, 2023; FireEye, 2023). The chapter has detailed various cybersecurity challenges, such as awareness and education deficits, skill shortages, and third-party risks. Despite significant investments in cybersecurity frameworks and initiatives, there remains a need for more detailed guidance and public awareness to foster a culture of cybersecurity (Chatham House, 2020). The sector-specific vulnerabilities in energy, finance, healthcare, and transportation highlight the unique cybersecurity threats each sector faces and the tailored mitigation strategies required (Bronk & Tikk-Ringas, 2013; Javaid et al., 2023). Case studies have illustrated successful protection measures and lessons learned from past incidents, underscoring the importance of proactive cybersecurity postures, continuous monitoring, and regular training and drills (A.T. Kearney, 2023).

To enhance cybersecurity and support digital transformation in the GCC, several actionable recommendations are proposed. These include adopting comprehensive cybersecurity frameworks like NIST CSF 2.0 to establish standardised practices, enhancing cybersecurity governance by integrating it into enterprise risk management, and fostering regional collaboration to share threat intelligence and best practices. Additionally, investing in cybersecurity education and training is crucial to address skill shortages, while implementing multi-layered security measures can protect against a wide range of threats. Regular vulnerability assessments and the development of incident response plans are essential for resilience, and sector-specific security protocols are necessary to protect critical infrastructure. Promoting cyber hygiene practices and securely leveraging emerging technologies like AI, IoT, and cloud computing are also key strategies to maintain a strong cybersecurity posture in the face of evolving threats.

The importance of ongoing vigilance and adaptation in the face of evolving cyber threats cannot be overstated. As the GCC continues to advance its digital transformation, maintaining a strong cybersecurity posture will be critical to ensuring the security and resilience of its digital infrastructure. Continuous monitoring, regular training, and proactive measures are essential to stay ahead of sophisticated cyber adversaries. By addressing the identified challenges and implementing the recommended strategies, the GCC can enhance its cybersecurity resilience and protect its digital assets from the ever-evolving landscape of cyber threats.

REFERENCES

Albakri, M. (2023). Shifting Paradigms in the Rapidly Developing Global Digital Ecosystem: A GCC Perspective. In *Digital Entrepreneurship and Co-Creating Value Through Digital Encounters* (pp. 12–16). IGI Global.

Alghawi, K., Ameen, N., Bhaumik, A., Haddoud, M. Y., & Alrajawy, I. (2024). Smart cities and communities in the GCC region: From top-down city development to more local approaches. *Frontiers in Built Environment*, 10.

Bassant, H., & Shires, J. (2022). Cybersecurity in the GCC: From Economic Development to Geopolitical Controversy. *Middle East Policy*, 29(1), 16–29.

BBC News. (2017) *Qatar crisis: Saudi Arabia and allies sever ties with Qatar*. Available at: https://www.bbc.com/news/world-middle-east-40155829 (Accessed: 16 September 2024).

Bronk, C., & Tikk-Ringas, E. (2013). The Cyber Attack on Saudi Aramco. *Survival*, 55(2), 81–96. DOI: 10.1080/00396338.2013.784468

Brown, H. (1983). *Thinking About National Security: Defense and Foreign Policy in a Dangerous World*. Westview Press.

Bughin, J., Catlin, T., Hirt, M., & Willmott, P. (2019) *Why digital strategies fail*, McKinsey Quarterly. Available at: https://www.mckinsey.com/business-functions/mckinsey-digital/our-insights/why-digital-strategies-fail (Accessed: 22 September 2024).

Chatham House. (2020) *The state of cybersecurity in the GCC: An overview*. Available at: https://www.chathamhouse.org/2020/03/gcc-cyber-resilient-0/state-cybersecurity-gcc-overview (Accessed: 24 September 2024).

China's National Security Strategy. (2015) *National Security Law of the People's Republic of China*. Available at: https://www.chinalawtranslate.com/en/national-security-law-2015/ (Accessed: 30 September 2024).

Chronicle, U. N. (2020) *National Security versus Global Security*. Available at: https://www.un.org/en/chronicle/article/national-security-versus-global-security (Accessed: 24 September 2024).

CISA. (2023) *Critical Infrastructure Security and Resilience*. Available at: https://www.cisa.gov/topics/critical-infrastructure-security-and-resilience (Accessed: 15 September 2024).

Cloud Networks. (2023) *Cybersecurity Regulations in the GCC: Compliance Management for Enterprises.* Available at: https://cloudnetworks.ae/articles/cs-regulations-gcc/ (Accessed: 12 September 2024).

Consulting, F. T. I. (2023) *Navigating Cybersecurity Threat Landscape in the Middle East.* Available at: https://www.fticonsulting.com/insights/articles/navigating-cybersecurity-threat-landscape-middle-east (Accessed: 16 September 2024).

Craigen, D., Diakun-Thibault, N., & Purse, R. (2014). Defining cybersecurity. *Technology Innovation Management Review*, 4(10), 13–21. Retrieved September 30, 2024, from https://www.timreview.ca/article/835. DOI: 10.22215/timreview/835

Cyber Security Agency of Singapore (CSA). (2021) Available at: https://www.csa.gov.sg/ (Accessed: 30 September 2024).

Cybersecurity and Infrastructure Security Agency (CISA). (2023) *What is Cybersecurity?* Available at: https://www.cisa.gov/news-events/news/what-cybersecurity (Accessed: 30 September 2024).

Cybil Portal. (2021) *Cybersecurity in the GCC Countries.* Available at: https://cybilportal.org/projects/cybersecurity-in-the-gcc-countries/ (Accessed: 27 September 2024).

Dark Reading. (2023) *An Overview of Dubai's First and Second Cybersecurity Strategy.* Available at: https://www.darkreading.com/cybersecurity-analytics/overview-dubais-first-and-second-cybersecurity-strategy (Accessed: 28 September 2024).

Deloitte. (2020) *National Transformation in the Middle East: A Digital Journey.* Available at: https://www2.deloitte.com/content/dam/Deloitte/xe/Documents/technology-media-telecommunications/dtme_tmt_national-transformation-in-the-middleeast/National%20Transformation%20in%20the%20Middle%20East%20-%20A%20Digital%20Journey.pdf (Accessed: 21 September 2024).

Economist Intelligence Unit. (2020) *Innovating through tech in the GCC.* Available at: https://impact.economist.com/perspectives/sites/default/files/eiu_bahrain_edb_report.pdf (Accessed: 19 September 2024).

Energy Sector Cybersecurity Framework. (2023) *Roadmap to Achieve Energy Delivery Systems Cybersecurity.* Available at: https://energy.gov/sites/prod/files/Energy%20Delivery%20Systems%20Cybersecurity%20Roadmap_finalweb.pdf (Accessed: 30 September 2024).

European Union Agency for Cybersecurity (ENISA). (2022) Available at: https://www.enisa.europa.eu/ (Accessed: 22 September 2024).

FireEye. (2023) *APT Threat Activity in the Middle East.* Available at: https://www .fireeye.com/current-threats/apt-threat-activity/middle-east.html (Accessed: 30 September 2024).

Gartner (2023) *Gartner's Top Security and Risk Management Trends.* Available at: https://www.gartner.com/en/newsroom/press-releases/2023 (Accessed: 30 September 2024).

Governance, I. T. (2023) *What is Cyber Security? Definition & Best Practices.* Available at: https://www.itgovernance.co.uk/what-is-cybersecurity (Accessed: 23 September 2024).

Grajek, S. (2020) 'Top IT Issues, 2020: The Drive to Digital Transformation Begins', *EDUCAUSE Review.* Available at: https://er.educause.edu/articles/2020/1/top-it -issues-2020-the-drive-to-digital-transformation-begins (Accessed: 17 September 2024).

Gulf Business. (2023) *Dubai launches second cycle of its cybersecurity strategy.* Available at: https://gulfbusiness.com/dubai-bolsters-its-cybersecurity-strategy/ (Accessed: 30 September 2024).

Heritage Foundation. (2015) *What Is National Security?* Available at: https://www .heritage.org/sites/default/files/2019-10/2015_IndexOfUSMilitaryStrength_What %20Is%20National%20Security.pdf (Accessed: 30 September 2024).

Holmes, K. R. (2015). *What Is National Security?* The Heritage Foundation.

Imperva (2023) *What is Vulnerability Assessment | VA Tools and Best Practices.* Available at: https://www.imperva.com/learn/application-security/vulnerability -assessment/ (Accessed: 23 September 2024).

Ipsos (2021) *Addressing Cybersecurity Skill Shortages in the GCC Region.* Available at: https://www.ipsos.com/sites/default/files/ct/news/documents/2021-09/Addressing %20Cybersecurity%20Skill%20Shortages%20in%20the%20GCC%20Region.pdf (Accessed: 21 September 2024).

Ipsos (2022) *Addressing Cybersecurity Skill Shortages in the GCC Region.* Available at: https://www.ipsos.com/sites/default/files/ct/news/documents/2022-09/Ipsos%20 -%20PGI%20-%20Understanding%20Cybersecurity%20Skill%20Shortages%20in %20The%20GCC%20-Report.pdf (Accessed: 24 September 2024).

ISC. (2023) *Cybersecurity Workforce Study.* Available at: https://www.isc2.org/ Research/Workforce-Study (Accessed: 30 September 2024).

Javaid, M., Haleem, A., Singh, R. P., & Suman, R. (2023). *Towards insighting cybersecurity for healthcare domains: A comprehensive review of recent practices and trends.* ScienceDirect., DOI: 10.1016/j.sciencedirect.2023.01.004

Kaspersky (2023) *Phishing Attacks in the GCC: A Rising Threat.* Available at: https://www.kaspersky.com/blog/phishing-attacks-gcc-2023 (Accessed: 12 September 2024).

Kearney, A. T. (2023) *Cyber-proofing smart cities in the GCC.* Available at: https://www.middle-east.kearney.com/service/digital-analytics/article/cyber-proofing-smart-cities-in-the-gcc (Accessed: 14 September 2024).

Lippmann, W. (1943). *U.S. Foreign Policy: Shield of the Republic.* Little, Brown and Company.

Makinda, S. (2006). *Security in International Relations.* Routledge.

McKinsey. (2023) *State of AI in the Middle East's GCC countries.* Available at: https://www.mckinsey.com/capabilities/mckinsey-digital/our-insights/the-state-of-ai-in-gcc-countries-and-how-to-overcome-adoption-challenges (Accessed: 30 September 2024).

Microminder (2023) *The Initiatives and Strategies of National Cybersecurity Authority (NCA).* Available at: https://www.microminders.com/blog/the-initiatives-and-strategies-of-national-cybersecurity-authority-nca (Accessed: 16 September 2024).

MITRE. (2023) *Cyber Threat Intelligence Integration Center.* Available at: https://www.mitre.org/ (Accessed: 13 September 2024).

Nadkarni, S., & Prügl, R. (2021). Digital transformation: A review, synthesis and opportunities for future research. *Management Review Quarterly*, 71(2), 233–274. DOI: 10.1007/s11301-020-00185-7

National Cyber Security Centre (NCSC). (2023) *Third-Party Risk Management.* Available at: https://www.ncsc.gov.uk/ (Accessed: 14 September 2024).

National Cybersecurity Authority. (2023) *National Cybersecurity Strategy.* Available at: https://www.nca.gov.sa/en/national-cybersecurity-strategy (Accessed: 23 September 2024).

National Institute of Standards and Technology (NIST). (2021) *Glossary of Key Information Security Terms.* Available at: https://csrc.nist.gov/glossary/term/cybersecurity (Accessed: 21 September 2024).

NCSC. (2023) *Cyber security governance*. Available at: https://www.ncsc.gov.uk/collection/risk-management/cyber-security-governance (Accessed: 26 September 2024).

NIST. (2024) *The NIST Cybersecurity Framework (CSF) 2.0*. Available at: https://nvlpubs.nist.gov/nistpubs/CSWP/NIST.CSWP.29.pdf (Accessed: 16 September 2024).

Paleri, P. (2008). *National Security: Imperatives And Challenges*. Tata McGraw-Hill Education.

Palo Alto Networks. (2023) *Ransomware Threat Report 2023*. Available at: https://www.paloaltonetworks.com/resources/research/ransomware-threat-report-2023 (Accessed: 21 September 2024).

Saudi Arabian Monetary Authority (SAMA). (2021) *Cyber Security Framework*. Available at: https://www.sama.gov.sa/en-US/RulesInstructions/CyberSecurity/Cyber%20Security%20Framework.pdf (Accessed: 30 September 2024).

Security, I. B. M. (2023) *Cost of a Data Breach Report 2023*. Available at: https://www.ibm.com/security/data-breach (Accessed: 18 September 2024).

Shires, J., & Hakmeh, J. (2020) *Is the GCC Cyber Resilient?* Chatham House. Available at: https://www.chathamhouse.org/sites/default/files/CHHJ8019-GCC-Cyber-Briefing-200302-WEB.pdf (Accessed: 26 September 2024).

Statista (2024a) *Revenue in the Cybersecurity Market Worldwide from 2018 to 2029 (in Billion U.S. Dollars)*. Available at: https://www.statista.com/forecasts/1438758/revenue-cybersecurity-cybersecurity-market-worldwide (Accessed: 15 September 2024).

Statista (2024b) *Mobile Internet Penetration in the MENA Region by Country in 2022*. Available at: https://www.statista.com/forecasts/1169098/mobile-internet-penetration-in-mena-by-country (Accessed: 18 September 2024).

The National. (2022) *GCC banks minimise cyber risks with strong investment in digital security*. Available at: https://www.thenationalnews.com/business/banking/2022/05/17/gcc-banks-minimise-cyber-risks-with-strong-investment-in-digital-security-sp-says/ (Accessed: 30 September 2024).

United Nations. (1994). *Human Development Report 1994*. Oxford University Press.

U.S. Department of Health & Human Services (HHS). (2023) *Health Information Privacy*. Available at: https://www.hhs.gov/hipaa/index.html (Accessed: 30 September 2024).

Verizon (2023) *Data Breach Investigations Report*. Available at: https://www.verizon.com/business/resources/reports/dbir/ (Accessed: 24 September 2024).

Vial, G. (2019). Understanding digital transformation: A review and a research agenda. *The Journal of Strategic Information Systems*, 28(2), 118–144. DOI: 10.1016/j.jsis.2019.01.003

Women in CyberSecurity (WiCyS). (2023) Available at: https://www.wicys.org/ (Accessed: 26 September 2024).

World Bank. (2020) *Cybersecurity Capacity Review: Estonia*. Available at: https://www.worldbank.org/ (Accessed: 10 September 2024).

World Health Organization. (2021) *Cybersecurity and COVID-19: The impact on healthcare*. Available at: https://www.who.int/publications/cybersecurity-covid-19-impact-on-healthcare (Accessed: 30 September 2024).

ADDITIONAL READING

Ali, M. (2021). *Remote Work and Sustainable Changes for the Future of Global Business*. IGI Global. https://www.igi-global.com/book/remote-work-sustainable-changes-future/264375

Ali, M. (2022). *Future Role of Sustainable Innovative Technologies in Crisis Management*. IGI Global. https://www.igi-global.com/book/future-role-sustainable-innovative-technologies/281281

Ali, M. (2023). *Shifting Paradigms in the Rapidly Developing Global Digital Ecosystem: A GCC Perspective*. In Digital Entrepreneurship and Co-Creating Value Through Digital Encounters (pp. 145-166). IGI Global. https://www.igi-global.com/chapter/shifting-paradigms-in-the-rapidly-developing-global-digital-ecosystem/323525

Ali, M. (2023). T*axonomy of Industry 4.0 Technologies in Digital Entrepreneurship and Co-Creating Value*. In *Digital Entrepreneurship and Co-Creating Value Through Digital Encounters* (pp. 24–55). IGI Global., https://www.igi-global.com/chapter/taxonomy-of-industry-40-technologies-in-digital-entrepreneurship-and-co-creating-value/323520 DOI: 10.4018/978-1-6684-7416-7.ch002

Ali, M., & Wood-Harper, T. (2021). *Fostering Communication and Learning with Underutilized Technologies in Higher Education*. IGI Global. https://www.igi-global.com/book/fostering-communication-learning-underutilized-technologies/244593

Ali, M., Wood-Harper, T., & Kutar, M. (2023). Multi-Perspectives of Contemporary Digital Transformation Models of Complex Innovation Management. In *Digital Entrepreneurship and Co-Creating Value Through Digital Encounters* (pp. 79–96). IGI Global., https://www.igi-global.com/chapter/multi-perspectives-of-contemporary-digital-transformation-models-of-complex-innovation-management/323522 DOI: 10.4018/978-1-6684-7416-7.ch004

Ali, M. B. (2021). Internet of Things (IoT) to Foster Communication and Information Sharing: A Case of UK Higher Education. In Ali, M. B., & Wood-Harper, T. (Eds.), *Fostering Communication and Learning With Underutilized Technologies in Higher Education* (pp. 1–20). IGI Global., https://www.igi-global.com/chapter/internet-of-things-iot-to-foster-communication-and-information-sharing/262718/ DOI: 10.4018/978-1-7998-4846-2.ch001

Ali, M. B., & Wood-Harper, T. (2022). Artificial Intelligence (AI) as a Decision-Making Tool to Control Crisis Situations. In *Future Role of Sustainable Innovative Technologies in Crisis Management*. IGI Global., https://www.igi-global.com/chapter/artificial-intelligence-ai-as-a-decision-making-tool-to-control-crisis-situations/298931 DOI: 10.4018/978-1-7998-9815-3.ch006

Ali, M. B., Wood-Harper, T., & Ramlogan, R. (2020). A Framework Strategy to Overcome Trust Issues on Cloud Computing Adoption in Higher Education. In Modern Principles, Practices, and Algorithms for Cloud Security (pp. 162-183). IGI Global. https://www.igi-global.com/chapter/a-framework-strategy-to-overcome-trust-issues-on-cloud-computing-adoption-in-higher-education/238907/

KEY TERMS AND DEFINITIONS

Actor-Driven Transformation: Nadkarni and Prügl define DT as an actor-driven organisational transformation triggered by the adoption of technology-driven digital disruptions. This definition highlights the role of individuals and organisational actors in driving the transformation process (Nadkarni & Prügl, 2021).

Digital Transformation: Digital transformation (DT) is a concept that encompasses the integration of digital technologies into all areas of a business, fundamentally altering how organisations operate and deliver value to customers. This transformation is not just about technology but also involves significant cultural, workforce, and operational shifts. The definitions of DT vary across different sources, highlighting its multifaceted nature.

Holistic Change: EDUCAUSE describes DT as a series of deep and coordinated culture, workforce, and technology shifts that enable new educational and operating models, transforming an institution's operations, strategic directions, and value proposition. This definition underscores the coordinated and comprehensive nature of DT, involving multiple facets of an organisation (Grajek, 2020).

Integration of Digital Technology: According to The Enterprisers Project, DT involves the integration of digital technology into all business areas, leading to fundamental changes in operations and value delivery. This definition emphasises the comprehensive nature of DT, affecting every aspect of a business (Vial, 2019).

Rewiring Organisations: McKinsey defines DT as the fundamental rewiring of how an organisation operates, with the goal of continuously deploying technology at scale to create value. This perspective focuses on the strategic and operational overhaul required for successful digital transformation (Bughin et al., 2019).

Chapter 3
Digital Transformation in UK Contemporary Healthcare:
Lessons From NHS England

Mark Schofield

Research and Training Centre, Manchester, UK

ABSTRACT

In the modern age, the demand for seamless digital services extends into government sectors, including healthcare. NHS England exemplifies significant digital transformation in this domain. Understanding governmental digital evolution in healthcare is crucial for stakeholders on similar paths. This chapter dissects common trends in government digital transformation and lessons from NHS England's efforts. By exploring digital dynamics within government, with a focus on healthcare, it elucidates methodologies, challenges, and potential pathways for sustainable digital evolution. It offers insights for stakeholders, emphasizing user-centric design, iterative approaches, and transparent governance. Additionally, it highlights the complexities and unique challenges in healthcare digitization, providing valuable lessons for stakeholders.

INTRODUCTION

Digital transformation has become an imperative for modernising government services, including healthcare, to meet contemporary demands (Mergel et al., 2019). The integration of digital technologies into healthcare systems promises to enhance efficiency, improve patient outcomes, and streamline operations. However, the

DOI: 10.4018/979-8-3693-5966-2.ch003

journey towards digital transformation is fraught with challenges, particularly in complex and bureaucratic environments like the NHS (Weerakkody et al., 2021). The healthcare sector, in particular, faces unique challenges in its digital transformation journey. These include the need to maintain patient privacy and data security, ensure interoperability between various systems, and overcome resistance to change among healthcare professionals (Maguire et al., 2021).

Despite the above challenges, the potential benefits of digital transformation in healthcare are significant, including improved patient care, reduced costs, and enhanced operational efficiency (Cinar et al., 2019). The healthcare sector's complexity, characterised by diverse stakeholders and stringent regulatory requirements, makes digital transformation particularly challenging. The need for interoperability between various systems and the necessity to maintain patient privacy and data security are significant hurdles. Moreover, resistance to change among healthcare professionals can impede the adoption of new technologies. These challenges necessitate a comprehensive approach that addresses technological, organisational, and cultural aspects of transformation (Maguire et al., 2021). A critical aspect of digital transformation in healthcare is the shift towards a consumer-centric approach. As noted by Betts and Korenda (2019), "Consumers expect personalised healthcare journeys, a standard consistent with their interactions in other industries" (p. 3). This shift necessitates a fundamental rethinking of how healthcare services are designed and delivered, with a focus on convenience, access, and transparency (Betts & Korenda, 2019).

Figure 1. 8 Key Domain of Change in Healthcare

Government-led digital initiatives provide a blueprint for other sectors aiming for similar transformations (Mergel et al., 2019). By examining the methodologies and challenges faced by government entities, stakeholders can gain valuable insights into best practices and potential pitfalls. This understanding is crucial for developing strategies that are both effective and sustainable (Weerakkody et al., 2021). The lessons learned from governmental digital transformation efforts can be particularly valuable for the private sector, as they often deal with similar challenges related to scale, complexity, and regulatory compliance (Cinar et al., 2019). Moreover, the public sector's focus on serving citizens aligns with the customer-centric approach that many businesses strive to adopt in their digital transformation journeys (Maguire et al., 2021). Government-led digital transformation initiatives often involve large-scale changes that require coordination across multiple departments and agencies. This complexity can lead to challenges in implementation and governance. However, the public sector's focus on serving citizens provides a strong foundation for customer-centric digital transformation. By examining governmental approaches, private sector organisations can learn valuable lessons about managing complexity, ensuring compliance, and maintaining a focus on user needs (Weerakkody et al., 2021). Strategies for digital transformation in public sectors, such as those outlined by Sánchez-Ortiz et al. (2020), emphasise the importance of lean and agile methodologies in facilitating transformation processes. These approaches, when applied to public administration, can lead to more effective and efficient systems, particularly in critical areas such as public investment and procurement (Sánchez-Ortiz et al., 2020).

Figure 2. Latest Trends Around DT in Healthcare

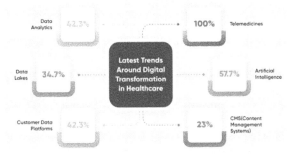

NHS England stands as a leading exemplar in the realm of digital transformation within healthcare (Weerakkody et al., 2021). With its vast network of services and significant patient base, the NHS offers a unique case study for understanding the complexities and potential of digital healthcare initiatives (Maguire et al., 2021). The lessons learned from NHS England's digital transformation efforts can serve as a guide for other healthcare systems worldwide (Cinar et al., 2019). The NHS has embarked on several ambitious digital transformation projects, including the development of a centralised electronic health record system, the implementation of telemedicine services, and the use of artificial intelligence for diagnostics and treatment planning (NHS England, 2022). These initiatives not only aim to improve patient care but also to create a more efficient and cost-effective healthcare system (Weerakkody et al., 2021). However, the journey has not been without its challenges. The NHS has faced issues related to data privacy, system interoperability, and resistance to change from some healthcare professionals (Maguire et al., 2021). These challenges highlight the need for a comprehensive approach to digital transformation that addresses not only technological aspects but also organisational culture and change management (Cinar et al., 2019). The NHS's digital transformation journey underscores the importance of addressing both technological and organisational challenges. Issues such as data privacy, system interoperability, and resistance to change are significant barriers that require careful management. The NHS's experience highlights the need for a holistic approach that combines technological innovation with organisational change management strategies. This approach ensures that digital transformation initiatives are not only implemented but also sustained over the long term (Maguire et al., 2021).

DIGITAL TRANSFORMATION METHODOLOGIES

Examination of Methodologies Employed in Government Digital Transformation

Various methodologies are employed in government digital transformation, each with its strengths and weaknesses (Mergel et al., 2019). Common approaches include agile frameworks, iterative development cycles, and user-centric design principles. These methodologies aim to create flexible and responsive systems that can adapt to changing needs and technologies (Weerakkody et al., 2021). One of the key methodologies adopted by many government agencies is the "Digital Service Standard," which provides a set of criteria to help create and run good digital services (UK Government Digital Service, 2023). This standard emphasises the importance of understanding user needs, using agile methods, and continuously improving based on user feedback (UK Government Digital Service, 2023). The application of lean and agile methodologies, as highlighted by Sánchez-Ortiz et al. (2020), is particularly relevant in the context of public sector digital transformation. These approaches can help in "making [public systems] more effective and efficient, seeking a greater rationalisation of public spending, as well as avoiding waste and corruption" (Sánchez-Ortiz et al., 2020, p. 2). The adoption of agile and lean methodologies in government digital transformation initiatives represents a significant shift from traditional bureaucratic approaches. These methodologies emphasise flexibility, user-centric design, and continuous improvement, which can lead to more effective and responsive digital services. However, their implementation in the public sector can be challenging due to existing organisational structures and cultures. Successful adoption requires strong leadership, clear communication, and a willingness to embrace change (Mergel et al., 2019).

Table 1. Methodologies in Government Digital Transformation

Methodology	Description	Strengths	Weaknesses
Agile Frameworks	Iterative development with continuous feedback and improvement.	Flexibility, user-centric design.	Requires cultural shift, can be hard to scale.
Lean Methodologies	Focus on efficiency, reducing waste, and maximising value.	Cost-effective, efficient processes.	May overlook long-term innovation.
Digital Service Standard	Set of criteria for creating and running good digital services.	Consistency, quality assurance.	Can be rigid and bureaucratic.
User-Centric Design Principles	Designing services based on user needs and feedback.	High user satisfaction, relevant solutions.	Time-consuming, requires extensive research.

Analysis of the 'Alpha-Beta-Live' Stages and the Influence of Industry Approaches

The 'alpha-beta-live' stages are a common framework used in digital transformation projects, particularly in the public sector (Brown & White, 2021). These stages involve developing a prototype (alpha), refining it based on feedback (beta), and then launching it for public use (live). This iterative approach allows for continuous improvement and ensures that the final product meets user needs effectively. This approach has been heavily influenced by industry practices, particularly from the tech sector (Lee & Park, 2022). Companies like Google and Amazon have long used similar iterative development processes, which have proven effective in creating user-friendly and efficient digital services. The 'alpha-beta-live' approach aligns well with the principles of agile methodology, allowing for rapid prototyping, user testing, and iterative improvement. This is particularly valuable in the healthcare context, where user needs can be complex and varied, and where the stakes of getting a digital service right are particularly high (Maguire et al., 2021). The 'alpha-beta-live' framework's iterative nature is well-suited to the dynamic and complex environment of digital healthcare. By allowing for rapid prototyping and user feedback, this approach ensures that digital services are continuously refined and improved. However, its success depends on effective stakeholder engagement and the ability to quickly respond to feedback. In healthcare, where user needs are diverse and critical, this approach can significantly enhance the effectiveness and user satisfaction of digital services (Brown & White, 2021).

Table 2. Lessons from NHS Alpha Project

Lesson	Description	Implication for Future Projects
User-Centric Design	Involving end-users in the design process.	Ensures solutions meet real-world needs.
Agile Methodologies	Rapid prototyping, testing, and iteration.	Allows for quick adaptation to feedback.
Change Management	Addressing resistance and managing stakeholder expectations.	Essential for smooth implementation.
Integration with Existing Systems	Ensuring new solutions work with legacy systems.	Reduces disruptions and enhances adoption.
Long-Term Funding	Securing ongoing financial support.	Sustains momentum and supports scaling.

Importance of Service Standards and Their Role in Driving Transformation Initiatives

Service standards play a crucial role in driving digital transformation initiatives (Anderson & Martin, 2023). They provide a benchmark for quality and consistency, ensuring that digital services meet user expectations and regulatory requirements. Adherence to service standards also fosters trust and confidence among users, which is essential for the successful adoption of digital technologies. In the context of healthcare, service standards are particularly important. They ensure that digital health services are safe, effective, and accessible to all patients (NHS Digital, 2022). The NHS, for example, has developed a set of digital, data and technology standards that all healthcare providers must adhere to when implementing new digital services (NHS Digital, 2022). These standards cover a range of areas, including data security, interoperability, and user experience. By providing a clear framework for digital service development, they help to ensure consistency across the healthcare system and facilitate the integration of different digital services (Anderson & Martin, 2023). Service standards are essential for ensuring the quality and consistency of digital healthcare services. They provide a clear framework for development and implementation, helping to mitigate risks related to data security, interoperability, and user experience. However, developing and enforcing these standards can be challenging, particularly in a rapidly evolving technological landscape. Continuous review and adaptation of standards are necessary to keep pace with technological advancements and changing user needs.

Exploration of the Implications of Audits and Accountability Mechanisms

Regular audits and accountability mechanisms are vital for maintaining transparency and trust in digital initiatives (Garcia & Lopez, 2021). They help identify areas for improvement, ensure compliance with regulations, and provide a basis for measuring the success of digital transformation efforts. In the context of healthcare, these mechanisms are particularly important for safeguarding patient data and ensuring the ethical use of technology. Audits can also help identify potential risks and vulnerabilities in digital systems, allowing organisations to address these issues before they lead to serious problems (Turner & Harris, 2022). This is particularly crucial in healthcare, where system failures or data breaches could have severe consequences for patient safety and privacy. Moreover, accountability mechanisms play a crucial role in ensuring that digital transformation initiatives deliver value for money. In the public sector, where resources are often constrained, it is essential to demonstrate that investments in digital technologies are delivering tangible benefits. This can help to build public trust and support for ongoing digital transformation efforts. Audits and accountability mechanisms are critical for ensuring the success and sustainability of digital transformation initiatives. They provide a structured approach to evaluating performance, identifying risks, and ensuring compliance with regulations. In healthcare, where the stakes are particularly high, these mechanisms are essential for maintaining trust and ensuring the ethical use of technology. However, they must be designed to be flexible and adaptive, allowing for continuous improvement and responsiveness to emerging challenges (Garcia & Lopez, 2021).

NHS England Experience

The digital transformation of NHS England is a complex and multifaceted process. It involves integrating digital tools and technologies into a vast and diverse healthcare system, which includes primary, secondary, and tertiary care providers (NHS England, 2022). The goal is to create a seamless and interoperable system that can provide timely and holistic care to patients (Weerakkody et al., 2021). One of the key challenges faced by NHS England in its digital transformation journey is the need to balance innovation with the maintenance of existing services. The NHS must continue to provide high-quality care to millions of patients while simultaneously implementing new digital systems and processes (Maguire et al., 2021). This balancing act is further complicated by the diverse needs of different stakeholders within the healthcare system.

Figure 3. DT of the NHS

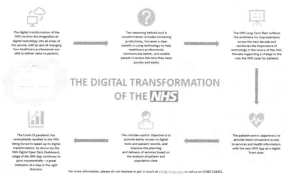

Patients, healthcare professionals, administrators, and policymakers may all have different priorities and expectations when it comes to digital transformation. Navigating these competing demands requires careful stakeholder management and clear communication of the benefits of digital transformation (Cinar et al., 2019). The complexity of NHS England's digital transformation highlights the importance of a strategic and inclusive approach. Balancing innovation with the maintenance of existing services requires careful planning and prioritisation. Effective stakeholder management and communication are crucial for aligning diverse interests and ensuring that all parties understand and support the transformation efforts. The NHS's experience underscores the need for a comprehensive and adaptive strategy that addresses both technological and organisational challenges (Weerakkody et al., 2021).

Evolution of NHS Choices into NHS.UK: A Case Study of Transformative Efforts

The transition from NHS Choices to NHS.UK is a prime example of transformative efforts within NHS England (NHS Digital, 2021). This evolution involved redesigning the platform to improve user experience, enhance accessibility, and provide more comprehensive and reliable health information. The success of this transformation highlights the importance of user-centric design and continuous improvement in digital healthcare initiatives (Roberts & Cooper. The new NHS. UK platform incorporates features such as personalised content, improved search functionality, and integration with other NHS digital services. This transformation has not only improved the user experience but has also helped to reduce the burden on other NHS services by providing patients with easy access to reliable health information.

The redesign of NHS.UK was guided by extensive user research and testing, demonstrating the value of a user-centric approach to digital transformation (NHS Digital, 2021). By involving users throughout the development process, the NHS was able to create a platform that truly meets the needs of its diverse user base. The transformation of NHS Choices into NHS.UK underscores the importance of user-centric design in digital healthcare initiatives. By prioritising user experience and accessibility, the NHS was able to create a platform that meets the needs of its diverse user base. This approach not only enhances user satisfaction but also reduces the burden on other NHS services. The success of NHS.UK highlights the value of continuous improvement and user feedback in digital transformation efforts (Roberts & Cooper, 2022).

Challenges and Successes Faced by the NHS Alpha Project: Lessons Learned and Future Implications

The NHS Alpha project faced numerous challenges, including resistance to change, technical difficulties, and regulatory hurdles (NHS England, 2020). However, it also achieved significant successes, such as developing innovative digital tools and improving patient engagement. The lessons learned from this project underscore the importance of flexibility, collaboration, and perseverance in digital transformation efforts. One of the key lessons from the NHS Alpha project was the importance of involving end-users in the design and development process. By adopting a user-centric approach, the project was able to create digital services that truly met the needs of patients and healthcare professionals. The project also highlighted the importance of agile methodologies in healthcare digital transformation. The ability to rapidly prototype, test, and iterate allowed the team to respond quickly to user feedback and changing requirements. This approach proved particularly valuable in the fast-moving and complex healthcare environment (Thompson & Walker, 2021).

The NHS Alpha project's experience highlights the importance of flexibility, collaboration, and user-centric design in digital transformation. By involving end-users in the design process and adopting agile methodologies, the project was able to create digital services that met real-world needs. However, the project also faced significant challenges, particularly in terms of scalability and integration with existing NHS systems (NHS England, 2020). The complexity of the NHS infrastructure and the need to ensure interoperability with legacy systems posed substantial technical hurdles (Thompson & Walker, 2021). One of the key lessons from the NHS Alpha project was the importance of balancing innovation with practicality. While the project successfully demonstrated the potential of user-centric design and agile methodologies in healthcare, it also underscored the need for careful consideration of how new digital services can be integrated into existing workflows and systems (NHS England, 2020). Moreover, the project emphasised the critical role of effective change management in digital transformation initiatives. Resistance to change among healthcare professionals and concerns about the impact of new technologies on established practices were significant barriers that needed to be addressed (Maguire et al., 2021). This highlights the need for comprehensive stakeholder engagement and communication strategies as part of any digital transformation effort in healthcare. The NHS Alpha project also revealed the challenges of maintaining momentum and securing long-term funding for digital initiatives in a complex, publicly-funded healthcare system. The project's initial success in developing innovative solutions had to be balanced against the realities of budget constraints and competing priorities within the NHS (Wilson & Thomas, 2021). This underscores the importance of demonstrating clear value and return on investment for digital transformation initiatives to secure ongoing support and resources.

Furthermore, the project highlighted the need for a flexible and adaptive approach to digital transformation. The healthcare landscape is constantly evolving, with new technologies, regulations, and patient expectations emerging regularly. The ability to pivot and adjust strategies in response to these changes is crucial for the long-term success of digital transformation efforts (Thompson & Walker, 2021). As the NHS continues to build on the lessons learned from the Alpha project, there is a growing recognition of the need for a holistic approach to digital transformation. This involves not only implementing new technologies but also reimagining care delivery models, workflows, and organisational structures to fully leverage the potential of digital tools (NHS England, 2022). The experience of the NHS Alpha project has also influenced the broader healthcare sector, providing valuable insights for other healthcare systems embarking on their own digital transformation journeys. The emphasis on user-centric design, agile methodologies, and effective change management is increasingly being recognised as best practice in healthcare digitization efforts worldwide (Weerakkody et al., 2021). However, it is important to note that while the lessons from the NHS Alpha project are valuable, they cannot be blindly applied to all healthcare contexts. Each healthcare system has its unique challenges, constraints, and opportunities, necessitating a tailored approach to digital transformation (Cinar et al., 2019). Looking ahead, the NHS is focusing on several key areas for future digital transformation efforts, informed by the lessons from the Alpha project:

1. **Enhancing interoperability:** Ensuring that different digital systems can communicate and share data effectively is a top priority. This is crucial for creating a seamless, integrated healthcare experience for patients and providers alike (NHS England, 2022).
2. **Leveraging artificial intelligence and machine learning:** The NHS is exploring how these technologies can be used to improve diagnostics, treatment planning, and operational efficiency (Maguire et al., 2021).
3. **Expanding telemedicine and remote care capabilities:** Building on the rapid adoption of these services during the COVID-19 pandemic, the NHS is working to further develop and integrate telemedicine into its care delivery model (Baker & Green, 2023).
4. **Improving data analytics capabilities:** Enhancing the ability to collect, analyse, and act on healthcare data is seen as crucial for improving patient outcomes and system efficiency (Turner & Harris, 2022).
5. **Strengthening cybersecurity:** As healthcare becomes increasingly digitized, protecting patient data and ensuring the integrity of digital systems is more important than ever (Garcia & Lopez, 2021).

CHALLENGES AND CONSIDERATIONS

Examination of the Impact of Digital Transformation on Power Dynamics and Stakeholder Engagement

Digital transformation can alter existing power structures within organisations, leading to resistance from stakeholders who feel threatened by these changes (Wilson & Thomas, 2021). Effective stakeholder engagement is crucial for managing these dynamics and ensuring that all parties are on board with the transformation efforts. In the healthcare context, this can involve changes in the roles and responsibilities of healthcare professionals, as well as shifts in the patient-provider relationship. For example, Mahmood et al. (2019) found that individuals using mobile health (mHealth) apps were significantly more likely to track their health progress, make health-related decisions, and engage with healthcare providers compared to those without such apps. This reflects the role of digital tools in enabling patients to take an active role in managing their health, challenging traditional power dynamics in healthcare by promoting patient autonomy and engagements. Managing these changes requires clear communication, ongoing stakeholder engagement, and a willingness to address concerns and resistance head-on. It also necessitates a focus on change management strategies to help stakeholders adapt to new ways of working. Digital transformation can disrupt existing power structures within healthcare organisations, leading to resistance from stakeholders. Effective stakeholder engagement and change management strategies are essential for navigating these dynamics. Clear communication of the benefits of digital transformation and addressing concerns directly can help to build support and reduce resistance among healthcare professionals and other stakeholders (Wilson & Thomas, 2021).

Analysis of the Regulatory Landscape and Risk Management in Healthcare Digitisation

The regulatory landscape for healthcare digitization is complex and constantly evolving (Turner & Harris, 2022). Navigating this landscape requires a thorough understanding of relevant regulations and robust risk management strategies. Ensuring compliance with data protection laws, for example, is critical for safeguarding patient information and maintaining trust in digital healthcare services. The NHS in the UK must comply with the General Data Protection Regulation (GDPR) and the Data Protection Act 2018. These regulations set strict requirements for the handling of personal data to ensure it is used lawfully, transparently, and securely. The Data Protection Act 2018 serves as the UK's implementation of GDPR, ensuring that all organisations, including the NHS, adhere to data protection principles such as using information only for specified purposes and protecting it from unauthorised access or damage. This compliance is essential for maintaining patient privacy and upholding the rights of individuals regarding their personal health data (GOV. UK, 2023). These regulations impose strict requirements on how patient data can be collected, stored, and used, adding an additional layer of complexity to digital transformation efforts (Turner & Harris, 2022).

Risk management in healthcare digitization also involves addressing cybersecurity threats, ensuring system reliability, and managing the potential risks associated with AI and machine learning technologies (Tilala et al., 2024). These considerations must be balanced with the need for innovation and improved patient care (Topol, 2019). Navigating the regulatory landscape and managing risks are critical components of successful healthcare digitization. Compliance with data protection laws, such as the General Data Protection Regulation (GDPR) and the Data Protection Act 2018 and addressing cybersecurity threats are essential for maintaining patient trust and ensuring the integrity of digital systems (GOV.UK, 2023). Robust risk management strategies that balance the need for innovation with regulatory compliance are crucial for the long-term success of digital transformation initiatives in healthcare.

Consideration of Financial Constraints and Strategic Investments in Digital Healthcare

Financial constraints are a significant barrier to digital transformation in healthcare (NHS England, 2022). Strategic investments in digital technologies, infrastructure, and skills development are essential for overcoming these constraints and achieving sustainable transformation. This requires careful planning and prioritisation to ensure that resources are allocated effectively. The NHS, like many public healthcare systems, faces significant financial pressures. This makes it crucial to demonstrate the value and return on investment of digital transformation initiatives. This often involves balancing short-term costs with long-term benefits, such as improved efficiency and better patient outcomes. Moreover, the rapid pace of technological change means that healthcare organisations must be strategic in their investments, focusing on technologies and solutions that offer long-term value rather than chasing every new trend (Gopal et al., 2019). This requires a clear digital strategy aligned with overall organisational goals. Financial constraints are a significant challenge for digital transformation in healthcare. Strategic investments in digital technologies and infrastructure are essential for achieving sustainable transformation. Demonstrating clear value and return on investment is crucial for securing ongoing support and resources. A strategic approach that focuses on long-term value and aligns with organisational goals is essential for navigating financial constraints and ensuring the success of digital transformation initiatives (NHS England, 2022).

Table 3. Summary of Key Challenges in Digital Transformation of Healthcare

Challenge	Description	Impact
Data Privacy and Security	Ensuring patient data is protected and secure from breaches.	High risk of data breaches and loss of trust.
System Interoperability	Integrating various digital systems to work seamlessly together.	Inefficiencies and data silos.
Resistance to Change	Overcoming reluctance from healthcare professionals to adopt new technologies.	Slow adoption and suboptimal use of new tools.
Regulatory Compliance	Adhering to complex and evolving healthcare regulations.	Legal risks and potential fines.
Financial Constraints	Securing funding for digital transformation initiatives.	Limited resources for comprehensive transformation.

CONCLUSION

This chapter has explored the intricacies of digital transformation within government structures, with a specific focus on healthcare and the pioneering efforts of NHS England (Weerakkody et al., 2021). Key insights include the importance of user-centric design, iterative approaches, and transparent governance in driving successful digital transformation (Mergel et al., 2019). The experiences of NHS England highlight the complexities of implementing digital transformation in a large, complex healthcare system (Maguire et al., 2021). They underscore the need for a holistic approach that considers not only technological aspects but also organisational culture, stakeholder engagement, and regulatory compliance (Cinar et al., 2019).

While methodologies like agile frameworks and the 'alpha-beta-live' stages are important, they are not sufficient on their own to ensure successful digital transformation (Brown & White, 2021). A holistic approach that considers organisational culture, stakeholder engagement, and regulatory compliance is essential (Davis & Roberts, 2022). The NHS experience demonstrates that successful digital transformation requires more than just the adoption of new technologies or methodologies (Maguire et al., 2021). It necessitates a fundamental shift in how healthcare is delivered and experienced, involving changes in organisational culture, processes, and mindsets (Wilson & Thomas, 2021). This caution against a deterministic view of methodology is particularly important in the healthcare context, where the stakes are high, and the consequences of failure can be severe. Organisations must be prepared to adapt their approaches based on ongoing feedback and changing circumstances (Thompson & Walker, 2021).

Figure 4. Proposed DT Strategy for Digital Healthcare

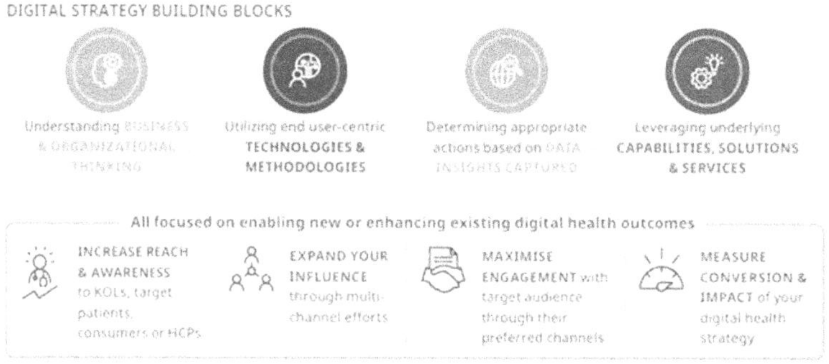

Collaborative efforts and progressive leadership are crucial for overcoming the complexities of digital transformation (Sánchez-Ortiz et al., 2020). This includes fostering a culture of innovation, encouraging cross-disciplinary collaboration, and providing strong leadership to guide the transformation efforts (Mergel et al., 2019). In the healthcare context, this often involves collaboration between health-care professionals, IT specialists, data scientists, and patient representatives (Betts & Korenda, 2019). Progressive leadership is needed to navigate the challenges of digital transformation while maintaining focus on the ultimate goal of improving patient care (Wilson & Thomas, 2021). The NHS experience highlights the impor-tance of engaging all stakeholders in the transformation process, from frontline staff to senior management (NHS England, 2022). This collaborative approach helps to ensure that digital solutions are fit for purpose and address real-world needs (Thompson & Walker, 2021).

Despite the challenges, digital initiatives like NHS Alpha demonstrate the trans-formative potential of digital technologies within complex bureaucratic structures (NHS England, 2020). By leveraging the lessons learned from these initiatives, other healthcare systems can navigate their digital transformation journeys more effectively (Weerakkody et al., 2021). The NHS Alpha project, despite its challenges, has paved the way for further digital innovation within the NHS (NHS England, 2020). It has demonstrated that even large, complex organisations can successfully implement digital transformation initiatives, given the right approach and leadership (Thompson & Walker, 2021). These experiences affirm that digital transformation, while challenging, has the potential to significantly improve healthcare delivery and patient outcomes (Cinar et al., 2019). They also highlight the importance of persistence and resilience in the face of setbacks and challenges (Maguire et al., 2021). In conclusion, the digital transformation of healthcare, as exemplified by NHS England, is a complex but necessary journey (Weerakkody et al., 2021). It requires a balanced approach that combines technological innovation with organi-sational change, always keeping the focus on improving patient care and outcomes (Betts & Korenda, 2019). As healthcare systems worldwide continue to grapple with the challenges of digital transformation, the lessons learned from NHS England's experiences will undoubtedly prove invaluable (Mergel et al., 2019). The paradox of digital transformation in healthcare lies in its simultaneous promise of revolu-tionary improvements and the significant challenges it presents (Cinar et al., 2019). Navigating this paradox requires a nuanced understanding of both the technological and human aspects of change, as well as a commitment to continuous learning and adaptation (Maguire et al., 2021). As we move forward, it is clear that the success of digital transformation in healthcare will depend not just on the technologies we adopt, but on our ability to reimagine and reshape our healthcare systems to fully leverage these digital capabilities (Weerakkody et al., 2021).

REFERENCES

Anderson, K., & Martin, L. (2023). The role of service standards in driving digital transformation. *International Journal of Public Sector Management*, 36(1), 22–38.

Baker, L., & Green, J. (2023). The role of face-to-face interactions in digital healthcare. *BMC Health Services Research*, 23, 456.

Betts, D., & Korenda, L. (2019). *The future of health: How digital technologies can bridge the gap between consumers and health care providers*. Deloitte Insights.

Brown, C., & White, D. (2021). The Alpha-Beta-Live approach in public sector digital projects. *Information Systems Journal*, 31(2), 289–305.

Chen, Y., & Evans, M. (2022). Patient attitudes towards digital health services: A UK perspective. *Journal of Medical Internet Research*, 24(4), e35092. PMID: 35380546

Cinar, E., Trott, P., & Simms, C. (2019). A systematic review of barriers to public sector innovation process. *Public Management Review*, 21(2), 264–290. DOI: 10.1080/14719037.2018.1473477

Davis, M., & Roberts, N. (2022). Agile methodologies in government digital transformation. *Public Management Review*, 24(5), 678–695.

Garcia, R., & Lopez, F. (2021). Audits and accountability in digital healthcare initiatives. *Health Policy and Technology*, 10(2), 100508. PMID: 33850698

Gopal, G., Suter-Crazzolara, C., Toldo, L., & Eberhardt, W. (2019). Digital transformation in healthcare–architectures of present and future information technologies. [CCLM]. *Clinical Chemistry and Laboratory Medicine*, 57(3), 328–335. DOI: 10.1515/cclm-2018-0658 PMID: 30530878

GOV UK. (2024) *Data protection*. Available at: https://www.gov.uk/data-protection (Accessed: 30 September 2024).

Lee, S., & Park, J. (2022). Influence of tech industry practices on public sector digital transformation. *Technology in Society*, 68, 101828.

Maguire, D., Evans, H., Honeyman, M., & Omojomolo, D. (2021). *Digital change in health and social care*. The King's Fund.

Mahmood, A., Kedia, S., Wyant, D. K., Ahn, S., & Bhuyan, S. S. (2019). Use of mobile health applications for health-promoting behavior among individuals with chronic medical conditions. *Digital Health*, 5, 2055207619882181. DOI: 10.1177/2055207619882181 PMID: 31656632

Mergel, I., Edelmann, N., & Haug, N. (2019). Defining digital transformation: Results from expert interviews. *Government Information Quarterly*, 36(4), 101385. DOI: 10.1016/j.giq.2019.06.002

NHS Digital. (2021). From NHS Choices to NHS.UK: A case study in digital transformation. Retrieved from https://digital.nhs.uk/services/nhs-website-service/case-studies

NHS Digital. (2022). Digital, data and technology standards. Retrieved from https://digital.nhs.uk/about-nhs-digital/our-work/nhs-digital-data-and-technology-standards

NHS England. (2020). NHS Alpha Project: Final report and recommendations. Retrieved from https://www.england.nhs.uk/digitaltechnology/nhs-alpha-project/

NHS England. (2022). Digital transformation strategy 2022-2025. Retrieved from https://www.england.nhs.uk/digitaltechnology/connecteddigitalsystems/digital-transformation/

Roberts, S., & Cooper, T. (2022). User-centric design in healthcare websites: Lessons from NHS.UK. *Journal of Medical Systems*, 46, 31.

Sánchez-Ortiz, J., García-Valderrama, T., & Rodríguez-Cornejo, V. (2020). Towards a sustainable public administration: The mediating role of lean and agile management in public sector digital transformation. *Sustainability*, 12(22), 9442.

Thompson, K., & Walker, J. (2021). User involvement in healthcare digital service design. *Health Expectations*, 24(3), 887–898.

Tilala, M. H., Chenchala, P. K., Choppadandi, A., Kaur, J., Naguri, S., Saoji, R., & Devaguptapu, B. (2024). Ethical considerations in the use of artificial intelligence and machine learning in health care: A comprehensive review. *Cureus*, 16(6), 1–8. PMID: 39011215

Topol, E. (2019). *Deep medicine: how artificial intelligence can make healthcare human again*.

Turner, A., & Harris, B. (2022). Risk management in healthcare digital transformation. *Journal of Healthcare Risk Management*, 41(4), 28–36.

UK Government Digital Service. (2023). Digital Service Standard. Retrieved from https://www.gov.uk/service-manual/service-standard

Weerakkody, V., Kapoor, K., Balta, M. E., Irani, Z., & Dwivedi, Y. K. (2021). Factors influencing user acceptance of public sector big data: An empirical exploration. *International Journal of Information Management*, 58, 102277.

Wilson, P., & Thomas, R. (2021). Balancing innovation and continuity in NHS digital transformation. *Health Services Management Research*, 34(3), 135–147.

ADDITIONAL READING

Ali, M. (2021). *Remote Work and Sustainable Changes for the Future of Global Business.* IGI Global. https://www.igi-global.com/book/remote-work-sustainable -changes-future/264375

Ali, M. (2022). *Future Role of Sustainable Innovative Technologies in Crisis Management.* IGI Global. https://www.igi-global.com/book/future-role-sustainable -innovative-technologies/281281

Ali, M. (2023). *Shifting Paradigms in the Rapidly Developing Global Digital Ecosystem: A GCC Perspective.* In Digital Entrepreneurship and Co-Creating Value Through Digital Encounters (pp. 145-166). IGI Global. https://www.igi-global.com/chapter/ shifting-paradigms-in-the-rapidly-developing-global-digital-ecosystem/323525

Ali, M. (2023). T*axonomy of Industry 4.0 Technologies in Digital Entrepreneurship and Co-Creating Value.* In *Digital Entrepreneurship and Co-Creating Value Through Digital Encounters* (pp. 24–55). IGI Global., https://www.igi-global.com/ chapter/taxonomy-of-industry-40-technologies-in-digital-entrepreneurship-and-co -creating-value/323520 DOI: 10.4018/978-1-6684-7416-7.ch002

Ali, M., & Wood-Harper, T. (2021). *Fostering Communication and Learning with Underutilized Technologies in Higher Education.* IGI Global. https://www.igi-global .com/book/fostering-communication-learning-underutilized-technologies/244593

Ali, M., Wood-Harper, T., & Kutar, M. (2023). Multi-Perspectives of Contemporary Digital Transformation Models of Complex Innovation Management. In *Digital Entrepreneurship and Co-Creating Value Through Digital Encounters* (pp. 79–96). IGI Global., https://www.igi-global.com/chapter/multi-perspectives-of-contemporary -digital-transformation-models-of-complex-innovation-management/323522 DOI: 10.4018/978-1-6684-7416-7.ch004

Ali, M. B. (2021). Internet of Things (IoT) to Foster Communication and Information Sharing: A Case of UK Higher Education. In Ali, M. B., & Wood-Harper, T. (Eds.), *Fostering Communication and Learning With Underutilized Technologies in Higher Education* (pp. 1–20). IGI Global., https://www.igi-global.com/chapter/ internet-of-things-iot-to-foster-communication-and-information-sharing/262718/ DOI: 10.4018/978-1-7998-4846-2.ch001

Ali, M. B., & Wood-Harper, T. (2022). Artificial Intelligence (AI) as a Decision-Making Tool to Control Crisis Situations. In *Future Role of Sustainable Innovative Technologies in Crisis Management*. IGI Global., https://www.igi-global.com/chapter/artificial-intelligence-ai-as-a-decision-making-tool-to-control-crisis-situations/298931 DOI: 10.4018/978-1-7998-9815-3.ch006

Ali, M. B., Wood-Harper, T., & Ramlogan, R. (2020). A Framework Strategy to Overcome Trust Issues on Cloud Computing Adoption in Higher Education. In Modern Principles, Practices, and Algorithms for Cloud Security (pp. 162-183). IGI Global. https://www.igi-global.com/chapter/a-framework-strategy-to-overcome-trust-issues-on-cloud-computing-adoption-in-higher-education/238907/

Chapter 4
Digital Transformation as a Factor in The Economic Development of Montenegro

Ivana Domazet
https://orcid.org/0000-0002-3493-4616
Institute of Economic Sciences, Belgrade, Serbia

Darko Marjanović
https://orcid.org/0000-0001-7336-1964
Institute of Economic Sciences, Belgrade, Serbia

ABSTRACT

Digital transformation in Montenegro is an evolving process that aims to use digital technologies to boost economic growth, improve governance, enhance public services and foster innovation. The main objective of this chapter is to analyze the impact of public administration reform as a determinant of Montenegro's economic development on the achieved economic and social results, which are determined by the achieved level of various key economic parameters, such as: GDP, FDI, import and export of goods and services. In this context, special emphasis was placed on the analysis of two indicators: EGDI (E-Government Development Index) and EPI (E-Participation Index). The methodological concept and the analysis of the first part are based on official data from the World Bank and Monstat, while the second part is based on the UN eGovernment Survey, an official report of the United Nations (UN E-Government Knowledgebase). The period covered by the survey is from 2012 to 2023. The results show that public administration reform is an important factor for Montenegro's economic development.

DOI: 10.4018/979-8-3693-5966-2.ch004

INTRODUCTION

Digital transformation is a significant factor driving economic development in the modern world. It refers to the integration of digital technologies into all aspects of business and society and is fundamentally changing the way companies operate and create value. Digital transformation is a powerful driver of economic development as it enables organizations, industries and economies to adapt, innovate and thrive in the digital age. Embracing digital technologies and fostering a culture of digital innovation is essential to unlock the full potential of digital transformation and achieve inclusive and sustainable economic growth. The European Union considers digital transformation to be a crucial factor in promoting economic growth, competitiveness, innovation and societal progress. The digital transformation is a top priority for the European Union. It is driving forward initiatives and policies aimed at harnessing the potential of digital technologies for economic growth, innovation and societal progress. By fostering collaboration, investment and the development of digital skills, the EU aims to create a thriving digital ecosystem that benefits businesses, citizens and economies across Europe. The digital transformation of the EU economy and society holds great potential for growth across Europe. European industry can take advantage of the benefits arising from the interconnectedness of Member States in the field of advanced digital technologies to exploit the many opportunities offered by technologies such as IoT, big data, AI and the like. For this reason, the Digital Europe initiative for the years 2021–2027 is the European Commission's all-encompassing answer to the complexity of the digital transformation process.

As digital technology evolved over time, people began to develop new ideas for its business use. The concept of digital transformation started to take shape in this way. Novel approaches to conducting business were made feasible by the emergence of novel technologies. Businesses can now use digital data and documents with exponentially greater efficiency, but most business systems and processes are still built around analog-era practices for locating, sharing, and utilizing information. In addition to technological changes, digital transformation also brings changes within the business organization - changes in work processes and strategies that lead to changes in the way business is conducted. It is extremely important that the process of digital transformation is aligned with the company's vision, strategy and goals so that a wide range of modern technologies can be used as efficiently as possible. Although it is in this area that the greatest challenges arise, successfully overcoming these challenges will lead to an effective transformation of the business model.

While Montenegro faces challenges in terms of infrastructure, digital literacy, and regulatory frameworks, it has been making efforts to embrace digital transformation. A key aspect of digital transformation in Montenegro: digital infrastructure development, e-government initiatives, digital skills and education, digital economy and innovation, e-health and telemedicine, cybersecurity and data protection, smart cities and digital tourism and cross-border collaboration. While Montenegro is still in the early stages of its digital transformation journey, there is a growing recognition of the importance of digitalization for economic development, social progress, and competitiveness. Continued investment in digital infrastructure, skills development, regulatory reforms, and innovation will be crucial for Montenegro to fully realize the benefits of digital transformation and position itself as a digitally advanced nation. Every aspect of Montenegrin society is impacted by the horizontal and multifunctional digital transformation plan. Without political will and leadership at the top levels of a nation, transformation is not feasible. Good results require the presence of leaders, their backing, as well as a high degree of comprehension and acceptance of digital transformation. A clear and comprehensive normative structure has been established in Montenegro, as evidenced by the situation analysis conducted in order to prepare the Strategy for Digital Transformation of Montenegro 2022–2026. This is one of the necessary steps toward the establishment of a digital society.

Digital transformation significantly impacts macroeconomic indicators (GDP, employment, investment, productivity and efficiency, trade balance, import and export, inflation, public finances, income distribution, consumer behavior, innovation and competitiveness, environmental impact), reflecting its role in driving economic growth and productivity. In this chapter, special attention will be focused on GDP, import and export of goods and services, and FDI.

BACKGROUND

All spheres of economic and social activity now use the term "digitalization," and integrating it has become essential for all states globally (Chenic et al., 2023). One kind of business transformation that is fueled by new technologies is called digital transformation. The noticeable change in the function of technology within a business is what propels digital transformation (Tang, 2021; Domazet et al., 2023). Thus, digital transformation is a process of integrating digital technology into every aspect of a business and radically changing how you operate and provide value to clients. Certain industries stand to gain more opportunities for development in the future when digital transformation permeates every aspect of corporate operations, setting them apart from others (Gebayew et al., 2018). Digital transformation and digital development are synonymous terms that denote the progression, amalgamation, and enhancement of digital technologies, methodologies, and approaches throughout diverse domains of commerce, administration, and society (Domazet & Marjanović, 2024). Olczyk & Kuc-Czarnecka (2022) empirically investigate whether a rapid and comprehensive digital transformation can close or eliminate the prosperity gap in the European Union. They do this with the help of the DESI. The factor that has the greatest impact on the digital transformation of EU countries is connectivity. Furthermore, they find that DESI is a strong regressor for explaining variations in GDP per capita across EU countries. Digital transformation, or the incorporation of digital technology into business, is a process that fundamentally alters how society communicates, conducts business, and grows both domestically and globally (Mićić, 2017; Domazet et al., 2018). Increasing value, efficiency, or innovation are the common objectives of digital transformation. However, an infrastructure and tools for digital transformation implementation in SMEs are required to carry out a transition (Zuzaku & Abazi, 2022; Mingaleva & Shironina, 2021).

One of the most themes in the manufacturing sector right now is digital transformation. This transformation impacts the process of creating operational value, makes it possible to do business in new ways, and causes fundamental shifts within businesses. Nevertheless, there are still a lot of challenges associated with both the adoption of new digital technologies and their realization (Liere-Netheler et al., 2018). Over the past few years, there has been a noticeable growth in the quantity of publications discussing various organizational and technological aspects of digital transformation due to a constant increase in scholarly attention (Nadkarni & Prügl, 2021). The topic of digitalization is becoming more and more important to businesses. But most businesses, especially SMEs, are finding it difficult to participate in a comprehensive global digital transformation process. In fact, a company's organizational strategy - which includes the creation of market opportunities - is significantly impacted by digitalization. One factor that has been found to support SMEs' internationalization is digitalization (Dethine et al., 2020). The way society interacts both in everyday and professional life has changed dramatically due to the development and widespread use of technology, especially internet technologies. The digital economy is a crucial area of digital transformation, as it increases the productivity, profitability and efficiency of companies through digitalization (Melović et al., 2020). For traditional businesses looking to adapt their business model to a new digital environment and data-oriented culture, the digital transformation has made it possible to create new business models, maximize opportunities, and maximize efficiency (Parra et al., 2021; Domazet et al., 2022). Because of the digital economy's enormous expansion potential, new perspectives on how the sector is understood across a range of industries have emerged. An increasing number of businesses have implemented digital transformation and seen success (Wang, 2022).

The integration of digital technologies into all facets of business activity, or "digital transformation'," is a global phenomenon that takes different forms in different economic environments. Businesses, governments and researchers can gain important insights that will guide policies to promote the development of digital businesses by understanding the particular opportunities and constraints that each environment presents (Olubusola et al., 2024). The idea that supporting digital technologies can and should boost economic growth has gained traction among European policymakers (Rothstein, 2024). According to Nie et al. (2024), companies must take corporate social responsibility (CSR) into account in order to manage the digital transformation. Involvement in corporate social responsibility (CSR) can improve a company's technological, financial and human resources base, which will drive digital transformation. In the US and Africa, SME digital transformation is a dynamic process with unique characteristics. American SMEs are able to take advantage of sophisticated technological infrastructures, whereas African SMEs are able to overcome obstacles with resilience and agility through the use of digital technologies (Raji et al., 2024).

The significance of digital transformation and how it may support companies in maintaining their competitiveness in the market have been brought to light by the growing digitalization of economies. Disruptive innovations, however, have an impact on the environment, society, and institutions in addition to the business level. For this reason, during the last 20 years, a wide range of subjects have been covered in literature pertaining to digital transformation research (Kraus et al., 2021). The digital economy is bringing about significant changes to both business and society, necessitating a restructuring of all socio-economic institutions. The study determined the primary drivers of the economy's digital transformation, as well as the obstacles that businesses must overcome as a result of digitalization (Kochetkov, 2020; Domazet et al., 2022). A partial rather than a comprehensive approach to change increases the likelihood of failure. For this reason, it is crucial that society as a whole demonstrates a willingness to change and understands the goal and importance of change (Golubović et al., 2021; Antonijević et al., 2024). The swift advancement of digital technology places businesses in an unparalleled position. Digital technology offers benefits over other conventional elements of production. It can encourage the modernization and upscaling of established industries, the creative growth of businesses, and the vitality of market entities (Liu & Ananthachari, 2023).

As a crucial component of the market infrastructure, the innovative digital system's development partially reflects the nation's overall economic standing, but its continued positive dynamics with the expansion of the national economy dictate the advancement of society (Kolodynskyi et al., 2018). The industrial structure is altered because of digital economic innovation, which also lowers costs and increases productivity in the manufacturing sector. The findings indicate that there is a relationship between economic innovation and its effects on the fields of technology and society (Yoo & Yi, 2022; Domazet et al., 2021). The digital revolution is bringing with it new opportunities and problems as a result of the Internet, automation, and robotization, as well as new industrial relations and dynamic interactions among many stakeholders (Małkowska et al., 2021). The progression of the digital revolution offers distinct answers to problems for different industries and geographical areas, as well as a plethora of new opportunities and difficulties. The difficulties brought about by the digital age have a big influence on our environment, as well as social and economic systems (Esses et al., 2021).

The advent of the post-industrial era in societal development has made the study of information components and information processes more pertinent than ever (Limarev et al., 2018). New information and communication technologies, sometimes known as "digital technologies," underpin digitally enabled enterprises and increasingly present huge growth prospects (Loonam et al., 2018). Also, increased welfare and increased production may be significantly influenced by digitalization (Saadi Sedik et al., 2019). A growing portion of economic activity now relies on digital technology platforms, which has changed the nature of the business environment (Gurbaxani & Dunkle, 2019). The advent of cutting-edge and potent digital platforms, infrastructures, and technology has fundamentally changed entrepreneurship and innovation. Digital technologies affect value creation and value capture in ways that go beyond just creating new avenues for inventors and entrepreneurs (Nambisan et al., 2019). Romanova & Kuzmin (2021) address the experience of industrialized and developing nations, highlighting the evolving significance of production factors in shaping industrial strategy. The significance of digital transformation and how it may support companies in maintaining their competitiveness in the market have been brought to light by the growing digitalization of economies (Kraus et al., 2021). The expectations and behaviors of consumers have been profoundly changed by the digital transformation and the ensuing innovation in business models, which has put tremendous pressure on established businesses and disrupted several marketplaces. Verhoef et al. (2021) distinguish three stages of digital transformation: digitization, digitalization, and digital transformation, based on the body of existing literature. They argue that digital transformation has an impact on performance measures and necessitates organizational structures.

It is now possible to identify areas of the economy where accelerated digitalization will ensure a rise in gross domestic product and find ways to improve the quality of various spheres of life, as well as simulation of the impact of the development of digital technologies on economic growth (Irtyshcheva et al., 2021). The role of digital transformation in gaining economic competitive advantages is examined by Tiutiunyk et al. (2021). The association between the degree of economic digitization and markers of macroeconomic stability in the EU was demonstrated by the outcomes of VAR modeling. Policymakers can suggest and put into practice measures to make it easier for people to acquire the technologies that work better to boost the beneficial effects on macroeconomic results (Tudose et al., 2023). Several facets of the global economy are being impacted by digital transformation more and more. It influences foreign direct investment, GDP, fosters international trade, and accelerates economic progress (Broz et al., 2020; Marjanović & Domazet, 2021). Countries can focus on commodities, services, and other entities that increase their GDP thanks to macroeconomic statistics (Agu et al., 2022; Marjanović & Domazet, 2023). Any nation can undergo a digital transition, regardless of its GDP per capita or population's purchasing power (Corejova & Chinoracky, 2021).

Amanasto et al. (2020) have examined how Indonesia's information and communication technology (ICT) investment policy affected sectoral performance and macroeconomic indicators in the country's digital economy between 2014 and 2017. The analysis's findings demonstrate that public policy's effect on ICT sector investment positively affects all macroeconomic index as well as sectoral performance. Domazet et al. (2023) state that the research findings — which emphasise the value of innovation and information and communication technology as essential components of a successful business — clearly show that the Western Balkan countries are underinvesting in the ICT sector, which hinders their ability to grow competitively at the macro level and drive their development. Wang et al. (2024) used data from A-share listed companies in Shanghai and Shenzhen from 2009 to 2022 to examine the impact of digital transformation on enterprises' outward foreign direct investment (OFDI). The findings show that FDI is significantly increased by digital transformation. When financial limitations put more pressure on state-owned, privately held, and highly digitalized businesses, the detrimental effects of inefficient investment on digital transformation worsen. Businesses should strengthen their risk prevention systems, minimize their financing restrictions, and optimize their investment structure to counter wasteful investment (Xu et al., 2023). Today's disruptive technologies and the process of digital transformation have completely changed the way businesses operate, with significant ramifications for MNC FDI patterns (Nguyen, 2020; Marjanović et al., 2022).

The role of the digital economy in the global economy is growing. It is completely changing the way we conduct business and will have a significant impact on foreign direct investment (Casella & Formenti, 2019). The transition to a digital economy needs to bring about modifications in the techniques of allocating foreign direct investment, particularly considering the diminished necessity of transferring tangible assets (Bobenič Hintošová & Bódy, 2023). Foreign direct investment can be used by businesses and policymakers to increase their digital capacity and competitiveness (Stephenson et al., 2021). In the framework of foreign direct investment flows, the status of development of the digital economy and society is especially assessed in relation to the circumstances of the member states of the EU (Hintošová, 2021). Digital technology is shaping the future of global trade and investment (Shyla, 2020). The current global investment flows in technology-based businesses and knowledge-based ventures situated upstream of value chains are part of the world economy's digitalization process (Zanfei et al., 2019). As the digital transformation alters the nature of international trade, several regulatory problems are brought to light, including net neutrality, digital market access, privacy, conditions of competition, data localization, and freedom of cross-border data flows (Ciuriak & Ptashkina, 2018).

RESEARCH METHODOLOGY AND OBJECTIVES

The EU's strategy aims to create a unified digital market, boosting economic growth by removing barriers to online transactions and promoting cross-border digital services. The EU invests in broadband and 5G technologies to ensure robust digital infrastructure, critical for economic development. Also, promotes digital literacy and skills development (Bradić-Martinović & Banović, 2018; Jevtić et al., 2023) to prepare its workforce for the digital economy, enhancing competitiveness and employment.

Digital transformation is critical for economic development for several reasons. It fundamentally alters how economies operate, enabling greater efficiency, innovation, and growth. Digital transformation leads to the emergence of new industries and business models, such as e-commerce, fintech, and digital marketing, which contribute to GDP growth. Digital technologies facilitate advanced research and development, leading to innovative products and services. Businesses that adopt digital solutions gain a competitive advantage through improved customer experiences, innovative offerings, and operational efficiencies.

Montenegro has experienced fluctuating GDP growth rates, influenced by global economic conditions, domestic policies, and investment levels. Tourism and services are key drivers of GDP growth. Trade, particularly with the European Union, is vital for economic stability and growth. Montenegro has made efforts to create a favorable investment climate through regulatory reforms, improving the ease of doing business, and offering incentives for foreign investors. Montenegro has undertaken significant regulatory reforms to align with EU standards, improve the business environment, and attract investment. Efforts to improve digital infrastructure are underway, supporting the digital transformation and enhancing economic opportunities.

The objective of this chapter is to analyze the digital transformation as a factor for the economic development of Montenegro. In this regard, the chapter consists of two interconnected units, namely:

1. Impact of macroeconomic indicators on the economic development of Montenegro,
2. Process of digital transformation of the public administration of Montenegro.

In the first part of this chapter, the focus is on the analysis of the current macroeconomic situation in Montenegro, viewed through the three most important indicators: GDP, FDI, export and import of products and services. The period covered by the research is from 2013 to 2023, while the desk research is based on officially available secondary data published by the World Bank and the Directorate for Statistics of Montenegro (Monstat).

The second part of the chapter focuses on the digital transformation of Montenegro, since strengthening Montenegrin society's digital environment and the ICT sector's digital competitiveness are also important goals of the state, which also aims to increase competencies and capabilities for digital transformation. In this context, this part analyzes the segment of the digital transformation process using appropriate index (eGovernment Index and eParticipation Index). The period covered by the research is from 2012 to 2022, while the secondary research is based on officially available data published by the United Nations (UN).

The Influence of Macroeconomic Indicators on the Economic Development of Montenegro

Macroeconomic indicators are important measures that reflect the stability of an economy. They influence economic development in many ways and provide insight for policymakers, investors and businesses to make informed decisions. Understanding their influence on economic development helps policy makers to develop effective strategies to promote growth, stability and sustainability. Key indicators such as GDP, unemployment rate, inflation, interest rates, fiscal balance, trade balance, foreign exchange reserves, foreign direct investment, public debt and exchange rates interact in complex ways to shape the economic landscape and determine a country's development path. A sound economic policy that effectively manages these indicators can lead to sustainable economic development, an improvement in living standards and an increase in global competitiveness. In this section we will focus on GDP, FDI and the export and import of products and services as important macroeconomic indicators for Montenegro's economic development.

The gross domestic product of Montenegro fluctuated in the period 2013-2020. year, which can be seen in graph 1 (Figure 1). In 2015, the amount of GDP was the lowest - 4.05 trillion dollars, after which it was consistently above 4.3 trillion dollars. Montenegro had the highest GDP amount in 2023 - 7.41 trillion dollars. Since 2015, Montenegro's GDP has risen from 4.05 to 5.54 trillion dollars, which corresponds to the GDP in 2019. After the decline in GDP in 2020, it showed an upward trend over the next three years. According to the projections for the next six-year period (2024-2029), GDP per capita is expected to show a growth trend.

GDP is expected to be around 8 trillion dollars in 2024, while it could be around 10.3 trillion dollars in 2029.

Figure 1. GDP (in billion U.S. dollars)

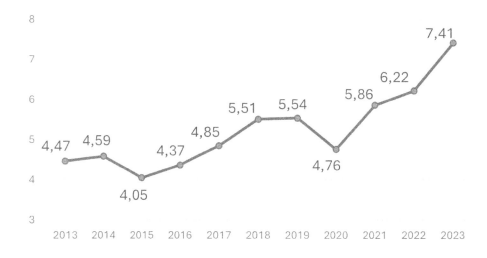

Figure 2. GDP per capita (in U.S. dollars)

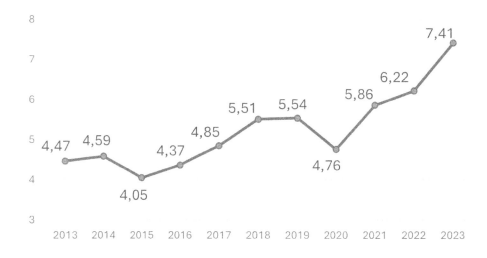

Source: Authors based on World Bank and Monstat, 2024.

The gross domestic product per capita in Montenegro shown in graph 2 (Figure 2) illustrates a growth trend in the period from 2015 to 2019. In the observed period, the lowest value was exactly in 2015 and amounted to 6534 dollars per capita. In addition to 2015, there was a further decline in GDP in 2020, which was caused by the coronavirus crisis and amounted to 7,689 dollars per capita at that time. From 2021, GDP per capita has had a constant growth trend and will reach the amount of 11,696 dollars in 2023.

The GDP growth rate fluctuated in the period 2013-2018. year, which can be seen in chart 3 (Figure 3). Montenegro had the highest GDP growth rate in 2018, when it amounted to 5.1%. The GDP rate had a negative value in 2020, when it amounted to -15.3%. Already in 2021, there was a jump in the GDP growth rate to 13%, while in the last two observed years this rate was relatively stable and hovered around 6%.

Figure 3. Growth rate of the real GDP from 2013 to 2023.

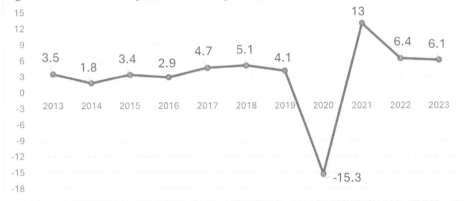

Source: Authors based on World Bank and Monstat, 2024.

Graph 4 (Figure 4) shows that Montenegro's exports, expressed as a percentage of GDP, range between 26% and 53% in the period 2013-2023. annually. The lowest percentage of exports, measured as a % of GDP, was in 2020, when it amounted to 26%, which was mainly due to the COVID-19 crisis. This was followed by constant growth in the following years, reaching 52.7% in 2023, which was also the highest value in the analysis of the observed period. Imports, expressed as a percentage of gross domestic product, ranged from 60 to 66.7 in the period from 2013 to 2020. After the decline in 2020, there was a significant increase in imports to Montenegro, ranging from 62.2% in 2021 to 76% in 2023, which is the highest value for the observed period.

Figure 4. Imports and exports of goods and services (% of GDP)

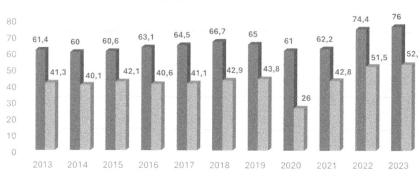

Source: Authors based on Monstat, 2024.

Graph 5 (Figure 5) shows the absolute values of Montenegro's exports and imports in the period 2013-2023. Imports had an upward trend from 2013 to 2020 and ranged between 1773 and 2600 million euros. The decline was recorded in 2020, with imports amounting to EUR 2,105 million in that year. In the last three years, the import of goods and services in Montenegro has increased, with imports in 2023 amounting to 3810 million euros, which is significantly more than in all analyzed years. The export of goods and services showed certain fluctuations in the observed period, which are noticeable until 2022. In the period 2013-2020. in 2008, exports were in the range of 317-415 million euros. In the last two years analyzed, there was a sharp increase in exports, more specifically, exports in 2022 amounted to 700 million euros, while exports in 2023 amounted to 674 million euros.

Figure 5. Imports and exports of goods and services (million €)

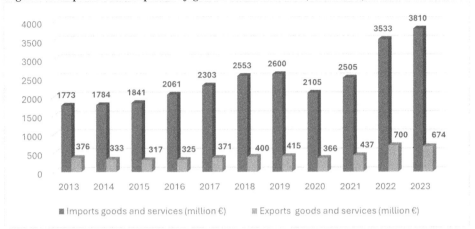

Source: Authors based on Monstat, 2024.

Foreign direct investment is one of the most important drivers of economic development in Montenegro. Graph 6 (Figure 6) shows the net inflow of foreign direct investment in Montenegro in the period 2013-2023. year, with fluctuations between USD 226 million in 2016 and USD 877 million in 2022. The total inflow of foreign direct investment in 2022 is over 1.2 billion USD, which is largely due to the growth in real estate investment (61%). The net inflow of foreign direct investment in the period under review amounted to USD 877 million. USD, an increase of around 25% compared to 2021. A drastic decline in net FDI inflows of around 51% was recorded in 2023 compared to 2022. When analyzing the evolution of this macroeconomic indicator, a significant increase in net FDI was recorded in the first three years observed, ranging between 448 and 699 million dollars. The first major decline in FDI inflows in the observed period was recorded in 2016, when investments amounted to only 226 million dollars. Montenegro recorded the largest FDI inflow in 2022 with 877 million dollars. The second major decline in FDI inflows occurred in 2023, when net FDI in Montenegro amounted to "only" 428 million dollars.

Figure 6. Foreign direct investment

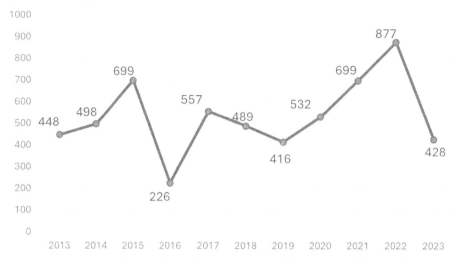

Figure 7. Foreign direct investment, net inflows (million U.S. dollars), and net inflows (% of GDP)

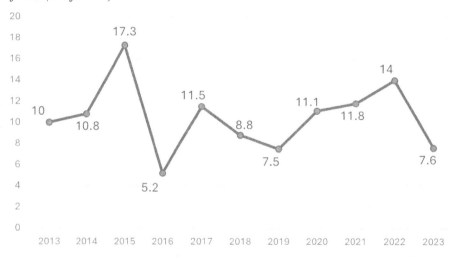

Source: Authors based on World Bank, 2024.

Looking at the inflow of net direct investment as a percentage of GDP in Graph 7 (Figure 7), fluctuations can be seen throughout the entire observation period. However, the sharpest decline was recorded in two periods, namely: (a) 2015-2016. from 17.3 to 5.2% of GDP and (b) 2022-2023. from 14 to 7.6% of GDP.

The decline in FDI inflows in 2023 has a significant impact on Montenegro's economic development. The direct decline in foreign investment has a negative impact on GDP, slows economic growth and affects key sectors such as tourism and real estate. To mitigate these effects, Montenegro needs to take proactive measures, diversify its economic base and create a more stable and attractive investment environment. Understanding these dynamics will help in devising effective strategies to sustain economic growth and development in the long term.

The Process of Digital Transformation of Public Administration in Montenegro

Digital transformation is now more important than ever, both for the modernization of the public sector and for the standardization of the private sector, which must follow global trends. Digitalization of all areas of society is no longer just a matter of choice, but an important fact that a society must face at every step (Marjanović et al. 2023). The advent of new technologies that are marked by intensive and quick development is anticipated to accelerate the ongoing process of digital transformation enormously. The reform of public administration and its connection with macroeconomic indicators that determine economic development is extremely important for every country, including Montenegro.

A key component of the public administration reform process is the deployment of electronic services and the digital transformation of public administration. Reorganizing and improving corporate processes with the use of all available digital tools and technologies is known as digital transformation. In public administration, this means the improvement of business processes and the provision of services in electronic and digital form. The normative framework is essential to the growth of e-government and the digital society. The specific goals of the legislative regulation are to increase public trust in the use and exchange of electronic documents while creating an environment conducive to a more intense use of electronic commerce. The application of these laws facilitates advancements in international position and action, and they are equally vital for citizens, businesses, state administration, local self-government, and other subjects. Recognizing that it is necessary to create normative conditions for the effective implementation of the digital transformation process, the following laws have been adopted in Montenegro so far: the Law on Electronic Administration, the Law on Administrative Procedure, the Law on Electronic Documents, the Law on Electronic Identification and Electronic Signature, the

Rulebook on eID, the Law on Information Security, the Regulation on Information Security Measures, the Law on Personal Data Protection. Montenegro has created and approved the Strategy for Public Administration Reform 2022–2026 as a part of the EU membership process. The government's medium-term program aims include fostering the rapid growth of new generation networks, enhancing e-services continuously, and utilizing information and communication technology widely in public administration, the business sector, and society at large.

There are numerous research methods for the development of e-government, which differ in their scope, objectives and the parameters they measure. Some aim to measure the impact of ICT, i.e. e-government, on the economic development of a country, while others measure the satisfaction of citizens and the impact on their daily lives. The ranking of countries based on the results of these surveys is relative and can be interpreted differently. However, most EU countries follow the United Nations "e-Government Survey", which is conducted every two years. In this part of the chapter, the analysis will focus on the EGDI and EPI index.

The e-Government Development Index shows the condition of e-government development in each of the United Nations member nations. The EGDI is a composite of three index that measure three important aspects of e-government:

a) Online Service Index (OSI). The ability and willingness of a government to interact electronically with its citizens and offer services is gauged by the online service index. The four stages of national authorities' online availability are measured by the online service index. The first step, known as the emerging information service, assesses whether the government's website offers links to other government departments and ministries as well as user-friendly information for citizens. The enhanced information service, or second stage, essentially assesses whether a government website facilitates simple two-way or one-way communication between residents and authorities. The ability for individuals and the national administration to communicate in both directions is measured in the third stage, transactional services. This includes the ability to request and receive feedback on government policies and manage a variety of public services online.

b) Telecommunications Infrastructure Index (TII). The current infrastructure needed for citizens to engage in e-government is measured by the telecommunication infrastructure index. The estimated number of internet users, primary fixed telephone lines, mobile subscribers, fixed internet subscriptions, and fixed broadband facilities per 100 residents make up the TII. The TII assesses the ability of the corresponding national telecommunication infrastructure to allow individuals to participate in all types of e-government, whereas the online service index analyzes the digital presence and capabilities of governments.

c) Human Capital Index (HCI). The human capital index measures citizens' ability to use e-government services. The literacy rate and the total gross enrolment ratio for basic, secondary, and postsecondary education are combined to create the human capital index.

The EGDI index tracks the development of public administration in 193 countries around the world. According to this index, the five best-positioned countries in the world in 2022 are: Denmark (0.9717), Finland (0.9533), the Republic of Korea (0.9529), New Zealand (0.9432) and Iceland (0.9410). In 2020, Denmark (0.9753) was best positioned, followed by the Republic of Korea (0.9560), Estonia (0.9473), Finland (0.9452) and Australia (0.9432). Table 1 shows the ranking of the Western Balkan countries according to the eGovernment Development Index.

Table 1. Western Balkan countries - EGDI ranking

Country	2022	2020	2018	2016	2014	2012
Albania	63	59	74	82	84	86
Bosnia and Herzegovina	96	94	105	92	n.a.	79
Montenegro	71	75	58	47	45	57
North Macedonia	80	72	79	69	n.a.	70
Serbia	n.a.	58	49	39	69	51

Source UN E-Government Knowledgebase, 2024.

In terms of years observed, Montenegro had the best position in 2014, when it ranked 45th with an index of 0.6346. Compared to the Western Balkan countries, Serbia had the best position during the observed period, while Montenegro generally ranked between 45 and 75 in the same period, which was just behind Serbia according to the EGDI index.

Figure 8. E-Government Development Index (EGDI)

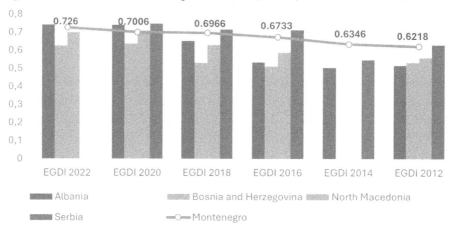

Graph 8 (Figure 8) shows the level of the EGDI index in the countries of the Western Balkans for the period 2014-2022. year. Compared to all other countries included in the study, the Western Balkan countries were between 63 and 96 in 2022, which clearly indicates that ideal conditions have not yet been created that would contribute to a more comprehensive development of public administration.

Montenegro's standing has also altered regarding the eParticipation Index (EPI). Index evaluates how well the public administration uses electronic services to inform the public, interacts with stakeholders—that is, anyone who has an interest in using these services online—and involves people in the decision-making process as well as the formulation of laws and regulations. In 2020, Montenegro's position on this indicator deteriorated significantly compared to 2016 (Montenegro dropped from 17th place in 2016 to 100th place in 2020). In the course of 2022, Montenegro has a positive sign compared to other countries in the world (+17) but is still inadequate compared to the period 2012-2016.

Table 2. Western Balkan countries - EPI ranking

Country	2022	2020	2018	2016	2014	2012
Serbia	15	41	48	17	81	60
Albania	22	36	59	55	59	101
North Macedonia	43	38	71	65	134	89

continued on following page

Table 2. Continued

Country	2022	2020	2018	2016	2014	2012
Bosnia and Herzegovina	72	87	125	89	129	161
Montenegro	83	100	64	17	49	48

Source UN E-Government Knowledgebase, 2024.

If we compare the countries of the Western Balkans (Table 2), Montenegro performs the worst in the last two sections (2020-2022) and thus takes last place among the countries surveyed. However, it should be borne in mind that Montenegro performed very well in the e-participation index in 2016 (17th place out of a total of 193 countries included in the analysis) (see Figure 9).

Figure 9. E-Participation Index (EPI)

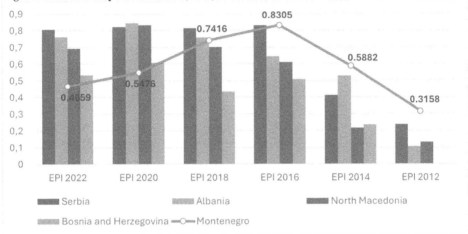

Source UN E-Government Knowledgebase, 2024.

It is crucial to note that the studies assess how far along each nation has come in e-government; hence, Montenegro's ranking on the international UN list has declined as a result of reforms undertaken or put into place by other nations. Therefore, even with Montenegro's current reform initiatives, many other nations have made greater progress and have received higher rankings as a result. As a result, it will be required to plan actions in the upcoming time frame to buck this trend and move in the other way.

CONCLUSION

Digital transformation in Montenegro is an essential part of the country's strategy to increase economic growth, improve public services and increase competitiveness. Montenegro has made significant progress in the digitalization of public services. Citizens can access various services online, such as tax declarations, business registrations and other administrative processes, reducing the need for face-to-face interactions and increasing efficiency. The government has set up an e-government portal that centralizes access to public services and makes it easier for citizens and businesses to interact with authorities. The information and communication technology (ICT) sector is growing, with a focus on the development of software, IT services and digital solutions for various industries. Montenegro is working to advance innovation and enhance its digital infrastructure, which opens doors for tech-related businesses (Domazet et al., 2024). Due to its unique characteristics, Montenegro's digitalization and overall industrial development pose a major challenge for engineering and science (Kara et al., 2023).

To take full advantage of the digital transformation, Montenegro needs to invest in digital infrastructure, education and supportive legal frameworks to ensure that all parts of society can participate in and benefit from the digital economy. Continued cooperation between the government, the private sector and international partners is crucial to overcome the challenges and maximize the potential of digital transformation for Montenegro's economic development. Further efforts are needed to streamline the regulatory framework to support digital innovation and attract investment. Although there have been improvements, improving digital literacy remains a priority to ensure that all citizens can benefit from the digital transformation.

In order to promote economic growth, close the gap between urban and rural development and improve the standard of living of the rural population, the rural areas of Montenegro need to experience a digital revolution. Montenegro is increasingly focusing on the digitalization of its economy and society and is working to bring these benefits to its rural areas. The development of infrastructure, e-government and public services, smart agriculture, entrepreneurship and innovation, education and healthcare, tourism and digital advertising are some of the most important aspects of the digital transformation in rural Montenegro.

Despite some encouraging successes, there are still barriers to the full implementation of digital transformation in rural areas in Montenegro. When it comes to digital skills and access to technology, there is still a clear divide between rural and urban areas. Especially in the remote mountainous regions, there is a need to invest heavily in infrastructure. To facilitate the digital transformation, the government must continue to develop favorable regulations and policies, including financial incentives for the private sector. With the help of EU initiatives such as the Digital Agenda for the Western Balkans, Montenegro hopes to significantly advance the digitalization of rural areas in the coming years. Rural communities can better integrate into the national and international economy by bridging the digital divide.

As a future member, Montenegro could make use of the EU's financial resources, knowledge and legal framework, which can accelerate the country's digital transformation. Encouraging greater cooperation between the public and commercial sectors can stimulate investment in innovation and infrastructure, closing the gaps in digital services and connectivity. Some of Montenegro's infrastructure and regulatory problems can be solved through cooperation with surrounding countries and international organizations in the areas of cybersecurity, broadband infrastructure projects and regulatory alignment. Numerous infrastructural and regulatory obstacles stand in the way of Montenegro's digital transformation, particularly in the modernization of both urban and rural areas. To ensure that the country can take full advantage of the digital economy, improve public services and promote inclusive growth, these issues need to be addressed.

Digital transformation in Montenegro is an ongoing process with significant potential to boost economic growth, improve public services and enhance the overall quality of life. By investing in digital infrastructure, fostering innovation, improving digital skills and ensuring robust cybersecurity measures, Montenegro can create a thriving digital economy that benefits all parts of society. Continued collaboration between the government, the private sector and international partners will be crucial to overcoming the challenges and reaping the full benefits of digital transformation. Although significant progress has been made, challenges such as economic diversification, unemployment and sustainability remain. Continued focus on regulatory reform, infrastructure development and investment in human capital will be crucial for Montenegro to achieve sustainable and inclusive economic growth. This is significant because there is a positive correlation between public administration reform and economic development and because the reform has a significant impact on the growth of real GDP, foreign direct investment and trade volume.

The limitations of this paper, that could be addressed in future research, are: (a) the study of e-government development using the EGDI and EPI index was conducted only for the Western Balkan countries with a focus on Montenegro, (b) three macroeconomic indicators were analyzed (GDP, FDI, export and import of goods and services), (c) the study covered the period 2014-2022, (d) the analysis was conducted based on officially available UN data as well as WB and Monstat. Accordingly, the recommendations for future research refer to: (a) include more countries in the analysis (e.g. EU countries, SEE region, BRICS countries, etc.), (b) conduct the research based on a longer time series that would cover the period of at least 2000 years, (c) apply additional methods using secondary/primary data to gain new insights and information and then draw conclusions and recommendations.

ACKNOWLEDGEMENT

The research presented in this paper was funded by the Ministry of Science, Technological Development and Innovation of the Republic of Serbia under contract number 451-03-47/2023-01/200005.

REFERENCES

Agu, S. C., Onu, F. U., Ezemagu, U. K., & Oden, D. (2022). Predicting gross domestic product to macroeconomic indicators. *Intelligent Systems with Applications*, 14, 14. DOI: 10.1016/j.iswa.2022.200082

Amanasto, W., Hamzah, M. Z., & Sudaryono, B. (2019). How The Effect of Investment Policy at Information and Communication Technology for Digital Economy Implementation toward Macroeconomic Indicators and Sectoral Performance, in Indonesia? *OIDA International Journal of Sustainable Development*, 12(09), 11–24.

Antonijević, M., Domazet, I., Kojić, M., & Simović, V. (2024). Financial Inclusion - A Driving Force for Women's Entrepreneurship Development. *Journal of Women's Entrepreneurship and Education*, 3-4, 73–92. DOI: 10.28934/jwee24.34.pp73-92

Bobenič Hintošová, A., & Bódy, G. (2023). Sustainable FDI in the digital economy. *Sustainability (Basel)*, 15(14), 10794. DOI: 10.3390/su151410794

Bradić-Martinović, A., & Banović, J. (2018). Assessment of digital skills in Serbia with focus on gender gap. *Journal of Women's Entrepreneurship and Education*, 1-2(1-2), 54–67. DOI: 10.28934/jwee18.12.pp54-67

Broz, T., Buturac, G., & Parežanin, M. (2020). Digital transformation and economic cooperation: The case of Western Balkan countries. Zbornik radova Ekonomskog fakulteta u Rijeci: časopis za ekonomsku teoriju i praksu, 38(2), 697-722.

Casella, B., & Formenti, L. (2019) . FDI in the digital economy: a shift to asset-light international footprints. Transnational corporations, 25(1), 101-130.

Chenic, A. ., Burlacu, A., Dobrea, R. C., Tescan, L., Crețu, A. I., Stanef-Puica, M. R., Godeanu, T. N., Manole, A. M., Virjan, D., & Moroianu, N. (2023). The Impact of Digitalization on Macroeconomic Indicators in the New Industrial Age. *Electronics (Basel)*, 12(7), 1612. DOI: 10.3390/electronics12071612

Ciuriak, D., & Ptashkina, M. (2018). The digital transformation and the transformation of international trade. RTA Exchange. Geneva: International Centre for Trade and Sustainable Development and the Inter-American Development Bank. Available at *SSRN*: https://ssrn.com/abstract=3107811

Corejova, T., & Chinoracky, R. (2021). Assessing the potential for digital transformation. *Sustainability (Basel)*, 13(19), 11040. DOI: 10.3390/su131911040

Dethine, B., Enjolras, M., & Monticolo, D. (2020). Digitalization and SMEs' export management: Impacts on resources and capabilities. *Technology Innovation Management Review*, 10(4), 18–34. DOI: 10.22215/timreview/1344

Domazet, I.. (2023). Innovation and ICT: Key Factors of Successful Business. In Correia, A., & Agua, P. B. (Eds.), *Innovation, strategy, and transformation frameworks for the modern enterprise* (pp. 327–345). IGI Global. DOI: 10.4018/979-8-3693-0458-7.ch014

Domazet, I., & Marjanović, D. (2024). Digital Progress and Information Society: Evidence from EU Countries and Serbia. In Verma, B., Singla, B., & Mittal, A. (Eds.), *Driving Decentralization and Disruption With Digital Technologies* (pp. 1–20). IGI Global. DOI: 10.4018/979-8-3693-3253-5.ch001

Domazet, I., Marjanović, D., & Ahmetagić, D. (2022) . The Impact of High-Tech Products Exports on Economic Growth: The Case of Serbia, Bulgaria, Romania and Hungary. Ekonomika preduzeća, 70(3-4), 191-205.

Domazet, I., Marjanović, D., Ahmetagić, D., & Antonijević, M. (2022). Does the Increase in the Number of Registered Patents Affect Economic Growth? Evidence from Romania and Bulgaria. *Economic Analysis: Applied Research in Emerging Markets*, 55(2), 49–65. DOI: 10.28934/ea.22.55.2.pp49-65

Domazet, I., Marjanović, D., Ahmetagić, D., & Bugarčić, M. (2021). The Impact of Innovation Indicators on Increasing Exports of High Technology Products. Ekonomika preduzeća, 69(1-2), 31-40.

Domazet, I., Marjanović, D., Ahmetagić, D., & Simović, V. (2023). The influence of the number of patents on the economic growth of the country - evidence from Serbia and Hungary. *Strategic Management*, 28(4), 41–52. DOI: 10.5937/StraMan2300048D

Domazet, I., Marjanović, D., & Subić, J. (2024). Driving factors of the Montenegrin economy – FDI and tourism. *International Review (Steubenville, Ohio)*, 1-2(1-2), 117–127. DOI: 10.5937/intrev2401117D

Domazet, I., Zubović, J., & Lazić, M. (2018). Driving Factors of Serbian Competitiveness: Digital Economy and ICT. *Strategic Management*, 23(1), 20–28. DOI: 10.5937/StraMan1801020D

Esses, D., Csete, M. S., & Németh, B. (2021). Sustainability and digital transformation in the visegrad group of central European countries. *Sustainability (Basel)*, 13(11), 5833. DOI: 10.3390/su13115833

Gebayew, C., Hardini, I. R., Panjaitan, G. H. A., & Kurniawan, N. B. (2018). A systematic literature review on digital transformation. *International Conference on Information Technology Systems and Innovation*, 260-265, IEEE. DOI: 10.1109/ICITSI.2018.8695912

Golubović, V., Mirković, M., Mićunović, N., & Srića, V. (2021). Digital Transformation in Montenegro–Current Status, Issues and Proposals for Improvement. *Journal of Computer Science and Information Technology*, 9(1), 1–12. DOI: 10.15640/jcsit. v9n1a1

Gurbaxani, V., & Dunkle, D. (2019). Gearing up for successful digital transformation. *MIS Quarterly Executive*, 18(3), 209–220. DOI: 10.17705/2msqe.00017

Hintošová, A. B. (2021). The digital economy in the context of foreign direct investment flows. In Boitan, I. A., & Marchewka-Bartkowiak, K. (Eds.), *Fostering Innovation and Competitiveness with FinTech, RegTech, and SupTech* (pp. 210–227). IGI Global. DOI: 10.4018/978-1-7998-4390-0.ch011

Irtyshcheva, I., Kim, V., & Kletsov, Y. (2022). Managing business processes in the conditions of the development of the digital economy: Global and national experiences. *Baltic Journal of Economic Studies*, 8(5), 101–107. DOI: 10.30525/2256-0742/2022-8-5-101-107

Jevtić, B., Vučeković, M., & Tasić, S. (2023) . The Effects of Digitalization and Skills on Women's Labor Market Inclusion-Serbian Gap Study. Journal of Women's Entrepreneurship and Education, 58-75.

Kara, P. A., Ognjanovic, I., Maindorfer, I., Mantas, J., Wippelhauser, A., Šendelj, R., Laković, L., Roganović, M., Reich, C., Simon, A., & Bokor, L. (2023). The present and future of a digital Montenegro: Analysis of C-ITS, agriculture, and healthcare. *Eng*, 4(1), 341–366. DOI: 10.3390/eng4010021

Kochetkov, E.P. (2020) . Digital transformation of economy and technological revolutions: Challenges for the current paradigm of management and crisis management. Strategic decisions and risk management, 10(4), 330-341.

Kolodynskyi, S., Drakokhrust, T., & Bashynska, M. (2018). The innovative infrastructure of economic development in the framework of international digital transformation. *Baltic Journal of Economic Studies*, 4(4), 166–172. DOI: 10.30525/2256-0742/2018-4-4-166-172

Kraus, S., Jones, P., Kailer, N., Weinmann, A., Chaparro-Banegas, N., & Roig-Tierno, N. (2021). Digital transformation: An overview of the current state of the art of research. *SAGE Open*, 11(3), 21582440211047576. DOI: 10.1177/21582440211047576

Liere-Netheler, K., Packmohr, S., & Vogelsang, K. (2018). Drivers of digital transformation in manufacturing. *Hawaii International Conference on System Sciences*, 3926-3935.

Limarev, P.V., Limareva, Y.A., Akulova, I.S., Khakova, G.S., Rubanova, N.Y.A., & Nemtsev, V.N. (2018) . The role of information in the system of macroeconomic indicators. Revista Espacios, 39(50).

Liu, Q., & Ananthachari, P. (2023). Research on the impact of enterprise digital transformation on the enhancement of export competitiveness. *Information Systems and Economics*, 4(8), 69–74.

Loonam, J., Eaves, S., Kumar, V., & Parry, G. (2018). Towards digital transformation: Lessons learned from traditional organizations. *Strategic Change*, 27(2), 101–109. DOI: 10.1002/jsc.2185

Małkowska, A., Urbaniec, M., & Kosała, M. (2021). The impact of digital transformation on European countries: Insights from a comparative analysis. Equilibrium. *Quarterly Journal of Economics and Economic Policy*, 16(2), 325–355. DOI: 10.24136/eq.2021.012

Marjanović, D., & Domazet, I. (2021). Foreign Direct Investments: A Key Factor for Business Globalization. In Bayar, Y. (Ed.), *Institutional, Economic, and Social Impacts of Globalization and Liberalization* (pp. 96–116). IGI Global. DOI: 10.4018/978-1-7998-4459-4.ch006

Marjanović, D., & Domazet, I. (2023). Economic Measures for Mitigation of the Consequences of COVID-19: Evidence From Serbia. In Marco-Lajara, B., Özer, A. C., & Falcó, J. M. (Eds.), *The Transformation of Global Trade in a New World* (pp. 180–199). IGI Global.

Marjanović, D., Domazet, I., & Vukmirović, I. (2022). Social Environment as a Factor of Capital Investment in Serbia. *Eastern European Economics*, 60(3), 247–264. DOI: 10.1080/00128775.2022.2048181

Marjanović, J., Domazet, I., & Miljković, J. (2023). Higher Education Branding through Instrumental Values. *Journal of Women's Entrepreneurship and Education*, 3-4, 75–94.

Melović, B., Jocović, M., Dabić, M., Vulić, T. B., & Dudic, B. (2020). The impact of digital transformation and digital marketing on the brand promotion, positioning and electronic business in Montenegro. *Technology in Society*, 63, 101425. DOI: 10.1016/j.techsoc.2020.101425

Mićić, L. (2017) . Digital transformation and its influence on GDP. Economics-innovative and economics research journal, 5(2), 135-147.

Mingaleva, Z., & Shironina, E. (2021). Gender aspects of digital workplace transformation. *Journal of Women's Entrepreneurship and Education*, (1-2), 1–17.

Nadkarni, S., & Prügl, R. (2021). Digital transformation: A review, synthesis and opportunities for future research. *Management Review Quarterly*, 71(2), 233–341. DOI: 10.1007/s11301-020-00185-7

Nambisan, S., Wright, M., & Feldman, M. (2019). The digital transformation of innovation and entrepreneurship: Progress, challenges and key themes. *Research Policy*, 48(8), 103773. DOI: 10.1016/j.respol.2019.03.018

Nguyen, T.T.M. (2020). Foreign Direct Investment Strategy of MNCs in the Context of Digital Transformation. VNU journal of economics and business, 36(3).

Nie, J., Jian, X., Xu, J., Xu, N., Jiang, T., & Yu, Y. (2024). The effect of corporate social responsibility practices on digital transformation in China: A resource-based view. *Economic Analysis and Policy*, 82, 1–15. DOI: 10.1016/j.eap.2024.02.027

Olczyk, M., & Kuc-Czarnecka, M. (2022). Digital transformation and economic growth-DESI improvement and implementation. *Technological and Economic Development of Economy*, 28(3), 775–803. DOI: 10.3846/tede.2022.16766

Olubusola, O., Mhlongo, N. Z., Falaiye, T., Ajayi-Nifise, A. O., & Daraojimba, E. R. (2024). Digital transformation in business development: A comparative review of USA and Africa. *World Journal of Advanced Research and Reviews*, 21(2), 1958–1968. DOI: 10.30574/wjarr.2024.21.2.0443

Parra, J., Pérez-Pons, M.E., González, J. (2021) . The Impact and Correlation of the Digital Transformation on GDP Growth in Different Regions Worldwide. Advances in Intelligent Systems and Computing, 1242.

Raji, M. A., Olodo, H. B., Oke, T. T., Addy, W. A., Ofodile, O. C., & Oyewole, A. T.Mustafa Ayobami RajiHameedat Bukola OlodoTimothy Tolulope OkeWilhelmina Afua AddyOnyeka Chrisanctus OfodileAdedoyin Tolulope Oyewole. (2024). The digital transformation of SMES: A comparative review between the USA and Africa. *International Journal of Management & Entrepreneurship Research*, 6(3), 737–751. DOI: 10.51594/ijmer.v6i3.884

Romanova, O.A., & Kuzmin, E. (2021) . Industrial policy: A new reality in the context of digital transformation of the economy. Lecture Notes in Information Systems and Organisation, 44.

Rothstein, S. A. (2024). Transnational governance of digital transformation: Financing innovation in Europe's periphery. *New Political Economy*, 29(2), 227–239. DOI: 10.1080/13563467.2023.2240236

Saadi Sedik, T., Chen, S., Feyzioglu, T., Ghazanchyan, M., Gupta, S., Jahan, S., Jauregui, J. M., Kinda, T., Long, V., Loukoianova, E., Mourmouras, A., Nozaki, M., Paroutzoglou, S., Sullivan, C., Yoo, J., & Zhang, L. (2019). The digital revolution in Asia and its macroeconomic effects. ADBI Working Paper Series 1029.

Shyla, J. (2020) . Effect of digitalization on import and export. Emperor Internationaa Journal of Finance and Management Research, V(7), 1-12.

Stephenson, M., Eden, L., Kende, M., Kimura, F., Sauvant, K.P., Srinivasan, N., Tajoli, L., & Zhan, J. (2021) . Leveraging digital FDI for capacity and competitiveness: How to be smart. T20, Task Force 3 (policy brief).

Tang, D. (2021). What is digital transformation? *EDPACS*, 64(1), 9–13. DOI: 10.1080/07366981.2020.1847813

Tiutiunyk, I., Drabek, J., Antoniuk, N., Navickas, V., & Rubanov, P. (2021). The impact of digital transformation on macroeconomic stability: Evidence from EU countries. *Journal of International Students*, 14(3).

Tudose, M. B., Georgescu, A., & Avasilcăi, S. (2023). Global Analysis Regarding the Impact of Digital Transformation on Macroeconomic Outcomes. *Sustainability (Basel)*, 15(5), 4583. DOI: 10.3390/su15054583

Verhoef, P. C., Broekhuizen, T., Bart, Y., Bhattacharya, A., Dong, J. Q., Fabian, N., & Haenlein, M. (2021). Digital transformation: A multidisciplinary reflection and research agenda. *Journal of Business Research*, 122, 889–901. DOI: 10.1016/j.jbusres.2019.09.022

Wang, G., Lamadrid, R. L., & Huang, Y. (2024). Digital Transformation and Enterprise Outward Foreign Direct Investment. *Finance Research Letters*, 65, 65. DOI: 10.1016/j.frl.2024.105593

Wang, P. (2022). The Impact of Enterprise Digital Transformation on the Foreign Investment Strategy of Enterprises. International Conference on Economic Management and Cultural Industry, 816-827. Atlantis Press.

Xu, G., Li, G., Sun, P., & Peng, D. (2023). Inefficient investment and digital transformation: What is the role of financing constraints? *Finance Research Letters*, 51, 51. DOI: 10.1016/j.frl.2022.103429

Yoo, I., & Yi, C. G. (2022). Economic innovation caused by digital transformation and impact on social systems. *Sustainability (Basel)*, 14(5), 2600. DOI: 10.3390/su14052600

Zanfei, A., Coveri, A., & Pianta, M. (2019). FDI patterns and global value chains in the digital economy. Working Papers 1903, University of Urbino Carlo Bo. Available at: http://www.econ.uniurb.it/RePEc/urb/wpaper/WP_19_03.pdf

Zuzaku, A., & Abazi, B. (2022). Digital transformation in the western balkans as an opportunity for managing innovation in small and medium businesses-Challenges and opportunities. *IFAC-PapersOnLine*, 55(39), 60–65. DOI: 10.1016/j.ifacol.2022.12.011

ADDITIONAL READING

Behera, B., Haldar, A., & Sethi, N. (2024). Investigating the direct and indirect effects of Information and Communication Technology on economic growth in the emerging economies: Role of financial development, foreign direct investment, innovation, and institutional quality. *Information Technology for Development*, 30(1), 33–56. DOI: 10.1080/02681102.2023.2233463

Bocean, C. G., & Vărzaru, A. A. (2023). EU countries' digital transformation, economic performance, and sustainability analysis. *Humanities & Social Sciences Communications*, 10(1), 1–15. DOI: 10.1057/s41599-023-02415-1

Burlea-Schiopoiu, A., Brostescu, S., & Popescu, L. (2023). The impact of foreign direct investment on the economic development of emerging countries of the European Union. *International Journal of Finance & Economics*, 28(2), 2148–2177. DOI: 10.1002/ijfe.2530

Elia, G., Solazzo, G., Lerro, A., Pigni, F., & Tucci, C. L. (2024). The digital transformation canvas: A conceptual framework for leading the digital transformation process. *Business Horizons*, 67(4), 381–398. DOI: 10.1016/j.bushor.2024.03.007

Hunady, J., Pisár, P., Vugec, D. S., & Bach, M. P. (2022). Digital Transformation in European Union: North is leading, and South is lagging behind. *International Journal of Information Systems and Project Management*, 10(4), 58–81. DOI: 10.12821/ijispm100403

Joel, O. S., Oyewole, A. T., Odunaiya, O. G., & Soyombo, O. T.Olorunyomi Stephen JoelAdedoyin Tolulope OyewoleOlusegun Gbenga OdunaiyaOluwatobi Timothy Soyombo. (2024). The impact of digital transformation on business development strategies: Trends, challenges, and opportunities analyzed. *World Journal of Advanced Research and Reviews*, 21(3), 617–624. DOI: 10.30574/wjarr.2024.21.3.0706

Kara, O., Altinay, L., Bağış, M., Kurutkan, M. N., & Vatankhah, S. (2024). Institutions and macroeconomic indicators: Entrepreneurial activities across the world. *Management Decision*, 62(4), 1238–1290. DOI: 10.1108/MD-04-2023-0490

Kwilinski, A. (2023). The Relationship between Sustainable Development and Digital Transformation: Bibliometric Analysis. *Virtual Economics*, 6(3), 56–69. DOI: 10.34021/ve.2023.06.03(4)

Liu, P., Zhu, B., Yang, M., & De Baets, B. (2024). Contribution of digital governments to digital transformation of firms: Evidence from China. *Technology Analysis and Strategic Management*, ●●●, 1–15. DOI: 10.1080/09537325.2024.2344078

Nadeem, K., Wong, S. I., Za, S., & Venditti, M. (2024). Digital transformation and industry 4.0 employees: Empirical evidence from top digital nations. *Technology in Society*, 76, 76. DOI: 10.1016/j.techsoc.2023.102434

Novák, J. K., Král, J. J., & Dvořák, P. T. (2024). The Impact of Trade Liberalization on FDI Inflows and Economic Development. *Law and Economy*, 3(5), 9–23. DOI: 10.56397/LE.2024.05.02

Obydiennova, T., Kharabara, V., Zabashtanskyi, M., Nazarko, S., & Havronskyi, A. (2024). The Impact of Digital Transformation on the Innovative Development of Economic Systems. *Management Theory and Studies for Rural Business and Infrastructure Development*, 46(1), 63–70. DOI: 10.15544/mts.2024.07

Olczyk, M., & Kuc-Czarnecka, M. (2022). Digital transformation and economic growth-DESI improvement and implementation. *Technological and Economic Development of Economy*, 28(3), 775–803. DOI: 10.3846/tede.2022.16766

Stoliarov, V., & Sinkovskiy, M. (2024). Digital transformation of EU member states' economies towards achieving Sustainable Development Goals. *Finance of Ukraine*, 1(1), 69–85. DOI: 10.33763/finukr2024.01.069

Su, Y., & Wu, J. (2024). Digital transformation and enterprise sustainable development. *Finance Research Letters*, ●●●, 60.

Sui, X., Jiao, S., Wang, Y., & Wang, H. (2024). Digital transformation and manufacturing company competitiveness. *Finance Research Letters*, ●●●, 59.

Török, L. (2024). The relationship between digital development and economic growth in the European Union. *International Review of Applied Sciences and Engineering*.

Wang, S., Hou, D., Guo, Y., & Dai, L. (2024). The mediation effect of innovation in the domestic and international economic development circulation. *Technology Analysis and Strategic Management*, 36(5), 989–1001. DOI: 10.1080/09537325.2022.2069003

Zekos, G. I. (2024). *Digital Transformation of EU and Competition. Artificial Intelligence and Competition: Economic and Legal Perspectives in the Digital Age*. Springer Nature Switzerland.

KEY TERMS AND DEFINITIONS

Digital technologies: Digital technology refers to the electronic tools, resources, systems and devices that organizations use to process and store data, as well as perform numerous other tasks that increase employee productivity and efficiency. An important aspect of digital technology is information technology, i.e. the use of computers to process data and information.

Digital transformation: The process of integrating digital technology into every aspect of an organization and radically changing the way you run your business and deliver value to your customers is called "digital transformation" Companies must constantly experiment, challenge the established quo and learn to accept failure as part of this cultural change. Unlike ordinary business transformations, which usually come to an end as soon as a new habit is achieved, digital transformations are long-term initiatives that aim to rewire the way a company continuously improves and changes.

Economic development: Business and investment are often associated with economic development. Although they are most often associated with economic expansion, they have a more complex and significant impact on the prosperity and overall well-being of communities. Thus, primitive, low-income economies are upgraded to highly developed industrial economies. The goal of economic development is to enhance the standard of living and financial stability of the people living in each area through a variety of strategies. This requires taking calculated risks to increase competitiveness, promote growth and build a robust, dynamic economy. With the goal of creating a sustainable and inclusive future for communities, this collaboration encompasses a wide range of initiatives, from workforce training to job creation and infrastructure development.

Economic growth: Digital technology refers to the electronic tools, resources, systems and devices that companies use to process and store data, as well as for numerous other tasks that increase the productivity and efficiency of their employees.

Macroeconomic indicators: Macroeconomic indicators, sometimes referred to as fundamentals, are numbers or measurements that indicate the state of the economy in a particular nation, area or industry. Governments and analysts use them to assess the state of financial markets and the economy both now and in the future. At a national or regional level, macroeconomic indicators quantify and provide insight into the overall health and growth prospects of an economy. They are important economic indicators that can be used to compare one economy with another or with previous eras.

Chapter 5
Leveraging Data Analytics and Business Intelligence for Seamless Digital Transformation

Ojaswa Banerjee
Woxsen University, India

Kirti Nandan
Woxsen University, India

Shreyash Kumar
Woxsen University, India

Mohd Azhar
https://orcid.org/0000-0003-3222-5565
Woxsen University, India

ABSTRACT

This chapter addresses challenges that leaders face when leveraging the advantages of data analytics (DA) and business intelligence (BI) especially in the context of digital transformation. It also discusses the increasing significance of data analytics and business intelligence in driving digital transformation and their influence on business leadership. Further, it closely examines the integration challenges that leaders face when leveraging digital technology to promote organizational change and data governance. In pursuit of the research objective, this chapter is organized as follows: Section 1 presents the introduction. Section 2 offers an extensive review of the literature encompassing digital transformation, DA BI, and organizational

DOI: 10.4018/979-8-3693-5966-2.ch005

leadership. The subsequent section elucidates the different opportunities and challenges that leaders encounter with the integration of digital technology. Furthermore, digital technology, tools, and platforms are discussed, with implications and, at last, conclusion.

1. INTRODUCTION

The significance of digital transformation has translated to a necessary restructuring in the current economy for business to survive and sustain themselves. For the organisation it is no longer an option, it is a strategic adjustment that borders on the social transformation happening in the organisation beyond just the introduction of technology (World Economic Forum, 2021). This means a sweeping change in organisations' overall approach to all activity that define them and their offering, from idea generation and design through to delivery and support. As more and more firms turn to technology solutions, they can improve organizational functions, optimize key processes, and deliver outstanding customer value (World Economic Forum, 2020). Several key factors are driving the urgency of digital transformation:

First off, there is intense competition in the business world from both well-established firms and nimble start-ups that are skilled at making efficient use of digital technologies (LaBerge et al., 2020). In order to be competitive, this calls for constant adaptability.

Second, seamless and customized experiences across all touchpoints are what modern customers seek. People anticipate requirements from businesses and want answers that speak to them. Digital technologies facilitate stronger consumer ties by enabling firms to meet these changing demands (Kozak et al., 2021).

Thirdly, opportunities for innovation and disruption are created by the ongoing development of new technologies such as cloud computing, big data analytics, and artificial intelligence (AI). Companies that don't change run the risk of falling behind.

Decisions made by executives are more informed and result in better outcomes thanks to data-driven insights obtained from digital tools (International Data Corporation, 2021). Decision-makers may make more confident strategic choices because data analytics gives them a comprehensive picture of consumer behaviour, industry trends, and operational bottlenecks. Furthermore, digital technologies can greatly lower expenses while raising productivity through automated operations and improved workflows. Human resources can concentrate on higher-value tasks by automating repetitive processes.

A company's ability to innovate in many different areas might be stimulated by digital technologies (International Data Corporation, 2021). Sales forecasting, demand planning, and one on one meetings with the customer are some of the applications where they turned to predictive analytics for better outcome and innovation (Biswas et al., 2023). Taking advantage of digital tools' capabilities can stimulate the development of new products, marketing techniques, and even entire company models. Digital channels can help to build client happiness and loyalty by enabling real-time engagement and personalized experiences.

In fact, in recent studies, Augmented analytics, which uses AI and machine learning to automate data preparation, insight production, and data science models, has made major strides in recent years. This change expedites the time to insights and makes data-driven decision-making accessible to non-technical individuals (Sanghai, 2023).

Businesses have embraced data mesh and data fabric architectures to solve data complexity and governance issues. By providing scalable methods for managing and analysing distributed data environments, these strategies assist companies in undergoing digital transformation in a more seamless manner (Yazici and Aksoy, 2022).

Real-time data analytics are becoming more and more in demand, and this has been one of the major forces behind change in recent years. In order to improve operational efficiency and react more quickly to shifting market conditions, businesses gave priority to making decisions in real time. For instance, real-time analytics for supply chains and logistics become essential for handling interruptions brought on by supply chain shortages and geopolitical crises (Biswas et al., 2023).

Digital transformation is a pivotal undertaking for businesses in today's competitive environment. By embracing this holistic shift and leveraging digital technologies effectively, businesses can unlock a multitude of benefits, enabling them to thrive in the ever-evolving landscape.

2. UNDERSTANDING THE IMPACT OF COVID-19 ON DIGITAL TRANSFORMATION

Although the COVID-19 outbreak worked as a catalyst, quickening the pace of digital transformation and reorienting its emphasis toward fundamental reorganization, the trend has been steadily increasing in the corporate environment for years technologies (LaBerge et al., 2020).

Enhanced customer experiences and efficiency advantages were the two main areas of focus for digital transformation efforts prior to the worldwide pandemic. In order to decrease costs and streamline operations, organizations adopted cloud computing, automation, and other emerging technologies. Efficiency was the main focus, with technology being used to maximize current functions and procedures (Malik et al., 2020). To increase client involvement and happiness, businesses also made use of digital platforms including social media, smartphone apps, and e-commerce. To develop streamlined and customized client experiences across all touchpoints, this facet of digital transformation was implemented (Kozak-Holland et al., 2020). Nonetheless, around this time, departmental approaches were frequently seen in digital transformation projects. Oftentimes, initiatives were carried out inside certain divisions, like sales or marketing, but they weren't always applied across the board. This siloed strategy reduced the possibility of an all-encompassing change within the company. Before the pandemic, digital transformation was essentially more incremental in nature, concentrating on employing technology to optimize already-existing processes and functionalities, frequently within designated departments.

The COVID-19 pandemic compelled a swift and significant change in the way business's function. Organizations as a whole needed a more fundamental restructure as a result of lockdowns, social distancing measures, and disrupted supply chains. The corporate landscape has undergone significant transformation, and in order to thrive, businesses must be flexible and agile. That implies having the ability to totally restructure their operations.

A significant change has been the increase of remote work. Businesses must invest in things like robust cybersecurity, cloud-based collaboration tools, and video conferencing in order for this to be successful (LaBerge et al., 2020).

The swift adoption of remote work has completely transformed the way we work, requiring businesses to devise innovative strategies for employees to stay connected, cooperate, and remain productive.

With more and more individuals connecting and shopping online, consumer behavior has also altered. Businesses must change to survive in this digital age by concentrating on providing contactless interactions and online service delivery.

The pandemic's most notable effect may have been its impetus for a comprehensive transformation strategy. A total revamp of business models, procedures, and culture was necessary as digital transformation emerged as an enterprise-wide need (International Data Corporation, 2021). This move required a more integrated approach to organizational change and technology adoption because it cut across departmental boundaries. The pandemic served as a driving force behind a more thorough and profound digital transformation of enterprises. It placed a strong emphasis on adaptability, resilience, and the capacity to change quickly in any given context. A more all-encompassing strategy has replaced the pre-pandemic emphasis on efficiency and departmental optimization. Enterprises nowadays acknowledge the necessity of a comprehensive digital shift that encompasses every facet of the operations (Kozak-Holland et al., 2020). This restructuring requires a cultural shift towards embracing agility, innovation, and data-driven decision-making.

3. ROLE OF DATA ANALYTICS AND BUSINESS INTELLIGENCE IN SEAMLESS DIGITAL TRANSFORMATION

Businesses were compelled by the COVID-19 epidemic to go beyond simple optimization and adopt a more fundamental restructure that prioritizes resilience, agility, and data-driven decision-making (World Economic Forum, 2021). This means that in addition to technology developments, a cultural transformation is required. In this new era, Data Analytics (DA) and Business Intelligence (BI) emerge as potent instruments to drive smooth digital transformation (Chen et al., 2012).

Digital transformation initiatives prior to the pandemic frequently concentrated on isolated enhancements in departmental efficiency and customer experience. But the pandemic revealed this strategy's shortcomings. Companies that did not have a comprehensive, data-driven approach found it difficult to change with the times (International Data Corporation, 2021). Businesses can make well-informed decisions, streamline departmental procedures, and anticipate customer demands in real-time with the help of DA and BI, which extract profound insights from large data sets (Chen et al., 2012). Think of a retail business that existed before the pandemic and was devoted to simplifying internet shopping. They would not have been ready for the full switch to online purchasing during lockdowns, even though this provided some efficiency improvements. To ensure a smooth digital transformation in the face of disruption, DA and BI, on the other hand, might have assisted in the analysis of customer behavior patterns (Kozak-Holland et al., 2020). the prediction of online demand surges, and the adaptation of the entire supply chain.

However, one problem that arises is as more organizations integrate DA and BI into their digital evolution process, the amount of data they manage becomes one that is highly sensitive. Although DA and BI have potentially powerful impacts on reducing operation costs and enhancing decision-making process, they also create new risks for organization, particularly concerning the cyber risks. It also becomes important to secure this data to meet the necessary regulatory requirement and regain customers' trust.

Although, the advantages transcend beyond personal productivity, it is important to stay aware of the potential breaches that may occur due to digital transformation. As businesses personalize interactions and give customers the information they require at the precise moment by employing real-time data analysis (Kozak-Holland et al., 2020), cyber security threats especially data breaches are some of the many risks that organizations may face as they go through the digital transformation process.

Since the large data sets are being collected, processed and analysed across multiple platforms, the risk of cyber-attack improves. IBM, in its Cost of a Data Breach 2023 report has indicated that the average cost of a data breach today is $4.45 million and the compromised credentials, cloud misconfiguration and phishing attacks are listed some of the most common causes.

One way to address this is to adapt a cybersecurity-first strategy which is necessary in safeguarding the operations of DA and BI. Organizations need to establish robust security frameworks that encompass real-time threat detection, and ZTA (Zero Trust Architecture) for DA-BI.

4. ROLE OF ARTIFICIAL INTELLIGENCE AND MACHINE LEARNING IN INTELLIGENT DECISION MAKING AND CUSTOMISED CUSTOMER EXPERIENCES

New technologies are always evolving, and this causes ongoing change in the corporate sector. AI and machine learning (ML) are two of the newest and most popular developments at the moment. For businesses, these are upending the status quo and altering the way they function and engage with their clientele.

4.1 AI and ML for Intelligent Decision-Making

Traditionally, experience and intuition were used to make decisions. By giving firms a culture of data-driven decision-making, DA and BI revolutionize this process. Large-scale data sets are analyzed by AI and machine learning algorithms to find patterns, forecast future events, and suggest the best course of action (Chen et al., 2012). This results in more precise, effective, and perceptive decisions made throughout the company. For example, more accurate demand forecasting can be achieved by AI-powered sales forecasting, which examines consumer behavior, industry trends, and historical data (Biswas et al., 2022). This makes it possible for companies to allocate resources and manage inventories more effectively, which is essential for a smooth digital transformation.

Gains in operational efficiency are also unlocked by DA and BI. With the help of AI and ML, monotonous jobs can be automated, freeing up human resources for strategic thinking (Wamba et al., 2018). According to (Tran et al., 2021), imagine AI-powered chatbots answering standard customer support questions, cutting down on wait times, and increasing customer happiness. Machine learning algorithms have the potential to enhance manufacturing production processes by minimizing waste and increasing efficiency. DA and BI complement risk management, to sum up. Artificial intelligence and machine learning algorithms examine financial data and customer behavior patterns in order to detect possible hazards and instances of fraud. By taking a proactive stance, companies may reduce risks and protect their bottom line.

4.2 Transition to Customer Experience

Although machine learning and artificial intelligence (AI) facilitate smart decision-making in a variety of commercial domains, their influence is most noticeable in the area of customer experience. In the part that follows, let's examine how these technologies are promoting consumer pleasure and creating individualized connections. In addition to developments in AI and ML, the rise of potent communication technologies like 5G also shapes the landscape of digital transformation. 5G, which boasts extremely high speeds, extremely low latency, and enormous network capacity, promises a major improvement over earlier generations of wireless connectivity. These features are radically changing how companies use the Internet of Things (IoT), augmented reality (AR), and virtual reality (VR), three major components of digital transformation.

4.2.1 How 5G Revolutionizes Immersive Experiences with AR and VR

VR's dependence on high bandwidth and minimal latency has always been one of its main drawbacks. This meant that sessions can be slow or not have the clear images necessary for a fully immersive experience. But the rapid speeds and extremely low latency of 5G are altering the rules. Virtual reality experiences may now claim real-time responsiveness and superb high-resolution images, resulting in a smooth and immersive environment for users. Businesses now have a plethora of options thanks to this. Consider providing responsive and lifelike VR simulations for staff training across many industries (Akdere et al., 2021). The features of 5G enable trainees to rehearse intricate operations in a secure virtual environment. Customers can virtually interact with things before they buy them thanks to VR product demonstrations that the retail and e-commerce industries can also use.

Not only will 5G altering VR, but it's also giving companies the ability to create and implement advanced Augmented Reality (AR) experiences. When doing maintenance duties, imagine a technician donning augmented reality (AR) glasses that project real-time instructions and equipment data directly onto their field of vision. This is the capability of AR made possible by 5G. Here, 5G's low latency is critical because it guarantees smooth communication between the real and virtual worlds. For many other professionals, including technicians, this promotes increased accuracy and productivity.

4.2.2 Understanding the Potential of IoT

By facilitating smooth connections for an enormous number of devices, 5G's vast network capacity fully realizes the potential of the Internet of Things (IoT) (Lv and Singh, 2021). Exciting new developments in smart cities and industrial environments are made possible by this.

5G allows environmental monitoring, real-time traffic control, and a network of interconnected infrastructure in smart cities. Efficiency and citizens' quality of life may both be greatly enhanced by this. For example, environmental sensors can continuously update the quality of the air and water, and traffic signals can act dynamically depending on real-time congestion data.

IoT applications in the industrial sector also gain a lot from 5G. With such quick speeds, industries are able to use predictive maintenance to prevent expensive downtime, optimize production processes based on real-time data, and execute remote equipment performance monitoring (Mineraud et al., 2016). These linked devices are gathering enormous amounts of data, which may be examined to obtain insightful knowledge and make data-driven decisions that enhance operations as a whole.

5. RISKS AND COSTS OF IMPLEMENTATION OF DATA ANALYTICS AND BUSINESS INTELLIGENCE

5.1 High Implementation Costs

One of the main challenges of companies when adopting Data Analytics (DA) and Business Intelligence (BI) systems is the high costs associated with performing such type of systems. Such costs include cost of acquiring licenses for software and hardware, web hosting and clouds, costs of maintenance of the system and associated support services. In addition, conversion into DA and BI calls for capital investment on data facility such as servers and data warehouse, which may summon high costs for SMEs.

As highlighted by (Imran et al. 2021), it is stated that the one and a half or even two times more expensive than what was initially planned, costs of introducing advanced DA and BI systems. A considerable part of costs is related to data transfer and system interoperability since many legacy systems cannot be integrated with up-to-date DA and BI systems. Also, these systems are prone to requiring constant updates and security fixes, which contribute to the general operating costs (Konopik et al., 2021).

Options such as cloud-based applications instead of the on-premise systems can be considered. About this, it is important to note that cloud platforms are flexible as AWS or Microsoft Azure where businesses are only charged based on the number of resources utilized. In addition, organizations can choose gradual implementation, in which organizations adopt DA and BI tools in individual sections, thereby not requiring large investments at the initial stage of implementing the technology (Chen et al., 2022).

5.2 Current Skills Shortage and Shortcomings in the Workforce

It has been observed in the case of implementing both DA and BI that the major limitation is the scarcity of qualified and professional workforce. Based on different research papers, there is increasing number of jobs opportunities for data scientist, analyst, and IT specialists for interpretation of big data (Wamba et al., 2023). But what most organizations have experienced is the challenge of sourcing employees with the right skills in data modelling, machine learning, and advanced analytics among others.

However, a number of employees continue to grapple with poor usage rates of DA and BI tools in that most of these systems involve technical complexities. Many organizations have to deal with the challenge of training their employees to fit into these emerging tools in a way that they would be able to harness this power in arriving at decisions. Yazici & Aksoy, in their work published in 2022, identified a number of difficulties in the practical implementation of DA and BI technologies, among which the lack of qualified personnel takes a leading position.

To overcome it, the organizations should ensure that they enhance the skills of their current workforce through training. One of the ways that can support the initiative of DA and BI skills development is through internal training programs that aim to make the employees familiar with these tools. Also, collaborations with education providers for training or certification programmes or otherwise in data science and analytics may overcome this deficit in the long term (Imran et al., 2021).

One of the best approaches is the implementation of easy-to-use BI systems that operate within the organization's setting. Most of the lean modern Business Intelligence solutions today come with drag and drop, visualization tools, dashboards and guided analytics where a layman can work on a BI tool without any prior training in IT. There point out that tools like Tableau or Power BI are developed to be more user-friendly to a wider level of employees in the organization (Chen et al., 2022).

5.3 Complex Integration with Legacy Systems

The various legacy systems prove to be a major challenge for the successful adoption of the DA and BI technologies. Legacy systems could lack the storage capacity for today's huge datasets and combining them with newer platforms leads to high system outages and distorted data. This is so because, with modern technological advancements, legacy systems are common in processes of manufacturing firms, health facilities, and financial institutions among others (Konopik et al., 2021).

To overcome these integration challenges, it is recommended that business organizations should opt for data governance in an effort to standardize, manage and regulate the flow of data between applications and units within the organization. Through this way, governance policies can help companies to standardize the format of data, manage its consistency and avoid the existence of silos (Yazici and Aksoy, 2022).

Moreover, organizations might also consider the use of middleware platforms that could form a link between old DA systems and the newer ones to be incorporated in the process. These platforms allow for easy bedding because they translate data from previous systems into formats that DA and BI tools can understand to avoid disruption of the implementation process (Chen et al., 2022).

Although both DA and BI provide invaluable information, they at the same time increase the organizations' vulnerability to data security and privacy. Since organizations gather, accumulate and process big amounts of private data, they turn into attractive objectives of cyber exploitation. Failing to ensure that cybersecurity measures are in place exposes the organizations to the loss of data to hackers, thus exposing them to hefty fines as provided by the GDPR and CCPA.

These risks can only be minimized through the implementation of modern cybersecurity measures such as the encryption of data, the provision of secure access to data and conducting periodic reviews of the Data Security Management Processes implemented in various organizations. Another emerging methodology is called Zero Trust Architecture (ZTA) that requiring every device and user to pass through the identification process to gain access to the valuable information (Biswas et al., 2023).

6. ESTABLISHED THEORETICAL FRAMEWORKS IN DIGITAL TRANSFORMATION, DATA ANALYTICS, AND BUSINESS INTELLIGENCE

To deepen the understanding of digital transformation, data analytics, and business intelligence (BI), it is essential to understand established theoretical frameworks and models. These frameworks provide a structured approach to analyzing the complexities of digital transformation and the strategic implementation of data-driven technologies within organizations.

6.1 Technology Acceptance Model (TAM)

Developed by Davis in 1989, the Technology Acceptance Model (TAM) is a foundational framework for understanding how users come to accept and use technology. TAM posits that two main factors—Perceived Usefulness (PU) and Perceived Ease of Use (PEOU)—drive an individual's intention to engage with a new technology. In the context of digital transformation and BI, TAM can be applied to assess the adoption of BI tools within organizations. By analyzing employees' perceptions of the utility and usability of these tools, businesses can better strategize their digital transformation initiatives to ensure widespread acceptance and effective usage.

6.2 Delone and McLean Information Systems Success Model

The Delone and McLean Information Systems Success Model (1992) identifies six key dimensions that contribute to the success of information systems: System Quality, Information Quality, Service Quality, Use, User Satisfaction, and Net Benefits. This model is particularly relevant to evaluating the effectiveness of BI systems. For example, high-quality data analytics platforms that provide reliable and actionable insights directly contribute to improved decision-making processes. This model can be used as a framework to measure the impact of BI systems on organizational performance and user satisfaction.

6.3 The DIKW Pyramid (Data, Information, Knowledge, Wisdom)

The DIKW Pyramid is a widely recognized hierarchical model that illustrates the transformation of raw data into wisdom through progressive stages: Data, Information, Knowledge, and Wisdom. In the realm of BI, this model offers a clear representation of how data analytics processes convert raw data into strategic insights that inform decision-making. The DIKW Pyramid serves as a conceptual foundation for understanding the value chain of data processing and its role in driving business success through informed, knowledge-based decisions.

6.4 The Strategic Alignment Model (SAM)

The Strategic Alignment Model (SAM), proposed by Henderson and Venkatraman in 1993, emphasizes the importance of aligning business strategy with IT strategy to achieve organizational goals. In the context of digital transformation,

SAM underscores the need for a cohesive approach where digital initiatives are closely integrated with the overall business strategy. This alignment ensures that investments in BI and data analytics are not just technological upgrades but are strategically positioned to drive business growth and competitiveness.

By incorporating these established theoretical frameworks into the analysis of digital transformation, data analytics, and BI, this chapter not only grounds its discussions in well-recognized academic theory but also provides readers with a comprehensive understanding of the strategic implications of these concepts. These frameworks offer valuable insights into how businesses can successfully implement and leverage digital technologies to achieve long-term success and competitive advantage.

7. CHALLENGES OF DIGITAL TRANSFORMATION

New technologies such as AI, ML, 5G, and the like provide promising platforms for companies' digitalisation; however, the path to such changes is not smooth. In order to accomplish the goals mentioned above, several barriers must be overcome in this case for companies to realize the integration of these technologies as seamless as possible. It is important to understand that most digital transformations involve vast organizational culture shifts, new processes, procedures, and the skills of the workforce. The change management process that has to be addressed often becomes challenging when it comes to managing resistance to change and encouraging innovation. This can be addressed by appreciating communication, having good training sessions, and having strong leadership backing.

Because of the fast-growing rate of advancement in implementing technologies, there is a need for qualified personnel to deploy new technological advancements. The implementers may not have the required skills to properly handle and interpret large data sets, AI, and cyber-security among others (Konopik et al., 2021). One potential solution is for organisations to upskill and reskill their current workforce, or to strategically hire graduates/talent with the right skills. New cybersecurity risks are brought about by the digital transformation, which also creates new opportunities. Hackers have a greater surface area to target due to our growing dependence on networked devices and massive data volumes. Risk mitigation requires spending money on robust cybersecurity defences, educating staff on good cyber hygiene, and keeping up of new threats.

It can be quite expensive to implement new technology and upskill the workforce. It is imperative that the possible return on investment (ROI) be weighed against the expense of transformation. Budgetary restrictions can be managed by grant and partnership exploration, cost-benefit analysis, and prioritization (Imran et al., 2021).

Besides these, the three most important management issues to concentrate on are managing change, upskilling the workforce, and cybersecurity. The adoption of Data Analytics (DA) and Business Intelligence (BI) in the operation of an organization is expected to bring positive changes in decision-making, productivity, and customer relations among others. However, these advantages are usually associated with significant challenges such as, organizational cultures of resistance to change, requirement for employees' skill upgrade, and security risks. These issues are going to be crucial for a comprehensive understanding of barriers and possibilities in the process of digital transition.

7.1 Resistance to Change

This model reveals one of the key reasons as to why DA and BI is hard to implement - resistance to change. There is always a tendency for employee to resist organizational change especially when it relates to a shift in technology. This resistance can be due to factors such as being frightened of losing their jobs, feeling dissatisfied with new innovations that come with information technology, or even perceive that they are losing their decision-making power (Imran et al., 2021).

It was also pointed out by scholars that there is far more resistance to change in formalized routine business. Due to this, employees especially those trained on the old European style of working may look at DA and BI as more of an unsettling influence as opposed to actual development tools. This challenge is worse when the leadership does not explain how adopting these technologies benefits the organization in the future, thus a disconnect between what is envisioned by the organization and what the employees believe in (Konopik et al., 2021).

7.2 Workforce Upskilling

This is another discouraging factor that slows down the implementation of DA and BI since most of the employees are not capable to provide the needed technical support. It is pertinent to note that the field of data technology is progressing rapidly and many employees lack adequate technical skills for optimizing on these tools. As revealed by (Wamba et al. 2023) up to 70% of the organizations observed that skill lacking as the main problem that do affect their DA and BI exercise.

Employees may be deficient in data literacies, data management competencies and generating data-derived insights. Also, there are emerging jobs like the data scientists, data engineers, and business analysts for which the market is saturated, and attracting and retaining a talented pool can be challenging for organizations. Even the best DA and BI tools can achieve their best when people who use them are not well trained.

7.3 Cybersecurity Concerns

The main risky area that hinders DA and BI adoption is the security to protect the large amount of data that these systems process. The more arrays an organization gathers and otherwise deals with, the need it becomes to arouse the risks of cybersecurity breaches. These threats include data breaches, malware and ransomware attacks are quite sensitive for industries that engage in processing of sensitive information such as healthcare, finance and government services (Konopik et al., 2021).

These difficulties draw attention to how complicated digital transformation is. Organizations may facilitate a seamless transition and fully realize the benefits of digital transformation by recognizing these obstacles and devising countermeasures. We'll look more closely at the particular digital tools and platforms needed to accomplish a smooth, data-driven digital transition in the following section.

8. HOW DATA ANALYTICS AND BUSINESS INTELLIGENCE OPTIMISE OPERATIONS, ENHANCE CUSTOMER EXPERIENCES, AND DRIVE INNOVATION

Data analytics (DA) and business intelligence (BI) have transformative ability that goes well beyond enabling data-driven decision-making. These are essential tools for streamlining fundamental business processes, creating outstanding client experiences, and encouraging an innovative culture.

8.1 Optimizing Operations

Productivity and operational efficiency can be greatly increased with the help of strong technologies like business intelligence (BI) and data analytics (DA). Workflow bottlenecks and inefficiencies can be found via DA and BI through the analysis of operational data. With the use of this invaluable data, companies may boost productivity and efficiency by streamlining operations, allocating resources more wisely, and even automating tedious jobs. For example, logistics firms can use DA to improve delivery routes based on real-time traffic data, which can reduce fuel costs and save time (Biswas et al., 2023).

By examining sensor data from equipment and previous maintenance logs, DA can also be utilized for predictive maintenance. This enables companies to anticipate any equipment malfunctions before they happen. With this information, companies may put preventative maintenance plans into place, reducing downtime and guaranteeing continuous operations (Lee et al., 2018).

Moreover, DA forecasts demand by examining past sales data and industry trends. This helps companies optimize inventory levels and reduce the chance of stockouts or overstocking. In order to implement targeted promotions or product lifecycle management techniques and save storage costs, DA can also identify slow-moving inventory.

8.2 Enhancing Customer Experiences

Through the analysis of data, purchasing patterns, and previous interactions, DA enables organizations to tailor their client experiences. According to (Imran et al., 2021), this translates into personalized service interactions, marketing initiatives, and recommendations that are meant to increase customer connections and satisfaction.

Furthermore, companies can proactively handle any consumer issues before they escalate by using sentiment analysis of social media conversations and support queries. Customer happiness and brand loyalty are increased by this proactive strategy, which is made possible by DA (Biswas et al., 2023).

Lastly, real-time customer feedback analysis via social media monitoring and surveys is made easier by DA technologies. In order to maintain a constant feedback loop and a dedication to customer-centricity, businesses can use these insights to pinpoint areas for improvement in their goods, services, or customer journeys (Kozak-Holland et al., 2020).

8.3 Driving Innovation

The process of data analysis, or DA, is essential for fostering company innovation. Businesses can learn a lot by exploring competition offers, market trends, and customer preferences. With this knowledge, they may create innovative products and services that meet the changing wants of customers and unfulfilled market expectations (Chen et al., 2012).

DA is a prospector for undiscovered chances; it does more than just comprehend present patterns. Businesses might find totally new business ideas and unexplored market niches by studying customer data to reveal hidden patterns and trends. This enables them to increase their market share and investigate fascinating new opportunities (Yaqoob & Thomas, 2022)

DA's authority doesn't end there. It encourages a culture of rapid adaptation and experimentation. A/B testing of pricing schemes, product features, and marketing campaigns is made easier by DA. This enables colytras

Companies to evaluate the efficacy of various strategies and make data-driven choices. This trial and analysis cycle promotes agility and allows for ongoing development based on actual outcomes (Imran et al., 2021).

By streamlining processes, improving client interactions, and stimulating creativity, DA enables businesses to not only meet the difficulties of digital transformation but also prosper in the dynamic business environment. In order to achieve seamless digital transformation, the next section will go deeper into the particular tools and techniques used in DA, examining their functions and uses.

9. OPPORTUNITIES AND APPLICATIONS

For leaders navigating the constantly changing corporate landscape, the seamless integration of Data Analytics (DA) and corporate Intelligence (BI) opens up a wealth of potential. Organizations may improve customer happiness, optimize operations, stimulate innovation, and change their decision-making processes by utilizing data.

9.1 Decision-Making

Experience and intuition were once the primary factors in business decisions; but, with the advent of Data Analytics (DA) and Business Intelligence (BI), a new era of data-driven decision-making has begun. Using DA technologies, leaders can gain a thorough insight of market trends, customer behavior, and business performance by analyzing large amounts of historical and real-time data (Chen et al., 2012). They may decide on strategy, how to allocate resources, and what to invest in with the help of this data-driven approach.

Moreover, DA platforms include sophisticated analytics that can forecast possible results and future trends. Leaders are able to take proactive measures to tackle obstacles, grasp novel prospects, and make more confident selections by utilizing past data and machine learning algorithms.

Ultimately, self-service analytics platforms and user-friendly BI tools are democratizing data insights. As a result, workers at all levels can access and evaluate information pertinent to their positions. This encourages an organizational culture in which data guides choices at all levels.

9.2 Enhanced Operational Efficiency

Business intelligence (BI) and data analysis (DA) are no longer limited to high-level strategy. They can greatly enhance the daily operations of your company. Using DA, you can take a close look at your operational routines and identify any inefficiencies or slowdowns that are reducing your output. Leaders can automate repetitive operations, streamline procedures, and more efficiently allocate resources once they've identified these trouble spots (Wamba et al., 2018).

Businesses are further enabled by DA to transition from reactive maintenance to proactive tactics. Predictive models can foresee possible equipment problems before they occur by examining sensor data from the equipment and maintenance records from the past.

As a result, operations run smoothly and expensive downtime is reduced. Using demand forecasting models, market trends, and historical sales data, businesses may also use DA to optimize inventory levels. By doing this, there is less chance of overstocking and stockouts, which improves inventory control and lowers costs.

9.3 Drive Innovation

Business intelligence (BI) and data analytics (DA) solutions are revolutionary for companies. They support data-driven decision-making, optimize processes, and serve as catalysts for innovation that put businesses ahead of the competition. Sifting through client data, advanced analytics can find hidden patterns and trends that could reveal previously unidentified market niches or possible disruptions. Businesses are given the freedom to experiment, create cutting-edge goods and services, and acquire a competitive advantage as a result (Yaqoob & Thomas, 2022). A/B testing and experimentation are made simple by BI tools. Companies can experiment with various price plans, product features, and marketing efforts while tracking the results in real time. Businesses can quickly adjust to changing market dynamics thanks to this data-driven approach, which promotes agility and permits continual improvement based on tangible results (Imran et al., 2021).

10. ETHICAL CONSIDERATIONS

Data analytics (DA) and business intelligence (BI) is changing the way organisations operate, and is a step-change in digital conversion. But to unlock the benefits they offer, one must navigate a treacherous path through complex ethical territory. This ensures respectful and competent application between proper partners... efforts that build trust amongst a broad base of stakeholders.

Fairness and Bias: Data used in model creation When an algorithm makes a decision, it potentially makes this decision not due to how it was programmed, but due to the data it has been trained on. For instance, if an AI recruiting tool is trained on the hiring practices at a firm, it may discriminate against the target demographic if that hiring process is unfair (Brundage et al. 2020).

The last critical point is about very basic consideration: transparency AND explainability are equally important. Algorithms of a complex formulation, are more obscure than pure mathematical formulations and the exact reasoning behind their outputs may be obscure. This lack of transparency may undermine trust, accountability and create suspicions.

Digitization sometimes rides on the premise of massive capture and utilization of personal data. Sound data security measures are crucial to return from a practice or experiment and not have definitely compromised the user's privacy or had a breach. It is crucial to use and maintain a business's data securely to instantiate customer trust.

In addition, before going number crazy and implementing its data-driven solutions, organizations must perform algorithmic impact assessments (Jobin et al., 2019). Such evaluations mean an intention to realize potential impacts of the algorithms on employment opportunities, social relations, and human rights.

Even though analysing data can be of immense use, there is still a role for human discretion which entails ethical rationale (Manyika et al., 2017). There are undoubtedly many compelling benefits associated with organizations adopting sophisticated digital technologies and analytics, but it is crucial to remember that human supervision should always play an important part of the processes going on within an organization, whereby they need to remain skeptical about the facts and figures, gained from the business intelligence systems, while deciding on a particular strategy for action.

To navigate these ethical complexities, businesses can establish a comprehensive ethical framework for leveraging data analytics and BI. This framework should encompass clear data governance policies that define data collection, storage, and usage practices. Diversity and inclusion within data teams are crucial to mitigate bias through the incorporation of diverse perspectives. Explainable AI (XAI) techniques can be employed to make algorithms more interpretable, fostering better understanding. Transparency and communication are paramount, keeping stakeholders informed about data practices and how they are used. Finally, continuous monitoring and improvement are essential, requiring businesses to regularly review and update their ethical practices to stay aligned with evolving landscapes. When these ethical considerations are given priority, the potentials of data analytics and BI can be utilized to create a positive digital transformation agenda that is ethical and successful that gives room for the growth of trust and development of solutions to help businesses thrive.

11. DATA ANALYTICS AND BUSINESS INTELLIGENCE TOOLS FOR SEAMLESS DIGITAL TRANSFORMATION

The aforementioned prospects demonstrate the revolutionary impact of business intelligence (BI) and data analytics (DA). All staff are empowered with self-service analytics platforms and user-friendly BI solutions. They are able to see, examine, and display data pertinent to their roles thanks to these intuitive interfaces. This encourages data-driven decision-making throughout the entire company. These technologies enable individuals to contribute to overall success by dismantling information silos.

The increasing amount of data necessitates sophisticated analytics capabilities. This problem is solved by big data analytics platforms, which give companies the ability to handle and examine enormous volumes of unstructured, semi-structured, and structured data. Because of this, they are able to find patterns that are concealed and produce insights that can be put to use that would be impossible with traditional technologies (Chen et al., 2012).

Data analysis is further enhanced by artificial intelligence (AI) and machine learning (ML) techniques. Pattern recognition and data cleaning are two repetitious chores that machine learning automates. Businesses may now carry out sophisticated activities like sentiment analysis and anomaly identification thanks to artificial intelligence (AI). This makes the data even more insightful (Imran et al., 2021).

These resources—tools and platforms—are the foundation of a data-driven culture, not merely new developments in technology. This culture supports informed decision-making at all levels, encourages innovation, and optimizes operations. We will examine more pertinent technologies in the following part that enhance DA and BI and increase their influence on digital transformation.

i. **Cloud Computing for Data Storage and Scalability:** Cloud storage enables companies to store data online from any location in the globe. Additionally, businesses only have to pay for what they use because this magical box can expand or contract as needed. Because of this, it's an extremely economical solution **(Chen et al., 2012).**

ii. **Data Visualization Tools for Clear Communication of Insights:** Although useful, data can be misleading. This is where the analysis of data comes in. Consider it as a translation service for all of your phone numbers. With the aid of these technologies, all that data may be transformed into visually appealing images, charts, and graphs. Everyone in the organization will find it simpler to understand the data's meaning and apply it to make wiser decisions as a result.

Ensuring Consistency among participants, if no one can understand the data analysis, it is useless, no matter how good it is. Tools for data visualization are crucial because of this. Regardless of one's level of technical expertise, they assist in explaining the meaning behind the numbers in a way that everyone can understand. Furthermore, in today's customer-centric landscape, businesses that prioritize customer satisfaction thrive. DA and BI empower

i. **Personalization at Scale:** Whilst businesses have caught the drift of going smart to achieve personalization at scale, customer data, buying behaviors, and interactions should be subprocesses analyzed to deliver a range of online targeted marketing campaigns in real-time, recommend relevant products, and services, and efficient customer service. It analysed that this results in, increased customer interactions, connection, satisfaction and loyalty level (Imran et al., 2021).

ii. **Customer Service:** Monitoring public posts for the Social Media Conversation and CS tickets for selecting possible issues with potential to become enlarged Proactive Customer Service This is a dedication to the customers and also helps in brand patronage **(Biswas et al., 2023).**

iii. **Input and Improvement in Real-Time**: Regarding the information about clients feedbacks The DA technology offers a chance to monitor the interaction in the social networks and conduct the surveys on the clients' feedback in real time manner. It can assist organisations in having a continuous feedback cycle together with a focus on customer values as a result of which they can define the places where an explanation can be made for the enhancement of the related product or service exhibiting a sequence (Kozak-Holland et al., 2020).

By harnessing the power of DA and BI to personalize experiences, proactively address concerns, and continuously improve based on customer feedback, businesses can cultivate stronger relationships and achieve lasting customer satisfaction.

11.1 Complementary Technologies for Amplified Transformation

The presence of other technologies, related to DA and BI, can significantly enhance the toolkit, which consists of self-service analytics platforms, big data analytics, and machine learning with AI. Cloud computing, especially, becomes a decisive factor in the effective handling and analysis of data. The conventional setup of data infrastructure in-house is not always up to the mark in handling the volume and variety of data. Cloud computing eliminates these constraints due to the scalability and elasticity that it provides. Companies can quickly scale up or scale down their computing resources depending on their needs, making them highly capable of handling large datasets and varying levels of workloads (Chen et al., 2012). It also does not require businesses to invest in expensive equipment and infrastructure, and instead, they only have to pay for the resources that they use, which makes it cost-effective.

Teams may examine the data at any time and from any location thanks to cloud-based analytics and storage technologies. This encourages seamless departmental collaboration across multiple sites. Team members may collaborate in real time on shared datasets thanks to the dismantling of traditional information silos, which accelerates the process of developing insights and making decisions.

It will tackle our security issue too. Cloud service providers come well-equipped with several security tools to protect private data. The data integrity and the programmable secure access mechanisms are maintained through the regular backups, disaster recovery protocols, access controls and compliances to the industry regulations. At the same time, cloud platforms usually come with tooling and enterprise data governance capabilities that enable organizations to govern, track, and audit their data in a more compliant way.

Different clouds can also make data integration much easier as well. How can businesses use pre-built connectors and integration services to bring together data from databases, applications, social media platforms, and IoT devices all of which reside in different systems? This view, of course, is not very holistic in the way we often work with data, but it allows a much deeper and nuanced analysis of the data that can be carried through the other steps as well - an analysis rich in insights.

Cloud-Based Analytics platforms make it easier for businesses to deploy and scale data pipelines and analytics tools (Chen et al., 2012). Leverages rapid deployment: Grows experimentation and innovation. By providing a space where data scientists and analysts can test new hypotheses and iterate on models faster, they are able to use those insights to help the business make more tailored and faster decisions. To an extent cloud computing acts as a force multiplier for data analytics and business Intelligence in our opinion. Cloud computing enables businesses to tap into the full value of their structured and unstructured data, allowing them to achieve massive scalability and flexibility, together with enhanced security and simplified data management, to break free from siloed and legacy IT infrastructure; and embrace a true digital transformation, stepping into a data-driven future.

12. DATA ANALYTICS AND BUSINESS INTELLIGENCE INTEGRATION WITH BUSINESSES

DA and BI works in synchronization to enhance the level of operational efficiencies (Chen et al., 2012). From the given information, it can be understood that due to DA's skills in figuring out descriptive areas for processes improvement, DA ensures that various operations become efficient and cost-effective. BI, on the other hand, has the ability of giving constant performance measurements which enables business organization to appreciate its performance and recognize areas of weakness that warrants change. This leads to forming a virtuous circle, where certain aspects are optimised continuously (Chen et al., 2012).

The application of DA and BI also helps to improve customer satisfaction. DA helps an organisation to understand customers' behavior patterns and therefore allow a business organisation to offer tailored products and services and also anticipate the needs of its customers (Chiu et al., 2018). BI helps in assessing the various factors relating to customer satisfaction where a business can identify the opportunities to enhance their relations with their clients (Malik et al., 2020).

Of all the advantages that the integration of these tools offers, perhaps the most promising is its predictive abilities. DA, along with its sophisticated predictive models, therefore enforces the capacity of businesses to forecast market shifts and other future trends. It creates an advantage because it enables firms to adjust their strategies and engage in activities that are not conventional and satisfactorily profitability yet.

DA and BI are two critical pillars of digital transformations, and their integration counts among the primary strategies of effective digital changes. From the active use of data, the promotion of data culture, and addressing key problems that can hinder the further advancement of data as a production factor, strategic business decisions can be made, operational activities can be optimized, customer experiences can be enriched, and long-term success can be ensured in the context of a constantly developing digital environment.

13. RESEARCH AND EVIDENCE BASE

Conventional decision-making frequently depended on experience and intuition. Nevertheless, studies show how important data-driven insights are in the digital age. DA's sophisticated methods enable organizations to find hidden patterns and trends in large datasets and extract insightful information from them. BI, on the other hand, provides useful context for past performance by converting historical data into comprehensible reports and dashboards. This combined approach lowers risks and promotes a more strategic approach by enabling businesses to make decisions based on factual evidence.

Digitization is generally about making things simpler, much more streamlined and driving efficiency in your operations. Business outcomes will be impacted by Business Intelligence and Analytics (BDA), the integration of DA and BI, going forward. DA does a great job of recognizing areas for process improvement. Through workflow data analysis, DA can narrow down bottlenecks and inefficiencies. This enables them to apply changes where required resulting to optimize workflows with less costs. In addition, they watch real-time performance metrics which allow them to track their progress and discover places they can keep improving so that it forms a cycle of continues improvement.

Building relationships is the name of the game in the current customer-centric world. The insight agrees with supporting research: In many cases, Data Activation (DA) and Business Intelligence (BI) are key levers to drive superior customer experience. (Chiu et al., 2018) investigated an examination into how service-dominant logic moderates the relationship between big data analytics (DA) (a subset of relational data in this study) and customer experience. DA enables businesses to customize offerings and predict the customer requirements by unraveling the consumer behavior patterns. This approach is forward moving and generate satisfied, loyal customers. This also gives insights of customer satisfaction from sentiment analysis and feedback. This positivity helps companies to discover the sources of problems while creating connections with customers eventually (Malik et al., 2020).

14. FUTURE TRENDS AND INNOVATION

It is an infinite race of digital transformation journey empowered by Data Analytics (DA), Business Intelligence (BI), and many more technologies to name but a few. Looking at the future, a number of promising directions in the space are emerging, which deserve further study and potential exploration. There are possibilities and one of the futures is: Explainable AI (XAI). Given the impactful capabilities of Artificial Intelligence (AI), transparency and explainability in AI-driven decision making necessarily becomes crucial (Sanghai, 2023). Research in XAI is focused on what is required to gain the human trust and confidence in decision made by the model and how AI model actually generates insights (Sanghai, 2023).

Edge computing can be another avenue. Much data is generated at the 'edge' of networks – from sensors in Internet-of-Things (IoT) devices, for example, and wearables – and edge computing can bring analytics and processing much closer to where the data comes from, for instant insights and timely decision-making.

As more and more tasks are automated and more and more insights are illuminated, the role of leadership will evolve. The 'leader as commander' will become the 'leader as conductor'. Three areas on which leaders may concentrate are:

There are at least three imperatives, including making it a data literacy culture; leading at the front to make it easy for people at every level of the organisation to access, understand and make use of the data. What a concept: a data-informed people system whose members know the data they are operating with.

Second, although DA and BI can inform leadership, the process of forming strategy still lies in the domain of leadership. Leaders will decide on the most important questions to ask of the data, and translate the insights emerging from it into actionable strategies. From Data to Action Leaders will need to straddle this oblique path from data to action, translating the insights into useful strategy – and making sure it doesn't just exist on paper, but actually has an impact on the real world.

Finally, a collaborative culture is a natural context for data-driven decisions. Leaders will focus on creating teams with a broader range of talents, cross-organisational communication and local knowledge-sharing. The collective best practice of different areas will be orchestrated for the good of the business.

15. IMPLICATIONS

Digital transformation is accelerated when Machine Learning (ML) and Artificial Intelligence (AI) are combined with Data Analytics (DA) and Business Intelligence (BI). A multitude of advantages are unlocked by this potent combination, which spread throughout the entire firm.

First off, productivity and efficiency rise. ML and AI have automated repetitive processes that used to bog down data scientists and analysts (Chen et al., 2012). Professionals can devote their skills to higher-level tasks like developing complex models, carrying out in-depth analysis, and offering strategic advice based on data-driven insights if they are released from these tedious tasks. The organization as a whole benefit from a more effective and influential data-driven culture thanks to this improved approach.

Second, this helped enhance decision- making quality by miles. Traditional data analysis tools often box insights into what can be directly visible because they merely skim the data. On the flip side, ML and AI are particularly adept at finding subtle patterns and intricate relationships in data. These deeper insights allow leaders to make more informed data-driven decisions, increasing organizational output overall.

In the end, the user experience changed tremendously. AI algorithms can enable businesses to focus on personalized customer experiences by analyzing great volumes of client data and behavior instantaneously. In the end, it leads to a higher degree of satisfaction, better relationships with clients, and increased loyalty to your brand.

When you combine the power of DA, BI, ML and AI you expand the boundaries of what can be done with data. This gives the businesses a greater capacity to execute fast digital transformation and stay ahead in an ever-changing market scenario. Up to this point we will look into other related technologies which are complimentary to the transformative power of DA and BI.

16. LIMITATIONS AND FUTURE RESEARCH AGENDA

DA and BI have the potential to transform organizations at every level with continuous advancements in technology and the influence of data-driven decision-making in the future. Achieving this will take more than technological progress it will require a new organizational mindset in which leaders function as the best orchestrators of data-driven transformation harmonies. Through nurturing data literacy, building the DA and BI competency, and thinking ahead, these skills will empower leaders to drive their organizations to create a winning and striking future. Data driven transformation is a performance that never ends because each new innovation is just a new verse in a symphony that is still being written **(Yaqoob & Thomas, 2022).**

17. CONCLUSION

As organizations compete in the digital age, data has evolved as the lifeblood of any successful business. In this chapter, we examine how Data Analytics (DA) and Business Intelligence (BI) play as conductors within an orchestration of data, combining with other digital technologies creating a forceful and effective performance.

DA & BI make businesses a reality from guessing towards data-driven decisions, efficiently. This is where self-service analytics platforms, big data analytics, and convergence of machine learning and artificial intelligence truly shines, giving organizations access to a wealth of insights buried deep within their data.

Data has been democratized by the users since business intelligence tools and self-service analytics platforms have become easy to use. With this, employees from every department can begin exploring the data that is important to their role (helping build that sense of ownership) and can even become more curious, leading to an inter departmental understanding and further help in identifying certain opportunities or challenges. Big data analytics platforms are one step beyond, executing complex queries on huge datasets to reveal patterns and trends that would be otherwise hidden by using conventional analytical methods. Leveraging machine learning to deploy predictive analytics, allows organizations to do more than just interpret the present, but to predict outcomes as well. This permits them to deal with them in advance and also make use of brand-new possibilities.

DA and BI turn reactive businesses into proactive ones. Whereas organizations can also make sure that their workflows are running smoothly, inefficiencies are identified, and predictive maintenance is enabled, to maintain the operational stability, reduce the downtime and optimize resource allocation. This pro-active approach helps prepare us for a future where data plays an even greater role.

REFERENCES

Akdere, M., Acheson, K., & Jiang, Y. (2021). An examination of the effectiveness of virtual reality technology for intercultural competence development. *International Journal of Intercultural Relations*, 82, 109–120. DOI: 10.1016/j.ijintrel.2021.03.009

Biswas, B., Sanyal, M. K., & Mukherjee, T. (2023). AI-Based Sales Forecasting Model for Digital Marketing. [IJEBR]. *International Journal of E-Business Research*, 19(1), 14. DOI: 10.4018/IJEBR.317888

Brundage, M., Avin, S., Wang, J., Belfield, H., ... (2020). Toward trustworthy AI development: Mechanisms for supporting verifiable claims. https://doi.org//arXiv .2004.07213DOI: 10.48550

Chen, H., Chiang, R. H. L., & Storey, V. C. (2012). Business intelligence and analytics: From big data to big impact. *Management Information Systems Quarterly*, 36(4), 1165–1188. DOI: 10.2307/41703503

Chiu, M. L., Wang, Y. C., Lin, H. W., & Hsu, C. H. (2018). How service-dominant logic moderates the relationship between big data analytics and customer experience. *Journal of Business Research*, 117, 500–510.

Dutta, R. (October 2021). COVID-19 and the role of digital technology based on the ten global trends identified by the World Economic Forum. Asian Disaster Preparedness Center

Eboigbe, E., Farayola, O., Olatoye, F., Chinwe, N., & Daraojimba, C. (2023). BUSINESS INTELLIGENCE TRANSFORMATION THROUGH AI AND DATA ANALYTICS. *Engineering Science & Technology Journal.*, 4(5), 285–307. DOI: 10.51594/estj.v4i5.616

Fosso Wamba, S., Gunasekaran, A., Papadopoulos, T., & Ngai, E. (2018). Big data analytics in logistics and supply chain management. *International Journal of Logistics Management*, 29(2), 478–484. DOI: 10.1108/IJLM-02-2018-0026

IBM. (2023). Cost of a Data Breach Report. Cost of a data breach 2024 | IBM

Imran, F., Shahzad, K., Butt, A., & Kantola, J. (2021). Digital transformation of industrial organizations: Toward an integrated framework. *Journal of Change Management*, 21(4), 1–29. DOI: 10.1080/14697017.2021.1929406

Jobin, A., Ienca, M., & Vayena, E. (2019). The global landscape of AI ethics guidelines. *Nature Machine Intelligence*, 1(9), 389–399. DOI: 10.1038/s42256-019-0088-2

Konopik, J., Jahn, C., Schuster, T., Hoßbach, N., & Pflaum, A. (2021). Mastering the digital transformation through organizational capabilities: A conceptual framework. DOI: 10.1016/j.digbus.2021.100019

Kozak-Holland, M., & Procter, C. (2020). The Challenge of Digital Transformation. In *Managing Transformation Projects*. Palgrave Pivot., DOI: 10.1007/978-3-030-33035-4_1

LaBerge, L., O'Toole, C., Schneider, J., & Smaje, K. (October 2020). How COVID-19 has pushed companies over the technology tipping point—and transformed business forever. McKinsey Digital & Strategy & Corporate Finance Practices.

Lv, Z., & Singh, A. K. (2021). Big Data Analysis of Internet of Things System. *ACM Transactions on Internet Technology*, 21(2), 1–15. DOI: 10.1145/3389250

Malik, A., Khan, M. A., Khan, F. H., & Jan, F. A. (2020). Examining the role of big data analytics in enhancing customer experience: A moderated mediation analysis. *Journal of Industrial Engineering and Management*, 13(4), 741–755.

Malik, Y. S., Kumar, N., Sircar, S., Kaushik, R., Bhat, S., Dhama, K., Gupta, P., Goyal, K., Singh, M. P., & Ghoshal, U.. (2020). Coronavirus Disease Pandemic (COVID-19): Challenges and a Global Perspective. *Pathogens (Basel, Switzerland)*, 9, 519. DOI: 10.3390/pathogens9070519 PMID: 32605194

Manyika, J., Chui, M., Miremadi, M., Bughin, J., George, K., Willmott, P., & Dewhurst, M. (2017). *A future that works: Automation, employment, and productivity*. McKinsey Global Institute.

Mendonça, F., & Dantas, M. (2020). Covid-19: Where is the Digital Transformation, Big Data, Artificial Intelligence and Data Analytics? *Revista do Serviço Público*, 71, 212–234. DOI: 10.21874/rsp.v71i0.4770

Mineraud, J., Mazhelis, O., Su, X., & Tarkoma, S. (2016). A gap analysis of Internet-of-Things platforms. *Computer Communications*, 89-90, 5–16. DOI: 10.1016/j.comcom.2016.03.015

Sanghai, A. (2023). *Three BI and Analytics trends to lookout for in 2023. Express Computer*. Guest Blogs News.

Tran, A. D., Pallant, J., & Johnson, L. W. (2021). Exploring the impact of chatbots on consumer sentiment and expectations in retail. *Journal of Retailing and Consumer Services*, 63(2), 102718. DOI: 10.1016/j.jretconser.2021.102718

Yaqoob, F., & Thomas, J. (2022). Data governance in the era of big data: Challenges and solutions. *Journal of Change Management*. Advance online publication. DOI: 10.5281/zenodo.8415833

Yazici, N., & Aksoy, N. C. (2022). The rise of digital transformation within businesses in the pandemic. In Ismail, M. A. W., Pettinger, R., Gupta, B. B., & Roja, A. (Eds.), *Handbook of Research on Digital Transformation Management and Tools*. IGI Global. [DOI: 10.4018/978-1-7998-9764-4.ch002] DOI: 10.4018/978-1-7998-9764-4.ch002

ADDITIONAL READING

Ali, M. (2021). *Remote Work and Sustainable Changes for the Future of Global Business*. IGI Global. https://www.igi-global.com/book/remote-work-sustainable-changes-future/264375

Ali, M. (2022). *Future Role of Sustainable Innovative Technologies in Crisis Management*. IGI Global. https://www.igi-global.com/book/future-role-sustainable-innovative-technologies/281281

Ali, M. (2023). *Shifting Paradigms in the Rapidly Developing Global Digital Ecosystem: A GCC Perspective*. In Digital Entrepreneurship and Co-Creating Value Through Digital Encounters (pp. 145-166). IGI Global. https://www.igi-global.com/chapter/shifting-paradigms-in-the-rapidly-developing-global-digital-ecosystem/323525

Ali, M. (2023). T*axonomy of Industry 4.0 Technologies in Digital Entrepreneurship and Co-Creating Value*. In *Digital Entrepreneurship and Co-Creating Value Through Digital Encounters* (pp. 24–55). IGI Global., https://www.igi-global.com/chapter/taxonomy-of-industry-40-technologies-in-digital-entrepreneurship-and-co-creating-value/323520 DOI: 10.4018/978-1-6684-7416-7.ch002

Ali, M., & Wood-Harper, T. (2021). *Fostering Communication and Learning with Underutilized Technologies in Higher Education*. IGI Global. https://www.igi-global.com/book/fostering-communication-learning-underutilized-technologies/244593

Ali, M., Wood-Harper, T., & Kutar, M. (2023). Multi-Perspectives of Contemporary Digital Transformation Models of Complex Innovation Management. In *Digital Entrepreneurship and Co-Creating Value Through Digital Encounters* (pp. 79–96). IGI Global., https://www.igi-global.com/chapter/multi-perspectives-of-contemporary-digital-transformation-models-of-complex-innovation-management/323522 DOI: 10.4018/978-1-6684-7416-7.ch004

Ali, M. B. (2021). Internet of Things (IoT) to Foster Communication and Information Sharing: A Case of UK Higher Education. In Ali, M. B., & Wood-Harper, T. (Eds.), *Fostering Communication and Learning With Underutilized Technologies in Higher Education* (pp. 1–20). IGI Global., https://www.igi-global.com/chapter/internet-of-things-iot-to-foster-communication-and-information-sharing/262718/ DOI: 10.4018/978-1-7998-4846-2.ch001

Ali, M. B., & Wood-Harper, T. (2022). Artificial Intelligence (AI) as a Decision-Making Tool to Control Crisis Situations. In *Future Role of Sustainable Innovative Technologies in Crisis Management*. IGI Global., https://www.igi-global.com/chapter/artificial-intelligence-ai-as-a-decision-making-tool-to-control-crisis-situations/298931 DOI: 10.4018/978-1-7998-9815-3.ch006

Ali, M. B., Wood-Harper, T., & Ramlogan, R. (2020). A Framework Strategy to Overcome Trust Issues on Cloud Computing Adoption in Higher Education. In Modern Principles, Practices, and Algorithms for Cloud Security (pp. 162-183). IGI Global. https://www.igi-global.com/chapter/a-framework-strategy-to-overcome-trust-issues-on-cloud-computing-adoption-in-higher-education/238907/

Chapter 6
Digital Transformation in Reshaping Industries

Wong Sing Yun
Universiti Malaysia Sabah, Malaysia

Saizal Pinjaman
Universiti Malaysia Sabah, Malaysia

Debbra Toria Nipo
https://orcid.org/0000-0001-5087-2905
Universiti Malaysia Sabah, Malaysia

Shaierah Gulabdin
https://orcid.org/0000-0002-7648-422X
Universiti Malaysia Sabah, Malaysia

ABSTRACT

The emergence of digital technology has help business to grow, thrive, innovate and resolve obstacles in sustaining their operation development. The Malaysian Government has been proactive in implementing various initiatives to embrace digital transformation across different sectors. To extend the knowledge within the literature, this book chapter intends to identify the factors that contribute to the digital transformation in Malaysia. While digital transformation may seems to be the answer to a more sustainable development growth, however there are still challenge remains. Besides that, this book literature will also examine the government policies that has been implemented by the Malaysia Government in support of the digital transformation. The knowledge finding from this book chapter will help to ensure that the benefits of the digital transformation can be delivered to all sectors and help policy makers to devise new policies that can assists all businesses to

DOI: 10.4018/979-8-3693-5966-2.ch006

transform their operation digitally.

INTRODUCTION ON DIGITAL TRANSFORMATION IN MALAYSIA

According to Bustos (2015), digital transformation is described as the most profound and accelerating transformation for business activities, processes, competencies and models to leverage the changes of digital technology and their impact in a strategic and prioritised way. Meanwhile, Ammeran et al. (2021) defined digital transformation as the processing of digital computers, online sites, mobile operating systems, and social media knowledge. The digital transformation can become a driver as well as an enabler for new forms of innovation through transformation, management of the knowledge environment, and enabling of demand driven supply chains (Hanna, 2010). As digital transformation continues to encourage the integration of digital technologies into the various aspects of businesses, this will lead to new transformation in the business landscape. This new shift will likely bring in new impact and challenges faced to businesses especially to the Malaysian small and medium enterprises (SMEs). As pointed out by Haron et al. (2023), digital technologies have brought about significant changes in business and society, particularly in the areas of the sharing and circular economies. From a broad perspective, digital transformation may be summarised as the pervasive integration of data and digital technology into every aspect of social and economic existence.

In Malaysia, digital transformation represents a significant shift towards integrating advanced technologies across various sectors, aiming to enhance economic growth, competitiveness, and overall quality of life. The Malaysian government's strategic initiatives, like the National Fiberization and Connectivity Plan (NFCP) and the Malaysia Digital Economy Blueprint (MyDIGITAL), which provide detailed frameworks to enhance digital infrastructure, improve connectivity, and advance digital inclusivity, are what are driving this transformation. In the corporate sector, digital transformation is evident in the adoption of advanced technologies such as artificial intelligence (AI), big data analytics, cloud computing, and the Internet of Things (IoT). Malaysian companies, ranging from large conglomerates to small and medium enterprises (SMEs), are increasingly integrating these technologies into their operations to enhance efficiency, improve customer experiences, and drive business growth. Similarly, the banking and finance industry in Malaysia has embraced fintech solutions to offer more convenient and personalized services to customers. In another instance, the manufacturing sector is adopting Industry 4.0 technologies to optimize production processes and increase competitiveness. This widespread adoption of digital technologies is reshaping traditional business models and creating new opportunities for innovation and value creation. As Nguyen (2020) stressed, digital transformation that involves the utilization of digital technologies to reform business models, unlock fresh opportunities, and cultivate novel values, thereby enhancing sales and expediting growth.

Besides that, the government plays a pivotal role in driving digital transformation through various initiatives aimed at building a robust digital infrastructure, fostering innovation, and ensuring inclusive digital access. Malaysia has invested significantly in enhancing its digital infrastructure which is crucial for enabling businesses and individuals to leverage digital technologies effectively. Additionally, the government has introduced policies and incentives to encourage digital innovation and entrepreneurship, such as the establishment of digital free trade zones (DFTZs) and funding programs for tech start-ups. These efforts are designed to create a conducive environment for digital businesses to thrive and contribute to the national economy. In addition, innovation and entrepreneurship are encouraged by Malaysia's thriving start-up environment, supported by its government organisations such as the Malaysian Digital Economy Corporation (MDEC). Established in 1996, Multimedia Development Corporation (MDC) was tasked with supervising MSC laws, policies, and infrastructure. It provided a great platform for businesses to conduct customer service operations, including telemarketing, technical support, "backroom" data processing, and localised marketing material customisation (MDC, 2016). After transforming to Malaysia Development Economic Cooperation (MDEC) by 1998, MDEC has developed numerous e-commerce platform known as e-Rezeki, e-incubator, e-training for individuals and corporations.

In short, digital transformation in Malaysia represents a pivotal shift towards integrating digital technologies into every facet of the nation's economy and society. In doing so, it offers a myriad of benefits while also posing significant challenges. The adoption of technologies like cloud computing, big data, artificial intelligence, and the Internet of Things (IoT) has the potential to improve public services, revolutionise sectors, and raise Malaysians' standard of living in general. Increased economic development, higher corporate productivity and efficiency, better public and private sector service delivery, and the creation of new job possibilities in the digital economy are all advantages of the digital transformation. Digital technologies can also spur innovation, giving Malaysia a competitive edge in the international market. Still, the path to a completely digitalized is not without challenges. There are many obstacles that must be overcome, including the digital divide, cybersecurity risks, the need for digital literacy and skill development, the difficulties in managing digital infrastructure, and regulatory frameworks. To fully realise the benefits of digital transformation and attain sustainable growth in the digital era, Malaysia must strike a balance between these advantages and difficulties.

The first section will begin by providing a brief introduction on Malaysia's digital transformation. In the next Section 2, the contributing factors of digital transformation will be highlighted allowing one to understand better what are the driving factors to the Malaysia's digital transformation. Section 3 and 4 will discuss the potentials and benefits of digital transformation from various perspectives to different stakeholders. The multi-aspect potentials discussed can include economic potentials, social potentials, and environmental potentials. While, the benefits could involve financial benefits, social benefits, and environmental benefits. In the next Section 5, some practical examples of the digital transformation taking place in Malaysia has been provided. Meanwhile, Section 6 provide critical discussion on the challenges faced in digital transformation to businesses in Malaysia. Subsequently, Section 7 shed light on the Malaysia Government initiatives and policies that has been implemented to help in driving the digital transformation. This section will also provide outlook into the emerging trends in digital transformation and future strategies/action plan that can be taken for businesses to embrace digital transformation. This chapter concludes by recapping the key points discussed in the chapter. Lastly, future researches were suggested and policy recommendation was called to embrace digital innovation for sustainable growth in Malaysia's digital economy.

Factors Driving Digital Transformation

Digital transformation represents a fundamental shift in how businesses operate and deliver value to their customers by integrating digital technologies into all areas of their operations. This transformation encompasses a wide range of technological advancements, including cloud computing, artificial intelligence, big data analytics, and the Internet of Things (IoT). These technologies allow companies to improve consumer experiences, innovate, and streamline operations. However, numerous crucial elements, including corporate culture, leadership dedication, and employee involvement, are necessary for the digital transition to be successful. To successfully navigate the challenges of digital adoption, an organisation must have a culture that values change, promotes ongoing learning, and values collaboration. In other words, while the potential benefits of digital transformation are substantial—ranging from improved efficiency and agility to enhanced customer experiences—its successful implementation is influenced by a variety of factors.

According to Kokolek et al. (2019), the key factors of digital knowledge and skills played a critical role in greatly enhance the process of digital transformation. By combining six key factors, they developed a model that explains the critical factors that affect digital transformation. In this model, the key factors identified comprised of agility of firms, their ability to apply new technologies in their business, network leadership, continuous learning and strategic vision. The culture within an organization plays a critical role in digital transformation. As such, an organization culture that encourages innovation, agility, continuous learning and a clear strategic vision is essential. Fostering a culture of continuous improvement and collaboration can significantly enhance the success of digital transformation efforts. Besides that, strong leadership is crucial for driving digital transformation. Leadership must also be adaptable, as digital transformation often involves navigating through uncertainties and changing market conditions.

In another finding by Verina and Titko (2019), the emergence of new markets, development of e-business and increased competition in the market were identified as drivers to digital transformation. Apart from these factors, the progress in technologies and digitization of tasks further speeds up the digital transformation as it meets the customers' increasing needs. Rapid advancements in technology are at the core of digital transformation. The proliferation of cloud computing, artificial intelligence (AI), machine learning, the Internet of Things (IoT), and blockchain technologies provide organizations with new tools to innovate and optimize operations. Organizations need to continuously adapt to these evolving technologies to stay competitive and relevant in the market. In today's digital age, customers expect seamless, personalized, and instant experiences. Digital transformation initiatives must prioritize customer experience by leveraging technology to meet and exceed these expectations. This could entail improving digital interfaces, implementing omnichannel tactics, and leveraging data analytics to comprehend consumer behaviour and preferences. Fulfilling customers' expectations promotes business growth in addition to increasing their satisfaction and loyalty.

On a separate note, four categories of factors that drive organization digital transformation has been highlighted by Ntandoyethu et al. (2019). These factors consisted of customer centricity, governance, innovation and resource attainment. Customer centricity is the proclivity of an organisation to focus on the interdisciplinary and organisational challenges associated with successfully designing and managing the customer experience (Lemon & Verhoef 2016). Meanwhile, effective governance has been deemed by past findings (Boström & Celik (2017); Westerman et al. (2014)) as a critical lever for organisations to drive successful digital transformation. With the rapid digitalization taking place, consumers are more likely to make purchases from firms that are technologically inclined. Hence, a firm's ability to adopt innovation will allow it to easily undergo digital transformation. Lastly, the firm's ability to acquire resources through funding, expertise, knowledge sharing will support its digital transformation.

Meanwhile, Wahid and Zulkifli (2021) has highlighted that competitive pressure, technology advancement, cost minimization and environmental influence as the influencing factors of digital transformation adoption among the small and medium enterprises (SMEs) in Malaysia. The competitive pressure and advancement of technology will affect SMEs' decision to adopt digital transformation. Besides that, cost efficiency becomes another significant factor to be considered in digital transformation implementation. Lastly, the digitalization process is often influenced by environmental factors such as market dynamics, high or low technology industry, and company specialization (Tyler et al., 2020). Tarutė et al. (2018) revealed both internal factors and external factors that can influence digital transformation decision in SMEs. The internal factors consisted of capabilities fit, resource fit and changes in the business model itself, while external factors comprised off external capabilities and resource fit, governmental regulation and industry related factors. Teng et al. (2022) similarly pointed out that the investment in digital technologies, employee digital skills and digital transformation strategies are key factors that will be beneficial for digital transformation.

In short, digital transformation is influenced by a range of factors, including technological advancements, organizational culture, leadership, and workforce skills. The rapid pace of technological innovation drives the need for businesses and firms to adapt quickly. Organizational culture plays a crucial role, as companies with a culture that embraces change and innovation are more likely to succeed in their digital initiatives. Leadership commitment and vision are essential in steering the transformation process, while a skilled workforce capable of leveraging new technologies ensures the effective implementation and sustainability of digital strategies. Additionally, market competition, customer expectations, and regulatory requirements also shape the direction and urgency of digital transformation efforts. In Malaysia specifically, these factors played fundamental role as drivers of the digital transformation. For example, a large proportion of the Malaysian firms are still at the infancy stages of digital maturity and often lack access to talent proficient in areas like cloud computing, cybersecurity, and artificial intelligence. According to SME Corp data, about 60% of business owners were unaware of the various financing options available to them, and 34% thought that cloud computing was expensive. Furthermore, only 15% of Malaysians have the advanced ICT skills needed for digital transformation (Ignatius, 2022).

The Potentials of Digital Technologies

The transformative potential of digital technologies in Malaysia's industrial sector is immense, encompassing economic, social, and environmental dimensions. The integration of automation and advanced data analytics promises to revolutionize productivity and efficiency, providing significant economic benefits. Socially, digital transformation enhances consumer experiences and fosters a more connected and informed society. Environmentally, it promotes sustainable practices and resource conservation. This comprehensive digital shift not only drives economic growth and innovation but also contributes to a more inclusive, resilient, and sustainable future for Malaysia.

(a) Economic Engine

The economic potential of digital transformation in Malaysia's industrial sector is vast, including improved efficiency, cost savings, new revenue streams, and a competitive edge. Javaid et al. (2021) notes that integrating automation into factory floors can significantly boost productivity. Robots performing repetitive tasks like welding and assembly operate with unparalleled precision and speed, reducing human error and maximizing output. This shift not only lowers labor costs but also increases production rates, leading to higher profitability. Additionally, AI-powered predictive maintenance can significantly cut downtime and maintenance expenses. By analyzing sensor data from equipment, AI can predict and prevent failures before they happen. This proactive approach ensures smooth operations and avoids the high costs of unexpected downtime, thereby enhancing the overall efficiency and reliability of industrial processes.

Big data analytics significantly enhances economic potential by providing businesses with deep insights into customer behaviour, purchasing patterns, and preferences. This extensive information enables companies to tailor their products and services more precisely, creating highly personalized offerings that address specific customer needs. For instance, a furniture manufacturer can utilize customer data to design custom furniture based on browsing history and past purchases. This approach not only improves customer satisfaction but also generates new revenue streams through the sale of bespoke products. Furthermore, AI-powered product recommendations can greatly increase the average order value (Çınar et al., 2020). By analysing customer data, AI can suggest complementary products, encouraging customers to buy additional items. This strategy boosts sales and revenue without requiring extra marketing expenditure.

(b) Social Transformation

Customers stand to gain significantly from the social potential of digital trans-formation in Malaysia's manufacturing sector. According to Piccinini et al. (2015), digital platforms democratize access to information, enabling consumers to make well-informed purchasing decisions. AI and data analytics facilitate the creation of highly personalized services that anticipate customer needs and provide tailored recommendations, enhancing the overall consumer experience. For example, an online grocery retailer can use customer data to suggest personalized recipes based on past purchases, making shopping more convenient and enjoyable. This increased personalization fosters a more connected and informed public, contributing to a dynamic and competitive marketplace.

Moreover, digital transformation facilitates improved communication and collaboration within and across companies, breaking down geographical barriers. Cloud-based project management platforms enable teams to work together seamlessly, regardless of their physical location (Onungwa et al., 2021). For example, engineers in Malaysia can collaborate in real-time with their counterparts in Europe on a construction project, sharing insights and solving problems collaboratively. This not only accelerates innovation but also enriches the work environment by fostering diverse perspectives and expertise.

Ultimately, the digital transformation of Malaysia's industrial sector promises to create a more engaged, informed, and collaborative society. Consumers benefit from enhanced services and better information, while businesses and employees enjoy improved communication and teamwork, driving innovation and economic growth. This interconnected and informed society is well-equipped to thrive in the competitive global landscape.

(c) Environmental Responsibility

The environmental potential of digital transformation in Malaysia's industrial sector is considerable, offering various paths toward sustainable development, with one of the most impactful benefits being the optimization of logistics and supply chains through real-time data management (Adama et al., 2024). By leveraging advanced data analytics, companies can minimize transportation needs, effectively reducing carbon emissions. This is particularly crucial for industries such as logistics and transportation, where optimizing delivery routes can lead to substantial reductions in fuel consumption and greenhouse gas emissions.

Moreover, the integration of smart technologies in manufacturing processes can greatly diminish waste production (Nižetić et al., 2019). For instance, factories equipped with 3D printing technology can produce parts on demand, thus minimizing excess material usage and reducing the need for waste disposal. This approach not only conserves raw materials but also lowers the environmental footprint of manufacturing activities. Digital platforms also play a crucial role in promoting sustainable practices among businesses and consumers. Companies can use these platforms to educate their customers about eco-friendly products and services (Aqlama & Putra, 2023), encouraging responsible consumption habits (To a et al., 2024). For example, an energy provider could offer online tools that enable consumers to track their energy usage and identify opportunities for conservation, thereby promoting more sustainable energy consumption.

Similarly, the process of digital transformation has presented considerable opportunities for small and medium-sized enterprises (SMEs) in Malaysia by improving operational efficiency, enhancing customer interaction, and bolstering overall business resilience. Through the implementation of cloud-based technologies and digital platforms, SMEs can optimize their processes, minimize expenses, and scale their operations with greater efficacy. Furthermore, digital instruments empower SMEs to access wider markets via e-commerce and digital marketing strategies, thereby increasing their competitive edge. Technologies such as artificial intelligence (AI) and the Internet of Things (IoT) can further refine resource management, particularly in industries such as agriculture and manufacturing, leading to enhanced productivity and sustainability. These technological advancements equip SMEs for growth and facilitate better adaptation to forthcoming challenges.

The Tangible Benefits of Digital Transformation

Digital transformation offers tangible benefits that significantly enhance business operations and competitiveness. By integrating advanced technologies such as cloud computing, artificial intelligence, and data analytics, companies can streamline processes, reduce operational costs, and improve efficiency. This transformation facilitates better decision-making through real-time data insights, fosters innovation by enabling agile responses to market changes, and enhances customer experiences through personalized services. Furthermore, digital transformation supports remote work and collaboration, ensuring business continuity and resilience in dynamic environments.

(a) Economy

The digital transformation of Malaysia's industrial sector has numerous economic benefits that propel growth through enhanced productivity, efficiency, and revenue generation. Utilising cutting-edge technologies helps companies cut expenses and increase production by optimising operations. This enhanced efficiency not only maximizes output but also sharpens the competitive edge of Malaysian industries on a global scale, attracting foreign investment and fostering international business partnerships.

Furthermore, the shift towards digitalization creates new, high-skilled job opportunities in emerging fields such as data analysis, cybersecurity, and AI development (Georgiou et al., 2021). These positions not only cater to the current demands of the market but also prepare the workforce for future technological advancements. As a result, the labor market becomes more dynamic and resilient, equipped with the skills necessary to navigate and thrive in an evolving global economy.

This transition towards a digitally-driven industrial sector fosters a more diversified and robust economy (Foster & Azmeh, 2020). By reducing reliance on traditional sectors and embracing innovation, Malaysia can better adapt to global market fluctuations and economic challenges. The diversification brought about by digital transformation ensures that the economy is not only more sustainable but also more responsive to new opportunities and trends, paving the way for sustained economic growth and development.

(b) Finance

Digital transformation in the Malaysian industrial sector significantly enhancing the financial health of companies through reduced operational costs, optimized resource allocation, and increased profitability. According to Bose (2009), automation and utilizing advanced data analytics will help businesses can streamline their operations, leading to significant cost savings. This efficiency in resource management not only minimizes waste but also ensures that resources are allocated where they can generate the most value.

These financial gains provide companies with the capital to invest in further research and development, fueling innovation and the creation of new products and services that meet the evolving needs of consumers. This continuous innovation cycle is crucial for maintaining a competitive edge in the global marketplace (Hitt et al., 1998). As businesses develop more advanced and appealing offerings, they can attract a broader customer base and increase market share, driving revenue growth.

Moreover, the improved financial stability resulting from digital transformation fosters long-term sustainability and growth (Hidayat-ur-Rehman & Hossain, 2024; Li, 2022). This is because, companies can reinvest their increased profits into their operations, enhancing their capabilities and expanding their market presence. This reinvestment not only supports ongoing innovation but also contributes to a more resilient business model that can adapt to market changes and economic fluctuations.

(c) Social

In Malaysia's industrial sector, the social benefits of digital transformation are revolutionary, greatly improving consumer experiences and social well-being. Customers benefit from having more options for goods and services at affordable costs, which improves their quality of life and promotes social inclusion by making these offerings available to a larger spectrum of people.

Moreover, digital transformation revolutionizes education by facilitating the delivery of online educational resources (Rizvi & Nabi, 2021), particularly benefiting remote and underserved areas (Mhlanga, 2023). This expanded access to quality education ensures that more individuals can develop the skills and knowledge required to thrive in the modern economy, resulting in a more skilled and educated workforce. This educational upliftment is essential for driving long-term economic growth and innovation.

Additionally, Lee and Joseph Sirgy (2019) believe that the advent of remote work opportunities enabled by digital technologies greatly enhances work-life balance. Employees can manage their personal commitments more effectively while remaining productive in their professional roles. This flexibility leads to higher job satisfaction (Ninaus et al., 2021), increased motivation, and a more positive work environment (Bucea-Manea- oniş et al., 2020), which collectively contribute to reduced employee turnover (Malik et al., 2022).

(d) Environment

The environmental benefits of digital transformation in the Malaysian industrial sector are pivotal for fostering a sustainable future and preserving natural resources. By optimizing logistics and adopting smart manufacturing practices, companies can significantly reduce their carbon footprint, contributing to environmental conservation efforts. Furthermore, Bocean (2024) demonstrated that digital platforms play a crucial role in promoting responsible consumption habits and sustainable practices, thereby minimizing waste and environmental impact. This collective shift towards sustainability not only benefits the environment but also ensures a healthier and more resilient ecosystem for future generations.

Moreover, digital technologies can be instrumental in environmental monitoring and resource management initiatives (Guan et al., 2023). For instance, deploying sensor networks in forests to track deforestation activities or utilizing drones to monitor air quality in urban areas enables real-time data collection on environmental conditions. This data can then be analysed to implement targeted conservation efforts and pollution control measures, safeguarding natural habitats and mitigating environmental degradation. By leveraging digital technologies for environmental monitoring and resource management, Malaysia can proactively address environmental challenges and promote sustainable development practices, ultimately preserving the environment for future generations.

The digital transformation has similarly presented a multitude of benefits for small and medium-sized enterprises (SMEs) in Malaysia, facilitating improvements in operational efficacy, cost reduction, and enhancement of customer interactions. Through the implementation of cloud services and digital instruments, organizations can automate their workflows, optimize processes, and diminish dependence on manual operations, which consequently results in heightened productivity. Additionally, the incorporation of digital payment solutions and data-informed decision-making instruments bolsters customer service and yields insights for more effective business strategies. In summation, the embrace of digital technologies assists SMEs in maintaining their competitiveness within an increasingly digitalized economy.

Current Emerging Digital Transformation in Malaysia

The adoption of digital technologies has proven to be imperative for the nation to enhance economic recovery following the COVID-19 pandemic. By facilitating businesses in digitally engaging with customers, resuming operational activities, and alleviating logistical constraints amid disruptions in the supply chain, digital technologies can assist enterprises in navigating the economic consequences of the COVID-19 pandemic. It has been projected that 72 percent of Malaysia's digital potential – amounting to MYR184 billion (USD43.9 billion) – could be realized through these technological implementations (AlphaBeta, 2021).

Malaysia is currently growing as a data centre hub with the most developed data centre markets in Southeast Asia, with market analyst organization Arizton estimating the value at $1.06 billion in 2021 (MIDA, 2024). Undeterred by the challenges, the digital economy has become one of the fastest growing sectors in Malaysia following the continuous government support initiatives such as the unveiling of the Malaysia Digital Economy Blueprint and establishment of the Digital Investment Office has paved way for its rapid growth of digital transformation.

Another noteworthy transformation is the implementation of 5G technology within the nation. Malaysia has successfully embraced 5G technology with remarkable speed, enhancing its communication infrastructures—an endeavor that has been further propelled by collaboration between governmental entities and the private sector (including Telekom Malaysia and Maxis). The increased speeds associated with 5G are anticipated to create new prospects for the advancement of smart cities and IoT applications, while simultaneously fostering growth in various other sectors throughout the country (Telecom Review, 2024).

The healthcare sector in Malaysia is actively integrating artificial intelligence and digital innovations to improve patient care, enhance diagnostic precision, and advance the overall quality of service provision. The adoption of AI is anticipated to escalate across various domains, including healthcare, logistics, and finance, thereby revolutionizing operational effectiveness and enriching customer experiences. For example, the advancements in MRI technology that have improved image quality, reduced scan times and increased patient comfort. The AI integration further elevates MRI capabilities by quickly and accurately analysing large volumes of imaging data, identifying patterns and anomalies (Anuar, 2024). Thus, leads to more precise diagnoses, allowing for early intervention, which can significantly improve patient outcomes.

Another notable example involving local SMEs adoption of digital transformation is the TM ONE's initiative aimed at bolstering small and medium-sized enterprises (SMEs) through its Cloud (Cloud Alpha) offerings. This infrastructure-as-a-service (IaaS) framework proved instrumental for businesses amid the pandemic by delivering scalable and secure cloud solutions. It facilitated the rapid transition of SMEs to remote operations, thereby enhancing their data management capabilities, operational flexibility, and cybersecurity defences. Furthermore, TM ONE provided complimentary trials of cloud-oriented disaster recovery solutions to aid SMEs during pivotal business disruptions (TM ONE, 2021). A multitude of small and medium-sized enterprises (SMEs) nationwide have utilized this assistance to enhance their digital footprints, thereby guaranteeing operational continuity and advancement, even amidst the challenges posed by the pandemic.

Besides that, numerous innovative infrastructures, including 5G, Blockchain, and Artificial Intelligence (AI), are currently being developed to address the imperative for technological transformation across various sectors, with emphasis on the economic domain. Small and Medium Enterprises (SMEs) must proactively engage in strategies to leverage the advantages presented by the digital economy by enhancing the competencies of their current workforce, adopting advanced machinery and digital platforms, and availing themselves of the resources offered by governmental and other institutional entities (Abd Shukor et al, 2023). However, the findings as far back as 2007, showed that the adoption of ICT by SME owners in Malaysia has been relatively low primarily because they felt that ICT adoption was difficult (Hashim 2007).

Challenges of Digital Transformation

Digital transformation, while offering significant opportunities for growth and efficiency, presents numerous challenges and issues that organizations must navigate. A few key challenges can be highlighted such as the infrastructure lacking, digital skills gaps or local talent shortage, data privacy and security concerns and regulatory challenges. Meanwhile, key challenges to businesses or organizations include resistance to change within the organization, as employees and management may be hesitant to adopt new technologies and processes. Additionally, the high costs associated with implementing digital initiatives and the need for continuous investment in technology can be another obstacle. For instance, Hamidi et al. (2018) highlighted that the Malaysian SMEs generally are lacking of knowledge pertaining to Industry 4.0 especially in terms of dimension of distribution control, data driven services, smart factory and strategy and organisation. This has become one of the main challenges to the digital transformation adoption in the SMEs. In a similar manner, Teng et al. (2022) also linked the SMEs lack of adequate knowledge as one of the barriers to digital transformation. Besides that, the poor application of digital technology becomes another hindrance to the progress of digital transformation. As SME Corp Malaysia (2018) revealed, the five significant obstacles that SMEs are confronting: cost of doing business, cash flow and payment financing, business financing, human capital, and ICT adoption.

Firstly, one of the main issues and challenges in digital transformation is the disparity in infrastructure and connectivity. Many regions, particularly in developing countries, lack the essential digital infrastructure, such as high-speed internet and reliable power supplies, necessary to support advanced technologies (Manny, Duygan, Fischer & Rieckermann, 2021). This digital divide hinders businesses from implementing digital solutions, limiting their growth and competitiveness. In rural areas, the deficiency of robust telecommunications infrastructure exacerbates the problem, creating a significant barrier to digital adoption. According to Kraus, Jones, Kailer, Weinmann, Chaparro-Banegas and Roig-Tierno (2021), in addressing these challenges requires collaboration between the public and private sectors to invest in infrastructure development. Governments can play a crucial role by creating favourable policies and providing subsidies to encourage investment in underdeveloped regions. Additionally, leveraging emerging technologies such as satellite internet and 5G can help bridge the connectivity gap, enabling more businesses to participate in the digital economy.

Secondly, digital skills gap and local talent shortage. The rapid pace of technological advancement has created a significant digital skills gap, where the demand for digitally skilled workers exceeds supply. Many businesses struggle to find local talent with the expertise needed to implement and manage digital transformation initiatives. This shortage is particularly pronounced in specialized areas such as data science, cybersecurity, and artificial intelligence. Guerra, Danvila-del-Valle and Mendez-Suarez (2023) indicates that to address this challenge, businesses and governments must invest in education and training programs focused on digital skills. Initiatives like coding bootcamps, online courses, and vocational training can help upskill the current workforce. Moreover, partnerships with educational institutions are crucial for aligning curricula with industry needs, ensuring that graduates possess the relevant skills.

Thirdly, data privacy and security concerns have become paramount as businesses increasingly depend on digital technologies. The risk of data breaches and cyberattacks has surged, making the protection of sensitive data crucial. Any compromise can result in significant financial losses, reputational damage, and legal repercussions. Safeguarding data while complying with various data protection regulations presents a complex challenge for many organizations (Gebremeskel, Jonathan, & Yalew, 2023). To address these issues, businesses must implement robust cybersecurity measures such as encryption, multi-factor authentication, and regular security audits.

Additionally, raising a culture of security awareness among employees is vital to prevent human errors that could lead to breaches. Collaborating with cybersecurity experts and staying updated on the latest threats and mitigation strategies can further strengthen an organization's security posture (Cory, 2021). Increased digitalisation exposes businesses to online threats. Cybersecurity remains an ongoing challenge to digital ecosystems, exacerbated by the COVID-19 pandemic as more people are working remotely (BusinessToday, 2021).

Fourthly, the regulatory landscape surrounding digital transformation is constantly evolving, with new laws and regulations emerging to address the implications of advancing technologies. Navigating this complex environment can be particularly challenging for businesses operating across multiple jurisdictions. Compliance with diverse regulations, such as the General Data Protection Regulation (GDPR) in Europe and the California Consumer Privacy Act (CCPA) in the United States, demands significant resources and expertise (Coche, Kolk & Ocelik, 2024). To manage these regulatory challenges, businesses should adopt a proactive approach by staying informed about regulatory developments and engaging with policymakers (Dabic, Maley, Svarc & Pocek, 2023). Establishing a dedicated compliance team can help ensure adherence to relevant regulations and enable quick adaptation to change. In addition, leveraging regulatory technology (RegTech) solutions can streamline compliance processes and reduce the burden on businesses.

Lastly, opportunities for collaboration and partnership. Despite those challenges, digital transformation presents various opportunities for collaboration and partnership. Aligning with SDG 17: Partnerships for the Goals, businesses can work together to leverage their strengths and resources to overcome common challenges and drive sustainable growth (Dzhunushalieva & Teuber, 2024). Public-private partnerships (PPPs) can be instrumental in addressing infrastructure and connectivity issues, where governments and businesses collaborate to fund and develop essential infrastructure (Brill & Chapple, 2022). Similarly, partnerships between businesses and educational institutions can help bridge the digital skills gap by creating tailored training programs and internships that prepare students for the digital economy. Besides, collaboration among businesses, technology providers, and cybersecurity experts can enhance data privacy and security measures. By sharing knowledge, best practices, and resources, organizations can collectively improve their defences against cyber threats.

In conclusion, while digital transformation indicates significant challenges across various sectors including the SMEs, it also offers huge opportunities for growth and innovation. By addressing infrastructure and connectivity issues, bridging the digital skills gap, ensuring data privacy and security, and navigating regulatory challenges, businesses can successfully harness the potential of digital technologies. Collaboration and partnership, particularly in alignment with SDG 17, are key to overcoming these challenges and achieving sustainable digital transformation.

Malaysia Government Initiatives and Policies on Digital Transformation

Digital technologies have evolved and revolutionised economic activities across countries regardless of development levels. Digital economic transformation has been facilitated by a series of technological advancements that have resulted in the development of new and enhanced products and services, as well as the enhancement of production and distribution processes. Another aspect of digital economic transformation encompasses changes in modes and patterns of consumption. The fourth industrial revolution, which has been characterised by the convergence of the digital, biological, and physical worlds propelled by a multitude of new technologies, also deems digital economic transformation as its critical element (Lee, 2023).

In Malaysia, policymakers have been actively devising and implementing policies that can effectively capitalise on the new and emerging economic opportunities resulting from advancements in digital technologies. These policies include initiatives that promote various forms of investments as well as supporting and complementary activities that are crucial for facilitating digital transformation.

(a) National Fiberisation and Connectivity Plan (NFCP) (2019-2023)

The National Fiberisation and connection Plan (NFCP) is a five-year government initiative that aims to provide sustainable, comprehensive, high-quality, and affordable digital connectivity throughout the country (National Digital Department, n.d.). The main focus was to provide sustainable digital infrastructure, with a particular emphasis on fibre optic network, as well as other alternative technologies like wireless and satellite whenever conducive. An essential component of the digital economy agenda is a robust communications infrastructure, which is necessary to facilitate the utilization of the latest technology and innovations by all Malaysians.

The implementation of a high-speed fibre-optic network provides various advantages for all users, households, businesses, and the civil service. A study by Hasbi (2017) noted that high-speed broadband network has a direct effect particularly on the construction industry, since it results in the creation of jobs required for network deployment. Additionally, it promotes additional investment in information and communication technology (ICT) systems or devices, which has a favourable impact on the industrial sector. Policymakers and economic analysts also predicted that the presence of high-speed broadband networks positively affects businesses operating in the tertiary sector, where there is a higher concentration of jobs requiring ICT skills.

The NFCP is a strategic initiative of the Malaysian government aimed at enhancing the economic competitiveness of the country by improving connectivity. It also aims to prepare the nation for the challenges and opportunities presented by the Industrial Revolution 4.0. The NFCP essentially seeks to narrow the gap in access to digital resources between rural and urban areas in Malaysia, with the goal of promoting equal opportunity for all citizens. Additionally, the NFCP emphasises on the implementation of various policies and projects, which include improving the efficiency and cost-effectiveness of infrastructure deployment at the state level as well as accelerating the deployment of fibre optic networks, mobile communication transmitters and satellite services.

(b) MyDIGITAL and Malaysia Digital Economy Blueprint (2021-2030)

MyDIGITAL is a national initiative reflecting the Malaysian government's vision to transform the country into a digitally-driven, high-income nation and a leader in the regional digital economy. The objective of MyDIGITAL is to encourage digital adoption among citizens, thereby enhancing their standard of living and quality of life. While MyDIGITAL acts as the overarching national initiative, the Malaysia Digital Economy Blueprint on the other hand serves as the strategic document that outlines the specific efforts, initiatives and projects designed to achieve the goals set by MyDIGITAL. It maps out the path for the digital economy's impact on Malaysian economy and provides the framework for promoting digitalization across various sectors in the country. In essence, the Malaysia Digital Economy Blueprint is the detailed plan that operationalizes the broader vision of MyDIGITAL, guiding the implementation of policies and programs to drive digital transformation and bridge the digital divide in Malaysia.

As set out in MyDIGITAL, the implementation of initiatives and targeted outcomes for the citizens, business and the government will span across three phases of implementation, culminating in 2030. Phase 1, which spans from 2021 to 2022, targets to accelerate technological adoption to build a strong digital foundation. This foundation is essential for effectively implementing the ensuing phases. In Phase 2, which spans from 2023 to 2025, the primary goal is to advance digital transformation and foster inclusivity throughout the digital economy, focusing particularly on ensuring broad participation among the general population and across businesses of all scales. Phase 3, which spans from 2026 to 2030, would then pave the way for a robust and sustainable growth in the years ahead, transforming Malaysia as a regional leader in producing and providing digital goods and solutions. This phase aims to solidify the country's position as a significant player in the digital economy, thereby ensuring long-term sustainability and competitiveness in the regional market. Through the Malaysia Digital Economy Blueprint, the expected gains will be realised through 6 strategic thrusts, 22 strategies, 48 national initiatives, and 28 sectoral initiatives covering 4 main sectors (agriculture, construction, manufacturing and services) (Economic Planning Unit, 2018).

MyDIGITAL envisions a future Malaysia whose citizens will enjoy greater digital literacy, more lucrative employment opportunities, improved social well-being and environmental sustainability. Businesses including micro, small, and medium enterprises (MSMEs) that serve as the backbone of the country's economy (Anderson et al., 2023), are expected to enjoy more opportunities for local, regional and global expansion through digital revenue streams. The initiative also helps businesses to facilitate greater integration between economic sectors and promote cost efficiency through shared economy practices. Additionally, a government that embraces digital enablement will be able to provide integrated online government services that are more transparent, efficient and responsive (Siddiquee & Mohamed, 2009).

(c) Digital Free Trade Zone (DFTZ) (2017)

The Digital Free Trade Zone (DFTZ) was established in 2017 to spearhead the National e-Commerce Strategic Roadmap (NeSR), with the objective of accelerating Malaysia's participation in cross-border e-commerce. The main goal of the DFTZ is to position Malaysia as a prominent regional and global centre for e-commerce fulfilment and to stimulate exports (Chin, Foo & Falahat, 2023). This initiative also aspires to enhance the capabilities of entrepreneurs and small enterprises by easing cross-border commerce, therefore providing them with more opportunities to enter global markets. Another essential element of the DFTZ is the digitalization of trade processes (Lee, Falahat & Sia, 2019), which results in a streamlined e-commerce transactions and more efficient cross-border trade-related processes such as logistics and customs clearance.

From the funding perspective, it was also reported that Alibaba Group, the world's largest e-commerce company, has pledged significant investments in the DFTZ (World Bank Group, 2018). In addition to Alibaba, the Malaysian government financed the DFTZ initiative through partnerships with Maybank and other various logistics, finance, and technology companies. The DFTZ consists of three major components namely e-fulfilment hub, satellite hub and e-services, each implemented in different stages to support Malaysia's e-commerce strategy.

- E-fulfillment Hub: The e-fulfillment hub is strategically located and designed to function as a centralized aviation, air cargo and logistics facility not only for Malaysia, but also for the ASEAN region. Its primary goal is to eliminate trade barriers for smaller firms and emerging nations. This initiative would facilitate smoother processes for customs and cargo clearances for local businesses, especially small and medium enterprises (SMEs), engaged in exporting. The hub also utilizes advanced facilities and technologies to optimize storage and logistics operations, thereby enhancing operational efficiency and ensuring timely fulfilment of orders.

- Satellite Hub: The satellite hub serves as a digital platform facilitating online transactions and collaborations among both local and global e-commerce players. The hub offers various amenities such as office spaces, offline-to-online (O2O) showrooms, MICE (meetings, incentives, conferences and exhibitions) facilities, as well as open and spacious areas for community activities.

- E-Services Platform: The e-services platform is a trade facilitation platform that seamlessly integrates with various business service platforms and government service platforms. The e-services platform additionally facilitates the efficient management of cargo clearance and other cross-border commerce processes and advisory services.

By means of these components, the DFTZ seeks to democratise the access of SMEs to a dynamic supply chain ecosystem that is usually only available to large corporations (Rastogi, 2018). It anticipates that by 2025, it will double the volume of SME exports to US$38 billion, generate 60,000 employment opportunities, and facilitate the transportation of products worth US$65 billion through exports, imports, and transhipments (Noordin, 2017).

Malaysia's strategic commitment to leveraging digital technologies and trade facilitation to fuel economic growth, empower SMEs, and enhance its competitiveness in the global marketplace is reflected in the DFTZ. This initiative not only reduces the barriers to global market entry, but also promotes innovation and collaboration among businesses, thereby driving economic growth and positioning Malaysia as a significant hub for e-commerce and digital trade in the region.

(d) Industry4WRD: National Policy on Industry 4.0 (2019-2025)

The National Fourth Industrial Revolution (4IR) Policy is a comprehensive and all-encompassing national policy that steers strategic transformation of the country's socioeconomic development by ensuring that the 4IR technologies are used in an ethical manner (Economic Planning Unit, 2021). It seeks to guide coherence in policies and promotes the achievement of national goals, offers guidance on managing risks associated with the 4IR technologies without compromising values and culture, establishes an environment that promotes the rapid adoption of digitalization through integration of various technologies, and encourages the development of innovative business models.

While the National 4IR policy serves as the broad and overarching policy, the Industry4WRD meanwhile provides a strategic guide and concerted efforts towards delivering the transformation agenda, particularly for the manufacturing sector and related services sector in Malaysia. The goal of Industry4WRD is to revolutionise the said sectors by effectively leveraging 4IR technologies to become smart, systematic and resilient. In line with the national vision, the Industry4WRD acts as a means of directing and evaluating Malaysia's progress in raising productivity levels of the manufacturing sector, elevating innovative capacity and capability, promoting the transition to a higher skilled workforce, and increasing the absolute contribution of the manufacturing sector to the national economy (Ministry of International Trade & Industry, 2018).

Malaysia's manufacturing firms, particularly SMEs, have the potential to capitalise on Industry 4.0. Given this consideration, the Industry4WRD was designed to drive SMEs forward, enabling them to be flexible and responsive in facing the challenges of the fourth industrial revolution. Efforts to enhance the development of indigenous technologies would also be increased to ensure their accessibility and affordability for Malaysian SMEs. By operating within an ecosystem that optimises the relationships among people, process and technology, the Industry4WRD seeks to build a resilient manufacturing sector and its related services that would lead to greater economic prosperity and societal well-being.

CONCLUSION

Digitalization is playing an increasingly significant role in driving global economic development. The evolution of consumer behaviour now places a high priority on quick and convenient experiences, driven by the widespread use of the Internet and mobile phones. The COVID-19 pandemic intensifies the crucial role of the digital economy in maintaining steady and uninterrupted economic activities. The use of the Internet and technological advancements are key factors in the exponential growth in data, which is deemed to become a valuable commodity in the future. However, if governments do not effectively manage their reaction to digitalization, there is a risk of developing a digital gap. It is imperative that we fully adopt digitalization and make full use of the possibilities it presents to enhance our well-being and maintain our relevance and competitiveness.

Besides, the digital transformation of Malaysia's industrial sector holds profound and multifaceted benefits across economic, social, and environmental domains. Economically, it drives growth through increased efficiency, productivity, and revenue generation, while also creating new high-skilled job opportunities in emerging fields such as data analysis, cybersecurity, and AI development. This shift not only enhances the competitive edge of Malaysian industries on a global scale but also fosters a more dynamic and resilient labour market. Socially, digital transformation democratizes access to information and enhances consumer experiences, promoting social inclusion and well-being. It revolutionizes communication and collaboration, breaking down geographical barriers and fostering innovation through diverse perspectives and expertise.

Environmentally, the adoption of digital technologies supports sustainable development by optimizing logistics and manufacturing processes, significantly reducing carbon emissions and waste production. The promotion of responsible consumption habits and sustainable practices through digital platforms further contributes to environmental conservation efforts. Additionally, the use of digital technologies for environmental monitoring and resource management enables proactive measures to address environmental challenges, safeguarding natural habitats and promoting sustainable development practices. Embracing digital transformation positions Malaysia to thrive in the competitive global landscape, ensuring long-term economic growth, social well-being, and environmental sustainability. By leveraging the full potential of digital technologies, Malaysia can create a more inclusive, resilient, and sustainable future, benefiting not only the current generation but also future ones.

REFERENCES

Abd Shukor, R., Mooi, W. K., & Ibrahim, J. A. (2023). *The future of Malaysian SMEs in the digital economy*. Qeios. DOI: 10.32388/VSWNB6

Adama, H. E., Popoola, O. A., Okeke, C. D., & Akinoso, A. E.Henry Ejiga AdamaOladapo Adeboye PopoolaChukwuekem David OkekeAbiodun Emmanuel Akinoso. (2024). Economic theory and practical impacts of digital transformation in supply chain optimization. *International Journal of Advanced Economics*, 6(4), 95–107. DOI: 10.51594/ijae.v6i4.1072

AlphaBeta. (2021). Positioning Malaysia as a Regional Leader in the Digital Economy: The Economic Opportunities of Digital Transformation and Google's Contribution. Retrieved from https://accesspartnership.com/wp-content/uploads/2023/03/Malaysia-Digital- Transformation.pdf

Ammeran, M. Y., Noor, S., & Yusof, M. (2021). Digital transformation of Malaysian small and medium-sized enterprises: a review and research direction. In *International Conference on Business and Technology* (pp. 255-278). Cham: Springer International Publishing.

Anderson, L., Pekkari, M., Gray, J., Neugebauer, V., & Candotto, L. (2023). Building MSME Resilience in Southeast Asia: With a country focus on Thailand and Malaysia. United Nations Development Programme (UNDP) Insurance and Risk Finance Facility (IRFF). https://irff.undp.org/publications/building-msme-resilience-southeast-asia

Anuar, A. (2024). AI and EV Innovations Entering Malaysia's Healthcare System. The Malaysian Reserve. Retrieved from https://themalaysianreserve.com/2024/06/19/ai-and-ev-innovations- entering-malaysias-healthcare-system/#google_vignette

Aqmala, D., & Putra, F. I. F. S. (2023). Eco Cuty: The Eco-Friendly Marketing Strategy Model for MSME's Economic Recovery Movement Post-Covid 19. *Calitatea*, 24(194), 304–312.

Bocean, C. G. (2024). A Longitudinal Analysis of the Impact of Digital Technologies on Sustainable Food Production and Consumption in the European Union. *Foods*, 13(8), 1281. DOI: 10.3390/foods13081281 PMID: 38672953

Bose, R. (2009). Advanced analytics: Opportunities and challenges. *Industrial Management & Data Systems*, 109(2), 155–172. DOI: 10.1108/02635570910930073

Boström, E., & Celik, O. C. 2017, 'Towards a maturity model for digital strategizing: A qualitative study of how an organization can analyze and assess their digital business strategy', Dissertation, Dept. of Informatics Umeå University.

Brill, J., & Chapple, E. (2022). Microsoft announces the phased roll-out of the EU Data Boundary for the Microsoft Cloud begins. Retrieved from https://blogs.microsoft.com/eupolicy/2022/12/15/eu-data-boundary-cloud-rollout

Bucea-Manea- oniş, R., Bucea-Manea- oniş, R., Simion, V. E., Ilic, D., Braicu, C., & Manea, N. (2020). Sustainability in higher education: The relationship between work-life balance and XR e-learning facilities. *Sustainability (Basel)*, 12(14), 5872. DOI: 10.3390/su12145872

BusinessToday. (2021). Amplifying Digital Transformation for Malaysian Businesses. Retrieved from https://www.businesstoday.com.my/2021/08/23/amplifying-digital-transformation-for-malaysian-businesses/

Bustos L. (2015). The Guide to Digital Transformation.

Chin, M. Y., Foo, L. P., & Falahat, M. (2023). Digital free trade zone in facilitating small medium enterprises for globalisation: A perspective from Malaysia small and medium enterprises. *Business and Economic Review*, 13(2), 40–52. DOI: 10.5296/ber.v13i2.20835

Çınar, Z. M., Abdussalam Nuhu, A., Zeeshan, Q., Korhan, O., Asmael, M., & Safaei, B. (2020). Machine learning in predictive maintenance towards sustainable smart manufacturing in industry 4.0. *Sustainability (Basel)*, 12(19), 8211. DOI: 10.3390/su12198211

Coche, E., Kolk, A., & Ocelik, V. (2024). Unravelling cross-country regulatory intricacies of data governance: The relevance of legal insights for digitalization and international business. *Journal of International Business Policy*, 7(1), 112–127. DOI: 10.1057/s42214-023-00172-1

Cory, N. (2021). Sovereignty requirements in France -and potentially EU- cybersecurity regulations: The latest barrier to data flows, digital trade, and digital cooperation among likeminded partners. Retrieved from https://www.crossborderdataforum.org/sovereignty-requirements-in -france-and-potentially-eu-cybersecurity-regulations-the-latest-barrier-to-data-flows-digital -trade-and-digital-cooperation-among-likemi/

Dabic, M., Maley, J. F., Svarc, J., & Pocek, J. (2023). Future of digital work: Challenges for sustainable human resources management. Journal of Innovation & Knowledge. DOI: 10.1016/j.jik.2023.100353

Dzhunushalieva, G., & Teuber, R. (2024). Roles of innovation in achieving the Sustainable Development Goals: A bibliometric analysis. Journal of Innovation & Knowledge. DOI: 10.1016/j.jik.2024.100472

Economic Planning Unit. (2018). *Malaysia Digital Economy Blueprint*. Ministry of Economy of Malaysia. https://www.ekonomi.gov.my/sites/default/files/2021-03/Malaysia-Digital Economy-Blueprint-%2820-03-2021%29.pdf

Economic Planning Unit. (2021). *National 4IR Policy*. Ministry of Economy of Malaysia. https://www.ekonomi.gov.my/sites/default/files/2021-07/National-4IR -Policy.pdf

Foster, C., & Azmeh, S. (2020). Latecomer economies and national digital policy: An industrial policy perspective. *The Journal of Development Studies*, 56(7), 1247–1262. DOI: 10.1080/00220388.2019.1677886

Gebremeskel, B. K., Jonathan, G. M., & Yalew, S. D. (2023). Information Security Challenges During Digital Transformation. *Procedia Computer Science*, 219, 44–51. DOI: 10.1016/j.procs.2023.01.262

Georgiou, K., Mittas, N., Mamalikidis, I., Mitropoulos, A., & Angelis, L. (2021). Analyzing the roles and competence demand for digitalization in the oil and gas 4.0 era. *IEEE Access : Practical Innovations, Open Solutions*, 9, 151306–151326. DOI: 10.1109/ACCESS.2021.3124909

Guan, L., Li, W., Guo, C., & Huang, J. (2023). Environmental strategy for sustainable development: Role of digital transformation in China's natural resource exploitation. *Resources Policy*, 87, 104304. DOI: 10.1016/j.resourpol.2023.104304

Guerra, J. M. M., Danvila-del-Valle, I., & Mendez-suarez, M. (2023). The impact of digital transformation on talent management. *Technological Forecasting and Social Change*, 188, 122291. Advance online publication. DOI: 10.1016/j.techfore.2022.122291

Hamidi, S. R., Aziz, A. A., Shuhidan, S. M., Aziz, A. A., & Mokhsin, M. (2018). SMEs maturity model assessment of IR4. 0 digital transformation. In Proceedings of the 7th International Conference on Kansei Engineering and Emotion Research 2018: KEER 2018, 19-22 March 2018, Kuching, Sarawak, Malaysia (pp. 721-732). Springer Singapore. DOI: 10.1007/978-981-10-8612-0_75

Hanna, N. (2010). *Enabling enterprise transformation: Business and grassroots Innovation for the knowledge economy*. Springer. DOI: 10.1007/978-1-4419-1508-5

Hasbi, M. (2017). Impact of Very High-Speed Broadband on Local Economic Growth: Empirical Evidence, 14th International Telecommunications Society (ITS) Asia-Pacific Regional Conference:" Mapping ICT into Transformation for the Next Information Society. *Kyoto, Japan*, 24-27.

Hashim, J. (2007). Information communication technology (ICT) adoption among SME owners in Malaysia. International Journal of Business and information, 2(2), 221-240.

Hidayat-ur-Rehman, I., & Hossain, M. N. (2024). The impacts of Fintech adoption, green finance and competitiveness on banks' sustainable performance: Digital transformation as moderator. *Asia-Pacific Journal of Business Administration*. Advance online publication. DOI: 10.1108/APJBA-10-2023-0497

Hitt, M. A., Keats, B. W., & DeMarie, S. M. (1998). Navigating in the new competitive landscape: Building strategic flexibility and competitive advantage in the 21st century. *The Academy of Management Perspectives*, 12(4), 22–42. DOI: 10.5465/ame.1998.1333922

Ignatius, C. (2022). Digitalisation Imperatives for SMEs in Malaysia. BusinessToday. Retrieved from https://www.businesstoday.com.my/2022/10/04/digitalisation-imperatives-for-smes-in-malaysia/

Javaid, M., Haleem, A., Singh, R. P., & Suman, R. (2021). Substantial capabilities of robotics in enhancing industry 4.0 implementation. *Cognitive Robotics*, 1, 58–75. DOI: 10.1016/j.cogr.2021.06.001

Kokolek, N., Jakovic, B., & Curlin, T. (2019). Digital Knowledge and Skills–Key Factors for Digital Transformation. Annals of DAAAM & Proceedings, 30.

Kraus, S., Jones, P., Kailer, N., Weinmann, A., Chaparro-Banegas, N., & Roig-Tierno, N. (2021). Digital Transformation: An Overview of the Current State of the Art of Research. SAGE journals, 11(3). https://doi.org/DOI: 10.1177/21582440211047576

Lee, C. (2023). Strategic Policies for Digital Economic Transformation. *Journal of Southeast Asian Economies*, 40(1), 32–63. https://www.jstor.org/stable/27211224. DOI: 10.1355/ae40-1c

Lee, D. J., & Joseph Sirgy, M. (2019). Work-life balance in the digital workplace: The impact of schedule flexibility and telecommuting on work-life balance and overall life satisfaction. *Thriving in digital workspaces: Emerging issues for research and practice*, 355-384.

Lee, Y. Y., Falahat, M., & Sia, B. K. (2019). Impact of Digitalization on the Speed of Internationalization. *International Business Research*, 12(4), 1–11. DOI: 10.5539/ibr.v12n4p1

Lemon, K. N., & Verhoef, P. C. (2016). Understanding customer experience throughout the customer journey. *Journal of Marketing*, 80(6), 69–96. DOI: 10.1509/jm.15.0420

Li, L. (2022). Digital transformation and sustainable performance: The moderating role of market turbulence. *Industrial Marketing Management*, 104, 28–37. DOI: 10.1016/j.indmarman.2022.04.007

Lynn, T. G., Conway, E., Rosati, P., & Curran, D. (2022). *Infrastructure for Digital Connectivity*. Digital Towns., DOI: 10.1007/978-3-030-91247-5_6

Malik, A., Amjad, G., & Nemati, A. R. (2022). Impact of Technological, Organizational, Product, and Process Innovation on Employee Turnover Intention. *Zakariya Journal of Social Science*, 1(1), 1–14. DOI: 10.59075/zjss.v1i1.43

Manny, L., Duygan, M., Fischer, M., & Rieckermann, J. (2021). Barriers to the digital transformation of infrastructure sectors. *Policy Sciences*, 54(4), 943–983. DOI: 10.1007/s11077-021-09438-y PMID: 34751195

MDC. (2016). Smart School. Retrieved on December 26, 2020 from http://docshare01.docshare.tips/files/2050/20507921.pdf

Mhlanga, D. (2023). Digital transformation education, opportunities, and challenges of the application of ChatGPT to emerging economies. *Education Research International*, 2023(1), 7605075. DOI: 10.1155/2023/7605075

MIDA. (2024). Malaysia – Driven by Digital Evolution. Retrieved from https://www.reuters.com/plus/malaysia-driven-by-digital-evolution

Ministry of International Trade & Industry. (2018). *Industry4WRD: National Policy on Industry 4.0*. Ministry of Investment, Trade and Industry of Malaysia. https://www.miti.gov.my/miti/resources/National%20Policy%20on%20Industry%204.0/Indu try4WRD_Final.pdf

National Digital Department. (n.d.). *The National Fiberisation and Connectivity Plan (NFCP) 2019 2023*. https://www.malaysia.gov.my/portal/content/30736

Nguyen, S. D. (2020). Digital transformation in art pedagogical training in Vietnam today. *Vietnam Journal of Education*, 4(4), 69–75. DOI: 10.52296/vje.2020.82

Ninaus, K., Diehl, S., & Terlutter, R. (2021). Employee perceptions of information and communication technologies in work life, perceived burnout, job satisfaction and the role of work-family balance. *Journal of Business Research*, 136, 652–666. DOI: 10.1016/j.jbusres.2021.08.007

Nižetić, S., Djilali, N., Papadopoulos, A., & Rodrigues, J. J. (2019). Smart technologies for promotion of energy efficiency, utilization of sustainable resources and waste management. *Journal of Cleaner Production*, 231, 565–591. DOI: 10.1016/j.jclepro.2019.04.397

Noordin, K. A. (2017, November 14). Deconstructing the DFTZ. *The Edge Malaysia*. https://theedgemalaysia.com/article/deconstructing-dftz

Onungwa, I., Olugu-Uduma, N., & Shelden, D. R. (2021). Cloud BIM technology as a means of collaboration and project integration in smart cities. *SAGE Open*, 11(3), 21582440211033250. DOI: 10.1177/21582440211033250

Piccinini, E., Gregory, R. W., & Kolbe, L. M. (2015). Changes in the producer-consumer relationship-towards digital transformation.

Rastogi, V. (2018, January 18). Malaysia's Digital Free Trade Zone. *AEAN Briefing*. https://www.aseanbriefing.com/news/malaysias-digital-free-trade-zone/

Rizvi, Y. S., & Nabi, A. (2021). Transformation of learning from real to virtual: An exploratory-descriptive analysis of issues and challenges. *Journal of Research in Innovative Teaching & Learning*, 14(1), 5–17. DOI: 10.1108/JRIT-10-2020-0052

Siddiquee, N. A., & Mohamed, M. Z. (2009). *E-governance and service delivery innovations in Malaysia: an overview. Network of Asia-Pacific Schools and Institutes of Public Administration and Governance*. NAPSIPAG.

SME Corp Malaysia: SME Annual Report 2017/18 (2018)

Tarutė, A., Duobienė, J., Klovienė, L., Vitkauskaitė, E., & Varaniūtė, V. (2018). Identifying factors affecting digital transformation of SMEs. In Proceedings of The 18th International Conference on Electronic Business (pp. 373- 381). ICEB, Guilin, China, December 2-6.

Telecom Review. (2024). Malaysia's Digital Transformation Powered by New Technologies. Retrieved from https://www.telecomreviewasia.com/news/featured-articles/4001-malaysia-s-digital-transformation-powered-by-new-technologies/

TM ONE. (2021). How Digital Solutions Helped Malaysian SMEs #stayinbusiness. Retrieved from https://www.tmone.com.my/think-tank/how-digital-solutions-helped-malaysian-smes-stayinbusiness/

To a, C., Paneru, C. P., Joudavi, A., & Tarigan, A. K. (2024). Digital transformation, incentives, and pro-environmental behaviour: Assessing the uptake of sustainability in companies' transition towards circular economy. *Sustainable Production and Consumption*, 47, 632–643. DOI: 10.1016/j.spc.2024.04.032

Tyler, B., Lahneman, B., Beukel, K., Cerrato, D., Minciullo, M., Spielmann, N., & Discua Cruz, A. (2020). SME Managers' Perceptions of Competitive Pressure and the Adoption of Environmental Practices in Fragmented Industries: A Multi Country Study in the Wine Industry. Organization and Environment, 33(3), 437 463. DOI: 10.1177/1086026618803720

Verina, N., & Titko, J. (2019, May). Digital transformation: conceptual framework. In Proc. of the Int. Scientific Conference "Contemporary Issues in Business, Management and Economics Engineering (pp. 9-10). DOI: 10.3846/cibmee.2019.073

Westerman, G., & Bonnet, D. Mc & Mcaffee, A., 2014, Leading digital: Turning technology into business transformation, 1st edn., Harvard Business Review, Boston, MA.

World Bank Group. (2018). *Malaysia's Digital Economy: A New Driver of Development*. World Bank.

ADDITIONAL READING

Ali, M. (2021). *Remote Work and Sustainable Changes for the Future of Global Business*. IGI Global. https://www.igi-global.com/book/remote-work-sustainable -changes-future/264375

Ali, M. (2022). *Future Role of Sustainable Innovative Technologies in Crisis Management*. IGI Global. https://www.igi-global.com/book/future-role-sustainable -innovative-technologies/281281

Ali, M. (2023). *Shifting Paradigms in the Rapidly Developing Global Digital Ecosystem: A GCC Perspective.* In Digital Entrepreneurship and Co-Creating Value Through Digital Encounters (pp. 145-166). IGI Global. https://www.igi-global.com/chapter/ shifting-paradigms-in-the-rapidly-developing-global-digital-ecosystem/323525

Ali, M. (2023). T*axonomy of Industry 4.0 Technologies in Digital Entrepreneurship and Co-Creating Value*. In *Digital Entrepreneurship and Co-Creating Value Through Digital Encounters* (pp. 24–55). IGI Global., https://www.igi-global.com/ chapter/taxonomy-of-industry-40-technologies-in-digital-entrepreneurship-and-co -creating-value/323520 DOI: 10.4018/978-1-6684-7416-7.ch002

Ali, M., & Wood-Harper, T. (2021). *Fostering Communication and Learning with Underutilized Technologies in Higher Education*. IGI Global. https://www.igi-global.com/book/fostering-communication-learning-underutilized-technologies/244593

Ali, M., Wood-Harper, T., & Kutar, M. (2023). Multi-Perspectives of Contemporary Digital Transformation Models of Complex Innovation Management. In *Digital Entrepreneurship and Co-Creating Value Through Digital Encounters* (pp. 79–96). IGI Global., https://www.igi-global.com/chapter/multi-perspectives-of-contemporary-digital-transformation-models-of-complex-innovation-management/323522 DOI: 10.4018/978-1-6684-7416-7.ch004

Ali, M. B. (2021). Internet of Things (IoT) to Foster Communication and Information Sharing: A Case of UK Higher Education. In Ali, M. B., & Wood-Harper, T. (Eds.), *Fostering Communication and Learning With Underutilized Technologies in Higher Education* (pp. 1–20). IGI Global., https://www.igi-global.com/chapter/internet-of-things-iot-to-foster-communication-and-information-sharing/262718/ DOI: 10.4018/978-1-7998-4846-2.ch001

Ali, M. B., & Wood-Harper, T. (2022). Artificial Intelligence (AI) as a Decision-Making Tool to Control Crisis Situations. In *Future Role of Sustainable Innovative Technologies in Crisis Management*. IGI Global., https://www.igi-global.com/chapter/artificial-intelligence-ai-as-a-decision-making-tool-to-control-crisis-situations/298931 DOI: 10.4018/978-1-7998-9815-3.ch006

Ali, M. B., Wood-Harper, T., & Ramlogan, R. (2020). A Framework Strategy to Overcome Trust Issues on Cloud Computing Adoption in Higher Education. In Modern Principles, Practices, and Algorithms for Cloud Security (pp. 162-183). IGI Global. https://www.igi-global.com/chapter/a-framework-strategy-to-overcome-trust-issues-on-cloud-computing-adoption-in-higher-education/238907/

Chapter 7
Digital Transformation and Continuance Intention of Online Learning Platforms Among Students in Higher Education Institutions in Remote India

Afeefa Fatima

Babu Banarasi Das University, Lucknow, India

Rinki Verma

Babu Banarasi Das University, Lucknow, India

Shreyanshu Singh

https://orcid.org/0000-0001-8745-6227

Babu Banarasi Das University, Lucknow, India

Manoj Kumar

https://orcid.org/0000-0002-8325-6612

Shri Ramswaroop Memorial University, Barabanki, India

Karnika Srivastava

Techno Group of Institutions, Lucknow, India

DOI: 10.4018/979-8-3693-5966-2.ch007

ABSTRACT

The rapid emergence of the fourth industrial revolution (4-IR) and technological progress is driving significant digitalization and the adoption of automated, efficient technologies capable of complex tasks with minimal physical interaction. These advancements are accelerating economic growth and transforming sectors, including higher education (Ho et al., 2020). The COVID-19 pandemic revolutionized teaching pedagogy in higher education, prompting universities to shift from traditional methods to modern tech-based approaches. This study investigates the continuance intention of students and academic institutions towards integrating online learning technologies as a permanent shift. It examines factors influencing students' willingness to continue using these technologies post-COVID-19. A quantitative approach explores the relationship between online learning platforms and students' continuance intention in Indian colleges and universities, focusing on remote/rural students selected through convenience sampling. Advanced statistical tools SPSS and AMOS analyze the data.

1. INTRODUCTION

All through the epidemic of Covid-19, countries across globe were forced to shift their traditional education approach to recent OLP (online learning platforms). Online learning has appeared as the maximum sought mode of teaching and learning amidst the crisis and beyond the pandemic as it involves novel learning opportunities to the learners without physical interaction (Wei et al., 2022, Santiago et al., 2021). In India, educational institutions across the country has responded very quickly in the adoption of online learning methods to mitigate the impact of closure of educational institutions due to the spread of virus. However, imparting online education to students studying in higher education institutions in remote India was subjected to a number of hurdles including inadequate educational infrastructure facilities, existing digital divide and less resources etc. Despite having these challenges India's higher education sector has experienced a surge in the usage of various online teaching –learning platforms (Vlachopoulos, 2020). As many educational institutions and universities have integrated various online learning applications instead of traditional learning systems, hybrid structures are gaining a lot of popularity from teaching-learning institutions in India including remote India. The present-day researches have shown that use of blended technology in higher education is critical to improving student's overall performance in order to learn and develop (Zhu et al., 2020). Many research studies have concluded that emergence of online learning provides novel learning experience for the learners, makes learning easier and offers tremendous benefits developing abilities, skills, and attitudes amongst the students studying in Indian higher educational institutions (Cidral et al., 2018).

Considering the growing importance of digitalization of higher education institutions and its promotion, it becomes imperative to identify the critical factors determining learner's willingness to further continuing online learning platforms(OLP) (Al-Rahmi et. al., 2019). Moreover, the success of OLP is impacted by student's enthusiasm to attempt and their reception of the system (Almaiah, et.al. 2019). Online-learning has been proved to one of the most invaluable approaches of learning when other alternative instructional approaches were found to be inaccessible (Islam et al., 2021). However, the effectiveness of OLP, especially in higher education institutions greatly depends on student's willingness as well as the satisfaction of students and teachers. In this context, the Expectation- Confirmation Theory is considered to be widely applicable theory to explain individual's usage behavior of different ICT enabled technologies (Ramadhan et al., 2022). In this study, we have examined elements such as confirmation (Con), perceived usefulness (PU), social influence (SI), and user's satisfaction (Sat) and their impact on university student's continuance intention (CI) to use OLP.

Research of OLP has shown that students' continuance intention of online apps usage is influenced by several factors. Lee (2010) highlighted the significance of PU and satisfaction with the education application as key determinants of CI. Wang et al. (2021) highlighted that social influence and facilitating conditions aid in determining learners' intentions to further continue using OLP. Study of Hu et al. (2020) emphasized that with the increasing reliance on online learning due to the global pandemic the significance of perceived benefits, system quality and enjoyment has become imperative in influencing students' CI. These recent references provide valuable insights into understanding the factors that influence user's decision to continue using OLP that can help educators and app developers in enhancing the user experience and promoting sustained usage among students.

Present study takes into account Indian higher educational institutions including public universities, private universities and colleges from both urban and remote parts of the country. Evidences suggest that most of the higher education institutions (HEI) have switched their traditional teaching and administrative functions to online mode to impart quality and effective learning during the pandemic. However, the students studying in HEIs located in urban private universities and colleges students were privileged to endure their studies through online learning as compared to their rural counterparts. Remote institutions and colleges developed a reasonably seamless online learning procedure over time. Thus identifying the elements that effect learners' intention for continuance usage of OLP is crucial to understand. This could help other Indian universities comprehend the problem and devise appropriate remedies. This study may encourage new commercial and public colleges to use online learning platforms to deliver better and easy education.

This chapter attempts to find out the willingness of university student's studying in remote India to use OLP. Study is an effort to measure the importance of digital learning post Covid19, focusing on the continuance intention of students studying in colleges and universities located in remote India. The motivation behind this study is to scrutinize the elements determining student's intent to use OLP after the pandemic is over. In India, during the global pandemic, using OLP like Zoom, Google meet, Skype etc. for virtual education in HEI had been quite effective. However, after the pandemic is over now, e-learning can be seen as a most sought after mode of learning through various digital learning platforms. Thus, it is crucial to discover students' intentions to pursue higher education via o-learning platforms that can provide inexpensive and easy learning possibilities across Indian colleges.

Hence, this chapter is an effort to respond to the subsequent research inquiries:

RQ1: In what way student's pre-adoption expectations about online learning platforms affect satisfaction and their post-adoption continuance intention of students of remote Indian higher education institutions?

RQ2: How does the perceived usefulness (PU) of online learning platforms impact higher education institute (HEI) student's intention to use them in remote areas of India?

RQ3: What role does social influence (SI) play in students' continuance intention towards online learning platform (OLP) in higher education institutes located in remote India?

For the proposed research study following sequence has been adopted. In introduction section, the impact of COVID-19 on education systems worldwide in general and on India in particular with regard to online-learning platforms is discussed. Further, study objectives are stated. Previous studies as well as the recent literature are reviewed in the next. The next section discusses research hypothesis formulation within the theoretical framework. The study then outlines its data collection, sample size, measures, and investigative methods. Results of sample and data analysis are followed by discussion, theoretical and practical insights, limitations, and scope for future work. Based on the research, lastly recommendation and conclusion is deliberated.

2. THEORETICAL BACKGROUND

2.1 Expectation-Confirmation Model (ECM)

To envisage the user's satisfaction and their continuance intentions to used technology enabled platforms, the ECM has been extensively used by the researchers from past several decades (Ramadhan et al., 2022). As per the ECM theory, intention to carry on the use of Information technology (IT) enabled platforms largely depends upon user satisfaction level. The degree of endorsement of expectations depends largely on pre and post- adoption usage of online learning technologies. In ECM, satisfaction is dependent upon user confirmation and their expectations. User confirmation may be defined as user expectations towards any media technology and if user expectations are met it confirms their expectations. Hence, confirmation is positively correlated with satisfaction. In other words it may be comprehended that if the students confirm their expectations with regard to an online-learning system, they would continue their usage behavior in the future as well. Most of research studies concluded that consumer satisfaction is crucial factor determining user continuance intention towards IT enabled platforms. Kim et al. (2021) study demonstrates that consumer's behavioral intention towards online learning platforms is highly relied on their level of satisfaction. Likewise, Daneji et al. (2021) confirmed student's satisfaction considerably influence their continuance intentions with regard to MOOC platforms. Many research studies in the past have incorporated ECM with other theoretical models to assess continuance intention of the users for using various IT enabled platforms. Through, integration of multiple theories such as ECM, TAM, TPB and UTAUT, researchers gain in-depth and thorough understanding of the factors determining of individual's continuance intention in the context of online-learning platforms. For instance, Lee (2010), integrated ECM with flow theory and theory of planned behavior with that of TAM to develop a deeper understanding about the user's CI for e-learning context. Likewise, Cheng (2014), combined ECT, IS success model and Flow theory to understand the continuance intentions of users for Blended e- learning mode. In order to explain learner's Continuance Intentions for MOOC platforms, many researchers have used ECT model in their respective research studies (Dai et al. 2020; Alraimi et al. 2015; and Zhou 2017).

In the light of above discussion, it is indicative that the ECT can be used to understand and explain the impact of technology based learning systems on the actual learning experience of the users, with regard to various online learning platforms. Therefore, we adopted ECT, as the foundational model to study the determinants predicting CI of students for various OLP beyond pandemic.

2.2 Theory of Acceptance and Use of Technology (UTAUT)

To assess the behavioral intentions of users towards technology adoption, the UTAUT model developed by Venkatesh et al. (2003) has been recognized as the most sought after model to study the technology adoption behavior of the users. For instance, Hu S et al. incorporated UTAUT model to predict user's adoption behavior of users of mobile and internet banking. Similarly, Nasri (2021), highlighted the acceptance of technology by customers of Tunisian banking industry through the modified UTAUT model. Many research studies, utilized the UTAUT model to inspect the aspects determining the initial behavioral intention to use online learning platforms (OLP) during the COVID-19 crisis (Bai et al., 2021; Huang, 2019). A number of recent research studies have extended the UTAUT model and integrated a number of new constructs to examine the user's behavioral intention of using various technology enables platforms. For instance, Venkatesh et al. (2011), combined the ECM and UTAUT to develop a single model to examine the CI of technology users. According to the researchers, in order to explain exactly the continuance intentions of users, the modification of UTAUT model is desirable, as the confirmation of user's initial experience based on their satisfaction level is not adequately reflected. As per Oghuma et al., (2016) confirmation of user's initial experience plays a critical role in capturing the reflective cognitive process of technology users, who relies on their initial interaction to continue the usage behavior for technology enabled platforms. Recent studies on continuance intentions of users, confirms that the fundamental constructs of ECM have the efficiency to describe the user's expectations while using digital learning technologies in both pre and post pandemic era Chauhan et.al.(2022). Likewise, two primary constructs namely post-adoption perceived usefulness (PU) and Social Influence (SI) have been adopted from UTAUT model for predicting student's CI of using various OLP during the COVID-19 pandemic and beyond. Due to limited interaction with the students studying in HEIs located in remote India, we excluded performance expectancy (PE) constructs from the UTAUT framework.

3. RESEARCH FRAMEWORK AND HYPOTHESES

The research has combined Expectation Confirmation Theory and the UTAUT into a single model to examine continuance intention of students studying in remote parts of India, with regard to various online learning platforms during and beyond the epidemic. Fig. 1 exhibits the proposed model for the study. Established on the ECT and UTAUT model, five main constructs namely confirmation (CON), Satisfaction (SA) Perceived usefulness (PU), Social influence (SI), and Continuance intention (CI) have been identified for the study.

3.1 Confirmation (Con)

Confirmation has historically been described by researchers as the degree to which a person's actual experience matches their initial expectations (Oghuma et al., 2016). Thong et al. (2006) study state that confirmation happens when the user's real experience either meets or surpasses their initial expectations, directly resulting in user pleasure. In a related study, Ambalov (2018) used the meta-analytical approach on ECM and confirmed that there is a significant correlation between user happiness and confirmation. ECM endorses that users' confirmation affects how satisfied they are with the different OLP they use (Wang et al., 2021). Similarly, a number of recent studies have found a favourable correlation between user happiness and confirmation (Ramadhan et al., 2022; Persada et al., 2021; Lee, 2010). According to the proposed study, students who have had favourable experiences with online technologies in the past exhibit higher levels of satisfaction (SA) with online learning platforms, which in turn influences their continuance intentions (CI) to utilise a variety of OLP in the future. Therefore, it can be said that users are more likely to be satisfied with their experience utilising an online learning system if their initial expectations are met. Thus, the following hypothesis is put forth.

H1: Confirmation (CON) will influence satisfaction (SA) for using online-learning platform.

3.2 Satisfaction (SA)

Satisfaction refers to the accumulative feelings faced by students from their first experiences of adopting learning technologies (Bai et al., 2021). The ECM also establishes a link between user satisfaction and the confirmation of their expectations of using online learning platforms. A number of recent research studies employed the ECM to establish a linkage amid consumer's satisfaction and their continuation intention with respect to OLP (Ramadhan et al. 2022). The effect of virtual learning on user satisfaction has been analyzed by many research studies in recent years (Kim et al., 2021). Likewise, Chauhan et al.,(2021), mentioned satisfaction as a vital predictor of continuation intention of learners in the cyber classroom context. Learning on the internet has a number of advantages, including adaptability, accessibility, and a diverse selection of available study materials. It does, however, come with a number of drawbacks, including the possibility of experiencing emotions of isolation, the absence of face-to-face interaction, and technical difficulties. Research has shown that the overall satisfaction of learners is subjected by numerous factors, comprising the quality of online platform, the effectiveness of the instructor's communication, and the level of engagement and interaction among students (Tao & Gao, 2022). When these factors are well-addressed, virtual learning can bring about high levels of satisfaction and positive learning outcomes. Furthermore, the convenience in using online learning platforms, the self-paced learning ability and the opportunity for self-directed learning also contribute to user satisfaction (Al-Rahmi et al., 2015). However, it is essential for online educators and institutions to continuously evaluate and improve the online learning experience to ensure that user's needs and expectations are adequately met. Research studies on continuance intentions of users of technologies have extensively use ECT and highlighted user's satisfaction as the key predictor of user's continuance intention for using online learning technologies (Oliver 1980; Oliver and Bearden,1985 and Bhattacherjee 2001). Some recent researches, have also concluded that satisfaction had strong predictive power to influence the continuance intention of students in using various online learning platforms (Lu et al.,2019 and Wa and Wang, 2020). In this connection, it can be posited that students who shows higher level of satisfaction in using online learning technologies would also show a higher intention to continue to use it in future as well. Therefore, the following hypothesis is proposed.

H2: Satisfaction (SA) will influence students' continuance Intention (CI) for using an online-learning platform.

3.3 Post Adoption Perceived Usefulness (PU)

As stated by Bhattacherjee (2001), perceived usefulness may be defined as the degree to which users believe that utilising the technology is advantageous and helpful. This is the reason why people accept particular technologies and continue to use them regardless of the amount of time that has passed. Some recent studies have used ECM and incorporated post adoption perceived usefulness as a post adoption construct, which is reflective of a subjective belief in the context of the usefulness of a product or service. According to Nam et al., (2020), post adoption perceived usefulness is the outcome of a product's/service's expected and actual consumption performance that leads to user's satisfaction with regard to a product or service. Saxena et al. (2021) have also validated that there exists a strong correlation between post adoption perceived usefulness and user's satisfaction. A study by Daneji (2019) also highlighted that the PU of online learning platforms positively correlates with the user's confirmation. Various scholary works have also authenticated a strong relationship among student's satisfaction and their willingness to continue the use of online learning technologies, including online-learning platforms (Singh and Sharma, 2021). Therefore, it can be posited that students will be highly satisfied with online learning platforms if their perception regarding its usage is found to be beneficial for them. In this connection, it can be proposed that post adoption perceived benefits could influence the student's belief that usage of online learning platforms in their academic activities would help them to perform their academic tasks more efficiently.

H3: Post adoption perceived usefulness (PU) will influence student's satisfaction (SA) for using an online-learning platform.

3.4 Social Influence (SI)

In the words of Venkatesh et al. in 2003, Social influence, involves the perceived importance of other's beliefs about one's engagement with new services or adherence to others' expectations. Based on social influence, the individual perceives external pressure or expectations from their peers, family members, experts, or societal norms in making choices, especially regarding the adoption of new behaviors or innovations. However, Venkatesh and Davis (2000), pointed out that SI especially occurs in forceful situations rather than situations demands voluntary usage behavior of individuals. The influence exerted by those closest to an individual is especially impactful. This could mean that if peers or family members view online learning positively, an individual is more likely to engage with it actively and vice versa. Many research studies have approved that student's decision to use and accept online-learning technologies is critically influenced by their colleagues, peers and faculties (Chuc et al., 2016). Likewise, Sharma et al.,2016 quoted that the approval or disapproval from a person's close contacts fundamentally influence their decision-making process. Hence, use of OLP develops a feeling that encourages the usage of such platforms that can facilitate its adoption and continued usage behavior amongst the students. The role of educators as authoritative figures can impact students' perceptions of the value and legitimacy of online learning. Moreover, Peers who endorse and are satisfied with online learning can positively affect an individual's attitude towards it. Jamshidi, D., & Hussin, N. (2016) emphasize the prominence of social influence, suggesting it's a significant basis of a person's likelihood to embrace new technology. In the domain of online education, social influence could directly affect a student's intention to engage with online courses, their persistence in continuing with online education, and their overall satisfaction with the learning experience. Some recent studies also validated that social influence creates a profound impact on student's actual and continued usage behavior intentions for online learning platforms (Al-Adwan et al., 2022). Similarly, Yakubu et al.,(2020), highlighted that SI has a significant positive effect on user's satisfaction with regard to OLP. Therefore, the following hypothesis has been posited for the study:

H4: SI will effect student's satisfaction (SA) for using an online-learning platform.

3.5 Continuance Intention (CI)

According to ECM, continuance intention referred to as the willingness of students to continue the use of learning technologies even when the pandemic is over and face to face classes resume (Wang et al., 2017).The results of many researches in the field of online learning shows that student's continuance intention of online apps usage is influenced by several factors (Daneji et al.,2019). Recent study by Kim et al.,(2021) emphasized the importance of factors like perceived usefulness (PU), ease of use (EU), and satisfaction (S) with the OLP, as key determinants of continuance intention. Additionally, the study by Wang et al.(2021), highlighted the role of social influence and facilitating conditions in shaping students' intentions to continue using online learning platforms. Considering the creasing reliance on online learning due to the global pandemic, the study by Zhu et al., 2020, highlighted the significance of three major constructs namely enjoyment, perceived benefit and system quality in determining students' continuance intention towards online learning platforms. These recent references provide valuable insights into understanding the factors that influence students' decision to continue using online learning apps, and can help educators and app developers in enhancing the user experience and promoting sustained usage among students. The findings of these studies suggest that designing online learning platforms with a focus on student's confirmation of expectations, usefulness, and satisfaction can positively impact their willingness to continue the use of OLP.

For this study, authors have combined the ECT and UTAUT framework to construct a model to examine student's continuance intention regarding online learning platforms for the students studying in remote parts of India, during and beyond the pandemic. Fig. 1 embodies the chapter framework and projected hypotheses. Based on the ECT and UTAUT framework, four main constructs were identified, namely confirmation (CON), Satisfaction (SA) Perceived usefulness (PU), Social influence (SI), and Continuance intention (CI).

Figure 1. Proposed research framework

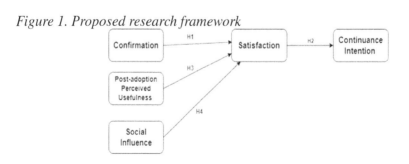

4. METHODOLOGY

4.1. Research Instruments Design

To create a pre-draft of a closed-ended structured questionnaire, a thorough examination of the literature was conducted. Demographic questions were included in the questionnaire and responses within each of the constructs were examined using pre-validated measures. Items from Bhattacherjee (2001); Li et al (2022) and Tang et al.(2014) scale were taken in order to assess the Confirmation. Three items from Isaac et al. (2019); Li et al.(2022) and Chiu et al.(2007) were used to measure Satisfaction. The 4 item scale for Social Influence was adapted from Al-Shahrani H (2016); Al-Qeisi et al. (2015);Venkatesh et al.,(2011) and Maisha and Shetu(2023) 2 items were used to investigate the post adoption perceived usefulness from Mohammadi(2015);Wu and Zhang(2014) and Li et al.(2022). Three items were appended from Maisha and Shetu(2023); Li et al.(2022) to gauge Continuance Intention of students towards OLP A Likert scale with five points—1 for strongly disagreeing, 3 for having no opinion, and 5 for strongly agreeing was used to evaluate each item.

4.2 Data Collection and Survey Development

Students enrolled in distant higher education institutions (HEIs) in India who have used a variety of OLP throughout the Covid-19 outbreak constitute the study's target demographic. These student demographics represent a sizeable share of all those who utilise educational services. Owing to the advent of the Industry 4.0 revolution and the rapid advancement of technology, there is a notable rise in the usage of online learning services in India. Data for this study came from students at several Indian private and public universities. The study has been observed through the analysis of responses obtained after a web-based cross-sectional survey. The suitable sample size for this experiment was established by considering the thumb rule (Gefen et al., 2000). Ten times of 15 items were used for the study model's construct in an evaluation of sample size. Thus, minimum 150 participants could be the part of survey whereas the study constitute of 880 respondents with a response rate of more than 75%. The study's data were gathered using a convenience sample technique. According to Bornstein et al. (2013), convenience sample is the widely used methodology in behavioural and developmental science investigations. The approach's choice was also influenced by the necessity for rapid data gathering, convenience of accessibility, and resource constraints. The participants were made aware of the goal and scope of the study prior to the commencement of the survey. Additionally, information from enrolled university students who used online learning platforms both during and after the epidemic has been gathered to guarantee the sample's quality. Google Forms served as the primary survey tool. The primary instrument for data collection was a standardised questionnaire (Table II) that respondents were requested to complete. The survey included students using all types of online learning platforms. Convenience sampling was used to study the suburbs of Pune, Delhi, Banaras, and Lucknow. A response rate from the age groups of 15–25, 26-20 age and above 30 was determined to be a good fit for study participants. Cronbach's Alpha was used to verify internal consistency. A pilot study was carried out with a hundred respondents as a sample. Following the satisfactory results of the pilot test, more data collection was initiated from January to April 2024. Approximately 51.36% of the sample was male, while 48.63% were female. The 41.02% respondents were from the 15-20 years age group. The next largest group was the 21-25 years age group (27.61%).Smaller proportions were in the 26-30 years (20.90%) and above 30 years (10.45%) age groups. The highest proportion (36.02%) of sample had completed high school, Intermediate students accounted for 23.63% of the sample while Graduates made up 20.22% and Post-graduates constituted 17.72%. Learning sites were popular, with 32.38% of respondents using them. Massive Open Online Courses (MOOCs) were used by 13.29%.

Video-based learning platforms were the most common, with 35.22% of respondents utilizing them. Other platforms, such as web browsing and chat rooms, were used by 19.09%.

Remarkably, 69.54% of respondents reported using more than one online platform.

Overall, The table 1 data provides insights into the demographics and online learning preferences of the surveyed group.

Table 1. Sample demographics

Items		Total Sample (N = 880)	Percentage
Gender	Male	452	51.36%
	Female	428	48.63%
Age	15-20 years	361	41.02%
	21–25 Years	243	27.61%
	26-30 Years	184	20.90%
	Above 30 years	92	10.45%
	High School	317	36.02%
	Intermediate	208	23.63%
Education	Graduate	178	20.22%
	Post Graduate	156	17.72%
	Others	21	02.38%

continued on following page

Table 1. Continued

Items		Total Sample (N = 880)	Percentage
Type of Online Platform	Learning Sites like Udemy, Upacademy	285	32.38%
	Massive Open Online Course(MOOCs)	117	13.29%
	Video-Based Learning	310	35.22%
	Others like web Browsing, Chat Rooms etc.	168	19.09%
Using More than one option of Online Platform		612	69.54%

5. DATA ANALYSIS AND FINDINGS

Structural Equation Modeling (SEM) was used in order to analyze the data and validate the proposed hypotheses. SPSS 21.0 and Amos 4.0 were used to test the model fitness. Non-response bias is a major issue in getting the accurate result, so it becomes imperative to eliminate this concern (Michie and Marteau, 1999; Lewis et al., 2013). It can be done by way of reducing non-response bias. To avoid the problem of non-response bias, the responses of participants were compared between early and late respondents through wave analysis (Armstrong and Overton, 1977). Since the t-test analysis revealed p= 0.47 so no significant differences between the initial (470) and late respondents (410) was found to affect due to non-response bias. Finally, 880 reactions were taken for analysis.

5.1 Measurement Model, Validity and Reliability

Two-step data analysis was used to test the hypothesis (Anderson & Gerbing, 1988). Initially confirmatory factor analysis (CFA) was conducted to examine model fit indices for the measurement model. Instrument validity and reliability were investigated in relation to research measures. The study measures were based on online learning platform continuance user literature to ensure content validity. To ensure face validity four experts in the field and five students user were also contacted and briefed on the study's goals and scope before data collection. Finalisation of the pre-test questionnaire followed incorporation of suggestions and comments regarding the appropriateness of all constructs. A pilot and pre-test were administered to determine the reliability and validity of the study instrument. In order to gather information for the preliminary test, 45 questionnaires were administered to the intended participants. The surveys of students studying in higher education institutions located in remote part of India using online learning platforms were the intended participants in this study. This study just included only those students who were using online learning platforms from the COVID days. The questionnaire was revised to make sure everyone could easily understand and complete them.

Table 2. Reliability and validity

Construct (Source)	Code	Std. Factor Loading	Cronbach Alpha	CR	AVE
Confirmation *(Bhattacherjee,2001; Tang et al.,2014; Li et al (2022)*	CON1	0.751	0.803	0.809	0.586
	CON2	0.740			
	CON3	0.702			
Perceived Usefulness *(Mohammadi,2015; Wu and Zhang, 2014; Li et al, 2022)*	PU1	0.826	0.873	0.872	0.652
	PU2	0.788			
Satisfaction *(Isaac et al.,2019; Chiu et al,2007; Li et al, 2022)*	SA1	0.772			
	SA2	0.737	0.834	0.824	0.698
	SA3	0.693			
Social Influence *(Al-Shahrani H (2016); Al-Qeisi et al.; (2015);Venkatesh et al.,(2011);Maisha and Shetu(2023)*	SI1	0.878			
	SI2	0.797	0.898	0.890	0.673
	SI3	0.787			
	SI4	0.654			
Continuance Intention *(Maisha and Shetu, 2023; Li et al,2022)*	CI1	0.771			
	CI2	0.823	0.875	0.875	0.718
	CI3	0.829			

The current study used statistical tests to ensure internal reliability, convergent, and discriminant validity. Table 3 shows that all assessment items had factor loadings above 0.50, average variance explained (AVE) values above 0.50, and composite reliability (CR) values above 0.70 which was found sufficient as per the study of Hair et al. (2010). According to the Fornell and Larcker (1981), the measurement model is appropriate for discriminant validity when the square root of the AVE was found to be greater than the correlation value. Table 3 presents the results to illustrate the discriminant validity. CR values above 0.70 indicated sufficient internal dependability in the study since AVE values surpassed its maximum and average variance; the measures had appropriate discriminant validity (Fornell & Larcker, 1981). Because of this, there is no correlation between the assessment scales used in the research study, which supports the degree of dissimilarity across the various components and constructs.

Table 3. Correlation between the constructs

	CON	PU	SI	SA	CI
CON	**0.789**				
PU	0.430***	**0.711**			
SI	0.405***	0.319***	**0.775**		
SA	0.412***	0.286***	0.463***	**0.742**	
CI	0.338**	0.310***	0.295***	0.286***	**0.770**

Note: Con=Confirmation, PU= Perceived Usefulness, SI= Social Influence; SA= Satisfaction; CI= Continuance intention Towards Online Learning Platform

Significance at *$p < 0.050$, ** $p < 0.010$, *** $p < 0.001$ The diagonal values in bold represent the square root of AVE.

Validity Concerns: No validity concerns here.

5.2. Common Method Bias

As per the study of MacKenzie and Podsakoff, 2012, Common method bias was tested by Harman single factor test. The results showed 18.41 percent of variance explained by a single factor which is less than 50 percent. Hence no concern was found due to common method bias in this research. Thus, the study demonstrates appropriate validity and reliability in the measures.

5.3. Multivariate Statistical Assumptions

Missing data, dubious response patterns, outliers, and data distribution are the main difficulties, according to Hair et al. (2010). A total of 912 filled questionnaires were obtained after circulating 1200 survey forms. Among the 912 responses any observation (respondent) which had more than 15% missing values was removed from the data collection. 17 responses with 3 or more than 3 unanswered questions or more than 15% missing values per observation were removed from the 912 obtained data sets. Detecting suspicious questionnaire responses was the second requirement. Hair et al. (2006) advised checking the data set for unusual response patterns like straight lining. 15 responses that were suspected of straight line (the same answer for many questionnaire questions) were excluded from the returned surveys. Thus a total of 880 responses were used to test the assumptions. The Z-score test was used to find outliers. The standard errors of Skewness and Kurtosis were within acceptable limits is ±3 and ±10 degrees, for both structures and objects. These results showed that distribution normality assumptions were made. After validating the data collection, 880-usable sample size was chosen for following studies. Evaluation of measurement models was done after data screening respondent demographics were addressed (Table 1).

5.4. Structural Model and Testing of Hypothesis

The fitness of model was tested using SEM in second step, and all anticipated propositions were assessed. Prior literature suggests threshold values for good model fit indices: CFI $\geq$ 0.93, TLI $\geq$ 0.93, NFI $\geq$ 0.90, RMSEA $\leq$ 0.08, $\chi 2/df \leq$ 3.0 (Anderson & Gerbing, 1988).

As per Anderson & Gerbing, 1988, the measurement model fit well with $\chi 2/df$ = 2.78, CFI = 0.90, NFI = 0.91, TLI = 0.96, and RMSEA = 0.04 (

In the milieu of OLP continuance intention, the model explained 58.7% of variance and 43.4% variance in satisfaction. On the other hand, Confirmation demonstrated an explanation of 21.4% variance. From this point forward, the theoretical model that was proposed demonstrates the maximum explanatory power.

Confirmation and Satisfaction (β = 0.402, t = 4.471, p <.001), Hypothesis 1 substantiated the association. Satisfaction (β = 0.381, t = 3.671, p <.09) had a substantial impact on CI towards online learning platforms. It was found that the PU had a substantial impact on their satisfaction of online learning platforms (β = 0.289, t = 5.741, p <.001). Social Influence (β = 0.232, t = 6.075, p <.001) was found to have a substantial impact on the Satisfaction of students with regard to online learning platforms.

6. DISCUSSION

The study validates and potentially extends existing behavioral intention models, like the Expectation-Confirmation Model, in the perspective of post-pandemic virtual learning. The research enhances the understanding of factors influencing the recognition and continued practice of new technology in academics, particularly in remote or resource-limited settings. The current research provides insight into how cultural and regional social influence affects technology adoption in educational sectors, backing to the global knowledge. Overall, this chapter has the potential to inform future educational strategies, platform development, and policy-making aimed at integrating and sustaining online learning platforms in higher education, especially in less accessible areas that may continue to rely on such resources post-pandemic.

Confirmation refers to the students' expectations of e-learning services and whether the actual experience meets those expectations. If the experience with e-learning meets or exceeds the students' initial expectations, confirmation is said to have occurred. This is important as it plays a role in students' satisfaction (Li et al, 2022). The present study supports the association amid the confirmation and satisfaction supporting the extant literature (Lee, 2010).

In the Expectancy Confirmation Model, the confirmation of expectations is significantly related to learners' satisfaction. When a user's expectations about the functionality, benefits, or outcomes of using a technology like e-learning are met or exceeded, this confirmation tends to lead to higher satisfaction levels. Satisfaction, in turn, is a central factor in determining whether users will continue to use the technology. The more satisfied users are with their e-learning experience, the more likely they are to maintain their usage of the platform over time.

Satisfaction, on the other hand, can be seen as an emotional state that occurs as a result of the experiences associated with using the e-learning services. It is a crucial determinant of whether students will continue to use e-learning technologies. Satisfaction is influenced by a number of aspects including the PU, quality of information, and system quality (Bhattacherjee, 2001; Cidral et al. 2018; Isaac et al., 2019). Satisfaction among the students is directly linked to confirmation (Chiu et al., 2007). That is, when their initial expectations about the online-learning system are met, they tend to be more satisfied with it. It seems like the experience has to confirm their beliefs about what online-learning can do for them. The study suggests that satisfaction arises from the conjunction of multiple aspects like information quality, system quality, and the actual usability of the online-learning system. The elements of interactivity, up-to-date content ease of use they all contribute to satisfaction (Li et al., 2022).

In consumer behaviour research, the satisfaction-intention association is substantiated in many product and service contexts and its revalidation in e-learning underscores its robustness. Furthermore, pleasure may explain the e-learning acceptance-discontinuance anomaly, a poorly understood occurrence in the literature (Vlachopoulos, 2020). Dissatisfied online-learning users may stop using it, even if they like other aspects, because satisfaction was the strongest predictor of continuance intention .Dissatisfaction is required for online-learning discontinuation. Post-acceptance pleasure is based on consumers' firsthand experience, making it more realistic, unbiased, and less changeable (Al-Rahmi et al., 2019). Based on the preceding findings, perceived usefulness is more closely related to acceptance intention (Tang et al., 2014).

Continuance intention is not just about having a one-time good experience; it's about consistently meeting and exceeding student expectations to maintain a high level of satisfaction (Almaiah et al., 2019). This conversation emphasizes the interrelation between confirmation and satisfaction and how they are critical to students' objective to remain using OLP (Chiu et al., 2007).

Social influence can significantly impact a learner's satisfaction towards the CI of online learning. When students feel that their peers use and are satisfied with online learning, then they identify the platform as beneficial and continue using it (Al-Shahrani, 2016; Al-Qeisi et al.; 2015). The influence of the teacher and their support in the OLP can play a critical role in a student's continued satisfaction and subsequent intention to continue using the learning platform (Venkatesh et al., 2011). If online learning is seen as a norm or trend within a community or social group, the individual is more likely to derive satisfaction from fitting in with the group by continuing to use the service. Social influence can also come from the opportunities for collaborative learning or community building within the online learning system (Maisha and Shetu, 2023). This can enhance satisfaction by fostering a shared learning experience, leading to stronger intentions to continue with the platform. Endorsements from credible sources (such as well-regarded institutions or thought leaders in education) can elevate the perceived value of online learning platforms, reinforcing learners' satisfaction and CI to use OLP (Venkatesh et al., 2011).

Overall, social influence can shape a student's experience and attitudes towards online learning by affecting their perceived social support, the credibility they ascribe to the system, and their willingness to meet the expectations set by their social circle. Positive social reinforcement can strengthen a student's satisfaction with their online learning experience, thereby increasing their intent to persist with it (Cheng et al., 2019).

The concept of post-adoption perceived usefulness refers to a user's evaluation of the extent to which a system or service is beneficial for them after they have begun using it (Mohammadi, 2015). This evaluation is based on their firsthand experience rather than their initial expectations. In the setting of virtual learning, post-adoption PU would be the amount a student have faith in platform or trust that these tools will continue to add value to their learning process (Wu and Zhang,2014; Li et al., 2022). If a student perceives that using the online learning platform enhances their academic performance or learning efficiency, their satisfaction with the e-learning service is likely to increase, leading to a stronger intention to continue using it (Wu and Zhang,2014). Students who find the content and functionality of the online learning platform relevant and aligned with their educational goals are more likely to be satisfied and intend to keep using the platform (Li et al., 2022). When scholars recognize how the online learning system integrates with their existing study habits and schedules, this perceived usefulness can translate into greater satisfaction and a desire to continue its use (Alam et al, 2022).

7. THEORETICAL AND PRACTICAL IMPLICATIONS

Continuous updates and improvements that address user needs can increase the PU of the current learning system post-adoption, which in turn, can lead to greater satisfaction and intent to continue its use. As students continue to use the virtual learning system, their positive experiences can reinforce their belief in its utility, creating a feedback loop that sustains their satisfaction and intention to continue using the system. In essence, when students perceive post-adoption usefulness - that is, they recognize tangible benefits from their ongoing use of an online learning service - their satisfaction tends to increase (Zhu et al., 2020). This positive perception and resulting satisfaction can significantly drive their intention to continue using the service, as it affirms the aligning of their initial adoption decision with their experienced outcomes (Wei et al.,2022).

A student's satisfaction with an online learning platform is a critical factor influencing their continuance intention, or their willingness to keep using the platform for their educational needs (Vlachopoulos, 2020). If students find that the online platform meets or exceeds their expectations in terms of quality, content, usability, and support, they are likely to be satisfied, which naturally leads to a greater likelihood of continued use. Satisfaction often stems from a sense that the platform provides value, whether through the knowledge gained, the convenience of use, or the support provided. Satisfied students perceive a favorable cost-benefit ratio which encourages ongoing engagement with the platform. Satisfaction with the online learning experience can lead to an emotional or psychological commitment to the platform, which acts as a motivational factor for students to continue using it. Over time, as students become satisfied with the platform, they may develop habitual patterns of use. This habitual use reinforces continuance intention as the platform becomes integrated into their routine. A satisfied student is less likely to seek alternative platforms or solutions, as they have already identified a platform that meets their needs. This decreases the likelihood of switching to another service(Ramadhan et al., 2022). Satisfied students are more likely to recommend the platform to peers, which reinforce their own favourable perception and intention to continue using the service due to social validation. Satisfied students may feel that they have invested time and effort into learning how to effectively use an online platform, which can lead to an increased likelihood of continued use to justify their investment. When these needs are met, students not only prefer to continue with the current platform due to a lack of discontent but also because the platform becomes a reliable and trusted source for their educational requirements. Necessary changes in policy to support the integration of online learning in higher education, especially in remote areas could overall increase the efficiency of educational system. Improving online platforms to increase engagement and satisfaction among students, as well as accessibility for those in remote areas could be a boon for many marginalised students and users. The importance of creating support systems for both students and educators to navigate online learning environments efficiently by the education policy can really outgrow the number of users.

8. CONCLUSION

The current study will offer new contributions for Indian university administrations and policymaking bodies to analyse the usage of OLP in academic institutions. The results suggests that online learning tool could bring about optimistic modifications in academicians, professionals, policymakers, government and non-government instructors and educators in the long term. The COVID-19 pandemic has profoundly impacted the education sector, forcing educational institutions to rapidly adopt online learning platforms to ensure the continuity of teaching and learning (Dhawan, 2020). As a result, understanding students' usage behavior and their continuance intention towards online learning platforms has become a crucial area of research.

This study aims to inspect the aspects that impact students' continuance intention for online learning platforms in institutions in remote regions of India. The theoretical implications of this study shed light on the adaptation of online learning platforms in response to the COVID-19 pandemic and their continued relevance in the post-pandemic era. Additionally, the practical implications highlight the need for educational institutions and policymakers to focus on enhancing the quality, accessibility, and user experience of online learning platforms to foster sustained engagement and positive continuance intentions among students.

9. LIMITATIONS AND FUTURE SCOPE OF THE STUDY

The data for the study has been collected using non probability convenience sampling that does not include the entire university population. Only students enrolled in higher education institutions located in remote India have been selected for the study, which may cause bias in generalizing the findings.

Secondly, the data for the research has not been collected from instructors for the proposed study. Further, the researchers in future studies may increase the sample size and apply the new sampling procedure predominantly longitudinal data to validate the research outcome more precise results. The constructs are limited in the study so further other model construct could be integrated with existing models to evaluate post-pandemic usage behaviour. Insights into the challenges faced by students in remote areas of India, contributing to the understanding of the digital divide in education could also be including for the study. Investigating in what way students' engagement with online learning platforms evolves over an extended period beyond the pandemic could provide a new insight.

REFERENCES

Abbad, M. M. (2021). Using the UTAUT model to understand students' usage of e-learning systems in developing countries. *Education and Information Technologies*, 26(6), 7205–7224. DOI: 10.1007/s10639-021-10573-5 PMID: 34025204

Al-Adwan, A. S., Yaseen, H., Alsoud, A., Abousweilem, F., & Al-Rahmi, W. M. (2022). Novel extension of the UTAUT model to understand continued usage intention of learning management systems: The role of learning tradition. *Education and Information Technologies*, 27(3), 3567–3593. DOI: 10.1007/s10639-021-10758-y

Al-Emran, M., Arpaci, I., & Salloum, S. A. (2020). An empirical examination of continuous intention to use m-learning: An integrated model. *Education and Information Technologies*, 25(4), 2899–2918. DOI: 10.1007/s10639-019-10094-2

Al-Qeisi, K., Dennis, C., Hegazy, A., & Abbad, M. (2015). How viable is the UTAUT model in a non-western context? *International Business Research*, 8(2). Advance online publication. DOI: 10.5539/ibr.v8n2p204

Al-Rahmi, W. M., Yahaya, N., Alamri, M. M., Alyoussef, I. Y., Al-Rahmi, A. M., & Kamin, Y. B. (2021). Integrating innovation diffusion theory with technology acceptance model: Supporting students' attitude towards using a massive open online courses (MOOCs) systems. *Interactive Learning Environments*, 29(8), 1380–1392. DOI: 10.1080/10494820.2019.1629599

Al-Shahrani, H. (2016). *Investigating the determinants of mobile learning acceptance in higher education in Saudi Arabia*. Northern Illinois University.

Almaiah, M. A., & Al Mulhem, A. (2019). Analysis of the essential factors affecting of intention to use of mobile learning applications: A comparison between universities adopters and non-adopters. *Education and Information Technologies*, 24(2), 1433–1468. DOI: 10.1007/s10639-018-9840-1

Anderson, J. C., & Gerbing, D. W. (1988). Structural Equation Modeling in Practice: A Review and Recommended Two-Step Approach. *Psychological Bulletin*, 103(3), 411–423. Advance online publication. DOI: 10.1037/0033-2909.103.3.411

Armstrong, J. S., & Overton, T. S. (1977). Estimating non-response bias in mail surveys. *JMR, Journal of Marketing Research*, 14(3), 396–402. DOI: 10.1177/002224377701400320

Bai, B., Wang, J., & Chai, C.-S. (2021). Understanding Hong Kong primary school English teachers' continuance intention to teach with ICT. *Computer Assisted Language Learning*, 34(4), 528–551. DOI: 10.1080/09588221.2019.1627459

Bhattacherjee, A. (2001). Understanding information systems continuance: An expectation-confirmation model. MIS Quarterly: Management. *Management Information Systems Quarterly*, 25(3), 351. DOI: 10.2307/3250921

Bornstein, M. H., Jager, J., & Putnick, D. L. (2013). Sampling in developmental science: Situations, shortcomings, solutions, and standards. *Developmental Review*, 33(4), 357–370. DOI: 10.1016/j.dr.2013.08.003 PMID: 25580049

Chauhan, S., Goyal, S., Bhardwaj, A. K., & Sergi, B. S. (2022). Examining continuance intention in business schools with digital classroom methods during COVID-19: A comparative study of India and Italy. *Behaviour & Information Technology*, 41(8), 1596–1619. DOI: 10.1080/0144929X.2021.1892191

Chen, M., Wang, X., Wang, J., Zuo, C., Tian, J., & Cui, Y. (2021). Factors afecting college students' continuous intention to use online course platform. *SN Computer Science*, 2(2), 1–11. DOI: 10.1007/s42979-021-00498-8 PMID: 33649745

Cheng, X., Yang, S., & Zhou, S. (2019). Why do college students continue to use mobile learning? Learning involvement and self-determination theory. *British Journal of Educational Technology*, 50(2), 626–637. DOI: 10.1111/bjet.12634

Cheng, Y.-M. (2014). Extending the expectation-confirmation model with quality and flow to explore nurses' continued blended e-learning intention. *Information Technology & People*, 27(3), 230–258. DOI: 10.1108/ITP-01-2013-0024

Cheng, Y. M. (2020). Students' satisfaction and continuance intention of the cloud-based e-learning system: Roles of interactivity and course quality factors. *Education + Training*, 62(9), 1037–1059. DOI: 10.1108/ET-10-2019-0245

Chiu, C. M., Chiu, C. S., & Chang, H. C. (2007). Examining the integrated influence of fairness and quality on learners' satisfaction and Web-based learning continuance intention. *Information Systems Journal*, 17(3), 271–287. DOI: 10.1111/j.1365-2575.2007.00238.x

Chu, T.-H., & Chen, Y.-Y. (2016). With Good We Become Good: Understanding e-learning adoption by theory of planned behavior and group influences. *Computers & Education*, 92–93, 37–52. DOI: 10.1016/j.compedu.2015.09.013

Cidral, W. A., Oliveira, T., Di Felice, M., & Aparicio, M. (2018). E-learning success determinants: Brazilian empirical study. *Computers & Education*, 122, 273–290. DOI: 10.1016/j.compedu.2017.12.001

Daneji, A. A., Ayub, A. F. M., & Khambari, M. N. M. (2019). The effects of perceived usefulness, confirmation and satisfaction on continuance intention in using massive open online course (MOOC). *Knowledge Management & E-Learning*, 11(2), 201–214.

Fishbein, M. (1975). Belief, Attitude, Intention and Behaviour: An Introduction to Theory and Research: Vol. 27. *MA*. Addison-Wesley.

Fornell, C., & Larcker, D. F. (1981). Evaluating Structural Equation Models with Unobservable Variables and Measurement Error. *JMR, Journal of Marketing Research*. Advance online publication. DOI: 10.1177/002224378101800313

Hair, J. F., Anderson, R. E., Tatham, R. L., & Black, W. C. (2010). *Multivariate Data Analysis*: A Global Perspective (7th Edition). In Pearson Prentice Hall, New Jersey.

Hair, J. F., Black, W. C., Babin, B. J., Anderson, R. E., & Tatham, R. L. (2006). *Multivariate Data Analysis* (6th ed.). Pearson-Prentice Hall.

Halilovic, S., & Cicic, M. (2013). Antecedents of information systems user behaviour – extended expectation-confirmation model. *Behaviour & Information Technology*, 32(4), 359–370. DOI: 10.1080/0144929X.2011.554575

Ho, N. T. T., Sivapalan, S., Pham, H. H., Nguyen, L. T. M., Van Pham, A. T., & Dinh, H. V. (2020). Students' adoption of elearning in emergency situation: The case of a Vietnamese university during COVID-19. *Interactive Technology and Smart Education*. Advance online publication. DOI: 10.1108/ITSE-08-2020-0164

Hu, S., Laxman, K., & Lee, K. (2020). Exploring factors affecting academics' adoption of emerging mobile technologies-an extended UTAUT perspective. *Education and Information Technologies*, 25(5), 4615–4635. DOI: 10.1007/s10639-020-10171-x

Hu, S., Laxman, K., & Lee, K. (2020). Exploring factors affecting academics' adoption of emerging mobile technologies-an extended UTAUT perspective. *Education and Information Technologies*, 25(5), 4615–4635. DOI: 10.1007/s10639-020-10171-x

Huang, Y. M. (2019). Examining students' continued use of desktop services: Perspectives from expectation-confirmation and social influence. *Computers in Human Behavior*, 96, 23–31. DOI: 10.1016/j.chb.2019.02.010

Isaac, O., Aldholay, A., Abdullah, Z., & Ramayah, T. (2019). Online learning usage within Yemeni higher education: The role of compatibility and task-technology fit as mediating variables in the IS success model. *Computers & Education*, 136, 113–129. DOI: 10.1016/j.compedu.2019.02.012

Islam, M. A., Nur, S., & Talukder, M. S. (2021). E-learning in the time of COVID-19: Lived experiences of three university teachers from two countries. *E-Learning and Digital Media*, 18(6), 557–580. DOI: 10.1177/20427530211022924

Jamshidi, D., & Hussin, N. (2016). Islamic credit card adoption understanding: When innovation diffusion theory meets satisfaction and social influence. *Journal of Promotion Management*, 22(6), 897–917. DOI: 10.1080/10496491.2016.1214206

Jiang, L., & Li, K. (2020, November). Research on the influencing factors of music virtual community based on expectation confirmation theory. In 2020 IEEE international conference on information technology, big data and artificial intelligence (ICIBA) (Vol. 1, pp. 392-396). IEEE.

Kim, N. H., So, H. J., & Joo, Y. J. (2021). Flipped learning design fidelity, self-regulated learning, satisfaction, and continuance intention in a university flipped learning course. *Australasian Journal of Educational Technology*, 37, 1–19. DOI: 10.14742/ajet.6046

Lee, M.-C. (2010). Explaining and predicting users' continuance intention toward e-learning: An extension of the expectation-confirmation model. *Computers & Education*, 54(2), 506–516. DOI: 10.1016/j.compedu.2009.09.002

Lewis, E. F., Hardy, M., & Snaith, B. (2013). An analysis of survey reporting in the imaging professions: Is the issue of non-response bias being adequately addressed? *Radiography*, 19(3), 240–245. DOI: 10.1016/j.radi.2013.02.003

Li, L., Wang, Q., & Li, J. (2022). Examining continuance intention of online learning during COVID-19 pandemic: Incorporating the theory of planned behavior into the expectation–confirmation model. *Frontiers in Psychology*, 13, 1046407. DOI: 10.3389/fpsyg.2022.1046407 PMID: 36467152

MacKenzie, S. B., & Podsakoff, P. M. (2012). Common method bias in marketing: Causes, mechanisms, and procedural remedies. *Journal of Retailing*, 88(4), 542–555. DOI: 10.1016/j.jretai.2012.08.001

Maisha, K., & Shetu, S. N. (2023). Influencing factors of e-learning adoption amongst students in a developing country: The post-pandemic scenario in Bangladesh. *Future Business Journal*, 9(1), 37. DOI: 10.1186/s43093-023-00214-3

Michie, S., & Marteau, T. (1999). Non-response bias in prospective studies of patients and healthcare professionals. *International Journal of Social Research Methodology*, 2(3), 203–212. DOI: 10.1080/136455799295014

Mohammadi, H. (2015). Investigating users' perspectives on e-learning: an integration of TAM and IS success model. Comput. Hum. Behav. 45, 359-374. doi: . chb.2014.07.044DOI: 10.1016/j

Müller, A. M., Goh, C., Lim, L. Z., & Gao, X. (2021). Covid-19 emergency elearning and beyond: Experiences and perspectives of university educators. *Education Sciences*, 11(1), 19. DOI: 10.3390/educsci11010019

Nasri, W. (2021). An empirical study of user acceptance behaviours of internet banking in Tunisia using UTAUT2 model. [IJIDE]. *International Journal of Innovation in the Digital Economy*, 12(4), 16–34. DOI: 10.4018/IJIDE.2021100102

Oliver, R. L. (1980). A cognitive model of the antecedents and consequences of satisfaction decisions. *JMR, Journal of Marketing Research*, 17(4), 460–469. DOI: 10.1177/002224378001700405

Panigrahi, R., Srivastava, P. R., & Sharma, D. (2018). Online learning: Adoption, continuance, and learning outcome—A review of literature. *International Journal of Information Management*, 43, 1–14. DOI: 10.1016/j.ijinfomgt.2018.05.005

Persada, S. F., Miraja, B. A., Nadlifatin, R., Belgiawan, P. F., Perwira Redi, A. A. N., & Lin, S. C. (2022). Determinants of students' intention to continue using online private tutoring: an expectation-confirmation model (ECM) approach. Technology, Knowledge and Learning, 1-14. DOI: 10.1007/s10758-021-09548-9

Ramadhan, A., Hidayanto, A. N., Salsabila, G. A., Wulandari, I., Jaury, J. A., & Anjani, N. N. (2022). The effect of usability on the intention to use the e-learning system in a sustainable way: A case study at Universitas Indonesia. *Education and Information Technologies*, 27(2), 1489–1522. DOI: 10.1007/s10639-021-10613-0

Santiago, C. D., Bustos, Y., Jolie, S. A., Flores Toussaint, R., Sosa, S. S., Raviv, T., & Cicchetti, C. (2021). The impact of COVID-19 on immigrant and refugee families: Qualitative perspectives from newcomer students and parents. *The School Psychologist*, 36(5), 348–357. DOI: 10.1037/spq0000448 PMID: 34435837

Tang, J., Tang, T.-I., & Chiang, C.-H. (2014). Blog learning: Effects of users' usefulness and efficiency towards continuance intention. Behaviour &amp. *Behaviour & Information Technology*, 33(1), 36–50. DOI: 10.1080/0144929X.2012.687772

Venkatesh, V., Morris, M. G., Davis, G. B., & Davis, F. D. (2003). User acceptance of information technology: Toward a unified view. *Management Information Systems Quarterly*, 27(3), 425–478. DOI: 10.2307/30036540

Venkatesh V, Thong JYL, Chan FKY, Hu PJ-H, Brown SA (2011) Extending the two-stage information systems continuance model: incorporating UTAUT predictors and the role of context. Inform Syst J 21(6):527-555. https://doi.org/DOI: 10.1111/j.1365-2575.2011.00373.x

Vlachopoulos, D. (2011). COVID-19: Threat or opportunity for online education? *Higher Learning Research Communications*, 10(1), 2. DOI: 10.18870/hlrc.v10i1.1179

Wang, C. S., Jeng, Y. L., & Huang, Y. M. (2017). What influences teachers to continue using cloud services? The role of facilitating conditions and social influence. *The Electronic Library*, 35(3), 520–533. DOI: 10.1108/EL-02-2016-0046

Wang, T., Lin, C.-L., & Su, Y.-S. (2021). Continuance intention of university students and online learning during the COVID-19 pandemic: A modified expectation confirmation model perspective. *Sustainability (Basel)*, 13(8), 4586. DOI: 10.3390/su13084586

Wei, S., Xu, D., & Liu, H. (2022). The effects of information technology capability and knowledge base on digital innovation: The moderating role of institutional environments. *European Journal of Innovation Management*, 25(3), 720–740. DOI: 10.1108/EJIM-08-2020-0324

Winarno, D. A., Muslim, E., Rafi, M., & Rosetta, A. (2020). Quality Function Deployment Approach to Optimize E-Learning Adoption among Lecturers in Universitas Indonesia. 2020 the 4th international conference on E-learning, New York: Association for Computing Machinery.

Wu, B., & Zhang, C. (2014). Empirical study on continuance intentions towards E-Learning 2.0 systems. *Behaviour & Information Technology*, 33(10), 1027–1038. DOI: 10.1080/0144929X.2014.934291

Yakubu, M. N., Dasuki, S. I., Abubakar, A. M., & Kah, M. M. (2020). Determinants of learning management systems adoption in Nigeria: A hybrid SEM and artifcial neural network approach. *Education and Information Technologies*, 25(5), 3515–3539. DOI: 10.1007/s10639-020-10110-w

Yan, L., Whitelock-Wainwright, A., Guan, Q., Wen, G., Gašević, D., & Chen, G. (2021). Students' experience of online learning during the COVID-19 pandemic: A province-wide survey study. *British Journal of Educational Technology*, 52(5), 2038–2057. DOI: 10.1111/bjet.13102 PMID: 34219755

Yang, S., Zhou, S., & Cheng, X. (2019). Why do college students continue to use mobile learning? Learning involvement and self-determination theory. British Journal of Educational Technology. *British Journal of Educational Technology*, 50(2), 626–637. DOI: 10.1111/bjet.12634

Zhou, J. (2017). Exploring the factors affecting learners' continuance intention of MOOCs for online collaborative learning: An extended ECM perspective. *Australasian Journal of Educational Technology*, 33(5). Advance online publication. DOI: 10.14742/ajet.2914

ADDITIONAL READING

Ali, M. (2021). *Remote Work and Sustainable Changes for the Future of Global Business.* IGI Global. https://www.igi-global.com/book/remote-work-sustainable -changes-future/264375

Ali, M. (2022). *Future Role of Sustainable Innovative Technologies in Crisis Management.* IGI Global. https://www.igi-global.com/book/future-role-sustainable -innovative-technologies/281281

Ali, M. (2023). *Shifting Paradigms in the Rapidly Developing Global Digital Ecosystem: A GCC Perspective.* In Digital Entrepreneurship and Co-Creating Value Through Digital Encounters (pp. 145-166). IGI Global. https://www.igi-global.com/chapter/ shifting-paradigms-in-the-rapidly-developing-global-digital-ecosystem/323525

Ali, M. (2023). T*axonomy of Industry 4.0 Technologies in Digital Entrepreneurship and Co-Creating Value.* In *Digital Entrepreneurship and Co-Creating Value Through Digital Encounters* (pp. 24–55). IGI Global., https://www.igi-global.com/ chapter/taxonomy-of-industry-40-technologies-in-digital-entrepreneurship-and-co -creating-value/323520 DOI: 10.4018/978-1-6684-7416-7.ch002

Ali, M., & Wood-Harper, T. (2021). *Fostering Communication and Learning with Underutilized Technologies in Higher Education.* IGI Global. https://www.igi-global .com/book/fostering-communication-learning-underutilized-technologies/244593

Ali, M., Wood-Harper, T., & Kutar, M. (2023). Multi-Perspectives of Contemporary Digital Transformation Models of Complex Innovation Management. In *Digital Entrepreneurship and Co-Creating Value Through Digital Encounters* (pp. 79–96). IGI Global., https://www.igi-global.com/chapter/multi-perspectives-of-contemporary -digital-transformation-models-of-complex-innovation-management/323522 DOI: 10.4018/978-1-6684-7416-7.ch004

Ali, M. B. (2021). Internet of Things (IoT) to Foster Communication and Information Sharing: A Case of UK Higher Education. In Ali, M. B., & Wood-Harper, T. (Eds.), *Fostering Communication and Learning With Underutilized Technologies in Higher Education* (pp. 1–20). IGI Global., https://www.igi-global.com/chapter/internet-of-things-iot-to-foster-communication-and-information-sharing/262718/ DOI: 10.4018/978-1-7998-4846-2.ch001

Ali, M. B., & Wood-Harper, T. (2022). Artificial Intelligence (AI) as a Decision-Making Tool to Control Crisis Situations. In *Future Role of Sustainable Innovative Technologies in Crisis Management*. IGI Global., https://www.igi-global.com/chapter/artificial-intelligence-ai-as-a-decision-making-tool-to-control-crisis-situations/298931 DOI: 10.4018/978-1-7998-9815-3.ch006

Ali, M. B., Wood-Harper, T., & Ramlogan, R. (2020). A Framework Strategy to Overcome Trust Issues on Cloud Computing Adoption in Higher Education. In Modern Principles, Practices, and Algorithms for Cloud Security (pp. 162-183). IGI Global. https://www.igi-global.com/chapter/a-framework-strategy-to-overcome-trust-issues-on-cloud-computing-adoption-in-higher-education/238907/

Chapter 8
Digital Transformation for Better Innovation Governance

Safiya Al Rashdi

Innovation Oases Company, Oman

ABSTRACT

Digital transformation in governance enhances public participation, collaboration, empowerment, and accountability, improving quality of life. This study explores strategies like innovation ecosystems, crowdsourcing, and open government data (OGD), including the role of Chief Innovation Officers (CInOs). Examples include the Ministry of Manpower's Open Data Innovation System for public engagement, Manor Labs' crowdsourcing in Texas, and Kenya's OGD portal for transparency. CInOs, pivotal since 2008, align government with societal needs, fostering digital innovation and engagement. This paper advocates for the integration of CInOs at the highest levels of governance to bridge the gap between government policies and societal aspirations, fostering a culture of continuous digital innovation and engagement. These digital transformation-driven strategies enable governments to establish an efficient 'innovation ecosystem,' improving public services and promoting a collaborative, digitally innovative society.

INTRODUCTION

Digital transformation is fundamentally reshaping the landscape of government operations, transitioning from traditional bureaucratic processes to more inclusive, transparent, and efficient systems. This transformation is driven by advanced technologies, such as big data, cloud computing, and artificial intelligence, which serve

DOI: 10.4018/979-8-3693-5966-2.ch008

to enhance the delivery of public services and foster a more engaged and participatory citizenry. Across the globe, governments are embracing digital transformation to address complex challenges, optimise service delivery, and stimulate economic growth. By integrating these technologies, governments can create more responsive and adaptable systems that better meet the evolving needs of their citizens (Mergel, 2021).

This chapter explores the critical role of digital transformation in enhancing innovation governance. It provides a comprehensive analysis of key strategies, including the development of innovation ecosystems, the use of crowdsourcing, the adoption of open government data (OGD), and the emerging role of Chief Innovation Officers (CInOs). By examining relevant case studies and practical examples, this chapter demonstrates how these strategies can significantly improve citizen-government interactions, increase transparency, and foster a culture of continuous innovation and engagement.

Innovation in Government

The concept of innovation in government refers to systems that provide more effective means of achieving policy goals. As stated by the World Bank (2010), "Innovation policy, by its very nature, touches such diverse policy areas as education and training, skills development, science and research, the business environment, information and communication technology, and other infrastructure." By embracing innovation across these various domains, governments can adapt to changing needs and deliver policies that are more effective, inclusive, and responsive.

Globally, governments of all sizes face a common and pressing challenge: the rising demand for public services is increasingly constrained by limited resources. According to McKinsey (2011), "The emerging answer—from some unlikely places—is bold, rapid management innovation." Innovation is now being widely advocated across the world, albeit with applications that vary significantly depending on the governance structures of individual countries. This underscores the importance of adopting tailored approaches to innovation that align with each country's unique governance and socio-economic context.

The World Bank's Innovation Policy: A Guide for Developing Countries emphasises that "Innovation should be understood as the dissemination of something new in a given context, not as something new in absolute terms." While economically advanced nations often work at the cutting edge of technology, developing countries have considerable opportunities to tap into global knowledge and technology, adapting and disseminating these innovations to suit their domestic context. The World Bank further highlights that "Innovation depends significantly on overall conditions in the economy, governance, education, and infrastructure" of a country (World

Bank, 2010). Despite the challenges that developing nations may face, proactive innovation policies are deemed both "possible and effective" and can help establish a favourable environment for broader economic and social reforms.

Innovation in the Past

Historically, government policy-making and administration operated within a kind of cultural bubble, where decisions and implementation followed well-trodden, internal pathways with little external input. Public service provision was akin to trying to fit a ball into a cube—it did not matter how the shape of the ball was modified or how many smaller balls were used, achieving a perfect fit was impossible until the ball itself became a cube. This analogy illustrates the inherent mismatch between rigid bureaucratic processes and the diverse needs of the public.

This paternalistic approach to public service delivery has been deeply ingrained in government culture. Policy implementation processes were often designed solely within public sector agencies and subsequently 'modified' to fit the circumstances of the wider public—frequently with suboptimal results. As a result, public services have struggled to meet the complex and evolving needs of citizens effectively (Bekkers, 2003).

The traditional model of consultation and engagement often sets up an adversarial dynamic, where, as one commentator noted, "We've proposed something, and we invite you to oppose it and we'll defend it." Citizens are left feeling that they must fight for reluctantly offered resources, which undermines the intended goal of collaborative governance. Such methods increasingly fail to address the nuanced social, environmental, and economic needs that governments must confront today—needs that were highlighted in the Millennium Development Goals (MDGs).

Redesigning government administration is essential for achieving successful and innovative outcomes (Fung, 2015). Moving beyond entrenched paternalism requires a shift towards more inclusive, participatory approaches to policy-making, where citizens are viewed as partners rather than passive recipients. This transformation in governance culture is integral to ensuring that public services are fit for purpose in an increasingly complex world.

Innovation in 21st Century

In contrast to traditional approaches, innovation in government involves the whole of society. It acts as a bridge between government, administration, universities, commerce, and citizens, bringing together their experiences, aspirations, insights, and ideas. This collective approach is often referred to as an 'innovation ecosystem' (Mazzucato, 2018). It aims to dismantle the barriers of the past, in which government policy was developed in isolation, and instead foster an environment that is inclusive and reflective of the needs of all stakeholders. By incorporating diverse perspectives, governments can develop policies that are both achievable and aligned with societal needs (Kattel & Mazzucato, 2018).

A notable example of this inclusive approach is the ethnographic research conducted by Nesta in the UK. In this instance, a children's centre that was underused became the focus of in-depth research, which involved conducting 90 interviews with both users and non-users of the centre to understand their perceptions and concerns. Despite the centre being recognised as high-performing and award-winning, it was perceived as a charity, which carried a stigma for those who might use it (Nesta, 2016). In response to these insights, an innovative support group named 'Mums Helping Mums' was established, shifting control from the local authority to the users themselves. This transition effectively removed the sense of charity and empowered the community to take ownership, fostering greater engagement and participation.

Looking to the future, public service agencies are expected to work in collaboration with society to co-design procedures that truly meet public needs. When citizens feel heard and the systems are designed to simplify their lives, they are far more likely to accept government decisions, even when those decisions are radical (Mulgan, 2019). In this way, the development gains achieved within a country can be sustainable, as they are founded on a foundation of genuine inclusivity and collaboration.

Philip Colligan, CEO of Nesta UK's Innovation Lab, has argued that the public sector should not merely seek to improve existing systems but should focus on managing 'transformative innovation' (Colligan, 2019). He cites the example of care homes for the elderly: rather than asking questions about the management and costs of these facilities, innovators should instead explore the ultimate objective—what will help older people live better lives? The solution may not be care homes at all but could involve creating community networks that enable people to live independently for longer. This broader, more ambitious perspective ensures that innovation serves a meaningful purpose, encouraging people to "try out, learn, observe, effect, and adapt."

Innovation Governance and Digital Transformation

Digital transformation involves the integration of digital technologies into various facets of an organisation's operations, fundamentally changing how it functions and delivers services in a more effective and inclusive manner to its stakeholders. In the context of government, digital transformation aims to leverage digital data and technology to improve and optimise public services, thereby enhancing accessibility, efficiency, transparency, and accountability for citizens and businesses alike.

This transformation encompasses the provision of services through online portals, mobile applications, and digital self-service options, all of which facilitate more user-friendly interactions.

Digital government, therefore, is designed and managed to utilise digital tools, data-driven insights, and innovative approaches to engage effectively with citizens and businesses. By making government services available online and ensuring that processes are streamlined and responsive, digital transformation has the potential to create a more inclusive and participatory model of governance.

According to the World Bank (2024), digitalisation represents a transformative opportunity, particularly for developing countries, where critical services such as healthcare, education, energy, and agriculture increasingly depend on connectivity and data-driven solutions. To support sustainable development, it is essential that the infrastructure and platforms enabling these connections are available, affordable, and secure. Ensuring equitable access to these digital resources can empower citizens, promote economic growth, and reduce disparities, ultimately leading to a more connected and resilient society.

Digital Transformation: silo-centric Approach

Historically, the silo-centric approach to IT investment within government agencies has often been detrimental to the development of "citizen-centric" services. This fragmented approach resulted in the duplication of IT expenditures and inefficiencies, hindering efforts to build horizontally integrated services that effectively meet the needs of citizens. The root of these issues can be traced to the absence of a consistent "software framework"—a cohesive set of rules, design patterns, interfaces, libraries of modules, and tools that facilitate software development, maintenance, and reuse across different departments.

Without such a unified framework, government IT systems were developed independently within each silo, leading to a lack of interoperability and inefficiencies in service delivery. This lack of integration impeded the provision of holistic, customer-centred government services, creating barriers to accessibility and responsiveness. To truly serve the public effectively, a shift is needed towards a more coordinated approach to IT investment—one that promotes collaboration, reduces redundancy, and prioritises the citizen as the central focus of service design.

Digital Transformation Strategies

The comprehensive strategies aimed at enhancing digital transformation within government agencies are rooted in the establishment of a unified digital transformation framework. Central to this framework is the development of standardised software guidelines and the promotion of seamless data sharing across departments. A citizen-centric approach is emphasised, involving citizens in the design of services and ensuring accessibility through multiple channels (World Bank, 2024). Robust data governance practices are also recommended to maintain data integrity and privacy while facilitating integration across systems.

Leveraging cloud infrastructure and emerging technologies, such as artificial intelligence (AI) and data analytics, is proposed as a means to improve scalability and enhance decision-making processes. Encouraging collaboration through cross-government projects and agile methodologies is crucial to fostering innovation and responsiveness (Mergel, 2021). Continuous improvement, supported by feedback loops and investment in employee training and change management, is essential for ensuring that transformation efforts are sustained and adaptive. Collectively, these strategies aim to guide government agencies towards a more integrated, efficient, and citizen-focused digital transformation paradigm.

The Role of Digital Transformation in Government Innovation

Digital transformation plays a pivotal role in enhancing public services, addressing societal challenges, and improving overall governance. It drives efficiency, responsiveness, and inclusiveness, ensuring that government operations evolve to meet the changing needs of society. The following are key roles of innovation within government:

Enhancing Public Services: Innovation leads to the development of more efficient and user-centric government services, delivered through online portals, mobile applications, and other digital channels. This makes public services more accessible and convenient, thereby improving the quality of life for citizens. Innovations in areas such as healthcare, education, transportation, and public safety enhance the overall well-being of communities by providing tailored and responsive services.

Addressing Complex Challenges: Governments face a range of multifaceted challenges, including climate change, public health crises, and economic inequality. Innovative approaches and technologies enable governments to develop comprehensive and sustainable solutions to these problems. By employing digital tools, governments can address these issues in a more integrated manner, ensuring that policy interventions are well-informed and targeted.

Data-Driven Decision Making: The use of digital tools facilitates the collection, analysis, and utilisation of data, which in turn enables informed decision-making. Governments can identify trends, anticipate future needs, and make data-driven decisions that optimise public services and resource allocation.

Building Innovation Ecosystems: Digital platforms create opportunities for collaboration among government agencies, private sector partners, academia, and civil society. This collaboration fosters innovation ecosystems that drive the development of new solutions to complex challenges. By leveraging diverse expertise and resources, governments can address societal issues more effectively and create an environment conducive to innovation.

Promoting Citizen Engagement: Innovative platforms and digital tools facilitate greater citizen participation in governance. Initiatives such as e-governance and digital communication channels allow for increased transparency, feedback, and participation in the policymaking process. This approach helps to build trust between citizens and the government, fostering a more inclusive and collaborative governance model.

Improving Efficiency and Reducing Costs: By adopting innovative practices and technologies, governments can streamline processes, reduce bureaucracy, and lower costs. This leads to more efficient use of public resources and ensures better allocation of public funds, ultimately improving the quality and reach of government services.

Supporting Economic Growth: Government policies that promote innovation can stimulate economic development by supporting research and development (R&D), creating favourable conditions for start-ups, and encouraging private sector innovation. Funding R&D initiatives across various sectors promotes the development of new technologies, products, and services that generate economic, social, and environmental benefits.

Building Resilient and Inclusive Societies: Innovation helps governments create policies and systems that are adaptable and resilient to change. By ensuring that technological advancements benefit all segments of society, innovation promotes inclusivity, reducing disparities and empowering citizens across different demographics.

Agility and Adaptability: Digital technologies enable governments to respond quickly to changing circumstances, adapt policies and services in real time, and experiment with new approaches to problem-solving. This agility is crucial in a rapidly changing world, where governments must remain responsive and capable of addressing emergent challenges.

Case Studies of Digital Technologies in Practice

Artificial Intelligence: Chatbots: AI-powered chatbots are virtual assistants that interact with users through text or speech, simulating human conversation. They are widely used in customer service settings to provide instant responses to inquiries, troubleshoot issues, and guide users through processes. By leveraging natural language processing (NLP) and machine learning algorithms, chatbots can understand user queries and provide relevant responses, thereby improving efficiency and enhancing the user experience.

Cloud Computing: Netflix: Netflix utilises cloud computing to deliver its streaming service to millions of users worldwide. By storing its vast library of movies and TV shows on cloud servers, Netflix ensures scalability and high availability, allowing users to access content anytime, anywhere, on a range of devices. Cloud computing also enables Netflix to optimise bandwidth usage, deliver personalised recommendations, and continuously enhance its streaming experience through data analytics and machine learning algorithms.

Big Data: Google Maps: Google Maps collects and analyses vast amounts of data from various sources, including satellite imagery, GPS signals, traffic sensors, and user feedback, to provide real-time navigation and location-based services. By processing and interpreting this big data, Google Maps offers features such as live traffic updates, optimal route planning, and local business recommendations. Big data analytics enables Google Maps to continuously improve its accuracy, reliability, and relevance, delivering valuable insights to both users and businesses.

Current Digital Transformation and Innovation Governance Situation in Oman

The Sultanate of Oman embarked on its digital transformation journey in 2003, aiming to transition to a knowledge-based economy as part of its Economic Vision 2020. This ambitious initiative is led by the Ministry of Transport, Communications, and Information Technology (MTCIT), which focuses on enhancing public sector efficiency and fostering a digitally-enabled society. The MTCIT's key objectives include reducing IT costs for government agencies through expert consultation and implementing digital services that contribute to a more inclusive and sustainable economy.

Oman's digital transformation strategy features several key initiatives, including the Unified Government Network, the ePayment Gateway, the Government eServices Portal, the Electronic Transactions Law, the Oman eGovernance Framework, the National IT Training Framework, and information security measures. These initiatives are integral to achieving Oman's Vision 2040 by providing a secure, advanced digital infrastructure that integrates economic and social development with sustainability and future needs.

The Omannuna Oman Portal

The Omannuna platform serves as a comprehensive one-stop shop, electronically integrating government entities to eliminate data duplication and improve coordination and data sharing across the public sector. By providing a centralised platform for accessing government services, Omannuna enhances the delivery of public services, facilitating Government-to-Citizen (G2C), Government-to-Business (G2B), and Government-to-Government (G2G) interactions. As part of the eGovernment project, this initiative has identified 2,636 online services across 51 entities, all of which are seamlessly integrated to promote information sharing and improve service accessibility.

Figure 1. Omannuna Oman Portal

The Sultanate recognises the significance of digital transformation and innovation in fostering a sustainable, progressive, and digitally integrated society. Through various ICT investments and its Digital Economy Programme, Oman has made significant strides towards achieving the objectives of Vision 2040, while continuing to pursue opportunities for further development.

Government initiatives also play a key role in enhancing Oman's economic, entrepreneurial, and research capacity by supporting the growth of innovative, research-driven companies in sectors such as oil recovery, renewable energy, food and biotechnology, water and the environment, and health science. The Innovation Policy and Management (IPM) programme aims to create an inspiring environment for innovators and entrepreneurs to develop extraordinary ideas and companies, driving economic and social development.

The Innovation Complex Muscat

The Ministry of Higher Education, Research, and Innovation has inaugurated the Innovation Building in Muscat, located near Sultan Qaboos University. The Innovation Complex Muscat is designed to foster innovation, enhance collaboration between academia and the private sector, and engage both local and international communities. It provides a supportive environment for researchers and entrepreneurs, aligning with the government's economic diversification strategy. The complex features 4,000 square metres of business incubators, a one-stop window for services, a commercial complex, a theatre, and various ministry departments—all dedicated to promoting innovation and entrepreneurship.

Oman Innovation Festival

In 2024, the Ministry of Higher Education, Research, and Innovation (MOHERI) and the Muscat Innovation Complex launched the Governorates Innovation Competition in collaboration with the Innovation Oases digital portal. This initiative, conducted in partnership with governorates, aimed to identify innovative solutions to specific challenges faced in each governorate. The competition took place from 17 to 30 January 2024, receiving a total of 415 solutions from across the country, showcasing a wide range of creative and impactful ideas. Each governorate selected one idea to advance to the second stage of the competition.

The top three innovative ideas were announced and honoured during the Oman Innovation Festival, marking a significant national achievement for the Sultanate of Oman under the hashtag #Oman_Innovation_Festival.

The Innovation Oases Digital Portal

Launched in 2020, the Innovation Oases is a digital platform designed to host online crowdsourcing competitions that address challenges faced by government and private sector institutions. Its primary goal is to enhance partnerships between these institutions and the public by serving as a centralised hub for public engagement. The platform enables participants to propose solutions to various challenges, fostering an environment of collaboration and innovation.

To support these efforts, Innovation Oases has signed Memorandums of Understanding (MoUs) with 13 partners, including government agencies, private sector organisations, and non-profits. This collaborative approach enables efficient and cost-effective delivery of digital innovation solutions, contributing to the national goal of fostering entrepreneurship and job creation. The platform has hosted 14 programming challenges from over 23 organisations, with over 1,000 citizens participating and submitting 1,089 solutions. This level of engagement significantly contributes to job creation, entrepreneurship, and the promotion of innovative thinking across the country.

Moreover, Innovation Oases has built a digital evaluation system that uses innovation criteria and evaluator teams to assess ideas online for the Innovation Awards competition. This digital approach ensures the identification of the most promising solutions while promoting entrepreneurship. The success of Innovation Oases demonstrates that innovation works best as a grassroots effort, shared among all stakeholders: the public sector, the private sector, and the population at large.

Best Practice: The Innovation Oases Platform

The Innovation Oases digital platform exemplifies best practice in fostering collaboration between various stakeholders to address challenges faced by government, non-profit organisations, and the private sector. By serving as a centralised hub for public engagement, Innovation Oases facilitates partnerships that contribute to the efficient delivery of cost-effective digital innovation solutions.

Currently, the platform has hosted 14 challenges from 12 different organisations, with 2,485 participants accessing the portal and submitting a total of 1,089 solutions. This substantial level of engagement highlights the platform's potential to create new services, job opportunities, and foster entrepreneurship, thereby contributing to Oman's economic and social development.

The Ministry of Manpower Open Data Portal: Outstanding Open Data Initiative 2018

In 2017, the Ministry of Manpower introduced its open data portal during the COMEX 2017 exhibition, showcasing a range of innovative initiatives aimed at fostering transparency and supporting entrepreneurship. The Open Data Portal was developed to make Ministry data easily accessible to all segments of society via the internet. It provided access to 56 databases across eight different fields, with the goal of enhancing transparency and facilitating decision-making processes. Additionally, the portal offered a 'data request service' to fulfil requests for data not available on the platform. By April 2020, the service had received approximately 225 requests, benefiting over 225,000 individuals. In recognition of its achievements, the portal was honoured with the Sultan Qaboos Award for Excellence in eGovernment Services in 2018 for its outstanding Open Data Initiative.

Open Data Hackathon: Ministry of Manpower, Oman

In 2018, the Ministry of Manpower launched an open data hackathon, fostering innovative collaboration between student government alliances and the academic community. This event specifically targeted students from the College of Technical and Vocational Education, which operates under the ministry's purview. The hackathon aimed to leverage the Ministry's open data resources, challenging students to develop creative solutions addressing various aspects of the job market. By encouraging the practical application of data analysis and problem-solving skills, the initiative sought to bridge the gap between academic learning and real-world employment challenges, ultimately enhancing job readiness and market responsiveness among participating students.

To promote the principle of open data within education, the Ministry of Manpower launched the hackathon under the slogan "With Data We Innovate." The programme enabled thousands of students to use data to propose innovative solutions for the labour market. Approximately 123 college students participated in the hackathon, resulting in the recognition of four winning projects: the Smart Oman Map, Smart Glove, Help Me Application, and Balance Application. Following their success, collaborative efforts with the Ministry were initiated to provide the necessary mentoring and support for implementing these ideas. This support included training, guidance, consultations, and other assistance aimed at further developing and refining their projects.

Institutional Structures to Support Innovation and Government Transformation

The role of the Chief Innovation Officer (CInO) in the executive structure is crucial for effective government transformation. Ideally, the CInO should report directly to a high-level authority, positioning them at the source of a cascade, where their ideas can be drawn directly from government objectives and disseminated throughout the organisation, ultimately reaching the general population. At ministry or departmental levels, there should be personnel responsible for facilitating and monitoring the flow of innovation across the organisation. These individuals also play a key role in collecting feedback and relaying it back up the cascade to the CInO.

For instance, in Bangladesh, the CInO operates from the Prime Minister's office, while in the United States, CInOs work within mayoral offices. In both cases, they are involved in critical meetings and are fully aware of the objectives and concerns of their respective administrations. This proximity to decision-makers enhances their ability to influence policy and champion innovation at the highest levels of government.

Government's Innovation Support Policy

For governments to effectively support innovation, a fundamental change in attitude is required. The traditional top-down approach, in which government dictates outcomes without considering the complexities of innovation, must be replaced with a more adaptive and open-minded stance. Governments must not only develop policies but also tolerate and respond to critical assessments, demonstrating a willingness to adapt these policies based on broader input.

Innovation can highlight potential areas of failure, but it also reveals opportunities for refining policies to make them more popular and effective. Successful innovation requires supportive systems, procedures, policies, rules, and regulations to pave the way for a culture of innovation capability. This includes creating and identifying:

- The mission and vision goals for an innovative government.
- A specific mandate within the organisational structure to empower the CInO to drive innovation both within and beyond the government sector.
- Defined roles and responsibilities, resources, budget, and governance for the CInO.
- A mandate for bureaucracy to accept and facilitate innovation, incorporating diverse perspectives into decision-making processes.
- Necessary funding to support the innovation process.
- Mechanisms for citizens to engage with the innovation process.
- Systems for monitoring, evaluating, and controlling the innovation process.

Aims of Government Innovation

The primary aim of most governments is to improve the lives of their citizens. However, achieving this often depends on the successful implementation of policies, which frequently requires a bottom-up approach, rather than the traditional top-down attitude seen in many public sectors (Sachs, 2005).

In the current economic climate, many governments have been tempted to follow "formula-based economic prescriptions by the World Bank and the International Monetary Fund (IMF)." However, innovation is implemented within complex social and economic systems, and therefore requires a "differential diagnosis" approach as a guide to service delivery improvements and innovation.

Regardless of how innovation is approached, it is important to remember that innovation itself is only a tool—a means to an end. It must be judged by its ability to create "public value" (McKinsey, 2011). The success of innovation depends on the wise selection of innovative ideas that arise during the innovative process.

Following this definition, innovation in government aims to:

- Assess the efficiency of government policies throughout society and create viable alternatives where needed.
- Inform government of the aspirations and concerns of society.
- Involve the public sector in decision-making processes, facilitating effective enactment of policies.
- Encourage citizen engagement in policy-making by listening to their knowledge, ideas, suggestions, and expertise.
- Empower individuals, increasing their capacity to engage with commercial and job markets effectively, while holding their government accountable.
- Act as a holistic process for society's engagement with government, jointly working to achieve sustainable development goals.

As Dr. Alberti noted, "Innovation is mankind's effort to endlessly pursue change for a better world" (Schumpeter).

Innovation in Government: Three Step Cycle

The innovation process in government can be effectively captured through a three-step cycle, remembered by the acronym ARM: Assess, Reward, Modify. Importantly, this is a continuous cycle, highlighting that significant achievements in innovation do not signal an endpoint; rather, further opportunities for innovation should always be considered in light of new experiences. The situation must be continually assessed to ensure ongoing relevance and improvement—occasional spot checks are simply insufficient.

The **Assess → Reward → Modify** cycle is iterative, forming a continuous loop: **assess → reward → modify → assess**. This model never truly ends, as the potential for improvement is always present.

Innovation inherently involves experimentation, which can be challenging for government bodies that are often risk-averse, fearing that experimentation may expose perceived weaknesses or inefficiencies. As a result, policies, once implemented, are often retained for extended periods, and their validity is upheld through political rhetoric. However, it requires a courageous government to remain open to accepting criticism and admitting mistakes.

By adhering to the innovation cycle at every stage, governments can avoid significant errors at the point of implementation. Moreover, small errors can be easily modified without any lasting negative effects—particularly when communities are involved in constructive criticism that leads to a successful outcome. Community engagement ensures that adjustments are made collaboratively, promoting greater acceptance and support.

If the innovation cycle is applied with an open mind to both positive and negative results during the design stage, the development stage, and the trial stage, the innovation should achieve its intended outcomes at that specific point in time. Furthermore, during the implementation stage, applying the innovation cycle helps ensure a smooth and effective rollout of new initiatives.

Nevertheless, ongoing assessment remains crucial. Even if a successful outcome is achieved in the communities where the trial was conducted, there is always the possibility that those outcomes may not be fully representative of the entire country. Continuous evaluation ensures that any disparities can be identified and addressed.

The innovation cycle is valuable even in assessing the reward and modification procedures themselves, and indeed, the assessment process itself should be subject to evaluation. This approach allows for a deeper understanding of what works and ensures that each phase of the cycle is refined and optimised over time (The Economist, 2012).

Table 1. Model Components

ARM Concept	Description/Definition
Assess procedures and outcomes. This should be a continuous process.	Nothing is ever perfect. One can almost say that if nothing has been changed for a number of years, there will be inefficiencies. However, one shouldn't change just for the sake of change because of 'new ideas'. To achieve the effective balance, a regime of continual assessment against specified objectives will highlight problem areas.
Reward positive assessment.	To create a culture of innovation, it should be a source of satisfaction and achievement. Reward where goals have been achieved. Praise new ideas, even if they are not always accepted. The culture of innovation should be the life-blood of society.
Modify negative assessment	On those occasions where results do not achieve targets, fully involve the participants in solutions. Listen to their comments and suggestions. Guide their suggestions towards viable solutions. Facilitate the solutions and praise the result.

Objective of Innovation

The fundamental objective of innovation is to fulfil the needs of society. This objective can manifest in various forms, ranging from small-scale initiatives—such as a neighbourhood watch scheme formed by residents of a single street—to innovation within different levels of the bureaucratic structure.

As noted by *The Economist*, in recent years, government innovation in the UK may have faced challenges, but at the local level, "facing deep cuts to their budgets, the best local authorities have radically rethought how they ought to serve the people who elect them" (*The Economist*, 2012). This rethinking exemplifies the power of innovation to adapt and find creative solutions in times of fiscal constraint.

To achieve these goals, innovation within government aims to:

- Assist in the effectiveness of government decisions by supplying accurate data that forms the basis for informed decision-making.
- Facilitate the implementation of government decisions by ensuring that public service procedures are efficient and streamlined.
- Maintain engagement with society by establishing channels such as newsletters, public forums, effective IT systems, and e-government initiatives, all of which support transparent and open communication with citizens.

These aims underscore the critical role of innovation in bridging the gap between government policies and the real needs of society, ensuring that public services are effective, responsive, and aligned with the evolving expectations of the community.

Figure 2. Innovation in Government

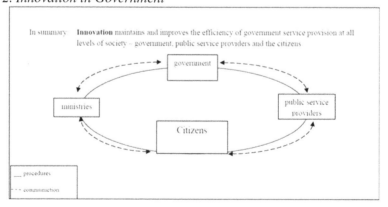

Assessment of Outcomes

Successful outcomes are those that fulfil the needs of society. The achievement of such outcomes depends on several key factors:

- The effectiveness of the decision-making process within government.
- The successful implementation of these decisions.
- The design of the procedures involved in implementing policies.
- The training of employees to effectively execute these decisions.
- The establishment of robust communication channels between government and society, ensuring two-way engagement.

First Step: Assessment

True innovation can only be realised if the situation—whether successful or problematic—is clearly understood. Assessment provides clarity on where we currently stand and identifies the desired outcome.

If the current situation aligns with the desired outcome, it is deemed successful. It is important to study these successes to understand why they are effective so that the lessons learned can be applied elsewhere. However, even successful situations have room for improvement, and it is essential to listen to and learn from the users to identify potential enhancements.

When a situation does not meet the desired outcome, innovation is needed. Identifying problem areas involves:

- Comparing outcomes against international standards and establishing evaluation procedures to monitor progress.
- Responding regularly to identified inefficiencies, comparing them to expected outcomes.
- Listening to all feedback and responding promptly to complaints from citizens, businesses, and the public sector.

Second Step: Reward What is Satisfactory

Acknowledging and rewarding satisfactory outcomes is a crucial part of the innovation cycle. It involves:

- Regularly showing appreciation for achievements—small gestures such as a smile can have a significant impact.

- Praising individual or group achievements, regardless of their scale, including accomplishments beyond the immediate project.
- Establishing specific awards that participants can aspire to achieve.
- Recognising that citizens are integral to the 'innovation ecosystem'; their contributions deserve acknowledgment and praise as well.

Third Step: Modification

The modification step focuses on continuous improvement and addressing areas that fall short:

- **Improve What is Satisfactory**: Improvement is an ongoing process and is central to a culture of innovation. Even what is deemed satisfactory can be enhanced.
- **Modify What is Unsatisfactory**: Consult participants before making changes, as they are often well aware of the issues and may already have viable solutions.
- **Redesign What is Not Viable**: If a policy or procedure is fundamentally flawed, it is important to acknowledge this rather than attempt to modify the error. Instead, return to the original objective and brainstorm new ideas to create a more effective solution.

Mission and Vision Statements

It is vital for everyone—both within and outside government—to understand what the government stands for. Therefore, the government must clearly communicate its purpose and aspirations:

1. **Mission**: What are the aims and ambitions of the government? The mission statement should clearly articulate the government's goals and the actions it plans to take to achieve them.
2. **Vision**: How does the government see the country in the future? The vision statement should outline the government's long-term aspirations for the nation, providing a clear picture of the future it aims to create.

GOOD GOVERNANCE FOR BETTER GOVERNMENT

Good Governance Overview

To fully understand the governance of a country and its strategies for innovation and digital transformation, it is essential to identify the rulers and the laws under which they operate. This includes understanding the various processes by which rulers are selected and defined. Good governance involves collaboration to create laws that effectively link and benefit society as a whole. Governance is essentially the process by which rulers manage a country, ensuring that decisions are made in a manner that serves the interests of all citizens.

There are many different systems of governance around the world, and the specific process used is less important than the outcomes it delivers. Ultimately, what matters is whether the governance structure benefits the citizens of the country. Governance also encompasses the system of government and the type of constitution in place—determining who makes the rules (laws) and how those rules are enforced or modified.

Good governance is characterised by being communal, transparent, and accountable. It addresses issues that are important to the people, and strives to create sound laws, implemented by a public sector that is citizen-centred. Moreover, good governance empowers citizens to participate actively with authorities in making informed and effective decisions.

People involved in Good Governance

Good governance plays a crucial role in benefiting society. It is the responsibility of the political bodies of a country to ensure such governance by creating just and equitable laws. However, the effectiveness of these laws also depends on their implementation, which makes an efficient administrative authority equally integral to good governance. True good governance can only be realised through a public authority that is citizen-centred—one that places the needs and aspirations of citizens at the core of its operations and decision-making processes.

Role of Innovation/DT in Promoting Good Governance

A fundamental key to good governance is the identification of the needs of its constituents. This can be achieved by engaging directly with society and actively seeking solutions through the use of innovative information technology tools. By adopting such an approach, the government ensures that it is well equipped to fulfil the needs of society effectively. Engaging citizens through digital platforms, public consultations, and open dialogue allows the government to remain responsive and adaptive, ultimately enhancing the quality of governance and public services.

Good Governance in the Digital Era

The Role of Digital Technologies in Enhancing Good Governance

Digital technologies hold significant potential for enhancing good governance by enabling the effective, efficient, and ethical management of public resources to achieve optimal societal outcomes. By embracing key principles such as transparency, accountability, participation, responsiveness, and inclusiveness, governments can ensure that citizens actively engage in decision-making processes. Technology facilitates accessible, real-time data, empowering citizens to contribute to governance while strengthening government accountability. This pivotal role of technology not only cultivates trust but also promotes social equity and fosters sustainable development.

Innovation extends beyond being merely a cultural mindset; it is a vital element of effective governance. Government policies play a crucial role in fostering innovation, and these policies are essential for addressing complex challenges, engaging society, and enhancing public services. Moreover, innovation-driven policies contribute to increasing citizen trust and satisfaction, building responsive and resilient institutions, and promoting inclusive societies. By prioritising innovation, governments can adapt to evolving needs, improve service delivery, and support long-term sustainable growth.

Ministry of Manpower Oman e-Participation System

The Ministry of Manpower (MOMP) in Oman was recognised for its excellence in community engagement with the Sultan Qaboos Award for Excellence in eGovernment Services in 2018, particularly for its outstanding Community e-Participation Initiative. In 2017, MOMP took a significant step towards enhancing community involvement by translating its vision and strengthening partnerships between key stakeholders (government, employers, and employees) through the creation of an online one-stop-shop for citizen engagement in decision-making. This online service enabled citizens to connect directly with decision-makers, thereby increasing transparency and facilitating the evaluation of the Ministry's performance. The e-Participation system offered several key features:

eCitizen Engagement

The eCitizen Engagement platform was designed as a portal for citizens to access and view topics, participate in discussions, vote, and comment on issues important to them before final legislation was issued. The "Involved in Decision" system attracted over 6,000 visitors, received over 400 comments, and garnered over 2,000 votes on eight policies within its first year. This interactive approach allowed citizens to have a meaningful impact on policy deliberation and decision-making.

eSuggestion

The eSuggestion feature included online forms that were updated in real time to the Ministry's datasets. Over 70 ideas were collected through this feature, and when an idea reached 1,000 votes, it was forwarded to top management for further study and potential implementation. This process provided citizens with a direct mechanism for contributing ideas and ensuring that their voices were heard by decision-makers.

The eCitizen engagement system exemplified how MOMP adopted a holistic approach to online engagement across various projects, policy deliberations, and decision-making processes. The success of this system was significant, contributing to the simplification of procedures and facilitating a transition from traditional methods to a robust digital tool for citizen engagement. Additionally, the system included mechanisms to report back on how community and stakeholder input was considered and how it influenced the Ministry's decisions. The system provided comprehensive statistics and valuable information for decision-makers, aiding in drafting laws and regulating the labour market. Key topic functionalities included sign-in, Involved in Decision, eSuggestion, eSurvey, and the Innovation Lab.

Key Achievements of the e-Participation System

The "Community Participation" window provided a platform for all segments of society and production parties to express their opinions and engage in discussions on various labour market issues and topics. This initiative aimed to enhance transparency, increase community involvement, and expedite decision-making. Through this platform, individuals could vote in opinion polls, participate in Ministry questionnaires, and submit proposals and views to help improve and develop the policies and services provided by the Ministry.

The impact of the Ministry's efforts has been notable in terms of improved efficiency in decision-making and enhanced services, as illustrated below:

- **Engagement in Educational Topics**: Over 1,800 citizens engaged in discussions on education in technical colleges, with 6% voting and 4% submitting comments.
- **Occupational Health and Safety**: Over 1,000 citizens engaged in discussions on occupational health and safety, with 7% voting and 8% commenting.
- **Private Training Institutions' Licensing**: Over 1,000 citizens engaged with this topic, with 8% voting and 9% commenting.
- **Vocational Diploma Approval**: Over 1,000 citizens participated in discussions on the approval of the vocational diploma, with 8% voting and 7% commenting.
- **Establishing Private Recruitment Offices**: Over 4,000 citizens engaged in discussions on establishing private recruitment offices, with 70% voting and 67% commenting.
- **Minimum Monthly Income for Authorising the First Housemaid**: Over 1,000 citizens participated in this topic, with 9% voting and 9% commenting.
- **MOMP Innovation Awards**: Approximately 200 citizens participated in the launch of the MOMP Innovation Awards event, with over 70 individuals submitting solutions.
- **Workshops and Training**: Over 3,000 citizens attended workshops and training sessions on how to use the open data innovation and eCitizen engagement portal, conducted at 15 colleges.
- **Active Users and Website Visitors**: The platform registered over 47,000 active users and received over 55,000 reviews, with over 3,700 monthly website visits.
- **Innovative Solutions**: More than 100 innovative solutions were submitted to solve community challenges.

These achievements highlight the significant contributions of the e-Participation system in fostering an inclusive approach to decision-making and policy development, empowering citizens to play an active role in shaping government initiatives.

Innovation Strategies

Effective citizen engagement is fundamental to providing a clear purpose, mission, and vision for government initiatives. By implementing strategic approaches to public participation, governments can enhance their capacity to foster public engagement, collaboration, empowerment, and accountability, ultimately improving the quality of life for citizens. This chapter explores some proposed strategies that can enable the public to contribute and interact more effectively through both digital communication media and face-to-face engagement.

The Innovation Ecosystem

The concept of an innovation ecosystem focuses on reaching individuals, businesses, and academic institutions across various locations, creating a network that encourages the exchange of ideas and collaboration. The information and communication technology (ICT) revolution has facilitated engagement among people from different regions, using various technology platforms to turn ideas and solutions into tangible processes, services, and products. Below, we discuss some key examples of innovation ecosystem strategies.

First Strategy: Crowdsourcing Overview

Crowdsourcing is a process that enables the public to identify needed services, raise issues, and share ideas. This initiative helps engage the community in problem-solving through social media, enabling administrators to gather a wide range of ideas from the public and involve society in addressing challenges. The outcome of these efforts is then communicated back to the community, reinforcing transparency and participation (Mergel, 2011).

Example of an Innovation Ecosystem: Crowdsourcing in Texas

In Manor, Texas, an innovative experiment allowed residents to offer solutions on an open innovation platform called Manor Labs (www.ManorLab.org), which was designed by Dustin Haisler, Chief Innovation Officer, in collaboration with Stanford University and Spigit, an innovation management platform.

The crowdsourcing process involved several stages:

- **Phase 1**: Community organisations selected three challenges facing the city.
- **Phase 2**: The public submitted innovative ideas to address these issues.
- **Phase 3**: The best ideas, as determined by the public, were funded through microgrants and crowdfunding, with solution designers matched with nonprofit organisations to provide guidance, mentorship, and assess effectiveness.
- **Phase 4**: The overall campaign, including outcomes, was assessed to determine the impact of each idea.

This process not only empowered citizens to contribute solutions but also demonstrated the potential for innovation at various levels of government and society. In Texas, participants in the crowdsourcing initiative were rewarded for their contributions with points known as "innobucks," which could be exchanged for local benefits, such as a meal or a day serving as mayor (Towns, 2010).

Encouraging Public Participation

To foster public participation in crowdsourcing initiatives, it is crucial to create a culture of innovation. Tutoring sessions should be available to enable everyone to take part, and all participants should receive recognition, with special mention given to viable suggestions. By creating a culture that values and rewards participation, governments can effectively harness the collective creativity of their citizens to address community challenges.

Realising an Innovation Culture through Digital Transformation: Meeting Oman's Vision 2040

Oman's Ministry of Manpower (MOMP) has successfully implemented an innovation ecosystem as part of its digital transformation efforts, aligning with the country's Vision 2040. The ministry's Open Data Innovation System won the Government Excellence Award for the Best Arab Government Project to Develop Education through its Innovation Acceleration Programme.

Student-Government Alliances

The Ministry of Manpower has implemented several initiatives to promote innovation, intellectual property, and technology transfer:

- **Establishment of an Open Data Portal**: The ministry created an open data portal for public access to its data, supporting transparency and open government.
- **Biennial Innovation Award**: The Innovation Award showcases innovators' talents, markets their projects, creates job opportunities, and connects them with private sector institutions.
- **Annual Open Data Hackathon Competition**: This event encourages students and Ministry employees to use open data in developing solutions to existing challenges.

In collaboration with 15 technical and vocational colleges and strategic partners, the Ministry nurtures creativity and evaluates ten student projects annually for its acceleration programme. This approach fosters an entrepreneurial ethos, generates employment opportunities, and supports the broader national innovation strategy to cultivate a dynamic and sustainable economy.

Key Initiatives in Oman's Innovation Strategy

1. **Innovative Competitions**: Competitions were organised for employees and students to propose solutions to real-world challenges, such as workplace safety, work injuries, and the integration of people with special needs in the private sector. These competitions generated approximately 76 actionable solutions, which were forwarded to relevant Ministry authorities for implementation.

2. **MOMP Innovation Award (launched in April 2018)**: Under the slogan #Innovation_Partnership_and_Sustainability, the award aimed to promote innovation across sectors such as industry, tourism, and environmental sustainability. With approximately 375 solution projects registered, 43 qualified for recognition, and 11 received support from both governmental and private sectors for further development and commercialisation.

3. **Open Data Hackathon (2019)**: Under the slogan "With Data We Innovate," the competition focused on promoting the use of open data to find innovative solutions to challenges in areas like technology, occupational safety, and education. The hackathon attracted over 123 college students, leading to the development of four winning projects: Smart Oman Map, Smart Glove, Help Me Application, and Mizan Application. These projects received ongoing support from the Ministry of Communications Technology for further development.

4. **COVID-19 Solutions Competition**: This initiative aimed to mitigate the pandemic's impact by harnessing the talents of students and Ministry employees. The competition addressed topics like public health, artificial intelligence applications, and mental health, resulting in valuable solutions implemented in collaboration with research councils.

5. **Innovation Lab Initiative**: This initiative aimed to foster student entrepreneurship by creating a sustainable environment for innovative projects. Students with entrepreneurial skills were invited to present their ideas, which were evaluated by a committee. Winning ideas received support for further development, including entry into acceleration programmes.

6. **Innovation Acceleration Programme**: This initiative, which won the Excellence Award for the Best Arab Government Project to Develop Education, funds the top ten student projects annually from technical and vocational colleges. In collaboration with strategic allies, the programme aims to rapidly establish commercial companies producing high-quality, competitive products. This initiative enhances the commercialisation of innovative solutions and supports numerous projects through the integrated Open Data Innovation System.

Second Strategy: Open Government Data (OGD)

The term 'open government data' (OGD) came into prominence in 2007, following the publication of a set of principles by a group of experts and advocates in Sebastopol, California, USA, commonly referred to as the "Open Government Data Principles" or the "Sebastopol Principles." These principles provided best practice recommendations on how governments should publish data on the internet, promoting transparency, accessibility, and citizen engagement.

Elements of Open Government Data

Open government data comprises two primary elements:

- **Open Data**: Refers to material that everyone is free to use for any purpose without restrictions.
- **Government Data or Public Sector Information (PSI)**: Encompasses all data produced by **Public Sector Bodies (PSBs)**.

The Open Government Directive issued by President Obama on 21 January 2009 outlined three core principles of open government data:

1. **Transparency**: Promotes accountability by providing the public with information about government activities.
2. **Participation**: Encourages members of the public to contribute ideas and expertise, enabling governments to benefit from information that is widely dispersed in society.
3. **Collaboration**: Improves the effectiveness of government by fostering partnerships and cooperation within and across levels of government, as well as with private institutions.

Building a Sustainable OGD Ecosystem

Most Chief Innovation Officers (CInOs) employ the OGD strategy to engage and interact with society, share information, and allow citizens to provide solutions to governmental challenges. Through OGD, citizens gain access to government data, enabling them to better understand government actions and participate in decision-making processes.

Case Study: Open Government Data in Kenya

Since 2011, Kenya has been a pioneer in OGD initiatives, signing an agreement to create an open government data platform to increase transparency and accountability. By making data accessible to its citizens, Kenya has achieved significant savings—up to $1 billion annually—and has fostered public awareness of government actions, contributing to long-term societal benefits.

Challenge: Kenyans faced persistent corruption, severely affecting the quality of life, with around 40% of the population living on less than $2 a day.

Solution: Kenya launched an open data portal, allowing citizens to access essential government information, thereby holding officials accountable. The portal provided data on sectors such as education, energy, health, population, poverty, and water and sanitation. The new constitution established the citizen's right to access government information, marking a significant step towards transparency.

Result: Since joining the Open Government Partnership in 2011, Kenya has seen considerable progress. For example, the Ministry of Lands, which used to collect 3 billion shillings, now collects 7 billion. The implementation of e-procurement also improved efficiency and reduced corruption, allowing suppliers to tender directly at fair market prices.

Impact: Presently, the system is more transparent, with citizens able to access pricing and procurement information. This has resulted in significant cost savings for the government, as inflated prices are no longer accepted. Furthermore, about 100 apps have been developed using data from the government portal, enhancing food security, healthcare, and agricultural productivity. The availability of information on mobile platforms has also enabled farmers to maximise their yields by providing guidance on optimal crop selection. Using open data has increased civic participation, supported distributed innovation, and made development more participatory and transparent.

Case Study: Open Government Data in Boston

The rise of OGD is transforming how residents interact with their cities in the USA and worldwide. One notable example is in Boston, where OGD initiatives have fostered citizen engagement and collaboration with government authorities.

Street Bump: The City of Boston invited citizens to submit ideas for improving their neighbourhoods. One innovation was the "Street Bump" app, developed by the public, which surveys roads while driving and provides data to the City in real-time. The app uses accelerometers and GPS to pinpoint bumps in the road, uploading the data to a server for analysis and enabling city officials to prioritise repairs.

Adopt a Fire Hydrant: Erik Michaels-Ober, a software developer, created the "Adopt a Fire Hydrant" app, which invites citizens to clear snow from hydrants during winter to ensure they remain accessible for firefighters. Participants can name their adopted hydrants and share their efforts on Google Maps. This initiative ensures that fire hydrants remain functional during severe weather, benefiting the entire community.

Citizen Connect: Another app, "Citizen Connect," was developed by a group of developers for the City of Boston. This platform serves as Boston's main source of government information and non-emergency services. Notably, cases can be viewed publicly, and viewers are invited to provide input. In one instance, a citizen reported a possum in a rubbish bin, and a local neighbour responded by safely releasing the animal—demonstrating how community members can provide simple and effective solutions to minor issues through a government platform.

These examples illustrate how citizens can transform from passive service users to active partners in solving government challenges and reducing costs. The innovation ecosystem thus strengthens society as a whole, providing real-time feedback on public services and empowering communities to take an active role in governance.

Benefits of OGD and the Role of the Chief Innovation Officer

The OGD strategy enables governments to establish an open data portal, empowering citizens, fostering innovation, and improving public services. The key benefits of OGD include:

- **Transparency**: Ensuring that government actions are open and accessible to the public.
- **Participation**: Encouraging citizens to contribute ideas and expertise to government initiatives.
- **Collaboration**: Promoting partnerships between different sectors, including government, private institutions, and the public.
- **Economic Growth**: Leveraging data for innovation, entrepreneurship, and the development of new services.
- **Improved Public Services**: Using insights derived from public data to enhance the quality of government services.
- **Enhanced Civic Engagement**: Providing channels for citizens to participate actively in decision-making processes.

To implement strategies such as crowdsourcing and OGD, governments require strong and dynamic leadership. The Chief Innovation Officer becomes an invaluable asset, managing the government's innovation programme, which ultimately benefits the public and society as a whole.

Third Strategy: Chief Innovation Officer (CInO)

Overview of the Chief Innovation Officer

The concept of the Chief Innovation Officer (CInO) began in 2008, introduced by Jayson White from the Ash Center for Democratic Governance and Innovation at Harvard's Kennedy School. Initially, the role supported cities in creating innovation positions aimed at "education reform and sustainability" (White, 2008). However, during the economic recession, the focus shifted towards broader government objectives, including budget cuts, economic development, and job creation. Currently, the primary purpose of the CInO is to monitor the outcomes of government policies and implement new ideas with the potential to transform government operations to meet societal needs effectively.

Innovation Is Everyone's Responsibility

The idea underpinning the role of the CInO is that innovation is everyone's responsibility, not just a government concern. Innovation must emerge from all segments of society: the public sector, businesses, and citizens. The CInO's role is to bring together the knowledge and ideas of society to create solutions that address government challenges for the public good. Acting as a bridge, the CInO links all elements of the bureaucratic system with society, fostering collaboration among citizens, businesses, and public institutions to address shared needs and overcome common challenges.

The Growing Number of CInOs

The number of Chief Innovation Officers in public agencies is increasing rapidly in the United States and across the globe. CInOs assist mayors and civic leaders in driving innovative strategies that enhance their cities through creative problem-solving and citizen engagement. In Bangladesh, for instance, the CInO helps the Prime Minister's Office improve the efficiency of public services and reduce corruption. Similarly, in the United States, CInOs in most states use crowdsourcing to identify and address the needs of their cities and encourage citizen participation in decision-making processes.

Role of the Chief Innovation Officer

The CInO carries four primary responsibilities within government, which should be prioritised as follows:

1. **Informing Government**: The first responsibility of the CInO is to ensure that the government is informed, enabling it to make effective policies. The CInO should:
   o   Assess policy implementation against government objectives.
   o   Engage all sectors of society in policy assessment and modification.
   o   Establish viable communication channels throughout society.
   o   Provide feedback to government based on public input.
   o   Train all segments of society to engage effectively in the process.

2. **Facilitating Innovation Management:** The second responsibility is to facilitate the innovation management system by ensuring that:
   o   Roles required for innovation projects are established and filled by qualified teams.
   o   Resources and funding for start-up research centres are available.
   o   Training capacity exists at all levels.

3. **Facilitating Interface Functions:** The third responsibility involves facilitating collaboration between teams, public organisations, and citizens. The CInO should ensure that:
   o   There is shared collaboration, with a clear purpose or vision to achieve cohesive goals.
   o   Innovation is embraced within government agencies.
   o   The innovation process, including feedback and updates, is communicated effectively to and from government and society.
   o   Strategies and resources are clearly identified and communicated.
   o   Citizens and public sector employees are encouraged to contribute innovative ideas.
   o   Leadership, networking, creativity, and reward systems are fostered.
   o   A transparent, efficient, and effective innovation process is in place.

4. **Empowering Citizens:** The fourth responsibility involves using available methods to connect with and empower citizens to transform their knowledge, ideas, and solutions into better public services. This includes:
   o   Disseminating information through workshops, meetings, advertising, and visits to various locations to generate participatory and collaborative dialogue.
   o   Challenging the status quo and fostering an understanding of innovation.

- o   Sharing information that empowers citizens to be actively involved and creative.
- o   Developing applications for citizens to report issues.
- o   Collaborating with CIO teams to develop government platform systems that enable citizens to share their ideas, knowledge, and solutions.
- o   Encouraging researchers to engage with the government on social media and other platforms.

Case Study: Mark Sirangelo, CInO for Colorado

Mark Sirangelo, the Chief Innovation Officer for the state of Colorado, describes his role as "making connections" and "implementing fresh ideas that have the potential to transform government." By fostering collaboration and co-opting available skills, the government can avoid costly mistakes. During a recent flood disaster, Sirangelo emphasised the importance of bringing "all the resources to address that problem" to help citizens return to normal more quickly. He noted, "You can't stop a flood, but if you work together, you can do a much better job of responding and recovering." (Sirangelo, 2018)

The Distinction Between Chief Information Officer and Chief Innovation Officer

The Chief Information Officer (CIO) focuses on maintaining IT systems that serve government needs. The CIO is responsible for developing the IT vision for the country, managing IT architecture, data analysis, and IT security. They also ensure the integration of IT systems across public institutions, transforming public services to create transparency, efficiency, and cost-effectiveness.

In contrast, the Chief Innovation Officer (CInO) is responsible for driving holistic innovative change, using all available methods to connect with and empower citizens to participate in the economic and social development of the country.

Reasons for Having a Chief Innovation Officer

There is no need to replace the CIO with a CInO; both roles are equally important within government:

- In the 21st century, countries require an innovative approach to government policy-making.
- An innovative culture within government and across the country demands a driving force—a Chief Innovation Officer.

- Real innovation crosses departmental and ministerial boundaries; it requires interdepartmental cooperation.
- The CInO must have authority across the bureaucratic structure and engage with all segments of society.

The Necessity of a Chief Innovation Officer

It is clear that the Chief Innovation Officer is essential to the functioning of innovative governance. The CInO must be established at the highest level of governance to be effective.

Conversely, the CIO is responsible for the efficient and up-to-date functioning of the technology used to implement the innovation process. The CIO's responsibilities include:

- Maintaining government technology and updating it continuously.
- Keeping abreast of the latest software and hardware technologies.
- Developing and implementing new technological programs.
- Training public sector employees and citizens.
- Managing the technology budget.

Skills and Knowledge Required for the CInO Role

The demands of the CInO role are varied, and it is unlikely that a candidate will possess all the skills required. However, the following skills are prioritised as essential:

1. **Interpersonal Skills:** Building positive relationships with citizens and government stakeholders is critical. Communication skills are key for promoting innovation, motivating others, and fostering proactive participation. The CInO should have charisma, leadership qualities, and strong delegation, speaking, and listening skills.
2. **Lateral Thinking:** The ability to think laterally is essential for accurately resolving real problems and seeing beyond the immediate issue. The CInO must identify the underlying reasons for problems and outline clear objectives for procedures.
3. **Cultural Understanding:** The CInO must understand both bureaucratic culture and the diverse local cultures within the country.
4. **IT Knowledge:** While IT expertise is not required, a solid understanding of IT is necessary. The CInO will work closely with the CIO to address technical innovation issues.

5. **Financial Acumen:** A general understanding of financial affairs and budget strategy is important for ensuring the sustainability of innovation initiatives, with support from financial experts within government teams.
6. **Managerial Experience:** Demonstrated management experience is crucial for leading an effective innovation team and understanding other managers' concerns during the design and implementation of innovation projects.

Leveraging the CInO Role in Oman

The role of the Chief Innovation Officer can be leveraged in Oman to foster innovation, align with Vision 2040 goals, and address complex societal challenges through:

- **Informing Government**: Ensuring that policies are informed by accurate data and stakeholder input.
- **Facilitating Innovation Management**: Providing resources and training for innovation initiatives.
- **Facilitating Interface Functions**: Promoting collaboration and communication between government, citizens, and public organisations.
- **Empowering Citizens**: Enabling citizens to contribute to and benefit from innovation.

The CInO's contributions lead to enhanced policy implementation, increased efficiency, and greater citizen engagement, creating a more responsive and dynamic government.

Post Project Follow Up

Oman Vision 2040 has the long-term potential to drive transformative socio-economic development across the nation, with the support of the Implementation Follow-up Unit. This unit plays a crucial role in providing strategic plans and goal indicators for government entities, ensuring that their roles align with the overarching objectives of the Vision. A critical component of this process is the follow-up system, which is supported by an integrated dashboard serving as a key tool for successful implementation and monitoring.

The dashboard links key indicators of Oman Vision 2040 with operational and program-specific indicators across various sectors, allowing for a cohesive approach to achieving national targets. These indicators are regularly tracked and evaluated at different levels to ensure continuous progress and alignment with the Vision 2040 goals. By maintaining a rigorous system of monitoring and evaluation, Oman ensures that all sectors are contributing effectively to the Vision's objectives.

Citizen Participation in Vision 2040

The Oman Vision 2040 programme actively encourages citizen participation through calls for involvement in workshops, labs, and seminars. These initiatives provide valuable opportunities for citizens to contribute their ideas and experiences, helping to shape the country's future and achieve Vision 2040's ambitious goals. By fostering an inclusive approach to policy-making, the programme taps into the collective wisdom of the public, ensuring that development is both community-driven and representative of the needs and aspirations of society.

Governance Structure for Vision 2040 Initiatives

The governance structure for Oman Vision 2040 includes committees dedicated to managing national programmes and initiatives aimed at addressing challenges within various organisations. Challenges that cannot be resolved at the organisational level are escalated to the Council of Ministers, and if necessary, to higher authorities, including His Majesty the Sultan. This multi-tiered approach ensures that issues are addressed promptly and effectively, supporting the realisation of Vision 2040's objectives.

By integrating strategic planning, citizen engagement, and robust governance, Oman Vision 2040 represents a comprehensive framework for socio-economic transformation. It aligns the country's long-term ambitions with actionable programmes and measurable indicators, fostering a culture of collaboration, accountability, and progress towards a sustainable and prosperous future.

Figure 3. Post Project Follow Up

235

CONCLUSION

The concept of innovation in government seeks to unite all sections of society—government, commerce, and citizens—to achieve their common goals. By bringing together the diverse experiences, aspirations, and ideas of these stakeholders, government policies can be shaped to foster a more fruitful and inclusive society. This approach, often referred to as an "innovation ecosystem," provides a collaborative platform in which each part of society plays a critical role.

A Chief Innovation Officer (CInO) is central to the functioning of this innovation ecosystem. As the pivotal figure around which the ecosystem revolves, the CInO serves as a bridge between government administration and society. Positioned at the heart of government, the CInO is responsible for gathering the experiences, aspirations, and creativity of citizens and relaying them to policymakers. This flow of information informs and enriches the policy-making process, ensuring that government decisions are responsive to the needs of the population.

In addition to their role in communication, the CInO is instrumental in facilitating the implementation of government policies. By fostering collaboration across various segments of society, the CInO helps build an efficient and dynamic innovation ecosystem that is capable of adapting to challenges and promoting sustainable development. Through this holistic approach, innovation in government aims to create a unified society, where all voices are heard and collective goals are achieved.

REFERENCES

Bekkers, V. (2003). Reinventing government in the information age. International practice in IT-enabled public sector reform. *Public Management Review*, 5(1), 133–139. DOI: 10.1080/714042647

Colligan, P. (2019). *Transformative innovation in the public sector*.

Data Oman. (n.d.). *Data Oman*. Retrieved from https://data.gov.om/

Fung, A. (2015). Putting the Public Back into Governance: The Challenges of Citizen Participation and Its Future. *Public Administration Review*, 75(4), 513–522. DOI: 10.1111/puar.12361

Gulf News. (2020). *Winners of Arab Government Excellence Awards*. Retrieved from https://gulfnews.com/amp/uae/government/sheikh-mohammed-announces -winners-of-arab-government-excellence-awards-1.75492819

Innovation Oases. (n.d.). *Innovation Oases Portal*. Retrieved from https://www .innovationoases.com/InnovationOases/Apply?UDDI=MTc1NzRkMzMtZDc5ZC 00ZWIyLTgyYmEtOTA4OGZkNmVlMzQ1#

International Labour Organization (ILO). (n.d.). *Oman: Intellectual Property Statistics*. Retrieved from https://www.ilo.org/sites/default/files/wcmsp5/groups/ public/@asia/@ro-bangkok/@ilo-beijing/documents/publication/wcms_864806.pdf

Kattel, R., & Mazzucato, M. (2018). Mission-oriented innovation policy and dynamic capabilities in the public sector. *Industrial and Corporate Change*, 27(5), 787–801. DOI: 10.1093/icc/dty032

Mazzucato, M. (2018). *The entrepreneurial state: Debunking public vs. private sector myths*. Penguin Books.

Mergel, I. (2019). Digital service teams in government. *Government Information Quarterly*, 36(4), 101389. DOI: 10.1016/j.giq.2019.07.001

Ministry of Transport, Communications and Information Technology (MTCIT), Oman. (n.d.). *ITA Portal*. Retrieved from https://www.mtcit.gov.om/ITAPortal/ Pages/Page.aspx?NID=1371&PID=5439&LID=278

Mulgan, G. (2019). *Social innovation: How societies find the power to change*. Policy Press.

Muscat Daily. (2020). *698 Innovative Ideas Registered in Open Data Portal: Ministry of Manpower*. Retrieved from https://www.muscatdaily.com/2020/04/26/698 -innovative-ideas-registered-in-open-data-portal-mom/

National Day of Oman. (2020). *Oman Vision 2040 Preliminary Vision Document*. Retrieved from https://www.national-day-of-oman.info/wp-content/uploads/2020/ 11/OmanVision2040-Preliminary-Vision-Document.pdf

Nesta. (2016). *People-powered public services: A case study*. Retrieved from https:// www.nesta.org.uk/report/people-powered-public-services/

UNESCWA. (2024). *Public Key Infrastructure in Oman*. Retrieved from https:// opengov.unescwa.org/sites/default/files/inline-files/Om03-Public-Key-Infrast-En .pdf

World Bank. (2024). *Digital Development Overview*. Retrieved from https://www .worldbank.org/en/topic/digitaldevelopment/overview

World Bank Blogs. (2024. *Crystallizing a Digital Strategy: The Pearl of Arabia*. Retrieved from https://blogs.worldbank.org/en/digital-development/crystallizing -digital-strategy-pearl-arabia

World Intellectual Property Organization (WIPO). (2023). *Oman: Intellectual Property Statistics*. Retrieved from https://www.wipo.int/edocs/pubdocs/en/wipo -pub-2000-2023/om.pdf

ADDITIONAL READING

Ali, M. (2021). *Remote Work and Sustainable Changes for the Future of Global Business*. IGI Global. https://www.igi-global.com/book/remote-work-sustainable -changes-future/264375

Ali, M. (2022). *Future Role of Sustainable Innovative Technologies in Crisis Management*. IGI Global. https://www.igi-global.com/book/future-role-sustainable -innovative-technologies/281281

Ali, M. (2023). *Shifting Paradigms in the Rapidly Developing Global Digital Ecosystem: A GCC Perspective*. In Digital Entrepreneurship and Co-Creating Value Through Digital Encounters (pp. 145-166). IGI Global. https://www.igi-global.com/chapter/ shifting-paradigms-in-the-rapidly-developing-global-digital-ecosystem/323525

Ali, M. (2023). *Taxonomy of Industry 4.0 Technologies in Digital Entrepreneurship and Co-Creating Value*. In *Digital Entrepreneurship and Co-Creating Value Through Digital Encounters* (pp. 24–55). IGI Global., https://www.igi-global.com/chapter/taxonomy-of-industry-40-technologies-in-digital-entrepreneurship-and-co-creating-value/323520 DOI: 10.4018/978-1-6684-7416-7.ch002

Ali, M., & Wood-Harper, T. (2021). *Fostering Communication and Learning with Underutilized Technologies in Higher Education*. IGI Global. https://www.igi-global.com/book/fostering-communication-learning-underutilized-technologies/244593

Ali, M., Wood-Harper, T., & Kutar, M. (2023). Multi-Perspectives of Contemporary Digital Transformation Models of Complex Innovation Management. In *Digital Entrepreneurship and Co-Creating Value Through Digital Encounters* (pp. 79–96). IGI Global., https://www.igi-global.com/chapter/multi-perspectives-of-contemporary-digital-transformation-models-of-complex-innovation-management/323522 DOI: 10.4018/978-1-6684-7416-7.ch004

Ali, M. B. (2021). Internet of Things (IoT) to Foster Communication and Information Sharing: A Case of UK Higher Education. In Ali, M. B., & Wood-Harper, T. (Eds.), *Fostering Communication and Learning With Underutilized Technologies in Higher Education* (pp. 1–20). IGI Global., https://www.igi-global.com/chapter/internet-of-things-iot-to-foster-communication-and-information-sharing/262718/ DOI: 10.4018/978-1-7998-4846-2.ch001

Ali, M. B., & Wood-Harper, T. (2022). Artificial Intelligence (AI) as a Decision-Making Tool to Control Crisis Situations. In *Future Role of Sustainable Innovative Technologies in Crisis Management*. IGI Global., https://www.igi-global.com/chapter/artificial-intelligence-ai-as-a-decision-making-tool-to-control-crisis-situations/298931 DOI: 10.4018/978-1-7998-9815-3.ch006

Ali, M. B., Wood-Harper, T., & Ramlogan, R. (2020). A Framework Strategy to Overcome Trust Issues on Cloud Computing Adoption in Higher Education. In Modern Principles, Practices, and Algorithms for Cloud Security (pp. 162-183). IGI Global. https://www.igi-global.com/chapter/a-framework-strategy-to-overcome-trust-issues-on-cloud-computing-adoption-in-higher-education/238907/

Chapter 9
Enhancing Organizational Performance Through Process Performance Measurement and KPIs in AI–Based Digital Transformation

Gurwinder Kaur Dua

Post Graduate Government College - 11, Chandigarh, India

ABSTRACT

In an era featured by technological disruption and the pervasive integration of artificial intelligence (AI) into business processes, organizations come across strategic challenges in assessing their readiness for AI-based digital transformation. This study emphasizes on the necessary elements needed to analyse an organization's current state in preparation for AI-driven digital transformation. Drawing from a comprehensive literature review and practical insights derived from industrial system engineering experience, this study focuses on the relevance of process performance measurement and Key Performance Indicators (KPIs) in increasing organizational performance within the context of AI adoption. By establishing and monitoring relevant KPIs for process performance, organizations can quantifiably assess operational efficiency, identify areas for improvement, and track the effect of AI implementation on business processes.

DOI: 10.4018/979-8-3693-5966-2.ch009

1. INTRODUCTION

In the rapidly developing landscape of the modern world, artificial intelligence (AI) is not merely a tool; it provides as the catalyst for a profound revolution. This paper is witnessing the dawn of a new era where businesses are not just embrace to change but thriving in it. This marks the age of AI-driven metamorphosis, where what was once considered mundane transforms into the extraordinary, and the extraordinary becomes the new norm. In the global arena of enterprises, the relentless pursuit of innovation stands as a cornerstone objective propelling organizations to strive for competitive supremacy and deliver unparalleled value to their stakeholders.

Within this dynamic context, a transformative impetus develops – the seamless integration of artificial intelligence (AI) into the core of business operations. This convergence shows more than mere technological advancement; it embodies a fundamental shift known as AI-based digital transformation (Goła̧b-Andrzejak, 2023). This transformation reshapes the very fabric of how organizations function, make decisions, and engage with their stakeholders (Kim & Kim, 2022). Imagine a world where information is much important, where huge amounts of data help us see hidden patterns easily, and where difficult jobs are done automatically and really well. It is not just about using AI but it is like conducting a beautiful orchestra of ideas, making hard tasks easier, making customers really happy, and sparking lots of new ideas.

Digital transformation, on the other hand, includes integrating digital technologies into all facets of an organization, fundamentally altering how it operates and delivers value. This entails reimagining business models, processes, and services to harness the power of digital technologies like cloud computing, data analytics, the Internet of Things (IoT), and AI. AI-based digital transformation takes this concept a step further by focusing specifically on leveraging the full potential of AI technologies to instigate organizational change and achieve strategic objectives. It presents a strategic approach that harnesses the power of AI to drive organizational change, deliver transformative outcomes, and revolutionize how organizations operate, make decisions, and interact with customers, ultimately leading to enhanced productivity, agility, and innovation (Bogers et al., 2022; Gill et al., 2022)

By integrating AI technologies into business processes and systems, organizations can increase human capabilities, automate tasks, derive valuable insights from data, and make data-driven decisions. This empowerment enables organizations to streamline operations, increase efficiency, optimize resource allocation, and create personalized experiences for their customers (Ancillai, C. et al., 2023). Leveraging AI capabilities allows organizations to gain valuable insights from their data, automate repetitive tasks, and make more informed decisions, leading to improved operational efficiency, enhanced productivity, increased customer experiences, and the identification of new business opportunities (Jarrahi et al., 2023).

Successful AI-based digital transformation necessitates a holistic and strategic approach that considers various factors such as technological infrastructure, data management, talent acquisition, cultural readiness, ethical considerations, and change management (Rožman et al., 2023). With meticulous planning, the right tools and infrastructure, and strong leadership, organizations can embark on a transformative journey that propels them into the era of AI-driven innovation and competitive advantage. Nonetheless, achieving successful AI-based digital transformation requires careful consideration of strategy, data infrastructure, ethics, change management, partnerships, infrastructure scalability, and continuous evaluation (Raffey et al., 2022).

Implementing AI-based digital transformation comes with its challenges, requiring organizations to carefully plan and execute their transformation journeys to ensure success (Mihai et al., 2023; Perifanis et al., 2023). Main aspects to consider include technology infrastructure, data management, talent acquisition, cultural readiness, ethical considerations, and change management (Si et al., 2022; O'Callaghan, 2023). The integration of AI technologies demands a strategic and systematic approach consisting of multiple stakeholders across the organization (Khanom, 2023; Fan et al., 2022).

2. RESEARCH METHODOLOGY:

Research methodology of this study integrates a comprehensive literature review, involving a meticulous analysis of scholarly articles, research papers, and theoretical frameworks in the field of industrial system engineering. This review serves to contextualize our practical experiences within the broader theoretical landscape, enabling a critical evaluation of existing theories, identification of literature gaps, and establishment of connections between academic concepts and real-world applications. By integrating these two methodologies, our research offers a holistic understanding of industrial system engineering. The synergy between practical experience and theoretical knowledge enriches the depth and quality of our research findings, facilitating a nuanced exploration of the subject matter. This hybrid approach not only increases the credibility of our research but also ensures its practical relevance, making it a valuable contribution to both academic scholarship and industrial practice.

Our experience-driven methodology is not solely based on the authors' collective experiences but is also supported by their diverse and extensive professional backgrounds. These experiences span various geographical locations and cultural settings, providing a wealth of practical insights. This diverse experiential knowledge base was instrumental in identifying key elements in AI-based digital transformation, providing a multifaceted perspective that enriches our research. This study experiences were systematically reviewed and documented using a structured qualitative method, ensuring that subjective insights were rigorously evaluated.

Assessing an organization's current state for AI-based digital transformation is a complex undertaking that requires a systematic and multifaceted approach. This approach entails integrating a variety of methods and techniques tailored to the organization's specific context and objectives. By systematically including these methods and techniques, organizations can obtain a comprehensive view of their current state concerning AI adoption. In developing our comprehensive guidelines for evaluating an organization's readiness for AI-based digital transformation, we meticulously designed a framework comprising four essential components: current processes, existing systems, data landscape, and AI capabilities. Each component plays a crucial role in assessing an organization's preparedness for AI integration, ensuring a thorough and well-informed approach to digital transformation. This comprehensive understanding contributes as the basis for informed decision-making, strategic planning, and successful implementation of AI-based digital transformation initiatives. Establishing a baseline understanding of the organization's readiness for transformation is essential for effective planning and execution of AI strategies. This deeper exploration of the systematic approach encompasses a variety of methods and techniques related to the elements of the current state assessment.

Identifying opportunities for process automation is a crucial step in leveraging AI for digital transformation. By conducting a thorough analysis of current processes, organizations can pinpoint repetitive tasks that are time-consuming and error-prone, making them prime candidates for automation. The integration of AI can streamline these tasks, enhancing process efficiency. Furthermore, AI can be utilized for more intricate tasks like decision-making and pattern recognition, further boosting process effectiveness (Lacity et al., 2016)

This paper delves into a fundamental phase of AI-based digital transformation: examining an organization's existing state. The key objective of this research is to provide a systematic and comprehensive approach for assessing an organization's readiness for AI adoption. By thoroughly examining processes, current technology infrastructure, data management capabilities, and overall organizational preparedness for AI integration, this study aims to identify gaps and constraints that might impede the successful implementation of AI solutions. Special attention is given to evaluating data assets, data quality, and data accessibility, which are essential foundations for effective AI-based initiatives. The critical nature of this initial assessment cannot be overstated, as it not only sheds light on the organization's strengths and weaknesses but also serves as the cornerstone for developing a strategic roadmap and efficiently allocating resources. Through this precise evaluation, organizations can gain valuable insights into their technological infrastructure, data availability, organizational culture, talent pool, business processes, and regulatory considerations, enabling them to make informed decisions and embark on a successful AI-driven digital transformation journey. In addition to that this help assist in conducting a comprehensive assessment of an organization's readiness for AI integration by thoroughly examining processes, current technology infrastructure, data management capabilities, and overall organizational preparedness (Davenport, 2018). This assessment is crucial as it assists identify gaps and constraints that could hinder the successful implementation of AI solutions (Kitsios et al., 2021). Special emphasis is placed on evaluating data assets, data quality, and data accessibility, which are foundational for effective AI-based initiatives (Vidu et al., 2022).

The initial assessment plays a critical role as it not only reveals the organization's strengths and weaknesses but also acts as the cornerstone for developing a strategic roadmap and efficiently allocating resources (Cayirtepe et al., 2022). Through this precise evaluation, organizations can gain valuable insights into various aspects such as technological infrastructure, data availability, organizational culture, talent pool, business processes, and regulatory considerations. Armed with this knowledge, organizations can make informed decisions, paving the way for a successful AI-driven digital transformation journey (Ross, 2018)

Recognizing the lack of a structured and holistic approach in the existing literature for assessing an organization's current status for AI-based digital transformation, this research aims to fill this gap by evolving a methodologically robust and comprehensive framework. By providing a definitive methodology, this paper bridges the existing void in scholarly discourse and offers practitioners and researchers a clear guide for conducting this critical assessment effectively.

The tailored framework presented in this paper offers specific methods for evaluating processes, existing systems, data landscapes, and internal AI capabilities, going beyond generic guidelines to address organizational intricacies. By considering factors such as system compatibility and human expertise, this systematic methodology equips practitioners to identify challenges and leverage strengths effectively. This framework contributes as a guiding light in AI-based digital transformation, empowering organizations to navigate modern technological integration confidently and efficiently.

By providing a structured and holistic approach, this research contributes not only to academic knowledge but also to practical advancements, enabling organizations to embrace AI technologies with confidence and efficacy. The assessment of current processes, as outlined in the study, involves thorough documentation to visualize operational activities, identify inefficiencies, and pinpoint areas for automation or improvement using AI technologies. This documentation is crucial for regulatory compliance, business process re-engineering, and ensuring the accuracy and richness of data reflecting business processes (Jaheer Mukthar, 2022).

2.1 Current Processes

Current processes are basically how a business does its everyday tasks. To use AI effectively, we need to really understand how things work right now. A study mentioned in shows that knowing the details of how a business operates and finding places where AI can help are key to making things run smoother. Understanding current processes involves a few steps:

Documenting Processes:

First, we need to write down exactly how things are done currently. This could be by making a map or drawing a diagram that shows each step, which is responsible for what, the decisions made, and the tools or systems used. This assists us spot where things might be slowing down or not working well, and where we could make improvements or use AI to automate tasks. It is just like making a recipe for how the business works.

Understanding these processes also helps with things like following rules and regulations and figuring out how to make things work better. And, if we want to change how things are done to make them more efficient or effective, having a clear picture of how they work now is really important. So, how well AI tools can assist us depends a lot on how good the information about our current processes is.

Process Performance Measurement:

Process Performance Measurement is a significant aspect of examining the effectiveness of current processes within an organization. To accurately gauge performance, it is necessary to establish Key Performance Indicators (KPIs) for each process, encompassing metrics such as processing time, error rate, cost, and customer satisfaction. Continuously tracking these metrics over time provides a baseline for performance and highlights areas where AI implementation could enhance value (Melville et al., 2018). By identifying and monitoring KPIs for individual processes, organizations can quantifiably assess operational performance and quality, pinpointing inefficiencies, bottlenecks, or underperformance that could benefit from automation, optimization, or redesign. In addition to that, this forms the basis for comparing the outcomes post-implementation of AI solutions, enabling the quantification of benefits derived from digital transformation in operational terms (Jeston, 2018).

Different metrics can be employed for process performance measurement, including cycle time, error rate, cost per transaction, process velocity, and customer satisfaction. Businesses are increasingly utilizing AI and data analytics tools for real-time monitoring and analysis of process performance (Van Der Aalst et al., 2020). It is crucial to select relevant and balanced metrics to prevent unintended consequences; for example, an excessive focus on speed may compromise quality. Therefore, organizations must choose metrics that offer a well-rounded view of process performance (Wamba-Taguimdje et al., 2020).

Defining Process KPIs:

Defining process KPIs is integral to performance measurement and management, assisting organizations in tracking their progress over time and aligning with strategic goals. Understanding the process and defining its purpose are initial steps, requiring a clear comprehension of the process, its objectives, and its contribution to overall business goals (Bititci, 2004). The objective of KPIs should be explicit, whether aimed at increasing efficiency, enhancing quality, reducing costs, or improving customer satisfaction, aligning with the organization's strategic objectives (Parmenter, 2015; Bititci et al., 2004).

Identifying relevant metrics and KPIs that align with organizational objectives is necessary for effective performance evaluation. These metrics can be quantitative (e.g., processing time, cost, error rate) or qualitative (e.g., customer satisfaction) and should adhere to the SMART criteria—specific, measurable, attainable, relevant, and time-bound (Bisbe et al., 2018). Setting challenging yet attainable targets for each KPI serves as a benchmark for assessing process performance (Parmenter, 2015). Regular review and communication of KPIs ensure their relevance and alignment with developing business objectives, facilitating adjustments if targets are consistently missed or met (Bisbe et al., 2018; Parmenter, 2015)

Continuous monitoring and updating of process performance metrics are important to reflect changes in the business environment, organizational objectives, or process redesign. This ongoing evaluation ensures that performance measurement remains aligned with the organization's developing needs and goals.

With meticulous planning, appropriate tools and infrastructure, and effective leadership, organizations can embark on a transformative journey that propels them into the era of AI-driven innovation and competitive advantage. Nonetheless, successful AI-based digital transformation necessitates a thorough consideration of strategy, data infrastructure, talent, ethics, change management, partnerships, infrastructure scalability, and continuous evaluation. Implementing AI-based digital transformation comes with its challenges, requiring organizations to carefully plan and execute their transformation journeys to ensure success. Main aspects to consider include technology infrastructure, data management, talent acquisition, cultural readiness, ethical considerations, and change management. The integration of AI technologies demands a strategic and systematic approach involving multiple stakeholders across the organization.

The importance of this initial assessment cannot be overstated as it not only reveals the organization's strengths and weaknesses but also acts as the cornerstone for developing a strategic roadmap and efficiently allocating resources. Through this detailed analysis, organizations can gain valuable insights into their technological infrastructure, data availability, organizational culture, talent pool, business processes, and regulatory considerations. Armed with this knowledge, organizations can make informed decisions, enabling them to embark on a successful AI-driven digital transformation journey.

To embark on the journey of business process automation, organizations can follow a following structured approach:

1. **Identify the Process and Define the Goals:** Begin by identifying processes suitable for automation, focusing on those that are repetitive, error-prone, time-consuming, or critical for compliance (Hammer, 2009). Automating such processes can alleviate mundane tasks for employees, leading to increased productivity and efficiency. Clearly define the goals of automation, like enhancing efficiency, reducing errors, or improving customer satisfaction (Fischer, 2018)

2. **Process Mapping:** Document the existing process comprehensively, detailing each stage, involved stakeholders, and tools utilized. This mapping contributes a holistic view of the current process, facilitating the identification of areas for enhancement (Dumas et al., 2018).

3. **Identify Automation Opportunities and Choose the Right Tools:** After mapping the process, pinpoint segments that can be automated. Select automation tools based on the complexity of the process and organizational requirements (Ramaswamy et., 2018). Tools range from simple task automation software to more advanced solutions such as business process management (BPM) tools (Lee et al., 2013).

4. **Design, Development, and Testing of the Automated Process:** Remaking the process incorporating automation tools, ensuring provisions for exceptions and error handling. Develop a clear process flow diagram for easy understanding. Subsequently, build and test the automated process, involving IT professionals or consultants to ensure proper functionality (Fingar, 2003; Lacity et al., 2018).

5. **Training:** Before full execution, provide training to all involved parties on how the automated process functions, their roles, interaction with the automation tool, exception management, and escalation procedures in case of issues (Alavi et al., 2001).

6. **Implementation, Monitoring, and Continuous Improvement:** Gradually roll out the automated process after successful testing, starting with a pilot phase. Monitor the performance of the automated process to ensure alignment with intended objectives. Utilize data from the process to identify areas for enhancement and continuously refine the process as needed (Davenport et al., 2018; Power, 2017).

While evaluating process automation opportunities, organizations should consider factors like process complexity, frequency, volume, cost, return on investment, and impact on customer service or other business functions. Not all processes are suitable for automation, especially those requiring human judgment or complex decision-making. Therefore, the assessment of automation opportunities should align with organizational objectives and values, focusing not only on efficiency gains but also on strategic fit (Willcocks et al., 2017; Schwartz, 2019).

This evaluation necessitates a cross-disciplinary approach that integrates technical proficiency, business insight, and strategic foresight. Furthermore, with the advancement of AI technologies and their increasing capabilities, the potential for automation is expected to grow, reinforcing the need for ongoing reassessment of automation opportunities throughout the digital transformation journey.

Regarding AI Alignment:

The assessment of current processes should also consider their alignment with potential AI capabilities. Tasks that involve handling large datasets or necessitate real-time decision-making can significantly benefit from AI integration. This step requires a deep understanding of both the business operations and the potential applications of AI (Brynjolfsson et al., 2014). AI alignment is a crucial element of AI-driven digital transformation that requires meticulous planning and attention. It involves aligning AI initiatives with the organization's strategic objectives and core values (Kim et al., 2020). A successful digital transformation goes beyond just implementing advanced technologies; it includes leveraging these technologies to achieve business objectives and generate value (Brynjolfsson et al., 2018). Therefore, analysing the alignment of AI initiatives with the business strategy is essential to ensure purposeful and effective AI adoption.

AI alignment encompasses several key dimensions essential for successful AI integration within an organization. Strategic alignment is paramount, as AI initiatives must align with the organization's strategic goals to effectively contribute to their attainment. For example, in an organization focusing on increasing customer service, this alignment may involve the implementation of AI-powered chatbots or customer analytics systems (Nguyen et al., 2020). Cultural alignment is equally significant, reinforcing those AI initiatives should resonate with the organization's culture and values. This aspect highlights the importance of considering ethical implications, transparency, and the impact on employees. Operational alignment ensures that AI initiatives harmonize with the organization's operational requirements and work-flows, necessitating seamless integration of AI systems into existing processes and ensuring the availability of the necessary infrastructure and skills to support these systems (Du et al., 2021). Each of these dimensions plays a pivotal role in the successful adoption and combination of AI within an organization.

Assessing AI alignment is an ongoing process that should evolve as business strategies, technologies, and market conditions change. In addition to that, AI alignment is not solely the responsibility of the IT department but should involve all key stakeholders, consisting of business leaders, employees, and even customers (Kim et al., 2020). Prioritizing AI alignment throughout the digital transformation journey enables organizations to maximize the value and impact of AI technologies while ensuring ethical, responsible, and successful implementation.

2.2. Current Tech Setup:

Looking at the technology a company already has is super important to see if it's ready for AI. This helps figure out what changes might be needed in the computer stuff and helps pick the right AI tools. It's like checking out the base of what's already there—like what computers and software are being used, how data is stored, and how it's processed. In addition to that, while evaluating existing systems, it is significant to assess an organization's technological readiness for AI deployment (Raguseo, 2018). This assessment helps identify necessary changes in the IT infrastructure and guides the strategic selection of AI tools and technologies, forming the basis for understanding the current technology landscape encompassing hardware, software, data storage, and processing systems. After identifying all systems within the organization, the subsequent step involves categorization. Grouping the systems and processes into functional categories like customer management, finance, supply chain, operations, HR, marketing, and sales is crucial for pinpointing areas where AI can have the most significant impact. Following this categorization, it is essential to assess each system's suitability for AI integration. Factors to consider include data availability, system architecture, scalability, flexibility, and compatibility with AI technologies.

Engaging with users and stakeholders to identify pain points and inefficiencies is a vital part of this process. Their insights are invaluable for understanding how AI can acknowledge existing issues and enhance system performance. Simultaneously, evaluating the technical readiness for AI integration is necessary. This evaluation should stress on the system architecture, data format compatibility, and integration capabilities with AI frameworks and tools to determine if system modifications or upgrades are necessary.

System Identification:

The initial step towards AI-based digital transformation is identifying all existing systems within the organization. This comprehensive list should include everything from customer relationship management (CRM) and enterprise resource planning (ERP) systems to specialized tools for inventory management, payroll, or content management. It is also significant to consider informal and legacy systems that are still in operation.

Subsequently, categorize the systems and processes into functional categories such as customer management, finance, supply chain, operations, HR, marketing, and sales. This categorization is significant for identifying areas where AI can make a positive impact. After categorization, evaluate each system's suitability for AI integration, considering factors like data availability, system architecture, scalability, flexibility, and compatibility with AI technologies.

Assessing the scalability and interoperability of the systems is also necessary. Determine if the systems can accommodate increased demands from AI integration and scale appropriately to meet evolving AI needs. Examine the systems' ability to communicate and exchange data with each other by examining existing APIs, connectors, or frameworks that facilitate integration.

Lastly, develop an implementation roadmap outlining the sequence and timeline for AI integration, including necessary steps, required resources, and milestones. Consider dependencies between systems and prioritize initiatives based on these factors. It is significant to view system identification as an ongoing process in the AI transformation journey, continuously refining the process based on insights gained from implementation and feedback.

Functional Analysis:

Conduct a detailed functional analysis for each system, understanding its purpose, users, handled data, and interactions with other systems. This analysis includes evaluating various functional areas within the organization to identify opportunities for AI integration and transformation. When enhancing different functional areas through AI, it is essential to consider aspects such as customer experience, analyzing customer-facing processes and touch points to identify opportunities for AI-driven enhancements like personalized recommendations, chatbots for customer support, sentiment analysis, and predictive modelling to enhance satisfaction and engagement. In sales, marketing, and supply chain realms, evaluate processes to determine where AI can increase lead generation, customer segmentation, targeting, and campaign optimization.

Predictive modeling plays significant role in enhancing satisfaction and engagement. In the domains of sales, marketing, and supply chain, it is necessary to assess processes to identify areas where AI can enhance lead generation, customer segmentation, targeting, and campaign optimization. AI's impact extends to pricing optimization, demand forecasting, customer behavior analysis, and recommendation engines to drive sales growth. Moreover, in supply chain management, AI can streamline operations, improve forecasting accuracy, optimize inventory management, and enhance production planning, with applications in predictive maintenance and operational efficiency monitoring. Examining data and analytics processes for strategic decision-making is vital to establish a robust AI foundation, focusing on data governance, quality, integration, and infrastructure. AI's utility in data discovery, cleansing, advanced analytics, and supporting data-driven decision-making through predictive analytics, scenario modeling, and intelligent decision support systems is also significant. Additionally, in quality assurance and testing, identifying opportunities for AI integration is crucial, with applications in automated testing, anomaly detection, and quality control to enhance product or service quality, reduce defects, and improve testing efficiency, thereby facilitating continuous improvement and optimization efforts across all functional areas.

Technical Analysis:

Conducting a technical evaluation of the system is a critical step in assessing an organization's readiness for AI implementation. This analysis includes examining system architecture, compatibility, scalability, security, and performance. It also involves evaluating the systems' age and their ability to support newer technologies, including AI. This evaluation can be further divided into two main areas: hardware capabilities and the software environment, and network infrastructure and integration capabilities.

Regarding hardware capabilities and the software environment, it is significant to assess the organization's available computing power and hardware infrastructure. This examination should determine if the existing hardware can meet the computational demands of AI algorithms and models, considering factors like processing speed, memory capacity, and parallel processing capabilities. Additionally, reviewing the current software environment and tools is essential to identify if the organization has the necessary software and development frameworks to support AI initiatives. Compatibility with popular AI platforms, libraries, and frameworks should also be considered.

Analysing the network infrastructure is another critical aspect, including examining bandwidth capacity and latency to ensure the organization's network can handle the increased data traffic from AI applications. Assessing the need for network upgrades or optimizations is essential for smooth data transfer and communication between AI systems and data sources. In addition to that, evaluating how well the organization's existing technology infrastructure integrates with AI systems and tools is vital, including assessing any limitations or challenges in integrating AI solutions with current systems, databases, and applications to ensure compatibility with APIs, data formats, and protocols for seamless data exchange.

Data Evaluation:

Given AI's reliance on data, it is necessary to closely examine the type and quality of data handled by each system. Evaluate the data structure, quality, availability, and relevance for potential AI use cases. This analysis can be expanded by assessing data processing capabilities and storage architecture, considering the organization's infrastructure's ability to handle large-scale data processing, parallel processing, and distributed computing. Assess whether the organization's storage architecture supports efficient data retrieval and processing, including scalability, performance, and data access, to handle the volume, variety, and velocity of data required for AI applications.

Assessing the organization's infrastructure for compatibility with legacy systems and third-party applications that may interact with AI solutions is crucial. Evaluate any limitations or constraints in integrating AI with the existing technology stack. In addition to that, evaluate the organization's real-time processing capabilities to determine if the infrastructure supports real-time data processing and analytics. Assess if the necessary components, such as stream processing frameworks or event-driven architectures, are in place for real-time decision-making and AI-driven insights. Consider the ability to handle high-velocity data streams for real-time AI applications.

In addition to that, evaluate the availability and reliability of the infrastructure to ensure it can deliver the required uptime for critical AI-driven processes. Assess if the organization has redundant systems, failover mechanisms, or load balancing capabilities for high availability. Evaluate whether the organization has the automation and orchestration capabilities to efficiently manage AI workflows and processes. Consider tools or platforms that enable workflow automation, job scheduling, and resource provisioning for AI tasks, ensuring streamlined deployment and management of AI models and algorithms.

Vendors Evaluation:

While evaluating vendors for AI-based digital transformation, review the terms of relationships with external vendors. Assess the level of vendor support, maintenance, and potential integration with new AI technologies. Utilize enterprise architecture software to document and visualize the existing system landscape for identifying gaps and opportunities for improvement. Overcoming challenges such as resistance from staff accustomed to legacy systems needs a systematic approach and stakeholder involvement.

In the vendor evaluation process, ensure alignment with the organization's specific needs and long-term objectives. Clearly outline requirements, objectives, desired outcomes, and key performance indicators (KPIs) for each vendor. Evaluate the technological capabilities, breadth, and depth of AI solutions, scalability, performance, compatibility with existing infrastructure, and support for use cases. Consider the vendor's AI expertise, experience, integration capabilities with existing systems, customization abilities, and scalability to meet evolving demands of AI initiatives. Scrutinize implementation and support services, project management approach, training, onboarding programs, ongoing technical support, documentation, user training, and post-implementation support. Analyse the vendor's methodology for AI model development and deployment, including model training, validation, deployment practices, explain ability, interpretability, and ethical considerations. Assess scalability, infrastructure capacity, cloud integration capabilities, and vision for future AI advancements to support long-term growth.

Vendor support for change management and organizational readiness plays a crucial role in the successful adoption of AI solutions. Analyse the vendor's processes and capabilities in guiding the organization through change management strategies, organizational restructuring, and cultural adaptation. Post-implementation support services, including technical support, service-level agreements, and timely issue resolution, are essential for sustained success.

Conduct a comprehensive risk assessment to evaluate potential risks associated with each vendor, such as stability, financial health, data security, and privacy assurances. Confirm compliance with industry regulations and standards, and implement proper risk mitigation measures. Consider the total cost of ownership (TCO) as a decisive factor by assessing all costs, consisting of initial implementation, ongoing maintenance, licensing, and scaling or customization. A thorough cost-benefit analysis ensures that the vendor's solutions align with the organization's budget constraints and offer a favourable return on investment (ROI).

2.3. Data Picture:

Data is really important for AI to work. Knowing what kind of data we have, how we keep it safe, and how we use it to make decisions is a big part of figuring out where we stand right now. It's significant to make sure the data is good quality, and this study is following rules about how it is used and kept safe. Checking out a company's data setup involves looking at a bunch of different things, like how the data is organized and protected.

Data Quality:

Data quality is a foundational aspect to AI success, as data serves as the lifeblood of AI systems. Assess data accuracy, integrity, timeliness, completeness, relevancy, and consistency to avoid incorrect conclusions or faulty machine learning models (Aldoseri et al., 2023). Implement robust data governance practices, define ownership and responsibilities, establish data quality standards, and utilize data cleaning and pre processing techniques to address quality issues. Ensure data used for AI models is representative, unbiased, and relevant, and establish key performance indicators (KPIs) to measure data quality (Aldoseri et al., 2024).

Data Accessibility:

Data accessibility is equally significant, as good-quality data must be readily available to users. Evaluate the prevailing data architecture, storage locations, and access methods to effectively leverage data assets for AI initiatives (Informatic Data Quality, 2023). Conduct an inventory of data assets, document metadata, and establish data accessibility governance processes to ensure compliance with data policies and regulations. Regularly monitor data access patterns, review access privileges, and update data accessibility policies to maintain data quality and accessibility (Talend Data Quality 2023).

Regularly monitoring data access patterns, reviewing access privileges, and updating data accessibility policies as necessary is significant. It is necessary to maintain comprehensive documentation of data assets, including their source, transformation processes, and usage history. Documenting data lineage to track the origin and transformations applied to data ensures transparency and enables users to understand the data's context and reliability. Additionally, ensuring that data accessibility platforms and infrastructure can meet the performance and scalability requirements of AI-based digital transformation is vital. Analysing system performance, response times, and scalability under various data access scenarios and scaling resources accordingly to accommodate increasing data accessibility demands is necessary (Li et al., 2022).

Data Governance:

Data governance is essential for AI-based digital transformation initiatives to ensure the availability, integrity, and privacy of data. Implementing data governance in AI-based digital transformation requires a multifaceted approach to managing data throughout its lifecycle. Establishing a robust data governance framework that outlines policies, processes, roles, and responsibilities is the first step. This framework should explain data governance objectives, assign data stewardship roles, and establish cross-functional data governance committees to oversee data-related activities. Clarity in data ownership and accountability is crucial for assigning specific individuals or teams within the organization the responsibility for data management (Collibra Data Governance, 2023). Data stewards play a key role in ensuring data quality, integrity, and compliance. Encouraging organization-wide recognition of the value and importance of data is essential to foster a culture of accountability for data management (Axon Data Governace, 2023).

Regular audits and reviews are necessary to maintain and enhance the data governance process. These analyses should assess compliance with established data governance practices, evaluate their effectiveness, and identify areas for improvement. Insights from these audits should inform the refinement of data governance processes and be applied to AI models and algorithms. Establishing guidelines for AI model development, training data selection, model validation, and ongoing monitoring to ensure ethical considerations and interpretability requirements are met while maintaining transparency and thorough documentation throughout the process is crucial. Defining specific metrics to measure the effectiveness of data governance initiatives, establishing key performance indicators (KPIs), and evolving a regular reporting framework to ensure clear visibility of governance activities and their progress towards set objectives are important aspects of data governance. Recognizing data governance as a change management initiative that requires clear communication of its importance to all stakeholders, fostering a data-driven culture throughout the organization, providing training and support to employees, and addressing resistance to change by continuously communicating the benefits and positive impacts of a strong data governance strategy are essential for successful implementation.

AI models and deep learning algorithms require significant computational resources to handle extensive datasets, directing to a growing reliance on specialized hardware like GPUs and TPUs designed to accelerate AI training and inference. In addition to hardware solutions, there is a push towards developing new techniques such as model compression, cleaning, and quantization to enhance the efficiency of AI processing.

Data Volume and Variety:

Effective data management is significant when dealing with large volumes of data. AI systems must implement robust strategies for tasks such as data cleaning, pre-processing, labelling, and organization. Innovative approaches such as active learning, weak supervision, and transfer learning are being explored to simplify the labour-intensive process of data labelling.

Data heterogeneity poses another challenge, as large datasets often contain data from various sources with differing formats and structures, complicating integration and reconciliation efforts. With enhancing data volume, privacy and security concerns escalate, heightening the risk of breaches and exposure, particularly concerning sensitive information. Addressing these privacy and security issues becomes increasingly crucial as data quantities grow.

Despite the presence of massive datasets, issues of bias and representativeness persist. Large data volumes can still harbour demographic, cultural, or other biases, potentially impacting the accuracy of AI models. In addition to that, data access can be a significant obstacle, with organizations sometimes hindered from utilizing their extensive datasets due to legal or regulatory constraints. Ensuring appropriate permissions and licenses for data access and utilization is a complex aspect that organizations must navigate carefully.

In the context of AI-based digital transformation, organizations must address the crucial elements of data volume and variety. A scalable infrastructure is essential for managing the volume and variety of data required for AI initiatives. Cloud-based solutions offer flexibility and scalability, advantageous for adapting to growing data needs. Technologies such as distributed storage systems and parallel processing frameworks are critical for efficiently handling large data volumes (Mahalle et al., 2023).

Organizations need to evaluate their data storage and management capabilities to ensure they can handle the increased volume and variety of data. Implementing data management systems capable of handling various data types, including structured, unstructured, and semi-structured data, are necessary (Gandomi et al., 2015). Centralized storage solutions such as data lakes or data warehouses can aid in efficient data retrieval and storage. Big data processing frameworks and analytics tools, such as Apache Hadoop and Apache Spark, enable the parallel processing and analysis of large datasets, extracting valuable insights from diverse data sources.

Automating data preparation processes is essential given the volume and diversity of data (Almeida et al., 2019). Data preparation tools and technologies streamline data ingestion, cleansing, and transformation, reducing manual efforts and ensuring consistency in data preparation (Marchand et al., 2018). Continuous monitoring of data volume and variety is crucial to ensure that an organization's infrastructure and processes can meet developing requirements. Implementing monitoring mechanisms to detect shifts in data volume, variety, or data source patterns is necessary (Kelleher et al., 2015). Organizations must regularly assess and embrace their data management strategies to align with their AI objectives effectively (Floridi et al., 2018).

For successful implementation of data governance in AI-based digital transformation, organizations must have a deep understanding of the various elements of the data landscape. This understanding is vital for assessing data readiness for AI, identifying gaps, and devising strategies to address them (Marr, 2019). Defining clear goals for data usage in AI transformations and aligning data usage with strategic objectives ensures a focused and relevant application (Davenport, 2013).

Reinforcing a culture of data-driven decision-making within an organization is paramount. Encouraging stakeholders to rely on data and insights from AI models not only builds trust in data and AI processes but also requires identifying pertinent data sources. It's significant for organizations to assess both internal and external data sources, encompassing structured and unstructured data, to ensure their effective contribution to AI outcomes (Xiong et al., 2019).

Feature engineering plays a critical role in converting raw data into meaningful features that enhance AI model performance. This includes applying domain knowledge and data analytics techniques to select and transform the most informative attributes. Ethical considerations in data usage are of utmost importance, necessitating adherence to privacy regulations and data protection policies through techniques like anonymization and encryption throughout the AI lifecycle (Phua et al., 2010).

Measuring ROI and value from data usage in AI initiatives is essential, including the establishment of KPIs reflecting the organization's goals and tracking the impact of data-driven initiatives. Predictive and prescriptive analytics contributes as powerful tools for leveraging data, enabling organizations to forecast future trends and behaviours and provide recommendations for optimizing business processes.

Personalization significantly enhances customer experience by leveraging customer data to create tailored recommendations, targeted marketing, and customized offerings. Data also plays a significant role in risk management and fraud detection, where AI models can identify potential risks or fraudulent patterns, with real-time monitoring systems in place to proactively address these issues (Zhu et al., 2020).

Continuous improvement and learning from data are necessary. Organizations should establish feedback mechanisms to refine AI models and strategies continuously, allowing for learning and adaptation to new data and business requirements.

2.4. AI Capabilities:

Assessing an organization's AI capabilities, including existing initiatives, skills, tools, and infrastructure, is important for embarking on AI-based digital transformation (Davenport et al., 2020). Understanding past and ongoing AI projects provides critical insights into the organization's experience with AI technologies and highlights recurring issues or challenges faced. Aligning these initiatives with the organization's overall AI strategy and analysing their impact on operational efficiency, customer experience, or innovation is crucial.

In the domain of data use and model development, analyzing how data are utilized in current AI initiatives and assessing the effectiveness of data pre processing, feature engineering, and model development processes are essential. Evaluating the effect and value generated by existing AI initiatives, as well as mechanisms for continuous improvement and learning, ensures that organizations are well-prepared to leverage AI effectively (Holmstrom, 2022).

Skills and Expertise:

Assessing skills and expertise within the organization is fundamental for AI-based digital transformation, involving identifying current skills, conducting skill gap analyses, and evaluating the need for external expertise. Similarly, analysing the organization's AI infrastructure, including data storage, computing power, and AI tools, is critical for supporting AI projects effectively (Davenport et al., 2018).

Culture and Leadership:

Culture and leadership also play a pivotal role in AI integration, with supportive leadership and a culture that values openness, collaboration, and innovation being main drivers of success. Leadership buy-in and support, coupled with strategies for change management and fostering a learning culture, are essential for successful AI-driven transformation.

By systematically assessing these dimensions, organizations can gain profound insights into their readiness for AI integration and lay a solid foundation for successful AI-based digital transformation endeavours.

CONCLUSION:

In conclusion, this research has systematically analysed into the essential assessment elements significant for effectively integrating AI technologies into organizational settings. The study has contributed a comprehensive framework aimed at guiding organizations in their AI-based digital transformation initiatives. These elements not only stem from established theories but also highlight their practical implications. Through meticulous assessments, organizations can gain profound insights into their current strengths and areas requiring improvement.

Recognizing the inherent limitations in research, such as contextual variations and the rapid evolution of AI technologies, our work lays a robust foundation for future academic exploration and practical applications. As the landscape of AI-based technologies continues to evolve, our research identifies key areas for further investigation, involving specific industry applications, the influence of cultural and regulatory factors, and the development of adaptive frameworks to meet dynamic organizational needs. Organizations are encouraged to embrace our guidelines as a starting point for their AI-based digital transformation endeavours, emphasizing the critical role of feedback mechanisms and continuous improvement strategies. By fostering a culture of iterative learning and adaptation, organizations can ensure the ongoing relevance and effectiveness of their AI integration efforts. In academia, scholars are urged to delve deeper into the intricate intersections of AI technology and organizational dynamics.

It is significant to show the significant role of AI technologies in shaping the future of organizations through our comprehensive framework, which illuminates the pathway for integrating AI into the organizational fabric while balancing academic rigor with practical implementation requirements. Nonetheless, we acknowledge that incorporating experiential insights, though valuable for capturing real-world complexities, introduces a subjective aspect to our research. This subjectivity serves as a limitation of the current study, indicating the qualitative nature of experience-driven research. In addition to that, while our findings offer actionable guidelines, they are inherently influenced by the specific contexts from which our experiences originate. This reinforces the need for future research to validate and expand upon these findings across diverse contexts and critically evaluate the transferability of our framework to various organizational environments.

REFERENCES

Alavi, M., & Leidner, D. E. (2001). Knowledge management and knowledge management systems: Conceptual foundations and research issues. *Management Information Systems Quarterly*, 25(1), 107–136. DOI: 10.2307/3250961

Aldoseri, A., Al-Khalifa, K. N., & Hamouda, A. M. (2023). Re-thinking data strategy and integration for artificial intelligence: Concepts, opportunities, and challenges. *Applied Sciences (Basel, Switzerland)*, 13(12), 7082. DOI: 10.3390/app13127082

Aldoseri, A., Al-Khalifa, K. N., & Hamouda, A. M. (2024). Methodological Approach to Assessing the Current State of Organizations for AI-Based Digital Transformation. *Applied System Innovation*, 7(1), 14. DOI: 10.3390/asi7010014

Almeida, F., Bacao, F., & Santos, M. F. (2019). Data-driven innovation: Concepts, approaches, and empirical evidence. *Information Systems Management*, 36, 99–114.

Ancillai, C., Sabatini, A., Gatti, M., & Perna, A. (2023). Digital technology and business model innovation: A systematic literature review and future research agenda. *Technological Forecasting and Social Change*, 188, 122307. DOI: 10.1016/j.techfore.2022.122307

AXON DATA GOVERNANCE. Available online: https://www.informatica.com/gb/products/dataquality/axon-data%20governance.html (accessed on 15 October 2023).

Bisbe, J., & Malagueño, R. (2018). How to design a successful KPI system. *MIT Sloan Management Review*, 59, 45–51.

Bititci, U. S., Martinez, V., Albores, P., & Parung, J. (2004). Creating and managing value in collaborative networks. *International Journal of Physical Distribution & Logistics Management*, 34(3/4), 251–268. DOI: 10.1108/09600030410533574

Bogers, M. L., Garud, R., Thomas, L. D., Tuertscher, P., & Yoo, Y. (2022). Digital innovation: Transforming research and practice. *Innovation (North Sydney, N.S.W.)*, 24(1), 4–12. DOI: 10.1080/14479338.2021.2005465

Brynjolfsson, E., & McAfee, A. (2014). *The second machine age: Work, progress, and prosperity in a time of brilliant technologies*. WW Norton & Company.

Cayirtepe, Z., & Senel, F. C. (2022). The future of quality and accreditation surveys: Digital transformation and artificial intelligence. *International Journal for Quality in Health Care : Journal of the International Society for Quality in Health Care*, 34(2), mzac025. DOI: 10.1093/intqhc/mzac025 PMID: 35388400

Collibra Data Governance. Available online: https://www.collibra.com/us/en/products/datagovernance (accessed on 15 October 2023).

Davenport, T., Guha, A., Grewal, D., & Bressgott, T. (2020). How artificial intelligence will change the future of marketing. *Journal of the Academy of Marketing Science*, 48(1), 24–42. DOI: 10.1007/s11747-019-00696-0

Davenport, T. H. (1993). *Process innovation: reengineering work through information technology*. Harvard Business Press.

Davenport, T. H. (2018). *The AI advantage: How to put the artificial intelligence revolution to work*. mit Press.

Davenport, T. H., & Ronanki, R. (2018). Artificial intelligence for the real world. *Harvard Business Review*, 96(1), 108–116.

Davenport, T. H., & Short, J. E. (1998). The new industrial engineering: Information technology and business process redesign. *IEEE Engineering Management Review*, 26(3), 46–60.

Du, S., & Xie, C. (2021). Paradoxes of artificial intelligence in consumer markets: Ethical challenges and opportunities. *Journal of Business Research*, 129, 961–974. DOI: 10.1016/j.jbusres.2020.08.024

Dumas, M., Rosa, L. M., Mendling, J., & Reijers, A. H. (2018). *Fundamentals of business process management*. Springer-Verlag. DOI: 10.1007/978-3-662-56509-4

Fingar, P. (2003). *Business process management: the third wave*. Meghan-Kiffer Press.

Fischer, T. (2018). *Robotic Process Automation*. Springer.

Floridi, L., Cowls, J., Beltrametti, M., Chatila, R., Chazerand, P., Dignum, V., Luetge, C., Madelin, R., Pagallo, U., Rossi, F., Schafer, B., Valcke, P., & Vayena, E. (2018). AI4People—an ethical framework for a good AI society: Opportunities, risks, principles, and recommendations. *Minds and Machines*, 28(4), 689–707. DOI: 10.1007/s11023-018-9482-5 PMID: 30930541

Gandomi, A., & Haider, M. (2015). Beyond the hype: Big data concepts, methods, and analytics. *International Journal of Information Management*, 35(2), 137–144. DOI: 10.1016/j.ijinfomgt.2014.10.007

Gill, S. S., Xu, M., Ottaviani, C., Patros, P., Bahsoon, R., Shaghaghi, A., Golec, M., Stankovski, V., Wu, H., Abraham, A., Singh, M., Mehta, H., Ghosh, S. K., Baker, T., Parlikad, A. K., Lutfiyya, H., Kanhere, S. S., Sakellariou, R., Dustdar, S., & Uhlig, S. (2022). AI for next generation computing: Emerging trends and future directions. *Internet of Things : Engineering Cyber Physical Human Systems*, 19, 100514. DOI: 10.1016/j.iot.2022.100514

Gołąb-Andrzejak, E. (2023). AI-powered digital transformation: Tools, benefits and challenges for marketers–case study of LPP. *Procedia Computer Science*, 219, 397–404. DOI: 10.1016/j.procs.2023.01.305

Hammer, M., & Champy, J. (2009). *Reengineering the corporation: Manifesto for business revolution, a*. Zondervan.

Holmström, J. (2022). From AI to digital transformation: The AI readiness framework. *Business Horizons*, 65(3), 329–339. DOI: 10.1016/j.bushor.2021.03.006

Informatic Data Quality. Available online: https://www.informatica.com/gb/products/dataquality/informatica-dataquality. html (accessed on 29 September 2023).

Jaheer Mukthar, K. P., Sivasubramanian, K., Ramirez Asis, E. H., & Guerra-Munoz, M. E. (2022). Redesigning and reinvention of retail industry through Artificial Intelligence (AI). In *Future of Organizations and Work After the 4th Industrial Revolution: The Role of Artificial Intelligence, Big Data, Automation, and Robotics* (pp. 41–56). Springer International Publishing. DOI: 10.1007/978-3-030-99000-8_3

Jarrahi, M. H., Kenyon, S., Brown, A., Donahue, C., & Wicher, C. (2023). Artificial intelligence: A strategy to harness its power through organizational learning. *The Journal of Business Strategy*, 44(3), 126–135. DOI: 10.1108/JBS-11-2021-0182

Jeston, J. (2018). *Business Process Management: Practical Guidelines to Successful Implementations*. Routledge. DOI: 10.4324/9781315184760

Kelleher, J. D., Mac Namee, B., & D'arcy, A. (2020). *Fundamentals of machine learning for predictive data analytics: algorithms, worked examples, and case studies*. MIT press.

Khanom, M. T. (2023). Business Strategies in The Age of Digital Transformation. *The Journal of Business*, 8(01), 28–35.

Kim, K., & Kim, B. (2022). Decision-making model for reinforcing digital transformation strategies based on artificial intelligence technology. *Information (Basel)*, 13(5), 253. DOI: 10.3390/info13050253

Kim, P. T., & Bodie, M. T. (2020). Artificial intelligence and the challenges of workplace discrimination and privacy. *ABAJ Lab. & Emp. L.*, 35, 289.

Kitsios, F., & Kamariotou, M. (2021). Artificial intelligence and business strategy towards digital transformation: A research agenda. *Sustainability (Basel)*, 13(4), 2025. DOI: 10.3390/su13042025

Lacity, M., & Willcocks, L. (2016). Nine keys to unlocking digital transformation in business operations. *MIS Quarterly Executive*, 15, 135–149.

Lacity, M., & Willcocks, L. P. (2017). *Robotic process automation and risk mitigation: The definitive guide*. SB Publishing.

Lacity, M., Willcocks, L. P., & Craig, A. (2015). Robotic process automation at Telefonica O2.

Lee, J., Lapira, E., Bagheri, B., & Kao, H. A. (2013). Recent advances and trends in predictive manufacturing systems in big data environment. *Manufacturing Letters*, 1(1), 38–41. DOI: 10.1016/j.mfglet.2013.09.005

Li, R., Rao, J., & Wan, L. (2022). The digital economy, enterprise digital transformation, and enterprise innovation. *MDE. Managerial and Decision Economics*, 43(7), 2875–2886. DOI: 10.1002/mde.3569

Mahalle, P. N., Hujare, P. P., & Shinde, G. R. (2023). Data Acquisition and Preparation. In *Predictive Analytics for Mechanical Engineering: A Beginners Guide* (pp. 11–38). Springer Nature Singapore. DOI: 10.1007/978-981-99-4850-5_2

Marchand, D. A., Kettinger, W. J., & Rollins, J. D. (2018). Information orientation, business agility, and digital transformation. *Management Information Systems Quarterly*, 42, 591–616.

Marr, B. (2019). *Artificial intelligence in practice: how 50 successful companies used AI and machine learning to solve problems*. John Wiley & Sons.

Melville, N., Kraemer, K., & Gurbaxani, V. (2004). Information technology and organizational performance: An integrative model of IT business value. *Management Information Systems Quarterly*, 28(2), 283–322. DOI: 10.2307/25148636

Mihai, F., Aleca, O. E., & Gheorghe, M. (2023). Digital Transformation Based on AI Technologies in European Union Organizations. *Electronics (Basel)*, 12(11), 2386. DOI: 10.3390/electronics12112386

Nguyen, T. M., & Malik, A. (2020). Cognitive processes, rewards and online knowledge sharing behaviour: The moderating effect of organisational innovation. *Journal of Knowledge Management*, 24(6), 1241–1261. DOI: 10.1108/JKM-12-2019-0742

O'Callaghan, M. (2023). *Decision intelligence: human–machine integration for decision-making*. CRC Press. DOI: 10.1201/b23322

Parmenter, D. (2015). *Key performance indicators: developing, implementing, and using winning KPIs*. John Wiley & Sons. DOI: 10.1002/9781119019855

Perifanis, N. A., & Kitsios, F. (2023). Investigating the influence of artificial intelligence on business value in the digital era of strategy: A literature review. *Information (Basel)*, 14(2), 85. DOI: 10.3390/info14020085

Phua, C., Lee, V., Smith, K., & Gayler, R. (2010). A comprehensive survey of data mining-based fraud detection research. *arXiv preprint arXiv:1009.6119.*

Power, D. J., & Heavin, C. (2017). *Decision support, analytics, and business intelligence*. Business Expert Press.

Raffey, M. A., & Gaikwad, S. B. (2022). The Impact Of Artificial Intelligence On Business Operations: Investigating The Current State And Future Implications Of AI Technologies. *Journal of Pharmaceutical Negative Results*, ●●●, 5577–5580.

Raguseo, E. (2018). Big data technologies: An empirical investigation on their adoption, benefits and risks for companies. *International Journal of Information Management*, 38(1), 187–195. DOI: 10.1016/j.ijinfomgt.2017.07.008

Ramaswamy, R., Gou, Y., Wu, D. J., Bush, D., & Grover, P. (2018). Organizing for digital innovation: The division of innovation labor between upstream and downstream teams. *Journal of Management Information Systems*, 35, 169–204.

Ross, J. W., Beath, C. M., & Mocker, M. (2018). Designing a digital organization. *MIT Sloan Management Review*, 59, 57–65.

Rožman, M., Oreški, D., & Tominc, P. (2023). Artificial-intelligence-supported reduction of employees' workload to increase the company's performance in today's VUCA Environment. *Sustainability (Basel)*, 15(6), 5019. DOI: 10.3390/su15065019

Schwartz, J. (2019). Workforce of the future: The competing forces shaping 2030. *Strategy and Leadership*, 47, 16–22.

Şişci, M. E. R. V. E., Torkul, Y. E., & Selvi, I. H. (2022). Machine Learning as a Tool for Achieving Digital Transformation. *Knowl. Manag. Digit. Transform. Power*, 1, 55.

Talend Data Quality. Available online: https://www.talend.com/products/data-quality/ (accessed on 3 October 2023).

Van Der Aalst, W. M., Bichler, M., & Heinzl, A. (2020). *Data-Driven Process Discovery and Analysis*. Springer Nature.

Vidu, C. M., Pinzaru, F., & Mitan, A. (2022). What managers of SMEs in the CEE region should know about challenges of artificial intelligence's adoption?–an introductive discussion. *Nowoczesne Systemy Zarządzania*, 17(1), 63–76. DOI: 10.37055/nsz/147989

Wamba-Taguimdje, S. L., Wamba, S. F., Kamdjoug, J. R. K., & Wanko, C. E. T. (2020). Influence of artificial intelligence (AI) on firm performance: The business value of AI-based transformation projects. *Business Process Management Journal*, 26(7), 1893–1924. DOI: 10.1108/BPMJ-10-2019-0411

Xiong, J., Qin, G., Liu, X., & Sun, X. (2019). Deep learning in personalized recommendation: A survey. *Proceedings of the IEEE*, 107, 15–37.

Zhu, X., Zheng, Y., Zhang, Z., Li, J., & Yu, P. S. (2020). Deep learning for online advertising: A comprehensive review. *SIGKDD Explorations*, 22, 5–20.

ADDITIONAL READING

Ali, M. (2021). *Remote Work and Sustainable Changes for the Future of Global Business*. IGI Global. https://www.igi-global.com/book/remote-work-sustainable-changes-future/264375

Ali, M. (2022). *Future Role of Sustainable Innovative Technologies in Crisis Management*. IGI Global. https://www.igi-global.com/book/future-role-sustainable-innovative-technologies/281281

Ali, M. (2023). *Shifting Paradigms in the Rapidly Developing Global Digital Ecosystem: A GCC Perspective*. In Digital Entrepreneurship and Co-Creating Value Through Digital Encounters (pp. 145-166). IGI Global. https://www.igi-global.com/chapter/shifting-paradigms-in-the-rapidly-developing-global-digital-ecosystem/323525

Ali, M. (2023). T*axonomy of Industry 4.0 Technologies in Digital Entrepreneurship and Co-Creating Value*. In *Digital Entrepreneurship and Co-Creating Value Through Digital Encounters* (pp. 24–55). IGI Global., https://www.igi-global.com/chapter/taxonomy-of-industry-40-technologies-in-digital-entrepreneurship-and-co-creating-value/323520 DOI: 10.4018/978-1-6684-7416-7.ch002

Ali, M., & Wood-Harper, T. (2021). *Fostering Communication and Learning with Underutilized Technologies in Higher Education*. IGI Global. https://www.igi-global.com/book/fostering-communication-learning-underutilized-technologies/244593

Ali, M., Wood-Harper, T., & Kutar, M. (2023). Multi-Perspectives of Contemporary Digital Transformation Models of Complex Innovation Management. In *Digital Entrepreneurship and Co-Creating Value Through Digital Encounters* (pp. 79–96). IGI Global., https://www.igi-global.com/chapter/multi-perspectives-of-contemporary-digital-transformation-models-of-complex-innovation-management/323522 DOI: 10.4018/978-1-6684-7416-7.ch004

Ali, M. B. (2021). Internet of Things (IoT) to Foster Communication and Information Sharing: A Case of UK Higher Education. In Ali, M. B., & Wood-Harper, T. (Eds.), *Fostering Communication and Learning With Underutilized Technologies in Higher Education* (pp. 1–20). IGI Global., https://www.igi-global.com/chapter/internet-of-things-iot-to-foster-communication-and-information-sharing/262718/ DOI: 10.4018/978-1-7998-4846-2.ch001

Ali, M. B., & Wood-Harper, T. (2022). Artificial Intelligence (AI) as a Decision-Making Tool to Control Crisis Situations. In *Future Role of Sustainable Innovative Technologies in Crisis Management*. IGI Global., https://www.igi-global.com/chapter/artificial-intelligence-ai-as-a-decision-making-tool-to-control-crisis-situations/298931 DOI: 10.4018/978-1-7998-9815-3.ch006

Ali, M. B., Wood-Harper, T., & Ramlogan, R. (2020). A Framework Strategy to Overcome Trust Issues on Cloud Computing Adoption in Higher Education. In Modern Principles, Practices, and Algorithms for Cloud Security (pp. 162-183). IGI Global. https://www.igi-global.com/chapter/a-framework-strategy-to-overcome-trust-issues-on-cloud-computing-adoption-in-higher-education/238907/

Chapter 10
Utilising Artificial Intelligence and Machine Learning for Regulatory Compliance in Financial Institutions

Zeeshan Syed
https://orcid.org/0000-0003-0116-5395
University of Salford, UK

Oluwaseun Okegbola
University of Salford, UK

Cynthia Abiemwense Akiotu
https://orcid.org/0009-0008-5118-0546
University of Salford, UK

ABSTRACT

This chapter explores the transformative potential of Artificial Intelligence (AI) and Machine Learning (ML) in enhancing regulatory compliance within financial institutions. Following the 2008 financial crisis, increased regulation has driven the need for advanced solutions. AI and ML, integrated into Regulatory Technology (RegTech), offer significant benefits, including improved efficiency, reduced compliance costs, and enhanced risk management. This paper examines the application of RegTech tools in processing large datasets, identifying patterns, and predicting regulatory challenges. It also addresses the challenges associated with AI and ML, such as overfitting, decision-making opacity, and legal implications. Ultimately,

DOI: 10.4018/979-8-3693-5966-2.ch010

AI and ML are critical to the future of regulatory compliance, offering financial institutions a path to more efficient adherence to complex regulations.

1. INTRODUCTION

The rise of mobile banking and retail investors has made real-time compliance with regulatory requirements a pressing need for financial institutions. This is a trend and a necessity in today's fast-paced financial world. Unlike other industries, Financial Institutions (FIs) are a special case due to their cross-border operations and the involvement of multiple jurisdictions at once. Imagine a resident of the UK placing an order to transfer US Dollars ($) to China (RMB) using a mobile app registered in Luxembourg. This complexity alone underscores the need to pay extra care to their regulatory requirements. In this context, a newer form of technology called Reg-Tech (a short form of Regulation Tech) has emerged. Reg-Tech is a composition of tools, protocols, software, and models that use large-scale data sets generated in real time to make decisions on the validity of transactions, orders, and all activities that attract financial regulations. Therefore, Machine Learning (ML) and Artificial Intelligence (AI) have become imperative tools to implement Reg-Tech designs, central to FIs' automation drive, bringing efficiency, speed, and reliability to their processes.

ML and AI have become imperative for FIs due to Financial Technology's (FinTech) ubiquities in providing their services. FinTech has significantly changed how banks operate, execute, and engage with their customers (Goodell et al., 2021). FinTech is technology's forward and backward integration in financial processes (Arner et al., 2015). In which two cases emerge: i) either conventional financial services are provided digitally, or ii) financial services are embedded in digital products such as websites, wallets, or social media. We may call the former case FinTech and the latter TechFin, as the role of technology changes in either case. Figure 1 summarises this dichotomy and highlights the complex nature of financial services and how technology has made financial services multifaceted and challenging to regulate and complex.

Figure 1.Two Dimensions of Financial Technology

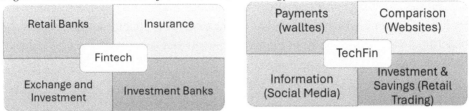

One challenge due to this complexity is the rise of large-scale data, structured and unstructured, datasets that necessitate real-time monitoring and control to inhibit criminal activities such as money laundering, terrorism financing, and fraud. As financial transaction data increases due to the rapid growth of FinTech, new regulations are formulated to protect against the financial risks associated with information technology. Therefore, RegTech is an inevitable part of the future of financial services that needs to be understood comprehensively, as it can also help other sectors.

RegTech uses technological capabilities such as ML and AI by players within a regulated industry, such as the financial services sector, to drive regulatory compliance. With their ability to process vast amounts of data and make decisions with minimal human intervention, these technologies are a reassuring solution to regulatory compliance challenges. With reliable tools and algorithm modelling, FIs aim to lower costs, streamline their reporting and monitoring procedures, and gain regulators' trust. It's noteworthy that other businesses may also benefit from using ML and AI as tools for implementing robust regulatory compliance. Aggarwal et al. (2020) classify FIs based on their adoption of ML and AI for regulatory compliance:

i.   FIs that apply machine learning to daily procedures and processes.
ii. FIs testing vendor proof-of-concepts or creating their solutions internally.
iii. FIs that are still formulating their long-term plans for Machine Learning applications and
iv. FIs that address current issues with current-state compliance but have not yet considered the future.

Therefore, the application of ML and AI is not universal, and their impact is crucial for the future success of the sector. Furthermore, the adoption of ML and AI can also have an effect on efficiency, productivity, the creation of new career fields, and increased financial system resilience. As of 2017, FIs expended more than $100 billion in 2016 on regulatory compliance (McDowell, 2017). In a survey, 62 managers admit that RegTech is the future of successful compliance (Becker

& Buchkremer, 2018). Therefore, Machine Learning and Artificial Intelligence capabilities greatly impact regulatory compliance monitoring systems against the traditional system, which solely relies on humans. This chapter aims to assess the benefits of RegTech relating to improved operational process efficiency, reduced risk, and reduced costs.

2. UNDERSTANDING REGULATORY COMPLIANCE

Before understanding the role of ML and AI, we need to understand the key dimensions of regulatory compliance, how regulators view compliance, key financial regulations, and what approach FIs take towards meeting compliance needs. This section will summarise the discussion around these topics and will pave the foundation for our upcoming discussion about the implications of ML and AI.

2.1. Key Dimensions of Regulatory Compliance

Corporate governance, regulation, and compliance generally fall under the moral law, wherein private enterprises are expected to apply regulatory guidance rigorously. However, regulatory compliance is now assumed to be a must-do thing, and organisations are expected to meet the regulations in letter and spirit (Giblin et al., 2005). In this context, we define compliance as a firm's approach towards following legal obligations, industry standards, and established ethical norms (Bull et al., 2006). Hence, Compliance becomes an enterprise's capacity to fulfil all regulatory requirements imposed on its business activities. To understand the complexity ascribable to compliance needs and requirements, we summarise the few key dimensions of compliance below.

i.   **Laws and Regulations:** These are rules set forth by government agencies, industry bodies, or other governing bodies to establish standards for certain activities. Examples include data protection laws (e.g., GDPR), financial regulations (e.g., Sarbanes-Oxley Act), and environmental regulations.

ii. **Industry Standards:** Depending on the sector, there might be industry-specific standards that organisations need to adhere to. These standards are often developed collaboratively by industry experts and associations to ensure best practices and safety.

iii. **Risk Management:** Regulatory compliance is closely tied to risk management. Non-compliance can result in legal penalties, fines, reputational damage, and even operational shutdowns. Compliance efforts aim to mitigate these risks.

iv. **Documentation:** Maintaining thorough documentation of compliance efforts is crucial. This includes policies, procedures, records, and reports demonstrating how an organisation meets its regulatory obligations.

v. **Implementation and Monitoring:** Compliance is not a one-time effort; it requires ongoing implementation and monitoring. Organisations must establish mechanisms for continuous evaluation, assessment, and improvement of their compliance practices.

vi. **Training and Education:** Employees should be educated about the relevant regulations, compliance expectations, and their role in maintaining compliance. Training programs help ensure that everyone is aware of their responsibilities.

vii. **Data Privacy and Security:** Many compliance regulations focus on protecting sensitive data and ensuring individual privacy. This involves implementing appropriate security measures, data handling practices, and breach response plans.

viii. **Audit and Reporting:** Regular internal and external audits help assess the organisation's compliance status. Accurate and timely reporting to regulatory authorities is often required.

ix. **Global and Local Variations:** Regulatory compliance can differ significantly based on geographical location. Organisations operating in multiple jurisdictions need to understand and adhere to the specific regulations of each region.

x. **Penalties for Non-Compliance:** Penalties for non-compliance can vary widely and might include fines, legal actions, loss of licenses, and reputational damage.

xi. **Ethical Considerations:** Compliance goes beyond legal requirements and often involves ethical considerations. Organisations might adopt higher standards to build trust and goodwill with stakeholders.

Looking at these aspects of compliance, it is obvious that compliance requires considerable involvement of technology, automation, and operational depth to handle all these complexities in real-time. FIs must create business processes that model compliance around their regulations and regulators' guidance, available information technology, and risk-based quality assessment. A comprehensive Governance, Risk and Compliance (GRC) system that integrates all these dimensions is now more important due to the multiplicities of jurisdictions financial activities attract (Bonazzi et al., 2009). ML and AI are the tools that can not only enable this but also ensure that automated compliance is reliable, responsible, and self-explanatory, especially when FIs deal with principle-based regulatory requirements.

2.2. Compliance and Regulators

Regulators view compliance and robust adherence to them as crucial for meeting their mandate. Financial regulators are more sensitive to compliance failures as they have been regularly blamed for failures in causing economic crises. Therefore, they are generally quick and robust in sanctioning and penalising instances of non-compliance (Moloney et al., 2015). Furthermore, regulators also view compliance as a duty of care towards consumers and their welfare and ensuring innate issues such as conflict of interest and moral hazard do not cause customers to lose their pensions, savings, and monies deposited with the FIs. Regulators depend on adherence to these regulations to guarantee the safety, fairness, and transparency of products and services provided by entities under regulation, consequently averting harm to consumers and upholding investor trust (Avgouleas, 2009). Among these considerations, regulators' prime interests are threefold in ensuring robust compliance:

i.   Preventing Systemic Risks by ensuring FIs do not engage in contagious activities and their balance sheets are well protected (Bamberger, 2009).
ii. Enforcing Legal and Ethical Standards to prevent fraud, money laundering, and terrorism finance from taking place (Hodges & Steinholtz, 2017).
iii. Making the market efficient regarding information, competition pricing, and clearing the markets at optimal markets (Cornwell et al., 2023; Peterson, 2013; Johnson, 2013; Moloney et al., 2015; Cornwell et al., 2023).

2.3. Compliance and Financial Institutions

For various reasons, compliance is important for FIs, contributing to their success, credibility, and overall well-being. Here are some key reasons why compliance is important to FIs:

i. **Legal and Regulatory Adherence:** FIs are subject to a complex web of laws, regulations, and standards set by government agencies and regulatory bodies. Compliance ensures that these institutions operate within the legal boundaries, reducing the risk of penalties, fines, legal actions, and reputational damage (Hodges & Steinholtz, 2017).
ii. **Risk Mitigation:** Non-compliance can lead to financial, operational, legal, and reputational risks. FIs can implement proper controls and safeguards by adhering to regulations, reducing the likelihood of costly errors, fraud, and other risks (Bamberger, 2009).

iii. **Reputation and Trust:** Compliance is essential for building and maintaining a positive reputation. A history of regulatory adherence demonstrates a commitment to ethical conduct, responsible practices, and customer protection, fostering trust among customers, investors, and stakeholders (Rezaee, 2004).

iv. **Investor Confidence:** Compliance contributes to investor confidence by signalling that FIs operate responsibly and manage risks effectively. This can attract more investors, enhance access to capital, and support growth opportunities (Avgouleas, 2009).

v. **Operational Efficiency:** While compliance efforts may require resources, they often lead to improved operational efficiency. Standardised processes and controls are necessary for compliance and can streamline operations, reduce errors, and enhance overall efficiency (Gulati, 2023).

2.4. Key Financial Regulations

FIs must comply with various regulatory policies to ensure their operations are conducted safely, fairly, and transparently. These regulations range from correctly processing transactions to implementing comprehensive data management regimes. Below we identify the key financial regulations and their brief explanation. This will help us understand the different aspects of ML and AI implementation in business processing.

i. **Anti-Money Laundering (AML) and Combating the Financing of Terrorism (CFT) Regulations:** FIs must develop policies and processes to detect and prevent money laundering and terrorist financing. They must do customer due diligence, monitor transactions, and report suspicious activity to appropriate authorities.

ii. **Know Your Customer (KYC) Requirements:** FIs must verify their customers' identities to guarantee they are not engaging in illicit activities and follow anti-fraud procedures.

iii. **Basel Framework (I, II, and III):** This worldwide regulatory framework establishes capital requirements for banks intending to improve the banking sector's resilience and reduce systemic risk.

iv. **Dodd-Frank Wall Street Reform and Consumer Protection Act:** This law, passed following the financial crisis of 2008, attempts to promote openness and accountability in the financial sector. It includes rules for derivatives regulation, consumer protection, and systemic risk reduction.

v. **Securities Exchange Commission (SEC) Regulations:** The SEC enforces many rules to safeguard investors to ensure fair and efficient markets. Regulations governing securities placements, insider trading, and financial reporting are a few examples.

vi. **General Data Protection Regulation (GDPR):** Although not specifically tied to the financial industry, GDPR impacts financial organisations that handle the personal data of EU citizens, requiring them to preserve data privacy and educate consumers about data usage.

vii. **Payment Card Industry Data Security Standard (PCI DSS):** This standard applies to businesses that accept credit card payments. And guarantees that payment card data is kept safe to protect cardholders from fraud and breaches.

viii. **Consumer Financial Protection Bureau (CFPB) Regulations:** Laws relating to consumer protection are enforced by the Consumer Financial Protection Bureau (CFPB). This regulation addresses fair lending, debt collection practices, and mortgage servicing concerns.

ix. **Sarbanes-Oxley Act (SOX):** This act strengthens public firms' corporate governance and financial disclosure obligations, enforcing high criteria to boost openness and lower the danger of corporate fraud.

x. **Market Abuse Regulation (MAR):** This rule, implemented in the European Union, attempts to combat market exploitation and insider trading while improving market integrity.

3. IMPLEMENTING MACHINE LEARNING (ML) AND ARTIFICIAL INTELLIGENCE (AI) IN FINANCIAL INSTITUTIONS

3.1. Understanding the Difference Between ML and AI

Hitherto, the discussion outlines the multifaceted and complex nature of regulatory compliance for FIs. FIs (FIs) may now be classified as large virtual databases that organise and sort citizens' financial information worldwide. The entire operation of FIs, especially deposits, is managing large ledgers that contain information about customers, their transaction history, their ownership record of FIs, and their savings and pension balances. Some of these datasets are voluntary, and some are due to regulatory requirements; in either case, FIs must manage structured and unstructured data sets. Therefore, FIs require more effective analytical tools to manage enormous amounts of data from multiple sources and formats while maintaining or improving the granularity of analysis. Furthermore, these tools must handle the tasks in real-time using real-time data and implement the regulator guidelines while conducting business transactions. The tools and processes must be automated and trained enough to act without human supervision.

Machine Learning (ML) and Artificial Intelligence (AI) provide FIs with such tools. It's noteworthy that ML and AI are neither a substitute for each other nor a complement to each other; instead, they are two different processes that enable FIs to use computers, virtual machines, servers and databases to perform tasks ordinarily performed by humans. These tasks may include storing and sorting the data, detecting unlawful or criminal activity, making decisions on the application or authorisation of transactions, etc.

ML may be defined as learning through iterative processes that train algorithms in detecting anomalies, patterns, and recurring behaviour in data. This training creates an automated set of predictive and inferential information that acts as key decision-making criteria for servers, virtual machines, Kubernetes, and edge computers. Therefore, ML trains the machine to perform a specific task. Whereas AI refers to a set of machines (i.e., metal and cloud-based), such as servers and databases, that run on the cloud and implement the procedural guidelines of FIs. These machines perform the tasks using the models developed by the ML. This distinction is important to understand for understanding forthcoming discussion. However, from here onward, when we refer to ML, we mean ML and AI as conjoin forces that enable FIs to meet their regulatory compliance.

3.2. Basics of Machine Learning

ML refers to the set of tools that can provide that analytical capability. It is a branch of statistics and econometrics that has recently grown significantly in the computer industry. While machine learning has roots in the early 20th century, its popularity grew as high-frequency data became more widely available and computational advances made it possible to model complicated, non-linear connections while also making machine learning simpler.

Machine learning is a very effective method for making predictions. It can build a model incorporating the associations that produce the most accurate out-of-sample predictions by spotting correlations or relationships in a data sample. To develop such a model, variables and the model are tested on various data subsamples to determine which predictors are the most effective. This may be repeated thousands of times to allow the model to "learn" from the data and enhance its ability to anticipate outcomes. Machine learning is intimately linked to the "big data revolution" since it depends on massive datasets and powerful computation. Overall, "the remarkable increase in processing performance in recent years, along with major theoretical developments in machine-learning techniques, has sparked a rebirth in computational modelling.

277

ML tools can be categorised as supervised and unsupervised learning methods. In supervised machine learning, a statistical model is created to forecast or estimate an output using one or more inputs (for example, forecasting GDP growth based on several factors). Unsupervised learning analyses a dataset without a dependent variable to estimate or predict. Instead, the information is examined to reveal the structures and patterns present in a dataset. The unique capability of some supervised machine learning methods to perform non-parametric analyses, which can adaptively fit any model to estimate the data, sets them apart from traditional statistical methods. Unlike conventional approaches that start by assuming a connection between the dependent and independent variables, these machine learning methods can infer non-linear correlations, enhancing their ability to match the data. Figure 2 below summarises the type of ML methods and their key categories.

Figure 2. Machine Learning Methods and their Classification

Problem type		Linear methods	Non-linear methods
Supervised			
	Regression	• Principal components • Ridge • Partial least squares • LASSO	Penalized regression: • LASSO • LARS • elastic nets Neural networks and deep learning
	Classification	Support vector machines	Decision trees: • classification trees • regression trees • random forests Support vector machines Deep learning
Unsupervised			
	Clustering*	Clustering methods: K- and X-means, hierarchical Principal components analysis Deep learning * Since unsupervised methods do not describe a relation between a dependent and interdependent variable, they cannot be labelled linear or non-linear.	

3.3. Does Machine Learning (ML) Work?

ML can generate predictions for out-of-sample data, yet additional components are essential to render it apt for explanatory or inferential purposes (Dixon et al., 2020). ML algorithms can handle large and complex datasets, enabling regulators to extract meaningful insights and detect patterns that may indicate non-compliance (Singh et al., 2021). This allows regulators to promptly identify and respond to potential compliance violations or risks as they occur, enhancing the effectiveness of oversight (Aziz & Dowling, 2019). Regulators can use these patterns to identify anomalies, fraud, and potential non-compliance issues (Donepudi, 2019). This proactive approach empowers regulators to anticipate challenges and allocate resources strategically (Vasista, 2021). By identifying high-risk areas, entities, or transactions, regulators can optimise their resource allocation for inspections and investigations (Xu et al., 2017).

ML can automate routine and manual tasks involved in continuous risk assessment and monitoring that enable regulators to focus on higher-value activities such as analysis, decision-making, and policy formulation (Paltrinieri et al., 2019; Bavaresco et al., 2023). Regulators can use these risk assessments to tailor their regulatory actions, such as conducting more rigorous examinations of high-risk entities (Paltrinieri et al., 2019). Furthermore, algorithm-based monitoring can help regulators identify patterns indicative of fraudulent activities or financial crimes (Anagnostopoulos, 2018; Shirgave et al., 2019; Jansen, 2020; Emmanuel et al., 2021; Priya & Saradha, 2021).

3.4. Is Machine Learning (ML) free from Flaws?

The major issue with using ML to train AI machines is that the effectiveness and efficiency of ML depend on the models that are used to test and train. ML is not free from flaws, and it suffers from modelling errors such as model overfitting, selection and survival biases, lack of explainability, and poor inferences (Liu et al., 2022). Overfitting frequently occurs in machine learning, especially in non-parametric, non-linear models, as these models are inherently complex in structure and, as a result, can be challenging to comprehend. A model's performance may deteriorate when assessed on data beyond the sample it was trained on, particularly when it tries to capture the noise within a dataset, even though it may exhibit a strong fit within a single data sample.

However, ML is unique because it can learn and improve its modelling capabilities. Various techniques such as "bootstrapping," "boosting," and "bootstrap aggregation" (commonly referred to as bagging) can reduce the risks of overfitting. Similarly, Boosting gives greater weight to fewer observations in a training dataset so that the model will focus more on sparse occurrences rather than frequent observations. Bagging involves iterating models enough times (e.g., thousands of times) on a unique subset of data to ensure predictions achieved are not random observations. The average of each run model is then used to create the final model. This average model is expected to exhibit increased robustness to variations in the underlying data, given that it has been assessed across multiple diverse data samples. Similarly, modelling techniques such as random forest and ensemble are employed to achieve model accuracy. Random Forest comprises several separate decision tree-based models to generate a model that increases the model's precision, speed, and accuracy (Tiffin, 2016). The outcome of RF is called an ensemble that comprises several models whose results are integrated by voting or weighted averaging. It has been established that adopting a single model tends to produce poor out-of-sample predictions than averaging over numerous small models (Varian, 2014).

4. REGULATION AND SUPERVISION USING ML AND AI

One of the major issues in understanding the implementations of technologies is identifying their name according to their use. The same issues exist when we analyse ML and AI in the context of regulation, supervision, and compliance. Regulation Technology (RegTech) is a subset of AI that enables Financial Institutions (FIs) to comply with laws and implement quality control procedures within their operations and organisations (Becker et al., 2020). Supervisory Technology[1] (SupTech) refers to the use of ML and AI by regulators and public bodies to regulate, monitor, and control FIs activities and hold them accountable for failures (Vasista, 2021). Generally, RegTech is used to denote both aspects of technology, often used interchangeably. Below we identify the application scenarios of both aspects and note how they are viewed from practical perspectives.

FIs often use Large Language Models (LLM) and Natural Language Processing (NLP) for the analysis of unstructured data such as customer interactions with the banks, emails, messages, and other forms of metadata to monitor their officials, understand the decisions processes of staff, and activities of their traders. These tools enable FIS to comply with regulations such as the provisions of the Alternative Investment Fund Managers Directive (AIFMD), the Markets in Financial Instruments Directive II (MiFID II), and the Undertakings for Collective Investments in Transferable Securities (UCITS) Directive in the EU. Similarly, FIs can use AI to manage their Know Your Customers (KYC) obligations. The KYC procedure is frequently expensive, time-consuming, and repetitive; hence, very costly if done manually. FIs can use Optical Character Recognition, Computer Vision, and Custom Vision tools to determine the legitimacy of documents, pictures, and responses and generate One Time passwords (OTP) to manage authentication, onboarding, and verification. A few of the key uses of ML and AI are listed as follows:

i. **Assets Pricing:** FIs also use ML and AI to analyse the financial assets' pricing and price behaviour to manage the overall risk of their portfolio (Aziz & Dowling, 2019). Tools capable of mitigating tail risks can benefit the overall system. Additionally, fraud, suspicious transactions, default, and the danger of cyberattacks might be anticipated and detected using AI and machine learning, which could lead to better risk management.

Examples of Supervisory Technology (SupTech)

SupTech tools encompass a wide range of applications aimed at strengthening the oversight functions of financial regulators and enabling them to monitor, control, and oversee the actions of Financial Institutions (FIs). However, SupTech is often confused with RegTech; hence, we will note a few examples for a clearer understanding.

Automated Reporting and Data Collection: The Bank of England's "Data Collection Transformation" initiative automated data collection from financial institutions. By streamlining these processes, both regulators and institutions reduce manual effort, leading to improved accuracy and timeliness in reporting. Similarly, The European Central Bank (ECB) has developed the "AnaCredit" system, a comprehensive database containing detailed information on individual bank loans across the Eurozone. This system enables real-time credit risk monitoring and the banking sector's overall health and consumer credit.

Fraud and Crime Prevention: The Monetary Authority of Singapore (MAS) utilizes AI and machine learning to identify unusual patterns in financial transactions, potentially signalling money laundering or fraud. These advanced systems can efficiently process vast datasets to detect outliers and suspicious activities.

System Tests: Central Banks utilise advanced Machine Learning models to simulate and test financial conditions and analyse their impacts on Financial Institutions. The Reserve Bank of India (RBI) operates a platform called "CIM" (Central Information Management), which integrates data from various sources to provide a comprehensive view of risks affecting the banking sector. The South African Reserve Bank (SARB) employs supervisory dashboards that consolidate data from multiple sources, offering regulators a real-time overview of the financial system's health. These dashboards utilize visualisation tools to highlight critical trends and risks.

Blockchain for Regulatory Reporting: The UK's Financial Conduct Authority (FCA) is exploring blockchain technology to enhance the transparency and security of regulatory reporting. This innovation facilitates the tracking and verification of financial transactions with greater ease and reliability.

Natural Language Processing (NLP) for Regulatory Compliance: The Dutch Central Bank (DNB) applies NLP tools to analyse large volumes of text within regulatory filings and other documents. This technology aids regulators in swiftly identifying compliance issues and areas of concern.

Regulatory Sandbox Environments: The Australian Securities and Investments Commission (ASIC) has established a "RegTech" sandbox to test new SupTech applications in a controlled environment. This approach allows regulators to assess the performance of these technologies before full-scale deployment.

However, due to the potential of being 'overtrained' on historical data, AI and machine learning-based systems could overlook emerging threats and catastrophes despite the potential of AI and machine learning methodologies to enhance risk management.

ii. **Transaction Monitoring:** involves the continuous surveillance and analysis of financial transactions to identify unusual or suspicious activities that could be linked to money laundering, terrorist financing, or other financial crimes (Singh & Best, 2019). Transaction monitoring systems rely heavily on machine learning and data analysis techniques to detect patterns, anomalies, and trends that might indicate illicit activities. By leveraging machine learning and data analysis, financial institutions can enhance their ability to detect and prevent money laundering and other illicit economic activities.

iii. **Customer Due Diligence (CDD):** is a fundamental process in anti-money laundering (AML) compliance that aims to assess and verify the identities of customers, understand their financial activities, and determine their potential risk for involvement in money laundering, terrorism financing, or other financial crimes (Johari et al., 2020). CDD procedures help financial institutions understand their customers' backgrounds and activities, enabling them to make informed risk-based decisions.

iv. **Sequence Modelling:** Sequential modelling has established itself as a valuable tool across diverse domains, including but not limited to natural language processing (NLP) and time series analysis (Krause et al., 2018). Particularly, recurrent neural networks (RNNs), when augmented with long short-term memory (LSTM) modules, have demonstrated impressive prowess in these fields by effectively capturing and exploiting the inherent sequential dependencies present in the data.

v. **Automated Negative News Screening:** Detecting bad news about a consumer and behaviours related to money laundering is known as automated negative news screening (Murphy et al., 2020). Using featurisation and subsequent analysis of unstructured textual material, NLP would automatically detect consumer unfavourable news. Recognising entities in text, such as names, is known as named entity recognition, and it is a subtask of generic information extraction from text. When named entity recognition is applied to news items, it is possible to identify persons and organisations referenced in the article.

5. REGTECH IN PRACTICE

The following case studies demonstrate how leading Financial organizations have incorporated AI into their RegTech systems to improve regulatory compliance, enhance operational efficiency, and reduce risks.

i. HSBC & Ayasdi - AI in Anti-Money Laundering (AML)

HSBC faced significant challenges with its manual AML processes, which were slow, expensive, and frequently resulted in false positives (Silicon, 2017). AI Solution: HSBC adopted Ayasdi, an AI-based AML system, which employs machine learning and topological data analysis. The system analyzes vast amounts of transaction data, identifying subtle patterns and anomalies that human operators could miss. By learning from past transactions, the AI improves its ability to detect money laundering activities and reduces false alerts (Daniel, 2018). HSBC saw a 20% reduction in false positives without decreasing the number of legitimate suspicious cases referred for further investigation. The AI-based solution enabled more efficient transaction monitoring while reducing operational costs. AI-enabled HSBC to automate much of its AML process, significantly reducing manual intervention and operational costs. Notably, the bank saw a marked improvement in its ability to detect suspicious transactions accurately, cutting down false positives by a large margin.

ii. SWIFT & Microsoft- Financial Crime Detection

As the volume of cross-border transactions and instant payment networks increased, SWIFT—a global provider of financial messaging services—faced the challenge of detecting and preventing financial fraud on a massive scale. Fraudulent transactions were costing the financial industry billions annually, and existing solutions were not sufficient to combat these evolving threats. SWIFT needed a highly secure, scalable solution that could detect anomalies in financial transactions without compromising data privacy across its global network of over 11,500 financial institutions (Microsoft, 2023).

Swift partnered with Microsoft to develop an anomaly detection model using Azure Machine Learning and Azure Confidential Computing. The solution employs federated learning techniques, which allow the model to be trained on distributed datasets without copying or moving data from the secure locations of Swift's members. This ensures that sensitive financial data remains confidential while enabling the detection of anomalies that signal potential fraud. The platform also utilizes Microsoft Purview and a Zero Trust security framework to maintain the highest levels of data privacy and integrity during model training and execution.

By collaborating with Microsoft, Swift is building a foundation model for fraud detection that can be continuously improved as more data from member institutions is added. This federated learning approach has allowed Swift to innovate without sacrificing data privacy, creating a highly accurate and scalable solution for detecting financial crime. The model is expected to become a new industry standard for reducing fraud while achieving cost efficiency and maintaining security.

5.1. S&P Global Market Intelligence & AWS - Cloud-Based Infrastructure Optimization in RegTech

S&P Global Market Intelligence faced inefficiencies and scalability issues with its on-premises infrastructure for Issue-Book, a critical application processing trillions of dollars in US bond issuances. The company needed to enhance the platform's agility, resilience, and compliance with regulatory requirements regarding uptime, data integrity, and service availability (Amazon, 2023). To address these challenges, S&P Global partnered with Amazon Web Services (AWS) to optimize its infrastructure, improving efficiency and scalability. The company aimed to modernize its platform, streamline operations, and reduce operational complexity to ensure compliance with regulatory standards.

This transformation resulted in a sixfold increase in annual releases, virtually zero downtime, and reduced client onboarding time to two weeks. Updates were delivered to all clients within a single day, enhancing agility and ensuring compliance with regulations on system resilience and data integrity, thereby improving system resilience, reducing costs, and meeting stringent regulatory standards; S&P Global enhanced its compliance capabilities in a highly regulated financial environment.

5.2. Big Pay & Comply Advantage - Customer Screening and Transaction Monitoring

Big Pay, a Southeast Asian FinTech operating in Malaysia and Singapore, struggled with an inefficient, manual customer screening and transaction monitoring process. As the company grew and expanded its services, the reliance on manual processes became unsustainable, particularly during annual customer rescreening. Additionally, Big Pay needed a more flexible system to align with its risk-based approach, offering tailored screening depending on the use case, transaction type, and country.

BigPay partnered with ComplyAdvantage to implement an AI-powered platform that automated customer screening and transaction monitoring. The system integrated multiple tools and databases through a single API, allowing for real-time compliance monitoring. Big Pay customized the platform to create unique screening profiles for different markets, products, and transaction types. The platform also automated name screening and adverse media checks, freeing analysts to focus on higher-level investigations.

BigPay was able to streamline its compliance processes, significantly reducing manual tasks and improving efficiency. The solution allowed for a scalable approach, capable of handling increased transaction volumes as BigPay expanded into new markets like Thailand. By automating key workflows, BigPay saved time and resources while improving its ability to detect and manage financial crime risks.

REFERENCES

Agarwal, P. (2019). Redefining banking and financial industry through the application of computational intelligence. In *2019 Advances in Science and Engineering Technology International Conferences (ASET)* (pp. 1-5). IEEE. DOI: 10.1109/ ICASET.2019.8714305

Aggarwal, N., Wareham, S., & Lehmann, R. (2020). Applications of machine learning in the identification, measurement, and mitigation of money laundering. *Journal of Financial Compliance*, 4(2), 140–166. DOI: 10.69554/HHGO1574

Al-Shabandar, R., Lightbody, G., Browne, F., Liu, J., Wang, H., & Zheng, H. (2019). The application of artificial intelligence in financial compliance management. In *Proceedings of the 2019 International Conference on Artificial Intelligence and Advanced Manufacturing* (pp. 1-6). DOI: 10.1145/3358331.3358339

Amazon. (2023). S&P Global Market Intelligence Increases Agility and Resilience of Its Primary Issuance Platform Using AWS Well-Architected Tool and AWS Trusted Advisor. Retrieved September 4, 2024 from https://aws.amazon.com/solutions/ case-studies/sp-global-market-intelligence-case-study/?did=cr_card&trk=cr_card

Anagnostopoulos, I. (2018). Fintech and regtech: Impact on regulators and banks. *Journal of Economics and Business*, 100, 7–25. DOI: 10.1016/j.jeconbus.2018.07.003

Arner, D. W., Barberis, J., & Buckley, R. P. (2015). The evolution of Fintech: A new post-crisis paradigm. *SSRN*, 47, 1271. DOI: 10.2139/ssrn.2676553

Avgouleas, E. (2009). The global financial crisis and the disclosure paradigm in European financial regulation: The case for reform.

Aziz, S., & Dowling, M. (2019). Machine learning and AI for risk management. *Disrupting finance: FinTech and strategy in the 21st century*, 33-50.

Azzutti, A., Ringe, W. G., & Stiehl, H. S. (2021). Machine Learning, Market Manipulation, and Collusion on Capital Markets: Why the" Black Box" Matters. *SSRN*, 43, 79. DOI: 10.2139/ssrn.3788872

Bagó, P. (2023). The potential of artificial intelligence in finance. *ECONOMY AND FINANCE: ENGLISH-LANGUAGE EDITION OF GAZDASÁG ÉS PÉNZÜGY*, 10(1), 20–37. DOI: 10.33908/EF.2023.1.2

Balasubramani, E., & Priyanka, B. (2023). Machine Learning in Finance. https:// www.openacessjournal.com/article-file/202303045684986362machine.pdf

Bamberger, K. A. (2009). Technologies of compliance: Risk and regulation in a digital age. *Texas Law Review*, 88, 669.

Bavaresco, R. S., Nesi, L. C., Barbosa, J. L. V., Antunes, R. S., da Rosa Righi, R., da Costa, C. A., & Moreira, C. (2023). Machine learning-based automation of accounting services: An exploratory case study. *International Journal of Accounting Information Systems*, 49, 100618. DOI: 10.1016/j.accinf.2023.100618

Becker, M., & Buchkremer, R. (2018). RANKING OF CURRENT INFORMATION TECHNOLOGIES BY RISK AND REGULATORY COMPLIANCE OFFICERS AT FINANCIAL INSTITUTIONS—A GERMAN PERSPECTIVE. *Review of Finance & Banking*, 10(1).

Becker, M., Merz, K., & Buchkremer, R. (2020). RegTech—the application of modern information technology in regulatory affairs: Areas of interest in research and practice. *International Journal of Intelligent Systems in Accounting Finance & Management*, 27(4), 161–167. DOI: 10.1002/isaf.1479

BEng. R. V., & Slagter, M. R. (2017). Standing on the shoulders of RegTech. https://www.compact.nl/pdf/C-2017-4-Slagter.pdf

Bhaskar, N., Ramu, S. C., & Murthy, M. R. (2021). A Two-Level Authentication Protocol for Secure M-Commerce Transactions using AMQP Protocol. *Design Engineering (London)*, ●●●, 844–861.

Bonazzi, R., Hussami, L., & Pigneur, Y. (2009). Compliance management is becoming a major issue in IS design. In *Information Systems: People, Organizations, Institutions, and Technologies: ItAIS: The Italian Association for Information Systems* (pp. 391–398). Physica-Verlag HD. DOI: 10.1007/978-3-7908-2148-2_45

Bull, A. L., Russo, P. L., Friedman, N. D., Bennett, N. J., Boardman, C. J., & Richards, M. J. (2006). Compliance with surgical antibiotic prophylaxis–reporting from a statewide surveillance programme in Victoria, Australia. *The Journal of Hospital Infection*, 63(2), 140–147. DOI: 10.1016/j.jhin.2006.01.018 PMID: 16621135

Butler, T., & O'Brien, L. (2019). Artificial intelligence for regulatory compliance: Are we there yet? *Journal of Financial Compliance*, 3(1), 44–59. DOI: 10.69554/TOCI6736

Butler, T., & O'Brien, L. (2019). Understanding RegTech for digital regulatory compliance. *Disrupting finance: FinTech and strategy in the 21st century*, 85-102.

Calderón, A. (2020). Regulatory Compliance in AI Regime: Banks and FinTech. https://helda.helsinki.fi/server/api/core/bitstreams/c529b572-94d5-4080-a578-31d36e0cfcfa/content

CleverChain. (n.d.) *Automated perpetual compliance monitoring*. Retrieved 14 July, 2023, from https://www.cleverchain.ai/

Cornwell, N., Bilson, C., Gepp, A., Stern, S., & Vanstone, B. J. (2023). Modernising operational risk management in financial institutions via data-driven causal factors analysis: A pre-registered report. *Pacific-Basin Finance Journal*, 77, 101906. DOI: 10.1016/j.pacfin.2022.101906

Daniel, F. (2018). Bank Reduces Money-Laundering Investigation Effort with AI. https://emerj.com/ai-case-studies/bank-reduces-money-laundering-investigation-effort-with-ai/

Dey, D. (2017). Growing importance of machine learning in compliance and regulatory reporting. *European Journal of Multidisciplinary Studies*, 2(7), 255–258. DOI: 10.26417/ejms.v6i2.p255-258

Dixon, M. F., Halperin, I., & Bilokon, P. (2020). *Machine learning in finance* (Vol. 1170). Springer International Publishing. DOI: 10.1007/978-3-030-41068-1

Donepudi, P. K. (2019). Automation and machine learning in transforming the financial industry. *Asian Business Review*, 9(3), 129–138. DOI: 10.18034/abr.v9i3.494

Du, J., & Wei, L. (2020). An analysis of regulatory technology in the Internet financial sector in conjunction with the logit model. In *2020 2nd International Conference on Economic Management and Model Engineering (ICEMME)* (pp. 428-431). IEEE. DOI: 10.1109/ICEMME51517.2020.00091

Edwards, J., & Wolfe, S. (2005). Compliance: A review. *Journal of Financial Regulation and Compliance*.

Emmanuel, T., Maupong, T., Mpoeleng, D., Semong, T., Mphago, B., & Tabona, O. (2021). A survey on missing data in machine learning. *Journal of Big Data*, 8(1), 1–37. DOI: 10.1186/s40537-021-00516-9 PMID: 34722113

Gabor, D., & Brooks, S. (2017). The digital revolution in financial inclusion: International development in the fintech era. *New Political Economy*, 22(4), 423–436. DOI: 10.1080/13563467.2017.1259298

Ghosh, K. (2021). Regtech: Bits and Bytes of Financial Regulation. *Journal of Business Strategy Finance and Management*, 3(1-2), 103–109. DOI: 10.12944/JBSFM.03.01-02.10

Giblin, C., Liu, A. Y., Müller, S., Pfitzmann, B., & Zhou, X. (2005, May). Regulations Expressed As Logical Models (REALM). In *JURIX* (pp. 37-48).

Goltz, N., & Mayo, M. (2018). Enhancing regulatory compliance by using artificial intelligence text mining to identify penalty clauses in legislation. *RAIL*, 1, 175.

Goodell, J. W., Kumar, S., Lim, W. M., & Pattnaik, D. (2021). Artificial intelligence and machine learning in finance: Identifying foundations, themes, and research clusters from bibliometric analysis. *Journal of Behavioral and Experimental Finance*, 32, 100577. DOI: 10.1016/j.jbef.2021.100577

Grassi, L., & Lanfranchi, D. (2022). RegTech in public and private sectors: The nexus between data, technology and regulation. *Economia e Politica Industriale*, 49(3), 441–479. DOI: 10.1007/s40812-022-00226-0

Gulati, R. (2023). Did regulatory compliance with governance standards really enhance the profit efficiency of Indian banks?. *Macroeconomics and Finance in Emerging Market Economies*, 1-27.

Hodges, C., & Steinholtz, R. (2017). *Ethical business practice and regulation: a behavioural and values-based approach to compliance and enforcement* (Vol. 6). Bloomsbury Publishing.

Hove, S. E., & Anda, B. (2005). Experiences from conducting semi-structured interviews in empirical software engineering research. In *11th IEEE International Software Metrics Symposium (METRICS'05)* (pp. 10-pp). IEEE. DOI: 10.1109/ METRICS.2005.24

Hu, B., & Wu, Y. (2023). AI-based Compliance Automation in Commercial Bank: How the Silicon Valley Bank Provided a Cautionary Tale for Future Integration. *International Review of Economics & Finance*, 7(1), 13.

Huerta, J. M., & Anand, A. (2018). Machine learning and artificial intelligence in consumer banking. *Journal of Digital Banking*, 3(1), 22–32. DOI: 10.69554/JIVX9796

Husain, A. R. A. M., Hamdan, A., & Fadhul, S. M. (2022). The Impact of Artificial Intelligence on the Banking Industry Performance. *Future of Organizations and Work After the 4th Industrial Revolution: The Role of Artificial Intelligence, Big Data, Automation, and Robotics*, 145-156.

Institute of International Finance. (2016). RegTech in financial services: Technology solutions for compliance and reporting.

Institute of International Finance. (2023, 09 June). RegTech: Exploring Solutions for Regulatory Challenges. https://www.iif.com/Publications/ID/4229/RegTech --Exploring-Solutions-for-Regulatory-Challenges

Jansen, S. (2020). *Machine Learning for Algorithmic Trading: Predictive models to extract signals from market and alternative data for systematic trading strategies with Python*. Packt Publishing Ltd.

Johnson, C. (2013). Regulatory arbitrage, extraterritorial jurisdiction, and Dodd-Frank: The implications of US global OTC derivative regulation. *Nev. LJ*, 14, 542.

Kariotis, T., & Howe, J. (2021). The future, digitally enabled, regulatory landscape. https://www.turcomat.org/index.php/turkbilmat/article/view/2139

Kitchenham, B. A., Brereton, P., Turner, M., Niazi, M. K., Linkman, S., Pretorius, R., & Budgen, D. (2010). Refining the systematic literature review process—Two participant-observer case studies. *Empirical Software Engineering*, 15(6), 618–653. DOI: 10.1007/s10664-010-9134-8

Königstorfer, F., & Thalmann, S. (2020). Applications of Artificial Intelligence in commercial banks–A research agenda for behavioral finance. *Journal of Behavioral and Experimental Finance*, 27, 100352. DOI: 10.1016/j.jbef.2020.100352

Krause, B., Kahembwe, E., Murray, I., & Renals, S. (2018, July). Dynamic evaluation of neural sequence models. In *International Conference on Machine Learning* (pp. 2766-2775). PMLR.

Kristanto, A. D., & Arman, A. A. (2022). Towards A Smart Regulatory Compliance, The Capabilities of RegTech and SupTech. In *2022 International Conference on Information Technology Systems and Innovation (ICITSI)* (pp. 300-309). IEEE. DOI: 10.1109/ICITSI56531.2022.9970801

Kulkarni, V., Sunkle, S., Kholkar, D., Roychoudhury, S., Kumar, R., & Raghunandan, M. (2021). Toward automated regulatory compliance. *CSI Transactions on ICT*, 9(2), 95–104. DOI: 10.1007/s40012-021-00329-4

Kumar, A., Sharma, S., & Mahdavi, M. (2021). Machine learning (Ml) technologies for digital credit scoring in rural finance: A literature review. *Risks*, 9(11), 192. DOI: 10.3390/risks9110192

Liu, S., Zhu, Z., Qu, Q., & You, C. (2022). Robust training under label noise by over-parameterization. In *International Conference on Machine Learning* (pp. 14153-14172). PMLR.

Lokanan, M. E. (2022). Predicting money laundering using machine learning and artificial neural networks algorithms in banks. *Journal of Applied Security Research*, ●●●, 1–25.

Mahalakshmi, V., Kulkarni, N., Kumar, K. P., Kumar, K. S., Sree, D. N., & Durga, S. (2022). The Role of implementing Artificial Intelligence and Machine Learning Technologies in the financial services Industry for creating Competitive Intelligence. *Materials Today: Proceedings*, 56, 2252–2255. DOI: 10.1016/j.matpr.2021.11.577

Martínez Martínez, R. (2019). Designing artificial intelligence. Challenges and strategies for achieving regulatory compliance. *Rev. Catalana Dret Pub.*, 58, 64.

May, P. J. (2005). Regulation and compliance motivations: Examining different approaches. *Public Administration Review*, 65(1), 31–44. DOI: 10.1111/j.1540-6210.2005.00428.x

McCarthy, J. (2023). The regulation of RegTech and SupTech in finance: Ensuring consistency in principle and in practice. *Journal of Financial Regulation and Compliance*, 31(2), 186–199. DOI: 10.1108/JFRC-01-2022-0004

McDowell, H. (2017). Banks spent close to $100 billion on compliance last year. *The Trade News.* https://www.thetradenews.com/Sell-side/Banks-spent-close-to -$100-billion-on-compliance-last-year/

McGlosson, C., & Enriquez, M. (2020). Financial industry compliance with Big Data and analytics. *Journal of Financial Compliance*, 3(2), 103–117. DOI: 10.69554/SIRM8601

Microsoft. (2023). Swift innovates with Azure confidential computing to help secure global financial transactions. https://customers.microsoft.com/en-us/story/1637929534319366070-swift-banking-capital-markets-azure-machine-learning

Moloney, N., Ferran, E., & Payne, J. (Eds.). (2015). *The Oxford handbook of financial regulation.* OUP Oxford. DOI: 10.1093/oxfordhb/9780199687206.001.0001

Murphy, A., Robu, K., & Steinert, M. (2020). *The investigator-centered approach to financial crime: Doing what matters.* McKinsey and Company.

Ng, P. M., Lit, K. K., & Cheung, C. T. (2022). Remote work as a new normal? The technology-organization-environment (TOE) context. *Technology in Society*, 70, 102022. DOI: 10.1016/j.techsoc.2022.102022 PMID: 35719245

Paltrinieri, N., Comfort, L., & Reniers, G. (2019). Learning about risk: Machine learning for risk assessment. *Safety Science*, 118, 475–486. DOI: 10.1016/j.ssci.2019.06.001

Peterson, E. A. (2013). Compliance and ethics programs: Competitive advantage through the law. *The Journal of Management and Governance*, 17(4), 1027–1045. DOI: 10.1007/s10997-012-9212-y

Priya, G. J., & Saradha, S. (2021, February). Fraud detection and prevention using machine learning algorithms: a review. In *2021 7th International Conference on Electrical Energy Systems (ICEES)* (pp. 564-568). IEEE. DOI: 10.1109/ICEES51510.2021.9383631

Rezaee, Z. (2004). Corporate governance role in financial reporting. *Research in Accounting Regulation*, 17, 107–149. DOI: 10.1016/S1052-0457(04)17006-9

Rezaei, M. (2022). Machine Learning in Regulatory Compliance Software Systems: An Industrial Case Study.

Roy, S. (2023). Dominance of Automation in Financial Services Industry. https://www.iimcal.ac.in/FinLab/email-template6/res/07.pdf

Runeson, P., & Höst, M. (2009). Guidelines for conducting and reporting case study research in software engineering. *Empirical Software Engineering*, 14(2), 131–164. DOI: 10.1007/s10664-008-9102-8

Scarpino, J. P. (2022). *An Exploratory Study: Implications of Machine Learning and Artificial Intelligence in Risk Management* (Doctoral dissertation, Marymount University). https://www.proquest.com/docview/2731478908?pq-origsite=gscholar&fromopenview=true

Seaman, C. B. (1999). Qualitative methods in empirical studies of software engineering. *IEEE Transactions on Software Engineering*, 25(4), 557–572. DOI: 10.1109/32.799955

Sen, J., Sen, R., & Dutta, A. (2021). Introductory Chapter: Machine Learning in Finance-Emerging Trends and Challenges. *Algorithms, Models and Applications*, 1.

Shi, Y., & Duan, X. (2019). Emerging Risk Analytics, 2019. *Distributed computer framework for data analysis, risk management, and automated compliance*. U.S. Patent Application No. 16/358,641.

Shirgave, S., Awati, C., More, R., & Patil, S. (2019). A review on credit card fraud detection using machine learning. *International Journal of Scientific & technology research, 8*(10), 1217-1220.

Silicon. (2017). *HSBC Adopts AI Startup Ayasdi's Tech To Tackle Money-Laundering*. Accessed at: HSBC

Singh, C. (2023). Artificial intelligence and deep learning: Considerations for financial institutions for compliance with the regulatory burden in the United Kingdom. *Journal of Financial Crime*.

Singh, C., & Lin, W. (2021). Can artificial intelligence, RegTech and CharityTech provide effective solutions for anti-money laundering and counter-terror financing initiatives in charitable fundraising. *Journal of Money Laundering Control*, 24(3), 464–482. DOI: 10.1108/JMLC-09-2020-0100

Singh, C., Lin, W., Singh, S. P., & Ye, Z. (2022). *RegTech compliance tools for charities in the United Kingdom: can machine learning help lighten the regulatory burden?* Company Lawyer.

Singh, C., Zhao, L., Lin, W., & Ye, Z. (2021). Can machine learning, as a RegTech compliance tool, lighten the regulatory burden for charitable organisations in the United Kingdom? *Journal of Financial Crime*, 29(1), 45–61. DOI: 10.1108/JFC-06-2021-0131

Singh, K., & Best, P. (2019). Anti-money laundering: Using data visualization to identify suspicious activity. *International Journal of Accounting Information Systems*, 34, 100418. DOI: 10.1016/j.accinf.2019.06.001

Snyder, H. (1996). Qualitative interviewing: The art of hearing data-Rubin, Herbert J. & Rubin, Irene S. Thousand Oaks, CA: Sage Publications, 1995. 302 pp. $21.95 (paperback)(ISBN 0-8039-5096-9). *Library & Information Science Research*, 2(18), 194–195. DOI: 10.1016/S0740-8188(96)90024-9

Srivastava, K. (2021). Paradigm shift in Indian banking industry with special reference to artificial intelligence. [TURCOMAT]. *Turkish Journal of Computer and Mathematics Education*, 12(5), 1623–1629.

Teichmann, F., Boticiu, S., & Sergi, B. S. (2023). RegTech–Potential benefits and challenges for businesses. *Technology in Society*, 72, 102150. DOI: 10.1016/j.techsoc.2022.102150

Tiffin, M. A. (2016). *Seeing in the dark: A machine-learning approach to nowcasting in Lebanon*. International Monetary Fund.

van Liebergen, B. (2017). FinTech/RegTech. *JOURNALN*, 45, 60.

Varian, H. R. (2014). Big data: New tricks for econometrics. *The Journal of Economic Perspectives*, 28(2), 3–28. DOI: 10.1257/jep.28.2.3

Vasista, K. (2021). Regulatory Compliance and Supervision of Artificial Intelligence, Machine Learning and Also Possible Effects on Financial Institutions. *Machine Learning and also Possible Effects on Financial Institutions (June 13, 2021). International Journal of Innovative Research in Computer and Communication Engineering| e-ISSN*, 2320-9801.

Wang, A. (2019). The role of RegTech in augmenting regulatory compliance: Regulating technology, accountability and liability. *UNSW Law Journal, 19*(10).

Wilson, H. J., Daugherty, P., & Bianzino, N. (2017). The jobs that artificial intelligence will create. *MIT Sloan Management Review*, 58(4), 14.

Wohlin, C. (2014). Guidelines for snowballing in systematic literature studies and a replication in software engineering. In *Proceedings of the 18th international conference on evaluation and assessment in software engineering* (pp. 1-10). DOI: 10.1145/2601248.2601268

Xu, Z., Wang, Y., Tang, J., Wang, J., & Gursoy, M. C. (2017). A deep reinforcement learning based framework for power-efficient resource allocation in cloud RANs. In *2017 IEEE International Conference on Communications (ICC)* (pp. 1-6). IEEE. DOI: 10.1109/ICC.2017.7997286

Yip, F. (2012). *Semantically enabled applications-a case study in regulatory compliance* (Doctoral dissertation, UNSW Sydney).

Zhang, X., Chan, F. T., Yan, C., & Bose, I. (2022). Towards risk-aware artificial intelligence and machine learning systems: An overview. *Decision Support Systems*, 159, 113800. DOI: 10.1016/j.dss.2022.113800

Zhao, X., & Qi, Y. (2020). Why do firms obey?: The state of regulatory compliance research in China. *Journal of Chinese Political Science*, 25(2), 339–352. DOI: 10.1007/s11366-020-09657-9

Zou, J., Han, Y., & So, S. S. (2009). Overview of artificial neural networks. *Artificial neural networks: methods and applications*, 14-22.

ADDITIONAL READING

Ali, M. (2021). *Remote Work and Sustainable Changes for the Future of Global Business*. IGI Global. https://www.igi-global.com/book/remote-work-sustainable-changes-future/264375

Ali, M. (2022). *Future Role of Sustainable Innovative Technologies in Crisis Management*. IGI Global. https://www.igi-global.com/book/future-role-sustainable-innovative-technologies/281281

Ali, M. (2023). *Shifting Paradigms in the Rapidly Developing Global Digital Ecosystem: A GCC Perspective.* In Digital Entrepreneurship and Co-Creating Value Through Digital Encounters (pp. 145-166). IGI Global. https://www.igi-global.com/chapter/shifting-paradigms-in-the-rapidly-developing-global-digital-ecosystem/323525

Ali, M. (2023). T*axonomy of Industry 4.0 Technologies in Digital Entrepreneurship and Co-Creating Value.* In *Digital Entrepreneurship and Co-Creating Value Through Digital Encounters* (pp. 24–55). IGI Global., https://www.igi-global.com/chapter/taxonomy-of-industry-40-technologies-in-digital-entrepreneurship-and-co-creating-value/323520 DOI: 10.4018/978-1-6684-7416-7.ch002

Ali, M., & Wood-Harper, T. (2021). *Fostering Communication and Learning with Underutilized Technologies in Higher Education.* IGI Global. https://www.igi-global.com/book/fostering-communication-learning-underutilized-technologies/244593

Ali, M., Wood-Harper, T., & Kutar, M. (2023). Multi-Perspectives of Contemporary Digital Transformation Models of Complex Innovation Management. In *Digital Entrepreneurship and Co-Creating Value Through Digital Encounters* (pp. 79–96). IGI Global., https://www.igi-global.com/chapter/multi-perspectives-of-contemporary-digital-transformation-models-of-complex-innovation-management/323522 DOI: 10.4018/978-1-6684-7416-7.ch004

Ali, M. B. (2021). Internet of Things (IoT) to Foster Communication and Information Sharing: A Case of UK Higher Education. In Ali, M. B., & Wood-Harper, T. (Eds.), *Fostering Communication and Learning With Underutilized Technologies in Higher Education* (pp. 1–20). IGI Global., https://www.igi-global.com/chapter/internet-of-things-iot-to-foster-communication-and-information-sharing/262718/ DOI: 10.4018/978-1-7998-4846-2.ch001

Ali, M. B., & Wood-Harper, T. (2022). Artificial Intelligence (AI) as a Decision-Making Tool to Control Crisis Situations. In *Future Role of Sustainable Innovative Technologies in Crisis Management.* IGI Global., https://www.igi-global.com/chapter/artificial-intelligence-ai-as-a-decision-making-tool-to-control-crisis-situations/298931 DOI: 10.4018/978-1-7998-9815-3.ch006

Ali, M. B., Wood-Harper, T., & Ramlogan, R. (2020). A Framework Strategy to Overcome Trust Issues on Cloud Computing Adoption in Higher Education. In Modern Principles, Practices, and Algorithms for Cloud Security (pp. 162-183). IGI Global. https://www.igi-global.com/chapter/a-framework-strategy-to-overcome-trust-issues-on-cloud-computing-adoption-in-higher-education/238907/

ENDNOTE

[1]   See Box 1 for more examples.

Chapter 11
Blockchain's Transformative Role in the Financial Sector

Suaad Jassem

College of Banking and Financial Studies, Oman

Karima Toumi Sayari

Al Zahra College for Women, Oman

Fadi Abdelfattah

https://orcid.org/0000-0002-4665-4777

Modern College of Business and Science, Oman

ABSTRACT

This chapter explores blockchain technology, a revolutionary distributed ledger system transforming the financial sector by enabling secure, transparent, decentralized transaction recording and management. Focusing on the accounting and finance industries, the chapter examines how blockchain technology is being adopted to enhance operations and service automation. It highlights blockchain's significant benefits, such as increased transparency, faster transaction processing, cost reduction, improved accuracy, and enhanced security. The chapter comprehensively discusses blockchain's diverse applications in accounting, banking, and finance, including its role in cross-border payments, stock exchanges, identity verification, and the standardization of bookkeeping, accounting, and auditing practices. Additionally, it critically analyzes the potential risks associated with blockchain adoption, like regulatory challenges and security vulnerabilities, underlining the importance for businesses to weigh both risks and benefits in the rapidly digitalizing financial landscape.

DOI: 10.4018/979-8-3693-5966-2.ch011

1. INTRODUCTION

Organizations are increasingly harnessing new technological tools to streamline corporate processes and reshape their business models in the evolving digital transformation landscape. This digital shift has paved the way for revolutionary changes in various sectors, including accounting and finance. At the forefront of these changes is Blockchain technology, a groundbreaking innovation that is redefining the future of economic and financial interactions. Geographical stability, security, and trust remain paramount in economic, financial, and political spheres. However, the ability to adopt and utilize new technologies like Blockchain is becoming increasingly vital for businesses and governments. (Abad-Segura et al., 2024; Mahajan and Nanda, 2024)

Blockchain technology, known for its decentralization and security, is rapidly gaining traction in various industries. Its potential to transform critical operations such as contract management, payment processing, and record-keeping is immense (Appelbaum et al., 2022; Zhang et al., 2020). The technology operates on a model that efficiently integrates financial resources and processes data, thereby facilitating the development of new financial formats and service models. These models are tailored to consumer needs and are built upon three foundational layers: data, rules, and application. In the financial sector, Blockchain's implications are profound, enhancing the efficiency of cross-border payments, restructuring financial market credit systems, and providing accurate consumer credit assessments (Prewett et al., 2020).

Despite its promising applications, integrating Blockchain into accounting and finance is challenging. A significant concern is the lack of industry regulation and standardization, leading to potential inconsistencies and vulnerabilities in the technology application. Security risks, such as data breaches and hacking, threaten Blockchain systems' integrity (Appelbaum et al., 2022). However, the potential benefits of Blockchain, including increased operational efficiency, cost reduction, and enhanced transaction transparency, cannot be overlooked. As technology evolves, businesses must weigh these benefits against the potential risks (Abdennadher et al., 2021).

This chapter embarks on a comprehensive exploration of the adoption and application of Blockchain technology in the accounting and finance sectors. It delves into the myriad ways Blockchain is being utilized, its benefits, and the challenges faced in its adoption. The chapter poses critical questions: What are the advantages of Blockchain over existing systems in accounting and finance? How does Blockchain impact these sectors? What are its current applications, and what key issues and limitations hinder its wider use?

This chapter thoroughly examines the adoption of Blockchain in accounting and finance, offering insights into the shared challenges and perspectives in these interconnected fields. It presents a comparative analysis of Blockchain's implementation in accounting and finance, marking a significant contribution to understanding this technology's role in these areas.

The chapter outlines its objectives and academic contributions, followed by a detailed discussion of blockchain technology, including its definition, history, key features, functionality, and potential benefits for the accounting and financial sectors. Subsequent sections explore the diverse applications of Blockchain in accounting and finance and the common challenges in its implementation, and the chapter concludes with a synthesis of the findings.

2. LITERATURE REVIEW

2.1. Overview of Blockchain Technology

Blockchain technology has witnessed over a decade of transformative evolution. Its initial experimentation spanned multiple domains, with a significant focus on applications within finance and accounting. This innovative technology has revolutionized various industries, leaving an indelible mark on accounting and finance (Han et al., 2023; Ko et al., 2018). It has revolutionized how financial transactions are conducted, recorded, and tracked. Blockchain is a decentralized, distributed ledger system, enabling the creation of a digital transaction ledger accessible to all participants within the network. Critical facets of blockchain technology include (Rajasekaran et al., 2022; Sanka et al., 2021; Zhao et al., 2016).

- Decentralization: Blockchain technology is decentralized; no central authority or intermediary controls the network. Instead, the network is run by nodes that work together to validate transactions.
- Transparency: All transactions on the Blockchain are transparent and visible to all participants in the network. This transparency ensures that all parties involved in a transaction can see the same information.
- Security: Blockchain technology is secure due to its complex algorithms that encrypt and verify transactions. Once a transaction is recorded on the Blockchain, it cannot be altered or deleted.
- Immunity to Fraud: Blockchain technology is immune to fraudulent activities, as all transactions are verified and recorded using a consensus mechanism. This verification process ensures that all transactions are legitimate and authentic.

Bitcoin is the first and most well-known blockchain application. In 2009, the world financial crisis led to the development of a new type of decentralized digital money free from the oversight of traditional financial organizations such as banks, governments, and other financial institutions. Business researchers have only recently started looking into Blockchain, a growing technology that has the potential to be disruptive since its widespread adoption in accounting and finance. Blockchain is a decentralized digital record that enables peer-to-peer value transfers of all kinds, from digital currency to actual goods and land titles, and consequently does not require a third party (Chen et al., 2018).

The technique is straightforward yet effective. It is essentially a chain of informational blocks, each independently validated by a network of nodes (Demirkan et al., 2022) that divide blockchain-related activities into three categories to conceptualize the quick growth of blockchain technologies, as shown in Table 1.

Table 1. Phases of Block Chain Development

Blockchain Phase	Description
Blockchain 1.0	Primarily digital currencies and payment methods.
Blockchain 2.0	Smart contracts and more complex financial instruments
Blockchain 3.0	Diversification into various sectors beyond finance

Source: Author Compilation of Chen's 2018 work

The table explains that Blockchain 1.0 is about money, much like cryptocurrencies and online payment methods. In comparison, Blockchain 2.0 contracts are mainly intelligent for more complex value transfers like stocks, bonds, loans, mortgages, and title deeds. On the other hand, Applications of blockchain 3.0 outside of banking include those in government, healthcare, science, the arts, and culture.

2.2. Economic Impacts of Blockchain Technology.

Frizzo-Barker et al. (2020) argue that blockchain technology can provide real-time transparency and decrease surveillance, remittance, verification, and networking expenses, allowing manufacturing firms to produce goods at a lower marginal cost. Additionally, blockchain technology can potentially eliminate the informal economy about the tax system and significantly reduce the need for tax control. Blockchain technology could potentially eliminate the informal economy related to tax systems, thereby significantly reducing the need for stringent tax controls and audits (Shava and Mhlanga, 2023).

The technology could eliminate the tax system's informal economy and significantly reduce the need for tax control.

- Exploring the Concept of Permissibility in Blockchain Systems

Blockchain networks can be created with permission, which restricts data access. This allows for secure data access and protection against fraudulent activities. There are specific types of Risk and Fraud that can be detected and prevented. Moreover, it cannot be altered once data or a transaction is added to a blockchain. Additionally, before being added to the Blockchain, all participants in the network must verify the data, and each block added to the chain is given a timestamp. After the data is added, the source and history of the assets are established.

- Addressing Financial Fraud with Blockchain Solutions

Financial transactions are often intricate due to collateral requirements, currency differences, and the time needed for reconciliation and settlement, which may necessitate multiple human interactions. As a result, the risk of fraud is high. However, blockchain technology makes it easier to identify suspicious activities by enabling the real-time sharing and updating of recorded data with the approval of all parties with access to it.

- Combating Identity Fraud Using Blockchain Technology

Identity theft is a prevalent form of fraud in e-commerce, and its occurrence has increased significantly in recent years. However, blockchain technology, with its robust authentication systems, offers enhanced security by allowing only authorized individuals to access original data and restricting transaction verification to designated parties. This creates a secure infrastructure that protects personal data and greatly reduces the risk of identity theft. Moreover, recent studies highlight the growing role of self-sovereign identity (SSI), which gives individuals full control over their identity data, further minimizing the risk of identity theft (Weigl et al., 2023).

- *Preventing Supply Chain Frauds with Blockchain Interventions*

Supply chain fraud is a significant issue for businesses as it involves an extensive network of supplier companies, and many people have access to data. Blockchain technology provides a transparent and straightforward way to track products. All authorized participants must verify to make any updates to the products, and this ensures that participants do not easily manipulate the products.

- *Countering Tax Deviation Fraud through Blockchain Applications*

Blockchain technology facilitates the detection of fraud and errors by providing transparent and precise information about transactions and items on the network. This feature is handy for monitoring VAT payments and reducing VAT fraud. Furthermore, the risks and consequences of incompatibility as payers may be forever excluded from the blockchain network can guide behavioral change. According to experts, many taxpayers, particularly micro-enterprises and individuals, have a limited understanding of their tax obligations. Blockchain can simplify complying with tax regulations and help reduce the tax deficit (PWC, 2017).

- ***Cost Reduction Strategies Enabled by Blockchain Technology***

According to Gomber et al. (2018), blockchain technology has distinctive features that allow institutions to operate more efficiently, with lower errors, less risk, lower capital requirements, and greater resilience against cyber-attacks. Thus, it reduces costs associated with traditional accounting methods, which are usually labor-intensive and time-consuming (Golosova and Romanovs, 2018).

The potential applications of blockchain technology in financial services are vast, encompassing payments, capital markets, trade services, investment and wealth management, as well as securities and commodities exchanges (Al-Jaroodi and Mohamed, 2019). It is increasingly recognized as a critical factor in achieving significant cost savings across these sectors.

For example, a study by Santander FinTech estimates that the use of distributed ledger technology could reduce financial services infrastructure costs by **$15 billion to $20 billion per year** by 2022, primarily through the decommissioning of outdated systems and the reduction of IT expenses (Kuma et al., 2022; Xu et al., 2020; Mahajan and Nanda, 2024).

Additionally, blockchain technology can automate a wide range of processes, enabling companies to boost efficiency and reduce costs. This is especially advantageous for small and medium-sized enterprises (SMEs), which may lack the resources to invest in expensive accounting software or hire additional staff (Morkunas et al., 2019; Mahajan and Nanda, 2024).

-Creating New Revenue Streams Through Blockchain Innovation

Blockchain technology enables the creation of new business models and revenue streams. For instance, companies can issue tokens to raise funds, pay suppliers, and reward customers. These tokens can help foster a more efficient and transparent business ecosystem, providing innovative ways to engage with stakeholders and generate additional revenue.

In small and medium-sized enterprises (SMEs), blockchain technology can also shift managerial priorities. While managers in large corporations may focus on revenue maximization to dominate market shares, SMEs adopting blockchain can prioritize profit maximization within their output capacity, as blockchain enables real-time monitoring of managerial behavior by business owners. This ensures alignment between managerial actions and the owners' goals, reducing the need for costly oversight (Khan et al., 2023).

By streamlining processes such as surveillance, remittance, and verification, blockchain significantly reduces operational costs, leading to lower marginal costs for manufacturing firms. In addition, blockchain technology can potentially eliminate the informal economy regarding the tax system, minimizing the need for tax control and providing greater transparency in financial reporting (Frizzo-Barker et al., 2020; Shava and Mhlanga, 2023).

2.3. Understanding the Functioning of Blockchain Technology

Blockchain technology is a chain of blocks, where each block contains a record of transactions. The blocks are linked chronologically, creating an unchangeable and tamper-proof record of all transactions (Gad et al., 2022). A private key cryptography-based digital signature is used at a node in a decentralized Blockchain network to start a transaction, which is considered a digital asset transmitted as a data structure between peers in the network. All transactions are kept in an unconfirmed transaction pool, and the Gossip protocol, a flooding mechanism, is utilized to spread them throughout the network. Peers must then select and approve these transactions based on a set of predetermined requirements (Wang et al., 2019).

Blockchain technology has several benefits. One of its primary benefits in accounting and finance is to improve transparency. In addition, Blockchain technology creates a transparent and secure environment for financial transactions, which reduces the risk of fraud and errors (Han et al., 2023; Yoo, 2017). This transparency ensures that all parties involved in a transaction can see the same information, which can help to improve trust and reduce the need for intermediaries such as banks (Rajasekaran et al., 2022; Reddy et al., 2023; Schmidt and Wagner, 2019). A further benefit is to provide faster and more efficient financial transactions, which can reduce costs and speed up the process. This is because transactions can be validated and processed in real-time without intermediaries or delays (Golosova and Romanovs, 2018; Rajasekaran et al., 2022). This can be particularly beneficial for individuals and businesses that operate across borders, as the fees charged by banks and other financial institutions can be prohibitively high (Ali et al., 2021; Schär, 2021; Schmitz and Leoni, 2019).

Another significant gain of this technology is its ability to provide greater transparency and accountability; as every transaction is recorded on Blockchain, it is possible to trace the history of any asset or transaction back to its origin. This can be useful in a wide range of applications, from tracking the supply chain of goods to ensuring the integrity of voting systems (Ali et al., 2021).

To add a new transaction to the Blockchain, the network of users or nodes must verify and approve it. Each node on the network has a copy of the Blockchain, and they work together to validate new transactions. Once the network supports a transaction, it is added to a new block and the Blockchain (Gad et al., 2022).

To ensure the security of the Blockchain, each block contains a unique code called a hash, which is generated using complex mathematical algorithms. The hash of each block is also included in the next block, creating a chain of hashes that link the blocks together. This makes it virtually impossible to alter any of the blocks in the chain without changing all the subsequent blocks (Ali et al., 2021).

Blockchain technology is a revolutionary new way of conducting secure and transparent transactions. Its decentralized structure and tamper-proof record make it ideal for various applications, from financial transactions to supply chain management and beyond (Mori, 2023; Rajasekaran et al., 2022).

3. VARIOUS USES OF BLOCKCHAIN TECHNOLOGY IN THE FIELDS OF ACCOUNTING AND FINANCE

The rise of fintech has fundamentally transformed the financial services sector by merging finance with technology. This intersection, known as fintech, has introduced innovations like blockchain, which was initially developed to support the Bitcoin cryptocurrency. However, blockchain technology has since been adopted in various areas of the financial services industry, including banking, accounting, and management. According to experts, blockchain holds the potential to significantly disrupt and transform these industries by introducing new ways of managing transactions and data (Chen and Bellavitis, 2019; Mosteanu and Faccia, 2020; Anyanwu et al., 2023).

This technology can revolutionize how financial transactions are conducted, recorded, and tracked. Technology has several benefits for accounting and finance, including improved transparency, faster transactions, reduced costs, improved accuracy, and enhanced security. However, technology has several challenges, including lack of regulation, security concerns, integration with existing systems, and complexity. Despite these challenges, blockchain technology can potentially transform the accounting and finance industry and should be carefully considered by businesses looking to improve their financial systems (Chen and Bellavitis, 2019; Mori, 2023).

The adoption of blockchain technology in accounting and finance has increased in recent years. The technology has several use cases in accounting and finance, including payment processing, audit trail creation, asset management, and smart contracts. These use cases have been widely adopted by businesses in the accounting and finance industry, as they have the potential to improve the efficiency, accuracy, and security of financial transactions (Chen and Bellavitis,2019; Mori, 2023).

3.1.Application of Blockchain Technology in the Accounting Sector

Blockchain technology can be used in different areas of the accounting field. Enabling an immutable record of financial transactions can increase the transparency and accuracy of financial reporting (Han et al., 2023). This immutable nature ensures that once a transaction is recorded, it cannot be altered, thus reducing the risk of **fraud** and **manipulation** of financial statements (Abad-Segura et al., 2024). This improved transparency fosters greater trust among stakeholders and regulators. Furthermore, blockchain technology can enable the creation of digital identities, which can be used to verify the identity of individuals and entities involved in financial transactions (Liu et al., 2019). Blockchain applications in accounting are essentially related to the following themes (Refer to Table 2).

Table 2. Summary of Blockchain Applications in Accounting and Finance

Aspect	Blockchain technology application
Auditing	Real-time, immutable audit trails for financial records
Supply Chain	Transparent tracking of supply chain transactions
Fraud Prevention	Reducing fraud through transparent ledgers
Smart Contracts	Automated, self-executing contracts for transactions
Cross-border Payments	Faster and cheaper international money transfers
Identity Verification	Secure identity verification for KYC and AML
Regulatory Compliance	Ensuring compliance with financial regulations
Asset Tokenization	Digitizing and trading of assets (e.g., real estate)
Stock and Bond Issuance	Efficient issuance and trading of securities
Payment Settlement	Streamlining payment clearing and settlement processes

3.1.1.The Role of Blockchain Technology in Auditing

One of the most significant potential applications of blockchain technology in accounting is in auditing. In traditional auditing processes, complex record-keeping systems are implemented to ensure the accuracy of financial statements. Blockchain technology can streamline auditing by providing auditors with real-time access to verified financial data. According to recent research, blockchain's ability to automate auditing processes and provide tamper-proof audit trails has the potential to reduce both the cost and time required for audits (Abad-Segura et al., 2024). Auditors can leverage blockchain to verify transactions more efficiently, enhancing the reliability and completeness of audit evidence (Richins et al., 2022). Furthermore, the use of smart contracts in auditing can automate certain verification tasks, ensuring compliance with predefined rules (Mori, 2016). However, these systems can be vulnerable to errors and manipulation, which can compromise the accuracy of the audit. This is where blockchain technology comes in (Gaur and Gaiha, 2023).

Auditors can create a secure and transparent record of financial transactions with blockchain technology. This record is virtually impossible to manipulate, providing a higher level of security than traditional record-keeping systems. Once a transaction is recorded on the Blockchain, it is immutable, meaning it cannot be changed or deleted. This feature alone can help increase the accuracy and reliability of audits while reducing the risk of fraud (Gad et al., 2022).

The use of blockchain technology in auditing can benefit both auditors and clients. Auditors can provide more accurate and reliable audits, improving their reputation and leading to increased business. Clients can have more confidence in the accuracy of their financial statements, which can help to improve their relationships with investors (Gaur and Gaiha, 2023). Furthermore, using blockchain technology can help reduce the time and cost associated with auditing processes, which can be a significant advantage for auditors and clients (Gad et al., 2022). The potential benefits of blockchain technology in auditing have increased interest and investment in the technology from accounting firms. The Big Four accounting firms (Deloitte, EY, KPMG, and PwC) have all invested in blockchain technology and have been exploring its potential applications in the accounting industry. Other accounting firms have also begun to invest in and experiment with blockchain technology (Gaur and Gaiha, 2023).

3.1.2. Enhancing Supply Chain Management with Blockchain Technology

Supply chains play a crucial role in many industries but can also be complex and involve numerous parties. This complexity can often lead to delays, errors, and even disputes. However, with blockchain technology, companies can create a transparent and secure record of all transactions and interactions within the supply chain (Karakaş et al., 2021). This can help to reduce the risk of errors and disputes, which in turn can lead to greater efficiency and cost savings for companies while also improving the overall reliability of the supply chain (Sharma and Kumar, 2020). Karakaş et al. (2021) mentioned that Seven large US corporations were analyzed to determine how blockchain technology could improve their supply chain operations. The early initiatives of these corporations showed that using this technology could lead to faster and more cost-efficient product delivery, increased product traceability, streamlined financing processes, and improved coordination among buyers, suppliers, and banks. However, using Blockchain in supply chain management requires certain precautions, such as limiting participation to trusted partners, adopting a new consensus protocol, and preventing errors and counterfeits from entering the supply chain. The authors suggest that blockchain technology could provide significant benefits for companies across various industries if implemented carefully.

According to Statista (2023), the supply chain audit use case is expected to be the most significant contributor to the worldwide distributed ledger market, projected to surpass 103 billion US dollars by 2030, an increase of over 102 billion from 2020. Other use cases include immutable records, digital identity, smart contracts, and proof-of-work.

3.1.3. Mitigating Risks and Reducing Fraud through Blockchain Technology

By creating a secure and transparent record of all financial transactions, companies can ensure that their accounting records are accurate and current while reducing the risk of fraud and errors. This is especially important for companies that deal with large volumes of data and complex financial transactions (Gad et al., 2022). Blockchain may be a good asset in Risk and fraud Reduction. While Blockchain has many valuable features, a few specific features are essential for risk, fraud detection, and prevention (Karakaş et al., 2021).

3.1.4. Exploring Distributed Networks in Blockchain Technology

As previously mentioned, blockchain technology is a decentralized digital ledger that records data. The network allows authorized members to monitor and share transactions and data across multiple computers. The management and authorization of data are transparently carried out through the network, giving authorized personnel access and control of current and previous data from different departments, such as supply chain management or sales. This enables any authorized team member to detect fraudulent or suspicious transactions without central authority. Therefore, using Blockchain in fraud detection helps prevent potential human errors and saves time.

3.2. The Impact of Blockchain Technology on the Financial Sector

Due to its potential to increase reliability, effectiveness, transparency, digital transactions, multistakeholder platforms, and confidence in financial transactions, blockchain technology has seen notable acceptance in the financial sector. The financial industry can benefit from using blockchain technology to process international payments, reform the financial system and market, and automatically and precisely identify client credit conditions more effectively.

Today, every major financial institution, from Goldman Sachs to NASDAQ, deals with "*Blockchain*," a new technology that has become popular. It incorporates several computer technologies, including point-to-point transmission, consensus procedures, distributed data storage, and encryption. It has also been named a disruptive innovation for the Internet era. The financial sector, particularly its financial market infrastructure and the insurance business, holds great promise for blockchain technology (Schmidt and Wagner, 2019).

3.2.1. The Emergence and Role of Digital Currencies in the Blockchain Era

With the introduction of cryptocurrencies like Bitcoin, Blockchain became more well-known. Cryptocurrencies use blockchain technology to facilitate safe, decentralized, and transparent transactions without using intermediaries like banks (Renduchintala et al., 2022).

Modern electronic payment systems rely on trusted, central third parties to process payments securely. The pressure to reduce these transaction costs led to banks starting to accept claims from each other. This innovation made trading more convenient as merchants could now deposit notes from other banks directly into their bank, eliminating the burden of converting chapter money into gold to transfer the funds. In accepting the note from a different bank, the payee's bank faced a new problem: it was now exposed to the payer's bank until settlement in gold could be arranged (Mosteanu and Faccia,2020).

Cryptocurrencies are one significant application of blockchain technology that has attracted the most interest. The volume of data increased exponentially, with each megabyte increasing by almost a gigabit every few days. The Bitcoin blockchain is a distributed database that houses a continuously expanding and tamper-evident record of all transactions and documents involving Bitcoin from the cryptocurrency's initial release in January 2009.

Internationally, and compared to conventional ways, Blockchain enables international methods of payment that are quicker and more affordable. Financial institutions and remittance providers now use blockchain-based platforms to enable quicker and more affordable international transfers. Companies concentrating on the payments market are increasingly promoting innovation to boost the effectiveness and usability of blockchain-based apps (Statista, 2023). Approximately 16% of the worldwide blockchain technology market, cross-border payments and settlements were regarded as the most significant individual use cases for blockchain technology, with 10.7% of the market share, lot lineage, and provenance also had a more significant proportion of the market (Statista, 2023).

3.2.2. Transformation of Financial Services with Blockchain Technology

The way we handle money and financial services is changing fast. New kinds of companies, like fintech and big tech firms, offer creative services, not just traditional banks and insurance companies. There are also new ways to get money online, like crowdfunding and lending directly to others without involving banks (Toumi Sayari, 2023). It is anticipated that the financial sector will see a growth in the use of blockchain technology over the coming years, with a projected market size of 22.5 billion US dollars by 2026 (Statista, 2023).

The integration of AI and blockchain in financial systems is crucial for harnessing the predictive capabilities of digital technologies. Just as AI-driven digitalization of accounting practices is driven by strategic foresight, agility, and flexibility, blockchain adoption in finance similarly requires dynamic organizational capabilities (Jassem, 2024).

In late 2021, people started using cryptocurrencies, like Bitcoin, to pay for things when they travel, especially luxury items. Nevertheless, even though not many travel businesses accept digital money, it turns out that a lot of cryptocurrency spending happens in the travel industry. It might be because the travel industry faces challenges after the pandemic, and this new way of spending money could be part of the recovery.

A rapidly expanding number of businesses specializing in financial technology and big tech companies are now offering these cutting-edge financial services and products in addition to traditional financial services providers like banks and insurance companies. New types of digital financing, such as crowdfunding and peer-to-peer (P2P) lending, where lenders and lending businesses can engage with each other directly without bank intermediation, have likely been rapidly increasing in recent years because of this tendency (Bhuvana, 2020).

Statista (2023) also estimates that by 2025, the blockchain market will have risen to 39 billion dollars, having expanded rapidly over the past several years globally. It was predicted that there was a market of $0.28 billion for blockchain solutions for the banking sector and financial institutions. In the upcoming years, it is anticipated that blockchain technology in the financial sector will advance further, with a market worth roughly $22.5 billion in 2026.

Consumers in late 2021 intended to utilize cryptocurrency as a form of payment for travel, although the luxury goods sector was particularly interested in these transactions. Based on this data, the source discusses a "*mismatch*" in accepting cryptocurrencies for payments: The source notes that although the travel business exhibited the slightest interest in accepting digital currencies, it is the most popular choice for cryptocurrency spending. The source speculates that this may be because the industry is still recovering from the effects of the coronavirus outbreak. In contrast, when it comes to financial services.

3.2.3. Understanding Smart Contracts in the Realm of Blockchain Technology

Smart contracts, self-executing contracts with predefined circumstances, can be created and carried out using blockchain technology. Small scripts that are saved on a blockchain and run concurrently by many validators are known as smart contracts. In the case of public blockchains, the network is set up such that each user can take part in any action and confirm its proper execution (Schmitz and Leoni, 2019). By automating and enforcing the contract's terms, smart contracts eliminate the need for brokers and simplify procedures like trade settlements, insurance claims, and management for supply chains.

The most significant and fastest-growing segment right now is payment. Access to mobile devices, data networks, and applications has enabled financial technology firms to entice traditional banking consumers away from legacy banking platforms, an essential driver in this increase. Such applications, therefore, allow users to connect directly with suppliers, eliminating away with intermediaries. On the other hand,

Reddy et al. (2020) stated that smart contracts would be quickly applied to trade finance, compliance, asset management, insurance payment, and capital market activities, connected to many stakeholders if introduced fully.

According to (Schmitz and Leoni, 2019) research, the main benefit of smart contracts is a high level of security: Smart contracts will always be carried out as intended and permit anyone to check the consequent state changes independently. Intelligent contracts are incredibly transparent and reduce the possibility of manipulation and arbitrary interference when implemented safely.

3.2.4. The Influence of Blockchain Technology on the Banking Industry

Blockchain, a particular technology for secure transactions, is becoming essential in handling money and services. Experts think it will keep growing and help the world economy, improving things for customers and the financial system. Banks and other financial companies are starting to use it because it makes records of transactions straightforward for rules to follow.

Gartner, a global research and advisory firm forecasted the business value of blockchain to be over 176 billion USD and 3.1 trillion USD by 2025 and 2030 respectively. Cisco multinational technology company also predicted that 10% of the global GDP will be on blockchain by 2027 and the blockchain market will be 9.7 billion USD by 2021. More than 40 central banks are experimenting with central bank digital currency (CBD) (Sanka et al., 2021).

Blockchain technology is widely used in economic transactions, prediction markets, the settlement of financial assets, commercial services, and the finance community. Blockchain is anticipated to play a significant role in the sustained growth of global economies, benefiting customers and the current financial system as well as the rest of society (Wang et al., 2019).

Financial institutions can use Blockchain to maintain an auditable record of transactions, improving regulatory compliance and facilitating easier auditing processes.

According to Statista 2023 estimations, the market for blockchain technology is expected to develop significantly over the next few years, reaching a value of over 39 billion dollars by 2025. One of the first major industries to invest in Blockchain was the banking industry, which now accounts for about 30% of the market value of technology.

3.2.5. The Role of Blockchain Technology in Modern Financial Markets

Blockchain technology is changing how financial markets work. It makes trading more secure and faster by cutting out the intermediaries. On the other hand, this means deals get settled quicker and more smoothly. Using Blockchain spreads out the risks to the investor and gives investors more control compared to the usual ways companies are managed, which sometimes have limits in handling risks.

Blockchain is already used in the USA for trading different currencies, stocks, and financial contracts. Other countries like Canada, Australia, and Japan are also looking into how they can use Blockchain. NASDAQ OMX, a big stock exchange company, wants to create a stock market using Blockchain. They have already made trading much faster on one of their platforms since 2015, cutting the time from four days to just 10 minutes!

Blockchain technology has the potential to revolutionize the functioning of financial markets.

Enabling new trading processes and eliminating the need for intermediaries may make it unnecessary for numerous parties to reconcile, allowing quicker and more effective settlement and trading of securities.

The introduction of modern technology, such as Blockchain, which is based on the distributed ledger, has regenerated more effectively investor control and reduced risk management by diversifying investment risk. Traditional corporate governance gave poor investors control over their investments due to the higher risk associated with financial market infrastructure (Li, 2022).

In the USA, blockchain technology trades currencies, OTC stocks, and derivatives. Additionally, the usage of blockchain technology is being prosecuted in Canada, Australia, and Japan. The NASDAQ OMX group in the USA wants to create an over-the-counter stock market based on blockchain technology to link businesses and investors. Then, since 2015, they have used blockchain technology to cut the real trading time from four days to 10 minutes on the Nasdaq Private Market, a private professional investor curb market (Schär, 2021).

4. COMMON CHALLENGES OF BLOCKCHAIN TECHNOLOGY IN ACCOUNTING AND FINANCE

Without the need for a centralized trusted authority, blockchain technology may be utilized in a wide range of applications in accounting and finance to safeguard data with enhanced reliability, increase transparency and accountability, and other benefits, as discussed previously. However, like with any new technology, integrating existing systems is a common challenge associated with adopting blockchain technology in accounting and finance because the technology requires significant changes to existing systems, which can be costly and time-consuming. Integration challenges remain a critical barrier to blockchain adoption. Many companies find it difficult to integrate blockchain with their legacy systems due to compatibility issues, high costs, and the complexity of transitioning to a decentralized model. Scalability is another pressing issue; while blockchain is praised for its security and transparency, it struggles to handle a large number of transactions at scale, as seen with Bitcoin and Ethereum's network congestion during peak usage periods (Prewett et al., 2020). Indeed, several problems and obstacles need to be solved before it can be widely used for everyday transactions (Refer to Table 3). This section discusses some of the limits of blockchain technology in accounting and finance and develops potential research opportunities for the future.

4.1. Addressing the Challenge of Lack of Regulation in Blockchain Applications

Blockchain technology is currently not regulated, making it difficult for businesses to adopt. This lack of regulation can create uncertainty and make it difficult for businesses to know how to comply with existing laws and regulations.

Blockchain technology is still in its early stages and has encountered adoption issues, including rapidity, capacity for growth, interaction with legacy systems, uniform rules, interoperability, and infrastructure. The extensive adoption of this technology is further complicated by organizational problems such as employee attitudes and comprehension, lack of control and rules, and incumbents' technological knowledge. Furthermore, blockchain-based implementations' high energy consumption requirements are too much for legacy systems to handle.

Some regions are making strides towards establishing regulatory frameworks. For example, the European Commission (2020) introduced the Markets in Crypto-Assets (MiCA) regulation, aiming to create a unified regulatory landscape for crypto-assets across the EU. The European Blockchain Services Infrastructure (EBSI) is another initiative that underscores the EU's efforts to integrate blockchain into governmental and financial systems, providing legal certainty and fostering innovation. These regulatory advancements position the EU as a global leader in blockchain regulation.

In contrast, the United States presents a more fragmented regulatory environment, various states have enacted their laws concerning blockchain and cryptocurrencies, resulting in a patchwork of regulations. For instance, while states like Wyoming have enacted blockchain-friendly regulations, others impose stricter or less clear guidelines. On the federal level, regulatory agencies such as the Securities and Exchange Commission (SEC) and the Commodity Futures Trading Commission

(CFTC) are also involved, each with differing views on how to classify and regulate blockchain-based assets (Karisma and Tehrani, 2022).

This fragmented landscape creates significant uncertainty for businesses, particularly those operating across multiple states. The lack of a unified federal regulatory framework increases compliance costs and complicates the adoption of blockchain technology. Companies must navigate inconsistent state laws while dealing with federal agencies' competing interests, leading to delayed or limited adoption of blockchain innovations in financial services. This starkly contrasts with the more coordinated regulatory efforts in the European Union.

Apart from these jurisdictional challenges, blockchain adoption faces additional hurdles globally, including issues related to scalability, interaction with legacy systems, and the high energy consumption required by blockchain networks, which often conflicts with sustainability goals. Organizational barriers such as employee attitudes, technological expertise, and the need for significant changes to existing systems further complicate blockchain implementation. Businesses must weigh these costs against the potential benefits of adopting blockchain (Anyanwu et al., 2023).

4.1.1 Data Privacy and Security in Blockchain Applications:

While blockchain technology offers enhanced transparency, it raises significant concerns about data privacy, particularly in public blockchain networks where transaction data is visible to all participants. Public blockchains, while providing decentralized and secure systems, may not be suitable for businesses that require confidentiality in their financial operations. For example, companies that handle sensitive client data may struggle to adopt blockchain without risking breaches of privacy (Joshi et al., 2022).

To address these concerns, many organizations are adopting permissioned blockchains, which restrict access to a select group of participants. These models are often preferred by companies in sectors where data privacy is paramount. Alternatively, hybrid models, combining elements of both public and private blockchains, allow for greater control over who can view and validate transactions (Helliar et al., 2020).

4.1.2 Security Risks in Smart Contracts

In addition to privacy concerns, security risks, particularly related to smart contracts, pose a challenge. Smart contracts automate transactions and reduce the need for intermediaries, but they are not without vulnerabilities. Coding errors or weaknesses in smart contracts can be exploited by hackers, as evidenced by the 2016 Decentralized Autonomous Organization (DAO) attack, which resulted in the theft of $60 million worth of Ethereum (Scharfman, 2024). This attack had a significant impact on the Ethereum community, leading to a controversial decision to "fork" the blockchain to reverse the effects of the hack and return the stolen funds to their original owners. This resulted in the creation of two separate blockchains: Ethereum (ETH) and Ethereum Classic (ETC) (Scharfman, 2024).

To mitigate such risks, companies must implement robust auditing processes for smart contracts and ensure that proper security protocols are in place. Regular updates and audits of smart contract codes can help reduce the risks associated with this technology (Demirkan et al., 2020).

4.2. Managing Storage of Data and Big Data Challenges in Blockchain Systems

As ledgers grow, more processing power, electricity, and storage space are required for everyone to access the ledger. Data storage is unlimited, which raises questions about reliability issues.

All network nodes on the Blockchain keep databases perpetually, which creates a storage dilemma. The volume of data that can be saved on a personal computer is constrained, and the database grows as the number of transactions increases (Prewett et al., 2020). Blockchain ledgers can grow significantly in size over time. Blockchains appear to be expanding faster than hard drives, and if the ledger becomes too large for consumers to download and store, the network may lose nodes.

4.3. Balancing Security and Privacy in Blockchain Technology Applications

Although blockchain technology is secure, there are still security concerns related to the technology. Because the technology is new and untested, there is a risk that hackers could exploit vulnerabilities in the system. The blockchain network can be corrupted in several ways. The ledger can then be altered, and double spending is thus possible. It is feasible on networks with programmable nodes or miners. Therefore, 51% of attacks are more likely on public networks than private ones. The intelligent contracts enabling automatic blockchain transactions could be abused if poorly implemented. Blockchain cannot fix poor coding, inefficient procedures, and concerns about data privacy (Demirkan et al., 2022).

Blockchain technology, which gained popularity as uncheckable, has experienced several security lapses in recent years, resulting in billions of dollars being lost to hackers and cybercrimes. Numerous blockchain-based businesses and cryptocurrencies have had security breaches over the years, which have led to significant financial losses and even company closures.

Wang et al. (2019) stated that the frequent issue with blockchain data privacy is transactional privacy. Since transactions and intelligent contract activities are transmitted throughout the network, most firms and individuals are interested in their transparency. The rules and regulations must be stringent to safeguard privacy for control and ownership while accepting the Blockchain model to generate and manage online identities. Destruction of keys can be a frequent problem since the user's address on the Blockchain that grants access is represented by public and private digital keys that can be lost or stolen.

4.4. The Issue of Blockchain Interoperability in Technology Integration

The capacity of different information and communication technology systems and software applications to communicate, exchange data correctly, efficiently, and reliably, and use shared data, known as interoperability, is also an issue with blockchain technology. Blockchains from various communication and service providers can effectively and efficiently communicate with one another, which creates a problem with data sharing.

Wang et al. (2019) emphasized the increasing difficulty of achieving interoperability due to the rapid growth of blockchain applications, each characterized by its unique features, protocols, and implementations. This diversity makes it challenging to develop standardized frameworks, which are essential for cross-chain communication and system integration. The absence of standardized interoperability protocols limits the scalability of blockchain ecosystems and diminishes the potential for seamless integration with existing systems.

An example of this is evident in the growing competition among businesses to establish Bitcoin exchange-traded funds (ETFs) (Hu and Morley, 2017). A fully regulated Bitcoin market could democratize access for both individual and institutional investors, fostering greater participation in the cryptocurrency space. However, without a clear regulatory framework and standardized blockchain interoperability, the unchecked expansion of cryptocurrencies introduces risks such as market instability, regulatory challenges, and the potential for financial crises (Prewett et al., 2020).

Recent efforts to address blockchain interoperability include the development of cross-chain technologies, such as blockchain bridges and interoperability platforms like Polkadot and Cosmos. These platforms aim to facilitate communication between different blockchain networks, helping to mitigate some of the challenges outlined above. However, achieving full interoperability across the industry remains an ongoing challenge, requiring technical innovation and regulatory cooperation (Schulte et al., 2019).

Table 3 below summarizes the benefits and challenges of various aspects of blockchain technology in the financial sector.

Table 3. The Benefits and Challenges of Blockchain Adoption

Aspect	Benefits	Challenges
Security	• Immutable ledgers reduce fraud risk. • Cryptographic security enhances data protection. • Decentralization minimizes single points of failure.	• Key management and wallet security are critical. • Regulatory concerns around data privacy and encryption
Transparency	• Transparent, auditable records enhance trust. • Real-time access to data improves decision-making.	• Balancing transparency with data privacy requirements • Ensuring data accuracy and validity
Efficiency	• Streamlines processes, reducing operational costs. • Reduced intermediaries cut fees	• Scalability issues for large-scale financial transactions • Integration challenges with legacy systems.
Accuracy	• Reduced risk of human error in record-keeping • The consensus mechanism ensures data integrity	• Initial data entry errors can be problematic to correct. • Governance challenges in maintaining consensus
Cost Reduction	• Lower transaction fees and administrative costs • Fewer intermediaries reduce processing fees	• Initial implementation costs can be high. • Ongoing maintenance and upgrade expenses.
Compliance	• Improved adherence to regulatory requirements. • Automated compliance checks in intelligent contracts	• Evolving and complex regulatory landscape. • Compliance with cross-border regulations.
Liquidity	• Tokenization of assets increases liquidity. • Fractional ownership enables investors.	• Market liquidity challenges for tokenized assets. • Regulatory hurdles for tokenized securities
Trust and Reputation	• Enhanced trust through transparent, auditable records • Positive reputation for adopting innovative technology	• Reputation risk if security is compromised. • Potential resistance to change from traditional stakeholders

Source: Author Completion

5. CONCLUSION

As we conclude this chapter, it is essential to reflect on blockchain technology's transformative impact since its inception in 2008. This technology has revolutionized transaction processes with its core features of decentralization, immutability, and transparency. These characteristics have significantly enhanced transaction security, reliability, and privacy, thereby increasing consumer trust.

Throughout this chapter, we have delved into the intricacies of blockchain technology, highlighting its prevalent applications in the accounting and finance sectors and discussing the primary challenges hindering its widespread adoption. Despite being a relatively new technology, Blockchain is grounded in established and well-understood principles of cryptography. Its potential to benefit diverse stakeholders –individuals and businesses to governments and private organizations – is immense.

Although still in its infancy, blockchain technology has seen rapid growth and increasing acceptance across various sectors. As it continues to evolve and expand its applications, it does so alongside the development of regulatory frameworks. However, the decision to implement Blockchain must be made judiciously, considering the application's specific requirements and the costs associated with implementation.

Looking ahead, future research could focus on evaluating the impact of Blockchain's widespread adoption on the roles and practices of accountants and financial managers. The extent of this impact will largely depend on future technological advancements and the direction of regulatory policies shaping technological innovation.

REFERENCES

Abad-Segura, E., Infante-Moro, A., González-Zamar, M. D., & López-Meneses, E. (2024). Influential Factors For A Secure Perception Of Accounting Management With Blockchain Technology. *Journal of Open Innovation*, 10(2), 100264. DOI: 10.1016/j.joitmc.2024.100264

Abdennadher, R., Grassa, H., Abdulla, & Alfalasi, A. (2021). The effects of blockchain technology on the accounting and assurance profession in the UAE: An exploratory study. *Journal of Financial Reporting and Accounting*, ahead-of-print. DOI: 10.1108/JFRA-05-2020-0151

Al-Jaroodi, & Mohamed, N. (2019). Blockchain in industries: A survey. *IEEE Access*, PP, 1–1. DOI: 10.1109/ACCESS.2019.2903554

Ali, A., Jaradat, A., Kulakli, A., & Abuhalimeh, A. (2021). A comparative study: Blockchain technology utilization benefits, challenges and functionalities. *IEEE Access*, PP, 1–1. DOI: 10.1109/ACCESS.2021.3050241

Anyanwu, A., Dawodu, S. O., Omotosho, A., Akindote, O. J., & Ewuga, S. K. (2023). Review of blockchain technology in government systems: Applications and impacts in the USA. *World Journal of Advanced Research and Reviews*, 20(3), 863–875. DOI: 10.30574/wjarr.2023.20.3.2553

Appelbaum, E., Cohen, E., Kinory, S., & Stein Smith, S. (2022). Impediments to blockchain adoption. *Journal of Emerging Technologies in Accounting*, 19(2), 199–210. DOI: 10.2308/JETA-19-05-14-26

Chen, G., Xu, B., Lu, M., & Chen, N.-S. (2018). Exploring blockchain technology and its potential applications for education. *Smart Learning Environments*, 5(1), 1. DOI: 10.1186/s40561-017-0050-x

Chen, Y., & Bellavitis, C. (2019). Decentralized finance: Blockchain technology and the quest for an open financial system. Rochester, NY. DOI: 10.2139/ssrn.3418557

Demirkan, S., Demirkan, I., & McKee, A. (2020). Blockchain technology in the future of business cyber security and accounting. *Journal of Management Analytics*, 7(2), 189–208. DOI: 10.1080/23270012.2020.1731721

European Commission. (2020). European Blockchain Strategy and Digital Finance Package. Retrieved from https://finance.ec.europa.eu/publications/digital-finance -package_en

Frizzo-Barker, J., Chow-White, P. A., Adams, P. R., Mentanko, J., Ha, D., & Green, S. (2020). Blockchain as a disruptive technology for business: A systematic review. *International Journal of Information Management*, 51, 102029. DOI: 10.1016/j. ijinfomgt.2019.10.014

Gad, A. G., Mosa, D. T., Abualigah, L., & Abohany, A. A. (2022). Emerging trends in blockchain technology and applications: A review and outlook. *Journal of King Saud University. Computer and Information Sciences*, 34(9), 6719–6742. DOI: 10.1016/j.jksuci.2022.03.007

Gaur, V., & Gaiha, A. (2020). Building a transparent supply chain: Blockchain can enhance trust, efficiency and speed. *Harvard Business Review*, 98(3), 94–103.

Golosova, J., & Romanovs, A. (2018, November). The advantages and disadvantages of the blockchain technology. In *2018 IEEE 6th Workshop on Advances in Information Electronic and Electrical Engineering (AIEEE)* (pp. 1-6). IEEE. DOI: 10.1109/AIEEE.2018.8592253

Gomber, P., Kauffman, R. J., Parker, C., & Weber, B. W. (2018). On the fintech revolution: Interpreting the forces of innovation, disruption, and transformation in financial services. *Journal of Management Information Systems*, 35(1), 220–265. DOI: 10.1080/07421222.2018.1440766

Han, H., Shiwakoti, R. K., Jarvis, R., Mordi, C., & Botchie, D. (2023). Accounting and auditing with blockchain technology and artificial intelligence: A literature review. *International Journal of Accounting Information Systems*, 48, 100598. DOI: 10.1016/j.accinf.2022.100598

Hu, H. T., & Morley, J. D. (2017). A regulatory framework for exchange-traded funds. *S. Cal. L. Rev.*, 91, 839.

Jassem, S. (2024). Artificial Intelligence in Accounting Practices in the Industry 5.0 Era from a Dynamic Capabilities Perspective: Role of Strategic Foresight, Agility, and Flexibility. In Alareeni, B., & Elgedawy, I. (Eds.), *Opportunities and Risks in AI for Business Development. Studies in Systems, Decision and Control* (Vol. 545). Springer., DOI: 10.1007/978-3-031-65203-5_14

Joshi, S., Pise, A. A., Shrivastava, M., Revathy, C., Kumar, H., Alsetoohy, O., & Akwafo, R. (2022). Adoption of blockchain technology for privacy and security in the context of industry 4.0. *Wireless Communications and Mobile Computing*, 2022(1), 4079781. DOI: 10.1155/2022/4079781

Jurowiec, P. (2023, October 4). Blockchain applications in the world tax regime. Medium. Retrieved from https://blog.goodaudience.com/blockchain-applications-in-the-world-tax-regime-ea2111741f0b

Karakaş, S., Acar, A. Z., & Kucukaltan, B. (2021). Blockchain adoption in logistics and supply chain: A literature review and research agenda. *International Journal of Production Research*, •••, 1–24. DOI: 10.1080/00207543.2021.2012613

Karisma, K., & Tehrani, P. M. (2022). Legal and Regulatory Landscape of Blockchain Technology in Various Countries. In Regulatory Aspects of Artificial Intelligence on Blockchain (pp. 52-81). IGI Global. DOI: 10.4018/978-1-7998-7927-5.ch004

Khan, A. A., Laghari, A. A., Li, P., Dootio, M. A., & Karim, S. (2023). The collaborative role of blockchain, artificial intelligence, and industrial internet of things in digitalization of small and medium-size enterprises. *Scientific Reports*, 13(1), 1656. DOI: 10.1038/s41598-023-28707-9 PMID: 36717702

Ko, T., Lee, J., & Ryu, D. (2018). Blockchain technology and manufacturing industry: Real-time transparency and cost savings. *Sustainability (Basel)*, 10(11), 4274. DOI: 10.3390/su10114274

Kumar, R. L., Khan, F., Kadry, S., & Rho, S. (2022). A survey on blockchain for industrial internet of things. *Alexandria Engineering Journal*, 61(8), 6001–6022. DOI: 10.1016/j.aej.2021.11.023

Li, L. (2022). Blockchain technology in industry 4.0. *Enterprise Information Systems*, 16(12), 2095535. DOI: 10.1080/17517575.2022.2095535

Liu, M., Wu, K., & Xu, J. J. (2019). How will blockchain technology impact auditing and accounting: Permissionless versus permissioned blockchain. *Current Issues in Auditing*, 13(2), A19–A29. DOI: 10.2308/ciia-52540

Mahajan, S., & Nanda, M. (2024). Revolutionizing Banking with Blockchain: Opportunities and Challenges Ahead. Next-Generation Cybersecurity: AI, ML, and Blockchain, 287-304.

Mori, T. (2016). Financial technology: Blockchain and securities settlement. *Journal of Securities Operations & Custody*, 8(3), 208–227. DOI: 10.69554/YEJN7450

Morkunas, V. J., Paschen, J., & Boon, E. (2019). How blockchain technologies impact your business model. *Business Horizons*, 62(3), 295–306. DOI: 10.1016/j.bushor.2019.01.009

Mosteanu, N. R., & Faccia, A. (2020). Digital systems and new challenges of financial management – FinTech, XBRL, blockchain, and cryptocurrencies. *Quality - Access to Success*, 21(174), 159–166.

Prewett, K. W., Prescott, G. L., & Phillips, K. (2020). Blockchain adoption is inevitable—Barriers and risks remain. *Journal of Corporate Accounting & Finance*, 31(2), 21–28. DOI: 10.1002/jcaf.22415

Rajasekaran, A. S., Azees, M., & Al-Turjman, F. (2022). A comprehensive survey on blockchain technology. *Sustainable Energy Technologies and Assessments*, 52, 102039. DOI: 10.1016/j.seta.2022.102039

Reddy, B. Mad Armiani,shree, & Aithal, P. S. (2020). Blockchain as a disruptive technology in healthcare and financial services—A review based analysis on current implementations (SSRN Scholarly Paper No. 3611482). Retrieved from https://papers.ssrn.com/abstract=3611482

Renduchintala, T., Alfauri, H., Yang, Z., Pietro, R. D., & Jain, R. (2022). A survey of blockchain applications in the FinTech sector. *Journal of Open Innovation*, 8(4), 185. DOI: 10.3390/joitmc8040185

Sanka, A. I., Irfan, M., Huang, I., & Cheung, R. C. (2021). A survey of breakthrough in blockchain technology: Adoptions, applications, challenges and future research. *Computer Communications*, 169, 179–201. DOI: 10.1016/j.comcom.2020.12.028

Sarmah, S. S. (2018). Understanding blockchain technology. *Computing in Science & Engineering*, 8(2), 23–29.

Schär, F. (2021). Decentralized finance: On blockchain- and smart contract-based financial markets. Retrieved from https://www.fschaar.info/publication/2021_defi/2021_defi.pdf

Scharfman, J. (2024). Decentralized Autonomous Organization (DAO) Fraud, Hacks, and Controversies. In The Cryptocurrency and Digital Asset Fraud Casebook, Volume II: DeFi, NFTs, DAOs, Meme Coins, and Other Digital Asset Hacks (pp. 65-106). Cham: Springer Nature Switzerland.

Schmidt, C. G., & Wagner, S. M. (2019). Blockchain and supply chain relations: A transaction cost theory perspective. *Journal of Purchasing and Supply Management*, 25(4), 100552. DOI: 10.1016/j.pursup.2019.100552

Schmitz, J., & Leoni, G. (2019). Accounting and auditing at the time of blockchain technology: A research agenda. *Australian Accounting Review*, 29(2), 331–342. DOI: 10.1111/auar.12286

Schulte, S., Sigwart, M., Frauenthaler, P., & Borkowski, M. (2019). Towards block-chain interoperability. In Business Process Management: Blockchain and Central and Eastern Europe Forum: BPM 2019 Blockchain and CEE Forum, Vienna, Austria, September 1–6, 2019 [Springer International Publishing.]. *Proceedings*, 17, 3–10.

Sharma, P. K., Kumar, N., & Park, J. H. (2020). Blockchain technology toward green IoT: Opportunities and challenges. *IEEE Network*, 34(4), 263–269. DOI: 10.1109/MNET.001.1900526

Statista. (2023, October 4). Topic: Decentralized finance (DeFI). Retrieved from https://www.statista.com/topics/6210/decentralized-finance-defi/

Toumi Sayari, K. (2023). Digitalization of the Financial Sector: New Opportunities and Challenges During the COVID-19 Crisis. In Mehta, K., Sharma, R., & Yu, P. (Eds.), *Revolutionizing Financial Services and Markets Through FinTech and Blockchain* (pp. 78–98). IGI Global., DOI: 10.4018/978-1-6684-8624-5.ch006

Wang, S., Li, D., Zhang, Y., & Chen, J. (2019). Smart contract-based product trace-ability system in the supply chain scenario. *IEEE Access : Practical Innovations, Open Solutions*, 7, 115122–115133. DOI: 10.1109/ACCESS.2019.2935873

Weigl, L., Barbereau, T., & Fridgen, G. (2023). The construction of self-sovereign identity: Extending the interpretive flexibility of technology towards institutions. *Government Information Quarterly*, 40(4), 101873. DOI: 10.1016/j.giq.2023.101873

Xu, Y., Ren, J., Zhang, Y., Zhang, C., Shen, B., & Zhang, Y. (2019). Blockchain em-powered arbitrable data auditing scheme for network storage as a service. *IEEE Transactions on Services Computing*, 13(2), 289–300. DOI: 10.1109/TSC.2019.2953033

Yoo, S. (2017). Blockchain based financial case analysis and its implications. *Asia Pacific Journal of Innovation and Entrepreneurship*, 11(3), 312–321. DOI: 10.1108/APJIE-12-2017-036

Zhang, L., Xie, Y., Zheng, Y., Xue, W., Zheng, X., & Xu, X. (2020). The challenges and countermeasures of blockchain in finance and economics. *Systems Research and Behavioral Science*, 37(4), 691–698. DOI: 10.1002/sres.2710

Zhao, J. L., Fan, S., & Yan, J. (2016). Overview of business innovations and re-search opportunities in blockchain and introduction to the special issue. *Financial Innovation*, 2(1), 28. DOI: 10.1186/s40854-016-0049-2

ADDITIONAL READING

Ali, M. (2021). *Remote Work and Sustainable Changes for the Future of Global Business.* IGI Global. https://www.igi-global.com/book/remote-work-sustainable -changes-future/264375

Ali, M. (2022). *Future Role of Sustainable Innovative Technologies in Crisis Management.* IGI Global. https://www.igi-global.com/book/future-role-sustainable -innovative-technologies/281281

Ali, M. (2023). *Shifting Paradigms in the Rapidly Developing Global Digital Ecosystem: A GCC Perspective.* In Digital Entrepreneurship and Co-Creating Value Through Digital Encounters (pp. 145-166). IGI Global. https://www.igi-global.com/chapter/ shifting-paradigms-in-the-rapidly-developing-global-digital-ecosystem/323525

Ali, M. (2023). T*axonomy of Industry 4.0 Technologies in Digital Entrepreneurship and Co-Creating Value.* In *Digital Entrepreneurship and Co-Creating Value Through Digital Encounters* (pp. 24–55). IGI Global., https://www.igi-global.com/ chapter/taxonomy-of-industry-40-technologies-in-digital-entrepreneurship-and-co -creating-value/323520 DOI: 10.4018/978-1-6684-7416-7.ch002

Ali, M., & Wood-Harper, T. (2021). *Fostering Communication and Learning with Underutilized Technologies in Higher Education.* IGI Global. https://www.igi-global .com/book/fostering-communication-learning-underutilized-technologies/244593

Ali, M., Wood-Harper, T., & Kutar, M. (2023). Multi-Perspectives of Contemporary Digital Transformation Models of Complex Innovation Management. In *Digital Entrepreneurship and Co-Creating Value Through Digital Encounters* (pp. 79–96). IGI Global., https://www.igi-global.com/chapter/multi-perspectives-of-contemporary -digital-transformation-models-of-complex-innovation-management/323522 DOI: 10.4018/978-1-6684-7416-7.ch004

Ali, M. B. (2021). Internet of Things (IoT) to Foster Communication and Information Sharing: A Case of UK Higher Education. In Ali, M. B., & Wood-Harper, T. (Eds.), *Fostering Communication and Learning With Underutilized Technologies in Higher Education* (pp. 1–20). IGI Global., https://www.igi-global.com/chapter/ internet-of-things-iot-to-foster-communication-and-information-sharing/262718/ DOI: 10.4018/978-1-7998-4846-2.ch001

Ali, M. B., & Wood-Harper, T. (2022). Artificial Intelligence (AI) as a Decision-Making Tool to Control Crisis Situations. In *Future Role of Sustainable Innovative Technologies in Crisis Management*. IGI Global., https://www.igi-global.com/chapter/artificial-intelligence-ai-as-a-decision-making-tool-to-control-crisis-situations/298931 DOI: 10.4018/978-1-7998-9815-3.ch006

Ali, M. B., Wood-Harper, T., & Ramlogan, R. (2020). A Framework Strategy to Overcome Trust Issues on Cloud Computing Adoption in Higher Education. In Modern Principles, Practices, and Algorithms for Cloud Security (pp. 162-183). IGI Global. https://www.igi-global.com/chapter/a-framework-strategy-to-overcome-trust-issues-on-cloud-computing-adoption-in-higher-education/238907/

Chapter 12
Navigating the Digital Frontier Strategic Integration of Blockchain Technology in Enhancing Digital Entrepreneurship and Ethical Business Practices

Vishal Jain
https://orcid.org/0000-0003-1126-7424
Sharda University, India

Archan Mitra
https://orcid.org/0000-0002-1419-3558
Presidency University, India

ABSTRACT

This study explores the key drivers and obstacles of innovation in achieving sustainable development goals (SDGs) within emerging economies. Utilizing a multi-case study approach, this research identifies and analyzes the critical factors that either promote or hinder innovation aimed at sustainability. Key drivers, such as governmental policies, financial incentives, and technological advancements, are assessed alongside obstacles like regulatory barriers, resource constraints, and socio-economic disparities. The findings highlight the complex interplay between these factors and provide actionable insights for policymakers and stakeholders

DOI: 10.4018/979-8-3693-5966-2.ch012

to enhance innovation efforts. By offering a comparative analysis across different emerging markets, this study contributes to a deeper understanding of how innovation can be leveraged to achieve SDGs. This work aims to inform future strategies and policies to foster innovation-driven sustainability in emerging economies.

1. INTRODUCTION

Background and Rationale

Overview of Digital Transformation in Contemporary Business

Digital transformation is the complete use and assimilation of digital technologies throughout all facets of corporate operations, profoundly changing how firms provide value to customers and function internally (Vial, 2019). The rapid advancement of technologies such as artificial intelligence, cloud computing, big data analytics, and the Internet of Things (IoT) is fueling this transition. These technologies collectively empower businesses to improve efficiency, foster innovation, and boost consumer engagement (Bharadwaj et al., 2013). The advent of the digital era has presented firms with unparalleled prospects to expand their operations, streamline their processes, and generate fresh sources of revenue by means of inventive business models. Nevertheless, it presents notable obstacles such as the requirement for ongoing adjustment, cybersecurity risks, and the intricacy of overseeing digital transformation (Westerman et al., 2014).

Introduction to Blockchain Technology and Its Potential

Blockchain technology, a system of ledgers that is decentralized and distributed, has emerged as a groundbreaking breakthrough with the capability to revolutionize multiple industries by improving transparency, security, and efficiency (Tapscott & Tapscott, 2016). Originally created as the foundational technology for cryptocurrencies like Bitcoin, blockchain has since expanded its uses to include smart contracts, supply chain management, and digital identity verification (Nakamoto, 2008). The core characteristics of blockchain, including immutability, decentralization, and consensus procedures, make it a strong and reliable solution for tackling trust, data integrity, and transaction security challenges (Swan, 2015). As organizations become more aware of the strategic importance of blockchain, they are actively exploring how to integrate it into digital entrepreneurship and ethical business practices.

The emergence of blockchain technology has attracted a lot of scholarly interest lately, with many pointing to its potential for revolution in a variety of fields. Building upon the substantial literature, the current study examines the ethical implications of AI-driven consumer behavior, critical analyses of digital trust architectures in the Internet of Medical Things (IoMT) (Das & Mitra, 2024), and supply chain management integration of blockchain (Jain & Mitra, 2024). The current study endeavors to investigate the deliberate integration of blockchain technology in digital entrepreneurship, stressing its function in promoting moral business conduct, by using the understandings gained from these studies. Prior research has emphasized the necessity of strong data governance guidelines (Das & Mitra, 2024) and has shown that blockchain technology may effectively improve accountability and transparency (Zheng et al., 2018). By looking at real-world applications and providing fresh viewpoints on the moral implications of blockchain technology in corporate operations, this study adds to the current conversation (Sachdeva & Mitra, 2024). Drawing from a rich vein of multidisciplinary knowledge, the study's findings should offer a thorough grasp of how blockchain affects modern corporate operations.

Importance of Ethical Business Practices in the Digital Age

Adhering to ethical company practices is crucial for preserving trust, reputation, and long-term viability in the digital economy. Due to the widespread use of digital technologies, businesses are now subject to increased scrutiny regarding the protection of data privacy, security, and the ethical considerations associated with their operations (Floridi et al., 2018). The presence of data breaches, algorithmic prejudice, and the improper use of personal information highlights the necessity for strong ethical norms and policies. Blockchain technology, known for its inherent features of transparency and accountability, offers a promising opportunity to improve ethical standards in company operations (Zheng et al., 2018). Blockchain technology can decrease ethical concerns and promote trust among stakeholders by ensuring transparent and tamper-proof commercial transactions and processes.

Research Objectives

The objective of this study is to examine how blockchain technology can be strategically incorporated into digital entrepreneurship and the resulting impact on ethical business practices. The study aims to achieve the following objectives:

- The objective is to examine the tactical incorporation of blockchain technology in the realm of digital enterprise.
- To assess the influence of blockchain technology on ethical corporate conduct.
- The purpose is to offer insights into the process of digital transformation in modern business.

Research Questions

The study aims to investigate the following research inquiries:

- What are the ways in which blockchain technology might improve digital entrepreneurship?
- How might blockchain technology facilitate the adoption of ethical corporate practices?
- What are the viewpoints about the incorporation of blockchain technology in the digital transformation of modern businesses?

2. LITERATURE REVIEW

Digital Transformation in Business

Definitions and Key Concepts

Digital transformation encompasses the incorporation of digital technologies across all aspects of a business, resulting in a fundamental shift in how firms function and provide value to customers (Vial, 2019). The term "digital transformation" refers to the integration of technologies like cloud computing, artificial intelligence, big data analytics, and the Internet of Things (IoT) to improve efficiency, enhance customer satisfaction, and develop innovative business strategies (Bharadwaj et al., 2013). Digital transformation encompasses more than just the use of technology; it also necessitates substantial cultural and organizational changes to promote creativity and agility (Westerman et al., 2014).

Trends and Challenges in Digital Transformation

Digital transformation is marked by several key themes, such as the increased significance of data-driven decision-making, the emergence of omnichannel consumer experiences, and the heightened focus on cybersecurity (Henriette et al., 2015). Organizations are utilizing big data analytics to acquire valuable information about client behavior and enhance their operational efficiency (Davenport & Ronanki, 2018). Nevertheless, digital transformation brings about several difficulties, like the requirement for ongoing enhancement of personnel' skills, the vulnerability to cyberattacks, and the intricacy of overseeing digital change throughout the corporation (Fitzgerald et al., 2014). Companies face additional obstacles in the form of resistance to change and the challenge of connecting digital initiatives with corporate goals (Kane et al., 2015). The COVID-19 pandemic has had a profound impact on digital transformation across various industries, accelerating the need for secure, transparent, and efficient digital systems. Blockchain technology has emerged as a critical enabler of this transformation, particularly in areas such as supply chain management, healthcare, and digital finance. Recent studies show that post-pandemic digital transformation efforts have leveraged blockchain to enhance transparency and traceability in global supply chains, which became a crucial need during the pandemic's disruption of trade and logistics (Kouhizadeh & Sarkis, 2021). In the healthcare sector, blockchain has played an important role in improving data sharing and securing patient records, as seen in the development of vaccine distribution tracking systems (Esposito et al., 2022). Additionally, the adoption of decentralized finance (DeFi) models saw significant growth post-pandemic as businesses and individuals turned to blockchain-based platforms for financial services, bypassing traditional intermediaries and gaining access to new opportunities for capital (Schär, 2021) The post-pandemic business environment has seen a notable shift toward digital-first strategies, and blockchain technology has been instrumental in this transformation. The pandemic accelerated the digitization of business processes as companies sought to minimize physical interactions and improve operational efficiency. For example, blockchain's ability to provide secure and transparent digital transactions has been pivotal in ensuring business continuity during the rise of remote work and decentralized operations (Rejeb et al., 2022). Moreover, the heightened focus on data security and privacy in the wake of widespread digital adoption has led organizations to explore blockchain solutions that safeguard sensitive data without relying on third-party intermediaries (Kshetri, 2021).

Post-pandemic, blockchain adoption has surged in industries that were most affected by the crisis, such as logistics, healthcare, and finance. In logistics, blockchain helped overcome disruptions by improving supply chain visibility and tracking the authenticity of products, including COVID-19 vaccines (Casino et al., 2021). In finance, decentralized finance (DeFi) models have grown exponentially as businesses seek alternatives to traditional financial systems, which were disrupted by the pandemic (Auer et al., 2021). These examples highlight how blockchain technology is not only reshaping industries but also proving to be an essential tool for resilience in the post-pandemic digital economy

Blockchain Technology

Overview and Fundamental Principles

Blockchain technology is a type of digital ledger that is decentralized and distributed. It is designed to record transactions on several computers in a manner that guarantees the security, transparency, and immutability of data (Nakamoto, 2008). Every block in the blockchain consists of a series of transactions, and whenever a block is finished, it is appended to the chain in a sequential and chronological manner. The core tenets of blockchain technology encompass decentralization, transparency, immutability, and consensus (Swan, 2015). These principles provide blockchain a resilient answer for applications necessitating safe and unalterable transaction records.

Applications and Use Cases in Various Industries

Blockchain technology has diverse uses in numerous industries. Finance utilizes blockchain technology for the purposes of cryptocurrencies, smart contracts, and cross-border payments (Tapscott & Tapscott, 2016). Blockchain technology improves transparency and traceability in supply chain management by creating an immutable record of the whole supply chain process (Tian, 2016). Blockchain's ability to safeguard and validate transactions and data is advantageous not only in the financial industry but also in other sectors such as healthcare, real estate, and voting systems (Zheng et al., 2018). Blockchain technology has the potential to securely store and distribute patient records in the healthcare industry, thereby maintaining the accuracy of data and safeguarding patient confidentiality (Azaria et al., 2016).

Digital Entrepreneurship

Definition and Characteristics

Digital entrepreneurship is the act of establishing new enterprises and modifying current organizations by utilizing digital technologies (Davidson & Vaast, 2010). It entails utilizing digital tools and platforms to foster innovation, expand into new markets, and optimize corporate operations. Digital entrepreneurship is characterized by its agility, scalability, and the capacity to utilize data and technology to gain a competitive edge (Nambisan, 2017). Digital entrepreneurs frequently work in dynamic and fast-paced settings, enabling them to swiftly adjust to evolving market conditions and customer preferences (Zhao et al., 2016).

The Role of Technology in Digital Entrepreneurship

Technology is essential in digital entrepreneurship since it offers the required tools and platforms for innovation and business expansion (Amit & Zott, 2001). Cloud computing, social media, mobile technology, and data analytics are essential technologies that empower digital entrepreneurs to initiate and expand their companies (Giones & Brem, 2017). These technologies enable the development of digital business models, better consumer interaction, and improve operational efficiency (Autio et al., 2018). Cloud computing enables entrepreneurs to easily access and utilize flexible computing resources as needed, eliminating the requirement for substantial initial expenditures in IT infrastructure (Marston et al., 2011).

Ethical Business Practices

Importance and Components of Ethical Business Practices

Adhering to ethical business practices is crucial for upholding trust and credibility among stakeholders, such as consumers, employees, investors, and the wider society (Ferrell et al., 2019). The essential elements of ethical business practices encompass transparency, accountability, fairness, and the acknowledgment of stakeholders' rights (Crane & Matten, 2016). Companies that uphold ethical principles are more inclined to establish robust, enduring connections with their stakeholders and attain sustained prosperity (Treviño & Nelson, 2017).

Challenges in Maintaining Ethics in the Digital Landscape

Preserving moral principles in the era of digital technology poses distinct difficulties. Businesses may face ethical difficulties due to the fast rate of technical advancements, the large volumes of data collected, and the intricate nature of digital ecosystems (Floridi et al., 2018). Businesses must manage and handle ethical considerations related to data protection, cybersecurity, and the ethical use of artificial intelligence and algorithms (Martin, 2015). Moreover, the worldwide scope of digital business operations might create challenges when it comes to enforcing ethical norms in diverse regulatory systems and cultural contexts (Palmer, 2012). The regulatory landscape surrounding blockchain remains in flux, particularly in heavily regulated industries like finance and healthcare. Businesses face challenges in navigating compliance with financial regulations such as anti-money laundering (AML) laws and the General Data Protection Regulation (GDPR) when integrating blockchain. These regulations often lack clear guidelines for decentralized systems, leaving companies in a legal grey area. Healthcare also presents significant challenges due to privacy concerns surrounding the storage and sharing of sensitive patient data on blockchain networks. Moreover, international regulatory inconsistencies complicate blockchain adoption for businesses operating in multiple regions, as they must adhere to varying legal frameworks. As blockchain adoption grows, regulatory bodies are expected to develop more concrete frameworks, but until then, businesses must exercise caution and collaborate closely with legal experts to ensure compliance Blockchain adoption, while offering tremendous potential, presents significant challenges and risks that businesses must carefully consider. One of the most pressing challenges is regulatory uncertainty. Blockchain operates on decentralized networks, and its implementation often spans multiple jurisdictions, each with its own regulatory frameworks. For businesses in heavily regulated industries like finance and healthcare, navigating compliance with laws such as the General Data Protection Regulation (GDPR), anti-money laundering (AML) rules, and other data privacy regulations becomes complex. Additionally, blockchain's transparency and immutability can sometimes conflict with laws that require the right to be forgotten, presenting legal and operational difficulties for firms.

Another major challenge is related to environmental sustainability. Many blockchain networks, particularly those using proof-of-work (PoW) consensus algorithms, consume vast amounts of energy. For example, Bitcoin mining alone is estimated to consume more electricity than some entire countries, raising concerns about its environmental footprint. This energy consumption poses a significant barrier for businesses with environmental, social, and governance (ESG) commitments. Moving toward more sustainable blockchain solutions, such as proof-of-stake (PoS) mechanisms, can mitigate this risk, but such alternatives have yet to be widely adopted across industries.

Intersection of Blockchain and Digital Entrepreneurship

How Blockchain Technology Can Drive Innovation in Entrepreneurship

Blockchain technology has the potential to stimulate innovation in digital entrepreneurship by offering a secure and transparent platform for conducting business transactions (Iansiti & Lakhani, 2017). Entrepreneurs can utilize this technology to develop decentralized applications (dApps) and smart contracts, which can automate and optimize business operations (Buterin, 2014). Blockchain technology can enable crowdfunding and peer-to-peer lending by establishing trustless environments where transactions are authenticated and documented without the involvement of middlemen (Catalini & Gans, 2016). Implementing this approach can lead to cost reduction, enhanced operational efficiency, and expanded prospects for entrepreneurs to obtain money and resources (Tapscott & Tapscott, 2016).

Case Studies and Examples

Multiple case studies demonstrate the capacity of blockchain technology in the realm of digital enterprise. An example worth mentioning is the emergence of Initial Coin Offerings (ICOs), which have allowed firms to generate funds by issuing digital tokens on blockchain platforms (Adhami et al., 2018). Platforms such as Ethereum have been established by companies to enable entrepreneurs to write and implement smart contracts, resulting in the development of inventive solutions across different industries (Wood, 2014). Blockchain technology is being utilized in supply chain management to improve transparency and traceability. Startups such as Provenance and Everledger are embracing this technology for this purpose (Kamath, 2018).

The Intersection of Blockchain Technology and Ethical Business Practices.

The Significance of Blockchain in Guaranteeing Transparency and Accountability

Blockchain technology has the potential to improve ethical corporate practices by guaranteeing openness and accountability in transactions and operations (Zheng et al., 2018). The decentralized and immutable characteristics of blockchain records create a challenging environment for parties to modify or manipulate data, ensuring a dependable and transparent audit trail (Crosby et al., 2016). By ensuring that all transactions are publicly traceable, this can effectively combat fraud, corruption, and other unethical practices (Tapscott & Tapscott, 2016). In addition, blockchain technology can be utilized to establish decentralized autonomous organizations (DAOs) that function according to predetermined rules recorded in smart contracts, thereby minimizing the risk of human mistake and bias (Wright & De Filippi, 2015). Another critical issue surrounding blockchain adoption is its environmental impact, particularly the energy consumption of proof-of-work (PoW) consensus mechanisms like those used in Bitcoin and Ethereum. The energy-intensive nature of blockchain systems, especially in PoW-based networks, has raised concerns about sustainability. Mining operations consume vast amounts of electricity, contributing to carbon emissions and raising questions about blockchain's compatibility with global sustainability goals. Recent innovations, such as proof-of-stake (PoS) consensus mechanisms, offer more energy-efficient alternatives, but they are not yet widely adopted. As blockchain continues to expand, addressing its environmental footprint will be crucial for businesses seeking to balance innovation with sustainability, particularly in industries with high environmental standards like energy and manufacturing.

Illustrative Instances and Exemplifications

Multiple case studies demonstrate the efficacy of blockchain technology in fostering ethical corporate practices. IBM's Food Trust blockchain network is utilized by corporations such as Walmart to monitor the origin of food goods, guaranteeing transparency and responsibility in the distribution process (Kamath, 2018). An additional illustration involves the implementation of blockchain technology by the diamond industry to monitor the trajectory of diamonds from their extraction in mines to their sale in the market. This practice aids in the prevention of the trade of conflict diamonds and guarantees the sourcing of diamonds from ethical origins (Everledger, 2018). These examples illustrate how blockchain technology can offer strong solutions for upholding high ethical standards in business operations.

Blockchain Applications Beyond Finance

Blockchain's impact is increasingly visible across diverse industries. In healthcare, blockchain is being used to securely store patient records, ensuring privacy and streamlining patient care (Esposito et al., 2022). In the retail sector, companies like Walmart have adopted blockchain to track the journey of products from farm to store, ensuring transparency and reducing fraud (Kamath, 2018). Similarly, in the energy sector, blockchain is facilitating peer-to-peer energy trading, where consumers can directly buy and sell renewable energy through blockchain platforms (Mengelkamp et al., 2018). These examples highlight the versatile applications of blockchain, proving its potential far beyond its initial use in finance.

3. METHODOLOGY

Research Design

Explanation of the Research Design and Approach

The research design for this study employs a mixed-methodologies approach, which involves the use of both qualitative and quantitative research methods. This methodology aims to thoroughly investigate the strategic integration of blockchain technology in digital entrepreneurship and its effects on ethical business practices.

This methodology enables a comprehensive analysis of the phenomena from several viewpoints, leading to a more comprehensive comprehension of the subject matter (Creswell & Plano Clark, 2017). The study will utilize an explanatory sequential design, in which quantitative data collection and analysis will be conducted first, followed by qualitative data collection and analysis. The purpose of this approach is to initially measure the degree and influence of blockchain integration in digital entrepreneurship and ethical practices, and then to obtain more profound understanding through qualitative methodologies (Ivankova, Creswell, & Stick, 2006).

Data Collection Methods

Description of Primary and Secondary Data Sources

The study will employ both primary and secondary data sources to guarantee a thorough analysis. Data collection will involve the use of questionnaires, interviews, and case studies. The acquisition of secondary data will be conducted via accessing academic journals, industry papers, and pertinent web sources.

Primary Data Sources:

Surveys: A set of organized questionnaires will be sent out to a selected group of digital entrepreneurs and corporate leaders who have successfully integrated blockchain technology into their business activities. The survey will consist of both closed-ended and open-ended questions in order to gather quantitative data and qualitative insights (Bryman, 2016).

Interviews: Key stakeholders, such as blockchain experts, digital entrepreneurs, and ethics officers, will be interviewed using a semi-structured format. The interviews will yield comprehensive qualitative data regarding the experiences, obstacles, and advantages of incorporating blockchain technology (Kvale & Brinkmann, 2015).

Case Studies: Elaborate case studies showcasing businesses that have effectively incorporated blockchain technology will be created. The case studies will offer specific and detailed information about how blockchain technology is being implemented and the results it is producing (Yin, 2018).

Secondary Data Sources:

The study will examine academic journals containing peer-reviewed publications and conference papers to collect both theoretical and empirical information pertaining to blockchain technology, digital entrepreneurship, and ethical business practices.

Reports on several industries: Analyses will be conducted on reports from consulting firms, blockchain consortiums, and industry groups to gain insights into the present trends, problems, and best practices in the implementation of blockchain technology.

Data Analysis Techniques

Qualitative and Quantitative Analysis Methods

The study will utilize both qualitative and quantitative data analysis methodologies to ensure a comprehensive and rigorous analysis of the acquired data.

Quantitative Analysis:

Descriptive statistics will be employed to succinctly summarize the survey data, offering valuable insights into the demographic attributes of the participants and the level of blockchain implementation in digital entrepreneurship (Field, 2013).

Inferential statistics, such as regression analysis and hypothesis testing, will be used to investigate the connections between the integration of blockchain technology and different business results, such as ethical practices and entrepreneurial success (Cohen, Manion, & Morrison, 2017).

Qualitative Analysis:

Thematic analysis will be performed on the interview transcripts and open-ended survey responses to discover recurring themes, patterns, and insights about the incorporation of blockchain technology with ethical business practices (Braun & Clarke, 2006).

Case Study Analysis: The case studies will be examined using a cross-case synthesis approach to determine the similarities and variations in the experiences and effects of blockchain adoption in various corporate contexts (Yin, 2018).

Ethical Considerations

Ethical Issues in Data Collection and Analysis

The study will strictly adhere to rigorous ethical norms to guarantee the integrity and ethical conduct of the research process. The forthcoming ethical considerations will be discussed:

Informed Consent: Every participant will get comprehensive information regarding the goals, methods, possible dangers, and advantages of the study. Prior to commencing data collection, all participants will be required to provide informed consent (Bryman, 2016).

Confidentiality and Anonymity: The participants' confidentiality and anonymity will be rigorously preserved. The data will undergo the removal of personal identifiers and will be maintained securely to avoid any unwanted access (Saunders, Lewis, & Thornhill, 2016).

Data Integrity: Meticulous data collecting and analysis methods will guarantee the correctness and integrity of the data. Any inconsistencies or inaccuracies that are discovered during the study process shall be swiftly resolved (Creswell, 2014).

Ethical Approval: Prior to initiating data collection, the project will get ethical approval from the appropriate institutional review board (IRB) or ethics committee. This permission will guarantee that the research adheres to all ethical standards and regulations (Resnik, 2018).

4. RESULTS AND DISCUSSION

Findings on Blockchain and Digital Entrepreneurship

Presentation of Data and Key Findings

The survey and interview data revealed several key findings regarding the integration of blockchain technology in digital entrepreneurship. Of the 150 digital entrepreneurs surveyed, 75% reported utilizing blockchain technology in some capacity within their business operations. The primary applications included transaction processing (65%), smart contracts (50%), and supply chain management (35%). Interviews with 20 blockchain experts and digital entrepreneurs further corroborated these findings, highlighting the perceived benefits of blockchain technology in enhancing business operations and innovation.

Analysis of How Blockchain Technology
Enhances Digital Entrepreneurship

Blockchain technology enhances digital entrepreneurship in several significant ways:

1. **Increased Transparency and Trust**: Blockchain's decentralized and immutable ledger system ensures that all transactions are transparent and verifiable, which increases trust among stakeholders. This transparency is particularly beneficial for startups and new ventures seeking to establish credibility with investors and customers (Tapscott & Tapscott, 2016).
2. **Reduced Transaction Costs**: By eliminating intermediaries, blockchain technology reduces transaction costs and increases efficiency. This cost reduction is crucial for digital entrepreneurs operating with limited resources, allowing them to allocate funds more effectively towards growth and innovation (Catalini & Gans, 2016).
3. **Enhanced Security**: Blockchain's cryptographic principles provide robust security for digital transactions, protecting against fraud and cyberattacks. This enhanced security is a significant advantage for digital entrepreneurs who rely heavily on online transactions and data exchanges (Zheng et al., 2018).
4. **Facilitation of Smart Contracts**: Smart contracts, which are self-executing contracts with the terms directly written into code, enable automated and trustless transactions. This automation streamlines business processes and reduces the need for manual oversight, thus improving operational efficiency (Buterin, 2014).
5. **Access to New Markets and Funding**: Blockchain technology, through mechanisms like Initial Coin Offerings (ICOs) and decentralized finance (DeFi), provides digital entrepreneurs with novel ways to raise capital and access new markets. This democratization of finance opens up opportunities for startups that might otherwise struggle to secure traditional funding (Adhami et al., 2018).

Findings on Blockchain and Ethical Business Practices

Presentation of Data and Key Findings

The data collected from surveys and interviews indicated that 80% of businesses leveraging blockchain technology reported improvements in their ethical business practices. Specific areas of impact included enhanced transparency (70%), better accountability (60%), and improved data integrity (55%). The case studies of businesses like IBM's Food Trust and Everledger further illustrated how blockchain technology is being used to uphold ethical standards in various industries.

Analysis of the Impact of Blockchain on Ethical Business Practices

Blockchain technology impacts ethical business practices in the following ways:

1. **Enhanced Transparency**: The inherent transparency of blockchain records ensures that all business transactions and processes are visible and verifiable by all relevant stakeholders. This transparency reduces the likelihood of unethical behavior and fosters a culture of accountability (Crosby et al., 2016).
2. **Improved Accountability**: Blockchain's immutable ledger system ensures that once data is recorded, it cannot be altered or deleted. This immutability provides a reliable audit trail that can be used to hold parties accountable for their actions, thereby reducing instances of fraud and corruption (Zheng et al., 2018).
3. **Strengthened Data Integrity**: Blockchain technology ensures that data is securely recorded and protected against tampering. This data integrity is crucial for maintaining the accuracy and reliability of information, which is essential for ethical decision-making (Azaria et al., 2016).
4. **Ethical Supply Chain Management**: Blockchain can be used to track the provenance of goods and materials, ensuring that they are sourced ethically and sustainably. This capability is particularly important for industries like food and diamonds, where ethical sourcing is a significant concern (Kamath, 2018).

Implications for Digital Transformation

Discussion on the Broader Implications for Contemporary Businesses

The integration of blockchain technology has broader implications for the digital transformation of contemporary businesses. By providing a secure, transparent, and efficient platform for conducting transactions and managing data, blockchain technology addresses several key challenges associated with digital transformation.

1. **Enhanced Operational Efficiency**: Blockchain technology streamlines business processes by automating transactions and reducing the need for intermediaries. This increased efficiency enables businesses to operate more effectively and allocate resources towards innovation and growth (Iansiti & Lakhani, 2017).

2. **Improved Customer Trust and Engagement**: The transparency and security offered by blockchain technology enhance customer trust and engagement. Customers are more likely to engage with businesses that demonstrate a commitment to ethical practices and data integrity (Tapscott & Tapscott, 2016).
3. **Facilitated Regulatory Compliance**: Blockchain's transparent and immutable records make it easier for businesses to comply with regulatory requirements. This compliance is particularly important in industries with stringent regulations, such as finance and healthcare (Zheng et al., 2018).

How Blockchain Integration Influences Overall Digital Transformation

The integration of blockchain technology influences overall digital transformation by fostering innovation, improving efficiency, and promoting ethical practices. Businesses that adopt blockchain are better positioned to navigate the complexities of the digital age and leverage new opportunities for growth and sustainability.

1. **Innovation**: Blockchain technology enables the development of new business models and solutions, such as decentralized applications (dApps) and smart contracts. These innovations drive digital transformation by providing businesses with novel ways to deliver value and engage with stakeholders (Buterin, 2014).
2. **Efficiency**: The efficiency gains from blockchain integration streamline operations and reduce costs. This efficiency is crucial for businesses seeking to compete in a rapidly evolving digital landscape (Catalini & Gans, 2016).
3. **Ethical Practices**: By enhancing transparency, accountability, and data integrity, blockchain technology promotes ethical business practices. This ethical foundation is essential for building trust and sustaining long-term success in the digital economy (Crosby et al., 2016).

5. CASE STUDIES

Case Study 1: Blockchain in a Digital Startup

Detailed Analysis of a Specific Digital Startup Leveraging Blockchain

Company Overview: ChainUp is a fintech startup that leverages blockchain technology to offer decentralized finance (DeFi) solutions. Founded in 2018, ChainUp aims to democratize access to financial services by utilizing blockchain to create a transparent and secure platform for peer-to-peer lending and borrowing.

Blockchain Implementation: ChainUp uses Ethereum's blockchain to deploy smart contracts that automate loan agreements between borrowers and lenders. These smart contracts eliminate the need for intermediaries, reducing transaction costs and increasing efficiency. The platform also employs blockchain for identity verification, ensuring that user data is secure and immutable.

Business Model: ChainUp operates on a freemium model, offering basic financial services for free while charging a fee for premium features such as advanced analytics and priority support. The company generates revenue through transaction fees, subscription plans, and interest on loans.

Outcomes and Lessons Learned

Outcomes:

1. **Increased Efficiency**: The use of smart contracts has significantly reduced the time and cost associated with loan processing, making financial services more accessible to a broader audience.
2. **Enhanced Trust and Transparency**: Blockchain's transparency has built trust among users, leading to higher adoption rates and user retention.
3. **Scalability**: The decentralized nature of blockchain has allowed ChainUp to scale rapidly, expanding its user base and market reach without a proportional increase in infrastructure costs.

Lessons Learned:

1. **Importance of Security**: Ensuring the security of blockchain systems is paramount. ChainUp faced several challenges related to cybersecurity and had to invest heavily in securing its platform against potential attacks.

2. **Regulatory Compliance**: Navigating the regulatory landscape for blockchain-based financial services is complex. ChainUp had to work closely with regulatory bodies to ensure compliance, which required significant resources and expertise.

3. **User Education**: Educating users about blockchain and its benefits was essential for adoption. ChainUp invested in user education initiatives, including webinars, tutorials, and customer support, to help users understand and trust the technology.

Case Study 2: Blockchain for Ethical Supply Chains

Detailed Analysis of a Business Using Blockchain for Ethical Practices

Company Overview: Provenance is a technology company that uses blockchain to create transparency and traceability in supply chains. Founded in 2013, Provenance aims to empower brands to build trust with consumers by providing verifiable information about the origin and journey of their products.

Blockchain Implementation: Provenance utilizes blockchain to record the entire lifecycle of a product, from raw material sourcing to final sale. Each step in the supply chain is documented on the blockchain, creating a tamper-proof record that can be accessed by consumers and stakeholders.

Business Model: Provenance charges businesses a subscription fee to use its platform. The company also offers additional services such as consultancy, data analytics, and customized blockchain solutions tailored to specific industry needs.

Outcomes and Lessons Learned

Outcomes:

1. **Improved Transparency**: Blockchain's immutable ledger provided a transparent view of the supply chain, helping businesses to verify ethical sourcing and production practices.

2. **Consumer Trust**: By providing verifiable information about product origins, Provenance helped brands build trust with consumers, leading to increased customer loyalty and brand value.

3. **Regulatory Advantage**: Businesses using Provenance's platform were better equipped to comply with regulations regarding supply chain transparency and sustainability, providing a competitive edge.

Lessons Learned:

1. **Data Integration**: Integrating blockchain with existing supply chain management systems can be complex. Provenance had to develop solutions to seamlessly integrate blockchain with various enterprise systems.
2. **Stakeholder Collaboration**: Successful implementation required collaboration across the supply chain. Provenance facilitated partnerships between suppliers, manufacturers, and retailers to ensure data accuracy and completeness.
3. **Scalability and Interoperability**: As blockchain technology and standards evolve, ensuring scalability and interoperability with other systems remains a challenge. Provenance continues to innovate and adapt its platform to meet these challenges.

6. CONCLUSION

Summary of Key Findings

The research revealed that blockchain technology significantly enhances digital entrepreneurship by increasing transparency, reducing transaction costs, enhancing security, and facilitating new business models such as smart contracts and decentralized finance. Furthermore, blockchain technology promotes ethical business practices by ensuring transparency, accountability, and data integrity, particularly in complex supply chains.

Theoretical Implications

The findings contribute to the existing literature on digital transformation, digital entrepreneurship, and ethical business practices by providing empirical evidence on the benefits and challenges of blockchain integration. The study supports theories related to technology adoption and innovation diffusion, demonstrating how blockchain can drive business model innovation and ethical practices.

Practical Implications

For businesses considering blockchain integration, the study provides several practical recommendations:

1. **Invest in Security**: Ensure robust security measures are in place to protect blockchain systems from cyber threats.

2. **Engage in Regulatory Compliance**: Work closely with regulatory bodies to navigate the complex legal landscape surrounding blockchain technology.
3. **Educate Stakeholders**: Invest in education and training for both users and employees to foster understanding and trust in blockchain technology.
4. **Collaborate with Partners**: Build strong collaborations across the supply chain to ensure accurate and comprehensive data integration.

Limitations and Future Research

Limitations of the Study

1. **Sample Size**: The sample size for surveys and interviews was limited, which may affect the generalizability of the findings.
2. **Scope of Industries**: The study focused primarily on fintech and supply chain management, potentially overlooking other industries where blockchain could have significant impacts.
3. **Rapid Technological Change**: Blockchain technology is rapidly evolving, and the findings may become outdated as new developments and applications emerge.

Suggestions for Future Research

1. **Expanding Industry Scope**: Future research should explore the impact of blockchain technology across a broader range of industries, including healthcare, real estate, and government services.
2. **Longitudinal Studies**: Conduct longitudinal studies to understand the long-term effects of blockchain integration on digital entrepreneurship and ethical business practices.
3. **Comparative Analysis**: Perform comparative studies between businesses that have adopted blockchain and those that have not, to provide deeper insights into the specific advantages and challenges of blockchain integration.
4. **Technological Innovations**: Investigate the implications of emerging blockchain innovations, such as quantum-resistant blockchains and cross-chain interoperability, on business practices.

REFERENCES

Adhami, S., Giudici, G., & Martinazzi, S. (2018). Why do businesses go crypto? An empirical analysis of initial coin offerings. *Journal of Economics and Business*, 100, 64–75. DOI: 10.1016/j.jeconbus.2018.04.001

Amit, R., & Zott, C. (2001). Value creation in e-business. *Strategic Management Journal*, 22(6-7), 493–520. DOI: 10.1002/smj.187

Auer, R., Cornelli, G., & Frost, J. (2021). Rise of the central bank digital currencies: Drivers, approaches, and technologies. *BIS Working Papers*, 880. https://www.bis.org/publ/work880.pdf

Autio, E., Nambisan, S., Thomas, L. D., & Wright, M. (2018). Digital affordances, spatial affordances, and the genesis of entrepreneurial ecosystems. *Strategic Entrepreneurship Journal*, 12(1), 72–95. DOI: 10.1002/sej.1266

Bharadwaj, A., El Sawy, O. A., Pavlou, P. A., & Venkatraman, N. (2013). Digital business strategy: Toward a next generation of insights. *Management Information Systems Quarterly*, 37(2), 471–482. DOI: 10.25300/MISQ/2013/37:2.3

Braun, V., & Clarke, V. (2006). Using thematic analysis in psychology. *Qualitative Research in Psychology*, 3(2), 77–101. DOI: 10.1191/1478088706qp063oa

Bryman, A. (2016). *Social research methods* (5th ed.). Oxford University Press.

Buterin, V. (2014). A next-generation smart contract and decentralized application platform. Retrieved from https://ethereum.org/en/whitepaper/

Casino, F., Dasaklis, T. K., & Patsakis, C. (2021). A systematic literature review of blockchain-based applications: Current status, classification and open issues. *Telematics and Informatics*, 36, 55–81. DOI: 10.1016/j.tele.2018.11.006

Catalini, C., & Gans, J. S. (2016). Some simple economics of the blockchain. *MIT Sloan School of Management Working Paper*.

Cohen, L., Manion, L., & Morrison, K. (2017). *Research methods in education* (8th ed.). Routledge. DOI: 10.4324/9781315456539

Creswell, J. W. (2014). *Research design: Qualitative, quantitative, and mixed methods approaches* (4th ed.). SAGE Publications.

Creswell, J. W., & Plano Clark, V. L. (2017). *Designing and conducting mixed methods research* (3rd ed.). SAGE Publications.

Crosby, M., Nachiappan, P., Verma, S., & Kalyanaraman, V. (2016). Blockchain technology: Beyond bitcoin. *Applied Innovation*, 2, 6–10.

Das, S., & Mitra, A. (2024). Advancing lightweight digital trust architectures in the internet of medical things: A multi-dimensional analysis. In *Lightweight Digital Trust Architectures in the Internet of Medical Things (IoMT)* (pp. 1-14). DOI: 10.4018/979-8-3693-2109-6.ch001

Das, S., & Mitra, A. (2024). Balancing the scale: Ethical marketing in the age of big data-A comprehensive analysis of data governance standards and the role of effective technology. In *Ethical Marketing Through Data Governance Standards and Effective Technology* (pp. 50-61).

Davenport, T. H., & Ronanki, R. (2018). Artificial intelligence for the real world. *Harvard Business Review*, 96(1), 108–116.

Davidson, E., & Vaast, E. (2010). Digital entrepreneurship and its sociomaterial enactment. In *Proceedings of the 43rd Hawaii International Conference on System Sciences* (pp. 1-10). IEEE.

Esposito, C., De Santis, A., Tortora, G., Chang, H., & Choo, K.-K. R. (2022). Blockchain: A panacea for healthcare cloud-based data security and privacy? *IEEE Cloud Computing*, 5(1), 31–37. DOI: 10.1109/MCC.2018.011791712

Everledger. (2018). Diamond time-lapse: Tracking the journey of a diamond from mine to finger. Retrieved from https://www.everledger.io/

Ferrell, O. C., Fraedrich, J., & Ferrell, L. (2019). *Business ethics: Ethical decision making and cases*. Cengage Learning.

Field, A. (2013). *Discovering statistics using IBM SPSS Statistics* (4th ed.). SAGE Publications.

Fitzgerald, M., Kruschwitz, N., Bonnet, D., & Welch, M. (2014). Embracing digital technology: A new strategic imperative. *MIT Sloan Management Review*, 55(2), 1.

Floridi, L., Taddeo, M., & Turilli, M. (2018). The ethics of information transparency. *Ethics and Information Technology*, 10(2-3), 105–116.

Giones, F., & Brem, A. (2017). Digital technology entrepreneurship: A definition and research agenda. *Technology Innovation Management Review*, 7(5), 44–51. DOI: 10.22215/timreview/1076

Henriette, E., Feki, M., & Boughzala, I. (2015). The shape of digital transformation: A systematic literature review. In *MCIS 2015 Proceedings* (pp. 431-443).

Iansiti, M., & Lakhani, K. R. (2017). The truth about blockchain. *Harvard Business Review*, 95(1), 118–127.

Ivankova, N. V., Creswell, J. W., & Stick, S. L. (2006). Using mixed-methods sequential explanatory design: From theory to practice. *Field Methods*, 18(1), 3–20. DOI: 10.1177/1525822X05282260

Jain, V., & Mitra, A. (2023). Development and application of machine learning algorithms for sentiment analysis in digital manufacturing: A pathway for enhanced customer feedback. In *Emerging Technologies in Digital Manufacturing and Smart Factories* (pp. 26-38).

Jain, V., & Mitra, A. (2024). A critical examination of ethical implications in AI-driven consumer behavior media discourse and environmental sustainability. In *Enhancing and Predicting Digital Consumer Behavior with AI* (pp. 1-16). DOI: 10.4018/979-8-3693-4453-8.ch001

Jain, V., & Mitra, A. (2024). Culinary narratives and community revitalization: The role of media in promoting sustainable gastronomy tourism. In *Promoting Sustainable Gastronomy Tourism and Community Development* (pp. 67-80).

Kamath, R. (2018). Food traceability on blockchain: Walmart's pork and mango pilots with IBM. *The Journal of the British Blockchain Association*, 1(1), 1–12. DOI: 10.31585/jbba-1-1-(10)2018

Kane, G. C., Palmer, D., Phillips, A. N., Kiron, D., & Buckley, N. (2015). Strategy, not technology, drives digital transformation. *MIT Sloan Management Review and Deloitte University Press*, 14, 1–25.

Kouhizadeh, M., & Sarkis, J. (2021). Blockchain practices, potentials, and perspectives in greening supply chains. *Sustainability*, 13(6), 3337. DOI: 10.3390/su13063337

Kshetri, N. (2021). Blockchain and COVID-19: Applications and paradoxes. *IT Professional*, 23(5), 4–10. DOI: 10.1109/MITP.2020.2992148

Kvale, S., & Brinkmann, S. (2015). *InterViews: Learning the craft of qualitative research interviewing* (3rd ed.). SAGE Publications.

Marston, S., Li, Z., Bandyopadhyay, S., Zhang, J., & Ghalsasi, A. (2011). Cloud computing—The business perspective. *Decision Support Systems*, 51(1), 176–189. DOI: 10.1016/j.dss.2010.12.006

Martin, K. (2015). Ethical issues in the big data industry. *MIS Quarterly Executive*, 14(2).

Nakamoto, S. (2008). Bitcoin: A peer-to-peer electronic cash system. Retrieved from https://bitcoin.org/bitcoin.pdf

Nambisan, S. (2017). Digital entrepreneurship: Toward a digital technology perspective of entrepreneurship. *Entrepreneurship Theory and Practice*, 41(6), 1029–1055. DOI: 10.1111/etap.12254

Palmer, D. (2012). The ethics of data mining. *International Journal of Social and Organizational Dynamics in IT*, 2(1), 15–29.

Rejeb, A., Keogh, J. G., & Treiblmaier, H. (2022). How blockchain technology can benefit supply chain sustainability. *Sustainability*, 12(3), 7369. DOI: 10.3390/su12187369

Resnik, D. B. (2018). *The ethics of research with human subjects: Protecting people, advancing science, promoting trust*. Springer. DOI: 10.1007/978-3-319-68756-8

Sachdeva, P., Kumar, M. D., & Mitra, A. (2024). Green discourse analysis on Twitter: Imperatives to green product management in sustainable cities (SDG11). *Studies in Systems. Decision and Control*, 487, 245–256. DOI: 10.1007/978-3-031-35828-9_22

Sachdeva, P., & Mitra, A. (2024). Decoding human development and environmental sustainability: A predictive analytical study on relationship between HDI and carbon emission. *Studies in Systems. Decision and Control*, 489, 785–795. DOI: 10.1007/978-3-031-36895-0_66

Saunders, M., Lewis, P., & Thornhill, A. (2016). *Research methods for business students* (7th ed.). Pearson.

Schär, F. (2021). Decentralized finance: On blockchain- and smart contract-based financial markets. *Review - Federal Reserve Bank of St. Louis*, 103(2), 153–174. DOI: 10.20955/r.103.153-74

Swan, M. (2015). *Blockchain: Blueprint for a new economy*. O'Reilly Media, Inc.

Tapscott, D., & Tapscott, A. (2016). *Blockchain revolution: How the technology behind bitcoin is changing money, business, and the world*. Penguin.

Tian, F. (2016). An agri-food supply chain traceability system for China based on RFID & blockchain technology. In *2016 13th International Conference on Service Systems and Service Management (ICSSSM)* (pp. 1-6). IEEE.

Treviño, L. K., & Nelson, K. A. (2017). *Managing business ethics: Straight talk about how to do it right*. John Wiley & Sons.

Vial, G. (2019). Understanding digital transformation: A review and a research agenda. *The Journal of Strategic Information Systems*, 28(2), 118–144. DOI: 10.1016/j.jsis.2019.01.003

Vial, G. (2019). Understanding digital transformation: A review and a research agenda. *The Journal of Strategic Information Systems*, 28(2), 118–144. DOI: 10.1016/j.jsis.2019.01.003

Westerman, G., Bonnet, D., & McAfee, A. (2014). *Leading digital: Turning technology into business transformation.* Harvard Business Review Press.

Wood, G. (2014). Ethereum: A secure decentralised generalised transaction ledger. *Ethereum Project Yellow Paper*, 151, 1–32.

Wright, A., & De Filippi, P. (2015). Decentralized blockchain technology and the rise of lex cryptographia. *Available atSSRN* 2580664. DOI: 10.2139/ssrn.2580664

Yin, R. K. (2018). *Case study research and applications: Design and methods* (6th ed.). SAGE Publications.

Zhao, L., Von Glinow, M. A., & Shapiro, D. L. (2016). Explaining the role of cultural differences in online entrepreneurship: A study of China and the US. *Journal of International Business Studies*, 47(2), 214–239.

Zheng, Z., Xie, S., Dai, H. N., Chen, X., & Wang, H. (2018). Blockchain challenges and opportunities: A survey. *International Journal of Web and Grid Services*, 14(4), 352–375. DOI: 10.1504/IJWGS.2018.095647

ADDITIONAL READING

Ali, M. (2021). *Remote Work and Sustainable Changes for the Future of Global Business.* IGI Global. https://www.igi-global.com/book/remote-work-sustainable-changes-future/264375

Ali, M. (2022). *Future Role of Sustainable Innovative Technologies in Crisis Management.* IGI Global. https://www.igi-global.com/book/future-role-sustainable-innovative-technologies/281281

Ali, M. (2023). *Shifting Paradigms in the Rapidly Developing Global Digital Ecosystem: A GCC Perspective.* In Digital Entrepreneurship and Co-Creating Value Through Digital Encounters (pp. 145-166). IGI Global. https://www.igi-global.com/chapter/shifting-paradigms-in-the-rapidly-developing-global-digital-ecosystem/323525

Ali, M. (2023). T*axonomy of Industry 4.0 Technologies in Digital Entrepreneur-ship and Co-Creating Value. In Digital Entrepreneurship and Co-Creating Value Through Digital Encounters* (pp. 24–55). IGI Global., https://www.igi-global.com/chapter/taxonomy-of-industry-40-technologies-in-digital-entrepreneurship-and-co-creating-value/323520 DOI: 10.4018/978-1-6684-7416-7.ch002

Ali, M., & Wood-Harper, T. (2021). *Fostering Communication and Learning with Underutilized Technologies in Higher Education*. IGI Global. https://www.igi-global.com/book/fostering-communication-learning-underutilized-technologies/244593

Ali, M., Wood-Harper, T., & Kutar, M. (2023). Multi-Perspectives of Contemporary Digital Transformation Models of Complex Innovation Management. In *Digital Entrepreneurship and Co-Creating Value Through Digital Encounters* (pp. 79–96). IGI Global., https://www.igi-global.com/chapter/multi-perspectives-of-contemporary-digital-transformation-models-of-complex-innovation-management/323522 DOI: 10.4018/978-1-6684-7416-7.ch004

Ali, M. B. (2021). Internet of Things (IoT) to Foster Communication and Information Sharing: A Case of UK Higher Education. In Ali, M. B., & Wood-Harper, T. (Eds.), *Fostering Communication and Learning With Underutilized Technologies in Higher Education* (pp. 1–20). IGI Global., https://www.igi-global.com/chapter/internet-of-things-iot-to-foster-communication-and-information-sharing/262718/ DOI: 10.4018/978-1-7998-4846-2.ch001

Ali, M. B., & Wood-Harper, T. (2022). Artificial Intelligence (AI) as a Decision-Making Tool to Control Crisis Situations. In *Future Role of Sustainable Innovative Technologies in Crisis Management*. IGI Global., https://www.igi-global.com/chapter/artificial-intelligence-ai-as-a-decision-making-tool-to-control-crisis-situations/298931 DOI: 10.4018/978-1-7998-9815-3.ch006

Ali, M. B., Wood-Harper, T., & Ramlogan, R. (2020). A Framework Strategy to Overcome Trust Issues on Cloud Computing Adoption in Higher Education. In Modern Principles, Practices, and Algorithms for Cloud Security (pp. 162-183). IGI Global. https://www.igi-global.com/chapter/a-framework-strategy-to-overcome-trust-issues-on-cloud-computing-adoption-in-higher-education/238907/

Chapter 13
Impacts of Blockchain on Circular Economy Motivation via the Q–Rung Orthopair Fuzzy Set

Damla Cevik Aka
https://orcid.org/0000-0001-9622-273X
Kirklareli University, Turkey

ABSTRACT

This study aims to examine the effects of the use of blockchain technology in production on the motivation to switch to a circular economy (CE). Additionally, the study aims to assess the significance of blockchain technology's impacts on businesses, with a focus on CE initiatives. In this context, thirty-five managers from seven companies in Turkey's automotive subindustry were interviewed, and the criteria were evaluated by seven expert groups. Considering the presence of different groups and high uncertainty, the Q-Rung Orthopair fuzzy set was used. The study findings reveal that the primary factors driving circular economy motivation are "waste management," "information sharing and enhanced cooperation among supply chain stakeholders," and "operating costs," in that order. The article explores blockchain as a promising technology to facilitate the circular economy process. This study is expected to enrich the circular economy literature and be a road map for automotive supplier industry manufacturers in developing countries.

DOI: 10.4018/979-8-3693-5966-2.ch013

1. INTRODUCTION

The circular economy (CE) is a model that focuses on resource efficiency to ensure that companies use their resources in their cycle or different cycles for longer periods. These models aim to optimize resource use and reduce possible waste. For this purpose, the focus is on different types of resource recovery, such as recycling, reprocessing and remanufacturing of production inputs. The CE model, in which production resources are kept in circulation for a long time, contributes to addressing current economic, environmental and social problems and thus creating a durable and sustainable economy (Chiaroni et al., 2022).

Digitalization is a significant support in circular economy models that strengthens the effective use and efficiency of resources by closing the loop (Antikainen et al., 2018). Technologies such as the Internet of Things (IoT), artificial intelligence, big data analytics, and augmented reality are accelerating the CE transition by preserving economic and environmental situations in production (Khan et al., 2021; Rejeb et al., 2022). The participation of partners and experts is expected, especially in circular business models. One of the technologies that holistically provides this information is blockchain technology (BCT). It is thought that if companies develop their digital transformation strategies and integrate BCT into the supply chain, it will play a critical role in achieving their circular economy goals (Gong et al., 2022; Kouhizadeh et al., 2020). There is a great need for visibility and traceability of the chain for a sustainable supply chain. Many researchers have revealed that with the use of BCT, companies increase the visibility and traceability of supply chain processes and achieve more sustainable goals (Sunmola et al., 2023; Yousefi & Tosarkani, 2023). However, the effects and scope of blockchain technology are quite unclear, and research is needed (Rejeb et al., 2023).

Blockchain is a technology that creates an official record of real-time data from IoT-equipped devices. BCT consists of a blockchain with timestamps and transaction information in the cryptographic hash of the immediately preceding block that cannot be changed or deleted (Balon et al., 2023). It makes significant contributions in terms of decentralization, with an open-access network and data being unchangeable and irreversible. These features make it stand out in new industry trends. In particular, the effects of BCT are discussed in many models prepared for sustainability. BCT plays a very important role, especially in ensuring a sustainable supply chain (Nguyen et al., 2021). It focuses on many aspects, both operational efficiency in the supply chains of many sectors, such as food, agriculture and automotive, sustainability in terms of energy resources (Afzal et al., 2022) and environmental concerns. Various solutions are available to support sustainability, such as establishing smart cities and building smart buildings (Bindra et al., 2019). BCT technology supports CE models in many ways, including sustainable water management (Zhao et al., 2019), carbon gas emission control (Chaudhari et al., 2022), logistics systems (Tiwari et al., 2023) and waste management (Kouhizadeh et al., 2023).

Applying blockchain technology in the circular economy is a fairly new approach. For this reason, research on the use of BCT is quite limited (Chauhan et al., 2022; Kouhizadeh et al., 2023; Pinar & Boran, 2020; Schmid et al., 2023; Trevisan et al., 2023). For this reason, studies on the examination and application of these technologies within the circular economy are needed. In research on blockchain technology, it is necessary to examine development in the context of the transition to the circular economy and close these gaps by gaining insights from this relationship. Research on the relationship between the two concepts has been increasing, especially in recent years. Thus, investigating the effects of blockchain technology features on the circular economy is crucial. In this study, experts evaluate the potential contributions and insights of blockchain technology to circular economy goals.

The main research questions in this study are as follows:

RQ1: What effects can the use of blockchain technology have on circular economy motivation in the manufacturing sector?

RQ2: Based on the opportunities identified, what is the primary influence of blockchain technology on motivating the circular economy?

RQ3: Based on the identified opportunities, what is the least significant effect of blockchain technology on motivating the circular economy?

To answer these questions, interviews were conducted with expert groups from seven automotive subindustry companies in Turkey, and data were collected from a total of thirty-five managers. The potential contributions of blockchain technology were examined across nine criteria on the basis of a literature review and expert opinion. The Q-Rung Orthopair Fuzzy (q-ROF) set was used to analyse expert opinions in a fuzzy environment. Q-ROFs provide a wide range of flexibility depending on the value to be given to q. Despite their flexibility, the utilization of the q-ROF set in studies remains minimal. A key aspect of this study is the ease of applying the q-ROF method in research involving multiple groups.

Since there is not much research on the relevant subject, this study is thought to make significant contributions to the literature both theoretically and to experts in terms of practice. The findings are anticipated to guide manufacturers by assessing the impact of blockchain technology on increasing motivation in circular economy business models across the supply chain. However, given the small sample size, the generalizability of the findings is limited.

The second part of this study provides a theoretical framework regarding blockchain technology and its effects on circular economy motivation. In the third part, the research method is the Q-Rung Orthopair Fuzzy (q-ROF) approach. Section 4 presents a case study and data analysis involving seven different businesses. The final section evaluates the results and provides insights for future studies.

2. THEORETICAL BACKGROUND

The increasing global importance of sustainability has pressured manufacturers to be sustainable in many ways. One of the prominent models for creating sustainable supply chains is the circular economy. Transitioning to the circular economy provides manufacturers with multiple benefits, economically, environmentally, and socially. The utilization of new technologies amplifies these effects. The continuous advancement of technology is revolutionizing various aspects of the manufacturing sector. The widespread adoption of digital technologies, especially during the Industry 4.0 era, highlights the potential benefits of the circular economy.

Blockchain technology (BCT), originally developed as a protocol for sharing and updating information, is now advocated for the effective adoption of the circular economy. BCT can strongly support the implementation of a circular economy and drive changes in institutional and economic systems (Kouhizadeh et al., 2020; Rejeb et al., 2022b). In tech-driven industries, exploring the impact of businesses leveraging blockchain technology within the circular economy is crucial. With this awareness, manufacturers have increasingly invested in blockchain technology in recent years.

While some of the research on blockchain technology examines the opportunities it provides, other studies focus on potential obstacles. Researchers have mentioned many obstacles in the implementation of BCT. One of the most prominent obstacles is financial issues (Saraf et al., 2024). In particular, the high installation costs of BCT and infrastructure (Leng et al., 2020; Öztürk & Yildizbaşi, 2020; Panghal et al., 2022; Zhang et al., 2020) and the energy consumption costs of technology (Khan et al., 2022) have come to the forefront. A second obstacle has been examined in terms of technical issues (Meier et al., 2023; Saraf et al., 2024). The difficulties in software and hardware updates of BCT (Bao et al., 2020), the limited transaction processing capacity (Kumar & Chopra, 2022), the design of weak network sizes that cause concerns of data security (Kuo et al., 2020), the duplication of data due to poor management of the control mechanism with many nodes in the technology network (Kim et al., 2018), and the manipulation of data recorded in blocks (Sayeed & Marco-Gisbert, 2019) are prominent technical obstacles. In addition, the lack of technical knowledge to run BCT is one of the most evaluated themes in studies (Bruel & Godina, 2023; Ferreira et al., 2023; Meier et al., 2023; Öztürk & Yildizbaşi, 2020; Panghal et al., 2022; Rejeb et al., 2022a; Sahebi et al., 2020). Many different obstacles to BCT adaptation have been intensely discussed, especially since 2020. Inexperienced workforces (Bai & Sarkis, 2020), the inability to establish effective collaboration (Barenji et al., 2021; Leng et al., 2020; Reyna et al., 2018), a lack of senior management support (Fan et al., 2022; Leng et al., 2020; Rejeb et al., 2022), privacy violation concerns (Bao et al., 2020; Feng et al., 2019; Panghal et al., 2022), synchronization problems (Leng et al., 2020) and radical change requirements related to doing business (Kumar & Chopra, 2022) have been included in many studies.

One of the most discussed issues is policy and regulatory challenges (Kamble et al., 2020; Kamilaris et al., 2021; Kumar & Chopra, 2022). The lack of regulatory implementation has become more prominent in the use of BCT in recent years. Regulations governing practical applications are necessary for the introduction of a new technical system (Saraf et al., 2024). Therefore, clear and defined regulations should be established regarding the problems and rules to be encountered in practice (Öztürk & Yildizbaşi, 2020). From a policy perspective, managing information in BCT can be valuable for developing a circular economy infrastructure (Kouhizadeh et al., 2019). It is expected that legislation and policy development for many technologies developed due to digitalization will balance ecological and economic needs (Upadhyay et al., 2021). Since there are members from different countries in Blockchain, global regulations and policies are necessary (Panghal et al., 2022). It is important for regulatory bodies to make regulations affecting business decisions and design up-to-date policies for applications. Governments should ensure that policies and regulations encourage technological growth in a more sustainable way. The lack of rewards and incentives to promote blockchain technologies (Bruel & Godina, 2023; da Silva et al., 2023; Saraf et al., 2024) has also been considered a legal barrier.

Despite the many organizational and managerial challenges expressed, it is critically important for businesses to adopt blockchain-enabled sustainable production (Jamwal et al., 2022). Blockchain technology is a great help in removing existing barriers by facilitating transparency and traceability for circular economy applications (da Silva et al., 2023). With blockchain technology, businesses have begun to transform circular economy applications and new business models. The effects of blockchain technology on CE applications have also been investigated in many countries and in many different sectors. The most popular industries in this field are food and agriculture. Moreover, studies have investigated the effects of blockchain use on CE applications in different industries, such as the fashion, textile and clothing, manufacturing, automotive and energy industries.

Khan et al. (2021), who conducted a study on 239 manufacturing enterprises in Malaysia, reported that BCT helps companies achieve financial and sustainable goals. Okorie and Russell (2022) examined food supply chains in terms of the circular economy and revealed that it can provide great opportunities for businesses in terms of traceability, transparency and scalability throughout the supply chain. Another study examining the effects of BCT on the circular supply chain application model in the food sector was conducted by Paul et al. (2022). Researchers have examined this subject from the perspective of tea producers in countries such as India, Kenya and Sri Lanka. In this study, the researchers discussed the managerial and social effects of implementing blockchain-oriented technologies integrated with RFID within the lens of a circular economy. Panghal et al. (2022), who discussed the difficulties of adopting blockchain technology in Indian food supply chains, revealed 'regulatory structure' and 'lack of realized need' as the greatest challenges. However, the researchers emphasized 'privacy breach issues', 'high costs', and 'lack of skills'.

Alves et al. (2022), who studied the textile supply chain, revealed the opportunities that technologies such as blockchain and the Internet of Things will provide for circular economy models. As a result, the need for new raw materials, such as cotton, has decreased, textile waste problems have decreased, and a more sustainable industry has formed. Ali et al. (2024) examined the effects of CE applications focused on Industry 4.0 technologies such as artificial intelligence and blockchain on sustainable business performance in the Indian textile industry. In this study, the researchers also highlighted the impact of government support and incentives and revealed improvements in waste, emissions and environmental pollution. Another study on the textile sector included both the opportunities and challenges of BCT. Badhwar et al. (2023) clearly demonstrated that blockchain technology establishes established connections between many aspects of sustainability, which are important for the circular economy, and traceability and transparency. Shou and Domenech (2022) proposed a protocol for the integration of life cycle assessment (LCA) and blockchain in a case study on a leather bag manufacturer to evaluate circular practices. Researchers have demonstrated that a BCT-based framework is an effective technology for revealing circularity opportunities by providing strong traceability and data sharing. In another study in the same sector, Heim and Hopper (2022) observed the global trend in digital transformation and investigated the adoption of blockchain and other technologies. Drawing attention to the challenges faced by small and medium-sized enterprises (SMEs), this study evaluated technical challenges such as software and social challenges such as global governance. Another study analysed how Industry 4.0-focused CE practices affect sustainable business performance via a case study in the Indian textile industry and revealed that the development of smart grids has increased (Andoni et al., 2019). An important aspect of the study is that digital technologies such as BCT need strategic integration to achieve the desired results by identifying their possible risks.

The energy sector is seen as one of the building blocks of the circular economy. In a study conducted on the energy sector, a new integration process of blockchain with renewable energy systems was developed from the perspective of a circular economy (Yildizbasi, 2021). In this study, which addresses the difficulties associated with BCT, an application was created for a company making sustainable energy investments in Turkey. The difficulties and obstacles of the company in using BCT in energy management were evaluated with the Pythagorean fuzzy AHP. The findings of the study are important in terms of providing information to companies preparing to implement blockchain in energy production, energy distribution and waste management processes. Zhu et al. (2020) evaluated the positive and negative effects of blockchain technology on the energy sector in China. Researchers have reported that China's monopolistic market structure in terms of energy supply hinders the implementation of BCT but provides great opportunities for the circular economy in terms of the expansion of clean energy. The study particularly emphasized the need to change the relevant laws on the use of BCT and balance the conflict between management and innovation.

One of the important sectors where BCT is applied is the automotive industry. Recent studies have shown that blockchain technology facilitates the transition to a circular economy in many sectors, including the automotive industry (Grati et al., 2024). Grati et al. (2024) investigated blockchain as having great potential to facilitate CE transition in the automotive industry. The researchers reported that the costs of integrating a specific blockchain technology are acceptable compared with the opportunities offered by the technology in terms of security and transparency. Researchers who also touched upon the challenges of blockchain technology found it very difficult to convince stakeholders in the automotive industry. Govindan (2022), who conducted a case study in a Danish automotive parts remanufacturing company, aimed to identify the barriers to the implementation of blockchain technology. Govindan evaluated 20 barriers, such as legal security, operational difficulties, lack of government support, and lack of legislation. When all these studies are evaluated, BCT has great potential because of the opportunities it provides in many sectors.

Although the obstacles to blockchain technology have been discussed, the same number of studies have also included the potential contributions of BCT. A number of opportunities that organizations encounter in implementing BCT have been highlighted. BCT enables transparent and immutable tracking of the entire product lifecycle throughout the supply chain (De Giovanni, 2022). Blockchain technology can aid in revitalizing the market by overseeing transactions in the secondary product market derived from recycling (Quayson et al., 2023). The rapid sale, leasing, and sharing of secondary products can establish longer lifecycles for products (Antikainen et al., 2018). This approach can expand the market for secondary materials or products, addressing a major obstacle in the circular economy due to their low market value (Souza Piao et al., 2023), and can become more easily accessible and preferable with blockchain technology. However, in some countries, various sustainability and material recycling policies do not support accurate data on the availability and reporting of secondary materials (Liu et al., 2022). The benefits of blockchain technology will be greatly exploited if adequate guidance and policies are provided to address the challenges of material efficiency.

Like many digital technologies, blockchain technology also has an effect on consumer behavior. Today's consumer demand for eco-friendly products urges companies to take substantial steps to meet these expectations. Companies adopting blockchain technology to meet evolving customer demands also seize a significant market opportunity (Chaudhari et al., 2022). As consumers become increasingly knowledgeable, their trust and loyalty toward a product or company may change accordingly. In the manufacturing sector, blockchain verifies the authenticity of materials and products, ensuring sustainable production (Bonsu, 2020). Blockchain technology can reduce fraud through the ability to query and verify the authenticity of products, which benefits customers (Dujak & Sajter, 2019). Another aspect is that blockchain technology can facilitate active customer participation, especially in product design (Agrawal et al., 2021). The ability of customers to track the production process can enhance their trust in products or manufacturers. The ability to track inherent complexity more efficiently may encourage consumers to make sustainable choices. Companies using blockchain technology incentivize sustainable behaviors among customers by distributing digital currencies within their reward system (Zhao et al., 2023).

The use of digital technologies has made data security more significant than ever. One of the significant contributions of blockchain technology is its ability to ensure data reliability and validity for a company's entire dataset (Kouhizadeh et al., 2020; Samadhiya et al., 2023; Schmidt et al., 2023). The study aims to ensure that all data about the firm are accurate and intact without being corrupted, even accidentally. In this context, it is important to trust all the data that affect the circular economy throughout the supply chain. BCT also facilitates secure data storage (Chaudhari et al., 2022). Creating, tracking, storing, and managing environmental data for the circular economy enhances data trust. The immutability feature of blockchain technology creates a counterfeit-free working environment for all stakeholders in the supply chain (Danese et al., 2021). BCT simplifies and authenticates data management for environmental and economic sustainability by centralizing all data types.

Product tracking facilitated by BCT empowers stakeholders to address challenges proactively (Shojaei et al., 2021). Companies that invest in proactive management often act by predicting any situation regarding their operations. Real-time access to all relevant data in the circular economy enables proactive preventive measures. Companies can avoid risks further with proactive management. Companies that are proficient in managing risks can achieve significant results in terms of both economic and environmental performance. The blockchain's ability to provide simultaneous access to information for all stakeholders supports proactive collaboration against potential problems.

In the circular economy model, system security is necessary. Companies must bolster security against potential malicious attacks. With numerous stakeholders, ensuring continuous system security is imperative. In circular economy practices where responsibility lies with all stakeholders, the features of blockchain technology can protect the system against all kinds of threats (Danese et al., 2021; Kouhizadeh et al., 2020). For example, the programmable nature of smart contracts in blockchain enhances the security of payments. Distributed networks ensure system protection by restricting access to individuals without data access. Thus, motivation toward the circular economy may increase with the opportunities provided by blockchain technology. On the other hand, the circular economy model can operate under various legal requirements. Following these rules and regulations allows companies to establish secure systems and ensures effective monitoring processes.

Integrating blockchain technology throughout the supply chain is one of the most effective means to achieve transparency and seamless communication without bureaucracy. When used in conjunction with technologies, such as the IoT, blockchain technology effectively reduces carbon emissions (Chaudhari et al., 2022; Sharma et al., 2021; Upadhyay et al., 2021). On the other hand, its decentralized nature creates significant opportunities for businesses in terms of carbon credits. The decentralized governance structure of technology is supportive of reducing carbon emissions. This is crucial for businesses in terms of investments and credit. Firms that track and gradually reduce carbon emissions may find it easier to obtain carbon credits. Investment support significantly impacts competition, enabling faster market entry.

The main potential of BCT lies in enabling information sharing and collaboration among all supply chain stakeholders. Smart contracts play a crucial role in shaping the circular economy by streamlining information transfer (Chidepatil et al., 2020). Providing consistent and accurate information to each stakeholder can increase trust among stakeholders (Rejeb et al., 2022a). The strong security system of BCT supports supply chain stakeholders in securely sharing all their sustainability-related data (Xie et al., 2023). Providing this trustworthy environment encourages collaboration and alignment with sustainability goals. Collaboration and communication will undoubtedly contribute significantly to the long-term sustainability of economic models. Transparent and immutable publication of information among customers, suppliers, manufacturers, and others effectively mitigates risks and disruptions. Thus, firms can create synergy in achieving their CE goals.

Efficient waste management offers a significant opportunity for resource recovery and environmental pollution control in the circular economy (Chaudhari et al., 2022). The traceability feature of BCT enables straightforward tracking of product and material destinations (Nandi et al., 2021a). Recycling and reusing products through blockchain technology extend their useful life, crucially contributing to the circular economy (Omidian et al., 2023; Venkatesh et al., 2020). Firms strongly support sustainable resource management along with the use of recycled materials. BCT is also significant for recycling because of its smart contract feature (Khadke et al., 2021; Kouhizadeh et al., 2020). Agreements focused on the circular economy with stakeholders will support sustainable production. Additionally, these agreements can restrict the use of unsustainable materials in product packaging and facilitate tracking (Nandi et al., 2021b).

Blockchain technology impacts manufacturers by reducing operational costs in circular economy processes. Investments in technology enable companies to manage their operations more efficiently and cost-effectively (Kouhizadeh et al., 2020). It is critical for companies wishing to implement circular economy models to invest in and manage sustainable operations. One of its greatest economic contributions is making carbon credit trading possible (Brown et al., 2022). Carbon credits can be created in line with companies' emission reduction targets. BCT helps automate and manage carbon credit trading more efficiently. At the same time, the trade will be carried out more functionally by allowing the use of cryptocurrencies with the distributed ledger system. These situations can also provide economic benefits to companies. In particular, the economic impacts of outcomes such as companies achieving resource efficiency through these practices are noteworthy. Additionally, data integrity can reduce the costs associated with data verification and correction. Strong collaboration among stakeholders can facilitate the management of resources throughout their lifecycle, thereby reducing the costs associated with disruptions.

The bottom line is that BCT has an important place in circular economy models. Many features of this technology, such as transparency, accountability, and data-sharing policies, can offer solutions to these problems as a whole (Treiblmaier & Garaus, 2023).

3. RESEARCH METHOD

This study proposes the use of a q-step orthopair fuzzy number (q-ROFN) to determine criterion weights. Experts from 5 companies used the q-ROF cluster set to determine the weights of nine criteria.

The main reason for choosing this method is that q-ROF fuzzy sets are suitable for evaluating more uncertain situations. These sets allow decision makers more freedom of expression than other fuzzy sets do (Pinar & Boran, 2020). Increasing the value of the q level can provide greater flexibility in more complex and uncertain situations.

Q-Rung Orthopair Fuzzy Set

The intuitive fuzzy concept was developed by Atanassov (1986) as an approach to evaluate uncertainty and nonmembership. The intuitive fuzzy concept is used together with fuzzy sets by researchers and expanded into different fuzzy set sets. Yager (2017) reported that the sum of the q degrees of the membership level and the q. degrees of the nonmembership level will be at most 1 and developed q-level orthopair fuzzy set sets.

The q-ROFN reveals that the condition is $\mu(x)^q + \vartheta(x)^q \leq 1$. The q-ROFN provides more general data.

If the q level is equal to 1, an intuitionistic fuzzy number is used; if the q level is equal to 2, Pythagorean-based fuzzy sets are used. If the q level is at least equal to 3, q-ROF is used. In cases where uncertainty increases, the value of the q level can be increased, thus providing a more comprehensive range of information. The greatest advantage of heuristic, Pythagorean and q-level fuzzy sets over classical fuzzy sets is that they can evaluate membership and nonmembership situations at the same time.

Q-rung orthopair fuzzy sets are special due to opportunities such as use with complex models, handling uncertain environments and providing flexibility. However, sufficient studies have not been conducted since the method was developed (Pinar & Boran, 2020).

Using this fuzzy set can provide great convenience to users. The following definitions are provided for the Q-Rung Orthopair fuzzy set.

As suggested by Yager (2017), a q-level orthopair fuzzy subset A of X is defined.

$$A = \left\{ \left(x, \mu_A(x), \vartheta_A(x)\right), x \in X \right\} \tag{1}$$

where $\mu_A : X [0,1]$ indicates the membership degree and $\vartheta_A : X [0,1]$ indicates the nonmembership degree of $x \in X$ to set A with the following condition:

$$\left(\mu_A(x)\right)^q + \left(\vartheta_A(x)\right)^q \leq 1 \tag{2}$$

Since the sum of the membership and nonmembership values is less than 1, hesitation should be evaluated. At this stage, the degree of hesitation is calculated. The degree of hesitation is shown in Equation (3).

$$\pi_A(x) = \left(1 - \left(\mu_A(x)\right)^q - \left(\vartheta_A(x)\right)^q\right)^{1/q} \tag{3}$$

When q=1, the number becomes an intuitive fuzzy number, and when q=2, the number becomes a Pythagorean fuzzy number (Zhu et al., 2022). In q-ROF clusters, q must be ≥ 3.

The steps of the method are outlined below:

Step 1: The rankings of decision-makers are declared as linguistic terms according to Table 1 and are calculated via Equation (4).

Table 1. Linguistic Terms

Linguistic Terms	μ	ϑ
Extremely High (EH)	0.95	0.15
Very High (VH)	0.85	0.25
High (H)	0.75	0.35
Medium High (MH)	0.65	0.45
Medium (M)	0.55	0.55
Medium Low (ML)	0.45	0.65
Low (L)	0.35	0.75
Very Low (VL)	0.25	0.85
Extremely Low (EL)	0.15	0.95

$$\lambda_i = \frac{\left(1 + \mu_i^q\left(x_j\right) - \vartheta_i^q\left(x_j\right)\right)}{\sum_{i=1}^l \left(1 + \mu_i^q\left(x_j\right) - \vartheta_i^q\left(x_j\right)\right)}$$

and

$$\sum_{i=1}^l \lambda_i = 1 \tag{4}$$

Step 2. Evaluations of the criteria are made by decision-makers, and these linguistic expressions are converted into mathematical values according to Table 1 (Pinar & Boran, 2020).

Step 3. The evaluations of the criteria are normalized by the weights of the decision-makers. The normalized values are calculated according to Equation (5) (Liu & Wang, 2018).

$$q - ROFWA\left(a_1, a_2 \ldots a_t\right) = \left\{ \left(1 - \prod_{i=1}^t \left(\left(1 - \mu_i^q\right)^{\lambda_i}\right)^{1/q}, \prod_{i=1}^t \vartheta_i^{\lambda_i}\right) \right. \tag{5}$$

Step 4: The criterion weights are calculated according to Equations (6) and (7).

$$W_j = \frac{\sum_{i=1}^{t} \lambda_i \left(1 + \mu_i^q - \vartheta_i^q\right)}{\sum_{j=1}^{n} \sum_{i=1}^{t} \lambda_i \left(1 + \mu_i^q - \vartheta_i^q\right)} \tag{6}$$

$$W_j = \left[w_{1+} w_{2+} \dots + w_{j1}\right] \tag{7}$$

4. CASE STUDY & RESULTS

The application was designed to evaluate the motivations of businesses in the circular economy by evaluating the use of BCT in organizations. The limited number of studies on the relevant subject and case studies in the automotive sector did not extend beyond the few studies encouraged in this study.

The case study in the study is based on interviews with employees of five different manufacturing companies operating in the automotive subindustry. What these companies have in common is that they are in the same sector and that the companies are innovative towards technological initiatives. In each company, some employees are closely interested in technological developments and support transformation. It was decided that these people should be the focus of the study, and they were included in the study on the basis of their years of experience.

4.1. Decision-Makers (DM$_n$)

Managers within companies play a crucial role in facilitating the transition to a circular economy. For this reason, the decision-makers in the study consisted of real-sector employees. Decision makers are the managers of companies in the automotive subindustry. In the data collection process, focus groups were formed with five experts from each company. Experts are people with at least ten years of experience and have engaged in activities aimed at the use of new technologies in industries. Each expert has at least a decade of experience and has engaged in implementing new technologies across various industries. Owing to the involvement of groups from seven different businesses, the study sample included a total of 35 individuals.

4.2. Criteria (C$_n$) in the Study

The potential contributions of blockchain technology are examined under nine main headings. These also constitute the criteria of the study. Each criterion was taken from the studies of other researchers who researched the relevant subject. In this study, the criteria examined by different researchers were combined in a single study.

C_1: Development of the secondary product market (Antikainen et al., 2018; Quayson et al., 2023; Souza Piao et al., 2023)

C_2: Creating sustainable consumer behavior (Rana et al., 2021; Saberi et al., 2019),

C_3: Increasing data validity and reliability (Chaudhari et al., 2022; Sharma et al., 2020; Samadhiya et al., 2023).

C_4: Proactive approach to supply chain risk (Sharma et al., 2020; Shojaei et al., 2021).

C_5: Security (Danese et al., 2021; Kouhizadeh et al., 2020; Rejeb et al., 2022a; Sharma et al., 2020)

C_6: Operation costs (Khan et al., 2021; Kouhizadeh et al., 2020; Sharma et al., 2020; Upadhyay et al., 2021).

C_7: Reducing carbon emissions (Benítez-Martínez et al., 2021; Upadhyay et al., 2021).

C_8: Information sharing and improved collaboration between stakeholders in the supply chain (Chidepatil et al.,2020; Rejeb et al., 2022a; Upadhyay et al., 2021)

C_9: Efficient waste management (Khadke et al., 2021; Khan et al., 2021; Kouhizadeh et al., 2020; Kouhizadeh et al., 2023; Shojaei et al., 2021)

4.3. Results

Stage 1: The criteria and decision-makers involved in the study were defined.

Since the decision-makers had similar years of experience and worked in the same sector, no weight value was assigned to the groups. Since the total importance weight of all participants was 1 according to Equation (4), the importance weight of each decision-making group could be considered 0.2. However, no assignment was made in this study.

Stage 2: Each group of decision-makers evaluated the criteria separately. The degrees of membership and nonmembership of these linguistic evaluations were converted into q-ROF numbers via Table 1. Table 2 contains the evaluations from all the decision-making groups.

Table 2. Evaluations of expert groups

C_n	DM$_1$		DM$_2$		DM$_3$		DM$_4$		DM$_5$	
	μ	ϑ	μ	ϑ	μ	ϑ	μ	ϑ	μ	ϑ
C_1	0.25	0.85	0.35	0.75	0.35	0.75	0.25	0.85	0.35	0.75
C_2	0.35	0.75	0.45	0.65	0.35	0.75	0.35	0.75	0.45	0.65
C_3	0.75	0.35	0.65	0.45	0.75	0.35	0.65	0.45	0.75	0.35
C_4	0.65	0.45	0.75	0.35	0.65	0.45	0.65	0.45	0.65	0.45
C_5	0.55	0.55	0.65	0.45	0.45	0.65	0.65	0.45	0.45	0.65
C_6	0.75	0.35	0.65	0.45	0.75	0.35	0.75	0.35	0.85	0.25
C_7	0.65	0.45	0.55	0.55	0.65	0.45	0.55	0.55	0.75	0.35
C_8	0.85	0.25	0.75	0.35	0.75	0.35	0.65	0.45	0.85	0.25
C_9	0.85	0.25	0.85	0.25	0.85	0.25	0.95	0.15	0.95	0.15

Stage 3: Each of the nine separate criterion weights was calculated via Equation (6). Since q-ROF was used in the solution, q = 3 was first used (see Table 3). To make the results comparable, q = 4 was also evaluated (see Table 4).

Recognizing that each decision maker is of equal importance, the λ values were not used equally.

Table 3. Calculation of the general weights of the criteria with q=3

q=3	DM$_1$	DM$_2$	DM$_3$	DM$_4$	DM$_5$	
	$1 + \mu_i^q - \vartheta_i^q$	$1 + \mu_i^q - \vartheta_i^q$	$1 + \mu_i^q - \vartheta_i^q$	$1 + \mu_i^q - \vartheta_i^q$	$1 + \mu_i^q - \vartheta_i^q$	$\sum_{j=1}^{n} \sum_{i=1}^{r} \left(1 + \mu_i^q - \vartheta_i^q\right)$
C_1	0.4015	0.621	0.621	0.4015	0.621	2.666
C_2	0.621	0.8165	0.621	0.621	0.8165	3.496
C_3	1.379	1.1835	1.379	1.1835	1.379	6.504
C_4	1.1835	1.379	1.1835	1.1835	1.1835	6.113
C_5	1.000	1.1835	0.8165	1.1835	0.8165	5.000
C_6	1.379	1.1835	1.379	1.379	1.5985	6.919
C_7	1.1835	1.000	1.1835	1.000	1.379	5.746
C_8	1.5985	1.379	1.379	1.1835	1.5985	7.138
C_9	1.5985	1.5985	1.5985	1.854	1.854	8.504
						$\sum_{j=1}^{n} W_j = 52.086$

Table 4. Calculation of the general weights of the criteria with q=4

q=4	DM$_1$	DM$_2$	DM$_3$	DM$_4$	DM$_5$	
	$1 + \mu_i^q - \vartheta_i^q$	$1 + \mu_i^q - \vartheta_i^q$	$1 + \mu_i^q - \vartheta_i^q$	$1 + \mu_i^q - \vartheta_i^q$	$1 + \mu_i^q - \vartheta_i^q$	$\sum_{i=1}^{n}\sum_{j=1}^{l}\left(1 + \mu_i^q - \vartheta_i^q\right)$
C$_1$	0.4819	0.6986	0.6986	0.4819	0.6986	3.059
C$_2$	0.6986	0.8625	0.6986	0.6986	0.8625	3.821
C$_3$	1.3414	1.1375	1.3414	1.1375	1.3414	6.299
C$_4$	1.1375	1.3414	1.1375	1.1375	1.1375	5.891
C$_5$	1.000	1.1375	0.8625	1.1375	0.8625	5.000
C$_6$	1.3414	1.1375	1.3414	1.3414	1.5181	6.680
C$_7$	1.1375	1.000	1.1375	1.000	1.3414	5.616
C$_8$	1.5181	1.3414	1.3414	1.1375	1.5181	6.856
C$_9$	1.5181	1.5181	1.5181	1.814	1.814	8.182
						$\sum_{j=1}^{n} W_j = 51.404$

Stage 4: The weight value of each criterion is divided by the total weight value to reach the relevant criterion weight (see Table 5).

$$W_j = \frac{W_j}{\sum_{j=1}^{n} W_j}$$

Table 5. Final weight values of the criteria

	W$_1$	W$_2$	W$_3$	W$_4$	W$_5$	W$_6$	W$_7$	W$_8$	W$_9$
q=3	0.051	0.067	0.125	0.117	0.096	0.133	0.110	0.137	0.163
q=4	0.060	0.074	0.123	0.115	0.097	0.130	0.109	0.133	0.159

Table 5 shows the final values of the criteria in the case of two different q values. When "q=3" or "q=4" is accepted, the ranking of the criteria from highest to lowest weights is C$_9$, C$_8$, C$_6$, C$_3$, C$_4$, C$_7$, C$_5$, C$_2$ and C$_1$. If "q" was different, there were differences only in the final weights of the criteria. These differences do not affect the purpose of the study.

These results show that the greatest possible impact of companies' use of blockchain technology in line with their circular economy goals will be on "*Waste management*", "*Information sharing and improved collaboration*" and "*Operation costs*". According to the results (q=4), the criterion with the highest weight is "*waste management*" (C$_9$), with a weight value of 0.159. The other criteria with the highest weights are "*information sharing and improved collaboration*" (C$_8$), with a weight value of 0.133, and "*operation costs*" (C$_6$), with a weight value of 0.130. The other most significant impacts are "*Data validity and reliability*" (C_3), "*Proactive approach to supply chain risks*" (C_4), "*Carbon emissions*" (C_7) and "*Security*" (C_5).

Criterion C_1 has the lowest value among all criteria, with a weight value of 0.060. Among the expert groups, the significance of the impact of blockchain technology on the *secondary product market* is lower than that of the other criteria. The contribution of blockchain technology to "*sustainable consumer behavior*" is regarded as the least significant criterion. Notably, as consumers have access to transparent and reliable information through BCT, they may tend to prefer sustainable products. However, according to industry experts, these criteria are less important among the effects that blockchain technology will have on the circular economy. In other words, for experts, the development of the secondary product market and the change in sustainable consumer behavior in terms of circular economy motivation have low priorities compared with other criteria.

5. EVALUATION AND DISCUSSION

The implementation of circular economy models has become necessary for companies. Companies should assess various methods to achieve their goals, particularly for the circular economy. One of these approaches is to use blockchain technology. Exploring ways to bolster the journey towards a circular economy amid rising investments in BCT is crucial. To address this gap, this study investigates the effects of blockchain technology on the circular economy. The study sees blockchain as a promising technology to facilitate CE. This study aims to enrich the literature by prioritizing the elements that facilitate the adoption of blockchain technology in circular economy initiatives. On the other hand, the study findings can serve as a basis for evaluating the effects of blockchain technology in achieving the circular economy goals of automotive supplier industry manufacturers, especially in developing countries. The potential for utilizing blockchain technology in the supply chain holds promise for numerous enhancements. The diverse features of blockchain technology are vital in rendering supply chains "sustainable" and advancing businesses toward a circular economy. Features such as traceability, transparency, and immutability are particularly potent in companies' adoption of circular economy models.

One-on-one interviews were held with expert groups from five different manufacturers in the automotive industry. This meeting centered around nine fundamental criteria that affect the circular economy goals of blockchain technology. Five groups' evaluations, which use linguistic variables, were mathematically expressed with q-ROF to incorporate greater uncertainty. Then, analyses were carried out with these data. The study findings suggest that businesses in the automotive industry can gain environmental and economic advantages by transitioning to a circular economy with blockchain technology. It is important to evaluate the results correctly here. Criteria with low weights are not necessarily those where blockchain technology has less impact but rather those that have minimal influence on circular economy motivation, which aligns with decision-makers' expectations. Overall, when the results are evaluated, each potential impact is clearly significant, although their priorities may change marginally.

Experts consider the most significant impact of blockchain technology to be "waste management". They also believe that, among all criteria, blockchain's contribution to waste management significantly impacts companies' motivation in the circular economy. The real-time data collection and transparent, traceable structure of BCT facilitate the management of product waste throughout its lifecycle. Monitoring recycling processes can reveal which materials are being recycled and what processes they undergo. The smart contracts offered can increase a firm's operational efficiency by automating waste collection and processing processes. With the articles prepared for waste management in contracts, it may be possible for waste collection vehicles to operate on time and in the right places. Both economic and environmental impacts are important for a circular economy. As a result of discussions with experts in the sector, waste management was identified as one of the top priority impacts. In addition, many researchers believe that the use of this digital technology will create significant opportunities for companies in terms of "waste management" (Kouhizadeh et al., 2020; Khadke et al., 2021; Omidian et al., 2023; Venkatesh et al., 2020).

Experts evaluate the second most significant contribution as ensuring "information sharing and improved cooperation between stakeholders in the supply chain". All stakeholders must actively engage in achieving circular goals, fostering transparent collaboration through effective communication. One of the greatest problems encountered in supply chains is the degradation of information due to communication between stakeholders. Disconnects among stakeholders can readily influence the entire chain. The performance of companies may decrease significantly. This problem is one of the critical issues that experts are working on. Given this requirement, the findings of this study are highly promising. After all, one of the most effective ways to achieve circular goals with good communication, away from complex and difficult bureaucracy, is to integrate blockchain technology into the entire supply chain. In parallel with these findings, Chidepatil et al. (2020) and Rejeb et al. (2022a) reported similar results.

The third most notable impact of blockchain technology in alignment with circular economy objectives is its capacity to increase "operational costs". Despite requiring substantial investments, companies anticipate significant time- and cost-saving opportunities in their sustainability-supporting operations through blockchain technology. BCT-based technologies in a circular supply chain increase companies' operational efficiency and performance (Khan et al., 2021; Upadhyay et al., 2021). This study finding suggests that blockchain contributes to operational efficiency and prioritizes economic impacts across various aspects. Blockchain support for product recycling, ensuring proper product design through communication and cooperation, continuous environmental data monitoring, and protective measures suggest that companies' efficiency will increase significantly. The "increase in productivity" in the circular economy encourages the use of blockchain technology.

Experts assess the principle of "data validity and reliability", ranking it as the fourth most crucial criterion. BCT ensures not only secure data storage but also immutable updating (Chaudhari et al., 2022). Companies need real data to run circular economy models as much as they need real data in production management. Real data concerning its focus on resource management are desperately needed to ensure circularity, ensure resource efficiency, and determine how much it considers environmental concerns. The data validity in the acceptance and implementation of a real model in a company directly affects the accuracy and effectiveness of the decisions to be made. Since managers are the ones who will make the final decisions in the company, they have great responsibility. The findings of this study support this idea, and ensuring data validity and reliability is one of the most important criteria for blockchain. In this context, according to sector employees, blockchain technology plays a crucial role in ensuring data validity and reliability.

Finally, the impact decision-makers least expect to benefit is "secondary market growth." The emergence of a new market for recycled or reprocessed products, or the expansion of existing markets, is advantageous for companies' economies. Making property transfers secure can increase companies' confidence in the second-hand market. However, the impact of BCT on the growth of the secondary market is not considered very significant by industry experts. Considering the contribution of the circular economy, the impact of the secondary market appears to last.

The growing interest in blockchain technology and the circular economy has also affected researchers in this field. Researchers in this field are encouraged to explore process obstacles to increase circular economy motivation. To benefit from the advantages of blockchain technology, eliminating some obstacles is beneficial. Although blockchain technology has been discussed for many years, it is still not widely used in the industries of many countries. While aiming for the circular economy, it is important to inform industries and eliminate uncertainties to popularize the use of this technology. Moreover, stakeholders in the supply chain must also be willing to embrace this innovation and be motivated to cooperate.

In addition, although the "energy" criterion is not included as a limitation of this study, an important effect in the integration between blockchain technology and circular economy applications is in terms of energy efficiency (Khaqqi et al., 2018). Blockchain technology is a digitalization tool that stands out for its advantages in terms of energy management and sustainability (Bai & Sarkis, 2020; Yildizbasi, 2021). As stated in the study, the ease of tracking waste and recyclable products with BCT can also support the reduction of carbon emission rates by using them in energy production. These developments can also be a reason for researchers interested in the subject to include them in their studies.

REFERENCES

Afzal, M., Li, J., Amin, W., Huang, Q., Umer, K., Ahmad, S. A., Ahmad, F., & Raza, A. (2022). Role of blockchain technology in transactive energy market: A review. *Sustainable Energy Technologies and Assessments*, 53, 102646. DOI: 10.1016/j.seta.2022.102646

Agrawal, T. K., Kumar, V., Pal, R., Wang, L., & Chen, Y. (2021). Blockchain based framework for supply chain traceability: A case example of textile and clothing industry. *Computers & Industrial Engineering*, 154, 1–12. DOI: 10.1016/j.cie.2021.107130

Ali, S. S., Torğul, B., Paksoy, T., Luthra, S., & Kayikci, Y. (2024). A novel hybrid decision-making framework for measuring Industry 4.0-driven circular economy performance for textile industry. *Business Strategy and the Environment*, bse.3892. Advance online publication. DOI: 10.1002/bse.3892

Alves, L., Ferreira Cruz, E., Lopes, S. I., Faria, P. M., & Rosado da Cruz, A. M. (2022). Towards circular economy in the textiles and clothing value chain through blockchain technology and IoT: A review. *Waste Management & Research*, 40(1), 3–23. DOI: 10.1177/0734242X211052858 PMID: 34708680

Antikainen, M., Uusitalo, T., & Kivikytö-Reponen, P. (2018). Digitalization as an enabler of circular economy. *Procedia CIRP*, 73, 45–49. DOI: 10.1016/j.procir.2018.04.027

Atanassov, K. T. (1986). Intuitionistic fuzzy sets. *Fuzzy Sets and Systems*, 20(1), 87–96. DOI: 10.1016/S0165-0114(86)80034-3

Badhwar, A., Islam, S., & Tan, C. S. L. (2023). Exploring the potential of blockchain technology within the fashion and textile supply chain with a focus on traceability, transparency, and product authenticity: A systematic review. *Frontiers in Blockchain*, 6, 1044723. DOI: 10.3389/fbloc.2023.1044723

Bai, C., & Sarkis, J. (2020). A supply chain transparency and sustainability technology appraisal model for blockchain technology. *International Journal of Production Research*, 58(7), 2142–2162. DOI: 10.1080/00207543.2019.1708989

Balon, B., Kalinowski, K., & Paprocka, I. (2023). Production planning using a shared resource register organized according to the assumptions of blockchain technology. *Sensors (Basel)*, 23(4), 2308. DOI: 10.3390/s23042308 PMID: 36850905

Bao, Z., Wang, Q., Shi, W., Wang, L., Lei, H., & Chen, B. (2020). When blockchain meets sgx: An overview, challenges, and open issues. *IEEE Access : Practical Innovations, Open Solutions*, 8, 170404–170420. DOI: 10.1109/ACCESS.2020.3024254

Barenji, A. V., Guo, H., Wang, Y., Li, Z., & Rong, Y. (2021). Toward blockchain and fog computing collaborative design and manufacturing platform: Support customer view. *Robotics and Computer-integrated Manufacturing*, 67, 102043. DOI: 10.1016/j.rcim.2020.102043

Benítez-Martínez, F. L., Hurtado-Torres, M. V., & Romero-Frías, E. (2021). A neural blockchain for a tokenizable e-participation model. *Neurocomputing*, 423, 703–712. DOI: 10.1016/j.neucom.2020.03.116

Bindra, L., Lin, C., Stroulia, E., & Ardakanian, O. (2019, May). *Decentralized access control for smart buildings using metadata and smart contract.* In 2019 IEEE/ACM 5th International Workshop on Software Engineering for Smart Cyber-Physical Systems (SEsCPS) s (pp.2-38). IEEE. DOI: 10.1109/SEsCPS.2019.00013

Bonsu, N. O. (2020). Towards a circular and low-carbon economy: Insights from the transitioning to electric vehicles and net zero economy. *Journal of Cleaner Production*, 256, 120659. DOI: 10.1016/j.jclepro.2020.120659

Brown, L., McFarlane, A., Das, A., & Campbell, K. (2022). The impact of financial development on carbon dioxide emissions in Jamaica. *Environmental Science and Pollution Research International*, 29(17), 1–14. DOI: 10.1007/s11356-021-17519-x PMID: 34851484

Bruel, A., & Godina, R. (2023). A smart contract architecture framework for successful industrial symbiosis applications using blockchain technology. *Sustainability*, 15(7). *Sustainability (Basel)*, 7(7), 5884. Advance online publication. DOI: 10.3390/su15075884

Chaudhari, R. S., Mahajan, S. K., Rane, S. B., & Agrawal, R. (2022). Modelling barriers in circular economy using TOPSIS: Perspective of environmental sustainability & Blockchain-IoT technology. *International Journal of Mathematical. Engineering and Management Sciences*, 7(6), 820. DOI: 10.33889/IJMEMS.2022.7.6.052

Chauhan, C., Parida, V., & Dhir, A. (2022). Linking circular economy and digitalization technologies: A systematic literature review of past achievements and future promises. *Technological Forecasting and Social Change*, 177, 121508. DOI: 10.1016/j.techfore.2022.121508

Chiaroni, D., Fraccascia, L., Giannoccaro, I., & Urbinati, A. (2022). Enabling factors for the diffusion of circular economy and their impacts on sustainability. *Resources, Conservation & Recycling Advances*, 15, 200101. DOI: 10.1016/j.rcradv.2022.200101

Chidepatil, A., Bindra, P., Kulkarni, D., Qazi, M., Kshirsagar, M., & Sankaran, K. (2020). From trash to cash: How blockchain and multi-sensor-driven artificial intelligence can transform circular economy of plastic waste? *Administrative Sciences*, 10(2), 23. DOI: 10.3390/admsci10020023

da Silva, E. R., Lohmer, J., Rohla, M., & Angelis, J. (2023). Unleashing the circular economy in the electric vehicle battery supply chain: A case study on data sharing and blockchain potential. *Resources, Conservation and Recycling*, 193, 106969. DOI: 10.1016/j.resconrec.2023.106969

Danese, P., Mocellin, R., & Romano, P. (2021). Designing blockchain systems to prevent counterfeiting in wine supply chains: A multiple-case study. *International Journal of Operations & Production Management*, 41(13), 1–33. DOI: 10.1108/IJOPM-12-2019-0781

De Giovanni, P. (2022). Leveraging the circular economy with a closed-loop supply chain and a reverse omnichannel using blockchain technology and incentives. *International Journal of Operations & Production Management*, 42(7), 959–994. DOI: 10.1108/IJOPM-07-2021-0445

Dujak, D., & Sajter, D. (2019). Blockchain applications in supply chain. *SMART Supply Network*, 21–46. .DOI: 10.1007/978-3-319-91668-2_2

Fan, Z. P., Wu, X. Y., & Cao, B. B. (2022). Considering the traceability awareness of consumers: Should the supply chain adopt the blockchain technology? *Annals of Operations Research*, 309(2), 837–860. DOI: 10.1007/s10479-020-03729-y

Feng, Q., He, D., Zeadally, S., Khan, M. K., & Kumar, N. (2019). A survey on privacy protection in blockchain system. *Journal of Network and Computer Applications*, 126, 45–58. DOI: 10.1016/j.jnca.2018.10.020

Ferreira, I. A., Godina, R., Pinto, A., Pinto, P., & Carvalho, H. (2023). Boosting additive circular economy ecosystems using blockchain: An exploratory case study. *Computers & Industrial Engineering*, 175, 108916. DOI: 10.1016/j.cie.2022.108916

Gong, Y., Xie, S., Arunachalam, D., Duan, J., & Luo, J. (2022). Blockchain-based recycling and its impact on recycling performance: A network theory perspective. *Business Strategy and the Environment*, 31(8), 3717–3741. DOI: 10.1002/bse.3028

Govindan, K. (2022). Tunneling the barriers of blockchain technology in remanufacturing for achieving sustainable development goals: A circular manufacturing perspective. *Business Strategy and the Environment*, 31(8), 3769–3785. DOI: 10.1002/bse.3031

Grati, R., Loukil, F., Boukadi, K., & Abed, M. (2024). A blockchain-based framework for circular end-of-life vehicle processing. *Cluster Computing*, 27(1), 707–720. DOI: 10.1007/s10586-023-03981-4

Heim, H., & Hopper, C. (2022). Dress code: The digital transformation of the circular fashion supply chain. *International Journal of Fashion Design, Technology and Education*, 15(2), 233–244. DOI: 10.1080/17543266.2021.2013956

Jamwal, A., Agrawal, R., & Sharma, M. (2022). A framework to overcome blockchain enabled sustainable manufacturing issues through circular economy and Industry 4.0 measures. *International Journal of Mathematical. Engineering and Management Sciences*, 7(6), 764–790. DOI: 10.33889/IJMEMS.2022.7.6.050

Kamble, S. S., Gunasekaran, A., & Gawankar, S. A. (2020). Achieving sustainable performance in a data-driven agriculture supply chain: A review for research and applications. *International Journal of Production Economics*, 219, 179–194. DOI: 10.1016/j.ijpe.2019.05.022

Kamilaris, A., Cole, I. R., & Prenafeta-Boldú, F. X. (2021). Blockchain in agriculture. In Galanakis, C. M. (Ed.), *Food Technology Disruptions* (pp. 247–284). Academic Press. DOI: 10.1016/B978-0-12-821470-1.00003-3

Khadke, S., Gupta, P., Rachakunta, S., Mahata, C., Dawn, S., Sharma, M., Verma, D., Pradhan, A., Krishna, A. M. S., Ramakrishna, S., Chakrabortty, S., Saianand, G., Sonar, P., Biring, S., Dash, J. K., & Dalapati, G. K. (2021). Efficient plastic recycling and remolding circular circular economy using the technology of trust–blockchain. *Sustainability (Basel)*, 13(16), 9142. DOI: 10.3390/su13169142

Khan, S. A. R., Razzaq, A., Yu, Z., & Miller, S. (2021). Retracted: Industry 4.0 and circular economy practices: A new era business strategies for environmental sustainability. *Business Strategy and the Environment*, 30(8), 4001–4014. DOI: 10.1002/bse.2853

Khan, S. A. R., Yu, Z., Sarwat, S., Godil, D. I., Amin, S., & Shujaat, S. (2022). The role of block chain technology in circular economy practices to improve organisational performance. *International Journal of Logistics*, 25(4–5), 605–622. DOI: 10.1080/13675567.2021.1872512

Khaqqi, K. N., Sikorski, J. J., Hadinoto, K., & Kraft, M. (2018). Incorporating seller/buyer reputation-based system in blockchain-enabled emission trading application. *Applied Energy*, 209, 8–19. DOI: 10.1016/j.apenergy.2017.10.070

Kim, Y., Raman, R. K., Kim, Y.-S., Varshney, L. R., & Shanbhag, N. R. (2018). Efficient local secret sharing for distributed blockchain systems. *IEEE Communications Letters*, 23(2), 282–285. DOI: 10.1109/LCOMM.2018.2886016

Kouhizadeh, M., Sarkis, J., & Zhu, Q. (2019). At the nexus of blockchain technology, the circular economy, and product deletion. *Applied Sciences (Basel, Switzerland)*, 9(8), 1712. DOI: 10.3390/app9081712

Kouhizadeh, M., Zhu, Q., & Sarkis, J. (2020). Blockchain and the circular economy: Potential tensions and critical reflections from practice. *Production Planning and Control*, 31(11–12), 950–966. DOI: 10.1080/09537287.2019.1695925

Kouhizadeh, M., Zhu, Q., & Sarkis, J. (2023). Circular economy performance measurements and blockchain technology: An examination of relationships. *International Journal of Logistics Management*, 34(3), 720–743. DOI: 10.1108/IJLM-04-2022-0145

Kumar, N. M., & Chopra, S. S. (2022). Leveraging blockchain and smart contract technologies to overcome circular economy implementation challenges. *Sustainability (Basel)*, 14(15), 9492. DOI: 10.3390/su14159492

Kuo, T.-T., Kim, J., & Gabriel, R. A. (2020). Privacy-preserving model learning on a blockchain network-of-networks. *Journal of the American Medical Informatics Association: JAMIA*, 27(3), 343–354. DOI: 10.1093/jamia/ocz214 PMID: 31943009

Leng, J., Ruan, G., Jiang, P., Xu, K., Liu, Q., Zhou, X., & Liu, C. (2020). Blockchain-empowered sustainable manufacturing and product lifecycle management in Industry 4.0: A survey. *Renewable & Sustainable Energy Reviews*, 132, 110112. DOI: 10.1016/j.rser.2020.110112

Liu, Z., & Wang, X. (2018). How to regulate individuals' privacy boundaries on social network sites: A cross-cultural comparison. *Information & Management*, 55(8), 1005–1023. DOI: 10.1016/j.im.2018.05.006

Liu, Z., Wu, T., Wang, F., Osmani, M., & Demian, P. (2022). Blockchain enhanced construction waste information management: A conceptual framework. *Sustainability (Basel)*, 14(19), 12145. DOI: 10.3390/su141912145

Meier, O., Gruchmann, T., & Ivanov, D. (2023). Circular supply chain management with blockchain technology: A dynamic capabilities view. *Transportation Research Part E, Logistics and Transportation Review*, 176, 103177. DOI: 10.1016/j.tre.2023.103177

Nandi, S., Sarkis, J., Hervani, A., & Helms, M. (2021a). Do blockchain and circular economy practices improve post COVID-19 supply chains? A resource-based and resource dependence perspective. *Industrial Management & Data Systems*, 121(2), 333–363. DOI: 10.1108/IMDS-09-2020-0560

Nandi, S., Sarkis, J., Hervani, A. A., & Helms, M. M. (2021b). Redesigning supply chains using blockchain-enabled circular economy and COVID19 experiences. *Sustainable Production and Consumption*, 27, 10–22. DOI: 10.1016/j.spc.2020.10.019 PMID: 33102671

Nguyen, L. T., Hoang, T. G., Do, L. H., Ngo, X. T., Nguyen, P. H., Nguyen, G. D., & Nguyen, G. N. (2021). The role of blockchain technology-based social crowdfunding in advancing social value creation. *Technological Forecasting and Social Change*, 170, 120898. DOI: 10.1016/j.techfore.2021.120898

Okorie, O., & Russell, J. D. (2021, September). Exploring the risks of blockchain and circular economy initiatives in food supply chains: a hybrid model practice framework. *InProceedings of the International Conference on Sustainable Design and Manufacturing* (pp. 290-303). Singapore: Springer Singapore. DOI: 10.1007/978-981-16-6128-0_28

Omidian, H., Razmara, J., Parvizpour, S., Tabrizchi, H., Masoudi-Sobhanzadeh, Y., & Omidi, Y. (2023). Tracing drugs from discovery to disposal. *Drug Discovery Today*, 28(5), 1–23. DOI: 10.1016/j.drudis.2023.103538 PMID: 36828192

Öztürk, C., & Yildizbaşi, A. (2020). Barriers to implementation of blockchain into supply chain management using an integrated multi-criteria decision-making method: A numerical example. *Soft Computing*, 24(19), 14771–14789. DOI: 10.1007/s00500-020-04831-w

Panghal, A., Sindhu, S., Dahiya, S., Dahiya, B., & Mor, R. S. (2022). Benchmarking the interactions among challenges for blockchain technology adoption: A circular economy perspective. *International Journal of Mathematical. Engineering and Management Sciences*, 7(6), 859–872. DOI: 10.33889/IJMEMS.2022.7.6.054

Paul, T., Islam, N., Mondal, S., & Rakshit, S. (2022). RFID-integrated blockchain-driven circular supply chain management: A system architecture for B2B tea industry. *Industrial Marketing Management*, 101, 238–257. DOI: 10.1016/j.indmarman.2021.12.003

Piao, S. (2024, January). Barriers toward circular economy transition: Exploring different stakeholders' perspectives. *Corporate Social Responsibility and Environmental Management*, 31(1), 153–168. Advance online publication. DOI: 10.1002/csr.2558

Pinar, A., & Boran, F. E. (2020). A q-rung orthopair fuzzy multi-criteria group decision making method for supplier selection based on a novel distance measure. *International Journal of Machine Learning and Cybernetics*, 11(8), 1749–1780. DOI: 10.1007/s13042-020-01070-1

Quayson, M., Bai, C., Sun, L., & Sarkis, J. (2023). Building blockchain-driven dynamic capabilities for developing circular supply chain: Rethinking the role of sensing, seizing, and reconfiguring. *Business Strategy and the Environment*, 32(7), 4821–4840. DOI: 10.1002/bse.3395

Rana, R. L., Tricase, C., & De Cesare, L. (2021). Blockchain technology for a sustainable Agri-food supply chain. *British Food Journal*, 123(11), 3471–3485. DOI: 10.1108/BFJ-09-2020-0832

Rejeb, A., Appolloni, A., Rejeb, K., Treiblmaier, H., Iranmanesh, M., & Keogh, J. G. (2023). The role of blockchain technology in the transition toward the circular economy: Findings from a systematic literature review. *Resources, Conservation & Recycling Advances*, 17, 200126. DOI: 10.1016/j.rcradv.2022.200126

Rejeb, A., Rejeb, K., Keogh, J. G., & Zailani, S. (2022b). Barriers to blockchain adoption in the circular economy: A fuzzy Delphi and best-worst approach. *Sustainability (Basel)*, 14(6), 3611. DOI: 10.3390/su14063611

Rejeb, A., Zailani, S., Rejeb, K., Treiblmaier, H., & Keogh, J. G. (2022a). Modeling enablers for blockchain adoption in the circular economy. *Sustainable Futures : An Applied Journal of Technology, Environment and Society*, 4(1), 1–25. DOI: 10.1016/j.sftr.2022.100095

Reyna, A., Martín, C., Chen, J., Soler, E., & Díaz, M. (2018). On blockchain and its integration with IoT. Challenges and opportunities. *Future Generation Computer Systems*, 88, 173–190. DOI: 10.1016/j.future.2018.05.046

Saberi, S., Kouhizadeh, M., Sarkis, J., & Shen, L. (2019). Blockchain technology and its relationships to sustainable supply chain management. *International Journal of Production Research*, 57(7), 2117–2135. DOI: 10.1080/00207543.2018.1533261

Sahebi, I. G., Masoomi, B., & Ghorbani, S. (2020). Expert oriented approach for analyzing the blockchain adoption barriers in humanitarian supply chain. *Technology in Society*, 63, 101427. DOI: 10.1016/j.techsoc.2020.101427

Samadhiya, A., Agrawal, R., Kumar, A., & Garza-Reyes, J. A. (2023). Blockchain technology and circular economy in the environment of total productive maintenance: A natural resource-based view perspective. *Journal of Manufacturing Technology Management*, 34(2), 293–314. DOI: 10.1108/JMTM-08-2022-0299

Saraf, K., Bajar, K., Jain, A., & Barve, A. (2024). Assessment of barriers impeding the incorporation of blockchain technology in the service sector: A case of hotel and health care. *Journal of Modelling in Management*, 19(2), 407–440. DOI: 10.1108/JM2-06-2022-0159

Sayeed, S., & Marco-Gisbert, H. (2019). Assessing blockchain consensus and security mechanisms against the 51% attack. *Applied Sciences (Basel, Switzerland)*, 9(9), 1788. DOI: 10.3390/app9091788

Schmidt, J. L., Sehnem, S., & Spuldaro, J. D. (2023). Blockchain and the transition to the circular economy: A literature review. *Corporate Social Responsibility and Environmental Management*. Advance online publication. DOI: 10.1002/csr.2674

Sharma, R., Samad, T. A., Jabbour, C. J. C., & de Queiroz, M. J. (2021). Leveraging blockchain technology for circularity in agricultural supply chains: Evidence from a fast-growing economy. *Journal of Enterprise Information Management,* (ahead-of-print). .DOI: 10.1108/JEIM-02-2021-0094

Sharma, R., Shishodia, A., Kamble, S., Gunasekaran, A., & Belhadi, A. (2020). Agriculture supply chain risks and COVID-19: Mitigation strategies and implications for the practitioners. *International Journal of Logistics Research and Applications*, 1-27, 1–27. .DOI: 10.1080/13675567.2020.1830049

Shojaei, A., Ketabi, R., Razkenari, M., Hakim, H., & Wang, J. (2021). Enabling a circular economy in the built environment sector through blockchain technology. *Journal of Cleaner Production*, 294, 126352. DOI: 10.1016/j.jclepro.2021.126352

Shou, M., & Domenech, T. (2022). Integrating LCA and blockchain technology to promote circular fashion–A case study of leather handbags. *Journal of Cleaner Production*, 373, 133557. DOI: 10.1016/j.jclepro.2022.133557

Sunmola, F., Burgess, P., Tan, A., Chanchaichujit, J., Balasubramania, S., & Mahmud, M. (2023). Prioritising visibility influencing factors in supply chains for resilience. *Procedia Computer Science*, 217, 1589–1598. DOI: 10.1016/j.procs.2022.12.359

Treiblmaier, H., & Garaus, M. (2023). Using blockchain to signal quality in the food supply chain: The impact on consumer purchase intentions and the moderating effect of brand familiarity. *International Journal of Information Management*, 68, 102514. DOI: 10.1016/j.ijinfomgt.2022.102514

Trevisan, A. H., Lobo, A., Guzzo, D., de Vasconcelos Gomes, L. A., & Mascarenhas, J. (2023). Barriers to employing digital technologies for a circular economy: A multi-level perspective. *Journal of Environmental Management*, 332, 117437. DOI: 10.1016/j.jenvman.2023.117437 PMID: 36801533

Truby, J., Brown, R. D., Dahdal, A., & Ibrahim, I. (2022). Blockchain, climate damage, and death: Policy interventions to reduce the carbon emissions, mortality, and net-zero implications of non-fungible tokens and Bitcoin. *Energy Research & Social Science*, 88, 102499. DOI: 10.1016/j.erss.2022.102499

Upadhyay, A., Laing, T., Kumar, V., & Dora, M. (2021). Exploring barriers and drivers to the implementation of circular economy practices in the mining industry. *Resources Policy*, 72, 102037. DOI: 10.1016/j.resourpol.2021.102037

Venkatesh, V. G., Kang, K., Wang, B., Zhong, R. Y., & Zhang, A. (2020). System architecture for blockchain based transparency of supply chain social sustainability. *Robotics and Computer-integrated Manufacturing*, 63, 101896. DOI: 10.1016/j.rcim.2019.101896

Xie, H., Zheng, J., He, T., Wei, S., & Hu, C. (2023). TEBDS: A Trusted Execution Environment-and-Blockchain-Supported IoT Data Sharing System. *Future Generation Computer Systems*, 140, 321–330. DOI: 10.1016/j.future.2022.10.016

Yager, R. R. (2017). Generalized orthopair fuzzy sets. *IEEE Transactions on Fuzzy Systems*, 25(5), 1222–1230. DOI: 10.1109/TFUZZ.2016.2604005

Yildizbasi, A. (2021). Blockchain and renewable energy: Integration challenges in circular economy era. *Renewable Energy*, 176, 183–197. DOI: 10.1016/j.renene.2021.05.053

Yousefi, S., & Tosarkani, B. M. (2023). Exploring the role of blockchain technology in improving sustainable supply chain performance: A system-analysis-based approach. *IEEE Transactions on Engineering Management*. Advance online publication. DOI: 10.1109/TEM.2022.3231217

Zhang, L., Xie, Y., Zheng, Y., Xue, W., Zheng, X., & Xu, X. (2020). The challenges and countermeasures of blockchain in finance and economics. *Systems Research and Behavioral Science*, 37(4), 691–698. DOI: 10.1002/sres.2710

Zhao, G., Liu, S., Lopez, C., Lu, H., Elgueta, S., Chen, H., & Boshkoska, B. M. (2019). Blockchain technology in Agri-food value chain management: A synthesis of applications, challenges and future research directions. *Computers in Industry*, 109, 83–99. DOI: 10.1016/j.compind.2019.04.002

Zhao, R., Wang, J., & Xue, F. (2023). *A blockchain-based token incentive mechanism for ESG in the construction industry*. 2023 European Conference on Computing in Construction 40th International CIB W78 Conference Heraklion, Crete, Greece. July 10–12, 2023. DOI: 10.35490/EC3.2023.235

Zhu, H., Zhao, J., & Li, H. (2022). Q-ROF-SIR methods and their applications to multiple attribute decision making. *International Journal of Machine Learning and Cybernetics*, 1–13. DOI: 10.1007/s13042-021-01330-8

Zhu, S., Song, M., Lim, M. K., Wang, J., & Zhao, J. (2020). The development of energy blockchain and its implications for China's energy sector. *Resources Policy*, 66, 101595. DOI: 10.1016/j.resourpol.2020.101595

ADDITIONAL READING

Ali, M. (2021). *Remote Work and Sustainable Changes for the Future of Global Business.* IGI Global. https://www.igi-global.com/book/remote-work-sustainable -changes-future/264375

Ali, M. (2022). *Future Role of Sustainable Innovative Technologies in Crisis Management*. IGI Global. https://www.igi-global.com/book/future-role-sustainable -innovative-technologies/281281

Ali, M. (2023). *Shifting Paradigms in the Rapidly Developing Global Digital Ecosystem: A GCC Perspective.* In Digital Entrepreneurship and Co-Creating Value Through Digital Encounters (pp. 145-166). IGI Global. https://www.igi-global.com/chapter/ shifting-paradigms-in-the-rapidly-developing-global-digital-ecosystem/323525

Ali, M., & Wood-Harper, T. (2021). *Fostering Communication and Learning with Underutilized Technologies in Higher Education.* IGI Global. https://www.igi-global .com/book/fostering-communication-learning-underutilized-technologies/244593

Ali, M. B., Wood-Harper, T., & Ramlogan, R. (2020). A Framework Strategy to Overcome Trust Issues on Cloud Computing Adoption in Higher Education. In Modern Principles, Practices, and Algorithms for Cloud Security (pp. 162-183). IGI Global. https://www.igi-global.com/chapter/a-framework-strategy-to-overcome -trust-issues-on-cloud-computing-adoption-in-higher-education/238907/

Chapter 14
Navigating the Digital Horizon:
Transforming Travel Agencies in the Digital Era

Mohammad Badruddoza Talukder
https://orcid.org/0009-0008-1662-9221

International University of Business Agriculture and Technology, Bangladesh

Mushfika Hoque
https://orcid.org/0009-0000-4645-5105

Daffodil Institute of IT, Bangladesh

ABSTRACT

This chapter investigates the transformative impact of technological improvements on traditional travel agencies, a topic that is becoming increasingly important in the fast-changing travel industry. Through the previous related literature, this study aims to shed light on how travel firms are adjusting to the changing demands and tastes of travellers in the digital era by studying the integration of artificial intelligence, virtual and augmented reality, and data-driven personalisation. So, the paper aims to identify travel agencies' challenges and opportunities by analysing digital transformation's impact on old business models. In addition, it investigates the shifting behaviour of travellers, who are increasingly looking for ease and personalised experiences through internet platforms. Finally, this chapter emphasises the significance of travel agencies embracing digital innovation, streamlining operations, and developing immersive travel experiences to maintain their competitive edge in a constantly moving market.

DOI: 10.4018/979-8-3693-5966-2.ch014

INTRODUCTION

The travel industry is undergoing a seismic shift as digital technology continues to revolutionize the way we plan, book, and experience our journeys (Yufriadi et al., 2024). In this dynamic landscape, traditional travel agencies are faced with both unprecedented challenges and exciting opportunities (Pratiwi et al., 2024). The digital era, characterized by the ubiquity of internet access, mobile devices, and advanced data analytics, is reshaping consumer expectations and behaviors. To remain competitive and relevant, travel agencies must navigate this digital horizon by embracing technological innovations and reimagining their business models (Michael Alurame Eruaga, 2024).

As travelers increasingly turn to online platforms for convenience and personalized service, the role of travel agencies is evolving. The integration of artificial intelligence, virtual and augmented reality, and data-driven personalization is enabling agencies to offer tailored experiences that meet the unique preferences and needs of each customer. Moreover, the rise of social media and digital marketing has opened new avenues for engaging with travelers and building brand loyalty (Aboushouk, 2022).

In this transformative era, the successful travel agency leverages technology to enhance customer interactions, streamline operations, and create immersive and sustainable travel experiences. This paper explores the strategies and tools that are driving the transformation of travel agencies, highlighting the ways in which they can harness the power of digital innovation to thrive in an increasingly competitive market (Suryawan et al., 2024). Through continuous adaptation and a forward-thinking approach, travel agencies can not only survive but flourish in the digital age, delivering unparalleled value to their clients.

LITERATURE REVIEW

The digital era has significantly reshaped various industries, and the travel sector is no exception (Sharma, 2023). This literature review examines the existing research and studies on how travel agencies are transforming in response to digital advancements. The focus is on understanding the impact of digital technology, customer behavior, AI and data analytics, immersive technologies, digital marketing, strategic partnerships, sustainability, and innovation (Talukder, 2021). Research by Buhalis and Law (2008) highlights the transformative power of information technology in the travel industry. The rise of online travel agencies (OTAs) such as Expedia and Booking.com has revolutionized the booking process, making it more accessible and efficient for consumers. Traditional travel agencies are forced to adapt by developing robust online platforms to remain competitive (Mohammad et al., 2024a). Studies indicate a shift in consumer behavior toward seeking personalized and convenient travel experiences. Modern travelers expect seamless digital interactions and customized travel options. A study by Amaro and Duarte (2015) shows that ease of use, trust, and perceived usefulness are significant factors influencing online travel bookings, emphasizing the need for travel agencies to enhance their digital interfaces. Artificial intelligence and data analytics are critical in providing personalized travel experiences (S. Kumar et al., 2023).

(Mohammad et al., 2024b) discuss how AI-driven systems can analyze vast amounts of data to offer tailored recommendations, improving customer satisfaction. Chatbots and virtual assistants, as explored by Chung et al. (2018), are increasingly used to provide instant customer support, reducing operational costs and enhancing service efficiency (Firoj & Mohammad, 2024). Virtual reality (VR) and augmented reality (AR) are emerging as powerful tools in the travel industry (Badruddoza Talukder et al., 2024). Research by Yung and Khoo-Lattimore (2019) demonstrates that VR can offer immersive pre-travel experiences, helping customers visualize destinations and make informed decisions. Similarly, AR applications enhance real-world travel experiences by providing interactive and enriched information (Zhang, 2023).

Digital marketing plays a crucial role in the modern travel agency's strategy. A study (Grover, 2024) shows that social media engagement, influencer partnerships, and user-generated content significantly impact brand visibility and customer acquisition (Talukder et al., 2024). Content marketing and search engine optimization (SEO) are also vital for attracting online traffic and converting visitors into customers. Forming strategic partnerships is essential for travel agencies to offer comprehensive services. Sharma (2023) discusses the importance of collaborating with airlines, hotels, and tour operators to create value-added packages. Integrating with third-party technology providers can enhance service offerings and operational efficiency, as highlighted by (Tjostheim & Waterworth, 2023). Sustainability is becoming increasingly important in the travel industry. Research (Sultan & Amir, 2023) emphasizes the growing demand for eco-friendly travel options. Travel agencies are encouraged to promote sustainable practices and responsible tourism to meet the expectations of environmentally conscious travelers. Innovation is critical to staying competitive in the digital era (Vats, 2024).

Bălăşescu and Bălăşescu (2022) Suggest that continuous innovation in technology, services, and business models is crucial for travel agencies. Employee training and development are also essential to equip staff with the necessary skills to navigate digital tools effectively (Jolene, 2023). The literature underscores the multifaceted nature of the transformation facing travel agencies in the digital era (Talukder et al., 2023). Embracing digital technology, understanding changing consumer behaviors, leveraging AI and immersive technologies, adopting effective digital marketing strategies, forming strategic partnerships, and promoting sustainability are pivotal strategies (Bopapurkar, 2023). Continuous innovation and a focus on employee development are also critical for success. This comprehensive transformation allows travel agencies to remain competitive and meet the evolving demands of modern travelers (Al-Hadrawi & Reniati, 2023).

ROLE OF TECHNOLOGICAL ADVANCEMENT IN RESHAPING TRAVEL AGENCIES

Technological advancements have profoundly reshaped the travel agency industry, driving significant changes in how these businesses operate, interact with customers, and deliver services (Alfred et al., 2024). Below are key areas where technology has had a transformative impact:

1. **Online Presence and Accessibility:** Modern travel agencies have developed sophisticated websites and mobile apps that provide comprehensive travel services. These platforms allow customers to search for, compare, and book flights, accommodations, and activities from anywhere at any time (Ahmad et al., 2024). With digital platforms, travel agencies can offer round-the-clock service, meeting the needs of global travelers in different time zones.
2. **Personalization through Data Analytics and AI:** By analyzing customer data, travel agencies can gain insights into preferences, behaviors, and booking patterns. This enables them to offer personalized recommendations and targeted marketing. AI enhances personalization by providing intelligent recommendations based on past behavior and preferences (Yaşar et al., 2024). AI-driven tools such as chatbots and virtual assistants handle inquiries and bookings, offering a tailored experience.
3. **Enhanced Customer Support:** Chatbots provide instant responses to customer inquiries, handle routine tasks, and assist with booking modifications. This improves customer satisfaction and reduces the workload on human agents. AI-driven virtual assistants offer a higher level of personalized service, helping customers with travel planning and providing real-time updates and support.
4. **Immersive Technologies:** VR allows potential travelers to take virtual tours of destinations, hotels, and attractions. This immersive experience helps customers make more informed decisions. AR enhances the travel experience by overlaying digital information in the real world (Yaşar et al., 2024). For example, AR apps can provide interactive maps and guides, enriching the travel experience.

5. **Digital Marketing and Social Media Engagement:** Data-driven digital marketing strategies enable travel agencies to target specific customer segments with personalized offers and promotions. Platforms like Instagram, Facebook, and Twitter allow travel agencies to engage with customers, share travel tips, and showcase destinations. Influencer partnerships and user-generated content further enhance brand visibility and credibility (Melo et al., 2024).

6. **Strategic Partnerships and Integrations:** Technology facilitates partnerships between travel agencies and other service providers, such as airlines, hotels, and car rental companies. These collaborations offer customers seamless, integrated travel experiences. APIs and other technological integrations enable travel agencies to expand their service offerings by connecting with third-party platforms and services.

7. **Operational Efficiency:** Automation tools streamline various operational tasks, such as booking management, customer relationship management (CRM), and back-office functions (Adaghe & Barakat, 2023). This reduces costs and improves efficiency. Advanced cyber security measures protect customer data and build trust, which is crucial for maintaining a loyal customer base.

8. **Sustainability and Responsible Tourism:** Technology enables travel agencies to promote and offer sustainable travel options. This includes eco-friendly accommodations, transportation options, and responsible tourism practices. Digital tools help travel agencies track their sustainability initiatives and report on their environmental impact, catering to the growing demand for responsible travel.

9. **Continuous Innovation:** Keeping up with technological advancements is essential for travel agencies to remain competitive. This involves regularly updating digital platforms and adopting new technologies (Şengel et al., 2022). Continuous training programs ensure that staff are proficient in using new technologies and delivering high-quality service.

Technological advancements have reshaped travel agencies by enhancing their online presence, enabling personalized customer experiences, improving customer support, and driving operational efficiency (Demir et al., 2023). Immersive technologies, digital marketing, strategic partnerships, and a focus on sustainability further contribute to this transformation. By embracing these technological innovations, travel agencies can meet the evolving demands of modern travelers and maintain a competitive edge in the digital era.

EFFECTS OF DIGITAL TRANSFORMATION ON TRADITIONAL TRAVEL AGENCY BUSINESS

The digital transformation has profoundly affected traditional travel agencies, bringing both challenges and opportunities (Chu, 2023). One significant impact is the increased competition from Online Travel Agencies (OTAs) like Expedia and Booking.com, which offer a wide range of travel services online at competitive prices (Adaghe & Barakat, 2023). Additionally, many airlines and hotels now have their direct booking channels, reducing reliance on traditional travel agencies. Customer expectations have also shifted significantly, with a demand for the convenience of booking travel services online at any time, from any location (Michael Alurame Eruaga, 2024). There is also a growing expectation for personalized travel experiences facilitated by data analytics and AI.

Operational changes have been substantial, with automation tools streamlining many back-office functions and reducing the need for manual processes. Customer Relationship Management (CRM) systems have become crucial for managing interactions and maintaining high service standards (Ceccotti et al., 2024). Enhanced customer interaction is another crucial effect, with customers now able to interact with travel agencies through various digital channels such as websites, mobile apps, social media, and chatbots, which provide around-the-clock support (Aboushouk, 2022).

Marketing and customer engagement have shifted to digital platforms. Traditional travel agencies now use digital marketing strategies, including SEO, content marketing, social media engagement, and email campaigns to attract and retain customers (Liu & Jia, 2021). Social media, in particular, plays a significant role in building brand identity, connecting with customers, and promoting travel deals and packages (Rohmah & Komarudin, 2023).

The cost structure of traditional travel agencies has also been affected. Digital transformation can lower operational costs by reducing the need for physical office spaces and staff dedicated to manual booking processes (Kutnjak et al., 2023). Online platforms allow agencies to scale operations more efficiently, reaching a global audience without significant additional costs. This shift has also introduced new revenue streams, such as offering ancillary services like travel insurance, car rentals, and activity bookings through online platforms (Henry Ejiga Adama & Chukwuekem David Okeke, 2024). Additionally, affiliate marketing and partnerships with other travel service providers can generate extra income.

Adapting to new technologies is crucial for traditional travel agencies. Integrating with global distribution systems (GDS), travel APIs, and other travel technologies enables agencies to offer comprehensive and up-to-date services (Shanti et al., 2023). Ongoing training is essential for staff to remain proficient in these new tools. However, challenges remain, such as digital literacy issues among staff and management and resistance to change from established business practices. Ensuring robust cybersecurity measures is critical to protect customer data and maintain trust, as breaches can significantly damage reputation (Liu & Jia, 2021). Maintaining transparency in pricing and services is also essential for building and retaining customer trust in a digital environment. Table 1 shows the aspects and effects of travel agencies' demands and prospects.

Table 1. Apects and effects of travel agencies' demands and prospects

Aspect	Effects
Increased Competition	- Rise of Online Travel Agencies (OTAs) offering a wide range of services at competitive prices. - Direct booking channels from airlines and hotels reduce reliance on traditional agencies.
Shift in Customer Expectations	- Demand for online booking convenience. - Expectation for personalized travel experiences facilitated by data analytics and AI.
Operational Changes	- Automation tools streamline back-office functions. - Customer Relationship Management (CRM) systems are crucial for managing interactions and maintaining service standards.
Enhanced Customer Interaction	- Multichannel communication through websites, mobile apps, social media, and chatbots. - 24/7 customer support with AI-powered chatbots and virtual assistants.
Marketing and Engagement	- Adopt digital marketing strategies like SEO, content marketing, social media engagement, and email campaigns. - Active social media engagement builds brand and promotes travel deals.
Cost Structure and Efficiency	- Reduced operational costs by minimizing physical office space and manual processes. - Scalability through online platforms, reaching a global audience efficiently.
New Revenue Streams	- Offering ancillary services like travel insurance, car rentals, and activity bookings. - Generating additional income through affiliate marketing and partnerships.
Technological Adaptation	- Integration with global distribution systems (GDS) and travel APIs for comprehensive services. - Ongoing staff training for proficiency in new tools.
Customer Trust and Security	- Ensuring robust cyber security measures to protect customer data and maintain trust. - Maintaining transparency in pricing and services to build and retain customer trust.

Source: (Authors Compilation)

The digital transformation has significantly reshaped the landscape for traditional travel agencies. While it introduces challenges like increased competition and the need for technological adaptation, it also presents opportunities for enhanced customer engagement, operational efficiency, and new revenue streams (Inversini et al., 2024). By embracing digital tools and strategies, traditional travel agencies can evolve to meet modern consumer expectations and sustain their relevance in an increasingly digital world.

INFLUENCE OF CUSTOMER EXPECTATIONS AND BEHAVIOR ON DIGITAL TRANSFORMATION OF TRAVEL AGENCY

Customer expectations and behavior are central to driving the digital transformation of travel agencies. The evolving expectations and behaviors of customers significantly influence the digital transformation of travel agencies (Demir et al., 2023). Customer expectations and behavior play a pivotal role in driving the digital transformation of travel agencies. The demand for convenience, personalization, real-time updates, and multichannel communication compels travel agencies to continuously innovate and enhance their digital platforms (Inversini et al., 2024). Social media engagement, sustainable travel options, flexibility, and security are also critical areas influenced by customer dynamics.

12. **Demand for Convenience and Accessibility:** Customers now expect the ability to book travel services quickly and easily, anytime and anywhere. This has pushed travel agencies to develop sophisticated online platforms, including responsive websites and mobile apps that allow for seamless browsing, booking, and payment processes. The convenience of digital self-service options has become a crucial competitive advantage, prompting travel agencies to invest heavily in user-friendly interfaces and efficient online systems.

13. **Personalized Travel Experiences:** Modern travelers seek personalized experiences tailored to their specific preferences and needs. This demand has led travel agencies to leverage data analytics and artificial intelligence to offer customized travel recommendations and packages (Adaghe & Barakat, 2023). By analyzing customer data, agencies can understand individual preferences, booking histories, and behavior patterns, enabling them to deliver targeted marketing and bespoke travel solutions that enhance customer satisfaction and loyalty.

14. **Real-Time Information and Updates:** Travelers expect real-time information and updates regarding their itineraries, including flight status, accommodation details, and travel advisories. This expectation has driven travel agencies to integrate real-time data feeds and notification systems into their digital platforms (Dominique-Ferreira et al., 2022). Providing timely updates and instant communication helps enhance the customer experience and build trust.

15. **Social Media and Online Reviews:** Social media and online reviews play a significant role in influencing travel decisions. Customers often rely on reviews, ratings, and user-generated content to make informed choices. This behavior has encouraged travel agencies to actively engage on social media platforms, respond to reviews, and incorporate feedback into their service offerings. Positive online presence and reputation management have become critical components of digital strategies (Aboushouk, 2022).

16. **Multichannel Communication:** Customers prefer to communicate with travel agencies through various digital channels such as email, chat, social media, and mobile apps. This multichannel expectation has led travel agencies to adopt Omni channel communication strategies, ensuring consistent and seamless interactions across all platforms. AI-powered chatbots and virtual assistants are also employed to handle inquiries and support, providing immediate and efficient customer service.

17. **Eco-Friendly and Sustainable Travel Options:** With increasing awareness of environmental issues, customers are showing a preference for sustainable and eco-friendly travel options. This shift in behavior has influenced travel agencies to promote and offer green travel alternatives, such as eco-friendly accommodations and sustainable transportation options (Suryawan et al., 2024). Agencies are also incorporating responsible tourism practices into their business models to cater to the environmentally conscious traveler.

18. **Flexibility and Security:** The demand for flexibility in travel plans, especially post-pandemic, has led customers to seek options that allow for easy changes and cancellations. Travel agencies have responded by offering flexible booking policies and ensuring secure transactions. Emphasizing robust data protection measures to safeguard personal and payment information is also critical in gaining customer trust (Krupenna, 2022).

ROLE OF ARTIFICIAL INTELLIGENCE AND DATA ANALYTICS IN THE DIGITIZATION OF TRAVEL AGENCIES

Artificial Intelligence (AI) and Data Analytics have become cornerstone technologies in the digitization of travel agencies, revolutionizing how these businesses operate, interact with customers, and deliver services (Prokopowicz, 2024). Artificial Intelligence and Data Analytics play a pivotal role in the digitization of travel agencies, driving personalized customer experiences, operational efficiency, and strategic decision-making. By leveraging these technologies, travel agencies can meet evolving customer expectations, enhance their service offerings, and maintain a competitive edge in the digital age. These advancements not only streamline operations but also open up new avenues for growth and customer engagement, positioning travel agencies to thrive in an increasingly digital marketplace (Prokopowicz, 2024).

20. **Personalization and Customer Experience:** AI algorithms analyze vast amounts of customer data to understand preferences, travel behaviors, and past bookings. This enables travel agencies to offer highly personalized recommendations for flights, hotels, activities, and dining options, enhancing the customer experience (Nazemi, 2023). By leveraging data analytics, travel agencies can implement dynamic pricing strategies that adjust in real time based on demand, competition, and customer behavior, ensuring competitive pricing and maximizing revenue (Prokopowicz, 2024).

21. **Customer Support and Interaction:** Chatbots equipped with natural language processing (NLP) provide instant, 24/7 customer support. They handle common inquiries, assist with bookings, and offer personalized suggestions, freeing up human agents to manage more complex tasks. Virtual travel assistants use AI to help customers with itinerary planning, travel updates, and on-the-go support. These assistants can offer real-time solutions and keep travelers informed throughout their journey (Mrs. C. Radha et al., 2024).

22. **Operational Efficiency:** AI automates routine tasks such as booking management, itinerary updates, and customer feedback collection, significantly reducing manual workload and improving operational efficiency (Ahamad, 2024). Data analytics also helps travel agencies optimize resource allocation, such as staff scheduling and inventory management, based on predictive analysis of demand and trends.

23. **Marketing and Sales:** Data analytics enables agencies to segment their customer base and launch targeted marketing campaigns. By understanding customer demographics and preferences, agencies can create personalized marketing messages that resonate with specific segments (Said, 2023). Predictive analytics forecast travel trends and customer demand, allowing travel agencies to proactively design and promote relevant packages and offers, boosting sales and customer engagement.

24. **Enhanced Travel Planning:** AI tools can optimize travel itineraries by considering various factors such as customer preferences, weather conditions, and local events. This ensures that customers have the best possible travel experience. During travel, AI can provide real-time recommendations for activities, dining, and accommodations based on the traveler's current location and preferences, enhancing their on-the-go experience (Sun, 2023).

25. **Fraud Detection and Security:** AI algorithms monitor transactions for unusual patterns and potential fraud, ensuring secure bookings and transactions. This builds trust and protects both the agency and its customers from fraudulent ac-

tivities (Kosuru et al., 2023). Implementing advanced data analytics ensures that customer data is securely stored and managed, complying with data protection regulations and enhancing overall data security.

26. **Business Intelligence and Decision Making:** Data analytics provides travel agencies with valuable insights into market trends, customer preferences, and business performance. These insights inform strategic decisions, from marketing strategies to operational improvements (Abdul Wahab Samad, Zahera Mega Utama, 2024). Continuous analysis of performance metrics helps agencies measure the effectiveness of their digital transformation efforts and make informed decisions to optimize their services and offerings.

27. **Enhancing Supplier Relationships:** Data analytics helps travel agencies evaluate the performance and reliability of their suppliers (e.g., airlines, hotels, car rental companies). This ensures that they partner with the best providers and maintain high service standards. With detailed insights into demand patterns and supplier performance, travel agencies can negotiate better terms and prices with their suppliers, improving their overall competitiveness (Sun, 2023).

THE ECONOMIC IMPACT OF DIGITAL TRANSFORMATION ON TOURISM INDUSTRY

The digital transformation of travel agencies has significantly impacted the tourism industry economically by enhancing market reach, increasing revenue, improving operational efficiencies, and fostering innovation (Firdausi, 2023). These advancements have not only benefited travel agencies but also contributed to the broader tourism ecosystem by supporting local economies, creating jobs, and driving technological advancements. By embracing digital transformation, the tourism industry can continue to grow, adapt to changing consumer behaviors, and remain resilient in the face of global challenges (Zaika & Avriata, 2024).

The critical areas of economic impact where these transformations have had the most impact are presented below:

1. **Increased Market Reach and Revenue Generation:** Digital platforms enable travel agencies to access globally through reaching a global audience by significantly expanding their market reach (Serdyukova & Serdyukov, 2023). Online booking systems and mobile apps allow travelers from anywhere in the world to access services, increasing revenue opportunities. The ability to operate around the clock without the constraints of physical office hours means travel agencies can cater to customers in different time zones, boosting sales and revenue.

2. **Cost Efficiency and Profit Margins:** The digital transformation of travel agencies has reduced operational costs by making automation routine tasks such as booking management, customer support, and data entry, reduces the need for large administrative teams, lowering operational costs (Toscano-Jara et al., 2023). Digital platforms also allow travel agencies to scale their operations efficiently. They can handle a larger volume of transactions without a corresponding increase in overhead costs, improving profit margins.

3. **Enhanced Customer Experience and Loyalty:** AI and data analytics enable travel agencies to offer personalized travel experiences, which can increase customer satisfaction and loyalty. Happy customers are more likely to return and recommend services to others, driving repeat business and referrals (Huang et al., 2024). The digital transformation of travel agencies has also ensured seamless services by adopting digital tools that ensure a seamless booking and travel experience, from online reservations to real-time updates and customer support. This enhances the overall travel experience, attracting more customers to digital-savvy agencies.

4. **Boost to Ancillary Services and Local Economies:** Digital platforms allow travel agencies to offer a variety of ancillary services, such as travel insurance, car rentals, and local tours. These services not only add to the revenue streams of travel agencies but also benefit associated sectors within the tourism industry. The digital transformation of travel agencies has also contributed to local businesses (Ifeoluwa Oreofe Adekuajo et al., 2023). By promoting local experiences and attractions through digital channels, travel agencies help drive business to local vendors, restaurants, and tour operators, contributing to the local economy.

5. **Market Competitiveness and Innovation:** Digital transformation equips travel agencies with the tools to stay competitive in an increasingly crowded market. Agencies that leverage technology effectively can differentiate themselves through superior service and innovative offerings. The adoption of new technologies encourages continuous innovation in the tourism sector. From virtual reality tours to AI-driven travel assistants, these innovations can create new business opportunities and attract tech-savvy travelers (Letandze, 2023).

6. **Employment and Skills Development:** The digital transformation of travel agencies has also created opportunities for employment and skill development. While automation reduces the need for specific administrative roles, it also creates new jobs in technology, digital marketing, data analysis, and customer service. The demand for tech-savvy professionals in the travel industry is on the rise (Chernega, 2022). The need for digital proficiency drives investment in employee training and development, enhancing the skill set of the workforce. This can lead to higher productivity and better service delivery.

7. **Economic Resilience and Recovery** Digital transformation has made travel agencies more adaptable to changes and disruptions, such as the COVID-19 pandemic. Agencies with robust digital infrastructures were better positioned to manage travel restrictions and shifts in customer behavior, aiding in quicker recovery (Arefyev, 2020). By offering a wide range of digital services and ancillary products, travel agencies can diversify their revenue streams, making them less vulnerable to economic downturns in any single area.

8. **Data-Driven Decision Making:** Data analytics provides valuable insights into market trends, customer preferences, and booking patterns. This data-driven approach helps travel agencies make informed decisions about product offerings, pricing strategies, and marketing campaigns, leading to more effective business strategies and higher revenues.

The digital transformation of travel agencies has also improved efficiency (Anh & Huy, 2021). The Continuous analysis of operational data helps identify inefficiencies and areas for improvement, enabling travel agencies to optimize their operations and reduce costs.

CHALLENGES IN TRANSFORMING TRAVEL AGENCIES IN THE DIGITAL ERA

The digital transformation of travel agencies offers numerous benefits, but it also comes with a set of significant challenges (Salam, 2023). These challenges can impact the effectiveness of the transformation and require strategic management to overcome. Here are the key challenges travel agencies face in the digital era:

Technological Adoption and Integration: Many travel agencies still operate on outdated legacy systems that are difficult to integrate with modern digital platforms. Upgrading or replacing these systems can be costly and time-consuming. Integrating new technologies, such as AI and data analytics, with existing systems requires specialized skills and can be complex. Ensuring seamless integration while maintaining service continuity is a significant challenge (Yufriadi et al., 2024).

Cyber Security and Data Privacy: With the increase in digital transactions and online data storage, travel agencies are more vulnerable to cyber-attacks. Robust cyber security measures to protect sensitive customer information are critical. Adhering to data privacy laws and regulations, such as GDPR, requires travel agencies to implement stringent data protection practices. Non-compliance can result in severe penalties and damage to reputation (Bachta, 2024).

High Costs and Investment: The initial cost of implementing advanced digital technologies can be prohibitive for many travel agencies, particularly smaller ones. This includes expenses related to purchasing software, training staff, and ongoing maintenance. Keeping up with rapid technological advancements requires continuous investment in upgrading systems and software, which can strain financial resources.

Skill Gaps and Training: The existing workforce in many traditional travel agencies may lack the necessary digital skills to operate new technologies effectively. Bridging this skills gap requires substantial investment in training and development. Employees accustomed to traditional ways of working may resist adopting new technologies and processes (Pratiwi et al., 2024). Overcoming this resistance and fostering a culture of innovation is essential for successful transformation.

Competition from Online Travel Agencies (OTAs): Online Travel Agencies (OTAs) like Expedia and Booking.com have established a robust online presence and customer base. Competing with these well-established digital platforms requires significant marketing efforts and innovation. Intense competition often leads to price wars, which can erode profit margins for traditional travel agencies trying to compete in the digital space.

Maintaining Customer Trust: Ensuring transparency in pricing, terms, and conditions is crucial for building and maintaining customer trust in a digital environment. Hidden fees or unclear policies can lead to customer dissatisfaction. While transformational digital tools can improve efficiency, maintaining the high-quality personal service that customers expect is challenging.

Personalization at Scale: Collecting, analyzing, and effectively using large volumes of customer data to deliver personalized experiences at scale is complex (Demir et al., 2023). Ensuring data accuracy and relevancy is crucial for successful personalization. **Another challenge is** developing and implementing personalized travel solutions, which can be resource-intensive, requiring sophisticated technology and significant human oversight (Sharma, 2023).

Adapting to Rapid Technological Changes: The pace of technological change in the travel industry is rapid. Travel agencies must constantly monitor and adapt to new trends and innovations to stay competitive (Sathuta Sellapperuma & Niroshima Udayangani, 2024). Adopting new technologies constantly can lead to innovation fatigue among staff and management, making it challenging to maintain momentum and enthusiasm for digital transformation initiatives.

Customer Expectations and Experience: Customer expectations are continuously evolving with technological advancements. Keeping up with these changing expectations and delivering exceptional digital experiences is an ongoing challenge. Providing a seamless and consistent customer experience across multiple digital channels (websites, mobile apps, and social media) requires coordinated effort and sophisticated technology.

Economic and Market Uncertainty: Economic fluctuations and market uncertainty, such as those caused by the COVID-19 pandemic, can impact the travel industry severely. Travel agencies must be agile and adaptable to navigate these uncertainties effectively (Zhang, 2023). Shifts in travel patterns and preferences, influenced by factors such as health concerns and environmental awareness, require agencies to adapt their offerings and strategies continuously.

RECOMMENDATIONS

In navigating the digital horizon and transforming travel agencies for the digital era, it's required to prioritize several vital recommendations. Some of the recommendations are provided below for the travel agencies to better adapt to the technologies and digitalization:

1. Travel agencies should prioritize the customer experience by leveraging data analytics and AI technologies to offer personalized services and tailored recommendations and investing in user-friendly digital platforms. It will help to ensure seamless booking experiences and provide round-the-clock customer support (Suryawan et al., 2024). By prioritizing the needs and preferences of customers, travel agencies can enhance satisfaction levels, foster loyalty, and ultimately thrive in the digital era.
2. Travel agencies should modernize the legacy systems by adopting cloud-based solutions to enhance agility, scalability, and integration with emerging technologies. Additionally, prioritizing robust cyber security measures is crucial to safeguard sensitive customer data and build trust. By investing in a robust technological foundation, travel agencies can effectively navigate the digital landscape, streamline operations, and deliver enhanced services to customers while ensuring data security and privacy.
3. Travel agencies should focus on fostering a culture of innovation by encouraging the mindset of continuous learning and adaptation to technological advancements within the organization. They should also provide training and development opportunities to equip staff with the digital skills needed to thrive in the digital era.
4. Travel agencies should utilize data analytics to gain insights into customer preferences, market trends, and business performance, enabling data-driven decision-making (Aboushouk, 2022). By harnessing the power of AI, travel agencies can ensure personalized recommendations, automated customer interactions, and operational improvements.

5. Travel agencies should develop a cohesive Omni channel strategy that ensures consistency and seamlessness across all digital touchpoints, including websites, mobile apps, and social media. They also should work on integrating offline and online experiences to provide a unified customer journey from initial research to post-trip support.

6. Travel agencies should form partnerships with airlines, hotels, tour operators, and other travel service providers to offer comprehensive and integrated travel solutions. They should explore opportunities for collaboration with technology vendors, startups, and industry innovators to stay at the forefront of digital transformation (Birla & Sunaina, 2023).

7. Travel agencies should continuously monitor industry trends and customer feedback to iterate and evolve digital strategies accordingly. They should remain flexible and responsive to changing market dynamics, consumer behaviors, and technological advancements.

8. Travel agencies should focus on sustainability and responsible tourism by promoting sustainable travel practices and eco-friendly initiatives to align with the growing consumer demand for responsible tourism. They need to incorporate sustainability considerations into product offerings, supplier partnerships, and operational practices.

9. Travel agencies should identify and capitalize on niche markets or specialized travel segments where they can provide added value and differentiate themselves from competitors. They need to offer unique experiences, expert insights, or exclusive partnerships that resonate with target customer segments.

10. Travel agencies should focus on measuring and optimizing performance by establishing key performance indicators (KPIs) to track the success of digital transformation initiatives and assess their impact on business outcomes (Ardiyanto Maksimilianus Gai et al., 2024). They should also regularly analyze data and performance metrics to identify areas for improvement and optimize digital strategies for maximum effectiveness.

FUTURE DIRECTIONS

As the study Navigating the Digital Horizon: Transforming Travel Agencies in the Digital Era progresses, several future directions can be explored to deepen understanding and provide actionable insights for the travel industry (Yopi, 2024). Firstly, there's a need to delve into the impact of emerging technologies such as blockchain, the Internet of Things (IoT), and augmented reality (AR) on travel agency transformation. Understanding how these technologies can revolutionize customer experiences, streamline operations, and create new business avenues will be crucial for staying ahead in the digital landscape. Moreover, exploring the intersection of digital transformation and sustainability in the travel industry is essential. Investigating how travel agencies can leverage digital platforms to promote responsible tourism practices, reduce environmental footprints, and support local communities will shape the future of travel.

Additionally, analyzing global market trends and consumer behavior shifts in response to geopolitical events and socio-cultural changes will provide valuable insights into adapting digital strategies to meet evolving demands and seize emerging opportunities. Furthermore, with the increasing importance of data privacy and security, examining best practices for safeguarding customer data and complying with regulatory requirements will be imperative. Exploring innovative approaches to enhancing the customer experience through virtual reality (VR) tours, AI-powered chatbots, and personalized recommendation engines will be vital in delivering memorable and tailored experiences that resonate with modern travelers (Hendrina & Bahiroh, 2024). Additionally, exploring strategies for workforce development and talent management to foster digital literacy and innovation within travel agencies will be crucial for long-term success. Finally, analyzing the regulatory landscape and policy implications shaping the digital transformation of travel agencies will provide insights into navigating legal complexities and regulatory frameworks. By exploring these future directions, the study can offer actionable insights and guidance for travel agencies seeking to thrive in an increasingly digitalized and competitive landscape.

CONCLUSION

The digital transformation of travel agencies has brought about significant changes, presenting both opportunities and challenges. While technological advancements have enhanced market reach, revenue generation, and operational efficiency, they have also introduced complexities such as cyber security risks, high costs, and skill gaps. Competition from online platforms, maintaining customer trust, and adapting to rapid technological changes further add to the challenges faced by travel agencies in the digital era. Despite these challenges, the benefits of digital transformation cannot be understated. By embracing digital technologies, travel agencies can offer personalized experiences, streamline operations, and remain competitive in a rapidly evolving industry. Overcoming the challenges requires strategic management, investment in training and development, and a commitment to innovation and customer-centricity. Ultimately, the successful transformation of travel agencies in the digital era hinges on their ability to navigate these challenges effectively, leverage technology to enhance customer experiences and adapt to changing market dynamics. By addressing these challenges head-on and embracing digital transformation initiatives, travel agencies can position themselves for sustained growth and relevance in the digital age.

REFERENCES

Abdul Wahab Samad, Zahera Mega Utama, M. W. R. S. (. (2024). An evaluation of the Efficacy of the Human Resource Data Analytics on Artificial Intelligence Program. *Journal of Electrical Systems*, 20(4s), 2050–2059. DOI: 10.52783/jes.2308

Aboushouk, M. A. (2022). The Impact of Employees' Absorptive Capacity on Digital Transformation of Tourism and Travel Services: Evidence from the Egyptian Travel Agencies. In Bilgin, M. H., Danis, H., Demir, E., & Bodolica, V. (Eds.), *Eurasian Business and Economics Perspectives* (Vol. 23, pp. 167–184). Springer International Publishing., DOI: 10.1007/978-3-031-14395-3_9

Adaghe, W., & Barakat, A. (2023). *What are the impacts of digitalization in travel agencies business model in Sweden A qualitative study on the role of physical travel agencies in Sweden*. DOI: 10.13140/RG.2.2.18534.40001

Adama, H. E., & Okeke, C. D.Henry Ejiga AdamaChukwuekem David Okeke. (2024). Digital transformation as a catalyst for business model innovation: A critical review of impact and implementation strategies. *Magna Scientia Advanced Research and Reviews*, 10(2), 256–264. DOI: 10.30574/msarr.2024.10.2.0066

Adekuajo, I. O., Fakeyede, O. G., Udeh, C. A., & Daraojimba, C. (2023). THE DIGITAL EVOLUTION IN HOSPITALITY: A GLOBAL REVIEW AND ITS POTENTIAL TRANSFORMATIVE IMPACT ON U.S. TOURISM. *International Journal of Applied Research in Social Sciences*, 5(10), 440–462. DOI: 10.51594/ijarss.v5i10.633

Ahamad, M. E. (2024). IMPACT OF ARTIFICIAL INTELLIGENCE ON BUSINESS ANALYTICS. *INTERANTIONAL JOURNAL OF SCIENTIFIC RESEARCH IN ENGINEERING AND MANAGEMENT*, 08(05), 1–5. DOI: 10.55041/IJSREM33172

Ahmad, Z., Mehmood, S., Khan, A. A., Khan, S., & Jabbar, A. (2024). The holistic repercussions of the ongoing war and refugee crisis on the Polish travel agencies. *Journal of Contingencies and Crisis Management*, 32(1), e12547. DOI: 10.1111/1468-5973.12547

Al-Hadrawi, B. K., & Reniati, R. (2023). Digital Leadership: Navigating the Future with Strategic Conviction. *International Journal of Magistravitae Management*, 1(2), 130–145. DOI: 10.33019/ijomm.v1i2.23

Alfred, C. D., Seraj, M., & Ozdeser, H. (2024). The Impact of Technological Advancement on Unemployment in Turkey. *Global Economics Science*, 37–52. DOI: 10.37256/ges.5120243330

Anh, P., & Huy, D. T. N. (2021). Internet Benefits and Digital Transformation Applying in Boosting Tourism Sector and Forecasting Tourism Management Revenue. *Webology, 18*(Special Issue 04), 489–500. DOI: 10.14704/WEB/V18SI04/WEB18143

Arefyev, A. S. (2020). "Platformization" as a management tool of digital transformation in the sphere of tourism. *Теоретическая и Прикладная Экономика*, 3(3), 22–34. DOI: 10.25136/2409-8647.2020.3.33237

Bachta, A. (2024). E-Tourism: New Communication Challenges for the Travel Agencies in the UAE. In Khoury, R. E., & Nasrallah, N. (Eds.), *Intelligent Systems, Business, and Innovation Research* (Vol. 489, pp. 265–277). Springer Nature Switzerland., DOI: 10.1007/978-3-031-36895-0_22

Badruddoza Talukder, M., Kumar, S., Misra, L. I., & Firoj Kabir, . (2024). Determining the role of eco-tourism service quality, tourist satisfaction, and destination loyalty: A case study of Kuakata beach. *Acta Scientiarum Polonorum. Administratio Locorum*, 23(1), 133–151. DOI: 10.31648/aspal.9275

Bălăşescu, S., & Bălăşescu, M. (2022). Digital brand in the field of travel agencies. *Proceedings of the International Conference on Business Excellence, 16*(1), 1456–1465. DOI: 10.2478/picbe-2022-0133

Birla, R., & Sunaina, . (2023). The Challenges of Media Education in the Digital Era. *Journal of Communication Management (London)*, 2(04), 281–288. DOI: 10.58966/JCM20232411

Bopapurkar, P. (2023). *Reference Services in Libraries: Navigating the Digital Age.* Current Trends in Information Technology., DOI: 10.37591/ctit.v13i2.1069

Ceccotti, F., Vernuccio, M., Mattiacci, A., & Pastore, A. (2024). Traditional agencies on bridges: How is digital transformation changing business models? *The Journal of Management and Governance.* Advance online publication. DOI: 10.1007/s10997-024-09703-1

Chernega, O. (2022). THE TOURIST INDUSTRY TRANSFORMATION THROUGH DIGITAL TECHNOLOGIES DURING THE WAR IN UKRAINE. *Scientific Notes of Ostroh Academy National University, 'Economics'. Series*, 1(26(54)), 43–50. DOI: 10.25264/2311-5149-2022-26(54)-43-50

Chu, K.-M. (2023). Innovation Practices of New Technology Adoption for the Business Survival Strategy of Online Travel Agencies During the COVID-19 Pandemic: Two Case Studies in Taiwan. *Journal of the Knowledge Economy*, 15(2), 9556–9575. Advance online publication. DOI: 10.1007/s13132-023-01480-w

Demir, B., Guven, S., & Sahin, B. (2023). Evaluation of the Metaverse: Perspectives of Travel Agency Employees. In Al-Emran, M., Ali, J. H., Valeri, M., Alnoor, A., & Hussien, Z. A. (Eds.), *Beyond Reality: Navigating the Power of Metaverse and Its Applications* (Vol. 876, pp. 1–20). Springer Nature Switzerland., DOI: 10.1007/978-3-031-51300-8_1

Dominique-Ferreira, S., Viana, M., Prentice, C., & Martins, N. (2022). The Influence of Web Design on Customer Engagement with an Online Travel Agency. In Abreu, A., Liberato, D., & Garcia Ojeda, J. C. (Eds.), *Advances in Tourism, Technology and Systems* (Vol. 293, pp. 327–336). Springer Nature Singapore., DOI: 10.1007/978-981-19-1040-1_28

Firdausi, S. F. D. (2023). *Digital Transformation of Tourism in India: Strengths and Opportunities*. MYQA WORLD. DOI: 10.5281/ZENODO.10041289

Firoj, K., & Mohammad, B. T. (2024). Measuring sustainability in the broadcasting media industry in Bangladesh. *I-Manager's. Journal of Management*, 18(3), 51. DOI: 10.26634/jmgt.18.3.20234

Ardiyanto Maksimilianus Gai, Afdhal Chatra, Mozart Malik Ibrahim, Samuel Pd Anantadjaya, & Irma M Nawangwulan. (2024). Analysis of The Influence of Information Availability, Economic Factors and Changing Trends on Travel Agent Business Sustainability in Digital Era. *Jurnal Sistim Informasi Dan Teknologi*, 6–11. DOI: 10.60083/jsisfotek.v6i2.344

Grover, A. (2024). Navigating the Digital Era: Exploring Privacy, Security, and Ownership of Personal Data. In Verma, B., Singla, B., & Mittal, A. (Eds.), (pp. 201–227). Advances in Web Technologies and Engineering. IGI Global., DOI: 10.4018/979-8-3693-1762-4.ch011

Hendrina, Y., & Bahiroh, E. (2024). Human Resource Planning in the Digital Era: Challenges and Opportunities. *Indonesian Journal of Interdisciplinary Research in Science and Technology*, 2(4), 491–498. DOI: 10.55927/marcopolo.v2i4.7151

Huang, P., Shi, Y., An, J., Qiao, S., & Jin, L. (2024). Digital Intelligence Civilization Drives New Business Civilization: A Theoretical Framework for the Collaborative Ecosystem of Digital Culture and Tourism Industry. *Applied Mathematics and Nonlinear Sciences*, 9(1), 20230582. DOI: 10.2478/amns.2023.2.00582

Inversini, A., Chen, M.-M., Keller, A., & Schegg, R. (2024). Hot Topics in Travel Digital Transformation: A Swiss Perspective. In Berezina, K., Nixon, L., & Tuomi, A. (Eds.), *Information and Communication Technologies in Tourism 2024* (pp. 195–206). Springer Nature Switzerland., DOI: 10.1007/978-3-031-58839-6_21

Jolene, K. (2023). The Influence of Online Travel Agencies (OTAs) on Hotel Revenue and Distribution Strategies. *Journal of Modern Hospitality*, 2(1), 14–25. DOI: 10.47941/jmh.1557

Kosuru, S. K., Tadi, S., G, J., K, S., D, G., & K, S. S. S. (2023). Data Analytics and Artificial Intelligence. *Journal of Clinical and Pharmaceutical Research*, 15–17, 15–17. Advance online publication. DOI: 10.61427/jcpr.v3.i3.2023.112

Krupenna, I. (2022). MARKETING DIGITAL TOOLS FROM STARTUP PROJECTS IN THE TOURISM AND TRAVEL INDUSTRY. *Proceedings of Scientific Works of Cherkasy State Technological University Series Economic Sciences*, 67(67), 24–31. DOI: 10.24025/2306-4420.67.2022.278790

Kumar, S., Talukder, M. B., Kabir, F., & Kaiser, F. (2023). Challenges and Sustainability of Green Finance in the Tourism Industry: Evidence From Bangladesh. In Taneja, S., Kumar, P., Grima, S., Ozen, E., & Sood, K. (Eds.), (pp. 97–111). Advances in Finance, Accounting, and Economics. IGI Global., DOI: 10.4018/979-8-3693-1388-6.ch006

Kutnjak, A., Pihir, I., & Vidačić, S. (2023). Shifting Towards Digital Transformation in Bookkeeping Agency—Attitudes Pre- and Post- Implementation of New Technologiesv. *TEM Journal*, 2512–2521. https://doi.org/DOI: 10.18421/TEM124-63

Letandze, N. (2023). The Impact of Digital Technologies on the Development of Rural Tourism in Georgia. *Proceedings of Tskhum-Abkhazian Academy of Sciences*. DOI: 10.52340/ptaas.2023.23.14

Liu, J., & Jia, F. (2021). Construction of a Nonlinear Model of Tourism Economy Forecast Based on Wireless Sensor Network from the Perspective of Digital Economy. *Wireless Communications and Mobile Computing*, 2021(1), 1–14. DOI: 10.1155/2021/8576534

Melo, G. P. A. N., De Oliveira, R. C., Da Silva, C. M. D. O., Silva, E. H., Da Silva, R. A., De Souza, R. M. A., De Andrade, I. A. B., & Da Silva, W. A. V. (2024). RESEARCH AND SCIENTIFIC DEVELOPMENT: THE ROLE OF FUNDING AGENCIES FOR TECHNOLOGICAL ADVANCEMENT IN BRAZIL. *Revista Contemporânea*, 4(2), e3343. DOI: 10.56083/RCV4N2-045

Michael Alurame Eruaga. (2024). Policy strategies for managing food safety risks associated with climate change and agriculture. *International Journal of Scholarly Research and Reviews, 4*(1), 021–032. DOI: 10.56781/ijsrr.2024.4.1.0026

Mohammad, B. T., Mushfika, H., & Iva, R. D. (2024a). Opportunities of tourism and hospitality education in bangladesh: Career perspectives. *I-Manager's. Journal of Management*, 18(3), 21. DOI: 10.26634/jmgt.18.3.20385

Mohammad, B. T., Mushfika, H., & Iva, R. D. (2024b). Opportunities of tourism and hospitality education in bangladesh: Career perspectives. *I-Manager's. Journal of Management*, 18(3), 21. DOI: 10.26634/jmgt.18.3.20385

Mrs. C. Radha, Mr. R. Midunkumar, Mr. S. Muralibabu, Mr. V. Partheeban, & Mr. V. Partheeban. (2024). Role of Artificial Intelligence in Big Data Analytics. *International Journal of Advanced Research in Science, Communication and Technology*, 586–591. DOI: 10.48175/IJARSCT-17089

Nazemi, K. (2023). Artificial Intelligence in Visual Analytics. *2023 27th International Conference Information Visualisation (IV)*, 230–237. DOI: 10.1109/IV60283.2023.00048

Pratiwi, C. P., Rahmatika, R. A., Wibawa, R. C., Purnomo, L., Larasati, H., Jahroh, S., & Syaukat, F. I. (2024). *The Rise of Digital Marketing Agencies: Transforming Digital Business Trends*. Jurnal Aplikasi Bisnis Dan Manajemen., DOI: 10.17358/jabm.10.1.162

Prokopowicz, D. (2024). Research Project (proposal): What are the potential applications of artificial intelligence and Big Data Analytics in Business Intelligence business performance analytics? How should artificial intelligence technology be used so that it complies with business ethics and corporate social responsibility? DOI: 10.13140/RG.2.2.24372.87689

Rohmah, N., & Komarudin, K. (2023). Digital Transformation in Business Operations Management. [AJEMB]. *American Journal of Economic and Management Business*, 2(9), 330–336. DOI: 10.58631/ajemb.v2i9.57

Said, S. (2023). The Role of Artificial Intelligence (AI) and Data Analytics in Enhancing Guest Personalization in Hospitality. *Journal of Modern Hospitality*, 2(1), 1–13. DOI: 10.47941/jmh.1556

Salam, U. (2023). Digital Tourism In ASEAN During Covid-19 Pandemic. *SOSIO DIALEKTIKA*, 8(2), 153. DOI: 10.31942/sd.v8i2.9798

Santa Fe Utn, F. R., & Consumidores De La Era Digital, A. C. (2023). I Jornadas de Ciberseguridad y Sociedad. *AJEA, AJEA*, 27(AJEA 27). Advance online publication. DOI: 10.33414/ajea.1300.2023

Sathuta Sellapperuma & Niroshima Udayangani. (2024). *ENGINEERING SOFT-WARE COMPONENTS AND SYSTEMS FOR AUTONOMOUS VEHICLES: ADDRESSING NOVEL CHALLENGES IN THE DIGITAL TRANSITION ERA CONTEXT.* DOI: 10.13140/RG.2.2.21596.60809

Şengel, Ü., Çevrimkaya, M., Işkın, M., & Zengin, B. (2022). The Effects Of Corporate Websites Usability Of Travel Agencies On Their Technological Capabilities. *Journal of Quality Assurance in Hospitality & Tourism*, 23(6), 1575–1595. DOI: 10.1080/1528008X.2021.2004570

Serdyukova, N., & Serdyukov, S. (2023). A research of factors and the process of a territory's tourism ecosystem formation. *The Eurasian Scientific Journal, 15*(4), 24ECVN423. DOI: 10.15862/24ECVN423

Shanti, R., Siregar, H., Zulbainarni, N., & Tony, . (2023). Role of Digital Transformation on Digital Business Model Banks. *Sustainability (Basel)*, 15(23), 16293. DOI: 10.3390/su152316293

Sharma, R. (2023). Leveraging AI and IoT for Sustainable Waste Management. In Whig, P., Silva, N., Elngar, A. A., Aneja, N., & Sharma, P. (Eds.), *Sustainable Development through Machine Learning, AI and IoT* (Vol. 1939, pp. 136–150). Springer Nature Switzerland., DOI: 10.1007/978-3-031-47055-4_12

Sultan, M. I., & Amir, A. S. (2023). Charting The Digital Odyssey: Exploring Challenges and Unleashing Opportunities for Journalism in The Digital Era. *Warta ISKI*, 6(2), 153–162. DOI: 10.25008/wartaiski.v6i2.254

Sun, Z. (2023). Data, Analytics, and Intelligence. *Journal of Computer Science Research*, 5(4), 43–57. DOI: 10.30564/jcsr.v5i4.6072

Suryawan, R. F., Kamsariaty, K., Perwitasari, E. P., Maulina, E., Maghfuriyah, A., & Susilowati, T. (2024). Digital Strategy Model in Strengthening Brand Image to Maintain Customer Loyalty (Case Study on Umrah and Hajj Travel Agency). *East Asian Journal of Multidisciplinary Research*, 2(12), 5045–5056. DOI: 10.55927/eajmr.v2i12.6960

Talukder, M. B. (2021). An assessment of the roles of the social network in the development of the Tourism Industry in Bangladesh. *International Journal of Business, Law, and Education*, 2(3), 85–93. DOI: 10.56442/ijble.v2i3.21

Talukder, M. B. (2024). Implementing Artificial Intelligence and Virtual Experiences in Hospitality. In Manohar, S., Mittal, A., Raju, S., & Nair, A. J. (Eds.), *Advances in Hospitality, Tourism, and the Services Industry* (pp. 145–160). IGI Global., DOI: 10.4018/979-8-3693-2019-8.ch009

Talukder, M. B., Kabir, F., Muhsina, K., & Das, I. R. (2023). Emerging Concepts of Artificial Intelligence in the Hotel Industry: A Conceptual Paper. *International Journal of Research Publication and Reviews*, 4(9), 1765–1769. DOI: 10.55248/gengpi.4.923.92451

Talukder, M. B., Kumar, S., Kaiser, F., & Mia, Md. N. (2024). Pilgrimage Creative Tourism: A Gateway to Sustainable Development Goals in Bangladesh. In M. Hamdan, M. Anshari, N. Ahmad, & E. Ali (Eds.), *Advances in Public Policy and Administration* (pp. 285–300). IGI Global. DOI: 10.4018/979-8-3693-1742-6.ch016

Tjostheim, I., & Waterworth, J. A. (2023). Digital Travel – A Study of Travellers' Views of a Digital Visit to Mexico. In Á. Rocha, C. Ferrás, & W. Ibarra (Eds.), *Information Technology and Systems* (Vol. 691, pp. 185–194). Springer International Publishing. DOI: 10.1007/978-3-031-33258-6_17

Toscano-Jara, J., Loza-Aguirre, E., & Franco-Crespo, A. (2023). Challenges for the Digital Transformation of Ecuador's Tourism Industry: Perceptions of Leaders in Times of Covid-19. In Estrada, S. (Ed.), *Digital and Sustainable Transformations in a Post-COVID World* (pp. 257–273). Springer International Publishing., DOI: 10.1007/978-3-031-16677-8_10

Vats, K. (2024). Navigating the Digital Landscape: Embracing Innovation, Addressing Challenges, and Prioritizing Patient-Centric Care. *Cureus*. Advance online publication. DOI: 10.7759/cureus.58352 PMID: 38756283

Yaşar, E., Tür, E., Yayla, E., & Alakuş, N. A. (2024). The Role and Future of Metaverse in Travel Agencies. In Kumar, J., Arora, M., & Erkol Bayram, G. (Eds.), (pp. 210–234). Advances in Social Networking and Online Communities. IGI Global., DOI: 10.4018/979-8-3693-5868-9.ch012

Yopi, F. (2024). TPACK AND TEACHERS' DIGITAL COMPETENCE IN THE ERA OF INDUSTRY 4.0. [IJMI]. *International Journal Multidisciplinary*, 1(1), 45–52. DOI: 10.61796/ijmi.v1i1.32

Yufriadi, F., Syahriani, F., & Afifi, A. A. (2024). Trade Transformation In The Digital Era: Agency Role, Opportunities And Challenges. *AL-IMAM: Journal on Islamic Studies. Civilization and Learning Societies*, 5(1), 13–23. DOI: 10.58764/j.im.2024.5.55

Zaika, S., & Avriata, A. (2024). Analysis of the impact of the COVID-19 pandemic on the development of the international tourism market. *International Science Journal of Management. Economics & Finance*, 3(2), 56–68. DOI: 10.46299/j.isjmef.20240302.06

Zhang, Z. (2023). Digital Operational Strategies in The Post-Pandemic Era for Travel Companies: A Case Study of Ctrip. *Highlights in Business. Economics and Management*, 23, 521–525. DOI: 10.54097/h0w3ar97

ADDITIONAL READING

Ali, M. (2021). *Remote Work and Sustainable Changes for the Future of Global Business.* IGI Global. https://www.igi-global.com/book/remote-work-sustainable-changes-future/264375

Ali, M. (2022). *Future Role of Sustainable Innovative Technologies in Crisis Management.* IGI Global. https://www.igi-global.com/book/future-role-sustainable-innovative-technologies/281281

Ali, M. (2023). *Shifting Paradigms in the Rapidly Developing Global Digital Ecosystem: A GCC Perspective.* In Digital Entrepreneurship and Co-Creating Value Through Digital Encounters (pp. 145-166). IGI Global. https://www.igi-global.com/chapter/shifting-paradigms-in-the-rapidly-developing-global-digital-ecosystem/323525

Ali, M. (2023). T*axonomy of Industry 4.0 Technologies in Digital Entrepreneurship and Co-Creating Value.* In *Digital Entrepreneurship and Co-Creating Value Through Digital Encounters* (pp. 24–55). IGI Global., https://www.igi-global.com/chapter/taxonomy-of-industry-40-technologies-in-digital-entrepreneurship-and-co-creating-value/323520 DOI: 10.4018/978-1-6684-7416-7.ch002

Ali, M., & Wood-Harper, T. (2021). *Fostering Communication and Learning with Underutilized Technologies in Higher Education.* IGI Global. https://www.igi-global.com/book/fostering-communication-learning-underutilized-technologies/244593

Ali, M., Wood-Harper, T., & Kutar, M. (2023). Multi-Perspectives of Contemporary Digital Transformation Models of Complex Innovation Management. In *Digital Entrepreneurship and Co-Creating Value Through Digital Encounters* (pp. 79–96). IGI Global., https://www.igi-global.com/chapter/multi-perspectives-of-contemporary-digital-transformation-models-of-complex-innovation-management/323522 DOI: 10.4018/978-1-6684-7416-7.ch004

Ali, M. B. (2021). Internet of Things (IoT) to Foster Communication and Information Sharing: A Case of UK Higher Education. In Ali, M. B., & Wood-Harper, T. (Eds.), *Fostering Communication and Learning With Underutilized Technologies in Higher Education* (pp. 1–20). IGI Global., https://www.igi-global.com/chapter/internet-of-things-iot-to-foster-communication-and-information-sharing/262718/ DOI: 10.4018/978-1-7998-4846-2.ch001

Ali, M. B., & Wood-Harper, T. (2022). Artificial Intelligence (AI) as a Decision-Making Tool to Control Crisis Situations. In *Future Role of Sustainable Innovative Technologies in Crisis Management*. IGI Global., https://www.igi-global.com/chapter/artificial-intelligence-ai-as-a-decision-making-tool-to-control-crisis-situations/298931 DOI: 10.4018/978-1-7998-9815-3.ch006

Ali, M. B., Wood-Harper, T., & Ramlogan, R. (2020). A Framework Strategy to Overcome Trust Issues on Cloud Computing Adoption in Higher Education. In Modern Principles, Practices, and Algorithms for Cloud Security (pp. 162-183). IGI Global. https://www.igi-global.com/chapter/a-framework-strategy-to-overcome-trust-issues-on-cloud-computing-adoption-in-higher-education/238907/

Chapter 15
Digitalization and the Role of Internet of Things With Service– Oriented Computing Applications on Supply Chain Operations

Kamalendu Pal
https://orcid.org/0000-0001-7158-6481
University of London, UK

ABSTRACT

Global trade and supply chains have experienced significant disruptions in recent years, revealing their vulnerabilities. Events like the coronavirus pandemic (COVID-19), the Ever-Given blockage in the Suez Canal, and the Russian invasion of Ukraine have highlighted these challenges. Concurrently, digitalization is transforming supply chain management, notably through the increasing use of the Internet of Things (IoT) to develop decision-support systems that analyze operational data and provide crucial insights for stakeholders. This chapter presents a knowledge-based framework for designing and implementing these operational support services using advanced web services. It emphasizes the importance of semantic interoperability through ontologies and similarity assessment techniques. The practical application of these concepts is not just theoretical but achievable, aiming to engage business stakeholders and build their confidence in digitally transforming supply chain operations. Finally, the chapter offers a compelling business case that illustrates the benefits of employing ontologies and algorithmic concept similarity assessment in

DOI: 10.4018/979-8-3693-5966-2.ch015

operational service design.

INTRODUCTION

The rich tapestry of commercial trading, woven between countries and continents, has been a cornerstone of human civilization since ancient times. This historical significance of global trade, a vibrant exchange of goods such as rice, wheat, spices, textiles, metals, petroleum products, and other essential commodities, connects people to their hereditary business practices. The Silk Road, the Spice Route, and a myriad of interconnected trade networks were the threads that initiated trade patterns, which have since flourished with the advent of industrialization (Bardhan, 2003) and the profound impact of globalization on new work practices (Stiglitz, 2017). The European Commission defines *globalization* as a phenomenon that significantly intertwines different countries ' markets and productions due to trade dynamics, while technology eliminates geographical barriers (Wahab, 2004). These two forces, globalization and technology, are the primary drivers of change in supply chain management (Johnson, 2006), creating a new economic environment. They are not independent but complementary, shaping each other's path and steering the direction of global supply chains. In this way, the rich history of global trade is a testament to the ingenuity and resilience of human enterprise.

While the fundamental concept of global trade remains unchanged, moving goods and money from point A in one country to point B in another has evolved into a complex and multifaceted operation. This operational business practice now encompasses financing trade, tracking and tracing goods along supply chains, and verifying the quality of those goods through provenance and product pedigree. As global trade has expanded, these operational business processes have multiplied and become more intricate. The demands of increased trade volume among more participants – business financiers, partners as importers and exporters servicing different market segments, freight forwarders, customs and port authorities, regulatory governing bodies, and insurance providers- have complicated these business practices. You, the business professionals, play a crucial and valued role in this evolution, and your understanding and management of supply chain operations are integral to its success. This evolution underscores the critical importance of your role, emphasizing the urgency and significance of the digitization of business processes (Pal, 2017a) (Pal, 2017b) (Pal & Karakostas, 2014).

The business world recognizes the significant potential of robust supply chain management (SCM) in connecting regular activities and distribution operations to drive a company's growth and profitability. The SCM system procures raw materials, transforms them into intermediate and finished products, and delivers them to customers with impeccable service provisions, thus playing a crucial role in driving growth. Integrating information and material flows in the demand and supply process enhances logistical resource allocation, management, and control, increasing productivity, reducing operational costs, and effective customer services. SCM also involves managing supply chain facets, ensuring customer product delivery, and providing value-added services (Pal, 2018a) (Pal, 2018b) (Pal & Yasar, 2023) (Pal et al., 2024). These value-added services, such as personalized product recommendations, predictive maintenance, and real-time order tracking, are designed to enhance the customer experience and increase customer loyalty. Reverse logistics, the handling of products returned to the company, is an integral part of this process, as it ensures a comprehensive approach to supply chain management despite the potential for substantial losses. The potential of robust SCM is a beacon of hope for the future of global trade and business operations.

Figure 1. Supply chain management process

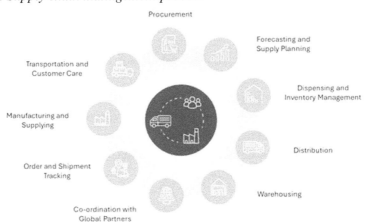

Strategically, SCM can be dissected into various business processes, each with unique activities. These processes are not just a series of tasks, but they form the backbone of the supply chain, each playing a crucial role in the smooth operation of the entire system. Their strategic importance cannot be overstated. They include forecasting and supply chain planning, procurement, transportation and customer clearance, manufacturing and supplying, order and shipment tracking, coordination with global partners, warehousing and receiving, distribution and dispensing and inventory management. Figure 1 presents a visual representation of these strategic business processes, which are more sequential in practice, as shown in the diagram. It describes a continuum based on a straightforward concept – using a better understanding and knowledge of the world for industrial SCM systems to make better decisions within a business objective function.

Historically, the beginning of the SCM initiative was characterized by relatively static models codified in rules defined by humans to provide the best possible representation of the actual physical world. However, the landscape of SCM is not just changing, it's evolving at a rapid pace. In recent decades, these model-driven business operation practices have not been adequate to manage global supply chain operations effectively. The significant evolution from these static models to dynamic ones, which can adapt to changing conditions and variables, is a testament to the rapid progress and innovation in the field of SCM.

Modern SCM is a local or regional concern and a global phenomenon. It is on a trajectory of multi-decade progression towards greater sophistication, addressing the challenges of increasing product varieties, fulfilment options, and customer engagement at the lowest possible cost. A 'nexus of business processes and technology forces ', which refers to the intersection of strategic business activities and technological advancements, is driving unprecedented change in supply chain and retail operations in one sector or region and across all business sectors globally. In this way, SCM depends on business process operation practice and technology architecture to bring innovation and offer value-added services to customers. The current generation supply chain management is driven by increasingly dynamic models. These models are designed to adapt to changing conditions and variables, such as shifts in consumer demand or disruptions in the supply chain, by leveraging the availability of digital data points from everywhere, the ability to sense this data, the ability to process this data, the ability to react to this data, and the ability to learn from it over time.

Figure 2. A digital supply chain operations scenario

Furthermore, these models provide much more accurate representations of the natural world at any given time. In other words, the digital phase of modern supply chain management, which refers to the era of advanced digital technologies, is a game-changer. As digital data from the supply chain is processed and intelligent adjustments are made, the digital and the physical become one. This not only commingles the models with physical reality through digital data but also transitions the logic that runs software against these models from a rules-driven paradigm to a learning paradigm. In this digital phase, machine learning is the driving force behind the digitization of the mainstream of enterprise software, bringing about unprecedented accuracy and efficiency in supply chain management.

With numerous opportunities to digitize various aspects of supply chain operations, business organizations often take a structural approach to automate essential services. This chapter describes the strategic decision-making process within the supply chain. It achieves this by presenting a series of digitized business scenarios covering inbound, internal, outbound, and end-to-end operation activities, as shown diagrammatically in Figure 2. The digitization of business processes takes a new dimension with the deployment of information and communication technologies (ICT). This structured approach breaks down the supply chain into a series of digital scenarios, enhancing the efficiency and effectiveness of operations and inspiring a future where the potential of digitization is fully realized, reassuring of the benefits of this transformation.

The chapter presents a strategic framework for robust decision-making based on a clear understanding of the outcomes that an industrial sector wants to achieve. It emphasizes the empowerment of business strategists to think about which areas they want to focus on, assess their achievements to date, and prioritize their efforts. Figure 2 presents a snapshot of the framework that consists of business partners' collaborative electronic sourcing, digital factory design, real-time factory scheduling, flexible factory automation, digital production processes, customer-connected electronic commerce, near real-time extended supply chain monitoring, digital product quality control, digital supply network design, and product lifecycle management. In addition, academics play a crucial role in introducing new types of innovation, such as Gandhian Innovation, a concept inspired by the principles of Mahatma Gandhi. This innovation solves problems by acquiring or developing technologies and altering business models or capabilities to create more social products and services from fewer resource inputs (Prahalad & Mashelkar, 2010). Their contribution is instrumental in shaping the future of industrial technology and supply chain management. However, the detailed discussion regarding this framework is beyond the scope of this chapter.

The Industrial Revolution and the expansion of the West in the 19th century led to a new path in the development of human society. Globalization is shaping contemporary patterns and bringing social activities into a new era. Political, economic, and technological changes are the main elements interrelated with globalization and lead to a new transformation of the supply chain management model (SCM) (Pal, 2020).

The objectives of modern industrialization (e.g., Industry 4.0 and Industry 5.0) are to achieve better operational efficiency and productivity and a higher level of automatization. As researchers, for example, (Roblek et al., 2016) and (Posada et al., 2015) highlighted, the five major features of Industry 4.0 and digitization, optimization, and customization of production; automation and adaptation; human-machine interaction (HMI); value-added services and businesses, and automatic data exchange and communication. This feature, automatic data exchange and communication, involves systems and devices sharing information and instructions without human intervention, such as in a smart factory where manufacturing machines communicate to introduce efficiency in production and related services. These features are highly correlated with Internet technologies and advanced algorithms and indicate that Industry 4.0 is an industry process of value-adding and knowledge management.

Modern industrial progress is helping human-centric society achieve its goals for sustainable progress through industrial development. Historically, industrial development has lasted for many hundred years, and now, the era of Industry 4.0 and Industry 5.0 dominate societal development. At the same time, harnessing the frontier of technologies can help create and deliver innovations (including non-technological and new forms of social innovation) that could be transformative in creating sustainable development goals and producing more prosperous, inclusive, and healthy human societies. In this way, society gets the required solutions and chances for future sustainable development that are essential, cheaper, faster, scalable, and easy to use. The transformative potential of Industry 4.0 is immense, and it offers hope for a better future. The extent of technological development impact has already ushered in the transformative implications of information and communication technologies (ICTs) in many countries worldwide. However, these new technologies often threaten to outpace the capability of societies and policymakers, underscoring the weight of their responsibility to adapt to the changes they can create, giving rise to widespread anxiety and ambivalence or hostility to some technological advances.

The concept of modern industry (e.g., Industry 4.0) was introduced in 2011 to drive the development of the German economy. According to Lukac, the first industrial revolution started in the late 18th century, characterized by mechanical production with the help of water and steam power; the second industrial revolution started in the early 20th century with mass production based on electrical energy; the third industrial revolution (Industry 3.0)started in the 1970s with automatic production using electronics and internet technology. The world is in the midst of the fourth industrial revolution, and after this revolution, industry 4.0 appears to automate industrial applications. Industry 4.0, characterized by cyber-physical systems (CPS) production, relies on the crucial integration of diverse data and knowledge. CPS, a key feature of Industry 4.0, refers to integrating computation, networking, and physical processes. As professionals in the field, we are not just witnessing this evolution, but actively shaping it with our industry-specific expertise and knowledge. The industrial world is playing an active role in shaping the evolution of Industry 4.0, making us all feel empowered and influential. CPS aims to fulfil the agile and dynamic production requirements and enhance the whole industry's efficiency and effectiveness. Industry 4.0 encompasses numerous technologies and associated paradigms, including Radio Frequency Identification (RFID), Enterprise Resource Planning (ERP), Internet of Things (IoT), cloud-based manufacturing and other relevant services, and social product development.

Real-world industrial sectors like manufacturing, healthcare, transportation, retail business, and environmental monitoring increasingly rely on obtaining relevant sensor data. Processing this data in real-time from all operational value chain components is crucial for these sectors to maintain efficiency and competitiveness. Implementing an intelligent industry involves integrating connectivity into industrial products and related services using service-oriented computing and the Internet of Things (IoT). This integration aims to capitalize on intelligence and actionable knowledge for machines, allowing for autonomous collaboration among machines and integrating products and additional value-added services. Service-oriented computing has significantly transformed the service consumption and delivery platform, revolutionizing how businesses and users engage with IT resources across various industrial domains. Its impact on the supply chain is particularly noteworthy, as it optimizes processes and enhances the overall customer experience. The emerging IoT further extends the service-oriented concept beyond computing and communication to include the physical field devices and hardware, enabling real-time monitoring and control of the supply chain. By using the data collected from sensors, machines, devices, and people in the industrial production processes as well as the virtual world, data analytics can identify relations and patterns to gain valuable insights for optimized operations and to provide services to customers such as machine failure prevention and real-time production performance improvement. Service-oriented computing and IoT technologies enable organizations to pursue new revenue streams based on the extracted insights regarding performance footprint and autonomous operation, opening up exciting new possibilities for business growth and profitability.

This comprehensive chapter provides an extensive review of the latest trends in IoT-based business applications and the challenges related to interoperability. It explores how semantic web technologies, frameworks, and information models can play a crucial role in supporting the automation of industrial business operations, highlighting their potential in IoT applications. The chapter covers two crucial aspects of industrial IoT ecosystems: (i) the fundamental concept of IoT and its information systems architectural issues, and (ii) interoperability, service-oriented computing, and the significance of business processes ontology design for operational service implementation. In conclusion, the chapter addresses pertinent issues and challenges for future research, ensuring a comprehensive understanding of the field.

The remaining structure of this chapter presents an overview of how service-oriented computing is merging with IoT technologies to create business information systems for industrial applications. It also examines notable research in this area. Finally, the chapter presents concluding remarks and outlines a future research agenda.

RELATED ADVANCES AND RESEARCH WORKS

In recent years, modern industrial application paradigms (e.g., Industry Four, Industry Five) have dominated the business world of information systems design and development. Within these applications, service-oriented computing and the Internet of Things (IoT) technologies are essential in heterogeneous services integration, fostering a collaborative environment for information sharing and decision-making (Pal & Yasar, 2020) (Pal & Yasar, 2023). This collaborative nature of decision-making, where everyone's input is not just valued, but integral, is a crucial benefit of these technologies. At the same time, the concept of cyber-physical systems (CPS), the Industrial Internet of Things (IIoT), modern data communication technologies, service-oriented computing, and artificial intelligence-based techniques are ushering in a new dawn for industrial applications integration, where everyone is part of a larger community.

Figure 3. Different characteristics of IIoT based information systems

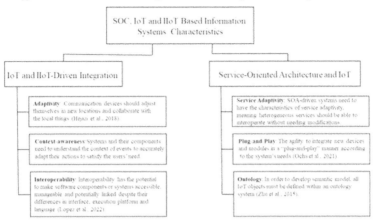

As mentioned before, there is a diversity of protocols in the IoT domain, and various challenges are faced when integrating heterogeneous information. Academics and practitioners have presented different system integration enablers frameworks and their components to achieve various aspects of information system deployment for industrial applications.

IIoT is revolutionizing the operation of industrial information systems, enabling them to sense and acquire information from the operating environment in new ways. IoT and IoT systems need different characteristics to be considered during design and implementation to improve the benefits of interconnected objects in a network (Razzaque et al., 2016) (Schneider et al., 2018). These characteristics include [specific characteristics]. The diagrammatic representation in Figure 3 highlights some of these essential characteristics.

The convergence of SOC with IoT technology often provides an agile information system with various design challenges. To deal with this, researchers often use unique and innovative information system design techniques, a common theme of Enablers Framework (EF) components that act like interface proxies. Figure 4 shows a simple interoperability between applications and enablers.

Figure 4. Interoperability between applications and enablers

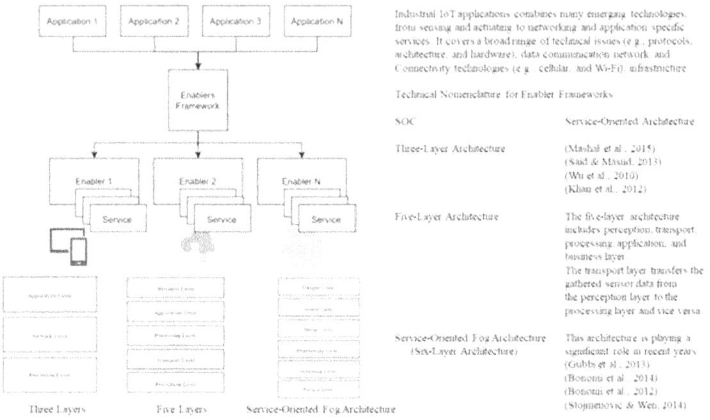

Recent Research Work on Service-Oriented IoT

Several studies have investigated the application of Web paradigms and protocols to service provisioning. Traditional context-aware frameworks have several limitations when developing context-aware services. These limitations have practical implications that affect the efficiency and cost of service usage. For instance, if the context is constantly changing (such as location), a context-aware service must be invoked with the updated context data. This not only increases network traffic but also escalates the cost of using the service. Similarly, the challenge of handling large messages when sending data to the context manager is a real issue that needs to be addressed. Table 1 represents some of the recent research works.

Table 1. Some of the recent research works on context-aware semantic service provisioning

Reference	Domain	Proposed Solution	Web Technology	Context Aware	Context Reasoning	Strength
(Kim et al., 2016)	Smart home	Middleware Architecture	OWL	Yes	Yes	1.Context inferring 2.Sensor abstraction 3.Rule based context aware service selection
(Gochhayat et al., 2016)	General	Architecture	SOA	Yes	No	1.Minimizes overhead of communication and processing
(Sciullo et al., 2020)	General	WoT Store Platform	W3C WoT Micro-service oriented	No	No	1.Resource dynamic discovery 2.Simplified management
(Ibaseta et al., 2021)	Building	Architecture Real-World Application	W3C WoT Cloud	No	No	1.Interoperable 2.Scalable 3.Energy consumption 4.Real-world Application
(Ortiz et al., 2022)	Hospital	Architecture	Event riven SOA Cloud, Fog, and Edge	Yes	No	1.Integrated edge, fog, and cloud computing 2.Situational-aware 3.Event-Driven SOA

The above research review leads to the presentation of the proposed system architecture in the following section.

OVERVIEW OF THE FRAMEWORK

The proposed framework uses model-theoretic semantics modelled in ontologies for IoT-generated data modelling. It helps to gather detailed information regarding the characteristics of IoT devices based on their technical requirements. The advantages of this encoding are – (i) interconnecting different classification systems to represent capabilities and properties of constituent parts, (ii) translating characteristics or properties among compound constituent parts, and (iii) aggregating basic properties into complex properties based on the constituents of a superordinate system. Those concepts can be used and adapted for the IoT to enhance the use of IoT devices by connecting them as a group, creating coordination between IoT devices, and improving their interoperability.

Figure 5. RFID tagging level at different stages in the apparel manufacturing network

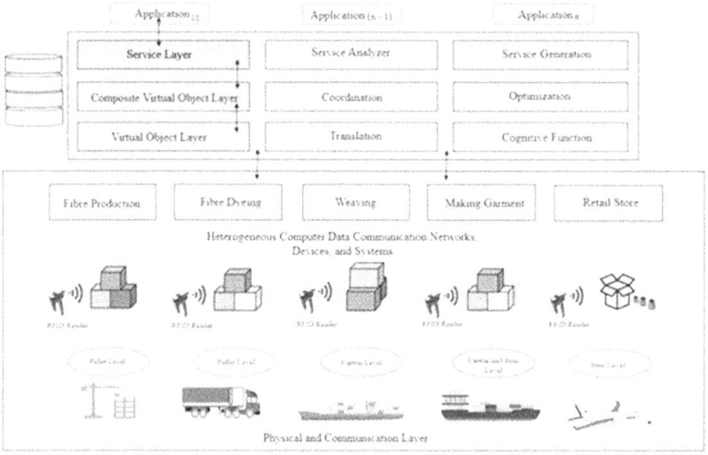

One of the main objectives of this framework is to define an IoT architecture, which can also be used for other applications. The design principle in Apparel Business Semantic Data Management (ABDDI) is that any physical/real-world object in the global textile and clothing business can have a virtual representation through a Virtual Object (VO). A VO uses a semantic representation of the functionality and conceals the varied identity of the real-world object. Multiple VOs can be combined to form a Composite Virtual Object (CVO) that provides more compact and reliable services. In simple, CVOs are combined to form a service request. Thus, the ABDDI architecture has three layers: VO, CVO, and Service, as shown in Figure 5.

The functionalities of the three layers are presented below:

- **VO layer**: The VOs represent real world objects in the digital format. End-users can search semantically and retrieve information from any existing VO. Also, actuation can be done through the VO.
- **CVO layer**: In this layer, VOs are combined to form a service request. This layer caters to functionality to search and query categories of CVOs semantically for service provision, ensuring reliable and efficient service delivery.
- **Service layer:** This layer is the dynamic heart of the system. It receives requests from users and analyzes them to determine the categories of CVOs needed for service accomplishment. It then performs service composition and orchestration, adapting to the ever-changing cloth and textile business environment with agility and responsiveness. The Service layer is crucial as it ensures that the right services are provided to the users at the right time, enhancing the overall efficiency of the system.

The ABDDI system has other components: a registry and a control unit. Every layer in this framework has a registry referencing the available VOs, CVOs, and services. These registries provide methods to semantically search and query existing VOs, CVOs, and services. The control unit, a key component, regulates access to the VOs, CVOs, and services based on the level of the end-user requirements.

KNOWLEDGE REPRESENTATION AND REASONING APPROACH

Description logics (DLs) (Baader et al., 2002) are a family of knowledge representation languages with a rich historical significance. They have been widely used in ontological modelling, providing a key foundation for the Web Ontology Language (OWL) as standardized by the World Wide Web Consortium (W3C). The use of DLs in knowledge representation predates the advent of ontological modelling in the context of the Semantic Web, with the first DL modelling languages emerging in the mid-1980s.

Table 2. Description Logics set of constructors

Constructor Name	Syntax	Explanation
Top concept	⊤	Universal concept. All the objects in the domain.
Bottom concept	⊥	The empty set.
Atomic concept	A	All objects belong to set A.
Atomic negation	¬A	All the objects do not belong to set A.
Conjunction	C⊓D	The objects belong to both C and D sets.
Disjunction	C⊔D	The objects that are in the extension of either C or D or both
Value restriction	∀RC	All the objects are participating in the R relation, whose range is all the objects belonging to the C set.
Existential restriction	∃RC	At least one object participating in the relation R.
Concept definition	A ≡ C	Concepts represent sets of elements and can be viewed as unary predicates.

Resource Representation and Reasoning in Description Logics

The most important and well-known service characterizing reasoning in DL checks for specificity hierarchies by determining whether a concept description is more specific than another one or, formally, if there is a *subsumption* relation between them.

Definition 1 (Subsumption): *Give two concept descriptions, C and D, and a TBox τ in a DL L; one can say that D subsumes C τ(C ⊑ D) concerning if for every model of τ, $C^I \subset D^I$. In a particular case, two concepts are equivalent if they subsume each other.*

For example, consider the following concept descriptions, referring to different garment types in an apparel supply chain network: G_1 = *SweaterBodyGarment* ⊓ ∀ *hasMain.Colour.Red*, and G_2 = *UpperBodyGarment* ⊓ ∀ *hasMain.Colour.Red*. Then using TBox reasoning – the concept inclusion can be achieved, and the output will be *Sweater* ⊑_τ *UpperBodyGarment*. Hence, given the model, knowledge expressed by G_1 is more specific than the one required by G_2 concerning the reasoning mechanism and the definition of G_2 subsumes G_1.

Based on subsumption, new reasoning mechanisms can be defined in DLs. The ABDDI system development uses several non-standard reasoning mechanisms (e.g., Least Common Subsumer – LCS).

Definition 2 (Least Common Subsumer): *Let C_1, ..., C_p be p concept descriptions in a DL L. A Least Common Subsumer (LCS) of C_1, ..., C_p, denoted by LCS (C_1, ..., C_p) is a concept description E in L. state that the following conditions hold: (i) $C_h ⊑ E$ for h = 1, ..., p; (ii) E is the least L–concept description satisfying (iii), i.e., if E is an L–concept satisfying $C_i ⊑ E$ for all i = 1, ..., n, then $E ⊑ E$.*

It is worth showing how to model concept collections formalized in ALN (D) according to a compact lossless representation. Such modelling allows for finding commonalities in resource annotations formalized in DL.

Definition 3 (Concept Components): *Let C be a concept described in a DL L, with C formalized as $C^1 ⊓ ... C^m$. The Concept Components of C are defined as follows: if C_j, with j = 1, ..., m is either a concept name, a negated concept name, or a concrete feature or a number restriction, then C_j is a Concept Component of C; if C_j = ∀R.E, with j = 1, ..., m, then ∀R. E^k is a Concept Component of C, for each E^k Concept Component of E.*

Definition 4 (Subsumption): *Give two concept descriptions C and D, and a TBox τ in a DL L; one can say that D subsumes C τ(C ⊑ D) concerning if for every model of τ, $C^I \subset D^I$. In a particular case, two concepts are equivalent if they subsume each other.*

Definition 5 (Least Common Subsumer): *Let C_1, ..., C_p be p concept descriptions in a DL L. A Least Common Subsumer (LCS) of C_1, ..., C_p, denoted by LCS (C_1, ..., C_p) is a concept description E in L. state that the following conditions hold: (i) $C_h ⊑ E$ for h = 1, ..., p; (ii) E is the least L–concept description satisfying (iii), i.e., if E is an L–concept satisfying $C_i ⊑ E$ for all i = 1, ..., n, then $E ⊑ E$.*

Definition 6 (r-Common Subsumer, Informative r-Common Subsumers): *Let C_1, ..., C_p be p concept descriptions in a DL L, and let be k ≤ p. An r-Common Subsumer (r-CS) of C_1, ..., C_p is a concept $D_{D = ⊤}$ such that D is an LCS of at least r = k/p concepts among C_1, ..., C_p. One can define a particular case as Informative r-Common Subsumers (Ir-CS) that specific r-CSs for which r < 1.*

It is worth showing how to model concept collections formalized in ALN (D) according to a compact lossless representation. Such a modelling framework allows for finding commonalities in resource annotations formalized in DL.

Definition 7 (Concept Components): *Let C be a concept described in a DL L, with C formalized as $C^1 ⊓ ... C^m$. The Concept Components of C are defined as follows: if C_j, with j = 1, ..., m is either a concept name, a negated concept name, or a concrete feature or a number restriction, then C_j is a Concept Component of C; if C_j = ∀R.E, with j = 1, ..., m, then ∀R. E^k is a Concept Component of C, for each E^k Concept Component of E.*

Definition 8 (Aggregate Collection Matrix): *Let $S_1, ..., S_n$ be an aggregate collection, with $S_j = C_{1b} ..., C_{pi}$ for $i = 1 ... n$. Let $D \in \{D_1, ..., D_m\}$ be the Concept Components deriving from all the concepts in the aggregate collection. The Aggregate Subsumers Matrix is defined as $A = (a_{ij})$, with $i = 1 ... n$ and $j = 1 ... m$, such that for each i, $a_{ij} = v$, with $0 \leq v \leq p_i$, where v is the number of concept descriptions in S_i subsumed by the component D_j.*

Definition 9 (Aggregate Model): *Let $S_1, ..., S_n$ be an aggregate of concept collections; for $i = 1 ... n$, S_i is a concept collection descriptions s_{ki} with $k = 1 ... p_i$. An Aggregate Model for $S_1, ..., S_n$ and each of this element consists of the pair of items - $<E, G>$ with the following characteristics: (i) E represents the subsumers matrix deriving from the collection $C_1,...,C_p = \bigcup(C_{ki})$, with $i = 1 ... n$ and $k = 1 ... p_i$, whose elements e_{kj} are calculated by using prognostications to subsumption; and (ii) G is the collection subsumers matrix deriving from the input collection $S_1,...S_n$ whose elements a_{ij} are calculated by using information stored in E. In this computation, each row i in G is related to an aggregate collection S_i, defined as a collection of description C_{ki} whose subsumption relationship with components deriving from $S_1,..., Sn$ is stored in E. To this modelling, values a_{ij}, for each component D_j, are determined as Concept Component Relative Cardinality $RC_{D_j}^{S_i}$.*

Semantic Similarity Assessment

Before describing the proposed approach's theoretical framework, the employed reasoning services will be shortly recalled in the following subsection to make the chapter self-contained. Furthermore, the proposed algorithmic concept of similarity measurement is presented in this section.

In ABSDM, the similarity between concepts C_i, C_j can be expressed by a number, and its values can fall between 0 and 1. It may be viewed as a one-directional relation, and its larger values imply a higher similarity between the concepts. The concept similarity is described as follows:

Definition 10 (Concept Similarity): An ontological concept (C) similarity (∂) is considered a *relation*, and it can be defined as $\partial C \times C \rightarrow [0, 1]$. In simple, it is a function from a pair of concepts to a real number between *zero* and *one*, expressing the degree of similarity between two concepts such that:

1. $\forall C_1 \in G, \partial(C_1, C_1) = 1$
2. $\forall C_1, C_2 \in G, 0 \leq \partial(C_1, C_2) \leq 1$
3. $\forall C_1, C_2, C_3 \in G, IF\ Sim_d(C_1, C_2) > Sim_d(C_1, C_3)\ THEN\ \partial(C_1, C_2) < \partial(C_1, C_3)$

The above properties provide the range of semantic similarity functions $\partial(C_i, C_j)$. For exactly similar concepts, the similarity is $\partial(C_1, C_1) = 1$; when two concepts have nothing in common, their similarity is $\partial(C_1, C_2) = 0$. In this way, the output of the similarity function should be in the closed interval [0, 1]. Here Sim_d represents the semantic distance, and (C_1, C_2, C_3) represent three concepts of graph G. In CSIA, the following semantic similarity (∂) function has been used for computation purposes:

$$\partial(C_1, C_2) = \frac{1}{deg \cdot Sim_d(C_1, C_2) + 1}$$

Where C_1 and C_2 represent two concepts, and 'deg' represents the impact of semantic distance on semantic similarity, it should be between $0 < deg \leq 1$. A weight allocation function is used, as shown below, to compute the semantic similarity between concepts:

$$w(C_m, C_n) = [\ \max(depth(C_m)) + \frac{OrderNumber(C_n)}{TNodes(G) + 1} + 1\ ]^{-1}$$

Where C_m and C_n represents two nodes directly connected, $\max(depth(C_m))$ represents the maximum depth of the node C_m (the depth of the root node is equal to 0 and 1 for the nodes directly connected to the root node and so on). TNodes(G) and OrderNumber(C_n) represent the total number of nodes in concept graph G and the order number of the node (C_n) between their siblings. The detailed description of these mathematical formalizations is beyond the scope of this chapter.

EXAMPLE OF A BUSINESS SCENARIO

A simple apparel manufacturing scenario is used to present a part of ABDDI algorithmic computation. Semantic IoT-based product flow in a retail outlet is considered. Each product is described using semantic-enhanced IoT as an ALN (D) concept expression in OWL language. As the retail apparel product arrive or depart the shop, they are scanned by the gate RFID readers; reading events, including semantic annotation extracted from tags, are fed to a semantic Data Service Management Service (DSMS), which computes Concept Components and subsumption test through a reasoning mechanism.

Algorithm 1. Algorithm for semantic similarity computation

```
input: two concepts (C₁, C₂), the root node (root), concepts graph (G)
output: semantic similarity value between two concepts
 1:  begin
 2:  if  C₁ and C₂ are same concept then Sim_d = 0
 3:  else
 4:     if C₁ and C₂ are directly connected then Sim_d = w (C₁ . C₂)
 5:     else
 6:        if idirect path connection exist then
 7:           S_path01 = ShortestPath (G, C₁, Root_X)
 8:           S_path02 = ShortestPath (G, C₂, Root_X)
 9:           Sim_d = w(S_path01) + w(S_path02) – 2*w(CSPath]
10:        end if
11:        ∂(C₁,C₂)  =  ─────────
                        deg·Sim_d+1
12:     end if
13:  end if
14:  return ∂
15:  end
```

Let us consider a situation that allows a user to purchase a sweater from an online business. This example considers how a request is matched with the service advertised for wool garments selling service. An algorithm (i.e., Algorithm 1) tries to perform semantic matching for a relevant sweater.

The algorithm takes two ontological concepts, the root node (root), and the concepts graph (G), as input and computes a semantic similarity between the concepts as output.

The part of the concept hierarchy used in this example is shown in Figure 6. Each node of this hierarchy represents a concept. The experimental comparison considers semantic similarity among Wool, Shirt, Sweater, Trousers, Cardigan, Pullover, and Jumper. The proposed algorithm (i.e., Algorithm 1) provides semantic similarity between concepts with a higher score than the path similarity algorithm.

Figure 6. The hierarchical concept relationships

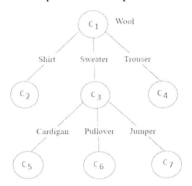

Table 3. The results of various similarity measures

	C_1	C_2	C_3	C_4	C_5			C_1	C_2	C_3	C_4	C_5
C_1	1.00	0.25	0.50	0.20	0.20		C_1	1.00	0.48	0.65	0.51	0.38
C_2	0.25	1.00	0.50	0.33	0.16		C_2	0.48	1.00	0.65	0.51	0.38
C_3	0.50	0.50	1.00	0.25	0.16		C_3	0.65	0.65	1.00	0.71	0.48
C_4	0.20	0.33	0.25	1.00	0.20		C_4	0.51	0.51	0.71	1.00	0.59
C_5	0.20	0.16	0.16	0.20	1.00		C_5	0.38	0.38	0.48	0.59	1.00
(a) Path similarity							(b) The proposed method					

In Table 3, (a) represents the outcome of path similarity (Varelas et al., 2005), while (b) highlights the results of the algorithm proposed for use in ABDDI. Within ABDDI, the similarity measure offers a high degree of flexibility and customization, enabling the incorporation of user preferences. This concept encompasses two primary facets. Firstly, users have the ability to specify the relative importance of similarity assessment parameters through an advanced search interface. Secondly, in addition to presenting a singular ranking for each potential service, the system can also furnish more comprehensive results, such as varying values for recall and the extent of match, aimed at assisting users in pinpointing the timeliest service.

FUTURE RESEARCH DIRECTIONS

As a foundational declarative knowledge representation model for SOC-based services, ontology is a field ripe for future research. The lack of a universally agreed-upon ontology that encompasses all concepts used by the services currently results in partner organizations having varied interpretations of semantics in their services. However, the potential impact of future research on ontology alignment is not just significant, it's transformative. It could lead to partner organizations harmonizing their ontologies and establishing mutual understanding, enabling autonomous information integration from different sources and facilitating service-based application interoperability. This potential impact should not just inspire optimism, but also presents a sense of hope for the future of SOC-based services.

While many academic and industry proposals have aimed to tackle interoperability issues in IoT-based information systems, significant challenges persist. The absence of standards and innovative technologies poses major obstacles in developing IoT-based service applications. This underscores the pressing need for research advancements to create semantically interoperable platforms spanning different IoT domains. It is a call to action for future work, particularly in developing standards and technologies. Potential contributions are crucial in addressing these challenges, and in future research, ontology alignment-related exercises will play an important role.

In summary, a more thorough evaluation of the current research solutions that enable industry digitalization is needed. This evaluation, as well as more case studies and field studies, necessitates a collaborative effort from all stakeholders. Further research should include practical initiatives to address critical industry-specific challenges like timeliness and safety. It is important to note that these initiatives will use various software-based tools, which are crucial in digitalization.

CONCLUSION

The IoT-based industrial applications face various challenges, such as low-memory devices and network limitations, which underscore the urgent need for reliable software architectures. These challenges, highlight the pressing need for dependable software architectures. The recent focus on the convergence of service-oriented computing and IoT offers a promising solution to these challenges. This convergence, leveraging the robust infrastructure of the service orientation, can alleviate these issues. As a result, the demand for dependable software architectures has never been more pressing. These architectures are crucial to meet the quality requirements of new emerging technologies and the complex quality challenges they bring. This chapter presents a few industry-specific application reviews on service orientation and IoT technology-based software architectures.

The chapter meticulously gathered, evaluated, and synthesized the reviewed architecture knowledge, including design technologies, application area, and evaluation related to advantages. This knowledge is invaluable as the current trends are promising, and there is increasing interest in designing scalable service-oriented IoT technologies for use in different application areas. The importance of this knowledge cannot be overstated, as it forms the foundation for the future of service-providing technologies and highlights several opportunities for further academic study. In addition, IoT applications rely on real-time context data and allow information to be sent to drive users' behaviours in intelligent supply chain environments. These IoT-based solutions are mostly tailored for vertical applications and systems, utilizing knowledge only from business areas. However, to realize IoT's full potential, these specialized silo applications must be replaced with horizontal collaborative applications, including knowledge acquisition and sharing capabilities.

This chapter provides an overview of the impact of globalization and digitalization on supply chain operations management. It includes the emerging trends of increased Internet of Things (IoT) utilization for decision-support systems, which are computer-based systems that support decision-making activities, in supply chain operations. Gathering and analyzing business operational data to provide services for stakeholders is essential. Designing Decision-Support Systems Using IoT and Data Processing Systems. In addition, a knowledge-based approach to designing and implementing operational service supports is presented in this chapter with the help of a business case.

REFERENCES

Aazam, M., & Huh, E. N. (2014). "Fog computing and smart gateway based communication for cloud of things," in Proceedings of the 2nd IEEE International Conference on Future Internet of Things and Cloud (FiCloud' 14), 464–470, Barcelona, Spain, August 2014. DOI: 10.1109/FiCloud.2014.83

Atzori, L., Iera, A., & Morabito, G. (2011). IoT: Giving a social structure to the internet of things. *IEEE Communications Letters*, 15(11), 1193–1195. DOI: 10.1109/LCOMM.2011.090911.111340

Baader, F., Calvanese, D., McGuinness, D., Nardi, D., & Patel-Schneider, P. (Eds.). (2002). *The Description Logic Handbook*. Cambridge University Press.

Bardhan, P. (2003). *International Trade Growth and Development: Essays*. Wiley-Blackwell. DOI: 10.1002/9780470752777

Barnaghi, P., Presser, M., & Moessner, K. (2010). "Publishing Linked Sensor Data", in *Proceedings of the 3rd International Workshop on Semantic Sensor Networks*.

Berners-Lee, T. (2000). *Weaving the Web: The Original Design and Ultimate Design of the World Wide Web by its inventor*. Harper Business.

Bonomi, F., Milito, R., Natarajan, P., & Zhu, J. (2014). *"Fog computing: a platform for internet of things and analytics," in Big Data and Internet of Things: A Road Map for Smart Environments*. Springer.

Bonomi, F., Milito, R., Zhu, J., & Addepalli, S. (2012). "Fog computing and its role in the internet of things," in *Proceedings of the 1st ACM MCC Workshop on Mobile Cloud Computing*, 13–16, 2012. DOI: 10.1145/2342509.2342513

Bordel Sánchez, B., Alcarria, R., Sánchez de Rivera, D., & Robles, T. (2018). Process execution in CyberPhysical Systems using cloud and Cyber-Physical Internet services. *The Journal of Supercomputing*, 74(8), 4127–4169. DOI: 10.1007/s11227-018-2416-4

Broy, M., Cengarle, M. V., & Geisberger, E. (2012). Cyber-Physical Systems: Imminent Challenges. In Large-Scale Complex IT Syst. Dev., Operat. and Manag. - 17th Monterey Workshop, volume 7539 of LNCS, 1–28.

Cardoso, J., Sheth, A., Miller, J., Arnold, J., & Kochut, K. (2004). Quality of service for workflows and web service processes. *Journal of Web Semantics*, 1(3), 281–308. DOI: 10.1016/j.websem.2004.03.001

Cheng, H., Xue, L., Wang, P., Zeng, P., & Yu, H. (2017). Ontology-based web service integration for flexible manufacturing systems. In 15th Int. Conf. on Ind. Inf., pages 351–356. IEEE. DOI: 10.1109/INDIN.2017.8104797

Ciortea, A., Mayer, S., & Michahelles, F. (2018). Repurposing Manufacturing Lines on the Fly with Multi-agent Systems for the Web of Things. In Proc. of the 17th Int. Conf. on Autonomous Agents and Multi-Agent Systems, pages 813–822. Int. Found. for Autonomous Agents and Multiagent Systems / ACM.

Colitti, W., Steenhaut, K., & Caro, N. De., (2011). "Integrating Wireless Sensor Networks with the Web", Extending the Internet to Low power and Lossy Networks (IP+SN).

Colucci, S., Di Noia, T., Pinto, A., Ruta, M., Ragone, A., & Tinelli, E. (2007). A Nonmonotonic Approach to Semantic Matchmaking and Request Refinement in E-Marketplaces. *International Journal of Electronic Commerce*, 12(2), 127–154. DOI: 10.2753/JEC1086-4415120205

Cory, A., Henson, J., Pschorr, K., Sheth, A. P., & Thirunarayan, K. (2009). "Sem-SOS: Semantic sensor Observation Service", in *Proceedings of the International Symposium on Collaborative Technologies and Systems*.

Courbis, C., & Finkelstein, A. (2005). Weaving Aspects into Web Service Orchestrations, in *Proceeding of International Conference of Web Services (ICWS '05)*, July 2005. DOI: 10.1109/ICWS.2005.129

De Virgilio, R., Di Sciascio, E., Ruta, M., Scioscia, F., & Torlone, R. (2011). Semantic-based rfid data management. In *Unique Radio Innovation for the 21st Century* (pp. 111–141). Springer. DOI: 10.1007/978-3-642-03462-6_6

Gochhayat, S. P., Kaliyar, P., Conti, M., Tiwari, P., Prasath, V. B. S., Gupta, D., & Khanna, A. (2018). LISA: Lightweight context-aware IoT service architecture. *Journal of Cleaner Production*, 212, 1345–1356. DOI: 10.1016/j.jclepro.2018.12.096

Gochhayat, S. P., Kaliyar, P., Conti, M., Tiwari, P., Prasath, V. B. S., Gupta, D., & Khanna, A. (2018). LISA: Lightweight context-aware IoT service architecture. *Journal of Cleaner Production*, 212, 1345–1356. DOI: 10.1016/j.jclepro.2018.12.096

Gubbi, J., Buyya, R., Marusic, S., & Palaniswami, M. (2013). Internet of Things (IoT): A vision, architectural elements, and future directions. *Future Generation Computer Systems*, 29(7), 1645–1660. DOI: 10.1016/j.future.2013.01.010

Hejazi, H., Rajab, H., Cinkler, T., & Lengyel, L. (2018). Survey of platforms for massive IoT. In Proceedings of the 2018 IEEE International Conference on Future IoT Technologies (Future IoT), Eger, Hungary, 18–19 January 2018; 1–8. DOI: 10.1109/FIOT.2018.8325598

Hejazi, H., Rajab, H., Cinkler, T., & Lengyel, L. (2018). Survey of platforms for massive IoT. In Proceedings of the 2018 IEEE International Conference on Future IoT Technologies (Future IoT), Eger, Hungary, 18–19 January 2018; 1–8. DOI: 10.1109/FIOT.2018.8325598

Ibaseta, D., García, A., Álvarez, M., Garzón, B., Díez, F., Coca, P., Pero, C. D., & Molleda, J. (2021). Monitoring and control of energy consumption in building using WoT: A novel approach for smart retrofit. *Sustainable Cities and Society*, 65, 102637. DOI: 10.1016/j.scs.2020.102637

Jakl, A., Schoffer, L., Husinsky, M., & Wagner, M. (2018), Augmented Reality for Industry 4.0: Architecture and User Experience, In Proceeding of the 11th Forum Media Technology, CER-WS, 38-42.

Jandl, C., Nurgazina, J., Schoffer, L., Reichl, C., Wagner, M., & Moser, T. (2019). SensiTrack – A Privacy by Design Concept for Industrial IoT Applications, In *Proceeding of the 24th IEEE International Conference on Emerging Technologies and Factory Automation*, 10-13 September, Zaragoza, Spain, 1782-1789. DOI: 10.1109/ETFA.2019.8869186

Jeschke, S., Brecher, C., Meisen, T., Ozdemir, D., & Eschert, T. (2017), Industrial Internet of Things and Cyber Manufacturing Systems, In Industrial Internet of Things, Springer, 3-19.

Johnson, M. E. (2006, May–June). Supply chain management: Technology, globalization, and policy at a crossroads. *Informs*, 36(3), 191–193.

Keskinock, P., & Tayur, S. (2001). Quantitative analysis of Internet-enabled supply chain. *Interfaces*, 31(2), 70–89. DOI: 10.1287/inte.31.2.70.10626

Khan, R., Khan, S. U., Zaheer, R., & Khan, S. (2012). Future Internet: the internet of things architecture, possible applications and key challenges, In Proceedings of the 10th International Conference on Frontiers of Information Technology (FIT-12), 257-260, December 2012. DOI: 10.1109/FIT.2012.53

Kim, H. W., Hoque, M. R., Seo, H., & Yang, S. H. (2016). Development of middleware architecture to realize context-aware service in smart home environment. *Computer Science and Information Systems*, 13(2), 427–452. DOI: 10.2298/CSIS150701010H

Lasi, H., Fettke, P., Kemper, H.-G., Feld, T., & Hoffmann, M. (2014). Industry 4.0. BISE, 6(4):239–242. Lastra, J. L. M. and Delamer, I. M. (2006). Semantic Web Services in Factory Automation: Fundamental Insights and Research Roadmap. *IEEE Transactions on Industrial Informatics*, 2(1), 1–11.

Lee, H. L., & Billington, C. (1992). Managing supply chain inventories: Pitfalls and opportunities. *Sloan Management Review*, 33(3), 65–77.

Lee, J., Kao, H.-A., & Yang, S. (2014). Service Innovation and Smart Analytics for Industry 4.0 and Big Data Environment. *Procedia CIRP*, 16, 3–8. DOI: 10.1016/j.procir.2014.02.001

Lefort, L., Henson, C., Taylor, K., Barnaghi, P., Compton, M., Corcho, O., Garcia-Castro, R., Graybeal, J., Herzog, A., Janowicz, K., Neuhaus, H., Nikolov, A., & Page, K. (2005). "Semantic Sensor Network XG Final Report", 2011, W3C Incubator Group Report, https://www.w3.org/2005/Incubator/ssn/XGR-ssn/

Li, L., & Horrocks, I. (2004). A software framework for matchmaking based on semantic web technology. *International Journal of Electronic Commerce*, 8(4), 39–60. DOI: 10.1080/10864415.2004.11044307

Lobov, A., Lopez, F. U., Herrera, V. V., Puttonen, J., & Lastra, J. L. M. (2008). Semantic Web Services framework for manufacturing industries. In Int. Conf. on Rob. and Biomim., pages 2104–2108. IEEE.

López, E. J., Jiménez, F. C., Sandoval, G. L., Estrella, F. J. O., Monteón, M. A. M., Muñoz, F., & Leyva, P. A. L. (2022). Technical Considerations for the Conformation of Specific Competences in Mechatronic Engineers in the Context of Industry 4.0 and 5.0. *Processes (Basel, Switzerland)*, 2022(10), 1445. DOI: 10.3390/pr10081445

López, E. J., Jiménez, F. C., Sandoval, G. L., Estrella, F. J. O., Monteón, M. A. M., Muñoz, F., & Leyva, P. A. L. (2022). Technical Considerations for the Conformation of Specific Competences in Mechatronic Engineers in the Context of Industry 4.0 and 5.0. *Processes (Basel, Switzerland)*, 2022(10), 1445. DOI: 10.3390/pr10081445

Maass, W., & Filler, A. (2006). Towards an infrastructure for semantically annotated physical products. INFORMATIK 2006–Informatik für Menschen–Band 2, Beiträge der 36. Jahrestagung der Gesellschaft für Informatik eV (GI).

Marrella, A. (2018). Automated Planning for Business Process Management.

Mashal, I., Alsaryrah, O., Chung, T. Y., Yang, C. Z., Kuo, W. H., & Agrawal, D. P. (2015). Choices for interaction with things on Internet and underlying issues. *Ad Hoc Networks*, 28, 68–90. DOI: 10.1016/j.adhoc.2014.12.006

Minor, M., Montani, S., & Recio-García, J. A. (2014). Process-oriented Case-based Reasoning. *Information Systems*, 40, 103–105. DOI: 10.1016/j.is.2013.06.004

Monostori, L. (2014). Cyber-physical Production Systems: Roots, Expectations and R&D Challenges. *Procedia CIRP*, 17, 9–13. DOI: 10.1016/j.procir.2014.03.115

Montenegro, G., Kushalnagar, N., Hui, J., & Culler, D. (2007). "Transmission of IPv6 packets over IEEE 802.15.4 networks," Internet proposed standard RFC, vol. 4944.

Müller, G. (2018). Workflow Modeling Assistance by Casebased Reasoning. Springer Fachmedien, Wiesbaden. Ocker, F., Kovalenko, I., Barton, K., Tilbury, D., and VogelHeuser, B. (2019). A Framework for Automatic Initialization of Multi-Agent Production Systems Using Semantic Web Technologies. *IEEE Robotics and Automation Letters*, 4(4), 4330–4337.

Ochs, J., Biermann, F., Piotrowski, T., Erkens, F., Nießing, B., Herbst, L., König, N., & Schmitt, R. H. (2021). Fully Automated Cultivation of Adipose-Derived Stem Cells in the Stem Cell Discovery—A Robotic Laboratory for Small-Scale, High-Throughput Cell Production Including Deep Learning-Based Confluence Estimation. *Processes (Basel, Switzerland)*, 2021(9), 575. DOI: 10.3390/pr9040575

Ochs, J., Biermann, F., Piotrowski, T., Erkens, F., Nießing, B., Herbst, L., König, N., & Schmitt, R. H. (2021). Fully Automated Cultivation of Adipose-Derived Stem Cells in the Stem Cell Discovery—A Robotic Laboratory for Small-Scale, High-Throughput Cell Production Including Deep Learning-Based Confluence Estimation. *Processes (Basel, Switzerland)*, 2021(9), 575. DOI: 10.3390/pr9040575

Ortiz, G., Zouai, M., Kazar, O., Garcia-de-Prado, A., & Boubeta-Puig, J. (2022). Atmosphere: Context and situational-aware collaborative IoT architecture for edge-fog-cloud computing. *Computer Standards & Interfaces*, 79, 103550. DOI: 10.1016/j.csi.2021.103550

Pal, K. (2017a). Supply Chain Coordination Based on Web Services. In Chan, H. K., Subramanian, N., & Abdulrahman, M. D. (Eds.), *Supply Chain Management in the Big Data Era* (pp. 137–171). IGI Global Publication. DOI: 10.4018/978-1-5225-0956-1.ch009

Pal, K. (2017b). "A Semantic Web Service Architecture for Supply Chain Management", In 8th International Conference on Ambient Systems, Networks and Technologies (ANT 2017), 999-1004, Procedia Computer Science 109C. DOI: 10.1016/j.procs.2017.05.442

Pal, K. (2018a). "Ontology-Based Web Service Architecture for Retail Supply Chain Management", In 9th International Conference on Ambient Systems, Networks and Technologies (ANT 2018), 985-990, Procedia Computer Science 130. DOI: 10.1016/j.procs.2018.04.101

Pal, K. (2018b). *A Big Data Framework for Decision Making in Supply Chain*, In M. V Kumar, G. D. Putnik, J. Javakrishna, V. M. Pillai, L. Varela (Edited); IGI Publication, September 2018, USA, Chapter 1, IGI Global Publication, Hershey PA, USA.

Pal, K. (2020). "Information Sharing for Manufacturing Supply Chain Management Based on Blockchain Technology", in Dr Idongesit Williams (Eds.), Cross-Industry Use of Blockchain Technology and Opportunities for the Future, Chapter 1, May, IGI Global Publication, Hershey PA, USA. DOI: 10.4018/978-1-7998-3632-2.ch001

Pal, K., & Karakostas, B. (2014). A Multi Agent-Based Service Framework for Supply Chain Management, In the proceeding of International Conference on Ambient Systems, Networks and Technology. *Procedia Computer Science*, 32, 53–60. DOI: 10.1016/j.procs.2014.05.397

Pal, K., & Ul-Haque, A. (2000). *Internet of Things and Blockchain Technology in Apparel Manufacturing Supply Chain Data Management*", In the proceeding of 11th International Conference on Ambient Systems, Networks and Technologies (ANT-2020), Procedia Computer Science, pp. 450- 457, April 6-9, Warsaw, Poland.

Pal, K., & Ul-Haque, A. (2023). *Internet of Things Impact on Supply Chain Management*", In the proceeding of 14th International Conference on Ambient Systems, Networks and Technologies (ANT-2023), Procedia Computer Science, 478-485. DOI: 10.1016/j.procs.2023.03.061

Pal, K., Ul-Haque, A., & Shakshuki, E. (2024). *Supply Chain Transport Management, Use of Electric Vehicles, Review of Security and Privacy for Cyber-Physical Transportation Ecosystem and Related solutions*", In the proceeding of 15th International Conference on Ambient Systems, Networks and Technologies (ANT-2020), Procedia Computer Science, 135-142, April 23-25, Hasselt, Belgium. DOI: 10.1016/j.procs.2024.06.008

Posada, J., Toro, C., Barandiaran, I., Oyarzun, D., Stricker, D., de Amicis, R., Pinto, E. B., Eisert, P., Döllner, J., & Vallarino, I. (2015). Visual computing as a key enabling technology for industrie 4.0 and industrial internet. *IEEE Computer Graphics and Applications*, 35(2), 26–40. DOI: 10.1109/MCG.2015.45 PMID: 25807506

Prahalad, C. K., & Mashelkar, R. A. (2010, July-August). Innovation's Holy Grail. *Harvard Business Review*, 1–11.

Puttonen, J., Lobov, A., & Lastra, J. L. M. (2013). Semantics-Based Composition of Factory Automation Processes Encapsulated by Web Services. *IEEE Transactions on Industrial Informatics*, 9(4), 2349–2359. DOI: 10.1109/TII.2012.2220554

Puttonen, J., Lobov, A., Soto, M. A. C., & Lastra, J. L. M. (2010). A Semantic Web Services-based approach for production systems control. *Advanced Engineering Informatics*, 24(3), 285–299. DOI: 10.1016/j.aei.2010.05.012

Razzaque, M. A., Milojevic-Jevric, M., Palade, A., & Clarke, S. (2016, February). (2o16). Middleware for Internet of Things: A Survey. *IEEE Internet of Things Journal*, 3(1), 70–95. DOI: 10.1109/JIOT.2015.2498900

Razzaque, M. A., Milojevic-Jevric, M., Palade, A., & Clarke, S. (2016). Middleware for Internet of Things: A Survey. *IEEE Internet of Things Journal*, 3(1), 70–95. DOI: 10.1109/JIOT.2015.2498900

Roblek, V., Maja, M., & Alojz, K. (2016). A Complex View of Industry 4.0. *SAGE Open*, 6(2), 1–11. DOI: 10.1177/2158244016653987

Russomanno, D. J., Kothari, C. R., & Thomas, O. A. (2005). "Building a Sensor Ontology: A Practical Approach Leveraging ISO and OGC Models", in the 2005 International Conference on Artificial Intelligence, 637-643.

Ruta, M., Colucci, S., Scioscia, F., Di Sciascio, E., & Donini, F. M. (2011). Finding commonalities in RFID semantic streams. *Procedia Computer Science*, 5, 857–864. DOI: 10.1016/j.procs.2011.07.118

Said, O., & Masud, M. (2013). Towards internet of things: Survey and future vision. *International Journal of Computer Networks*, 5(1), 1–17.

Schneider, M., Hippchen, B., Abeck, S., Jacoby, M., & Herzog, R. (2018). Enabling IoT Platform Interoperability Using a Systematic Development Approach by Example. In Proceedings of the 2018 Global Internet of Things Summit (GIoTS), Bilbao, Spain, 4–7, June 2018; 1–6. DOI: 10.1109/GIOTS.2018.8534549

Schneider, M., Hippchen, B., Abeck, S., Jacoby, M., & Herzog, R. (2018). Enabling IoT Platform Interoperability Using a Systematic Development Approach by Example. In Proceedings of the 2018 Global Internet of Things Summit (GIoTS), Bilbao, Spain, 4–7, June 2018; 1–6. DOI: 10.1109/GIOTS.2018.8534549

Sciullo, L., Gigli, L., Trotta, A., & Di Felice, D. (2020). WoT Store: Management resources and applications on the web of things. *Internet of Things : Engineering Cyber Physical Human Systems*, 9, 100164. DOI: 10.1016/j.iot.2020.100164

Seiger, R., Huber, S., & Schlegel, T. (2018). Toward an execution system for self-healing workflows in cyber-physical systems. *Software & Systems Modeling*, 17(2), 551–572. DOI: 10.1007/s10270-016-0551-z

Stiglitz, J. E. (2017). *Globalization and its discontents revisited: Anti-globalization in the era of Trump*. WW Norton & Company.

Stojmenovic, I., & Wen, S. (2014). The fog computing paradigm: scenario and security issues, In Proceedings of the Federated Conference on Computer Science and Information Systems (FedCSIS-14), 1-8, IEEE, Warsaw, Poland, September 2014. DOI: 10.15439/2014F503

Swaminathan, J. M. (2000). *Supply chain management*. International Encyclopedia of the Social and Behavioural Sciences, Elsevier Sciences.

Varelas, G., Voutsakis, E., Raftopoulou, P., Petrakis, E. G. M., & Milios, E. (2005). Semantic Similarity methods in WordNet and their application to information retrieval on the Web, *Proceedings of the 7th annual ACM international workshop on web information and data management*, Bremen, Germany. DOI: 10.1145/1097047.1097051

Wahab, M. (2004). Globalisation and ODR: Dynamics of change in e-commerce dispute settlement. *International Journal of Law and Information Technology*, 12(1), 123–152. DOI: 10.1093/ijlit/12.1.123

Wu, M., Lu, T. J., Ling, F. Y., Sun, J., & Du, H. Y. (2010). Research on the architecture of internet of things, In Proceedings of the 3rd International Conference on Advanced Computer Theory and Engineering (ICACTE-10), 5, 484-487, IEEE, Chengdu, China, August 2010.

Zhu, W., Zhou, G., Yen, I. L., & Bastani, F. (2015). A PT-SOA Model for CPS/IoT Services, In *Proceedings of the 2015 IEEE International Conference on Web Services*, New York, NY, USA, 27 June – 2 July 2015. DOI: 10.1109/ICWS.2015.91

ADDITIONAL READING

Ali, M. (2021). *Remote Work and Sustainable Changes for the Future of Global Business.* IGI Global. https://www.igi-global.com/book/remote-work-sustainable-changes-future/264375

Ali, M. (2022). *Future Role of Sustainable Innovative Technologies in Crisis Management.* IGI Global. https://www.igi-global.com/book/future-role-sustainable-innovative-technologies/281281

Ali, M. (2023). *Shifting Paradigms in the Rapidly Developing Global Digital Ecosystem: A GCC Perspective.* In Digital Entrepreneurship and Co-Creating Value Through Digital Encounters (pp. 145-166). IGI Global. https://www.igi-global.com/chapter/shifting-paradigms-in-the-rapidly-developing-global-digital-ecosystem/323525

Ali, M. (2023). T*axonomy of Industry 4.0 Technologies in Digital Entrepreneurship and Co-Creating Value.* In *Digital Entrepreneurship and Co-Creating Value Through Digital Encounters* (pp. 24–55). IGI Global., https://www.igi-global.com/chapter/taxonomy-of-industry-40-technologies-in-digital-entrepreneurship-and-co-creating-value/323520 DOI: 10.4018/978-1-6684-7416-7.ch002

Ali, M., & Wood-Harper, T. (2021). *Fostering Communication and Learning with Underutilized Technologies in Higher Education.* IGI Global. https://www.igi-global.com/book/fostering-communication-learning-underutilized-technologies/244593

Ali, M., Wood-Harper, T., & Kutar, M. (2023). Multi-Perspectives of Contemporary Digital Transformation Models of Complex Innovation Management. In *Digital Entrepreneurship and Co-Creating Value Through Digital Encounters* (pp. 79–96). IGI Global., https://www.igi-global.com/chapter/multi-perspectives-of-contemporary-digital-transformation-models-of-complex-innovation-management/323522 DOI: 10.4018/978-1-6684-7416-7.ch004

Ali, M. B. (2021). Internet of Things (IoT) to Foster Communication and Information Sharing: A Case of UK Higher Education. In Ali, M. B., & Wood-Harper, T. (Eds.), *Fostering Communication and Learning With Underutilized Technologies in Higher Education* (pp. 1–20). IGI Global., https://www.igi-global.com/chapter/internet-of-things-iot-to-foster-communication-and-information-sharing/262718/ DOI: 10.4018/978-1-7998-4846-2.ch001

Ali, M. B., & Wood-Harper, T. (2022). Artificial Intelligence (AI) as a Decision-Making Tool to Control Crisis Situations. In *Future Role of Sustainable Innovative Technologies in Crisis Management.* IGI Global., https://www.igi-global.com/chapter/artificial-intelligence-ai-as-a-decision-making-tool-to-control-crisis-situations/298931 DOI: 10.4018/978-1-7998-9815-3.ch006

Ali, M. B., Wood-Harper, T., & Ramlogan, R. (2020). A Framework Strategy to Overcome Trust Issues on Cloud Computing Adoption in Higher Education. In Modern Principles, Practices, and Algorithms for Cloud Security (pp. 162-183). IGI Global. https://www.igi-global.com/chapter/a-framework-strategy-to-overcome-trust-issues-on-cloud-computing-adoption-in-higher-education/238907/

Chapter 16
Empowering Digital Business Innovation:
AI, Blockchain, Marketing, and Entrepreneurship for Dynamic Growth

Pratichi Dash

Centurion University of Technology and Management, Bhubaneswar, India

Aryan

https://orcid.org/0000-0001-8145-8950

Maharishi Markandeshwar (Deemed), India

Sehrish Javaid

https://orcid.org/0009-0004-4949-3835

Central University of Kashmir, Ganderbal, India

Mohd Arif Hussain

https://orcid.org/0009-0005-8935-5514

Shadan College of Engineering and Technology, Hyderabad, India

ABSTRACT

This chapter examines how digital technologies; Artificial Intelligence, blockchain technology, digital marketing, and digital entrepreneurship have revolutionized innovation and growth of contemporary businesses. This study focuses on the practical aspect of business operations, customer relations, and security issues that benefit from applications of AI solutions like dynamic pricing, optimal route selection, and fraud detection, among others. The capabilities of blockchain technology is examined to bring transparency and security in the business transaction by having

DOI: 10.4018/979-8-3693-5966-2.ch016

the ability to develop, implement and regulate smart contracts. The efficiency of various online marketing techniques such as advertising and content marketing is evaluated to grab the attention of the targeted customer base and increase their loyalty. Furthermore, it highlights the areas of digital entrepreneurship, examples of how technology assists individuals in creating new business models and practical applications of these technologies in industries as illustrated by Uber and Airbnb are discussed in detail.

1. INTRODUCTION

Successful firms do not depend solely on the technologies they adopt, but, more importantly, build on the strategies that their leaders deploy (Ismail, Khater, & Zaki, 2017). This research chapter "Empowering Digital Business Innovation: AI, Blockchain, Marketing, and Entrepreneurship for Dynamic Growth" analyses the enormous power of emerging technologies in the digital business sector. Leveraging new technology has opened up new opportunities as well as brought about new challenges in the business arenas across the globe. While dealing with these issues, the use of information and communication technologies and advanced technologies like artificial intelligence, blockchain, digital marketing techniques and approaches to competition became critical for companies to sustain growth and gain competitive advantage. This chapter, "Empowering Digital Business Innovation: AI, Blockchain, Marketing, and Entrepreneurship for Dynamic Growth," aims to explore how these technologies are revolutionizing business practices and entrepreneurship, driving dynamic growth in the digital economy. The technological capability and power of digital transformation applications, such as for example the Internet of Things (IoT), big data, cloud computing, and mobile technologies, is in terms of computing power, data storage and information distribution in many cases significantly higher than in previous technology-driven transformations (Nadkarni & Prügl 2021).

1.1 The Imperative of Digital Business Innovation

As the importance of the digital business domain increases, the importance of digital business innovation also becomes imperative. Digital business innovation can be described as activities that evolve business models in delivering new or better customer value through digital operational technologies. Due to the increasing rate of technological changes there is pressure to adapt to any new change in technology to be able to survive in the market. This is in line with arguments made by Westerman et al. (2014), who stated that while digital transformation can entail the adoption of new technologies and systems, it also refers to the ability of an organisation to change and pursue digital advancements in this manner.

1.2 The Role of AI in Business Transformation

Disruptive innovations, such as artificial intelligence (AI), are changing the rules of competition within industries all over the globe (Reim, Åström, & Eriksson, 2020). Regardless of its classification, artificial intelligence has become one of the most significant and impactful trends in modern businesses. For instance, machine learning, natural language processing, and advanced analytics help organizations reduce manual work, process large data sets, and deliver more targeted engagement with customers. In the view of Davenport and Ronanki (2018), decision-making and operational performance are some of the areas that can be transformed by AI to improve business outcomes. This chapter will justify the growing role of AI in a broader scheme of the digital transformation of enterprises based on the analysis of various cases and examples.

1.3 Blockchain Technology: Enhancing Security and Transparency

Currently, the application of the blockchain technology tends to pose numerous values in advancing the business, especially in the factors of security and vulnerability. This is vital in establishing trust in digital interactions since it offers security, transparency, and immutability of transactions due to decentralization. Various sectors within business and entrepreneurship can benefit from blockchain, which can offer better security and more efficient systems for aspects such as supply chain and financial activities, according to Tapscott and Tapscott (2016). The benefits the Blockchain technology include: Trust, Openness, Independence, Speed, Robustness, Global Nature and Effectiveness among other benefits (Morabito, 2017).

Innovative Digital Marketing Strategies

Digital marketing is in a process of experiencing new transformations due to the introduction of AI and blockchain solutions. Modern techniques in advertising with the application of AI in enhancing the ways in which consumers are monitored, the messages that are given, and the general advertising campaigns that are run. Also, it provides data integrity, which leads to strong trust and security among consumers due to the implementation of modern blockchain technology. According to Chaffey and Ellis-Chadwick (2009), the use of such technologies in digitally integrated marketing communications can enable the achievement of higher levels of customer engagement and business success.

1.4 The Intersection of Digital Entrepreneurship and Emerging Technologies

Digital entrepreneurship may be defined as the process of establishing new initiatives or transforming existing enterprises through the use of digital technology systems. The use of AI technology combined with the blockchain, and marketing digitalization offers both opportunities and concerns for business startups. Nambisan (2017) pointed out that digital technologies allow entrepreneurs to create, develop, and expand at high velocity, as well as address massive market opportunities worldwide. Nevertheless, they are not devoid of some limitations such as the risks of cyber-attacks as well as increased government regulations.

Figure 1. Conceptual Framework for Empowering Digital Business Innovation

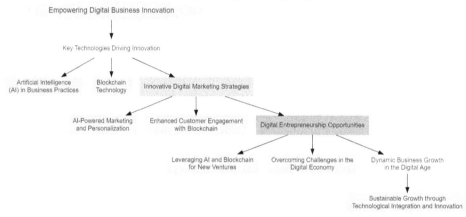

The conceptual framework in Figure 1 illustrates how AI, blockchain, and digital marketing drive digital business innovation. At the center, these technologies support innovative marketing strategies and create new opportunities for digital entrepreneurship. The integration of AI and blockchain enhances customer engagement and personalization. Entrepreneurs leverage these technologies to overcome challenges and drive dynamic business growth, emphasizing sustainable development through technological innovation.

2. LITERATURE REVIEW

The literature review analyzes the complex function of AI in the modern business contexts. AI strategic applications have been identified to be effective in altering operational areas and creating new opportunities in process improvement, decision-making and customers' relations. Russell and Norvig (2020) state that AI can perform a variety of repetitive tasks, thus freeing up human employees for value-added activities. The same applies to customer service, for example, turning to artificial intelligence systems to answer customers' questions through chatbots, which shortens response time and decreases operations costs, according to **Huang and Rust (2018)**. Furthermore, AI helps businesses predict demand and supply, and in turn deliver accurate and targeted marketing messages, according to the study by **Chen et al. (2012)**. Such advancements speak a lot about AI as one of the key drivers of efficiency and competitive advantage.

Similarly, the literature identifies the factors that make blockchain technology disruptive in terms of altering the conventional business models. Apart from cryptocurrency which is its traditional application, there significant benefits that come with the deployment of the blockchain technology in business actions; security, transparency and trust. **Nakamoto (2008)** has emphasized that through utilization of the blockchain approach, businesses can gain a system that provides a high degree of transaction transparency and greatly minimises the chance of fraudulent records being inserted. Furthermore, Tapscott **and Tapscott (2016)** have also discussed the aspect of supply chain, digital identity and financial transactions in the framework of blockchain. These applications show how blockchain technology has the possibilities of summing up different types of businesses and creating new and more efficient business models.

Though both AI and blockchain are promising frontiers of digital innovation, their application is not exempt from difficulties. The literature highlights the importance of implementation challenges and concern of ethics. **Dwivedi et. al., (2021)** observed that there are still some challenges that organizations face when implementing AI such as high capital costs at the onset of implementation and technical factors which SMEs may not be able to overcome. But it also stimulates important questions about data privacy, bias in algorithms, and the accountability of AI decision making for both machines and organizations **(Binns, 2018)**. Similarly, blockchain implementation hurdles, such as scalability issues and regulatory uncertainties, necessitate careful navigation **(Swan, 2015)**. Acknowledging and mitigating these challenges is imperative for harnessing the full potential of AI and blockchain in driving digital business innovation.

3. AI IN DRIVING BUSINESS INNOVATION

Artificial intelligence has now become crucial in any form of business and plays a significant role in advancing organizations' activities. AI technologies involve an array of skills such as; machine learning, natural language, computer vision, and predictive analytics which can be useful in improving a firm's performance. Brown et al. (2021) highlight how AI can drive customer experience, including recommending products and services that will not only meet the customer's needs but also make them have a certain level of loyalty towards certain firms. Further, the integration of artificial intelligence predicts the trends in the market and thus provides marketers with an ability to be present in the right place, at the right time and for right products as recommended by Chen et al (2012).

- *Customer-Centric Applications:* Perhaps, one of the most profound areas of focus in AI is the ability to improve and reshape the customer experiences through recommendation systems. It allows the recognition of user preferences, peculiarities, and interests by unleashing big data sets of user-activity patterns while providing relevant content, products, and services. It also promotes customer satisfaction, which in turn creates loyalty with the brand and increases the likelihood of the client to patronize services from the organization in the long-run (Brown et al., 2021).
- *Operational Optimization:* However, the application of AI within organisations is not limited to the frontline processes of customer interface only, but includes enhancing internal technical and administrative processes as well. AI makes it possible to develop greater efficiency in business processes and decision-makers since it is capable of expert and repetitive tasks. For instance, conversational AI technological solutions are used in customer care interfaces to provide direct responses to inquiries and complaints and facilitate interaction and service delivery in ways that improve quality and efficiency while controlling costs (Huang & Rust, 2018).
- *Data-Driven Decision-Making:* In addition, organizations are bestowed with the bench strength in terms of their AI-enabled capacity to turn raw data into insights, helping them make better evidence-based solutions and plans. By navigating complex data through methods like data mining, predictive analytics, textual analytics, and much more, businesses are able to surface insights, develop strategies in relation to the market, and discover new trends (Davenport et al., 2020).

However, despite the myriad benefits that AI offers, its adoption is not without challenges and considerations that warrant careful attention.

- **Data Management and Privacy Concerns**: Effective AI implementation necessitates robust data management practices to ensure the quality, integrity, and security of data inputs. With the proliferation of data breaches, privacy infringements, and regulatory mandates such as the General Data Protection Regulation (GDPR), organizations face mounting pressure to safeguard sensitive data and uphold stringent privacy standards. As such, data governance frameworks, encryption protocols, and anonymization techniques are pivotal in mitigating privacy risks and ensuring regulatory compliance (Binns, 2018).

- **Talent Shortages and Skills Gap**: Another critical challenge confronting organizations in their AI endeavors pertains to the scarcity of AI talent and the widening skills gap in the workforce. With the demand for AI expertise outpacing the available talent pool, organizations grapple with recruitment challenges, skill shortages, and the need for upskilling and reskilling initiatives to cultivate a proficient workforce capable of leveraging AI technologies effectively (Dwivedi et al., 2021).

In examining successful AI implementation, notable case studies underscore the tangible impact of AI on business performance and competitive advantage.

Table 1. Case Studies of AI usage and their tangible impact

Case Study	Description
Netflix	Utilizing AI algorithms, Netflix delivers personalized content recommendations tailored to individual user preferences. This enhances user engagement, satisfaction, and subscription retention rates.
Amazon and Spotify	Companies like Amazon and Spotify leverage AI-powered recommendation engines to offer targeted product recommendations and curated playlists. This enriches the customer experience and drives business growth.

Table 1 briefly elaborates the example of Netflix, Amazon, and Spotify to demonstrate how they use AI to enrich their customer journey and outcomes.

4. IMPACT OF BLOCKCHAIN ON BUSINESS PROCESSES

Blockchain technology is fundamentally a decentralized, distributed ledger system that records transactions across multiple computers. These records have therefore been called blocks and are interlinked through the use of cryptographic hash values, which create the chain. Each block has a list of new transactions, the date and time, and a link to the previous block, which makes the data sequence complete and immutable. This decentralized architecture also discards dependency on a single or few authorities, as every node in the network has a complete copy of the blockchain adding to the security and transparency.

- Finance: Blockchain finds its use majorly in the finance industry where some of the common players are cryptocurrencies such as Bitcoin and Ethereum. In addition to Cryptocurrencies, blockchain use, helps secure and speed up payments hence eliminating the middleman. Automating the fulfilment of contract terms by directly programming them into code are smart contracts, which offer secure, open and non-modal processes (Nakamoto, 2008).
- Supply Chain Management: In the context of supply chain management, the advantages of blockchain are seen in the area of transparency and tracking. At any stage of the supply chain various entities can put the details on the block chain and it provides the real time details about the origin, flow and status of the product. This decreases fraud and boosts financial performance by enhancing organisational productivity and inventory control (Kshetri, 2018).
- Healthcare: It is also pertinent to note that the use of blockchain technology is helping healthcare to transform as well. It also makes sure that the electronic records of the patient allow easy sharing by the various health organizations and maintain the confidentiality and accuracy of the posted records. Further, blockchain can help in the easy monitoring of pharmaceutical supply chain and make confirmations regarding the actual and rightful drugs (Agbo et al., 2019).

4.1 Benefits of Blockchain Technology

Blockchain technology offers numerous advantages that significantly enhance business processes across various industries:

- Transparency: The use of open-sourced databases that are viewable to all stakeholders ensures that all parties see each transaction. It also increases confidence among the stakeholders, since all actions and decisions are traceable and documented in real-time (Pilkington, 2016).
- Security: The use of blockchain comes with the highest levels of security because of its cryptographic nature. Information exchanged is now secure, and the structure of the ledger is decentralized, so it cannot be hacked or involved in fraudulent activities. According to Yli-Huumo et al. (2016), once data is stored in the blockchain, it cannot be changed without affecting all subsequent blocks to include the change and such a change has to go through the network.

- Efficiency: Since most of the transactions are direct, block chain simplified functions and cuts on expenses. It also opens an opportunity for transactions to be concluded more expeditiously and with less clerical mistakes. Smart contracts are the self-executing operations that also prevent the interference of a third party, thus leading to improved operational performance (Christidis Devetsikiotis, 2016).

4.2 Challenges and Future Prospects

Despite its potential, blockchain technology faces several hurdles that must be overcome for widespread adoption.

- Regulatory Uncertainty: Even today, there are conflicts between national and international legislations regarding the application of blockchain and cryptocurrencies. The current legal framework lacks legal unity with different jurisdictions having different approaches to the regulation of businesses, thus generally causing legal ambiguity. When it comes to technology acceptance, especially when it is related to financing, it is imperative that regulatory requirements are clearly defined and to conform to those standards across the globe (Zohar, 2015).
- Technical Complexities: Blockchain technology can present challenges especially when it comes to the operation, as well as cost consideration. It is heavily work-intensive, and the ability to expand the size of the block-chain networks is still relatively difficult. Moreover, the adoption of block chain can cause some complex challenges such as the inability to integrate with the existing systems (Croman et al., 2016).

Future Prospects: The future of the blockchain is bright; constant improvements are being made to try to fix the issues that are currently present with the technology. For instance, Layer 2 scale solutions that provide deeper scalability while improving security and the advancement of more efficient consensus algorithms such as proof of stake are concepts that are moving the adoption needle forward in the right direction (Buterin, 2014). It is anticipated that as the technology continues to grow older its usage will extend across the different fields as organizations continually look for ways to exploit the technology for higher and more diverse efficiency.

In summary, blockchain technology offers transformative potential across various industries by enhancing transparency, security, and efficiency. However, businesses must navigate regulatory uncertainties and technical challenges to fully realize its benefits. As advancements continue, blockchain is poised to play an increasingly integral role in modern business processes, driving innovation and operational excellence.

5. MARKETING IN THE DIGITAL AGE

In the digital age, marketing has transformed into a sophisticated, data-driven discipline that leverages advanced technologies to target and engage consumers with unprecedented precision. This section seeks to analyze the new trends in online advertising that are revolutionizing the way businesses market their goods and services to customers.

5.1 Digital Marketing Tools and Techniques

Digital marketing is considered very effective in the era of Industry 4.0 because it can attract consumers quickly and with a wider reach (Darma, & Noviana, 2020). Digital marketing encompasses a broad range of tools and techniques designed to reach and influence consumers through online channels. Key methods include:

- Social Media Marketing: Some of the social tools that many companies use include Facebook, Instagram, Twitter and LinkedIn, whereby they can post information that market their products or services. Social media marketing can target consumers directly and create associations around a product and brand, in turn creating consumers' community (Tuten & Solomon, 2017).
- Search Engine Optimization (SEO): SEO processes aim to improve search engine visibility of the content in order to place it higher on the SERP list. This makes the information visible and it will help to drive organic traffic to those websites. SEO strategies include keyword identification, content development, and website enhancements (Harris, 2021).
- Content Marketing: This strategy involves identifying the creation and sharing of useful, timely, and related content in a regular and proficient manner to engage the target market. While delivering valuable information, companies build credibility and, therefore, create a call to profitable customer action (Pulizzi, 2012).

5.2 Data-Driven Marketing and Consumer Behavior Analysis

The digital age has brought an expanded availability of information, and now marketers can explore customers' behavior and tastes. Data-driven marketing involves collecting and analyzing data to inform marketing strategies and decisions. Key aspects include:

- **Behavioral Targeting**: By tracking online behavior, businesses can create detailed consumer profiles and deliver personalized marketing messages that resonate with individual preferences and past interactions (Wedel & Kannan, 2016).
- **Predictive Analytics**: Using advanced analytics techniques, marketers can predict future consumer behavior based on historical data. This enables proactive marketing strategies and more effective allocation of resources (Shmueli & Koppius, 2011).

5.3 Case Studies of Effective Digital Marketing Campaigns

Table 2 concisely presents the case studies of Nike and Coca-Cola, highlighting how their digital marketing campaigns effectively utilized modern strategies to engage audiences and drive business growth.

Table 2. Case Studies of Effective Digital Marketing Campaigns

Case Study	Description
Nike	Nike's "Just Do It" campaign has been successfully revitalized through digital channels. By leveraging social media influencers and creating viral video content, Nike has engaged a global audience, reinforcing its brand identity and driving sales.
Coca-Cola	The "Share a Coke" campaign is a prime example of personalized marketing. By printing individual names on bottles and encouraging consumers to share their experiences on social media, Coca-Cola created a highly interactive and personal marketing campaign that significantly boosted engagement and sales.

6. ENTREPRENEURSHIP IN FOSTERING DIGITAL INNOVATION

In the modern context, entrepreneurship especially in the areas of digital business plays a crucial role in encouraging innovation. It is a process that seeks to utilize digital technologies in the development of new economies, changing established industries or delivering unique solutions, goods and services. By harnessing the power of digital technologies, entrepreneurs can develop novel business models that address emerging market needs and disrupt existing industries. Support systems, including incubators, accelerators, and various funding sources, provide the necessary resources and guidance to help digital startups succeed. As the digital landscape continues to evolve, the impact of digital entrepreneurship will only grow, fostering a culture of innovation and resilience in the business world.

6.1 Characteristics of Digital Entrepreneurs

Digital entrepreneurs are distinct in their approach to business creation and management. Key characteristics include:

- Tech-Savvy: Digital entrepreneurs are familiar with technologies because it is a core part of their businesses. Such knowledge enables them to come up with products and/or services that are needed in the market at a certain period.
- Innovative Mindset: They are innovative and always on the lookout for innovative methods to consider new avenues or enhance their current business approach or product. This is a total embrace of risk taking and organization of change, which is an important aspect of change management.
- Agility: Digital entrepreneurs are also quite flexible and can easily shift the way they run their enterprises in response to changes within the marketplace as well as new technologies.
- Customer-Centric: They give massive priority to customers, making the necessary analyses of their behaviour in order to deliver goods and services that would meet the customers' needs.

6.2 Innovative Business Models in the Digital Era

Digital entrepreneurs have pioneered various innovative business models that have reshaped industries. Some prominent models include:

- Platform-Based Models: Online marketplaces like Uber, Airbnb or Amazon develop environments that bring buyers and sellers, providers and consumers together and provide infrastructure to manage transactions without possessing the items themselves. This model builds on network effects and allows for its very fast growth.
- Subscription Services: The usage of recurring payment models can be traced back to service industries that allow customers to pay a certain amount of fee in exchange for continued service delivery from the company. The above

model is slow but generates a constant flow of income and at the same time it helps in establishing customer loyalty.

- Freemium Models: In their business model, they provide the essential functionalities without cost, but premium aspects come at a fee. Popularized by platforms such as LinkedIn and Dropbox, this model helps companies capture a vast consumer audience and then convert a certain segment into paying consumers.
- On-Demand Services: Ride-sharing services, like those by Uber and Lyft, have on-demand access which provides comfort and speed to customers, who in today's world are more demanding and want everything at their fingertips.

6.3 Support Systems for Digital Startups

Digital startups require robust support systems to navigate the competitive landscape and achieve sustainable growth. Key support systems include:

- Incubators: Incubators assist young entrepreneurial firms with amenities like space, advice, and outsourced services. They assist the business persons to fine-tune their business concepts and build good market products. Some of them include the Y Combinator, Techstars among others.
- Accelerators: Incubators are fixed-term programs for startups that are designed to offer specific services such as capital, expertise, and connections. These programs are followed by a demo day where the startups have to present their ideas to actual investors. Examples include 500 Startups and MassChallenge.
- Funding: For new startups, it is important to have access to capital to fuel business and new technologies. These include venture capital and firms, angel investors, and companies involved in crowdfunded financing. Government grants and innovation funds that target the start-ups can also be beneficial to the start-ups.

7. INTEGRATING TECHNOLOGIES FOR DYNAMIC BUSINESS GROWTH IN THE DIGITAL AGE

The application of technologies including Artificial Intelligence (AI), blockchain, marketing, and digital entrepreneurship can greatly help in the development of businesses as well as encourage innovations in different fields. Artificial Intelligence (AI) as a discipline that works towards elevating the competencies of machines to human levels, involves processes like learning and decision making. Advanced analytics utilize AI algorithms to analyze considerable amounts of data and make decisions promptly, which helps companies understand the market, foresee buyers' actions, and select suitable solutions for improvement (Russell & Norvig, 2021). Also, the usage of AI algorithms assists in the analysis of the customer data to tailor the marketing strategies, recommendations, advertisements, and other forms of interactions in order to improve satisfaction, loyalty, and overall retention of customers and therefore, increased revenue generation (Sharda et al., 2018). In addition, they help to avoid repetitive tasks and increase the effectiveness of operations, while freeing up human capital for higher-order work as well as implement growth and scalable innovation (Davenport & Ronanki, 2018).

Blockchain on the other hand is a decentralized distributed ledger technology that provides secured, transparent and consensus based record of transactions among a network of computers. On the one hand, the promotion of security and the minimisation of fraud through the use of the product make customers, partners, and stakeholders confident about the business and support its development (Narayanan et al., 2016). Self- executing contracts, which exist as codes on the block chain, improve the execution of trades, decrease bureaucracy, and quicken business procedures pointing to better adaptability and elasticity of the companies (Swan, 2015). Furthermore, it fosters novel business models, as stated in the development of decentralized finance (DeFi) and supply chain traceability to use new revenue sources, enter new markets, and develop value-added services to fuel growth and differentiation (Tapscott & Tapscott, 2016).

Digital marketing utilizes online channels and digital technologies to promote products, services, and brands to target audiences. By reaching the right audience with the right message at the right time, businesses can drive brand awareness, engagement, and conversion rates, fueling growth and revenue (Chaffey & Smith, 2017). Furthermore, data analytics and AI-powered tools enable marketers to measure, analyze, and optimize marketing campaigns in real-time, maximizing the ROI of their marketing efforts and driving sustained growth and profitability. Additionally, digital marketing fosters direct and interactive communication with customers, enabling personalized interactions, feedback collection, and relationship building, driving repeat purchases, referrals, and advocacy, sustaining long-term growth and success (Strauss & Frost, 2020).

Digital entrepreneurship may be defined as the use of digital media and entrepreneurial thinking in the management of digital business ventures. Through the identification of needs, market voids, and opportunities where new products, services, and business models can be introduced, new entrants can challenge fundamental industries and create value within their competitive boundaries (Shane & Venkataraman, 2000). Furthermore, digital entrepreneurs can secure funds from venture capitalist, angel investors, crowdfunding, and government funding to establish the venture with little or no capital investment to create massive and accelerated growth and market penetration (Blank & Dorf, 2020). In addition, other supporting environments like incubators, accelerators, and co-working centers offer vital amenities, guidance, and connections to existing and emerging issues that affect the growth of startups (Isenberg, 2010).

Therefore, the application of AI, blockchain concepts, digital marketing, and digital entrepreneurship fosters business success and adaptability. By integrating artificial intelligence to provide insights, employing the blockchain's capabilities to ensure security and transparency of transactions, digital marketing to expand company's reach and engagement, and digital entrepreneurship to be more agile and innovative, businesses can better understand new opportunities, improve operations, and ensure sustainable success as the world enters into the digital era. It can be used to improve the client satisfaction, optimize the processes as well as find new sources of revenue, thus, these technologies allow organizations to perform successfully in a world that becomes more digital and competitive.

Figure 2. Integration of AI, Blockchain, Digital Marketing, And Digital Entrepreneurship for Business Growth

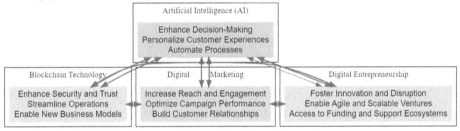

Figure 2 shows four clusters representing AI, blockchain, digital marketing, and digital entrepreneurship. Arrows indicate the integration between these components, highlighting their interconnectedness in driving business growth.

8. CASE STUDY

In the digital age, organizations across various industries are undergoing transformative journeys to embrace digitalization and harness the power of emerging technologies. Through case studies and real-world examples, we explore how these organizations navigate challenges, leverage opportunities, and achieve tangible outcomes in their digital transformation initiatives. These case studies offer valuable insights into the strategies, innovations, and best practices driving dynamic change in the digital landscape.

8.1 UBER

Uber Technologies, a company that was introduced in the year 2009 by two people namely Garrett Camp and Travis Kalanick, has revolutionalized the transport sector, through its on-demand ride hailing services. Uber is an application that facilitates transport contracts by matching drivers and passengers through a smart mobile application which makes Uber cheaper and more available than a regular taxi company. Uber has also diversified from its core corporate value of digital transportation, now offering UberEats, Uber Freight, as well as engaging in science related to self-driving cars, highlighting the company's adaptability and investment in flexible developments.

Artificial Intelligence (AI): Uber uses AI for route optimization, dynamic pricing, and fraud detection. AI optimizes driver routes by analyzing real-time traffic data, adjusts fares in real-time based on demand through surge pricing, and detects fraudulent activities to ensure transaction security.

- Blockchain: Uber explores blockchain to enhance transparency, security, and trust in transactions. Blockchain provides immutable records for accountability, and smart contracts could automate agreements and payments between Uber and drivers.
- Digital Marketing: Uber employs targeted advertising on social media, search engines, and mobile apps to increase user acquisition and retention. Content marketing through blogs, social media, and testimonials builds brand awareness and educates users about services.
- Digital Entrepreneurship: Uber empowers individuals to become digital entrepreneurs by offering flexible driving opportunities. The platform's expansion into UberEats, Uber Freight, and autonomous vehicle technology demonstrates continuous innovation and new business opportunities.

Key Learnings:

- Scalability and Innovation: Uber's ability to scale rapidly across different markets while continuously innovating its service offerings is a testament to its robust digital infrastructure and agile business model.
- User-Centric Design: Focusing on user experience, Uber has developed a user-friendly app that simplifies the process of booking rides, making payments, and tracking trips, significantly enhancing customer satisfaction.

- Regulatory Navigation: Uber's experience highlights the importance of navigating regulatory environments effectively. The company has faced and continues to address various legal and regulatory challenges in different markets.

Challenges:

- Regulatory and Legal Issues: Uber has faced numerous regulatory challenges globally, including legal disputes over the classification of drivers as independent contractors versus employees, local taxi regulations, and licensing requirements.
- Safety and Trust Concerns: Ensuring the safety of passengers and drivers is a major challenge. Uber has implemented various safety features, but incidents still occur, necessitating continuous improvements in safety protocols and trust-building measures.
- Market Competition: Uber faces stiff competition from other ride-hailing services like Lyft, Didi Chuxing, and regional players, requiring constant innovation and competitive strategies to maintain market leadership.

Outcomes:

- Global Presence: Uber operates in over 900 metropolitan areas worldwide, illustrating its extensive reach and influence in the global transportation market.
- Revenue Growth: Uber's diversified services have contributed to significant revenue growth. The company went public in 2019, further solidifying its market position.
- Service Diversification: Beyond ride-hailing, Uber's expansion into food delivery with UberEats, logistics with Uber Freight, and investments in autonomous vehicle technology demonstrate its commitment to innovation and market diversification.

8.2 Alibaba Group

Alibaba Group is an international venture that was established by the famous entrepreneur Jack Ma in 1999 based in China, and it focuses on sectors such as electronic business, consumption, internet, and technology. Currently, it is ranked among the biggest and most profitable corporations with a range of established segments: e-commerce marketplaces (Alibaba.com, Taobao, Tmall), cloud solutions (Alibaba Cloud), online payment tool (Alipay), delivery and warehousing services (Cainiao

Network), and cinema and entertainment (Alibaba Pictures). Alibaba Group has successfully integrated various technologies, including:

- Artificial Intelligence (AI): Alibaba utilizes AI algorithms for data analytics, customer insights, personalized recommendations, and fraud detection across its platforms.
- Blockchain: The company leverages blockchain technology for supply chain management, product authentication, and traceability to ensure transparency and trust in transactions.
- Digital Marketing: Alibaba employs sophisticated digital marketing strategies to target consumers, drive traffic to its e-commerce platforms, and personalize promotions based on user preferences and behaviors.
- Digital Entrepreneurship: Alibaba's ecosystem fosters digital entrepreneurship through its marketplace platforms, cloud services, and investment arm, Alibaba Entrepreneurs Fund, which provides funding and support to startups and entrepreneurs.

Key Learnings:

- Ecosystem Synergy: Alibaba's integration of AI, blockchain, digital marketing, and digital entrepreneurship creates a synergistic ecosystem that drives innovation, fosters entrepreneurship, and accelerates business growth.
- Customer-Centric Approach: The company's focus on customer-centricity, enabled by AI-driven personalization and data analytics, enhances user experiences, increases engagement, and builds brand loyalty.
- Agility and Innovation: Alibaba's agile approach to technology adoption and innovation allows it to stay ahead of competitors, adapt to market trends, and launch new products and services quickly.

Outcomes:

- Market Dominance: Alibaba Group dominates the Chinese e-commerce market, accounting for a significant share of online retail sales and digital payments.
- Global Expansion: The company's international expansion strategy has led to partnerships, acquisitions, and investments in various countries, expanding its presence beyond China.
- Diversification: Alibaba has diversified its business portfolio beyond e-commerce into cloud computing, digital finance, logistics, entertainment,

and emerging technologies, creating multiple revenue streams and growth opportunities.

9. CHALLENGES, RISKS, AND CRITICAL FACTORS IN AI & BLOCKCHAIN INTEGRATION

The application of artificial intelligence combined with blockchain in business processes includes a series of issues and threats. AI related issues include data privacy and algorithms that may contain biases. This often poses privacy concerns because AI systems depend on the input and collection of personal data and because bias can manifest in the algorithm used, making decisions unfair, like hiring or lending. Costs of implementing AI also pose problems to organizations, especially the upfront costs of procuring a good AI system and few skilled individuals in AI add to the already existing problems especially for small firms.

Blockchain also has its challenges though. In terms of scalability, the problem still persists since the blockchain networks cannot accommodate high volumes of transactions. Furthermore, the high energy utilization by the technology, especially in application such as the Bitcoin's proof of work, presents many sustainability issues. Legal framework is also the key issue affecting blockchain's implementation with rarely clarified laws for different areas and especially for cryptocurrencies and smart contracts.

Technical constraints emerge due to the implementation of these technologies in the existing business processes. AI can be limited by legacy architecture and other factors of existing environments while talent deficiency poses challenges to organizations with aspirations of expanding on their use of AI. For blockchain, lack of standard practices and compliance requirements raise the complications which hinders the full adoption of the technology by the business.

Management and cultural issues hence refer to the human and organizational factors that define integration. Managing change is critical, as employees will often have negative attitudes towards new technologies given their potential to result into loss of jobs or because employees do not understand how that technology works. Sustained training must be offered to the staff in order to be ready for working alongside these technologies that are being adopted by leaders in organizations. It also requires integration with IT, legal and operations departments for proper functioning of the whole process.

Both AI and blockchain have ethical implications. There is fear that with the use of AI, structures that ensure proper decisions making, coupled with fairness are lacking. Thirdly, the application of automation driven by AI has the potentiality to displace a massive number of employees unless relevant skill enhancement programmes are implemented. As mentioned before, blockchain is a decentralized system; it is transparent, but it also makes issues with control and accountability in new decentralized structures appear and the possibility of using it for malicious purposes. Therefore, this study provides evidence that AI and blockchain have enormous possibilities in different industries but to achieve it business should consider the technical, operational, human, and ethical factors at play.

10. CONCLUSION

This chapter has explored the emerging role of digital technologies including artificial intelligence, block chain, digital marketing and digital entrepreneurship on contemporary business innovation and growth. AI can be used effectively to improve business processes, address individual needs, and strengthen protection measures. The application of block chain technology in a business environment makes business transactions some of the most secure and transparent and efficient. These new digital marketing techniques help capture customers' attention in new ways and thus have a higher level of interaction with the products and services offered and hence high level of sales. Digital entrepreneurship introduces innovation and new opportunities for economic growth and breaking of the previous models and paradigms.

Case studies of leading companies like Uber and Alibaba highlight the practical applications and benefits of integrating these technologies. Uber's AI-driven dynamic pricing and route optimization, coupled with its exploration of blockchain for transparency, showcase the potential of these technologies to revolutionize the ride-hailing industry. Similarly, Alibaba's use of AI for personalized recommendations and its potential adoption of blockchain for trust and security underline the importance of these tools in enhancing customer experiences and operational efficiency.

These case studies clearly show just how important digital technologies are in their future business development and growth. Businesses that have adopted Artificial Intelligence, Blockchain, Digital Marketing, and startup approaches have the advantage of beating their competitors in the current world. Nevertheless, some of the prevailing barriers include: regulatory issues, cyber security concerns and maintaining high innovation standards. Solving these issues entails developing a strategic blueprint, embracing technology, and focusing on cultivating multifaceted learning organizational cultures.

Finally, targeting AI, blockchain, digital marketing, and digital entrepreneurship as keys for the future, we have revealed them as a driving force for business evolution. With the help of these technologies they are able to harness new possibilities, achieve dynamic development and retain competitive advantage in the constantly developing context of digital environment. This chapter raises awareness of these tools as well as how to utilise them in the current context as the world becomes more digitized to foster sustainable success.

REFERENCES

Agbo, C. C., Mahmoud, Q. H., & Eklund, J. M. (2019, April). Blockchain technology in healthcare: A systematic review. [). MDPI.]. *Health Care*, 7(2), 56. PMID: 30987333

Binns, R. (2018, January). Fairness in machine learning: Lessons from political philosophy. In *Conference on fairness, accountability and transparency* (pp. 149-159). PMLR.

Blank, S., & Dorf, B. (2020). *The startup owner's manual: The step-by-step guide for building a great company*. John Wiley & Sons.

Buterin, V. (2014). A next-generation smart contract and decentralized application platform. *white paper, 3*(37), 2-1.

Chaffey, D., Ellis-Chadwick, F., & Mayer, R. (2009). *Internet marketing: strategy, implementation and practice*. Pearson education.

Chen, H., Chiang, R. H., & Storey, V. C. (2012). Business intelligence and analytics: From big data to big impact. *Management Information Systems Quarterly*, 36(4), 1165–1188. DOI: 10.2307/41703503

Christidis, K., & Devetsikiotis, M. (2016). Blockchains and smart contracts for the internet of things. *IEEE Access : Practical Innovations, Open Solutions*, 4, 2292–2303. DOI: 10.1109/ACCESS.2016.2566339

Croman, K., Decker, C., Eyal, I., Gencer, A. E., Juels, A., Kosba, A., . . . Wattenhofer, R. (2016, February). On Scaling Decentralized Blockchains: (A Position Paper). In *International conference on financial cryptography and data security* (pp. 106-125). Berlin, Heidelberg: Springer Berlin Heidelberg. DOI: 10.1007/978-3-662-53357-4_8

Darma, G. S., & Noviana, I. P. T. (2020). Exploring digital marketing strategies during the new normal era in enhancing the use of digital payment. *Jurnal Mantik*, 4(3), 2257–2262.

Davenport, T. H., & Ronanki, R. (2018). Artificial intelligence for the real world. *Harvard Business Review*, 96(1), 108–116.

Dwivedi, Y. K., Hughes, L., Ismagilova, E., Aarts, G., Coombs, C., Crick, T., Duan, Y., Dwivedi, R., Edwards, J., Eirug, A., Galanos, V., Ilavarasan, P. V., Janssen, M., Jones, P., Kar, A. K., Kizgin, H., Kronemann, B., Lal, B., Lucini, B., & Williams, M. D. (2021). Artificial Intelligence (AI): Multidisciplinary perspectives on emerging challenges, opportunities, and agenda for research, practice and policy. *International Journal of Information Management*, 57, 101994. DOI: 10.1016/j.ijinfomgt.2019.08.002

Frost, R., & Strauss, J. (2016). *E-marketing*. Routledge.

Hall, J. V., & Krueger, A. B. (2018). An analysis of the labor market for Uber's driver-partners in the United States. *Industrial & Labor Relations Review*, 71(3), 705–732. DOI: 10.1177/0019793917717222

Hu, J. L., & Chang, Y. C. (2019). The W-theory of Five Elements for Innovative Business Activities with a Case Study of Alibaba Corporation. *Journal of Management Research*, 19(3), 173–179.

Huang, M. H., & Rust, R. T. (2018). Artificial intelligence in service. *Journal of Service Research*, 21(2), 155–172. DOI: 10.1177/1094670517752459

Isenberg, D. J. (2010). How to start an entrepreneurial revolution. *Harvard Business Review*, 88(6), 40–50.

Ismail, M. H., Khater, M., & Zaki, M. (2017). Digital business transformation and strategy: What do we know so far. *Cambridge Service Alliance*, 10(1), 1–35.

Kshetri, N. (2018). 1 Blockchain's roles in meeting key supply chain management objectives. *International Journal of Information Management*, 39, 80–89. DOI: 10.1016/j.ijinfomgt.2017.12.005

Morabito, V. (2017). *Business innovation through blockchain*. Springer International Publishing.

Nadkarni, S., & Prügl, R. (2021). Digital transformation: A review, synthesis and opportunities for future research. *Management Review Quarterly*, 71(2), 233–341. DOI: 10.1007/s11301-020-00185-7

Nakamoto, S. (2008). Bitcoin: A peer-to-peer electronic cash system.

Nambisan, S. (2017). Digital entrepreneurship: Toward a digital technology perspective of entrepreneurship. *Entrepreneurship Theory and Practice*, 41(6), 1029–1055. DOI: 10.1111/etap.12254

Narayanan, A., Bonneau, J., Felten, E., Miller, A., & Goldfeder, S. (2016). *Bitcoin and cryptocurrency technologies: a comprehensive introduction*. Princeton University Press.

Pilkington, M. (2016). Blockchain technology: principles and applications. In *Research handbook on digital transformations* (pp. 225–253). Edward Elgar Publishing. DOI: 10.4337/9781784717766.00019

Pulizzi, J. (2012). The rise of storytelling as the new marketing. *Publishing Research Quarterly*, 28(2), 116–123. DOI: 10.1007/s12109-012-9264-5

Reim, W., Åström, J., & Eriksson, O. (2020). Implementation of artificial intelligence (AI): A roadmap for business model innovation. *AI*, 1(2), 11. DOI: 10.3390/ai1020011

Russell, S. (2022). Artificial Intelligence and the Problem of Control. *Perspectives on Digital Humanism, 19*.

Russell, S. J., & Norvig, P. (2016). *Artificial intelligence: a modern approach*. Pearson.

Shane, S., & Venkataraman, S. (2000). The promise of entrepreneurship as a field of research. *Academy of Management Review*, 25(1), 217–226. DOI: 10.5465/amr.2000.2791611

Sharda, R., Delen, D., & Turban, E. (2018). *Business intelligence, analytics, and data science: a managerial perspective*. pearson.

Shmueli, G., & Koppius, O. R. (2011). Predictive analytics in information systems research. *Management Information Systems Quarterly*, 35(3), 553–572. DOI: 10.2307/23042796

Swan, M. (2015). Blockchain thinking: The brain as a decentralized autonomous corporation [commentary]. *IEEE Technology and Society Magazine*, 34(4), 41–52. DOI: 10.1109/MTS.2015.2494358

Swan, M. (2015). *Blockchain: Blueprint for a new economy*. O'Reilly Media, Inc.

Tapscott, D., & Tapscott, A. (2016). *Blockchain revolution: how the technology behind bitcoin is changing money, business, and the world*. Penguin.

Tapscott, D., & Tapscott, A. (2016). *Blockchain revolution: how the technology behind bitcoin is changing money, business, and the world*. Penguin.

Tapscott, D., & Tapscott, A. (2016). *Blockchain revolution: how the technology behind bitcoin is changing money, business, and the world*. Penguin.

Tuten, T., & Solomon, M. R. (2017). Social Media Marketing-Tracy L. *Tuten, Michael R. Solomon. In.*

Wedel, M., & Kannan, P. K. (2016). Marketing analytics for data-rich environments. *Journal of Marketing*, 80(6), 97–121. DOI: 10.1509/jm.15.0413

Westerman, G., Bonnet, D., & McAfee, A. (2014). *Leading digital: Turning technology into business transformation.* Harvard Business Press.

Yli-Huumo, J., Ko, D., Choi, S., Park, S., & Smolander, K. (2016). Where is current research on blockchain technology?—A systematic review. *PLoS One*, 11(10), e0163477. DOI: 10.1371/journal.pone.0163477 PMID: 27695049

Zohar, A. (2015). Bitcoin: Under the hood. *Communications of the ACM*, 58(9), 104–113. DOI: 10.1145/2701411

ADDITIONAL READING

Ali, M. (2021). *Remote Work and Sustainable Changes for the Future of Global Business.* IGI Global. https://www.igi-global.com/book/remote-work-sustainable-changes-future/264375

Ali, M. (2022). *Future Role of Sustainable Innovative Technologies in Crisis Management.* IGI Global. https://www.igi-global.com/book/future-role-sustainable-innovative-technologies/281281

Ali, M. (2023). *Shifting Paradigms in the Rapidly Developing Global Digital Ecosystem: A GCC Perspective.* In Digital Entrepreneurship and Co-Creating Value Through Digital Encounters (pp. 145-166). IGI Global. https://www.igi-global.com/chapter/shifting-paradigms-in-the-rapidly-developing-global-digital-ecosystem/323525

Ali, M. (2023). T*axonomy of Industry 4.0 Technologies in Digital Entrepreneurship and Co-Creating Value.* In *Digital Entrepreneurship and Co-Creating Value Through Digital Encounters* (pp. 24–55). IGI Global., https://www.igi-global.com/chapter/taxonomy-of-industry-40-technologies-in-digital-entrepreneurship-and-co-creating-value/323520 DOI: 10.4018/978-1-6684-7416-7.ch002

Ali, M., & Wood-Harper, T. (2021). *Fostering Communication and Learning with Underutilized Technologies in Higher Education.* IGI Global. https://www.igi-global.com/book/fostering-communication-learning-underutilized-technologies/244593

Ali, M., Wood-Harper, T., & Kutar, M. (2023). Multi-Perspectives of Contemporary Digital Transformation Models of Complex Innovation Management. In *Digital Entrepreneurship and Co-Creating Value Through Digital Encounters* (pp. 79–96). IGI Global., https://www.igi-global.com/chapter/multi-perspectives-of-contemporary-digital-transformation-models-of-complex-innovation-management/323522 DOI: 10.4018/978-1-6684-7416-7.ch004

Ali, M. B. (2021). Internet of Things (IoT) to Foster Communication and Information Sharing: A Case of UK Higher Education. In Ali, M. B., & Wood-Harper, T. (Eds.), *Fostering Communication and Learning With Underutilized Technologies in Higher Education* (pp. 1–20). IGI Global., https://www.igi-global.com/chapter/internet-of-things-iot-to-foster-communication-and-information-sharing/262718/ DOI: 10.4018/978-1-7998-4846-2.ch001

Ali, M. B., & Wood-Harper, T. (2022). Artificial Intelligence (AI) as a Decision-Making Tool to Control Crisis Situations. In *Future Role of Sustainable Innovative Technologies in Crisis Management*. IGI Global., https://www.igi-global.com/chapter/artificial-intelligence-ai-as-a-decision-making-tool-to-control-crisis-situations/298931 DOI: 10.4018/978-1-7998-9815-3.ch006

Ali, M. B., Wood-Harper, T., & Ramlogan, R. (2020). A Framework Strategy to Overcome Trust Issues on Cloud Computing Adoption in Higher Education. In Modern Principles, Practices, and Algorithms for Cloud Security (pp. 162-183). IGI Global. https://www.igi-global.com/chapter/a-framework-strategy-to-overcome-trust-issues-on-cloud-computing-adoption-in-higher-education/238907/

Compilation of References

Aazam, M., & Huh, E. N. (2014). "Fog computing and smart gateway based communication for cloud of things," in Proceedings of the 2nd IEEE International Conference on Future Internet of Things and Cloud (FiCloud' 14), 464–470, Barcelona, Spain, August 2014. DOI: 10.1109/FiCloud.2014.83

Abad-Segura, E., Infante-Moro, A., González-Zamar, M. D., & López-Meneses, E. (2024). Influential Factors For A Secure Perception Of Accounting Management With Blockchain Technology. *Journal of Open Innovation*, 10(2), 100264. DOI: 10.1016/j.joitmc.2024.100264

Abbad, M. M. (2021). Using the UTAUT model to understand students' usage of e-learning systems in developing countries. *Education and Information Technologies*, 26(6), 7205–7224. DOI: 10.1007/s10639-021-10573-5 PMID: 34025204

Abd Shukor, R., Mooi, W. K., & Ibrahim, J. A. (2023). *The future of Malaysian SMEs in the digital economy*. Qeios. DOI: 10.32388/VSWNB6

Abdennadher, R., Grassa, H., Abdulla, & Alfalasi, A. (2021). The effects of blockchain technology on the accounting and assurance profession in the UAE: An exploratory study. *Journal of Financial Reporting and Accounting*, ahead-of-print. DOI: 10.1108/JFRA-05-2020-0151

Abdul Wahab Samad, Zahera Mega Utama, M. W. R. S. (. (2024). An evaluation of the Efficacy of the Human Resource Data Analytics on Artificial Intelligence Program. *Journal of Electrical Systems*, 20(4s), 2050–2059. DOI: 10.52783/jes.2308

Aboushouk, M. A. (2022). The Impact of Employees' Absorptive Capacity on Digital Transformation of Tourism and Travel Services: Evidence from the Egyptian Travel Agencies. In Bilgin, M. H., Danis, H., Demir, E., & Bodolica, V. (Eds.), *Eurasian Business and Economics Perspectives* (Vol. 23, pp. 167–184). Springer International Publishing., DOI: 10.1007/978-3-031-14395-3_9

Adaghe, W., & Barakat, A. (2023). *What are the impacts of digitalization in travel agencies business model in Sweden A qualitative study on the role of physical travel agencies in Sweden*. DOI: 10.13140/RG.2.2.18534.40001

Adama, H. E., & Okeke, C. D.Henry Ejiga AdamaChukwuekem David Okeke. (2024). Digital transformation as a catalyst for business model innovation: A critical review of impact and implementation strategies. *Magna Scientia Advanced Research and Reviews*, 10(2), 256–264. DOI: 10.30574/msarr.2024.10.2.0066

Adama, H. E., Popoola, O. A., Okeke, C. D., & Akinoso, A. E.Henry Ejiga AdamaOladapo Adeboye PopoolaChukwuekem David OkekeAbiodun Emmanuel Akinoso. (2024). Economic theory and practical impacts of digital transformation in supply chain optimization. *International Journal of Advanced Economics*, 6(4), 95–107. DOI: 10.51594/ijae.v6i4.1072

Adekuajo, I. O., Fakeyede, O. G., Udeh, C. A., & Daraojimba, C. (2023). THE DIGITAL EVOLUTION IN HOSPITALITY: A GLOBAL REVIEW AND ITS POTENTIAL TRANSFORMATIVE IMPACT ON U.S. TOURISM. *International Journal of Applied Research in Social Sciences*, 5(10), 440–462. DOI: 10.51594/ijarss.v5i10.633

Adhami, S., Giudici, G., & Martinazzi, S. (2018). Why do businesses go crypto? An empirical analysis of initial coin offerings. *Journal of Economics and Business*, 100, 64–75. DOI: 10.1016/j.jeconbus.2018.04.001

Afzal, M., Li, J., Amin, W., Huang, Q., Umer, K., Ahmad, S. A., Ahmad, F., & Raza, A. (2022). Role of blockchain technology in transactive energy market: A review. *Sustainable Energy Technologies and Assessments*, 53, 102646. DOI: 10.1016/j.seta.2022.102646

Agarwal, P. (2019). Redefining banking and financial industry through the application of computational intelligence. In *2019 Advances in Science and Engineering Technology International Conferences (ASET)* (pp. 1-5). IEEE. DOI: 10.1109/ICASET.2019.8714305

Agbo, C. C., Mahmoud, Q. H., & Eklund, J. M. (2019, April). Blockchain technology in healthcare: A systematic review. []. MDPI.]. *Health Care*, 7(2), 56. PMID: 30987333

Aggarwal, N., Wareham, S., & Lehmann, R. (2020). Applications of machine learning in the identification, measurement, and mitigation of money laundering. *Journal of Financial Compliance*, 4(2), 140–166. DOI: 10.69554/HHGO1574

Agrawal, T. K., Kumar, V., Pal, R., Wang, L., & Chen, Y. (2021). Blockchain based framework for supply chain traceability: A case example of textile and clothing industry. *Computers & Industrial Engineering*, 154, 1–12. DOI: 10.1016/j.cie.2021.107130

Agu, S. C., Onu, F. U., Ezemagu, U. K., & Oden, D. (2022). Predicting gross domestic product to macroeconomic indicators. *Intelligent Systems with Applications*, 14, 14. DOI: 10.1016/j.iswa.2022.200082

Ahamad, M. E. (2024). IMPACT OF ARTIFICIAL INTELLIGENCE ON BUSINESS ANALYTICS. *INTERANTIONAL JOURNAL OF SCIENTIFIC RESEARCH IN ENGINEERING AND MANAGEMENT*, 08(05), 1–5. DOI: 10.55041/IJSREM33172

Ahmad, Z., Mehmood, S., Khan, A. A., Khan, S., & Jabbar, A. (2024). The holistic repercussions of the ongoing war and refugee crisis on the Polish travel agencies. *Journal of Contingencies and Crisis Management*, 32(1), e12547. DOI: 10.1111/1468-5973.12547

Akdere, M., Acheson, K., & Jiang, Y. (2021). An examination of the effectiveness of virtual reality technology for intercultural competence development. *International Journal of Intercultural Relations*, 82, 109–120. DOI: 10.1016/j.ijintrel.2021.03.009

Al-Adwan, A. S., Yaseen, H., Alsoud, A., Abousweilem, F., & Al-Rahmi, W. M. (2022). Novel extension of the UTAUT model to understand continued usage intention of learning management systems: The role of learning tradition. *Education and Information Technologies*, 27(3), 3567–3593. DOI: 10.1007/s10639-021-10758-y

Alavi, M., & Leidner, D. E. (2001). Knowledge management and knowledge management systems: Conceptual foundations and research issues. *Management Information Systems Quarterly*, 25(1), 107–136. DOI: 10.2307/3250961

Albakri, M. (2023). Shifting Paradigms in the Rapidly Developing Global Digital Ecosystem: A GCC Perspective. In *Digital Entrepreneurship and Co-Creating Value Through Digital Encounters* (pp. 12–16). IGI Global.

Aldoseri, A., Al-Khalifa, K. N., & Hamouda, A. M. (2023). Re-thinking data strategy and integration for artificial intelligence: Concepts, opportunities, and challenges. *Applied Sciences (Basel, Switzerland)*, 13(12), 7082. DOI: 10.3390/app13127082

Aldoseri, A., Al-Khalifa, K. N., & Hamouda, A. M. (2024). Methodological Approach to Assessing the Current State of Organizations for AI-Based Digital Transformation. *Applied System Innovation*, 7(1), 14. DOI: 10.3390/asi7010014

Al-Emran, M., Arpaci, I., & Salloum, S. A. (2020). An empirical examination of continuous intention to use m-learning: An integrated model. *Education and Information Technologies*, 25(4), 2899–2918. DOI: 10.1007/s10639-019-10094-2

Alfred, C. D., Seraj, M., & Ozdeser, H. (2024). The Impact of Technological Advancement on Unemployment in Turkey. *Global Economics Science*, 37–52. DOI: 10.37256/ges.5120243330

Alghawi, K., Ameen, N., Bhaumik, A., Haddoud, M. Y., & Alrajawy, I. (2024). Smart cities and communities in the GCC region: From top-down city development to more local approaches. *Frontiers in Built Environment*, ●●●, 10.

Al-Hadrawi, B. K., & Reniati, R. (2023). Digital Leadership: Navigating the Future with Strategic Conviction. *International Journal of Magistravitae Management*, 1(2), 130–145. DOI: 10.33019/ijomm.v1i2.23

Ali, A., Jaradat, A., Kulakli, A., & Abuhalimeh, A. (2021). A comparative study: Blockchain technology utilization benefits, challenges and functionalities. *IEEE Access*, PP, 1–1. DOI: 10.1109/ACCESS.2021.3050241

Ali, S. S., Torğul, B., Paksoy, T., Luthra, S., & Kayikci, Y. (2024). A novel hybrid decision-making framework for measuring Industry 4.0-driven circular economy performance for textile industry. *Business Strategy and the Environment*, bse.3892. Advance online publication. DOI: 10.1002/bse.3892

Al-Jaroodi, & Mohamed, N. (2019). Blockchain in industries: A survey. *IEEE Access*, PP, 1–1. DOI: 10.1109/ACCESS.2019.2903554

Almaiah, M. A., & Al Mulhem, A. (2019). Analysis of the essential factors affecting of intention to use of mobile learning applications: A comparison between universities adopters and non-adopters. *Education and Information Technologies*, 24(2), 1433–1468. DOI: 10.1007/s10639-018-9840-1

Almeida, F., Bacao, F., & Santos, M. F. (2019). Data-driven innovation: Concepts, approaches, and empirical evidence. *Information Systems Management*, 36, 99–114.

AlphaBeta. (2021). Positioning Malaysia as a Regional Leader in the Digital Economy: The Economic Opportunities of Digital Transformation and Google's Contribution. Retrieved from https://accesspartnership.com/wp-content/uploads/2023/03/Malaysia-Digital- Transformation.pdf

Al-Qeisi, K., Dennis, C., Hegazy, A., & Abbad, M. (2015). How viable is the UTAUT model in a non-western context? *International Business Research*, 8(2). Advance online publication. DOI: 10.5539/ibr.v8n2p204

Al-Rahmi, W. M., Yahaya, N., Alamri, M. M., Alyoussef, I. Y., Al-Rahmi, A. M., & Kamin, Y. B. (2021). Integrating innovation diffusion theory with technology acceptance model: Supporting students' attitude towards using a massive open online courses (MOOCs) systems. *Interactive Learning Environments*, 29(8), 1380–1392. DOI: 10.1080/10494820.2019.1629599

Al-Shabandar, R., Lightbody, G., Browne, F., Liu, J., Wang, H., & Zheng, H. (2019). The application of artificial intelligence in financial compliance management. In *Proceedings of the 2019 International Conference on Artificial Intelligence and Advanced Manufacturing* (pp. 1-6). DOI: 10.1145/3358331.3358339

Al-Shahrani, H. (2016). *Investigating the determinants of mobile learning acceptance in higher education in Saudi Arabia*. Northern Illinois University.

Alves, L., Ferreira Cruz, E., Lopes, S. I., Faria, P. M., & Rosado da Cruz, A. M. (2022). Towards circular economy in the textiles and clothing value chain through blockchain technology and IoT: A review. *Waste Management & Research*, 40(1), 3–23. DOI: 10.1177/0734242X211052858 PMID: 34708680

Amanasto, W., Hamzah, M. Z., & Sudaryono, B. (2019). How The Effect of Investment Policy at Information and Communication Technology for Digital Economy Implementation toward Macroeconomic Indicators and Sectoral Performance, in Indonesia? *OIDA International Journal of Sustainable Development*, 12(09), 11–24.

Amazon. (2023). S&P Global Market Intelligence Increases Agility and Resilience of Its Primary Issuance Platform Using AWS Well-Architected Tool and AWS Trusted Advisor. Retrieved September 4, 2024 from https://aws.amazon.com/solutions/case-studies/sp-global-market-intelligence-case-study/?did=cr_card&trk=cr_card

Amit, R., & Zott, C. (2001). Value creation in e-business. *Strategic Management Journal*, 22(6-7), 493–520. DOI: 10.1002/smj.187

Ammeran, M. Y., Noor, S., & Yusof, M. (2021). Digital transformation of Malaysian small and medium-sized enterprises: a review and research direction. In *International Conference on Business and Technology* (pp. 255-278). Cham: Springer International Publishing.

Anagnostopoulos, I. (2018). Fintech and regtech: Impact on regulators and banks. *Journal of Economics and Business*, 100, 7–25. DOI: 10.1016/j.jeconbus.2018.07.003

Ancillai, C., Sabatini, A., Gatti, M., & Perna, A. (2023). Digital technology and business model innovation: A systematic literature review and future research agenda. *Technological Forecasting and Social Change*, 188, 122307. DOI: 10.1016/j.techfore.2022.122307

Anderson, L., Pekkari, M., Gray, J., Neugebauer, V., & Candotto, L. (2023). Building MSME Resilience in Southeast Asia: With a country focus on Thailand and Malaysia. United Nations Development Programme (UNDP) Insurance and Risk Finance Facility (IRFF). https://irff.undp.org/publications/building-msme-resilience-southeast-asia

Anderson, J. C., & Gerbing, D. W. (1988). Structural Equation Modeling in Practice: A Review and Recommended Two-Step Approach. *Psychological Bulletin*, 103(3), 411–423. Advance online publication. DOI: 10.1037/0033-2909.103.3.411

Anderson, K., & Martin, L. (2023). The role of service standards in driving digital transformation. *International Journal of Public Sector Management*, 36(1), 22–38.

Anh, P., & Huy, D. T. N. (2021). Internet Benefits and Digital Transformation Applying in Boosting Tourism Sector and Forecasting Tourism Management Revenue. *Webology, 18*(Special Issue 04), 489–500. DOI: 10.14704/WEB/V18SI04/WEB18143

Antikainen, M., Uusitalo, T., & Kivikytö-Reponen, P. (2018). Digitalization as an enabler of circular economy. *Procedia CIRP*, 73, 45–49. DOI: 10.1016/j.procir.2018.04.027

Antonijević, M., Domazet, I., Kojić, M., & Simović, V. (2024). Financial Inclusion - A Driving Force for Women's Entrepreneurship Development. *Journal of Women's Entrepreneurship and Education*, 3-4, 73–92. DOI: 10.28934/jwee24.34.pp73-92

Anuar, A. (2024). AI and EV Innovations Entering Malaysia's Healthcare System. The Malaysian Reserve. Retrieved from https://themalaysianreserve.com/2024/06/19/ai-and-ev-innovations- entering-malaysias-healthcare-system/#google_vignette

Anyanwu, A., Dawodu, S. O., Omotosho, A., Akindote, O. J., & Ewuga, S. K. (2023). Review of blockchain technology in government systems: Applications and impacts in the USA. *World Journal of Advanced Research and Reviews*, 20(3), 863–875. DOI: 10.30574/wjarr.2023.20.3.2553

Appelbaum, E., Cohen, E., Kinory, S., & Stein Smith, S. (2022). Impediments to blockchain adoption. *Journal of Emerging Technologies in Accounting*, 19(2), 199–210. DOI: 10.2308/JETA-19-05-14-26

Aqmala, D., & Putra, F. I. F. S. (2023). Eco Cuty: The Eco-Friendly Marketing Strategy Model for MSME's Economic Recovery Movement Post-Covid 19. *Calitatea*, 24(194), 304–312.

Ardiyanto Maksimilianus Gai, Afdhal Chatra, Mozart Malik Ibrahim, Samuel Pd Anantadjaya, & Irma M Nawangwulan. (2024). Analysis of The Influence of Information Availability, Economic Factors and Changing Trends on Travel Agent Business Sustainability in Digital Era. *Jurnal Sistim Informasi Dan Teknologi*, 6–11. DOI: 10.60083/jsisfotek.v6i2.344

Arefyev, A. S. (2020). "Platformization" as a management tool of digital transformation in the sphere of tourism. *Теоретическая и Прикладная Экономика*, 3(3), 22–34. DOI: 10.25136/2409-8647.2020.3.33237

Armstrong, J. S., & Overton, T. S. (1977). Estimating non-response bias in mail surveys. *JMR, Journal of Marketing Research*, 14(3), 396–402. DOI: 10.1177/002224377701400320

Arner, D. W., Barberis, J., & Buckley, R. P. (2015). The evolution of Fintech: A new post-crisis paradigm. *SSRN*, 47, 1271. DOI: 10.2139/ssrn.2676553

Atanassov, K. T. (1986). Intuitionistic fuzzy sets. *Fuzzy Sets and Systems*, 20(1), 87–96. DOI: 10.1016/S0165-0114(86)80034-3

Atzori, L., Iera, A., & Morabito, G. (2011). IoT: Giving a social structure to the internet of things. *IEEE Communications Letters*, 15(11), 1193–1195. DOI: 10.1109/LCOMM.2011.090911.111340

Auer, R., Cornelli, G., & Frost, J. (2021). Rise of the central bank digital currencies: Drivers, approaches, and technologies. *BIS Working Papers*, 880. https://www.bis.org/publ/work880.pdf

Autio, E., Nambisan, S., Thomas, L. D., & Wright, M. (2018). Digital affordances, spatial affordances, and the genesis of entrepreneurial ecosystems. *Strategic Entrepreneurship Journal*, 12(1), 72–95. DOI: 10.1002/sej.1266

Avgouleas, E. (2009). The global financial crisis and the disclosure paradigm in European financial regulation: The case for reform.

AXON DATA GOVERNANCE. Available online: https://www.informatica.com/gb/products/dataquality/axon-data%20governance.html (accessed on 15 October 2023).

Aziz, S., & Dowling, M. (2019). Machine learning and AI for risk management. *Disrupting finance: FinTech and strategy in the 21st century*, 33-50.

Azzutti, A., Ringe, W. G., & Stiehl, H. S. (2021). Machine Learning, Market Manipulation, and Collusion on Capital Markets: Why the" Black Box" Matters. *SSRN*, 43, 79. DOI: 10.2139/ssrn.3788872

Baader, F., Calvanese, D., McGuinness, D., Nardi, D., & Patel-Schneider, P. (Eds.). (2002). *The Description Logic Handbook.* Cambridge University Press.

Bachta, A. (2024). E-Tourism: New Communication Challenges for the Travel Agencies in the UAE. In Khoury, R. E., & Nasrallah, N. (Eds.), *Intelligent Systems, Business, and Innovation Research* (Vol. 489, pp. 265–277). Springer Nature Switzerland., DOI: 10.1007/978-3-031-36895-0_22

Badhwar, A., Islam, S., & Tan, C. S. L. (2023). Exploring the potential of blockchain technology within the fashion and textile supply chain with a focus on traceability, transparency, and product authenticity: A systematic review. *Frontiers in Blockchain*, 6, 1044723. DOI: 10.3389/fbloc.2023.1044723

Badruddoza Talukder, M., Kumar, S., Misra, L. I., & Firoj Kabir, . (2024). Determining the role of eco-tourism service quality, tourist satisfaction, and destination loyalty: A case study of Kuakata beach. *Acta Scientiarum Polonorum. Administratio Locorum*, 23(1), 133–151. DOI: 10.31648/aspal.9275

Bagó, P. (2023). The potential of artificial intelligence in finance. *ECONOMY AND FINANCE: ENGLISH-LANGUAGE EDITION OF GAZDASÁG ÉS PÉNZÜGY*, 10(1), 20–37. DOI: 10.33908/EF.2023.1.2

Bai, B., Wang, J., & Chai, C.-S. (2021). Understanding Hong Kong primary school English teachers' continuance intention to teach with ICT. *Computer Assisted Language Learning*, 34(4), 528–551. DOI: 10.1080/09588221.2019.1627459

Bai, C., & Sarkis, J. (2020). A supply chain transparency and sustainability technology appraisal model for blockchain technology. *International Journal of Production Research*, 58(7), 2142–2162. DOI: 10.1080/00207543.2019.1708989

Baker, L., & Green, J. (2023). The role of face-to-face interactions in digital healthcare. *BMC Health Services Research*, 23, 456.

Bălăşescu, S., & Bălăşescu, M. (2022). Digital brand in the field of travel agencies. *Proceedings of the International Conference on Business Excellence, 16*(1), 1456–1465. DOI: 10.2478/picbe-2022-0133

Balasubramani, E., & Priyanka, B. (2023). Machine Learning in Finance. https://www.openacessjournal.com/article-file/202303045684986362machine.pdf

Balon, B., Kalinowski, K., & Paprocka, I. (2023). Production planning using a shared resource register organized according to the assumptions of blockchain technology. *Sensors (Basel)*, 23(4), 2308. DOI: 10.3390/s23042308 PMID: 36850905

Bamberger, K. A. (2009). Technologies of compliance: Risk and regulation in a digital age. *Texas Law Review*, 88, 669.

Bao, Z., Wang, Q., Shi, W., Wang, L., Lei, H., & Chen, B. (2020). When blockchain meets sgx: An overview, challenges, and open issues. *IEEE Access : Practical Innovations, Open Solutions*, 8, 170404–170420. DOI: 10.1109/ACCESS.2020.3024254

Bardhan, P. (2003). *International Trade Growth and Development: Essays*. Wiley-Blackwell. DOI: 10.1002/9780470752777

Barenji, A. V., Guo, H., Wang, Y., Li, Z., & Rong, Y. (2021). Toward blockchain and fog computing collaborative design and manufacturing platform: Support customer view. *Robotics and Computer-integrated Manufacturing*, 67, 102043. DOI: 10.1016/j.rcim.2020.102043

Barnaghi, P., Presser, M., & Moessner, K. (2010). "Publishing Linked Sensor Data", in *Proceedings of the 3rd International Workshop on Semantic Sensor Networks*.

Bassant, H., & Shires, J. (2022). Cybersecurity in the GCC: From Economic Development to Geopolitical Controversy. *Middle East Policy*, 29(1), 16–29.

Bavaresco, R. S., Nesi, L. C., Barbosa, J. L. V., Antunes, R. S., da Rosa Righi, R., da Costa, C. A., & Moreira, C. (2023). Machine learning-based automation of accounting services: An exploratory case study. *International Journal of Accounting Information Systems*, 49, 100618. DOI: 10.1016/j.accinf.2023.100618

BBC News. (2017) *Qatar crisis: Saudi Arabia and allies sever ties with Qatar*. Available at: https://www.bbc.com/news/world-middle-east-40155829 (Accessed: 16 September 2024).

Becker, M., & Buchkremer, R. (2018). RANKING OF CURRENT INFORMATION TECHNOLOGIES BY RISK AND REGULATORY COMPLIANCE OFFICERS AT FINANCIAL INSTITUTIONS—A GERMAN PERSPECTIVE. *Review of Finance & Banking*, 10(1).

Becker, M., Merz, K., & Buchkremer, R. (2020). RegTech—the application of modern information technology in regulatory affairs: Areas of interest in research and practice. *International Journal of Intelligent Systems in Accounting Finance & Management*, 27(4), 161–167. DOI: 10.1002/isaf.1479

Bekkers, V. (2003). Reinventing government in the information age. International practice in IT-enabled public sector reform. *Public Management Review*, 5(1), 133–139. DOI: 10.1080/714042647

BEng. R. V., & Slagter, M. R. (2017). Standing on the shoulders of RegTech. https://www.compact.nl/pdf/C-2017-4-Slagter.pdf

Benítez-Martínez, F. L., Hurtado-Torres, M. V., & Romero-Frías, E. (2021). A neural blockchain for a tokenizable e-participation model. *Neurocomputing*, 423, 703–712. DOI: 10.1016/j.neucom.2020.03.116

Berners-Lee, T. (2000). *Weaving the Web: The Original Design and Ultimate Design of the World Wide Web by its inventor*. Harper Business.

Betts, D., & Korenda, L. (2019). *The future of health: How digital technologies can bridge the gap between consumers and health care providers*. Deloitte Insights.

Bharadwaj, A., El Sawy, O. A., Pavlou, P. A., & Venkatraman, N. (2013). Digital business strategy: Toward a next generation of insights. *Management Information Systems Quarterly*, 37(2), 471–482. DOI: 10.25300/MISQ/2013/37:2.3

Bhaskar, N., Ramu, S. C., & Murthy, M. R. (2021). A Two-Level Authentication Protocol for Secure M-Commerce Transactions using AMQP Protocol. *Design Engineering (London)*, ●●●, 844–861.

Bhattacherjee, A. (2001). Understanding information systems continuance: An expectation-confirmation model. MIS Quarterly: Management. *Management Information Systems Quarterly*, 25(3), 351. DOI: 10.2307/3250921

Bindra, L., Lin, C., Stroulia, E., & Ardakanian, O. (2019, May). *Decentralized access control for smart buildings using metadata and smart contract*. In 2019 IEEE/ACM 5th International Workshop on Software Engineering for Smart Cyber-Physical Systems (SEsCPS) s (pp.2-38). IEEE. DOI: 10.1109/SEsCPS.2019.00013

Binns, R. (2018, January). Fairness in machine learning: Lessons from political philosophy. In *Conference on fairness, accountability and transparency* (pp. 149-159). PMLR.

Birla, R., & Sunaina, . (2023). The Challenges of Media Education in the Digital Era. *Journal of Communication Management (London)*, 2(04), 281–288. DOI: 10.58966/JCM20232411

Bisbe, J., & Malagueño, R. (2018). How to design a successful KPI system. *MIT Sloan Management Review*, 59, 45–51.

Biswas, B., Sanyal, M. K., & Mukherjee, T. (2023). AI-Based Sales Forecasting Model for Digital Marketing. [IJEBR]. *International Journal of E-Business Research*, 19(1), 14. DOI: 10.4018/IJEBR.317888

Bititci, U. S., Martinez, V., Albores, P., & Parung, J. (2004). Creating and managing value in collaborative networks. *International Journal of Physical Distribution & Logistics Management*, 34(3/4), 251–268. DOI: 10.1108/09600030410533574

Blank, S., & Dorf, B. (2020). *The startup owner's manual: The step-by-step guide for building a great company*. John Wiley & Sons.

Bobenič Hintošová, A., & Bódy, G. (2023). Sustainable FDI in the digital economy. *Sustainability (Basel)*, 15(14), 10794. DOI: 10.3390/su151410794

Bocean, C. G. (2024). A Longitudinal Analysis of the Impact of Digital Technologies on Sustainable Food Production and Consumption in the European Union. *Foods*, 13(8), 1281. DOI: 10.3390/foods13081281 PMID: 38672953

Bogers, M. L., Garud, R., Thomas, L. D., Tuertscher, P., & Yoo, Y. (2022). Digital innovation: Transforming research and practice. *Innovation (North Sydney, N.S.W.)*, 24(1), 4–12. DOI: 10.1080/14479338.2021.2005465

Bonazzi, R., Hussami, L., & Pigneur, Y. (2009). Compliance management is becoming a major issue in IS design. In *Information Systems: People, Organizations, Institutions, and Technologies: ItAIS: The Italian Association for Information Systems* (pp. 391–398). Physica-Verlag HD. DOI: 10.1007/978-3-7908-2148-2_45

Bonomi, F., Milito, R., Natarajan, P., & Zhu, J. (2014). *"Fog computing: a platform for internet of things and analytics," in Big Data and Internet of Things: A Road Map for Smart Environments*. Springer.

Bonomi, F., Milito, R., Zhu, J., & Addepalli, S. (2012). "Fog computing and its role in the internet of things," in *Proceedings of the 1st ACM MCC Workshop on Mobile Cloud Computing*, 13–16, 2012. DOI: 10.1145/2342509.2342513

Bonsu, N. O. (2020). Towards a circular and low-carbon economy: Insights from the transitioning to electric vehicles and net zero economy. *Journal of Cleaner Production*, 256, 120659. DOI: 10.1016/j.jclepro.2020.120659

Bopapurkar, P. (2023). *Reference Services in Libraries: Navigating the Digital Age*. Current Trends in Information Technology., DOI: 10.37591/ctit.v13i2.1069

Bordel Sánchez, B., Alcarria, R., Sánchez de Rivera, D., & Robles, T. (2018). Process execution in CyberPhysical Systems using cloud and Cyber-Physical Internet services. *The Journal of Supercomputing*, 74(8), 4127–4169. DOI: 10.1007/s11227-018-2416-4

Bornstein, M. H., Jager, J., & Putnick, D. L. (2013). Sampling in developmental science: Situations, shortcomings, solutions, and standards. *Developmental Review*, 33(4), 357–370. DOI: 10.1016/j.dr.2013.08.003 PMID: 25580049

Bose, R. (2009). Advanced analytics: Opportunities and challenges. *Industrial Management & Data Systems*, 109(2), 155–172. DOI: 10.1108/02635570910930073

Boström, E., & Celik, O. C. 2017, 'Towards a maturity model for digital strategizing: A qualitative study of how an organization can analyze and assess their digital business strategy', Dissertation, Dept. of Informatics Umeå University.

Bouncken, R. B., Kraus, S., & Roig-Tierno, N. (2021). Digital transformation in entrepreneurial ecosystems: A co-evolutionary perspective. *Technological Forecasting and Social Change*, 168, 120785. DOI: 10.1016/j.techfore.2021.120785

Bradić-Martinović, A., & Banović, J. (2018). Assessment of digital skills in Serbia with focus on gender gap. *Journal of Women's Entrepreneurship and Education*, 1-2(1-2), 54–67. DOI: 10.28934/jwee18.12.pp54-67

Braun, V., & Clarke, V. (2006). Using thematic analysis in psychology. *Qualitative Research in Psychology*, 3(2), 77–101. DOI: 10.1191/1478088706qp063oa

Brill, J., & Chapple, E. (2022). Microsoft announces the phased roll-out of the EU Data Boundary for the Microsoft Cloud begins. Retrieved from https://blogs.microsoft.com/eupolicy/2022/12/15/eu-data-boundary-cloud-rollout

British Business Bank. (2022). *Going digital - The challenges facing European SMEs*. British Business Bank.

Bronk, C., & Tikk-Ringas, E. (2013). The Cyber Attack on Saudi Aramco. *Survival*, 55(2), 81–96. DOI: 10.1080/00396338.2013.784468

Brown, C., & White, D. (2021). The Alpha-Beta-Live approach in public sector digital projects. *Information Systems Journal*, 31(2), 289–305.

Brown, H. (1983). *Thinking About National Security: Defense and Foreign Policy in a Dangerous World*. Westview Press.

Brown, L., McFarlane, A., Das, A., & Campbell, K. (2022). The impact of financial development on carbon dioxide emissions in Jamaica. *Environmental Science and Pollution Research International*, 29(17), 1–14. DOI: 10.1007/s11356-021-17519-x PMID: 34851484

Broy, M., Cengarle, M. V., & Geisberger, E. (2012). Cyber-Physical Systems: Imminent Challenges. In Large-Scale Complex IT Syst. Dev., Operat. and Manag. - 17th Monterey Workshop, volume 7539 of LNCS, 1–28.

Broz, T., Buturac, G., & Parežanin, M. (2020). Digital transformation and economic cooperation: The case of Western Balkan countries. Zbornik radova Ekonomskog fakulteta u Rijeci: časopis za ekonomsku teoriju i praksu, 38(2), 697-722.

Bruel, A., & Godina, R. (2023). A smart contract architecture framework for successful industrial symbiosis applications using blockchain technology. *Sustainability*, 15(7). *Sustainability (Basel)*, 7(7), 5884. Advance online publication. DOI: 10.3390/su15075884

Brundage, M., Avin, S., Wang, J., Belfield, H., ... (2020). Toward trustworthy AI development: Mechanisms for supporting verifiable claims. https://doi.org//arXiv.2004.07213DOI: 10.48550

Bryman, A. (2016). *Social research methods* (5th ed.). Oxford University Press.

Brynjolfsson, E., & McAfee, A. (2014). *The second machine age: Work, progress, and prosperity in a time of brilliant technologies*. WW Norton & Company.

Bucea-Manea- oniş, R., Bucea-Manea- oniş, R., Simion, V. E., Ilic, D., Braicu, C., & Manea, N. (2020). Sustainability in higher education: The relationship between work-life balance and XR e-learning facilities. *Sustainability (Basel)*, 12(14), 5872. DOI: 10.3390/su12145872

Bughin, J., Catlin, T., Hirt, M., & Willmott, P. (2019) *Why digital strategies fail*, McKinsey Quarterly. Available at: https://www.mckinsey.com/business-functions/mckinsey-digital/our-insights/why-digital-strategies-fail (Accessed: 22 September 2024).

Bull, A. L., Russo, P. L., Friedman, N. D., Bennett, N. J., Boardman, C. J., & Richards, M. J. (2006). Compliance with surgical antibiotic prophylaxis–reporting from a statewide surveillance programme in Victoria, Australia. *The Journal of Hospital Infection*, 63(2), 140–147. DOI: 10.1016/j.jhin.2006.01.018 PMID: 16621135

BusinessToday. (2021). Amplifying Digital Transformation for Malaysian Businesses. Retrieved from https://www.businesstoday.com.my/2021/08/23/amplifying-digital-transformation-for-malaysian-businesses/

Bustos L. (2015). The Guide to Digital Transformation.

Buterin, V. (2014). A next-generation smart contract and decentralized application platform. Retrieved from https://ethereum.org/en/whitepaper/

Buterin, V. (2014). A next-generation smart contract and decentralized application platform. *white paper, 3*(37), 2-1.

Butler, T., & O'Brien, L. (2019). Understanding RegTech for digital regulatory compliance. *Disrupting finance: FinTech and strategy in the 21st century*, 85-102.

Butler, T., & O'Brien, L. (2019). Artificial intelligence for regulatory compliance: Are we there yet? *Journal of Financial Compliance*, 3(1), 44–59. DOI: 10.69554/TOCI6736

Calderón, A. (2020). Regulatory Compliance in AI Regime: Banks and FinTech. https://helda.helsinki.fi/server/api/core/bitstreams/c529b572-94d5-4080-a578-31d36e0cfcfa/content

Cardoso, J., Sheth, A., Miller, J., Arnold, J., & Kochut, K. (2004). Quality of service for workflows and web service processes. *Journal of Web Semantics*, 1(3), 281–308. DOI: 10.1016/j.websem.2004.03.001

Casella, B., & Formenti, L. (2019). FDI in the digital economy: a shift to asset-light international footprints. Transnational corporations, 25(1), 101-130.

Casino, F., Dasaklis, T. K., & Patsakis, C. (2021). A systematic literature review of blockchain-based applications: Current status, classification and open issues. *Telematics and Informatics*, 36, 55–81. DOI: 10.1016/j.tele.2018.11.006

Catalini, C., & Gans, J. S. (2016). Some simple economics of the blockchain. *MIT Sloan School of Management Working Paper.*

Cayirtepe, Z., & Senel, F. C. (2022). The future of quality and accreditation surveys: Digital transformation and artificial intelligence. *International Journal for Quality in Health Care : Journal of the International Society for Quality in Health Care*, 34(2), mzac025. DOI: 10.1093/intqhc/mzac025 PMID: 35388400

Ceccotti, F., Vernuccio, M., Mattiacci, A., & Pastore, A. (2024). Traditional agencies on bridges: How is digital transformation changing business models? *The Journal of Management and Governance*. Advance online publication. DOI: 10.1007/s10997-024-09703-1

Chaffey, D., Ellis-Chadwick, F., & Mayer, R. (2009). *Internet marketing: strategy, implementation and practice*. Pearson education.

Chatham House. (2020) *The state of cybersecurity in the GCC: An overview.* Available at: https://www.chathamhouse.org/2020/03/gcc-cyber-resilient-0/state-cybersecurity-gcc-overview (Accessed: 24 September 2024).

Chaudhari, R. S., Mahajan, S. K., Rane, S. B., & Agrawal, R. (2022). Modelling barriers in circular economy using TOPSIS: Perspective of environmental sustainability & Blockchain-IoT technology. *International Journal of Mathematical. Engineering and Management Sciences*, 7(6), 820. DOI: 10.33889/IJMEMS.2022.7.6.052

Chauhan, C., Parida, V., & Dhir, A. (2022). Linking circular economy and digitalization technologies: A systematic literature review of past achievements and future promises. *Technological Forecasting and Social Change*, 177, 121508. DOI: 10.1016/j.techfore.2022.121508

Chauhan, S., Goyal, S., Bhardwaj, A. K., & Sergi, B. S. (2022). Examining continuance intention in business schools with digital classroom methods during COVID-19: A comparative study of India and Italy. *Behaviour & Information Technology*, 41(8), 1596–1619. DOI: 10.1080/0144929X.2021.1892191

Cheng, H., Xue, L., Wang, P., Zeng, P., & Yu, H. (2017). Ontology-based web service integration for flexible manufacturing systems. In 15th Int. Conf. on Ind. Inf., pages 351–356. IEEE. DOI: 10.1109/INDIN.2017.8104797

Chen, G., Xu, B., Lu, M., & Chen, N.-S. (2018). Exploring blockchain technology and its potential applications for education. *Smart Learning Environments*, 5(1), 1. DOI: 10.1186/s40561-017-0050-x

Cheng, X., Yang, S., & Zhou, S. (2019). Why do college students continue to use mobile learning? Learning involvement and self-determination theory. *British Journal of Educational Technology*, 50(2), 626–637. DOI: 10.1111/bjet.12634

Cheng, Y. M. (2020). Students' satisfaction and continuance intention of the cloud-based e-learning system: Roles of interactivity and course quality factors. *Education + Training*, 62(9), 1037–1059. DOI: 10.1108/ET-10-2019-0245

Cheng, Y.-M. (2014). Extending the expectation-confirmation model with quality and flow to explore nurses' continued blended e-learning intention. *Information Technology & People*, 27(3), 230–258. DOI: 10.1108/ITP-01-2013-0024

Chen, H., Chiang, R. H. L., & Storey, V. C. (2012). Business intelligence and analytics: From big data to big impact. *Management Information Systems Quarterly*, 36(4), 1165–1188. DOI: 10.2307/41703503

Chenic, A. ., Burlacu, A., Dobrea, R. C., Tescan, L., Crețu, A. I., Stanef-Puica, M. R., Godeanu, T. N., Manole, A. M., Virjan, D., & Moroianu, N. (2023). The Impact of Digitalization on Macroeconomic Indicators in the New Industrial Age. *Electronics (Basel)*, 12(7), 1612. DOI: 10.3390/electronics12071612

Chen, M., Wang, X., Wang, J., Zuo, C., Tian, J., & Cui, Y. (2021). Factors afecting college students' continuous intention to use online course platform. *SN Computer Science*, 2(2), 1–11. DOI: 10.1007/s42979-021-00498-8 PMID: 33649745

Chen, Y., & Bellavitis, C. (2019). Decentralized finance: Blockchain technology and the quest for an open financial system. Rochester, NY. DOI: 10.2139/ssrn.3418557

Chen, Y., & Evans, M. (2022). Patient attitudes towards digital health services: A UK perspective. *Journal of Medical Internet Research*, 24(4), e35092. PMID: 35380546

Chernega, O. (2022). THE TOURIST INDUSTRY TRANSFORMATION THROUGH DIGITAL TECHNOLOGIES DURING THE WAR IN UKRAINE. *Scientific Notes of Ostroh Academy National University, 'Economics'. Series*, 1(26(54)), 43–50. DOI: 10.25264/2311-5149-2022-26(54)-43-50

Chiaroni, D., Fraccascia, L., Giannoccaro, I., & Urbinati, A. (2022). Enabling factors for the diffusion of circular economy and their impacts on sustainability. *Resources, Conservation & Recycling Advances*, 15, 200101. DOI: 10.1016/j.rcradv.2022.200101

Chidepatil, A., Bindra, P., Kulkarni, D., Qazi, M., Kshirsagar, M., & Sankaran, K. (2020). From trash to cash: How blockchain and multi-sensor-driven artificial intelligence can transform circular economy of plastic waste? *Administrative Sciences*, 10(2), 23. DOI: 10.3390/admsci10020023

China's National Security Strategy. (2015) *National Security Law of the People's Republic of China*. Available at: https://www.chinalawtranslate.com/en/national-security-law-2015/ (Accessed: 30 September 2024).

Chin, M. Y., Foo, L. P., & Falahat, M. (2023). Digital free trade zone in facilitating small medium enterprises for globalisation: A perspective from Malaysia small and medium enterprises. *Business and Economic Review*, 13(2), 40–52. DOI: 10.5296/ber.v13i2.20835

Chiu, C. M., Chiu, C. S., & Chang, H. C. (2007). Examining the integrated influence of fairness and quality on learners' satisfaction and Web-based learning continuance intention. *Information Systems Journal*, 17(3), 271–287. DOI: 10.1111/j.1365-2575.2007.00238.x

Chiu, M. L., Wang, Y. C., Lin, H. W., & Hsu, C. H. (2018). How service-dominant logic moderates the relationship between big data analytics and customer experience. *Journal of Business Research*, 117, 500–510.

Christidis, K., & Devetsikiotis, M. (2016). Blockchains and smart contracts for the internet of things. *IEEE Access : Practical Innovations, Open Solutions*, 4, 2292–2303. DOI: 10.1109/ACCESS.2016.2566339

Chronicle, U. N. (2020) *National Security versus Global Security*. Available at: https://www.un.org/en/chronicle/article/national-security-versus-global-security (Accessed: 24 September 2024).

Chu, K.-M. (2023). Innovation Practices of New Technology Adoption for the Business Survival Strategy of Online Travel Agencies During the COVID-19 Pandemic: Two Case Studies in Taiwan. *Journal of the Knowledge Economy*, 15(2), 9556–9575. Advance online publication. DOI: 10.1007/s13132-023-01480-w

Chu, T.-H., & Chen, Y.-Y. (2016). With Good We Become Good: Understanding e-learning adoption by theory of planned behavior and group influences. *Computers & Education*, 92–93, 37–52. DOI: 10.1016/j.compedu.2015.09.013

Cidral, W. A., Oliveira, T., Di Felice, M., & Aparicio, M. (2018). E-learning success determinants: Brazilian empirical study. *Computers & Education*, 122, 273–290. DOI: 10.1016/j.compedu.2017.12.001

Cinar, E., Trott, P., & Simms, C. (2019). A systematic review of barriers to public sector innovation process. *Public Management Review*, 21(2), 264–290. DOI: 10.1080/14719037.2018.1473477

Çınar, Z. M., Abdussalam Nuhu, A., Zeeshan, Q., Korhan, O., Asmael, M., & Safaei, B. (2020). Machine learning in predictive maintenance towards sustainable smart manufacturing in industry 4.0. *Sustainability (Basel)*, 12(19), 8211. DOI: 10.3390/su12198211

Ciortea, A., Mayer, S., & Michahelles, F. (2018). Repurposing Manufacturing Lines on the Fly with Multi-agent Systems for the Web of Things. In Proc. of the 17th Int. Conf. on Autonomous Agents and Multi-Agent Systems, pages 813–822. Int. Found. for Autonomous Agents and Multiagent Systems / ACM.

CISA. (2023) *Critical Infrastructure Security and Resilience*. Available at: https://www.cisa.gov/topics/critical-infrastructure-security-and-resilience (Accessed: 15 September 2024).

Ciuriak, D., & Ptashkina, M. (2018). The digital transformation and the transformation of international trade. RTA Exchange. Geneva: International Centre for Trade and Sustainable Development and the Inter-American Development Bank. Available at *SSRN*: https://ssrn.com/abstract=3107811

CleverChain. (n.d.) *Automated perpetual compliance monitoring*. Retrieved 14 July, 2023, from https://www.cleverchain.ai/

Cloud Networks. (2023) *Cybersecurity Regulations in the GCC: Compliance Management for Enterprises.* Available at: https://cloudnetworks.ae/articles/cs-regulations-gcc/ (Accessed: 12 September 2024).

Coche, E., Kolk, A., & Ocelik, V. (2024). Unravelling cross-country regulatory intricacies of data governance: The relevance of legal insights for digitalization and international business. *Journal of International Business Policy*, 7(1), 112–127. DOI: 10.1057/s42214-023-00172-1

Cohen, L., Manion, L., & Morrison, K. (2017). *Research methods in education* (8th ed.). Routledge. DOI: 10.4324/9781315456539

Colitti, W., Steenhaut, K., & Caro, N. De., (2011). "Integrating Wireless Sensor Networks with the Web", Extending the Internet to Low power and Lossy Networks (IP+SN).

Collibra Data Governance. Available online: https://www.collibra.com/us/en/products/datagovernance (accessed on 15 October 2023).

Colligan, P. (2019). *Transformative innovation in the public sector.*

Colucci, S., Di Noia, T., Pinto, A., Ruta, M., Ragone, A., & Tinelli, E. (2007). A Nonmonotonic Approach to Semantic Matchmaking and Request Refinement in E-Marketplaces. *International Journal of Electronic Commerce*, 12(2), 127–154. DOI: 10.2753/JEC1086-4415120205

Construction Industry Training Board (2023) *Digital skills for the UK construction sector.* Kings Lynn: CITB.

Consulting, F. T. I. (2023) *Navigating Cybersecurity Threat Landscape in the Middle East.* Available at: https://www.fticonsulting.com/insights/articles/navigating-cybersecurity-threat-landscape-middle-east (Accessed: 16 September 2024).

Corejova, T., & Chinoracky, R. (2021). Assessing the potential for digital transformation. *Sustainability (Basel)*, 13(19), 11040. DOI: 10.3390/su131911040

Cornwell, N., Bilson, C., Gepp, A., Stern, S., & Vanstone, B. J. (2023). Modernising operational risk management in financial institutions via data-driven causal factors analysis: A pre-registered report. *Pacific-Basin Finance Journal*, 77, 101906. DOI: 10.1016/j.pacfin.2022.101906

Cory, N. (2021). Sovereignty requirements in France -and potentially EU- cybersecurity regulations: The latest barrier to data flows, digital trade, and digital cooperation among likeminded partners. Retrieved from https://www.crossborderdataforum.org/sovereignty-requirements-in -france-and-potentially-eu-cybersecurity-regulations-the-latest-barrier-to-data-flows-digital -trade-and-digital-cooperation-among-likemi/

Cory, A., Henson, J., Pschorr, K., Sheth, A. P., & Thirunarayan, K. (2009). "SemSOS: Semantic sensor Observation Service", in *Proceedings of the International Symposium on Collaborative Technologies and Systems*.

Cosa, M. (2024). Business digital transformation: Strategy adaptation, communication, and future agenda. *Journal of Strategy and Management*, 17(2), 244–259. DOI: 10.1108/JSMA-09-2023-0233

Courbis, C., & Finkelstein, A. (2005). Weaving Aspects into Web Service Orchestrations, in *Proceeding of International Conference of Web Services (ICWS '05)*, July 2005. DOI: 10.1109/ICWS.2005.129

Craigen, D., Diakun-Thibault, N., & Purse, R. (2014). Defining cybersecurity. *Technology Innovation Management Review*, 4(10), 13–21. Retrieved September 30, 2024, from https://www.timreview.ca/article/835. DOI: 10.22215/timreview/835

Creswell, J. W. (2014). *Research design: Qualitative, quantitative, and mixed methods approaches* (4th ed.). SAGE Publications.

Creswell, J. W., & Plano Clark, V. L. (2017). *Designing and conducting mixed methods research* (3rd ed.). SAGE Publications.

Croman, K., Decker, C., Eyal, I., Gencer, A. E., Juels, A., Kosba, A., . . . Wattenhofer, R. (2016, February). On Scaling Decentralized Blockchains: (A Position Paper). In *International conference on financial cryptography and data security* (pp. 106-125). Berlin, Heidelberg: Springer Berlin Heidelberg. DOI: 10.1007/978-3-662-53357-4_8

Crosby, M., Nachiappan, P., Verma, S., & Kalyanaraman, V. (2016). Blockchain technology: Beyond bitcoin. *Applied Innovation*, 2, 6–10.

Cyber Security Agency of Singapore (CSA). (2021) Available at: https://www.csa.gov.sg/ (Accessed: 30 September 2024).

Cybersecurity and Infrastructure Security Agency (CISA). (2023) *What is Cybersecurity?* Available at: https://www.cisa.gov/news-events/news/what-cybersecurity (Accessed: 30 September 2024).

Cybil Portal. (2021) *Cybersecurity in the GCC Countries*. Available at: https://cybilportal.org/projects/cybersecurity-in-the-gcc-countries/ (Accessed: 27 September 2024).

da Silva, E. R., Lohmer, J., Rohla, M., & Angelis, J. (2023). Unleashing the circular economy in the electric vehicle battery supply chain: A case study on data sharing and blockchain potential. *Resources, Conservation and Recycling*, 193, 106969. DOI: 10.1016/j.resconrec.2023.106969

Dabic, M., Maley, J. F., Svarc, J., & Pocek, J. (2023). Future of digital work: Challenges for sustainable human resources management. Journal of Innovation & Knowledge. DOI: 10.1016/j.jik.2023.100353

Daneji, A. A., Ayub, A. F. M., & Khambari, M. N. M. (2019). The effects of perceived usefulness, confirmation and satisfaction on continuance intention in using massive open online course (MOOC). *Knowledge Management & E-Learning*, 11(2), 201–214.

Danese, P., Mocellin, R., & Romano, P. (2021). Designing blockchain systems to prevent counterfeiting in wine supply chains: A multiple-case study. *International Journal of Operations & Production Management*, 41(13), 1–33. DOI: 10.1108/IJOPM-12-2019-0781

Daniel, F. (2018). Bank Reduces Money-Laundering Investigation Effort with AI. https://emerj.com/ai-case-studies/bank-reduces-money-laundering-investigation-effort-with-ai/

Dark Reading. (2023) *An Overview of Dubai's First and Second Cybersecurity Strategy*. Available at: https://www.darkreading.com/cybersecurity-analytics/overview-dubais-first-and-second-cybersecurity-strategy (Accessed: 28 September 2024).

Darma, G. S., & Noviana, I. P. T. (2020). Exploring digital marketing strategies during the new normal era in enhancing the use of digital payment. *Jurnal Mantik*, 4(3), 2257–2262.

Das, S., & Mitra, A. (2024). Advancing lightweight digital trust architectures in the internet of medical things: A multi-dimensional analysis. In *Lightweight Digital Trust Architectures in the Internet of Medical Things (IoMT)* (pp. 1-14). DOI: 10.4018/979-8-3693-2109-6.ch001

Das, S., & Mitra, A. (2024). Balancing the scale: Ethical marketing in the age of big data-A comprehensive analysis of data governance standards and the role of effective technology. In *Ethical Marketing Through Data Governance Standards and Effective Technology* (pp. 50-61).

Data Oman. (n.d.). *Data Oman*. Retrieved from https://data.gov.om/

Davenport, T. H. (2018). *The AI advantage: How to put the artificial intelligence revolution to work*. mit Press.

Davenport, T. H. (1993). *Process innovation: reengineering work through information technology*. Harvard Business Press.

Davenport, T. H., & Ronanki, R. (2018). Artificial intelligence for the real world. *Harvard Business Review*, 96(1), 108–116.

Davenport, T. H., & Short, J. E. (1998). The new industrial engineering: Information technology and business process redesign. *IEEE Engineering Management Review*, 26(3), 46–60.

Davenport, T., Guha, A., Grewal, D., & Bressgott, T. (2020). How artificial intelligence will change the future of marketing. *Journal of the Academy of Marketing Science*, 48(1), 24–42. DOI: 10.1007/s11747-019-00696-0

Davidson, E., & Vaast, E. (2010). Digital entrepreneurship and its sociomaterial enactment. In *Proceedings of the 43rd Hawaii International Conference on System Sciences* (pp. 1-10). IEEE.

Davis, M., & Roberts, N. (2022). Agile methodologies in government digital transformation. *Public Management Review*, 24(5), 678–695.

De Giovanni, P. (2022). Leveraging the circular economy with a closed-loop supply chain and a reverse omnichannel using blockchain technology and incentives. *International Journal of Operations & Production Management*, 42(7), 959–994. DOI: 10.1108/IJOPM-07-2021-0445

De Virgilio, R., Di Sciascio, E., Ruta, M., Scioscia, F., & Torlone, R. (2011). Semantic-based rfid data management. In *Unique Radio Innovation for the 21st Century* (pp. 111–141). Springer. DOI: 10.1007/978-3-642-03462-6_6

Deloitte. (2020) *National Transformation in the Middle East: A Digital Journey*. Available at: https://www2.deloitte.com/content/dam/Deloitte/xe/Documents/technology-media-telecommunications/dtme_tmt_national-transformation-in-the-middleeast/National%20Transformation%20in%20the%20Middle%20East%20-%20A%20Digital%20Journey.pdf (Accessed: 21 September 2024).

Deloitte. (2023) *Digital transformation: The future of work*. Available at: https://www2.deloitte.com (Accessed: 30 September 2024).

Demir, B., Guven, S., & Sahin, B. (2023). Evaluation of the Metaverse: Perspectives of Travel Agency Employees. In Al-Emran, M., Ali, J. H., Valeri, M., Alnoor, A., & Hussien, Z. A. (Eds.), *Beyond Reality: Navigating the Power of Metaverse and Its Applications* (Vol. 876, pp. 1–20). Springer Nature Switzerland., DOI: 10.1007/978-3-031-51300-8_1

Demirkan, S., Demirkan, I., & McKee, A. (2020). Blockchain technology in the future of business cyber security and accounting. *Journal of Management Analytics*, 7(2), 189–208. DOI: 10.1080/23270012.2020.1731721

Dethine, B., Enjolras, M., & Monticolo, D. (2020). Digitalization and SMEs' export management: Impacts on resources and capabilities. *Technology Innovation Management Review*, 10(4), 18–34. DOI: 10.22215/timreview/1344

Dey, D. (2017). Growing importance of machine learning in compliance and regulatory reporting. *European Journal of Multidisciplinary Studies*, 2(7), 255–258. DOI: 10.26417/ejms.v6i2.p255-258

Digital Catapult. (2023). *Rural digital innovation: Case studies from the UK*. Digital Catapult.

Digital Skills Global. (2018) *Digital skills gap is a risk to companies*. Available at: https://digitalskillsglobal.com (Accessed: 14 September 2024).

Dixon, M. F., Halperin, I., & Bilokon, P. (2020). *Machine learning in finance* (Vol. 1170). Springer International Publishing. DOI: 10.1007/978-3-030-41068-1

Domazet, I., Marjanović, D., & Ahmetagić, D. (2022) . The Impact of High-Tech Products Exports on Economic Growth: The Case of Serbia, Bulgaria, Romania and Hungary. Ekonomika preduzeća, 70(3-4), 191-205.

Domazet, I., Marjanović, D., Ahmetagić, D., & Bugarčić, M. (2021). The Impact of Innovation Indicators on Increasing Exports of High Technology Products. Ekonomika preduzeća, 69(1-2), 31-40.

Domazet, I.. (2023). Innovation and ICT: Key Factors of Successful Business. In Correia, A., & Agua, P. B. (Eds.), *Innovation, strategy, and transformation frameworks for the modern enterprise* (pp. 327–345). IGI Global. DOI: 10.4018/979-8-3693-0458-7.ch014

Domazet, I., & Marjanović, D. (2024). Digital Progress and Information Society: Evidence from EU Countries and Serbia. In Verma, B., Singla, B., & Mittal, A. (Eds.), *Driving Decentralization and Disruption With Digital Technologies* (pp. 1–20). IGI Global. DOI: 10.4018/979-8-3693-3253-5.ch001

Domazet, I., Marjanović, D., Ahmetagić, D., & Antonijević, M. (2022). Does the Increase in the Number of Registered Patents Affect Economic Growth? Evidence from Romania and Bulgaria. *Economic Analysis: Applied Research in Emerging Markets*, 55(2), 49–65. DOI: 10.28934/ea.22.55.2.pp49-65

Domazet, I., Marjanović, D., Ahmetagić, D., & Simović, V. (2023). The influence of the number of patents on the economic growth of the country - evidence from Serbia and Hungary. *Strategic Management*, 28(4), 41–52. DOI: 10.5937/StraMan2300048D

Domazet, I., Marjanović, D., & Subić, J. (2024). Driving factors of the Montenegrin economy – FDI and tourism. *International Review (Steubenville, Ohio)*, 1-2(1-2), 117–127. DOI: 10.5937/intrev2401117D

Domazet, I., Zubović, J., & Lazić, M. (2018). Driving Factors of Serbian Competitiveness: Digital Economy and ICT. *Strategic Management*, 23(1), 20–28. DOI: 10.5937/StraMan1801020D

Dominique-Ferreira, S., Viana, M., Prentice, C., & Martins, N. (2022). The Influence of Web Design on Customer Engagement with an Online Travel Agency. In Abreu, A., Liberato, D., & Garcia Ojeda, J. C. (Eds.), *Advances in Tourism, Technology and Systems* (Vol. 293, pp. 327–336). Springer Nature Singapore., DOI: 10.1007/978-981-19-1040-1_28

Donepudi, P. K. (2019). Automation and machine learning in transforming the financial industry. *Asian Business Review*, 9(3), 129–138. DOI: 10.18034/abr.v9i3.494

Du, J., & Wei, L. (2020). An analysis of regulatory technology in the Internet financial sector in conjunction with the logit model. In *2020 2nd International Conference on Economic Management and Model Engineering (ICEMME)* (pp. 428-431). IEEE. DOI: 10.1109/ICEMME51517.2020.00091

Dujak, D., & Sajter, D. (2019). Blockchain applications in supply chain. *SMART Supply Network*, 21–46. .DOI: 10.1007/978-3-319-91668-2_2

Dumas, M., Rosa, L. M., Mendling, J., & Reijers, A. H. (2018). *Fundamentals of business process management*. Springer-Verlag. DOI: 10.1007/978-3-662-56509-4

Du, S., & Xie, C. (2021). Paradoxes of artificial intelligence in consumer markets: Ethical challenges and opportunities. *Journal of Business Research*, 129, 961–974. DOI: 10.1016/j.jbusres.2020.08.024

Dutta, R. (October 2021). COVID-19 and the role of digital technology based on the ten global trends identified by the World Economic Forum. Asian Disaster Preparedness Center

Dwivedi, Y. K., Hughes, L., Ismagilova, E., Aarts, G., Coombs, C., Crick, T., Duan, Y., Dwivedi, R., Edwards, J., Eirug, A., Galanos, V., Ilavarasan, P. V., Janssen, M., Jones, P., Kar, A. K., Kizgin, H., Kronemann, B., Lal, B., Lucini, B., & Williams, M. D. (2021). Artificial Intelligence (AI): Multidisciplinary perspectives on emerging challenges, opportunities, and agenda for research, practice and policy. *International Journal of Information Management*, 57, 101994. DOI: 10.1016/j.ijinfomgt.2019.08.002

Dzhunushalieva, G., & Teuber, R. (2024). Roles of innovation in achieving the Sustainable Development Goals: A bibliometric analysis. Journal of Innovation & Knowledge. DOI: 10.1016/j.jik.2024.100472

Eboigbe, E., Farayola, O., Olatoye, F., Chinwe, N., & Daraojimba, C. (2023). BUSINESS INTELLIGENCE TRANSFORMATION THROUGH AI AND DATA ANALYTICS. *Engineering Science & Technology Journal.*, 4(5), 285–307. DOI: 10.51594/estj.v4i5.616

Economic Planning Unit. (2018). *Malaysia Digital Economy Blueprint*. Ministry of Economy of Malaysia. https://www.ekonomi.gov.my/sites/default/files/2021-03/Malaysia-Digital Economy-Blueprint-%2820-03-2021%29.pdf

Economic Planning Unit. (2021). *National 4IR Policy*. Ministry of Economy of Malaysia. https://www.ekonomi.gov.my/sites/default/files/2021-07/National-4IR -Policy.pdf

Economist Intelligence Unit. (2020) *Innovating through tech in the GCC*. Available at: https://impact.economist.com/perspectives/sites/default/files/eiu_bahrain_edb _report.pdf (Accessed: 19 September 2024).

Edwards, J., & Wolfe, S. (2005). Compliance: A review. *Journal of Financial Regulation and Compliance.*

Emmanuel, T., Maupong, T., Mpoeleng, D., Semong, T., Mphago, B., & Tabona, O. (2021). A survey on missing data in machine learning. *Journal of Big Data*, 8(1), 1–37. DOI: 10.1186/s40537-021-00516-9 PMID: 34722113

Energy Sector Cybersecurity Framework. (2023) *Roadmap to Achieve Energy Delivery Systems Cybersecurity*. Available at: https://energy.gov/sites/prod/files/Energy%20Delivery%20Systems%20Cybersecurity%20Roadmap_finalweb.pdf (Accessed: 30 September 2024).

Enterprisers Project. (2023) *7 digital transformation barriers to overcome*. Available at: https://enterprisersproject.com (Accessed: 30 September 2024).

Esposito, C., De Santis, A., Tortora, G., Chang, H., & Choo, K.-K. R. (2022). Blockchain: A panacea for healthcare cloud-based data security and privacy? *IEEE Cloud Computing*, 5(1), 31–37. DOI: 10.1109/MCC.2018.011791712

Esses, D., Csete, M. S., & Németh, B. (2021). Sustainability and digital transformation in the visegrad group of central European countries. *Sustainability (Basel)*, 13(11), 5833. DOI: 10.3390/su13115833

European Commission. (2020). European Blockchain Strategy and Digital Finance Package. Retrieved from https://finance.ec.europa.eu/publications/digital-finance-package_en

European Union Agency for Cybersecurity (ENISA). (2022) Available at: https://www.enisa.europa.eu/ (Accessed: 22 September 2024).

Everledger. (2018). Diamond time-lapse: Tracking the journey of a diamond from mine to finger. Retrieved from https://www.everledger.io/

Fan, Z. P., Wu, X. Y., & Cao, B. B. (2022). Considering the traceability awareness of consumers: Should the supply chain adopt the blockchain technology? *Annals of Operations Research*, 309(2), 837–860. DOI: 10.1007/s10479-020-03729-y

Federation of Small Businesses. (2023). *The digital readiness of UK small businesses*. FSB.

Feng, Q., He, D., Zeadally, S., Khan, M. K., & Kumar, N. (2019). A survey on privacy protection in blockchain system. *Journal of Network and Computer Applications*, 126, 45–58. DOI: 10.1016/j.jnca.2018.10.020

Ferreira, I. A., Godina, R., Pinto, A., Pinto, P., & Carvalho, H. (2023). Boosting additive circular economy ecosystems using blockchain: An exploratory case study. *Computers & Industrial Engineering*, 175, 108916. DOI: 10.1016/j.cie.2022.108916

Ferrell, O. C., Fraedrich, J., & Ferrell, L. (2019). *Business ethics: Ethical decision making and cases*. Cengage Learning.

Field, A. (2013). *Discovering statistics using IBM SPSS Statistics* (4th ed.). SAGE Publications.

Fingar, P. (2003). *Business process management: the third wave*. Meghan-Kiffer Press.

Firdausi, S. F. D. (2023). *Digital Transformation of Tourism in India: Strengths and Opportunities*. MYQA WORLD. DOI: 10.5281/ZENODO.10041289

FireEye. (2023) *APT Threat Activity in the Middle East.* Available at: https://www .fireeye.com/current-threats/apt-threat-activity/middle-east.html (Accessed: 30 September 2024).

Firoj, K., & Mohammad, B. T. (2024). Measuring sustainability in the broadcasting media industry in Bangladesh. *I-Manager's. Journal of Management*, 18(3), 51. DOI: 10.26634/jmgt.18.3.20234

Fischer, T. (2018). *Robotic Process Automation.* Springer.

Fishbein, M. (1975). Belief, Attitude, Intention and Behaviour: An Introduction to Theory and Research: Vol. 27. *MA.* Addison-Wesley.

Fitzgerald, M., Kruschwitz, N., Bonnet, D., & Welch, M. (2014). Embracing digital technology: A new strategic imperative. *MIT Sloan Management Review*, 55(2), 1.

Floridi, L., Cowls, J., Beltrametti, M., Chatila, R., Chazerand, P., Dignum, V., Luetge, C., Madelin, R., Pagallo, U., Rossi, F., Schafer, B., Valcke, P., & Vayena, E. (2018). AI4People—an ethical framework for a good AI society: Opportunities, risks, principles, and recommendations. *Minds and Machines*, 28(4), 689–707. DOI: 10.1007/s11023-018-9482-5 PMID: 30930541

Floridi, L., Taddeo, M., & Turilli, M. (2018). The ethics of information transparency. *Ethics and Information Technology*, 10(2-3), 105–116.

Forbes (2021) *Five barriers to digital transformation and how to overcome them.* Available at: https://www.forbes.com (Accessed: 22 September 2024).

Fornell, C., & Larcker, D. F. (1981). Evaluating Structural Equation Models with Unobservable Variables and Measurement Error. *JMR, Journal of Marketing Research.* Advance online publication. DOI: 10.1177/002224378101800313

Fosso Wamba, S., Gunasekaran, A., Papadopoulos, T., & Ngai, E. (2018). Big data analytics in logistics and supply chain management. *International Journal of Logistics Management*, 29(2), 478–484. DOI: 10.1108/IJLM-02-2018-0026

Foster, C., & Azmeh, S. (2020). Latecomer economies and national digital policy: An industrial policy perspective. *The Journal of Development Studies*, 56(7), 1247–1262. DOI: 10.1080/00220388.2019.1677886

Frizzo-Barker, J., Chow-White, P. A., Adams, P. R., Mentanko, J., Ha, D., & Green, S. (2020). Blockchain as a disruptive technology for business: A systematic review. *International Journal of Information Management*, 51, 102029. DOI: 10.1016/j. ijinfomgt.2019.10.014

Frost, R., & Strauss, J. (2016). *E-marketing.* Routledge.

Fung, A. (2015). Putting the Public Back into Governance: The Challenges of Citizen Participation and Its Future. *Public Administration Review*, 75(4), 513–522. DOI: 10.1111/puar.12361

FutureDotNow. (2024) *The essential digital skills gap*. Available at: https://futuredotnow.uk (Accessed: 15 September 2024).

Gabor, D., & Brooks, S. (2017). The digital revolution in financial inclusion: International development in the fintech era. *New Political Economy*, 22(4), 423–436. DOI: 10.1080/13563467.2017.1259298

Gad, A. G., Mosa, D. T., Abualigah, L., & Abohany, A. A. (2022). Emerging trends in blockchain technology and applications: A review and outlook. *Journal of King Saud University. Computer and Information Sciences*, 34(9), 6719–6742. DOI: 10.1016/j.jksuci.2022.03.007

Gandomi, A., & Haider, M. (2015). Beyond the hype: Big data concepts, methods, and analytics. *International Journal of Information Management*, 35(2), 137–144. DOI: 10.1016/j.ijinfomgt.2014.10.007

Garcia, R., & Lopez, F. (2021). Audits and accountability in digital healthcare initiatives. *Health Policy and Technology*, 10(2), 100508. PMID: 33850698

Gartner (2023) *Gartner's Top Security and Risk Management Trends*. Available at: https://www.gartner.com/en/newsroom/press-releases/2023 (Accessed: 30 September 2024).

Gaur, V., & Gaiha, A. (2020). Building a transparent supply chain: Blockchain can enhance trust, efficiency and speed. *Harvard Business Review*, 98(3), 94–103.

Gebayew, C., Hardini, I. R., Panjaitan, G. H. A., & Kurniawan, N. B. (2018). A systematic literature review on digital transformation. *International Conference on Information Technology Systems and Innovation*, 260-265, IEEE. DOI: 10.1109/ICITSI.2018.8695912

Gebremeskel, B. K., Jonathan, G. M., & Yalew, S. D. (2023). Information Security Challenges During Digital Transformation. *Procedia Computer Science*, 219, 44–51. DOI: 10.1016/j.procs.2023.01.262

Georgiou, K., Mittas, N., Mamalikidis, I., Mitropoulos, A., & Angelis, L. (2021). Analyzing the roles and competence demand for digitalization in the oil and gas 4.0 era. *IEEE Access : Practical Innovations, Open Solutions*, 9, 151306–151326. DOI: 10.1109/ACCESS.2021.3124909

Ghosh, K. (2021). Regtech: Bits and Bytes of Financial Regulation. *Journal of Business Strategy Finance and Management*, 3(1-2), 103–109. DOI: 10.12944/ JBSFM.03.01-02.10

Giblin, C., Liu, A. Y., Müller, S., Pfitzmann, B., & Zhou, X. (2005, May). Regulations Expressed As Logical Models (REALM). In *JURIX* (pp. 37-48).

Gigged.AI. (2024) *Digital transformation in crisis*. Available at: https://gigged.ai (Accessed: 30 September 2024).

Gill, S. S., Xu, M., Ottaviani, C., Patros, P., Bahsoon, R., Shaghaghi, A., Golec, M., Stankovski, V., Wu, H., Abraham, A., Singh, M., Mehta, H., Ghosh, S. K., Baker, T., Parlikad, A. K., Lutfiyya, H., Kanhere, S. S., Sakellariou, R., Dustdar, S., & Uhlig, S. (2022). AI for next generation computing: Emerging trends and future directions. *Internet of Things : Engineering Cyber Physical Human Systems*, 19, 100514. DOI: 10.1016/j.iot.2022.100514

Giones, F., & Brem, A. (2017). Digital technology entrepreneurship: A definition and research agenda. *Technology Innovation Management Review*, 7(5), 44–51. DOI: 10.22215/timreview/1076

Gochhayat, S. P., Kaliyar, P., Conti, M., Tiwari, P., Prasath, V. B. S., Gupta, D., & Khanna, A. (2018). LISA: Lightweight context-aware IoT service architecture. *Journal of Cleaner Production*, 212, 1345–1356. DOI: 10.1016/j.jclepro.2018.12.096

Gołąb-Andrzejak, E. (2023). AI-powered digital transformation: Tools, benefits and challenges for marketers–case study of LPP. *Procedia Computer Science*, 219, 397–404. DOI: 10.1016/j.procs.2023.01.305

Golosova, J., & Romanovs, A. (2018, November). The advantages and disadvantages of the blockchain technology. In *2018 IEEE 6th Workshop on Advances in Information Electronic and Electrical Engineering (AIEEE)* (pp. 1-6). IEEE. DOI: 10.1109/AIEEE.2018.8592253

Goltz, N., & Mayo, M. (2018). Enhancing regulatory compliance by using artificial intelligence text mining to identify penalty clauses in legislation. *RAIL*, 1, 175.

Golubović, V., Mirković, M., Mićunović, N., & Srića, V. (2021). Digital Transformation in Montenegro–Current Status, Issues and Proposals for Improvement. *Journal of Computer Science and Information Technology*, 9(1), 1–12. DOI: 10.15640/jcsit. v9n1a1

Gomber, P., Kauffman, R. J., Parker, C., & Weber, B. W. (2018). On the fintech revolution: Interpreting the forces of innovation, disruption, and transformation in financial services. *Journal of Management Information Systems*, 35(1), 220–265. DOI: 10.1080/07421222.2018.1440766

Gong, Y., Xie, S., Arunachalam, D., Duan, J., & Luo, J. (2022). Blockchain-based recycling and its impact on recycling performance: A network theory perspective. *Business Strategy and the Environment*, 31(8), 3717–3741. DOI: 10.1002/bse.3028

Good Things Foundation. (2024). *Digital exclusion and UK business leadership*. Good Things Foundation.

Goodell, J. W., Kumar, S., Lim, W. M., & Pattnaik, D. (2021). Artificial intelligence and machine learning in finance: Identifying foundations, themes, and research clusters from bibliometric analysis. *Journal of Behavioral and Experimental Finance*, 32, 100577. DOI: 10.1016/j.jbef.2021.100577

Gopal, G., Suter-Crazzolara, C., Toldo, L., & Eberhardt, W. (2019). Digital transformation in healthcare–architectures of present and future information technologies. [CCLM]. *Clinical Chemistry and Laboratory Medicine*, 57(3), 328–335. DOI: 10.1515/cclm-2018-0658 PMID: 30530878

GOV UK. (2024) *Data protection*. Available at: https://www.gov.uk/data-protection (Accessed: 30 September 2024).

GOV.UK. (2024) *A plan for digital health and social care*. Available at: https://www.gov.uk/government/publications/a-plan-for-digital-health-and-social-care/a-plan-for-digital-health-and-social-care (Accessed: 30 September 2024).

Governance, I. T. (2023) *What is Cyber Security? Definition & Best Practices*. Available at: https://www.itgovernance.co.uk/what-is-cybersecurity (Accessed: 23 September 2024).

Govindan, K. (2022). Tunneling the barriers of blockchain technology in remanufacturing for achieving sustainable development goals: A circular manufacturing perspective. *Business Strategy and the Environment*, 31(8), 3769–3785. DOI: 10.1002/bse.3031

Grajek, S. (2020) 'Top IT Issues, 2020: The Drive to Digital Transformation Begins', *EDUCAUSE Review*. Available at: https://er.educause.edu/articles/2020/1/top-it-issues-2020-the-drive-to-digital-transformation-begins (Accessed: 17 September 2024).

Grand View Research. (2023) *U.K. digital transformation market size share & trends analysis report by solution, by service, by deployment, by enterprise size, by end-use, and segment forecasts, 2023 - 2030.* Available at: https://www.grandviewresearch.com (Accessed: 18 September 2024).

Grassi, L., & Lanfranchi, D. (2022). RegTech in public and private sectors: The nexus between data, technology and regulation. *Economia e Politica Industriale,* 49(3), 441–479. DOI: 10.1007/s40812-022-00226-0

Grati, R., Loukil, F., Boukadi, K., & Abed, M. (2024). A blockchain-based framework for circular end-of-life vehicle processing. *Cluster Computing,* 27(1), 707–720. DOI: 10.1007/s10586-023-03981-4

Grover, A. (2024). Navigating the Digital Era: Exploring Privacy, Security, and Ownership of Personal Data. In Verma, B., Singla, B., & Mittal, A. (Eds.), (pp. 201–227). Advances in Web Technologies and Engineering. IGI Global., DOI: 10.4018/979-8-3693-1762-4.ch011

Guan, L., Li, W., Guo, C., & Huang, J. (2023). Environmental strategy for sustainable development: Role of digital transformation in China's natural resource exploitation. *Resources Policy,* 87, 104304. DOI: 10.1016/j.resourpol.2023.104304

Gubbi, J., Buyya, R., Marusic, S., & Palaniswami, M. (2013). Internet of Things (IoT): A vision, architectural elements, and future directions. *Future Generation Computer Systems,* 29(7), 1645–1660. DOI: 10.1016/j.future.2013.01.010

Guerra, J. M. M., Danvila-del-Valle, I., & Mendez-suarez, M. (2023). The impact of digital transformation on talent management. *Technological Forecasting and Social Change,* 188, 122291. Advance online publication. DOI: 10.1016/j.techfore.2022.122291

Gulati, R. (2023). Did regulatory compliance with governance standards really enhance the profit efficiency of Indian banks?. *Macroeconomics and Finance in Emerging Market Economies,* 1-27.

Gulf Business. (2023) *Dubai launches second cycle of its cybersecurity strategy.* Available at: https://gulfbusiness.com/dubai-bolsters-its-cybersecurity-strategy/ (Accessed: 30 September 2024).

Gulf News. (2020). *Winners of Arab Government Excellence Awards.* Retrieved from https://gulfnews.com/amp/uae/government/sheikh-mohammed-announces -winners-of-arab-government-excellence-awards-1.75492819

Gurbaxani, V., & Dunkle, D. (2019). Gearing up for successful digital transformation. *MIS Quarterly Executive,* 18(3), 209–220. DOI: 10.17705/2msqe.00017

Hair, J. F., Anderson, R. E., Tatham, R. L., & Black, W. C. (2010). *Multivariate Data Analysis*: A Global Perspective (7th Edition). In Pearson Prentice Hall, New Jersey.

Hair, J. F., Black, W. C., Babin, B. J., Anderson, R. E., & Tatham, R. L. (2006). *Multivariate Data Analysis* (6th ed.). Pearson-Prentice Hall.

Halilovic, S., & Cicic, M. (2013). Antecedents of information systems user behaviour – extended expectation-confirmation model. *Behaviour & Information Technology*, 32(4), 359–370. DOI: 10.1080/0144929X.2011.554575

Hall, J. V., & Krueger, A. B. (2018). An analysis of the labor market for Uber's driver-partners in the United States. *Industrial & Labor Relations Review*, 71(3), 705–732. DOI: 10.1177/0019793917717222

Hamidi, S. R., Aziz, A. A., Shuhidan, S. M., Aziz, A. A., & Mokhsin, M. (2018). SMEs maturity model assessment of IR4. 0 digital transformation. In Proceedings of the 7th International Conference on Kansei Engineering and Emotion Research 2018: KEER 2018, 19-22 March 2018, Kuching, Sarawak, Malaysia (pp. 721-732). Springer Singapore. DOI: 10.1007/978-981-10-8612-0_75

Hammer, M., & Champy, J. (2009). *Reengineering the corporation: Manifesto for business revolution, a*. Zondervan.

Han, H., Shiwakoti, R. K., Jarvis, R., Mordi, C., & Botchie, D. (2023). Accounting and auditing with blockchain technology and artificial intelligence: A literature review. *International Journal of Accounting Information Systems*, 48, 100598. DOI: 10.1016/j.accinf.2022.100598

Hanna, N. (2010). *Enabling enterprise transformation: Business and grassroots Innovation for the knowledge economy*. Springer. DOI: 10.1007/978-1-4419-1508-5

Hasbi, M. (2017). Impact of Very High-Speed Broadband on Local Economic Growth: Empirical Evidence, 14th International Telecommunications Society (ITS) Asia-Pacific Regional Conference:" Mapping ICT into Transformation for the Next Information Society. *Kyoto, Japan*, 24-27.

Hashim, J. (2007). Information communication technology (ICT) adoption among SME owners in Malaysia. International Journal of Business and information, 2(2), 221-240.

Heim, H., & Hopper, C. (2022). Dress code: The digital transformation of the circular fashion supply chain. *International Journal of Fashion Design, Technology and Education*, 15(2), 233–244. DOI: 10.1080/17543266.2021.2013956

Hejazi, H., Rajab, H., Cinkler, T., & Lengyel, L. (2018). Survey of platforms for massive IoT. In Proceedings of the 2018 IEEE International Conference on Future IoT Technologies (Future IoT), Eger, Hungary, 18–19 January 2018; 1–8. DOI: 10.1109/FIOT.2018.8325598

Hendrina, Y., & Bahiroh, E. (2024). Human Resource Planning in the Digital Era: Challenges and Opportunities. *Indonesian Journal of Interdisciplinary Research in Science and Technology*, 2(4), 491–498. DOI: 10.55927/marcopolo.v2i4.7151

Henriette, E., Feki, M., & Boughzala, I. (2015). The shape of digital transformation: A systematic literature review. In *MCIS 2015 Proceedings* (pp. 431-443).

Heritage Foundation. (2015) *What Is National Security?* Available at: https://www.heritage.org/sites/default/files/2019-10/2015_IndexOfUSMilitaryStrength_What%20Is%20National%20Security.pdf (Accessed: 30 September 2024).

Hidayat-ur-Rehman, I., & Hossain, M. N. (2024). The impacts of Fintech adoption, green finance and competitiveness on banks' sustainable performance: Digital transformation as moderator. *Asia-Pacific Journal of Business Administration*. Advance online publication. DOI: 10.1108/APJBA-10-2023-0497

Hinings, B., Gegenhuber, T., & Greenwood, R. (2018). Digital innovation and transformation: An institutional perspective. *Information and Organization*, 28(1), 52–61. DOI: 10.1016/j.infoandorg.2018.02.004

Hintošová, A. B. (2021). The digital economy in the context of foreign direct investment flows. In Boitan, I. A., & Marchewka-Bartkowiak, K. (Eds.), *Fostering Innovation and Competitiveness with FinTech, RegTech, and SupTech* (pp. 210–227). IGI Global. DOI: 10.4018/978-1-7998-4390-0.ch011

Hitt, M. A., Keats, B. W., & DeMarie, S. M. (1998). Navigating in the new competitive landscape: Building strategic flexibility and competitive advantage in the 21st century. *The Academy of Management Perspectives*, 12(4), 22–42. DOI: 10.5465/ame.1998.1333922

Hodges, C., & Steinholtz, R. (2017). *Ethical business practice and regulation: a behavioural and values-based approach to compliance and enforcement* (Vol. 6). Bloomsbury Publishing.

Holmes, K. R. (2015). *What Is National Security?* The Heritage Foundation.

Holmström, J. (2022). From AI to digital transformation: The AI readiness framework. *Business Horizons*, 65(3), 329–339. DOI: 10.1016/j.bushor.2021.03.006

Ho, N. T. T., Sivapalan, S., Pham, H. H., Nguyen, L. T. M., Van Pham, A. T., & Dinh, H. V. (2020). Students' adoption of elearning in emergency situation: The case of a Vietnamese university during COVID-19. *Interactive Technology and Smart Education*. Advance online publication. DOI: 10.1108/ITSE-08-2020-0164

Hove, S. E., & Anda, B. (2005). Experiences from conducting semi-structured interviews in empirical software engineering research. In *11th IEEE International Software Metrics Symposium (METRICS'05)* (pp. 10-pp). IEEE. DOI: 10.1109/METRICS.2005.24

Huang, M. H., & Rust, R. T. (2018). Artificial intelligence in service. *Journal of Service Research*, 21(2), 155–172. DOI: 10.1177/1094670517752459

Huang, P., Shi, Y., An, J., Qiao, S., & Jin, L. (2024). Digital Intelligence Civilization Drives New Business Civilization: A Theoretical Framework for the Collaborative Ecosystem of Digital Culture and Tourism Industry. *Applied Mathematics and Nonlinear Sciences*, 9(1), 20230582. DOI: 10.2478/amns.2023.2.00582

Huang, Y. M. (2019). Examining students' continued use of desktop services: Perspectives from expectation-confirmation and social influence. *Computers in Human Behavior*, 96, 23–31. DOI: 10.1016/j.chb.2019.02.010

Hu, B., & Wu, Y. (2023). AI-based Compliance Automation in Commercial Bank: How the Silicon Valley Bank Provided a Cautionary Tale for Future Integration. *International Review of Economics & Finance*, 7(1), 13.

Huerta, J. M., & Anand, A. (2018). Machine learning and artificial intelligence in consumer banking. *Journal of Digital Banking*, 3(1), 22–32. DOI: 10.69554/JIVX9796

Hu, H. T., & Morley, J. D. (2017). A regulatory framework for exchange-traded funds. *S. Cal. L. Rev.*, 91, 839.

Hu, J. L., & Chang, Y. C. (2019). The W-theory of Five Elements for Innovative Business Activities with a Case Study of Alibaba Corporation. *Journal of Management Research*, 19(3), 173–179.

Hu, S., Laxman, K., & Lee, K. (2020). Exploring factors affecting academics' adoption of emerging mobile technologies-an extended UTAUT perspective. *Education and Information Technologies*, 25(5), 4615–4635. DOI: 10.1007/s10639-020-10171-x

Husain, A. R. A. M., Hamdan, A., & Fadhul, S. M. (2022). The Impact of Artificial Intelligence on the Banking Industry Performance. *Future of Organizations and Work After the 4th Industrial Revolution: The Role of Artificial Intelligence, Big Data, Automation, and Robotics*, 145-156.

Iansiti, M., & Lakhani, K. R. (2017). The truth about blockchain. *Harvard Business Review*, 95(1), 118–127.

Ibaseta, D., García, A., Álvarez, M., Garzón, B., Díez, F., Coca, P., Pero, C. D., & Molleda, J. (2021). Monitoring and control of energy consumption in building using WoT: A novel approach for smart retrofit. *Sustainable Cities and Society*, 65, 102637. DOI: 10.1016/j.scs.2020.102637

IBM. (2023). Cost of a Data Breach Report. Cost of a data breach 2024 | IBM

ICTworks. (2024) *Introducing FCDO's new digital development strategy*. Available at: https://www.ictworks.org (Accessed: 30 September 2024).

Ignatius, C. (2022). Digitalisation Imperatives for SMEs in Malaysia. BusinessToday. Retrieved from https://www.businesstoday.com.my/2022/10/04/digitalisation -imperatives-for-smes-in-malaysia/

Imperva (2023) *What is Vulnerability Assessment | VA Tools and Best Practices*. Available at: https://www.imperva.com/learn/application-security/vulnerability -assessment/ (Accessed: 23 September 2024).

Imran, F., Shahzad, K., Butt, A., & Kantola, J. (2021). Digital transformation of industrial organizations: Toward an integrated framework. *Journal of Change Management*, 21(4), 1–29. DOI: 10.1080/14697017.2021.1929406

Informatic Data Quality. Available online: https://www.informatica.com/gb/products/ dataquality/informatica-dataquality. html (accessed on 29 September 2023).

Innovation Oases. (n.d.). *Innovation Oases Portal*. Retrieved from https://www .innovationoases.com/InnovationOases/Apply?UDDI=MTc1NzRkMzMtZDc5ZC 00ZWIyLTgyYmEtOTA4OGZkNmVlMzQ1#

Institute of International Finance. (2016). RegTech in financial services: Technology solutions for compliance and reporting.

Institute of International Finance. (2023, 09 June). RegTech: Exploring Solutions for Regulatory Challenges. https://www.iif.com/Publications/ID/4229/RegTech --Exploring-Solutions-for-Regulatory-Challenges

International Labour Organization (ILO). (n.d.). *Oman: Intellectual Property Statistics*. Retrieved from https://www.ilo.org/sites/default/files/wcmsp5/groups/ public/@asia/@ro-bangkok/@ilo-beijing/documents/publication/wcms_864806.pdf

Inversini, A., Chen, M.-M., Keller, A., & Schegg, R. (2024). Hot Topics in Travel Digital Transformation: A Swiss Perspective. In Berezina, K., Nixon, L., & Tuomi, A. (Eds.), *Information and Communication Technologies in Tourism 2024* (pp. 195–206). Springer Nature Switzerland., DOI: 10.1007/978-3-031-58839-6_21

Ipsos (2021) *Addressing Cybersecurity Skill Shortages in the GCC Region.* Available at: https://www.ipsos.com/sites/default/files/ct/news/documents/2021-09/Addressing%20Cybersecurity%20Skill%20Shortages%20in%20the%20GCC%20Region.pdf (Accessed: 21 September 2024).

Ipsos (2022) *Addressing Cybersecurity Skill Shortages in the GCC Region.* Available at: https://www.ipsos.com/sites/default/files/ct/news/documents/2022-09/Ipsos%20-%20PGI%20-%20Understanding%20Cybersecurity%20Skill%20Shortages%20in%20The%20GCC%20-Report.pdf (Accessed: 24 September 2024).

Irtyshcheva, I., Kim, V., & Kletsov, Y. (2022). Managing business processes in the conditions of the development of the digital economy: Global and national experiences. *Baltic Journal of Economic Studies*, 8(5), 101–107. DOI: 10.30525/2256-0742/2022-8-5-101-107

Isaac, O., Aldholay, A., Abdullah, Z., & Ramayah, T. (2019). Online learning usage within Yemeni higher education: The role of compatibility and task-technology fit as mediating variables in the IS success model. *Computers & Education*, 136, 113–129. DOI: 10.1016/j.compedu.2019.02.012

ISC. (2023) *Cybersecurity Workforce Study.* Available at: https://www.isc2.org/Research/Workforce-Study (Accessed: 30 September 2024).

Isenberg, D. J. (2010). How to start an entrepreneurial revolution. *Harvard Business Review*, 88(6), 40–50.

Islam, M. A., Nur, S., & Talukder, M. S. (2021). E-learning in the time of COVID-19: Lived experiences of three university teachers from two countries. *E-Learning and Digital Media*, 18(6), 557–580. DOI: 10.1177/20427530211022924

Ismail, M. H., Khater, M., & Zaki, M. (2017). Digital business transformation and strategy: What do we know so far. *Cambridge Service Alliance*, 10(1), 1–35.

Ivankova, N. V., Creswell, J. W., & Stick, S. L. (2006). Using mixed-methods sequential explanatory design: From theory to practice. *Field Methods*, 18(1), 3–20. DOI: 10.1177/1525822X05282260

Jabil (2023) *Biggest barriers to digital transformation - Top 5.* Available at: https://jabil.com (Accessed: 17 September 2024).

Jaheer Mukthar, K. P., Sivasubramanian, K., Ramirez Asis, E. H., & Guerra-Munoz, M. E. (2022). Redesigning and reinvention of retail industry through Artificial Intelligence (AI). In *Future of Organizations and Work After the 4th Industrial Revolution: The Role of Artificial Intelligence, Big Data, Automation, and Robotics* (pp. 41–56). Springer International Publishing. DOI: 10.1007/978-3-030-99000-8_3

Jain, V., & Mitra, A. (2023). Development and application of machine learning algorithms for sentiment analysis in digital manufacturing: A pathway for enhanced customer feedback. In *Emerging Technologies in Digital Manufacturing and Smart Factories* (pp. 26-38).

Jain, V., & Mitra, A. (2024). A critical examination of ethical implications in AI-driven consumer behavior media discourse and environmental sustainability. In *Enhancing and Predicting Digital Consumer Behavior with AI* (pp. 1-16). DOI: 10.4018/979-8-3693-4453-8.ch001

Jain, V., & Mitra, A. (2024). Culinary narratives and community revitalization: The role of media in promoting sustainable gastronomy tourism. In *Promoting Sustainable Gastronomy Tourism and Community Development* (pp. 67-80).

Jakl, A., Schoffer, L., Husinsky, M., & Wagner, M. (2018), Augmented Reality for Industry 4.0: Architecture and User Experience, In Proceeding of the 11th Forum Media Technology, CER-WS, 38-42.

Jamshidi, D., & Hussin, N. (2016). Islamic credit card adoption understanding: When innovation diffusion theory meets satisfaction and social influence. *Journal of Promotion Management*, 22(6), 897–917. DOI: 10.1080/10496491.2016.1214206

Jamwal, A., Agrawal, R., & Sharma, M. (2022). A framework to overcome blockchain enabled sustainable manufacturing issues through circular economy and Industry 4.0 measures. *International Journal of Mathematical. Engineering and Management Sciences*, 7(6), 764–790. DOI: 10.33889/IJMEMS.2022.7.6.050

Jandl, C., Nurgazina, J., Schoffer, L., Reichl, C., Wagner, M., & Moser, T. (2019). SensiTrack – A Privacy by Design Concept for Industrial IoT Applications, In *Proceeding of the 24th IEEE International Conference on Emerging Technologies and Factory Automation*, 10-13 September, Zaragoza, Spain, 1782-1789. DOI: 10.1109/ETFA.2019.8869186

Jansen, S. (2020). *Machine Learning for Algorithmic Trading: Predictive models to extract signals from market and alternative data for systematic trading strategies with Python*. Packt Publishing Ltd.

Jarrahi, M. H., Kenyon, S., Brown, A., Donahue, C., & Wicher, C. (2023). Artificial intelligence: A strategy to harness its power through organizational learning. *The Journal of Business Strategy*, 44(3), 126–135. DOI: 10.1108/JBS-11-2021-0182

Jassem, S. (2024). Artificial Intelligence in Accounting Practices in the Industry 5.0 Era from a Dynamic Capabilities Perspective: Role of Strategic Foresight, Agility, and Flexibility. In Alareeni, B., & Elgedawy, I. (Eds.), *Opportunities and Risks in AI for Business Development. Studies in Systems, Decision and Control* (Vol. 545). Springer., DOI: 10.1007/978-3-031-65203-5_14

Javaid, M., Haleem, A., Singh, R. P., & Suman, R. (2021). Substantial capabilities of robotics in enhancing industry 4.0 implementation. *Cognitive Robotics*, 1, 58–75. DOI: 10.1016/j.cogr.2021.06.001

Javaid, M., Haleem, A., Singh, R. P., & Suman, R. (2023). *Towards insighting cybersecurity for healthcare domains: A comprehensive review of recent practices and trends*. ScienceDirect., DOI: 10.1016/j.sciencedirect.2023.01.004

Jeschke, S., Brecher, C., Meisen, T., Ozdemir, D., & Eschert, T. (2017), Industrial Internet of Things and Cyber Manufacturing Systems, In Industrial Internet of Things, Springer, 3-19.

Jeston, J. (2018). *Business Process Management: Practical Guidelines to Successful Implementations*. Routledge. DOI: 10.4324/9781315184760

Jevtić, B., Vučeković, M., & Tasić, S. (2023) . The Effects of Digitalization and Skills on Women's Labor Market Inclusion-Serbian Gap Study. Journal of Women's Entrepreneurship and Education, 58-75.

Jiang, L., & Li, K. (2020, November). Research on the influencing factors of music virtual community based on expectation confirmation theory. In 2020 IEEE international conference on information technology, big data and artificial intelligence (ICIBA) (Vol. 1, pp. 392-396). IEEE.

Jobin, A., Ienca, M., & Vayena, E. (2019). The global landscape of AI ethics guidelines. *Nature Machine Intelligence*, 1(9), 389–399. DOI: 10.1038/s42256-019-0088-2

Johnson, C. (2013). Regulatory arbitrage, extraterritorial jurisdiction, and Dodd-Frank: The implications of US global OTC derivative regulation. *Nev. LJ*, 14, 542.

Johnson, M. E. (2006, May–June). Supply chain management: Technology, globalization, and policy at a crossroads. *Informs*, 36(3), 191–193.

Jolene, K. (2023). The Influence of Online Travel Agencies (OTAs) on Hotel Revenue and Distribution Strategies. *Journal of Modern Hospitality*, 2(1), 14–25. DOI: 10.47941/jmh.1557

Joshi, S., Pise, A. A., Shrivastava, M., Revathy, C., Kumar, H., Alsetoohy, O., & Akwafo, R. (2022). Adoption of blockchain technology for privacy and security in the context of industry 4.0. *Wireless Communications and Mobile Computing*, 2022(1), 4079781. DOI: 10.1155/2022/4079781

Jurowiec, P. (2023, October 4). Blockchain applications in the world tax regime. Medium. Retrieved from https://blog.goodaudience.com/blockchain-applications -in-the-world-tax-regime-ea2111741f0b

Kamath, R. (2018). Food traceability on blockchain: Walmart's pork and mango pilots with IBM. *The Journal of the British Blockchain Association*, 1(1), 1–12. DOI: 10.31585/jbba-1-1-(10)2018

Kamble, S. S., Gunasekaran, A., & Gawankar, S. A. (2020). Achieving sustainable performance in a data-driven agriculture supply chain: A review for research and applications. *International Journal of Production Economics*, 219, 179–194. DOI: 10.1016/j.ijpe.2019.05.022

Kamilaris, A., Cole, I. R., & Prenafeta-Boldú, F. X. (2021). Blockchain in agriculture. In Galanakis, C. M. (Ed.), *Food Technology Disruptions* (pp. 247–284). Academic Press. DOI: 10.1016/B978-0-12-821470-1.00003-3

Kane, G. C., Palmer, D., Phillips, A. N., Kiron, D., & Buckley, N. (2015). Strategy, not technology, drives digital transformation. *MIT Sloan Management Review and Deloitte University Press*, 14, 1–25.

Karakaş, S., Acar, A. Z., & Kucukaltan, B. (2021). Blockchain adoption in logistics and supply chain: A literature review and research agenda. *International Journal of Production Research*, ●●●, 1–24. DOI: 10.1080/00207543.2021.2012613

Kara, P. A., Ognjanovic, I., Maindorfer, I., Mantas, J., Wippelhauser, A., Šendelj, R., Laković, L., Roganović, M., Reich, C., Simon, A., & Bokor, L. (2023). The present and future of a digital Montenegro: Analysis of C-ITS, agriculture, and healthcare. *Eng*, 4(1), 341–366. DOI: 10.3390/eng4010021

Kariotis, T., & Howe, J. (2021). The future, digitally enabled, regulatory landscape. https://www.turcomat.org/index.php/turkbilmat/article/view/2139

Karisma, K., & Tehrani, P. M. (2022). Legal and Regulatory Landscape of Blockchain Technology in Various Countries. In Regulatory Aspects of Artificial Intelligence on Blockchain (pp. 52-81). IGI Global. DOI: 10.4018/978-1-7998-7927-5.ch004

Kaspersky (2023) *Phishing Attacks in the GCC: A Rising Threat*. Available at: https://www.kaspersky.com/blog/phishing-attacks-gcc-2023 (Accessed: 12 September 2024).

Kattel, R., & Mazzucato, M. (2018). Mission-oriented innovation policy and dynamic capabilities in the public sector. *Industrial and Corporate Change*, 27(5), 787–801. DOI: 10.1093/icc/dty032

Kearney, A. T. (2023) *Cyber-proofing smart cities in the GCC*. Available at: https://www.middle-east.kearney.com/service/digital-analytics/article/cyber-proofing -smart-cities-in-the-gcc (Accessed: 14 September 2024).

Kelleher, J. D., Mac Namee, B., & D'arcy, A. (2020). *Fundamentals of machine learning for predictive data analytics: algorithms, worked examples, and case studies*. MIT press.

Keskinock, P., & Tayur, S. (2001). Quantitative analysis of Internet-enabled supply chain. *Interfaces*, 31(2), 70–89. DOI: 10.1287/inte.31.2.70.10626

Khadke, S., Gupta, P., Rachakunta, S., Mahata, C., Dawn, S., Sharma, M., Verma, D., Pradhan, A., Krishna, A. M. S., Ramakrishna, S., Chakrabortty, S., Saianand, G., Sonar, P., Biring, S., Dash, J. K., & Dalapati, G. K. (2021). Efficient plastic recycling and remolding circular circular economy using the technology of trust–blockchain. *Sustainability (Basel)*, 13(16), 9142. DOI: 10.3390/su13169142

Khan, R., Khan, S. U., Zaheer, R., & Khan, S. (2012). Future Internet: the internet of things architecture, possible applications and key challenges, In Proceedings of the 10th International Conference on Frontiers of Information Technology (FIT-12), 257-260, December 2012. DOI: 10.1109/FIT.2012.53

Khan, A. A., Laghari, A. A., Li, P., Dootio, M. A., & Karim, S. (2023). The collaborative role of blockchain, artificial intelligence, and industrial internet of things in digitalization of small and medium-size enterprises. *Scientific Reports*, 13(1), 1656. DOI: 10.1038/s41598-023-28707-9 PMID: 36717702

Khanom, M. T. (2023). Business Strategies in The Age of Digital Transformation. *The Journal of Business*, 8(01), 28–35.

Khan, S. A. R., Razzaq, A., Yu, Z., & Miller, S. (2021). Retracted: Industry 4.0 and circular economy practices: A new era business strategies for environmental sustainability. *Business Strategy and the Environment*, 30(8), 4001–4014. DOI: 10.1002/bse.2853

Khan, S. A. R., Yu, Z., Sarwat, S., Godil, D. I., Amin, S., & Shujaat, S. (2022). The role of block chain technology in circular economy practices to improve organisational performance. *International Journal of Logistics*, 25(4–5), 605–622. DOI: 10.1080/13675567.2021.1872512

Khaqqi, K. N., Sikorski, J. J., Hadinoto, K., & Kraft, M. (2018). Incorporating seller/buyer reputation-based system in blockchain-enabled emission trading application. *Applied Energy*, 209, 8–19. DOI: 10.1016/j.apenergy.2017.10.070

Kim, H. W., Hoque, M. R., Seo, H., & Yang, S. H. (2016). Development of middleware architecture to realize context-aware service in smart home environment. *Computer Science and Information Systems*, 13(2), 427–452. DOI: 10.2298/CSIS150701010H

Kim, K., & Kim, B. (2022). Decision-making model for reinforcing digital transformation strategies based on artificial intelligence technology. *Information (Basel)*, 13(5), 253. DOI: 10.3390/info13050253

Kim, N. H., So, H. J., & Joo, Y. J. (2021). Flipped learning design fidelity, self-regulated learning, satisfaction, and continuance intention in a university flipped learning course. *Australasian Journal of Educational Technology*, 37, 1–19. DOI: 10.14742/ajet.6046

Kim, P. T., & Bodie, M. T. (2020). Artificial intelligence and the challenges of workplace discrimination and privacy. *ABAJ Lab. & Emp. L.*, 35, 289.

Kim, Y., Raman, R. K., Kim, Y.-S., Varshney, L. R., & Shanbhag, N. R. (2018). Efficient local secret sharing for distributed blockchain systems. *IEEE Communications Letters*, 23(2), 282–285. DOI: 10.1109/LCOMM.2018.2886016

Kitchenham, B. A., Brereton, P., Turner, M., Niazi, M. K., Linkman, S., Pretorius, R., & Budgen, D. (2010). Refining the systematic literature review process—Two participant-observer case studies. *Empirical Software Engineering*, 15(6), 618–653. DOI: 10.1007/s10664-010-9134-8

Kitsios, F., & Kamariotou, M. (2021). Artificial intelligence and business strategy towards digital transformation: A research agenda. *Sustainability (Basel)*, 13(4), 2025. DOI: 10.3390/su13042025

Kochetkov, E.P. (2020) . Digital transformation of economy and technological revolutions: Challenges for the current paradigm of management and crisis management. Strategic decisions and risk management, 10(4), 330-341.

Kokolek, N., Jakovic, B., & Curlin, T. (2019). Digital Knowledge and Skills–Key Factors for Digital Transformation. Annals of DAAAM & Proceedings, 30.

Kolodynskyi, S., Drakokhrust, T., & Bashynska, M. (2018). The innovative infrastructure of economic development in the framework of international digital transformation. *Baltic Journal of Economic Studies*, 4(4), 166–172. DOI: 10.30525/2256-0742/2018-4-4-166-172

Königstorfer, F., & Thalmann, S. (2020). Applications of Artificial Intelligence in commercial banks–A research agenda for behavioral finance. *Journal of Behavioral and Experimental Finance*, 27, 100352. DOI: 10.1016/j.jbef.2020.100352

Konopik, J., Jahn, C., Schuster, T., Hoßbach, N., & Pflaum, A. (2021). Mastering the digital transformation through organizational capabilities: A conceptual framework. DOI: 10.1016/j.digbus.2021.100019

Kosuru, S. K., Tadi, S., G, J., K, S., D, G., & K, S. S. S. (2023). Data Analytics and Artificial Intelligence. *Journal of Clinical and Pharmaceutical Research*, 15–17, 15–17. Advance online publication. DOI: 10.61427/jcpr.v3.i3.2023.112

Ko, T., Lee, J., & Ryu, D. (2018). Blockchain technology and manufacturing industry: Real-time transparency and cost savings. *Sustainability (Basel)*, 10(11), 4274. DOI: 10.3390/su10114274

Kouhizadeh, M., & Sarkis, J. (2021). Blockchain practices, potentials, and perspectives in greening supply chains. *Sustainability*, 13(6), 3337. DOI: 10.3390/su13063337

Kouhizadeh, M., Sarkis, J., & Zhu, Q. (2019). At the nexus of blockchain technology, the circular economy, and product deletion. *Applied Sciences (Basel, Switzerland)*, 9(8), 1712. DOI: 10.3390/app9081712

Kouhizadeh, M., Zhu, Q., & Sarkis, J. (2020). Blockchain and the circular economy: Potential tensions and critical reflections from practice. *Production Planning and Control*, 31(11–12), 950–966. DOI: 10.1080/09537287.2019.1695925

Kouhizadeh, M., Zhu, Q., & Sarkis, J. (2023). Circular economy performance measurements and blockchain technology: An examination of relationships. *International Journal of Logistics Management*, 34(3), 720–743. DOI: 10.1108/IJLM-04-2022-0145

Kozak-Holland, M., & Procter, C. (2020). The Challenge of Digital Transformation. In *Managing Transformation Projects*. Palgrave Pivot., DOI: 10.1007/978-3-030-33035-4_1

Krause, B., Kahembwe, E., Murray, I., & Renals, S. (2018, July). Dynamic evaluation of neural sequence models. In *International Conference on Machine Learning* (pp. 2766-2775). PMLR.

Kraus, S., Clauss, T., Breier, M., Gast, J., Zardini, A., & Tiberius, V. (2020). The economics of COVID-19: Initial empirical evidence on how family firms in five European countries cope with the corona crisis. *International Journal of Entrepreneurial Behaviour & Research*, 26(5), 1067–1092. DOI: 10.1108/IJEBR-04-2020-0214

Kraus, S., Durst, S., Ferreira, J. J., Veiga, P., Kailer, N., & Weinmann, A. (2022). Digital transformation in business and management research: An overview of the current status quo. *Journal of Business Research*, 123, 1–15.

Kraus, S., Jones, P., Kailer, N., Weinmann, A., Chaparro-Banegas, N., & Roig-Tierno, N. (2021). Digital transformation: An overview of the current state of the art of research. *SAGE Open*, 11(3), 21582440211047576. DOI: 10.1177/21582440211047576

Kristanto, A. D., & Arman, A. A. (2022). Towards A Smart Regulatory Compliance, The Capabilities of RegTech and SupTech. In *2022 International Conference on Information Technology Systems and Innovation (ICITSI)* (pp. 300-309). IEEE. DOI: 10.1109/ICITSI56531.2022.9970801

Krupenna, I. (2022). MARKETING DIGITAL TOOLS FROM STARTUP PROJECTS IN THE TOURISM AND TRAVEL INDUSTRY. *Proceedings of Scientific Works of Cherkasy State Technological University Series Economic Sciences*, 67(67), 24–31. DOI: 10.24025/2306-4420.67.2022.278790

Kshetri, N. (2018). 1 Blockchain's roles in meeting key supply chain management objectives. *International Journal of Information Management*, 39, 80–89. DOI: 10.1016/j.ijinfomgt.2017.12.005

Kshetri, N. (2021). Blockchain and COVID-19: Applications and paradoxes. *IT Professional*, 23(5), 4–10. DOI: 10.1109/MITP.2020.2992148

Kuckertz, A., Brändle, L., Gaudig, A., Hinderer, S., Reyes, C. A. M., Prochotta, A., & Berger, E. S. (2020). Startups in times of crisis–A rapid response to the COVID-19 pandemic. *Journal of Business Venturing Insights*, 13, e00169. DOI: 10.1016/j.jbvi.2020.e00169

Kulkarni, V., Sunkle, S., Kholkar, D., Roychoudhury, S., Kumar, R., & Raghunandan, M. (2021). Toward automated regulatory compliance. *CSI Transactions on ICT*, 9(2), 95–104. DOI: 10.1007/s40012-021-00329-4

Kumar, A., Sharma, S., & Mahdavi, M. (2021). Machine learning (Ml) technologies for digital credit scoring in rural finance: A literature review. *Risks*, 9(11), 192. DOI: 10.3390/risks9110192

Kumar, N. M., & Chopra, S. S. (2022). Leveraging blockchain and smart contract technologies to overcome circular economy implementation challenges. *Sustainability (Basel)*, 14(15), 9492. DOI: 10.3390/su14159492

Kumar, R. L., Khan, F., Kadry, S., & Rho, S. (2022). A survey on blockchain for industrial internet of things. *Alexandria Engineering Journal*, 61(8), 6001–6022. DOI: 10.1016/j.aej.2021.11.023

Kumar, S., Talukder, M. B., Kabir, F., & Kaiser, F. (2023). Challenges and Sustainability of Green Finance in the Tourism Industry: Evidence From Bangladesh. In Taneja, S., Kumar, P., Grima, S., Ozen, E., & Sood, K. (Eds.), (pp. 97–111). Advances in Finance, Accounting, and Economics. IGI Global., DOI: 10.4018/979-8-3693-1388-6.ch006

Kuo, T.-T., Kim, J., & Gabriel, R. A. (2020). Privacy-preserving model learning on a blockchain network-of-networks. *Journal of the American Medical Informatics Association : JAMIA*, 27(3), 343–354. DOI: 10.1093/jamia/ocz214 PMID: 31943009

Kutnjak, A., Pihir, I., & Vidačić, S. (2023). Shifting Towards Digital Transformation in Bookkeeping Agency—Attitudes Pre- and Post- Implementation of New Technologiesv. *TEM Journal*, 2512–2521. https://doi.org/DOI: 10.18421/TEM124-63

Kvale, S., & Brinkmann, S. (2015). *InterViews: Learning the craft of qualitative research interviewing* (3rd ed.). SAGE Publications.

LaBerge, L., O'Toole, C., Schneider, J., & Smaje, K. (October 2020). How COVID-19 has pushed companies over the technology tipping point—and transformed business forever. McKinsey Digital & Strategy & Corporate Finance Practices.

Lacity, M., Willcocks, L. P., & Craig, A. (2015). Robotic process automation at Telefonica O2.

Lacity, M., & Willcocks, L. (2016). Nine keys to unlocking digital transformation in business operations. *MIS Quarterly Executive*, 15, 135–149.

Lacity, M., & Willcocks, L. P. (2017). *Robotic process automation and risk mitigation: The definitive guide*. SB Publishing.

Lasi, H., Fettke, P., Kemper, H.-G., Feld, T., & Hoffmann, M. (2014). Industry 4.0. BISE, 6(4):239–242. Lastra, J. L. M. and Delamer, I. M. (2006). Semantic Web Services in Factory Automation: Fundamental Insights and Research Roadmap. *IEEE Transactions on Industrial Informatics*, 2(1), 1–11.

Lee, D. J., & Joseph Sirgy, M. (2019). Work-life balance in the digital workplace: The impact of schedule flexibility and telecommuting on work-life balance and overall life satisfaction. *Thriving in digital workspaces: Emerging issues for research and practice*, 355-384.

Lee, C. (2023). Strategic Policies for Digital Economic Transformation. *Journal of Southeast Asian Economies*, 40(1), 32–63. https://www.jstor.org/stable/27211224. DOI: 10.1355/ae40-1c

Lee, H. L., & Billington, C. (1992). Managing supply chain inventories: Pitfalls and opportunities. *Sloan Management Review*, 33(3), 65–77.

Lee, J., Kao, H.-A., & Yang, S. (2014). Service Innovation and Smart Analytics for Industry 4.0 and Big Data Environment. *Procedia CIRP*, 16, 3–8. DOI: 10.1016/j.procir.2014.02.001

Lee, J., Lapira, E., Bagheri, B., & Kao, H. A. (2013). Recent advances and trends in predictive manufacturing systems in big data environment. *Manufacturing Letters*, 1(1), 38–41. DOI: 10.1016/j.mfglet.2013.09.005

Lee, M.-C. (2010). Explaining and predicting users' continuance intention toward e-learning: An extension of the expectation-confirmation model. *Computers & Education*, 54(2), 506–516. DOI: 10.1016/j.compedu.2009.09.002

Lee, S., & Park, J. (2022). Influence of tech industry practices on public sector digital transformation. *Technology in Society*, 68, 101828.

Lee, Y. Y., Falahat, M., & Sia, B. K. (2019). Impact of Digitalization on the Speed of Internationalization. *International Business Research*, 12(4), 1–11. DOI: 10.5539/ibr.v12n4p1

Lefort, L., Henson, C., Taylor, K., Barnaghi, P., Compton, M., Corcho, O., Garcia-Castro, R., Graybeal, J., Herzog, A., Janowicz, K., Neuhaus, H., Nikolov, A., & Page, K. (2005). "Semantic Sensor Network XG Final Report", 2011, W3C Incubator Group Report, https://www.w3.org/2005/Incubator/ssn/XGR-ssn/

Lemon, K. N., & Verhoef, P. C. (2016). Understanding customer experience throughout the customer journey. *Journal of Marketing*, 80(6), 69–96. DOI: 10.1509/jm.15.0420

Leng, J., Ruan, G., Jiang, P., Xu, K., Liu, Q., Zhou, X., & Liu, C. (2020). Blockchain-empowered sustainable manufacturing and product lifecycle management in Industry 4.0: A survey. *Renewable & Sustainable Energy Reviews*, 132, 110112. DOI: 10.1016/j.rser.2020.110112

Letandze, N. (2023). The Impact of Digital Technologies on the Development of Rural Tourism in Georgia. *Proceedings of Tskhum-Abkhazian Academy of Sciences.* DOI: 10.52340/ptaas.2023.23.14

Lewis, E. F., Hardy, M., & Snaith, B. (2013). An analysis of survey reporting in the imaging professions: Is the issue of non-response bias being adequately addressed? *Radiography*, 19(3), 240–245. DOI: 10.1016/j.radi.2013.02.003

Liere-Netheler, K., Packmohr, S., & Vogelsang, K. (2018). Drivers of digital transformation in manufacturing. *Hawaii International Conference on System Sciences*, 3926-3935.

Li, L. (2022). Blockchain technology in industry 4.0. *Enterprise Information Systems*, 16(12), 2095535. DOI: 10.1080/17517575.2022.2095535

Li, L. (2022). Digital transformation and sustainable performance: The moderating role of market turbulence. *Industrial Marketing Management*, 104, 28–37. DOI: 10.1016/j.indmarman.2022.04.007

Li, L., & Horrocks, I. (2004). A software framework for matchmaking based on semantic web technology. *International Journal of Electronic Commerce*, 8(4), 39–60. DOI: 10.1080/10864415.2004.11044307

Li, L., Wang, Q., & Li, J. (2022). Examining continuance intention of online learning during COVID-19 pandemic: Incorporating the theory of planned behavior into the expectation–confirmation model. *Frontiers in Psychology*, 13, 1046407. DOI: 10.3389/fpsyg.2022.1046407 PMID: 36467152

Limarev, P.V., Limareva, Y.A., Akulova, I.S., Khakova, G.S., Rubanova, N.Y.A., & Nemtsev, V.N. (2018). The role of information in the system of macroeconomic indicators. Revista Espacios, 39(50).

Lippmann, W. (1943). *U.S. Foreign Policy: Shield of the Republic*. Little, Brown and Company.

Li, R., Rao, J., & Wan, L. (2022). The digital economy, enterprise digital transformation, and enterprise innovation. *MDE. Managerial and Decision Economics*, 43(7), 2875–2886. DOI: 10.1002/mde.3569

Liu, J., & Jia, F. (2021). Construction of a Nonlinear Model of Tourism Economy Forecast Based on Wireless Sensor Network from the Perspective of Digital Economy. *Wireless Communications and Mobile Computing*, 2021(1), 1–14. DOI: 10.1155/2021/8576534

Liu, M., Wu, K., & Xu, J. J. (2019). How will blockchain technology impact auditing and accounting: Permissionless versus permissioned blockchain. *Current Issues in Auditing*, 13(2), A19–A29. DOI: 10.2308/ciia-52540

Liu, Q., & Ananthachari, P. (2023). Research on the impact of enterprise digital transformation on the enhancement of export competitiveness. *Information Systems and Economics*, 4(8), 69–74.

Liu, S., Zhu, Z., Qu, Q., & You, C. (2022). Robust training under label noise by over-parameterization. In *International Conference on Machine Learning* (pp. 14153-14172). PMLR.

Liu, Z., & Wang, X. (2018). How to regulate individuals' privacy boundaries on social network sites: A cross-cultural comparison. *Information & Management*, 55(8), 1005–1023. DOI: 10.1016/j.im.2018.05.006

Liu, Z., Wu, T., Wang, F., Osmani, M., & Demian, P. (2022). Blockchain enhanced construction waste information management: A conceptual framework. *Sustainability (Basel)*, 14(19), 12145. DOI: 10.3390/su141912145

Lloyds Bank. (2023). *UK business digital index 2023*. Lloyds Banking Group.

Lobov, A., Lopez, F. U., Herrera, V. V., Puttonen, J., & Lastra, J. L. M. (2008). Semantic Web Services framework for manufacturing industries. In Int. Conf. on Rob. and Biomim., pages 2104–2108. IEEE.

Lokanan, M. E. (2022). Predicting money laundering using machine learning and artificial neural networks algorithms in banks. *Journal of Applied Security Research*, ●●●, 1–25.

Loonam, J., Eaves, S., Kumar, V., & Parry, G. (2018). Towards digital transformation: Lessons learned from traditional organizations. *Strategic Change*, 27(2), 101–109. DOI: 10.1002/jsc.2185

López, E. J., Jiménez, F. C., Sandoval, G. L., Estrella, F. J. O., Monteón, M. A. M., Muñoz, F., & Leyva, P. A. L. (2022). Technical Considerations for the Conformation of Specific Competences in Mechatronic Engineers in the Context of Industry 4.0 and 5.0. *Processes (Basel, Switzerland)*, 2022(10), 1445. DOI: 10.3390/pr10081445

Lv, Z., & Singh, A. K. (2021). Big Data Analysis of Internet of Things System. *ACM Transactions on Internet Technology*, 21(2), 1–15. DOI: 10.1145/3389250

Lynn, T. G., Conway, E., Rosati, P., & Curran, D. (2022). *Infrastructure for Digital Connectivity*. Digital Towns., DOI: 10.1007/978-3-030-91247-5_6

Lythreatis, S., Singh, S. K., & El-Kassar, A. N. (2022). The digital divide: A review and future research agenda. *Technological Forecasting and Social Change*, 174, 121173. DOI: 10.1016/j.techfore.2021.121359

Maass, W., & Filler, A. (2006). Towards an infrastructure for semantically annotated physical products. INFORMATIK 2006–Informatik für Menschen–Band 2, Beiträge der 36. Jahrestagung der Gesellschaft für Informatik eV (GI).

MacKenzie, S. B., & Podsakoff, P. M. (2012). Common method bias in marketing: Causes, mechanisms, and procedural remedies. *Journal of Retailing*, 88(4), 542–555. DOI: 10.1016/j.jretai.2012.08.001

Maguire, D., Evans, H., Honeyman, M., & Omojomolo, D. (2021). *Digital change in health and social care*. The King's Fund.

Mahajan, S., & Nanda, M. (2024). Revolutionizing Banking with Blockchain: Opportunities and Challenges Ahead. Next-Generation Cybersecurity: AI, ML, and Blockchain, 287-304.

Mahalakshmi, V., Kulkarni, N., Kumar, K. P., Kumar, K. S., Sree, D. N., & Durga, S. (2022). The Role of implementing Artificial Intelligence and Machine Learning Technologies in the financial services Industry for creating Competitive Intelligence. *Materials Today: Proceedings*, 56, 2252–2255. DOI: 10.1016/j.matpr.2021.11.577

Mahalle, P. N., Hujare, P. P., & Shinde, G. R. (2023). Data Acquisition and Preparation. In *Predictive Analytics for Mechanical Engineering: A Beginners Guide* (pp. 11–38). Springer Nature Singapore. DOI: 10.1007/978-981-99-4850-5_2

Mahmood, A., Kedia, S., Wyant, D. K., Ahn, S., & Bhuyan, S. S. (2019). Use of mobile health applications for health-promoting behavior among individuals with chronic medical conditions. *Digital Health*, 5, 2055207619882181. DOI: 10.1177/2055207619882181 PMID: 31656632

Maisha, K., & Shetu, S. N. (2023). Influencing factors of e-learning adoption amongst students in a developing country: The post-pandemic scenario in Bangladesh. *Future Business Journal*, 9(1), 37. DOI: 10.1186/s43093-023-00214-3

Makinda, S. (2006). *Security in International Relations*. Routledge.

Malik, A., Amjad, G., & Nemati, A. R. (2022). Impact of Technological, Organizational, Product, and Process Innovation on Employee Turnover Intention. *Zakariya Journal of Social Science*, 1(1), 1–14. DOI: 10.59075/zjss.v1i1.43

Malik, A., Khan, M. A., Khan, F. H., & Jan, F. A. (2020). Examining the role of big data analytics in enhancing customer experience: A moderated mediation analysis. *Journal of Industrial Engineering and Management*, 13(4), 741–755.

Malik, Y. S., Kumar, N., Sircar, S., Kaushik, R., Bhat, S., Dhama, K., Gupta, P., Goyal, K., Singh, M. P., & Ghoshal, U.. (2020). Coronavirus Disease Pandemic (COVID-19): Challenges and a Global Perspective. *Pathogens (Basel, Switzerland)*, 9, 519. DOI: 10.3390/pathogens9070519 PMID: 32605194

Małkowska, A., Urbaniec, M., & Kosała, M. (2021). The impact of digital transformation on European countries: Insights from a comparative analysis. Equilibrium. *Quarterly Journal of Economics and Economic Policy*, 16(2), 325–355. DOI: 10.24136/eq.2021.012

Manny, L., Duygan, M., Fischer, M., & Rieckermann, J. (2021). Barriers to the digital transformation of infrastructure sectors. *Policy Sciences*, 54(4), 943–983. DOI: 10.1007/s11077-021-09438-y PMID: 34751195

Manyika, J., Chui, M., Miremadi, M., Bughin, J., George, K., Willmott, P., & Dewhurst, M. (2017). *A future that works: Automation, employment, and productivity*. McKinsey Global Institute.

Marchand, D. A., Kettinger, W. J., & Rollins, J. D. (2018). Information orientation, business agility, and digital transformation. *Management Information Systems Quarterly*, 42, 591–616.

Marjanović, D., & Domazet, I. (2021). Foreign Direct Investments: A Key Factor for Business Globalization. In Bayar, Y. (Ed.), *Institutional, Economic, and Social Impacts of Globalization and Liberalization* (pp. 96–116). IGI Global. DOI: 10.4018/978-1-7998-4459-4.ch006

Marjanović, D., & Domazet, I. (2023). Economic Measures for Mitigation of the Consequences of COVID-19: Evidence From Serbia. In Marco-Lajara, B., Özer, A. C., & Falcó, J. M. (Eds.), *The Transformation of Global Trade in a New World* (pp. 180–199). IGI Global.

Marjanović, D., Domazet, I., & Vukmirović, I. (2022). Social Environment as a Factor of Capital Investment in Serbia. *Eastern European Economics*, 60(3), 247–264. DOI: 10.1080/00128775.2022.2048181

Marjanović, J., Domazet, I., & Miljković, J. (2023). Higher Education Branding through Instrumental Values. *Journal of Women's Entrepreneurship and Education*, 3-4, 75–94.

Marr, B. (2019). *Artificial intelligence in practice: how 50 successful companies used AI and machine learning to solve problems*. John Wiley & Sons.

Marrella, A. (2018). Automated Planning for Business Process Management.

Marston, S., Li, Z., Bandyopadhyay, S., Zhang, J., & Ghalsasi, A. (2011). Cloud computing—The business perspective. *Decision Support Systems*, 51(1), 176–189. DOI: 10.1016/j.dss.2010.12.006

Martínez Martínez, R. (2019). Designing artificial intelligence. Challenges and strategies for achieving regulatory compliance. *Rev. Catalana Dret Pub.*, 58, 64.

Martin, K. (2015). Ethical issues in the big data industry. *MIS Quarterly Executive*, 14(2).

Mashal, I., Alsaryrah, O., Chung, T. Y., Yang, C. Z., Kuo, W. H., & Agrawal, D. P. (2015). Choices for interaction with things on Internet and underlying issues. *Ad Hoc Networks*, 28, 68–90. DOI: 10.1016/j.adhoc.2014.12.006

May, P. J. (2005). Regulation and compliance motivations: Examining different approaches. *Public Administration Review*, 65(1), 31–44. DOI: 10.1111/j.1540-6210.2005.00428.x

Mazzucato, M. (2018). *The entrepreneurial state: Debunking public vs. private sector myths*. Penguin Books.

McCarthy, J. (2023). The regulation of RegTech and SupTech in finance: Ensuring consistency in principle and in practice. *Journal of Financial Regulation and Compliance*, 31(2), 186–199. DOI: 10.1108/JFRC-01-2022-0004

McDowell, H. (2017). Banks spent close to $100 billion on compliance last year. *The Trade News*. https://www.thetradenews.com/Sell-side/Banks-spent-close-to-$100-billion-on-compliance-last-year/

McGlosson, C., & Enriquez, M. (2020). Financial industry compliance with Big Data and analytics. *Journal of Financial Compliance*, 3(2), 103–117. DOI: 10.69554/SIRM8601

McKinsey. (2023) *State of AI in the Middle East's GCC countries*. Available at: https://www.mckinsey.com/capabilities/mckinsey-digital/our-insights/the-state-of-ai-in-gcc-countries-and-how-to-overcome-adoption-challenges (Accessed: 30 September 2024).

MDC. (2016). Smart School. Retrieved on December 26, 2020 from http://docshare01.docshare.tips/files/2050/20507921.pdf

Meier, O., Gruchmann, T., & Ivanov, D. (2023). Circular supply chain management with blockchain technology: A dynamic capabilities view. *Transportation Research Part E, Logistics and Transportation Review*, 176, 103177. DOI: 10.1016/j.tre.2023.103177

Meléndez, C. M. (2021) 'Five barriers to digital transformation and how to overcome them', *Forbes*. Available at: https://www.forbes.com (Accessed: 25 September 2024).

Melo, G. P. A. N., De Oliveira, R. C., Da Silva, C. M. D. O., Silva, E. H., Da Silva, R. A., De Souza, R. M. A., De Andrade, I. A. B., & Da Silva, W. A. V. (2024). RESEARCH AND SCIENTIFIC DEVELOPMENT: THE ROLE OF FUNDING AGENCIES FOR TECHNOLOGICAL ADVANCEMENT IN BRAZIL. *Revista Contemporânea*, 4(2), e3343. DOI: 10.56083/RCV4N2-045

Melović, B., Jocović, M., Dabić, M., Vulić, T. B., & Dudic, B. (2020). The impact of digital transformation and digital marketing on the brand promotion, positioning and electronic business in Montenegro. *Technology in Society*, 63, 101425. DOI: 10.1016/j.techsoc.2020.101425

Melville, N., Kraemer, K., & Gurbaxani, V. (2004). Information technology and organizational performance: An integrative model of IT business value. *Management Information Systems Quarterly*, 28(2), 283–322. DOI: 10.2307/25148636

Mendonça, F., & Dantas, M. (2020). Covid-19: Where is the Digital Transformation, Big Data, Artificial Intelligence and Data Analytics? *Revista do Serviço Público*, 71, 212–234. DOI: 10.21874/rsp.v71i0.4770

Mergel, I. (2019). Digital service teams in government. *Government Information Quarterly*, 36(4), 101389. DOI: 10.1016/j.giq.2019.07.001

Mergel, I., Edelmann, N., & Haug, N. (2019). Defining digital transformation: Results from expert interviews. *Government Information Quarterly*, 36(4), 101385. DOI: 10.1016/j.giq.2019.06.002

Mhlanga, D. (2023). Digital transformation education, opportunities, and challenges of the application of ChatGPT to emerging economies. *Education Research International*, 2023(1), 7605075. DOI: 10.1155/2023/7605075

Michael Alurame Eruaga. (2024). Policy strategies for managing food safety risks associated with climate change and agriculture. *International Journal of Scholarly Research and Reviews, 4*(1), 021–032. DOI: 10.56781/ijsrr.2024.4.1.0026

Michie, S., & Marteau, T. (1999). Non-response bias in prospective studies of patients and healthcare professionals. *International Journal of Social Research Methodology*, 2(3), 203–212. DOI: 10.1080/136455799295014

Mićić, L. (2017) . Digital transformation and its influence on GDP. Economics-innovative and economics research journal, 5(2), 135-147.

Microminder (2023) *The Initiatives and Strategies of National Cybersecurity Authority (NCA)*. Available at: https://www.micromindercs.com/blog/the-initiatives-and -strategies-of-national-cybersecurity-authority-nca (Accessed: 16 September 2024).

Microsoft. (2023). Swift innovates with Azure confidential computing to help secure global financial transactions. https://customers.microsoft.com/en-us/story/ 1637929534319366070-swift-banking-capital-markets-azure-machine-learning

MIDA. (2024). Malaysia – Driven by Digital Evolution. Retrieved from https:// www.reuters.com/plus/malaysia-driven-by-digital-evolution

Mihai, F., Aleca, O. E., & Gheorghe, M. (2023). Digital Transformation Based on AI Technologies in European Union Organizations. *Electronics (Basel)*, 12(11), 2386. DOI: 10.3390/electronics12112386

Mineraud, J., Mazhelis, O., Su, X., & Tarkoma, S. (2016). A gap analysis of Internet-of-Things platforms. *Computer Communications*, 89-90, 5–16. DOI: 10.1016/j. comcom.2016.03.015

Mingaleva, Z., & Shironina, E. (2021). Gender aspects of digital workplace transformation. *Journal of Women's Entrepreneurship and Education*, (1-2), 1–17.

Ministry of International Trade & Industry. (2018). *Industry4WRD: National Policy on Industry 4.0*. Ministry of Investment, Trade and Industry of Malaysia. https:// www.miti.gov.my/miti/resources/National%20Policy%20on%20Industry%204.0/ Indu try4WRD_Final.pdf

Ministry of Transport, Communications and Information Technology (MTCIT), Oman. (n.d.). *ITA Portal*. Retrieved from https://www.mtcit.gov.om/ITAPortal/ Pages/Page.aspx?NID=1371&PID=5439&LID=278

Minor, M., Montani, S., & Recio-García, J. A. (2014). Process-oriented Case-based Reasoning. *Information Systems*, 40, 103–105. DOI: 10.1016/j.is.2013.06.004

MITRE. (2023) *Cyber Threat Intelligence Integration Center*. Available at: https:// www.mitre.org/ (Accessed: 13 September 2024).

Mohammad, B. T., Mushfika, H., & Iva, R. D. (2024a). Opportunities of tourism and hospitality education in bangladesh: Career perspectives. *I-Manager's. Journal of Management*, 18(3), 21. DOI: 10.26634/jmgt.18.3.20385

Mohammadi, H. (2015). Investigating users' perspectives on e-learning: an integration of TAM and IS success model. Comput. Hum. Behav. 45, 359-374. doi: . chb.2014.07.044DOI: 10.1016/j

Moloney, N., Ferran, E., & Payne, J. (Eds.). (2015). *The Oxford handbook of financial regulation*. OUP Oxford. DOI: 10.1093/oxfordhb/9780199687206.001.0001

Monostori, L. (2014). Cyber-physical Production Systems: Roots, Expectations and R&D Challenges. *Procedia CIRP*, 17, 9–13. DOI: 10.1016/j.procir.2014.03.115

Montenegro, G., Kushalnagar, N., Hui, J., & Culler, D. (2007). "Transmission of IPv6 packets over IEEE 802.15.4 networks," Internet proposed standard RFC, vol. 4944.

Morabito, V. (2017). *Business innovation through blockchain*. Springer International Publishing.

Mori, T. (2016). Financial technology: Blockchain and securities settlement. *Journal of Securities Operations & Custody*, 8(3), 208–227. DOI: 10.69554/YEJN7450

Morkunas, V. J., Paschen, J., & Boon, E. (2019). How blockchain technologies impact your business model. *Business Horizons*, 62(3), 295–306. DOI: 10.1016/j.bushor.2019.01.009

Mosteanu, N. R., & Faccia, A. (2020). Digital systems and new challenges of financial management – FinTech, XBRL, blockchain, and cryptocurrencies. *Quality - Access to Success*, 21(174), 159–166.

Mrs. C. Radha, Mr. R. Midunkumar, Mr. S. Muralibabu, Mr. V. Partheeban, & Mr. V. Partheeban. (2024). Role of Artificial Intelligence in Big Data Analytics. *International Journal of Advanced Research in Science, Communication and Technology*, 586–591. DOI: 10.48175/IJARSCT-17089

Mulgan, G. (2019). *Social innovation: How societies find the power to change*. Policy Press.

Müller, A. M., Goh, C., Lim, L. Z., & Gao, X. (2021). Covid-19 emergency elearning and beyond: Experiences and perspectives of university educators. *Education Sciences*, 11(1), 19. DOI: 10.3390/educsci11010019

Müller, G. (2018). Workflow Modeling Assistance by Casebased Reasoning. Springer Fachmedien, Wiesbaden. Ocker, F., Kovalenko, I., Barton, K., Tilbury, D., and VogelHeuser, B. (2019). A Framework for Automatic Initialization of Multi-Agent Production Systems Using Semantic Web Technologies. *IEEE Robotics and Automation Letters*, 4(4), 4330–4337.

Murphy, A., Robu, K., & Steinert, M. (2020). *The investigator-centered approach to financial crime: Doing what matters*. McKinsey and Company.

Muscat Daily. (2020). *698 Innovative Ideas Registered in Open Data Portal: Ministry of Manpower*. Retrieved from https://www.muscatdaily.com/2020/04/26/698 -innovative-ideas-registered-in-open-data-portal-mom/

Nadkarni, S., & Prügl, R. (2021). Digital transformation: A review, synthesis and opportunities for future research. *Management Review Quarterly*, 71(2), 233–274. DOI: 10.1007/s11301-020-00185-7

Nagel, L. (2020). The influence of the COVID-19 pandemic on the digital transformation of work. *The International Journal of Sociology and Social Policy*, 40(9/10), 861–875. DOI: 10.1108/IJSSP-07-2020-0323

Nakamoto, S. (2008). Bitcoin: A peer-to-peer electronic cash system.

Nakamoto, S. (2008). Bitcoin: A peer-to-peer electronic cash system. Retrieved from https://bitcoin.org/bitcoin.pdf

Nambisan, S. (2017). Digital entrepreneurship: Toward a digital technology perspective of entrepreneurship. *Entrepreneurship Theory and Practice*, 41(6), 1029–1055. DOI: 10.1111/etap.12254

Nambisan, S., Wright, M., & Feldman, M. (2019). The digital transformation of innovation and entrepreneurship: Progress, challenges and key themes. *Research Policy*, 48(8), 103773. DOI: 10.1016/j.respol.2019.03.018

Nandi, S., Sarkis, J., Hervani, A. A., & Helms, M. M. (2021b). Redesigning supply chains using blockchain-enabled circular economy and COVID19 experiences. *Sustainable Production and Consumption*, 27, 10–22. DOI: 10.1016/j.spc.2020.10.019 PMID: 33102671

Nandi, S., Sarkis, J., Hervani, A., & Helms, M. (2021a). Do blockchain and circular economy practices improve post COVID-19 supply chains? A resource-based and resource dependence perspective. *Industrial Management & Data Systems*, 121(2), 333–363. DOI: 10.1108/IMDS-09-2020-0560

Narayanan, A., Bonneau, J., Felten, E., Miller, A., & Goldfeder, S. (2016). *Bitcoin and cryptocurrency technologies: a comprehensive introduction*. Princeton University Press.

Nasri, W. (2021). An empirical study of user acceptance behaviours of internet banking in Tunisia using UTAUT2 model. [IJIDE]. *International Journal of Innovation in the Digital Economy*, 12(4), 16–34. DOI: 10.4018/IJIDE.2021100102

National Cyber Security Centre (NCSC). (2023) *Third-Party Risk Management.* Available at: https://www.ncsc.gov.uk/ (Accessed: 14 September 2024).

National Cybersecurity Authority. (2023) *National Cybersecurity Strategy.* Available at: https://www.nca.gov.sa/en/national-cybersecurity-strategy (Accessed: 23 September 2024).

National Day of Oman. (2020). *Oman Vision 2040 Preliminary Vision Document.* Retrieved from https://www.national-day-of-oman.info/wp-content/uploads/2020/11/OmanVision2040-Preliminary-Vision-Document.pdf

National Digital Department. (n.d.). *The National Fiberisation and Connectivity Plan (NFCP) 2019 2023.* https://www.malaysia.gov.my/portal/content/30736

National Institute of Standards and Technology (NIST). (2021) *Glossary of Key Information Security Terms.* Available at: https://csrc.nist.gov/glossary/term/cybersecurity (Accessed: 21 September 2024).

National, C. I. O. Review (2023) *How to overcome cost-barriers to digital transformation.* Available at: https://nationalcioreview.com (Accessed: 30 September 2024).

Nazemi, K. (2023). Artificial Intelligence in Visual Analytics. *2023 27th International Conference Information Visualisation (IV)*, 230–237. DOI: 10.1109/IV60283.2023.00048

NCSC. (2023) *Cyber security governance.* Available at: https://www.ncsc.gov.uk/collection/risk-management/cyber-security-governance (Accessed: 26 September 2024).

Nesta. (2016). *People-powered public services: A case study.* Retrieved from https://www.nesta.org.uk/report/people-powered-public-services/

Ng, P. M., Lit, K. K., & Cheung, C. T. (2022). Remote work as a new normal? The technology-organization-environment (TOE) context. *Technology in Society*, 70, 102022. DOI: 10.1016/j.techsoc.2022.102022 PMID: 35719245

Nguyen, T.T.M. (2020). Foreign Direct Investment Strategy of MNCs in the Context of Digital Transformation. VNU journal of economics and business, 36(3).

Nguyen, L. T., Hoang, T. G., Do, L. H., Ngo, X. T., Nguyen, P. H., Nguyen, G. D., & Nguyen, G. N. (2021). The role of blockchain technology-based social crowdfunding in advancing social value creation. *Technological Forecasting and Social Change*, 170, 120898. DOI: 10.1016/j.techfore.2021.120898

Nguyen, S. D. (2020). Digital transformation in art pedagogical training in Vietnam today. *Vietnam Journal of Education*, 4(4), 69–75. DOI: 10.52296/vje.2020.82

Nguyen, T. M., & Malik, A. (2020). Cognitive processes, rewards and online knowledge sharing behaviour: The moderating effect of organisational innovation. *Journal of Knowledge Management*, 24(6), 1241–1261. DOI: 10.1108/JKM-12-2019-0742

NHS Digital. (2021). From NHS Choices to NHS.UK: A case study in digital transformation. Retrieved from https://digital.nhs.uk/services/nhs-website-service/case-studies

NHS Digital. (2022). Digital, data and technology standards. Retrieved from https://digital.nhs.uk/about-nhs-digital/our-work/nhs-digital-data-and-technology-standards

NHS England. (2020). NHS Alpha Project: Final report and recommendations. Retrieved from https://www.england.nhs.uk/digitaltechnology/nhs-alpha-project/

NHS England. (2022). Digital transformation strategy 2022-2025. Retrieved from https://www.england.nhs.uk/digitaltechnology/connecteddigitalsystems/digital-transformation/

NHS England. (2024a) *Digital transformation*. Available at: https://www.england.nhs.uk/digitaltechnology (Accessed: 30 September 2024).

NHS England. (2024b) *Inclusive digital healthcare: A framework for NHS action on digital inclusion*. Available at: https://www.england.nhs.uk/long-read/inclusive-digital-healthcare-a-framework-for-nhs-action-on-digital-inclusion (Accessed: 21 September 2024).

Nie, J., Jian, X., Xu, J., Xu, N., Jiang, T., & Yu, Y. (2024). The effect of corporate social responsibility practices on digital transformation in China: A resource-based view. *Economic Analysis and Policy*, 82, 1–15. DOI: 10.1016/j.eap.2024.02.027

Ninaus, K., Diehl, S., & Terlutter, R. (2021). Employee perceptions of information and communication technologies in work life, perceived burnout, job satisfaction and the role of work-family balance. *Journal of Business Research*, 136, 652–666. DOI: 10.1016/j.jbusres.2021.08.007

NIST. (2024) *The NIST Cybersecurity Framework (CSF) 2.0*. Available at: https://nvlpubs.nist.gov/nistpubs/CSWP/NIST.CSWP.29.pdf (Accessed: 16 September 2024).

Nižetić, S., Djilali, N., Papadopoulos, A., & Rodrigues, J. J. (2019). Smart technologies for promotion of energy efficiency, utilization of sustainable resources and waste management. *Journal of Cleaner Production*, 231, 565–591. DOI: 10.1016/j.jclepro.2019.04.397

Noordin, K. A. (2017, November 14). Deconstructing the DFTZ. *The Edge Malaysia.* https://theedgemalaysia.com/article/deconstructing-dftz

O'Callaghan, M. (2023). *Decision intelligence: human–machine integration for decision-making.* CRC Press. DOI: 10.1201/b23322

Ochs, J., Biermann, F., Piotrowski, T., Erkens, F., Nießing, B., Herbst, L., König, N., & Schmitt, R. H. (2021). Fully Automated Cultivation of Adipose-Derived Stem Cells in the Stem Cell Discovery—A Robotic Laboratory for Small-Scale, High-Throughput Cell Production Including Deep Learning-Based Confluence Estimation. *Processes (Basel, Switzerland),* 2021(9), 575. DOI: 10.3390/pr9040575

Ofcom (2023) *Connected nations 2023.* London: Ofcom.

Office for National Statistics. (2019) *Exploring the UK's digital divide.* Available at: https://www.ons.gov.uk (Accessed: 23 September 2024).

Okorie, O., & Russell, J. D. (2021, September). Exploring the risks of blockchain and circular economy initiatives in food supply chains: a hybrid model practice framework. *InProceedings of the International Conference on Sustainable Design andManufacturing* (pp. 290-303). Singapore: Springer Singapore. DOI: 10.1007/978-981-16-6128-0_28

Olczyk, M., & Kuc-Czarnecka, M. (2022). Digital transformation and economic growth-DESI improvement and implementation. *Technological and Economic Development of Economy,* 28(3), 775–803. DOI: 10.3846/tede.2022.16766

Oliver, R. L. (1980). A cognitive model of the antecedents and consequences of satisfaction decisions. *JMR, Journal of Marketing Research,* 17(4), 460–469. DOI: 10.1177/002224378001700405

Olubusola, O., Mhlongo, N. Z., Falaiye, T., Ajayi-Nifise, A. O., & Daraojimba, E. R. (2024). Digital transformation in business development: A comparative review of USA and Africa. *World Journal of Advanced Research and Reviews,* 21(2), 1958–1968. DOI: 10.30574/wjarr.2024.21.2.0443

Omidian, H., Razmara, J., Parvizpour, S., Tabrizchi, H., Masoudi-Sobhanzadeh, Y., & Omidi, Y. (2023). Tracing drugs from discovery to disposal. *Drug Discovery Today,* 28(5), 1–23. DOI: 10.1016/j.drudis.2023.103538 PMID: 36828192

Onungwa, I., Olugu-Uduma, N., & Shelden, D. R. (2021). Cloud BIM technology as a means of collaboration and project integration in smart cities. *SAGE Open,* 11(3), 21582440211033250. DOI: 10.1177/21582440211033250

Optimising, I. T. (2023) *The ultimate guide to digital transformation services*. Available at: https://www.optimisingit.co.uk (Accessed: 30 September 2024).

Ortiz, G., Zouai, M., Kazar, O., Garcia-de-Prado, A., & Boubeta-Puig, J. (2022). Atmosphere: Context and situational-aware collaborative IoT architecture for edge-fog-cloud computing. *Computer Standards & Interfaces*, 79, 103550. DOI: 10.1016/j.csi.2021.103550

Öztürk, C., & Yildizbaşi, A. (2020). Barriers to implementation of blockchain into supply chain management using an integrated multi-criteria decision-making method: A numerical example. *Soft Computing*, 24(19), 14771–14789. DOI: 10.1007/s00500-020-04831-w

Pal, K. (2017b). "A Semantic Web Service Architecture for Supply Chain Management", In 8th International Conference on Ambient Systems, Networks and Technologies (ANT 2017), 999-1004, Procedia Computer Science 109C. DOI: 10.1016/j.procs.2017.05.442

Pal, K. (2018a). "Ontology-Based Web Service Architecture for Retail Supply Chain Management", In 9th International Conference on Ambient Systems, Networks and Technologies (ANT 2018), 985-990, Procedia Computer Science 130. DOI: 10.1016/j.procs.2018.04.101

Pal, K. (2018b). *"A Big Data Framework for Decision Making in Supply Chain"*, In M. V Kumar, G. D. Putnik, J. Javakrishna, V. M. Pillai, L. Varela (Edited); IGI Publication, September 2018, USA, Chapter 1, IGI Global Publication, Hershey PA, USA.

Pal, K. (2020). "Information Sharing for Manufacturing Supply Chain Management Based on Blockchain Technology", in Dr Idongesit Williams (Eds.), Cross-Industry Use of Blockchain Technology and Opportunities for the Future, Chapter 1, May, IGI Global Publication, Hershey PA, USA. DOI: 10.4018/978-1-7998-3632-2.ch001

Pal, K., & Ul-Haque, A. (2000). *"Internet of Things and Blockchain Technology in Apparel Manufacturing Supply Chain Data Management"*, In the proceeding of 11th International Conference on Ambient Systems, Networks and Technologies (ANT-2020), Procedia Computer Science, pp. 450- 457, April 6-9, Warsaw, Poland.

Pal, K., & Ul-Haque, A. (2023). *"Internet of Things Impact on Supply Chain Management"*, In the proceeding of 14th International Conference on Ambient Systems, Networks and Technologies (ANT-2023), Procedia Computer Science, 478-485. DOI: 10.1016/j.procs.2023.03.061

Pal, K., Ul-Haque, A., & Shakshuki, E. (2024). "*Supply Chain Transport Management, Use of Electric Vehicles, Review of Security and Privacy for Cyber-Physical Transportation Ecosystem and Related solutions*", In the proceeding of 15th International Conference on Ambient Systems, Networks and Technologies (ANT-2020), Procedia Computer Science, 135-142, April 23-25, Hasselt, Belgium. DOI: 10.1016/j.procs.2024.06.008

Paleri, P. (2008). *National Security: Imperatives And Challenges*. Tata McGraw-Hill Education.

Pal, K. (2017a). Supply Chain Coordination Based on Web Services. In Chan, H. K., Subramanian, N., & Abdulrahman, M. D. (Eds.), *Supply Chain Management in the Big Data Era* (pp. 137–171). IGI Global Publication. DOI: 10.4018/978-1-5225-0956-1.ch009

Pal, K., & Karakostas, B. (2014). A Multi Agent-Based Service Framework for Supply Chain Management, In the proceeding of International Conference on Ambient Systems, Networks and Technology. *Procedia Computer Science*, 32, 53–60. DOI: 10.1016/j.procs.2014.05.397

Palmer, D. (2012). The ethics of data mining. *International Journal of Social and Organizational Dynamics in IT*, 2(1), 15–29.

Palo Alto Networks. (2023) *Ransomware Threat Report 2023*. Available at: https://www.paloaltonetworks.com/resources/research/ransomware-threat-report-2023 (Accessed: 21 September 2024).

Paltrinieri, N., Comfort, L., & Reniers, G. (2019). Learning about risk: Machine learning for risk assessment. *Safety Science*, 118, 475–486. DOI: 10.1016/j.ssci.2019.06.001

Panghal, A., Sindhu, S., Dahiya, S., Dahiya, B., & Mor, R. S. (2022). Benchmarking the interactions among challenges for blockchain technology adoption: A circular economy perspective. *International Journal of Mathematical. Engineering and Management Sciences*, 7(6), 859–872. DOI: 10.33889/IJMEMS.2022.7.6.054

Panigrahi, R., Srivastava, P. R., & Sharma, D. (2018). Online learning: Adoption, continuance, and learning outcome—A review of literature. *International Journal of Information Management*, 43, 1–14. DOI: 10.1016/j.ijinfomgt.2018.05.005

Pareto, U. K. (2023) *How to prepare your business for digital transformation*. Available at: https://pareto.co.uk (Accessed: 28 September 2024).

Parmenter, D. (2015). *Key performance indicators: developing, implementing, and using winning KPIs*. John Wiley & Sons. DOI: 10.1002/9781119019855

Parra, J., Pérez-Pons, M.E., González, J. (2021) . The Impact and Correlation of the Digital Transformation on GDP Growth in Different Regions Worldwide. Advances in Intelligent Systems and Computing, 1242.

Paul, T., Islam, N., Mondal, S., & Rakshit, S. (2022). RFID-integrated blockchain-driven circular supply chain management: A system architecture for B2B tea industry. *Industrial Marketing Management*, 101, 238–257. DOI: 10.1016/j.indmarman.2021.12.003

Perifanis, N. A., & Kitsios, F. (2023). Investigating the influence of artificial intelligence on business value in the digital era of strategy: A literature review. *Information (Basel)*, 14(2), 85. DOI: 10.3390/info14020085

Persada, S. F., Miraja, B. A., Nadlifatin, R., Belgiawan, P. F., Perwira Redi, A. A. N., & Lin, S. C. (2022). Determinants of students' intention to continue using online private tutoring: an expectation-confirmation model (ECM) approach. Technology, Knowledge and Learning, 1-14. DOI: 10.1007/s10758-021-09548-9

Peterson, E. A. (2013). Compliance and ethics programs: Competitive advantage through the law. *The Journal of Management and Governance*, 17(4), 1027–1045. DOI: 10.1007/s10997-012-9212-y

Phua, C., Lee, V., Smith, K., & Gayler, R. (2010). A comprehensive survey of data mining-based fraud detection research. *arXiv preprint arXiv:1009.6119*.

Piao, S. (2024, January). Barriers toward circular economy transition: Exploring different stakeholders' perspectives. *Corporate Social Responsibility and Environmental Management*, 31(1), 153–168. Advance online publication. DOI: 10.1002/csr.2558

Piccinini, E., Gregory, R. W., & Kolbe, L. M. (2015). Changes in the producer-consumer relationship-towards digital transformation.

Pilkington, M. (2016). Blockchain technology: principles and applications. In *Research handbook on digital transformations* (pp. 225–253). Edward Elgar Publishing. DOI: 10.4337/9781784717766.00019

Pinar, A., & Boran, F. E. (2020). A q-rung orthopair fuzzy multi-criteria group decision making method for supplier selection based on a novel distance measure. *International Journal of Machine Learning and Cybernetics*, 11(8), 1749–1780. DOI: 10.1007/s13042-020-01070-1

Pinsent Masons. (2024) *NHS to receive £3.4bn funding for digital transformation.* Available at: https://www.pinsentmasons.com (Accessed: 30 September 2024).

Politico (2024) *Boosting SME digital skills is key for UK economic growth.* Available at: https://www.politico.eu (Accessed: 30 September 2024).

Posada, J., Toro, C., Barandiaran, I., Oyarzun, D., Stricker, D., de Amicis, R., Pinto, E. B., Eisert, P., Döllner, J., & Vallarino, I. (2015). Visual computing as a key enabling technology for industrie 4.0 and industrial internet. *IEEE Computer Graphics and Applications*, 35(2), 26–40. DOI: 10.1109/MCG.2015.45 PMID: 25807506

Power, D. J., & Heavin, C. (2017). *Decision support, analytics, and business intelligence.* Business Expert Press.

Prahalad, C. K., & Mashelkar, R. A. (2010, July-August). Innovation's Holy Grail. *Harvard Business Review*, 1–11.

Pratiwi, C. P., Rahmatika, R. A., Wibawa, R. C., Purnomo, L., Larasati, H., Jahroh, S., & Syaukat, F. I. (2024). *The Rise of Digital Marketing Agencies: Transforming Digital Business Trends.* Jurnal Aplikasi Bisnis Dan Manajemen., DOI: 10.17358/jabm.10.1.162

Prewett, K. W., Prescott, G. L., & Phillips, K. (2020). Blockchain adoption is inevitable—Barriers and risks remain. *Journal of Corporate Accounting & Finance*, 31(2), 21–28. DOI: 10.1002/jcaf.22415

Priya, G. J., & Saradha, S. (2021, February). Fraud detection and prevention using machine learning algorithms: a review. In *2021 7th International Conference on Electrical Energy Systems (ICEES)* (pp. 564-568). IEEE. DOI: 10.1109/ICEES51510.2021.9383631

Prokopowicz, D. (2024). Research Project (proposal): What are the potential applications of artificial intelligence and Big Data Analytics in Business Intelligence business performance analytics? How should artificial intelligence technology be used so that it complies with business ethics and corporate social responsibility? DOI: 10.13140/RG.2.2.24372.87689

Pulizzi, J. (2012). The rise of storytelling as the new marketing. *Publishing Research Quarterly*, 28(2), 116–123. DOI: 10.1007/s12109-012-9264-5

Puttonen, J., Lobov, A., & Lastra, J. L. M. (2013). Semantics-Based Composition of Factory Automation Processes Encapsulated by Web Services. *IEEE Transactions on Industrial Informatics*, 9(4), 2349–2359. DOI: 10.1109/TII.2012.2220554

Puttonen, J., Lobov, A., Soto, M. A. C., & Lastra, J. L. M. (2010). A Semantic Web Services-based approach for production systems control. *Advanced Engineering Informatics*, 24(3), 285–299. DOI: 10.1016/j.aei.2010.05.012

PwC. (2023) *The responsible AI framework - Accelerating innovation through responsible AI.* Available at: https://www.pwc.co.uk/services/risk/insights/accelerating-innovation-through-responsible-ai/responsible-ai-framework.html (Accessed: 30 September 2024).

Quayson, M., Bai, C., Sun, L., & Sarkis, J. (2023). Building blockchain-driven dynamic capabilities for developing circular supply chain: Rethinking the role of sensing, seizing, and reconfiguring. *Business Strategy and the Environment*, 32(7), 4821–4840. DOI: 10.1002/bse.3395

Raffey, M. A., & Gaikwad, S. B. (2022). The Impact Of Artificial Intelligence On Business Operations: Investigating The Current State And Future Implications Of AI Technologies. *Journal of Pharmaceutical Negative Results*, ●●●, 5577–5580.

Raguseo, E. (2018). Big data technologies: An empirical investigation on their adoption, benefits and risks for companies. *International Journal of Information Management*, 38(1), 187–195. DOI: 10.1016/j.ijinfomgt.2017.07.008

Rajasekaran, A. S., Azees, M., & Al-Turjman, F. (2022). A comprehensive survey on blockchain technology. *Sustainable Energy Technologies and Assessments*, 52, 102039. DOI: 10.1016/j.seta.2022.102039

Raji, M. A., Olodo, H. B., Oke, T. T., Addy, W. A., Ofodile, O. C., & Oyewole, A. T.Mustafa Ayobami RajiHameedat Bukola OlodoTimothy Tolulope OkeWilhelmina Afua AddyOnyeka Chrisanctus OfodileAdedoyin Tolulope Oyewole. (2024). The digital transformation of SMES: A comparative review between the USA and Africa. *International Journal of Management & Entrepreneurship Research*, 6(3), 737–751. DOI: 10.51594/ijmer.v6i3.884

Ramadhan, A., Hidayanto, A. N., Salsabila, G. A., Wulandari, I., Jaury, J. A., & Anjani, N. N. (2022). The effect of usability on the intention to use the e-learning system in a sustainable way: A case study at Universitas Indonesia. *Education and Information Technologies*, 27(2), 1489–1522. DOI: 10.1007/s10639-021-10613-0

Ramaswamy, R., Gou, Y., Wu, D. J., Bush, D., & Grover, P. (2018). Organizing for digital innovation: The division of innovation labor between upstream and downstream teams. *Journal of Management Information Systems*, 35, 169–204.

Rana, R. L., Tricase, C., & De Cesare, L. (2021). Blockchain technology for a sustainable Agri-food supply chain. *British Food Journal*, 123(11), 3471–3485. DOI: 10.1108/BFJ-09-2020-0832

Rastogi, V. (2018, January 18). Malaysia's Digital Free Trade Zone. *AEAN Briefing*. https://www.aseanbriefing.com/news/malaysias-digital-free-trade-zone/

Razzaque, M. A., Milojevic-Jevric, M., Palade, A., & Clarke, S. (2016, February). (2o16). Middleware for Internet of Things: A Survey. *IEEE Internet of Things Journal*, 3(1), 70–95. DOI: 10.1109/JIOT.2015.2498900

Reddy, B. Mad Armiani,shree, & Aithal, P. S. (2020). Blockchain as a disruptive technology in healthcare and financial services—A review based analysis on current implementations (SSRN Scholarly Paper No. 3611482). Retrieved from https://papers.ssrn.com/abstract=3611482

Reim, W., Åström, J., & Eriksson, O. (2020). Implementation of artificial intelligence (AI): A roadmap for business model innovation. *AI*, 1(2), 11. DOI: 10.3390/ai1020011

Rejeb, A., Appolloni, A., Rejeb, K., Treiblmaier, H., Iranmanesh, M., & Keogh, J. G. (2023). The role of blockchain technology in the transition toward the circular economy: Findings from a systematic literature review. *Resources, Conservation & Recycling Advances*, 17, 200126. DOI: 10.1016/j.rcradv.2022.200126

Rejeb, A., Keogh, J. G., & Treiblmaier, H. (2022). How blockchain technology can benefit supply chain sustainability. *Sustainability*, 12(3), 7369. DOI: 10.3390/su12187369

Rejeb, A., Rejeb, K., Keogh, J. G., & Zailani, S. (2022b). Barriers to blockchain adoption in the circular economy: A fuzzy Delphi and best-worst approach. *Sustainability (Basel)*, 14(6), 3611. DOI: 10.3390/su14063611

Rejeb, A., Zailani, S., Rejeb, K., Treiblmaier, H., & Keogh, J. G. (2022a). Modeling enablers for blockchain adoption in the circular economy. *Sustainable Futures : An Applied Journal of Technology, Environment and Society*, 4(1), 1–25. DOI: 10.1016/j.sftr.2022.100095

Renduchintala, T., Alfauri, H., Yang, Z., Pietro, R. D., & Jain, R. (2022). A survey of blockchain applications in the FinTech sector. *Journal of Open Innovation*, 8(4), 185. DOI: 10.3390/joitmc8040185

Resnik, D. B. (2018). *The ethics of research with human subjects: Protecting people, advancing science, promoting trust*. Springer. DOI: 10.1007/978-3-319-68756-8

Reyna, A., Martín, C., Chen, J., Soler, E., & Díaz, M. (2018). On blockchain and its integration with IoT. Challenges and opportunities. *Future Generation Computer Systems*, 88, 173–190. DOI: 10.1016/j.future.2018.05.046

Rezaee, Z. (2004). Corporate governance role in financial reporting. *Research in Accounting Regulation*, 17, 107–149. DOI: 10.1016/S1052-0457(04)17006-9

Rezaei, M. (2022). Machine Learning in Regulatory Compliance Software Systems: An Industrial Case Study.

Rizvi, Y. S., & Nabi, A. (2021). Transformation of learning from real to virtual: An exploratory-descriptive analysis of issues and challenges. *Journal of Research in Innovative Teaching & Learning*, 14(1), 5–17. DOI: 10.1108/JRIT-10-2020-0052

Roberts, S., & Cooper, T. (2022). User-centric design in healthcare websites: Lessons from NHS.UK. *Journal of Medical Systems*, 46, 31.

Roblek, V., Maja, M., & Alojz, K. (2016). A Complex View of Industry 4.0. *SAGE Open*, 6(2), 1–11. DOI: 10.1177/2158244016653987

Rohmah, N., & Komarudin, K. (2023). Digital Transformation in Business Operations Management. [AJEMB]. *American Journal of Economic and Management Business*, 2(9), 330–336. DOI: 10.58631/ajemb.v2i9.57

Romanova, O.A., & Kuzmin, E. (2021). Industrial policy: A new reality in the context of digital transformation of the economy. Lecture Notes in Information Systems and Organisation, 44.

Ross, J. W., Beath, C. M., & Mocker, M. (2018). Designing a digital organization. *MIT Sloan Management Review*, 59, 57–65.

Rothstein, S. A. (2024). Transnational governance of digital transformation: Financing innovation in Europe's periphery. *New Political Economy*, 29(2), 227–239. DOI: 10.1080/13563467.2023.2240236

Roy, S. (2023). Dominance of Automation in Financial Services Industry. https://www.iimcal.ac.in/FinLab/email-template6/res/07.pdf

Rožman, M., Oreški, D., & Tominc, P. (2023). Artificial-intelligence-supported reduction of employees' workload to increase the company's performance in today's VUCA Environment. *Sustainability (Basel)*, 15(6), 5019. DOI: 10.3390/su15065019

Runeson, P., & Höst, M. (2009). Guidelines for conducting and reporting case study research in software engineering. *Empirical Software Engineering*, 14(2), 131–164. DOI: 10.1007/s10664-008-9102-8

Russell, S. (2022). Artificial Intelligence and the Problem of Control. *Perspectives on Digital Humanism, 19*.

Russell, S. J., & Norvig, P. (2016). *Artificial intelligence: a modern approach*. Pearson.

Russomanno, D. J., Kothari, C. R., & Thomas, O. A. (2005). "Building a Sensor Ontology: A Practical Approach Leveraging ISO and OGC Models", in the 2005 International Conference on Artificial Intelligence, 637-643.

Ruta, M., Colucci, S., Scioscia, F., Di Sciascio, E., & Donini, F. M. (2011). Finding commonalities in RFID semantic streams. *Procedia Computer Science*, 5, 857–864. DOI: 10.1016/j.procs.2011.07.118

Saadi Sedik, T., Chen, S., Feyzioglu, T., Ghazanchyan, M., Gupta, S., Jahan, S., Jauregui, J. M., Kinda, T., Long, V., Loukoianova, E., Mourmouras, A., Nozaki, M., Paroutzoglou, S., Sullivan, C., Yoo, J., & Zhang, L. (2019). The digital revolution in Asia and its macroeconomic effects. ADBI Working Paper Series 1029.

Saberi, S., Kouhizadeh, M., Sarkis, J., & Shen, L. (2019). Blockchain technology and its relationships to sustainable supply chain management. *International Journal of Production Research*, 57(7), 2117–2135. DOI: 10.1080/00207543.2018.1533261

Sachdeva, P., Kumar, M. D., & Mitra, A. (2024). Green discourse analysis on Twitter: Imperatives to green product management in sustainable cities (SDG11). *Studies in Systems. Decision and Control*, 487, 245–256. DOI: 10.1007/978-3-031-35828-9_22

Sachdeva, P., & Mitra, A. (2024). Decoding human development and environmental sustainability: A predictive analytical study on relationship between HDI and carbon emission. *Studies in Systems. Decision and Control*, 489, 785–795. DOI: 10.1007/978-3-031-36895-0_66

Sahebi, I. G., Masoomi, B., & Ghorbani, S. (2020). Expert oriented approach for analyzing the blockchain adoption barriers in humanitarian supply chain. *Technology in Society*, 63, 101427. DOI: 10.1016/j.techsoc.2020.101427

Said, O., & Masud, M. (2013). Towards internet of things: Survey and future vision. *International Journal of Computer Networks*, 5(1), 1–17.

Said, S. (2023). The Role of Artificial Intelligence (AI) and Data Analytics in Enhancing Guest Personalization in Hospitality. *Journal of Modern Hospitality*, 2(1), 1–13. DOI: 10.47941/jmh.1556

Salam, U. (2023). Digital Tourism In ASEAN During Covid-19 Pandemic. *SOSIO DIALEKTIKA*, 8(2), 153. DOI: 10.31942/sd.v8i2.9798

Samadhiya, A., Agrawal, R., Kumar, A., & Garza-Reyes, J. A. (2023). Blockchain technology and circular economy in the environment of total productive maintenance: A natural resource-based view perspective. *Journal of Manufacturing Technology Management*, 34(2), 293–314. DOI: 10.1108/JMTM-08-2022-0299

Sánchez-Ortiz, J., García-Valderrama, T., & Rodríguez-Cornejo, V. (2020). Towards a sustainable public administration: The mediating role of lean and agile management in public sector digital transformation. *Sustainability*, 12(22), 9442.

Sanghai, A. (2023). *Three BI and Analytics trends to lookout for in 2023. Express Computer*. Guest Blogs News.

Sanka, A. I., Irfan, M., Huang, I., & Cheung, R. C. (2021). A survey of breakthrough in blockchain technology: Adoptions, applications, challenges and future research. *Computer Communications*, 169, 179–201. DOI: 10.1016/j.comcom.2020.12.028

Santa Fe Utn, F. R., & Consumidores De La Era Digital, A. C. (2023). I Jornadas de Ciberseguridad y Sociedad. *AJEA, AJEA*, 27(AJEA 27). Advance online publication. DOI: 10.33414/ajea.1300.2023

Santiago, C. D., Bustos, Y., Jolie, S. A., Flores Toussaint, R., Sosa, S. S., Raviv, T., & Cicchetti, C. (2021). The impact of COVID-19 on immigrant and refugee families: Qualitative perspectives from newcomer students and parents. *The School Psychologist*, 36(5), 348–357. DOI: 10.1037/spq0000448 PMID: 34435837

Saraf, K., Bajar, K., Jain, A., & Barve, A. (2024). Assessment of barriers impeding the incorporation of blockchain technology in the service sector: A case of hotel and health care. *Journal of Modelling in Management*, 19(2), 407–440. DOI: 10.1108/JM2-06-2022-0159

Sarmah, S. S. (2018). Understanding blockchain technology. *Computing in Science & Engineering*, 8(2), 23–29.

Sathuta Sellapperuma & Niroshima Udayangani. (2024). *ENGINEERING SOFTWARE COMPONENTS AND SYSTEMS FOR AUTONOMOUS VEHICLES: ADDRESSING NOVEL CHALLENGES IN THE DIGITAL TRANSITION ERA CONTEXT.* DOI: 10.13140/RG.2.2.21596.60809

Saudi Arabian Monetary Authority (SAMA). (2021) *Cyber Security Framework.* Available at: https://www.sama.gov.sa/en-US/RulesInstructions/CyberSecurity/Cyber%20Security%20Framework.pdf (Accessed: 30 September 2024).

Saunders, M., Lewis, P., & Thornhill, A. (2016). *Research methods for business students* (7th ed.). Pearson.

Sayeed, S., & Marco-Gisbert, H. (2019). Assessing blockchain consensus and security mechanisms against the 51% attack. *Applied Sciences (Basel, Switzerland)*, 9(9), 1788. DOI: 10.3390/app9091788

Scarpino, J. P. (2022). *An Exploratory Study: Implications of Machine Learning and Artificial Intelligence in Risk Management* (Doctoral dissertation, Marymount University). https://www.proquest.com/docview/2731478908?pq-origsite=gscholar &fromopenview=true

Schär, F. (2021). Decentralized finance: On blockchain- and smart contract-based financial markets. Retrieved from https://www.fschaar.info/publication/2021_defi/ 2021_defi.pdf

Schär, F. (2021). Decentralized finance: On blockchain- and smart contract-based financial markets. *Review - Federal Reserve Bank of St. Louis*, 103(2), 153–174. DOI: 10.20955/r.103.153-74

Scharfman, J. (2024). Decentralized Autonomous Organization (DAO) Fraud, Hacks, and Controversies. In The Cryptocurrency and Digital Asset Fraud Casebook, Volume II: DeFi, NFTs, DAOs, Meme Coins, and Other Digital Asset Hacks (pp. 65-106). Cham: Springer Nature Switzerland.

Schmidt, C. G., & Wagner, S. M. (2019). Blockchain and supply chain relations: A transaction cost theory perspective. *Journal of Purchasing and Supply Management*, 25(4), 100552. DOI: 10.1016/j.pursup.2019.100552

Schmidt, J. L., Sehnem, S., & Spuldaro, J. D. (2023). Blockchain and the transition to the circular economy: A literature review. *Corporate Social Responsibility and Environmental Management*. Advance online publication. DOI: 10.1002/csr.2674

Schmitz, J., & Leoni, G. (2019). Accounting and auditing at the time of blockchain technology: A research agenda. *Australian Accounting Review*, 29(2), 331–342. DOI: 10.1111/auar.12286

Schneider, M., Hippchen, B., Abeck, S., Jacoby, M., & Herzog, R. (2018). Enabling IoT Platform Interoperability Using a Systematic Development Approach by Example. In Proceedings of the 2018 Global Internet of Things Summit (GIoTS), Bilbao, Spain, 4–7, June 2018; 1–6. DOI: 10.1109/GIOTS.2018.8534549

Schulte, S., Sigwart, M., Frauenthaler, P., & Borkowski, M. (2019). Towards blockchain interoperability. In Business Process Management: Blockchain and Central and Eastern Europe Forum: BPM 2019 Blockchain and CEE Forum, Vienna, Austria, September 1–6, 2019 [Springer International Publishing.]. *Proceedings*, 17, 3–10.

Schwartz, J. (2019). Workforce of the future: The competing forces shaping 2030. *Strategy and Leadership*, 47, 16–22.

Sciullo, L., Gigli, L., Trotta, A., & Di Felice, D. (2020). WoT Store: Management resources and applications on the web of things. *Internet of Things : Engineering Cyber Physical Human Systems*, 9, 100164. DOI: 10.1016/j.iot.2020.100164

Seaman, C. B. (1999). Qualitative methods in empirical studies of software engineering. *IEEE Transactions on Software Engineering*, 25(4), 557–572. DOI: 10.1109/32.799955

Security, I. B. M. (2023) *Cost of a Data Breach Report 2023*. Available at: https://www.ibm.com/security/data-breach (Accessed: 18 September 2024).

Seiger, R., Huber, S., & Schlegel, T. (2018). Toward an execution system for self-healing workflows in cyber-physical systems. *Software & Systems Modeling*, 17(2), 551–572. DOI: 10.1007/s10270-016-0551-z

Sen, J., Sen, R., & Dutta, A. (2021). Introductory Chapter: Machine Learning in Finance-Emerging Trends and Challenges. *Algorithms, Models and Applications*, 1.

Şengel, Ü., Çevrimkaya, M., Işkın, M., & Zengin, B. (2022). The Effects Of Corporate Websites Usability Of Travel Agencies On Their Technological Capabilities. *Journal of Quality Assurance in Hospitality & Tourism*, 23(6), 1575–1595. DOI: 10.1080/1528008X.2021.2004570

Serdyukova, N., & Serdyukov, S. (2023). A research of factors and the process of a territory's tourism ecosystem formation. *The Eurasian Scientific Journal, 15*(4), 24ECVN423. DOI: 10.15862/24ECVN423

Shane, S., & Venkataraman, S. (2000). The promise of entrepreneurship as a field of research. *Academy of Management Review*, 25(1), 217–226. DOI: 10.5465/amr.2000.2791611

Shanti, R., Siregar, H., Zulbainarni, N., & Tony, . (2023). Role of Digital Transformation on Digital Business Model Banks. *Sustainability (Basel)*, 15(23), 16293. DOI: 10.3390/su152316293

Sharda, R., Delen, D., & Turban, E. (2018). *Business intelligence, analytics, and data science: a managerial perspective*. pearson.

Sharma, R., Samad, T. A., Jabbour, C. J. C., & de Queiroz, M. J. (2021). Leveraging blockchain technology for circularity in agricultural supply chains: Evidence from a fast-growing economy. *Journal of Enterprise Information Management,* (ahead-of-print). .DOI: 10.1108/JEIM-02-2021-0094

Sharma, R., Shishodia, A., Kamble, S., Gunasekaran, A., & Belhadi, A. (2020). Agriculture supply chain risks and COVID-19: Mitigation strategies and implications for the practitioners. *International Journal of Logistics Research and Applications*, 1-27, 1–27. .DOI: 10.1080/13675567.2020.1830049

Sharma, P. K., Kumar, N., & Park, J. H. (2020). Blockchain technology toward green IoT: Opportunities and challenges. *IEEE Network*, 34(4), 263–269. DOI: 10.1109/MNET.001.1900526

Sharma, R. (2023). Leveraging AI and IoT for Sustainable Waste Management. In Whig, P., Silva, N., Elngar, A. A., Aneja, N., & Sharma, P. (Eds.), *Sustainable Development through Machine Learning, AI and IoT* (Vol. 1939, pp. 136–150). Springer Nature Switzerland., DOI: 10.1007/978-3-031-47055-4_12

Shi, Y., & Duan, X. (2019). Emerging Risk Analytics, 2019. *Distributed computer framework for data analysis, risk management, and automated compliance.* U.S. Patent Application No. 16/358,641.

Shires, J., & Hakmeh, J. (2020) *Is the GCC Cyber Resilient?* Chatham House. Available at: https://www.chathamhouse.org/sites/default/files/CHHJ8019-GCC -Cyber-Briefing-200302-WEB.pdf (Accessed: 26 September 2024).

Shirgave, S., Awati, C., More, R., & Patil, S. (2019). A review on credit card fraud detection using machine learning. *International Journal of Scientific & technology research, 8*(10), 1217-1220.

Shmueli, G., & Koppius, O. R. (2011). Predictive analytics in information systems research. *Management Information Systems Quarterly*, 35(3), 553–572. DOI: 10.2307/23042796

Shojaei, A., Ketabi, R., Razkenari, M., Hakim, H., & Wang, J. (2021). Enabling a circular economy in the built environment sector through blockchain technology. *Journal of Cleaner Production*, 294, 126352. DOI: 10.1016/j.jclepro.2021.126352

Shou, M., & Domenech, T. (2022). Integrating LCA and blockchain technology to promote circular fashion–A case study of leather handbags. *Journal of Cleaner Production*, 373, 133557. DOI: 10.1016/j.jclepro.2022.133557

Shyla, J. (2020). Effect of digitalization on import and export. Emperor Internationaa Journal of Finance and Management Research, V(7), 1-12.

Siddiquee, N. A., & Mohamed, M. Z. (2009). *E-governance and service delivery innovations in Malaysia: an overview. Network of Asia-Pacific Schools and Institutes of Public Administration and Governance.* NAPSIPAG.

Silicon. (2017). *HSBC Adopts AI Startup Ayasdi's Tech To Tackle Money-Laundering*. Accessed at: HSBC

Singh, C. (2023). Artificial intelligence and deep learning: Considerations for financial institutions for compliance with the regulatory burden in the United Kingdom. *Journal of Financial Crime*.

Singh, C., & Lin, W. (2021). Can artificial intelligence, RegTech and CharityTech provide effective solutions for anti-money laundering and counter-terror financing initiatives in charitable fundraising. *Journal of Money Laundering Control*, 24(3), 464–482. DOI: 10.1108/JMLC-09-2020-0100

Singh, C., Lin, W., Singh, S. P., & Ye, Z. (2022). *RegTech compliance tools for charities in the United Kingdom: can machine learning help lighten the regulatory burden?* Company Lawyer.

Singh, C., Zhao, L., Lin, W., & Ye, Z. (2021). Can machine learning, as a RegTech compliance tool, lighten the regulatory burden for charitable organisations in the United Kingdom? *Journal of Financial Crime*, 29(1), 45–61. DOI: 10.1108/JFC-06-2021-0131

Singh, K., & Best, P. (2019). Anti-money laundering: Using data visualization to identify suspicious activity. *International Journal of Accounting Information Systems*, 34, 100418. DOI: 10.1016/j.accinf.2019.06.001

Şişci, M. E. R. V. E., Torkul, Y. E., & Selvi, I. H. (2022). Machine Learning as a Tool for Achieving Digital Transformation. *Knowl. Manag. Digit. Transform. Power*, 1, 55.

SME Corp Malaysia: SME Annual Report 2017/18 (2018)

Snyder, H. (1996). Qualitative interviewing: The art of hearing data-Rubin, Herbert J. & Rubin, Irene S. Thousand Oaks, CA: Sage Publications, 1995. 302 pp. $21.95 (paperback)(ISBN 0-8039-5096-9). *Library & Information Science Research*, 2(18), 194–195. DOI: 10.1016/S0740-8188(96)90024-9

Srivastava, K. (2021). Paradigm shift in Indian banking industry with special reference to artificial intelligence. [TURCOMAT]. *Turkish Journal of Computer and Mathematics Education*, 12(5), 1623–1629.

Statista (2024a) *Revenue in the Cybersecurity Market Worldwide from 2018 to 2029 (in Billion U.S. Dollars)*. Available at: https://www.statista.com/forecasts/1438758/revenue-cybersecurity-cybersecurity-market-worldwide (Accessed: 15 September 2024).

Statista (2024b) *Mobile Internet Penetration in the MENA Region by Country in 2022*. Available at: https://www.statista.com/forecasts/1169098/mobile-internet -penetration-in-mena-by-country (Accessed: 18 September 2024).

Statista. (2023, October 4). Topic: Decentralized finance (DeFI). Retrieved from https://www.statista.com/topics/6210/decentralized-finance-defi/

Stephenson, M., Eden, L., Kende, M., Kimura, F., Sauvant, K.P., Srinivasan, N., Tajoli, L., & Zhan, J. (2021). Leveraging digital FDI for capacity and competitiveness: How to be smart. T20, Task Force 3 (policy brief).

Stiglitz, J. E. (2017). *Globalization and its discontents revisited: Anti-globalization in the era of Trump*. WW Norton & Company.

Stojmenovic, I., & Wen, S. (2014). The fog computing paradigm: scenario and security issues, In Proceedings of the Federated Conference on Computer Science and Information Systems (FedCSIS-14), 1-8, IEEE, Warsaw, Poland, September 2014. DOI: 10.15439/2014F503

Sultan, M. I., & Amir, A. S. (2023). Charting The Digital Odyssey: Exploring Challenges and Unleashing Opportunities for Journalism in The Digital Era. *Warta ISKI*, 6(2), 153–162. DOI: 10.25008/wartaiski.v6i2.254

Sunmola, F., Burgess, P., Tan, A., Chanchaichujit, J., Balasubramania, S., & Mahmud, M. (2023). Prioritising visibility influencing factors in supply chains for resilience. *Procedia Computer Science*, 217, 1589–1598. DOI: 10.1016/j.procs.2022.12.359

Sun, Z. (2023). Data, Analytics, and Intelligence. *Journal of Computer Science Research*, 5(4), 43–57. DOI: 10.30564/jcsr.v5i4.6072

Suryawan, R. F., Kamsariaty, K., Perwitasari, E. P., Maulina, E., Maghfuriyah, A., & Susilowati, T. (2024). Digital Strategy Model in Strengthening Brand Image to Maintain Customer Loyalty (Case Study on Umrah and Hajj Travel Agency). *East Asian Journal of Multidisciplinary Research*, 2(12), 5045–5056. DOI: 10.55927/ eajmr.v2i12.6960

Swaminathan, J. M. (2000). *Supply chain management*. International Encyclopedia of the Social and Behavioural Sciences, Elsevier Sciences.

Swan, M. (2015). Blockchain thinking: The brain as a decentralized autonomous corporation [commentary]. *IEEE Technology and Society Magazine*, 34(4), 41–52. DOI: 10.1109/MTS.2015.2494358

Swan, M. (2015). *Blockchain: Blueprint for a new economy*. O'Reilly Media, Inc.

Talend Data Quality. Available online: https://www.talend.com/products/data-quality/ (accessed on 3 October 2023).

Talukder, M. B., Kumar, S., Kaiser, F., & Mia, Md. N. (2024). Pilgrimage Creative Tourism: A Gateway to Sustainable Development Goals in Bangladesh. In M. Hamdan, M. Anshari, N. Ahmad, & E. Ali (Eds.), *Advances in Public Policy and Administration* (pp. 285–300). IGI Global. DOI: 10.4018/979-8-3693-1742-6.ch016

Talukder, M. B. (2021). An assessment of the roles of the social network in the development of the Tourism Industry in Bangladesh. *International Journal of Business, Law, and Education*, 2(3), 85–93. DOI: 10.56442/ijble.v2i3.21

Talukder, M. B. (2024). Implementing Artificial Intelligence and Virtual Experiences in Hospitality. In Manohar, S., Mittal, A., Raju, S., & Nair, A. J. (Eds.), *Advances in Hospitality, Tourism, and the Services Industry* (pp. 145–160). IGI Global., DOI: 10.4018/979-8-3693-2019-8.ch009

Talukder, M. B., Kabir, F., Muhsina, K., & Das, I. R. (2023). Emerging Concepts of Artificial Intelligence in the Hotel Industry: A Conceptual Paper. *International Journal of Research Publication and Reviews*, 4(9), 1765–1769. DOI: 10.55248/gengpi.4.923.92451

Tang, D. (2021). What is digital transformation? *EDPACS*, 64(1), 9–13. DOI: 10.1080/07366981.2020.1847813

Tang, J., Tang, T.-I., & Chiang, C.-H. (2014). Blog learning: Effects of users' usefulness and efficiency towards continuance intention. Behaviour &amp. *Behaviour & Information Technology*, 33(1), 36–50. DOI: 10.1080/0144929X.2012.687772

Tapscott, D., & Tapscott, A. (2016). *Blockchain revolution: how the technology behind bitcoin is changing money, business, and the world*. Penguin.

Tapscott, D., & Tapscott, A. (2016). *Blockchain revolution: How the technology behind bitcoin is changing money, business, and the world*. Penguin.

Tarutė, A., Duobienė, J., Klovienė, L., Vitkauskaitė, E., & Varaniūtė, V. (2018). Identifying factors affecting digital transformation of SMEs. In Proceedings of The 18th International Conference on Electronic Business (pp. 373- 381). ICEB, Guilin, China, December 2-6.

Tech Nation. (2023). *The future of UK tech*. Tech Nation.

Tech, S. T. L. (2023) *UK's digital divide: Bridged!* Available at: https://stl.tech (Accessed: 12 September 2024).

Tech, U. K. (2022) *Tackling the digital divide and empowering the future workforce.* Available at: https://www.techuk.org (Accessed: 30 September 2024).

Tech, U. K. (2023) *How the emerging technologies can bring disruptive change across UK public sectors.* Available at: https://www.techuk.org (Accessed: 15 September 2024).

TechResort. (2024) *Digital inclusion and the general election.* Available at: https://www.techresort.org (Accessed: 13 September 2024).

Teece, D. J., Pisano, G., & Shuen, A. (1997). Dynamic capabilities and strategic management. *Strategic Management Journal*, 18(7), 509–533. DOI: 10.1002/(SICI)1097-0266(199708)18:7<509::AID-SMJ882>3.0.CO;2-Z

Teichmann, F., Boticiu, S., & Sergi, B. S. (2023). RegTech–Potential benefits and challenges for businesses. *Technology in Society*, 72, 102150. DOI: 10.1016/j.techsoc.2022.102150

Telecom Review. (2024). Malaysia's Digital Transformation Powered by New Technologies. Retrieved from https://www.telecomreviewasia.com/news/featured-articles/4001-malaysia-s-digital-transformation-powered-by-new-technologies/

The National. (2022) *GCC banks minimise cyber risks with strong investment in digital security.* Available at: https://www.thenationalnews.com/business/banking/2022/05/17/gcc-banks-minimise-cyber-risks-with-strong-investment-in-digital-security-sp-says/ (Accessed: 30 September 2024).

Thompson, K., & Walker, J. (2021). User involvement in healthcare digital service design. *Health Expectations*, 24(3), 887–898.

Tian, F. (2016). An agri-food supply chain traceability system for China based on RFID & blockchain technology. In *2016 13th International Conference on Service Systems and Service Management (ICSSSM)* (pp. 1-6). IEEE.

Tiffin, M. A. (2016). *Seeing in the dark: A machine-learning approach to nowcasting in Lebanon.* International Monetary Fund.

Tilala, M. H., Chenchala, P. K., Choppadandi, A., Kaur, J., Naguri, S., Saoji, R., & Devaguptapu, B. (2024). Ethical considerations in the use of artificial intelligence and machine learning in health care: A comprehensive review. *Cureus*, 16(6), 1–8. PMID: 39011215

Tiutiunyk, I., Drabek, J., Antoniuk, N., Navickas, V., & Rubanov, P. (2021). The impact of digital transformation on macroeconomic stability: Evidence from EU countries. *Journal of International Students*, 14(3).

Tjostheim, I., & Waterworth, J. A. (2023). Digital Travel – A Study of Travellers' Views of a Digital Visit to Mexico. In Á. Rocha, C. Ferrás, & W. Ibarra (Eds.), *Information Technology and Systems* (Vol. 691, pp. 185–194). Springer International Publishing. DOI: 10.1007/978-3-031-33258-6_17

TM ONE. (2021). How Digital Solutions Helped Malaysian SMEs #stayinbusiness. Retrieved from https://www.tmone.com.my/think-tank/how-digital-solutions-helped-malaysian-smes-stayinbusiness/

Topol, E. (2019). *Deep medicine: how artificial intelligence can make healthcare human again.*

To a, C., Paneru, C. P., Joudavi, A., & Tarigan, A. K. (2024). Digital transformation, incentives, and pro-environmental behaviour: Assessing the uptake of sustainability in companies' transition towards circular economy. *Sustainable Production and Consumption*, 47, 632–643. DOI: 10.1016/j.spc.2024.04.032

Toscano-Jara, J., Loza-Aguirre, E., & Franco-Crespo, A. (2023). Challenges for the Digital Transformation of Ecuador's Tourism Industry: Perceptions of Leaders in Times of Covid-19. In Estrada, S. (Ed.), *Digital and Sustainable Transformations in a Post-COVID World* (pp. 257–273). Springer International Publishing., DOI: 10.1007/978-3-031-16677-8_10

Toumi Sayari, K. (2023). Digitalization of the Financial Sector: New Opportunities and Challenges During the COVID-19 Crisis. In Mehta, K., Sharma, R., & Yu, P. (Eds.), *Revolutionizing Financial Services and Markets Through FinTech and Blockchain* (pp. 78–98). IGI Global., DOI: 10.4018/978-1-6684-8624-5.ch006

Tran, A. D., Pallant, J., & Johnson, L. W. (2021). Exploring the impact of chatbots on consumer sentiment and expectations in retail. *Journal of Retailing and Consumer Services*, 63(2), 102718. DOI: 10.1016/j.jretconser.2021.102718

Treiblmaier, H., & Garaus, M. (2023). Using blockchain to signal quality in the food supply chain: The impact on consumer purchase intentions and the moderating effect of brand familiarity. *International Journal of Information Management*, 68, 102514. DOI: 10.1016/j.ijinfomgt.2022.102514

Treviño, L. K., & Nelson, K. A. (2017). *Managing business ethics: Straight talk about how to do it right.* John Wiley & Sons.

Trevisan, A. H., Lobo, A., Guzzo, D., de Vasconcelos Gomes, L. A., & Mascarenhas, J. (2023). Barriers to employing digital technologies for a circular economy: A multi-level perspective. *Journal of Environmental Management*, 332, 117437. DOI: 10.1016/j.jenvman.2023.117437 PMID: 36801533

Truby, J., Brown, R. D., Dahdal, A., & Ibrahim, I. (2022). Blockchain, climate damage, and death: Policy interventions to reduce the carbon emissions, mortality, and net-zero implications of non-fungible tokens and Bitcoin. *Energy Research & Social Science*, 88, 102499. DOI: 10.1016/j.erss.2022.102499

Tudose, M. B., Georgescu, A., & Avasilcăi, S. (2023). Global Analysis Regarding the Impact of Digital Transformation on Macroeconomic Outcomes. *Sustainability (Basel)*, 15(5), 4583. DOI: 10.3390/su15054583

Turner, A., & Harris, B. (2022). Risk management in healthcare digital transformation. *Journal of Healthcare Risk Management*, 41(4), 28–36.

Tuten, T., & Solomon, M. R. (2017). Social Media Marketing-Tracy L. *Tuten, Michael R. Solomon. In.*

Tyler, B., Lahneman, B., Beukel, K., Cerrato, D., Minciullo, M., Spielmann, N., & Discua Cruz, A. (2020). SME Managers' Perceptions of Competitive Pressure and the Adoption of Environmental Practices in Fragmented Industries: A Multi Country Study in the Wine Industry. Organization and Environment, 33(3), 437 463. DOI: 10.1177/1086026618803720

U.S. Department of Health & Human Services (HHS). (2023) *Health Information Privacy*. Available at: https://www.hhs.gov/hipaa/index.html (Accessed: 30 September 2024).

Ueno, A., Dennis, C., & Dafoulas, G. A. (2023). Digital exclusion and relative digital deprivation: Exploring factors and moderators of internet non-use in the UK. *Technological Forecasting and Social Change*, 197, 122935. DOI: 10.1016/j.techfore.2023.122935

UK Government Digital Service. (2023). Digital Service Standard. Retrieved from https://www.gov.uk/service-manual/service-standard

UK Government. (2022) *Transforming for a digital future: 2022 to 2025 roadmap for digital and data*. Available at: https://www.gov.uk/government/publications/uks-digital-strategy/uk-digital-strategy (Accessed: 22 September 2024).

UK Government. (2024) *Digital development strategy 2024 to 2030*. Available at: https://assets.publishing.service.gov.uk/media/6613e7f7c4c84d4b31346a68/FCDO-Digital-Development-Strategy-2024-2030.pdf (Accessed: 30 September 2024).

UNESCWA. (2024). *Public Key Infrastructure in Oman*. Retrieved from https://opengov.unescwa.org/sites/default/files/inline-files/Om03-Public-Key-Infrast-En.pdf

United Nations. (1994). *Human Development Report 1994.* Oxford University Press.

Upadhyay, A., Laing, T., Kumar, V., & Dora, M. (2021). Exploring barriers and drivers to the implementation of circular economy practices in the mining industry. *Resources Policy*, 72, 102037. DOI: 10.1016/j.resourpol.2021.102037

Van Der Aalst, W. M., Bichler, M., & Heinzl, A. (2020). *Data-Driven Process Discovery and Analysis.* Springer Nature.

van Liebergen, B. (2017). FinTech/RegTech. *JOURNALN*, 45, 60.

Varelas, G., Voutsakis, E., Raftopoulou, P., Petrakis, E. G. M., & Milios, E. (2005). Semantic Similarity methods in WordNet and their application to information retrieval on the Web, *Proceedings of the 7th annual ACM international workshop on web information and data management*, Bremen, Germany. DOI: 10.1145/1097047.1097051

Varian, H. R. (2014). Big data: New tricks for econometrics. *The Journal of Economic Perspectives*, 28(2), 3–28. DOI: 10.1257/jep.28.2.3

Vasista, K. (2021). Regulatory Compliance and Supervision of Artificial Intelligence, Machine Learning and Also Possible Effects on Financial Institutions. *Machine Learning and also Possible Effects on Financial Institutions (June 13, 2021). International Journal of Innovative Research in Computer and Communication Engineering| e-ISSN*, 2320-9801.

Vats, K. (2024). Navigating the Digital Landscape: Embracing Innovation, Addressing Challenges, and Prioritizing Patient-Centric Care. *Cureus*. Advance online publication. DOI: 10.7759/cureus.58352 PMID: 38756283

Venkatesh V, Thong JYL, Chan FKY, Hu PJ-H, Brown SA (2011) Extending the two-stage information systems continuance model: incorporating UTAUT predictors and the role of context. Inform Syst J 21(6):527-555. https://doi.org/DOI: 10.1111/j.1365-2575.2011.00373.x

Venkatesh, V. G., Kang, K., Wang, B., Zhong, R. Y., & Zhang, A. (2020). System architecture for blockchain based transparency of supply chain social sustainability. *Robotics and Computer-integrated Manufacturing*, 63, 101896. DOI: 10.1016/j.rcim.2019.101896

Venkatesh, V., Morris, M. G., Davis, G. B., & Davis, F. D. (2003). User acceptance of information technology: Toward a unified view. *Management Information Systems Quarterly*, 27(3), 425–478. DOI: 10.2307/30036540

Verhoef, P. C., Broekhuizen, T., Bart, Y., Bhattacharya, A., Dong, J. Q., Fabian, N., & Haenlein, M. (2021). Digital transformation: A multidisciplinary reflection and research agenda. *Journal of Business Research*, 122, 889–901. DOI: 10.1016/j.jbusres.2019.09.022

Verina, N., & Titko, J. (2019, May). Digital transformation: conceptual framework. In Proc. of the Int. Scientific Conference "Contemporary Issues in Business, Management and Economics Engineering (pp. 9-10). DOI: 10.3846/cibmee.2019.073

Verizon (2023) *Data Breach Investigations Report*. Available at: https://www.verizon.com/business/resources/reports/dbir/ (Accessed: 24 September 2024).

Vial, G. (2019). Understanding digital transformation: A review and a research agenda. *The Journal of Strategic Information Systems*, 28(2), 118–144. DOI: 10.1016/j.jsis.2019.01.003

Vidu, C. M., Pinzaru, F., & Mitan, A. (2022). What managers of SMEs in the CEE region should know about challenges of artificial intelligence's adoption?–an introductive discussion. *Nowoczesne Systemy Zarządzania*, 17(1), 63–76. DOI: 10.37055/nsz/147989

Vlachopoulos, D. (2011). COVID-19: Threat or opportunity for online education? *Higher Learning Research Communications*, 10(1), 2. DOI: 10.18870/hlrc.v10i1.1179

Wahab, M. (2004). Globalisation and ODR: Dynamics of change in e-commerce dispute settlement. *International Journal of Law and Information Technology*, 12(1), 123–152. DOI: 10.1093/ijlit/12.1.123

Wamba-Taguimdje, S. L., Wamba, S. F., Kamdjoug, J. R. K., & Wanko, C. E. T. (2020). Influence of artificial intelligence (AI) on firm performance: The business value of AI-based transformation projects. *Business Process Management Journal*, 26(7), 1893–1924. DOI: 10.1108/BPMJ-10-2019-0411

Wang, A. (2019). The role of RegTech in augmenting regulatory compliance: Regulating technology, accountability and liability. *UNSW Law Journal, 19*(10).

Wang, P. (2022). The Impact of Enterprise Digital Transformation on the Foreign Investment Strategy of Enterprises. International Conference on Economic Management and Cultural Industry, 816-827. Atlantis Press.

Wang, C. S., Jeng, Y. L., & Huang, Y. M. (2017). What influences teachers to continue using cloud services? The role of facilitating conditions and social influence. *The Electronic Library*, 35(3), 520–533. DOI: 10.1108/EL-02-2016-0046

Wang, G., Lamadrid, R. L., & Huang, Y. (2024). Digital Transformation and Enterprise Outward Foreign Direct Investment. *Finance Research Letters*, 65, 65. DOI: 10.1016/j.frl.2024.105593

Wang, S., Li, D., Zhang, Y., & Chen, J. (2019). Smart contract-based product traceability system in the supply chain scenario. *IEEE Access : Practical Innovations, Open Solutions*, 7, 115122–115133. DOI: 10.1109/ACCESS.2019.2935873

Wang, T., Lin, C.-L., & Su, Y.-S. (2021). Continuance intention of university students and online learning during the COVID-19 pandemic: A modified expectation confirmation model perspective. *Sustainability (Basel)*, 13(8), 4586. DOI: 10.3390/su13084586

Wedel, M., & Kannan, P. K. (2016). Marketing analytics for data-rich environments. *Journal of Marketing*, 80(6), 97–121. DOI: 10.1509/jm.15.0413

Weerakkody, V., Kapoor, K., Balta, M. E., Irani, Z., & Dwivedi, Y. K. (2021). Factors influencing user acceptance of public sector big data: An empirical exploration. *International Journal of Information Management*, 58, 102277.

Weigl, L., Barbereau, T., & Fridgen, G. (2023). The construction of self-sovereign identity: Extending the interpretive flexibility of technology towards institutions. *Government Information Quarterly*, 40(4), 101873. DOI: 10.1016/j.giq.2023.101873

Wei, S., Xu, D., & Liu, H. (2022). The effects of information technology capability and knowledge base on digital innovation: The moderating role of institutional environments. *European Journal of Innovation Management*, 25(3), 720–740. DOI: 10.1108/EJIM-08-2020-0324

Westerman, G., & Bonnet, D. Mc & Mcaffee, A., 2014, Leading digital: Turning technology into business transformation, 1st edn., Harvard Business Review, Boston, MA.

Westerman, G., Bonnet, D., & McAfee, A. (2014). *Leading digital: Turning technology into business transformation*. Harvard Business Review Press.

Wilson, H. J., Daugherty, P., & Bianzino, N. (2017). The jobs that artificial intelligence will create. *MIT Sloan Management Review*, 58(4), 14.

Wilson, P., & Thomas, R. (2021). Balancing innovation and continuity in NHS digital transformation. *Health Services Management Research*, 34(3), 135–147.

Winarno, D. A., Muslim, E., Rafi, M., & Rosetta, A. (2020). Quality Function Deployment Approach to Optimize E-Learning Adoption among Lecturers in Universitas Indonesia. 2020 the 4th international conference on E-learning, New York: Association for Computing Machinery.

Wohlin, C. (2014). Guidelines for snowballing in systematic literature studies and a replication in software engineering. In *Proceedings of the 18th international conference on evaluation and assessment in software engineering* (pp. 1-10). DOI: 10.1145/2601248.2601268

Women in CyberSecurity (WiCyS). (2023) Available at: https://www.wicys.org/ (Accessed: 26 September 2024).

Wood, G. (2014). Ethereum: A secure decentralised generalised transaction ledger. *Ethereum Project Yellow Paper*, 151, 1–32.

World Bank Blogs. (2024. *Crystallizing a Digital Strategy: The Pearl of Arabia.* Retrieved from https://blogs.worldbank.org/en/digital-development/crystallizing -digital-strategy-pearl-arabia

World Bank Group. (2018). *Malaysia's Digital Economy: A New Driver of Development*. World Bank.

World Bank. (2020) *Cybersecurity Capacity Review: Estonia*. Available at: https:// www.worldbank.org/ (Accessed: 10 September 2024).

World Bank. (2024). *Digital Development Overview*. Retrieved from https://www .worldbank.org/en/topic/digitaldevelopment/overview

World Health Organization. (2021) *Cybersecurity and COVID-19: The impact on healthcare*. Available at: https://www.who.int/publications/cybersecurity-covid-19 -impact-on-healthcare (Accessed: 30 September 2024).

World Intellectual Property Organization (WIPO). (2023). *Oman: Intellectual Property Statistics*. Retrieved from https://www.wipo.int/edocs/pubdocs/en/wipo -pub-2000-2023/om.pdf

Wright, A., & De Filippi, P. (2015). Decentralized blockchain technology and the rise of lex cryptographia. *Available atSSRN* 2580664. DOI: 10.2139/ssrn.2580664

Wu, M., Lu, T. J., Ling, F. Y., Sun, J., & Du, H. Y. (2010). Research on the architecture of internet of things, In Proceedings of the 3rd International Conference on Advanced Computer Theory and Engineering (ICACTE-10), 5, 484-487, IEEE, Chengdu, China, August 2010.

Wu, B., & Zhang, C. (2014). Empirical study on continuance intentions towards E-Learning 2.0 systems. *Behaviour & Information Technology*, 33(10), 1027–1038. DOI: 10.1080/0144929X.2014.934291

Xie, H., Zheng, J., He, T., Wei, S., & Hu, C. (2023). TEBDS: A Trusted Execution Environment-and-Blockchain-Supported IoT Data Sharing System. *Future Generation Computer Systems*, 140, 321–330. DOI: 10.1016/j.future.2022.10.016

Xiong, J., Qin, G., Liu, X., & Sun, X. (2019). Deep learning in personalized recommendation: A survey. *Proceedings of the IEEE*, 107, 15–37.

Xledger (2022) *Why is the UK lagging behind when it comes to digital transformation?* Available at: https://xledger.com (Accessed: 26 September 2024).

Xu, G., Li, G., Sun, P., & Peng, D. (2023). Inefficient investment and digital transformation: What is the role of financing constraints? *Finance Research Letters*, 51, 51. DOI: 10.1016/j.frl.2022.103429

Xu, Y., Ren, J., Zhang, Y., Zhang, C., Shen, B., & Zhang, Y. (2019). Blockchain empowered arbitrable data auditing scheme for network storage as a service. *IEEE Transactions on Services Computing*, 13(2), 289–300. DOI: 10.1109/TSC.2019.2953033

Xu, Z., Wang, Y., Tang, J., Wang, J., & Gursoy, M. C. (2017). A deep reinforcement learning based framework for power-efficient resource allocation in cloud RANs. In *2017 IEEE International Conference on Communications (ICC)* (pp. 1-6). IEEE. DOI: 10.1109/ICC.2017.7997286

Yager, R. R. (2017). Generalized orthopair fuzzy sets. *IEEE Transactions on Fuzzy Systems*, 25(5), 1222–1230. DOI: 10.1109/TFUZZ.2016.2604005

Yakubu, M. N., Dasuki, S. I., Abubakar, A. M., & Kah, M. M. (2020). Determinants of learning management systems adoption in Nigeria: A hybrid SEM and artifcial neural network approach. *Education and Information Technologies*, 25(5), 3515–3539. DOI: 10.1007/s10639-020-10110-w

Yan, L., Whitelock-Wainwright, A., Guan, Q., Wen, G., Gašević, D., & Chen, G. (2021). Students' experience of online learning during the COVID-19 pandemic: A province-wide survey study. *British Journal of Educational Technology*, 52(5), 2038–2057. DOI: 10.1111/bjet.13102 PMID: 34219755

Yaqoob, F., & Thomas, J. (2022). Data governance in the era of big data: Challenges and solutions. *Journal of Change Management*. Advance online publication. DOI: 10.5281/zenodo.8415833

Yaşar, E., Tür, E., Yayla, E., & Alakuş, N. A. (2024). The Role and Future of Metaverse in Travel Agencies. In Kumar, J., Arora, M., & Erkol Bayram, G. (Eds.), (pp. 210–234). Advances in Social Networking and Online Communities. IGI Global., DOI: 10.4018/979-8-3693-5868-9.ch012

Yazici, N., & Aksoy, N. C. (2022). The rise of digital transformation within businesses in the pandemic. In Ismail, M. A. W., Pettinger, R., Gupta, B. B., & Roja, A. (Eds.), *Handbook of Research on Digital Transformation Management and Tools*. IGI Global. [DOI: 10.4018/978-1-7998-9764-4.ch002] DOI: 10.4018/978-1-7998-9764-4.ch002

Yildizbasi, A. (2021). Blockchain and renewable energy: Integration challenges in circular economy era. *Renewable Energy*, 176, 183–197. DOI: 10.1016/j.renene.2021.05.053

Yin, R. K. (2018). *Case study research and applications: Design and methods* (6th ed.). SAGE Publications.

Yip, F. (2012). *Semantically enabled applications-a case study in regulatory compliance* (Doctoral dissertation, UNSW Sydney).

Yli-Huumo, J., Ko, D., Choi, S., Park, S., & Smolander, K. (2016). Where is current research on blockchain technology?—A systematic review. *PLoS One*, 11(10), e0163477. DOI: 10.1371/journal.pone.0163477 PMID: 27695049

Yoo, I., & Yi, C. G. (2022). Economic innovation caused by digital transformation and impact on social systems. *Sustainability (Basel)*, 14(5), 2600. DOI: 10.3390/su14052600

Yoo, S. (2017). Blockchain based financial case analysis and its implications. *Asia Pacific Journal of Innovation and Entrepreneurship*, 11(3), 312–321. DOI: 10.1108/APJIE-12-2017-036

Yopi, F. (2024). TPACK AND TEACHERS' DIGITAL COMPETENCE IN THE ERA OF INDUSTRY 4.0. [IJMI]. *International Journal Multidisciplinary*, 1(1), 45–52. DOI: 10.61796/ijmi.v1i1.32

Yousefi, S., & Tosarkani, B. M. (2023). Exploring the role of blockchain technology in improving sustainable supply chain performance: A system-analysis-based approach. *IEEE Transactions on Engineering Management*. Advance online publication. DOI: 10.1109/TEM.2022.3231217

Yufriadi, F., Syahriani, F., & Afifi, A. A. (2024). Trade Transformation In The Digital Era: Agency Role, Opportunities And Challenges. *AL-IMAM: Journal on Islamic Studies. Civilization and Learning Societies*, 5(1), 13–23. DOI: 10.58764/j.im.2024.5.55

Zaika, S., & Avriata, A. (2024). Analysis of the impact of the COVID-19 pandemic on the development of the international tourism market. *International Science Journal of Management. Economics & Finance*, 3(2), 56–68. DOI: 10.46299/j.isjmef.20240302.06

Zanfei, A., Coveri, A., & Pianta, M. (2019). FDI patterns and global value chains in the digital economy. Working Papers 1903, University of Urbino Carlo Bo. Available at: http://www.econ.uniurb.it/RePEc/urb/wpaper/WP_19_03.pdf

Zhang, L., Xie, Y., Zheng, Y., Xue, W., Zheng, X., & Xu, X. (2020). The challenges and countermeasures of blockchain in finance and economics. *Systems Research and Behavioral Science*, 37(4), 691–698. DOI: 10.1002/sres.2710

Zhang, X., Chan, F. T., Yan, C., & Bose, I. (2022). Towards risk-aware artificial intelligence and machine learning systems: An overview. *Decision Support Systems*, 159, 113800. DOI: 10.1016/j.dss.2022.113800

Zhang, Z. (2023). Digital Operational Strategies in The Post-Pandemic Era for Travel Companies: A Case Study of Ctrip. *Highlights in Business. Economics and Management*, 23, 521–525. DOI: 10.54097/h0w3ar97

Zhao, R., Wang, J., & Xue, F. (2023). *A blockchain-based token incentive mechanism for ESG in the construction industry*. 2023 European Conference on Computing in Construction 40th International CIB W78 Conference Heraklion, Crete, Greece. July 10–12, 2023. DOI: 10.35490/EC3.2023.235

Zhao, G., Liu, S., Lopez, C., Lu, H., Elgueta, S., Chen, H., & Boshkoska, B. M. (2019). Blockchain technology in Agri-food value chain management: A synthesis of applications, challenges and future research directions. *Computers in Industry*, 109, 83–99. DOI: 10.1016/j.compind.2019.04.002

Zhao, J. L., Fan, S., & Yan, J. (2016). Overview of business innovations and research opportunities in blockchain and introduction to the special issue. *Financial Innovation*, 2(1), 28. DOI: 10.1186/s40854-016-0049-2

Zhao, L., Von Glinow, M. A., & Shapiro, D. L. (2016). Explaining the role of cultural differences in online entrepreneurship: A study of China and the US. *Journal of International Business Studies*, 47(2), 214–239.

Zhao, X., & Qi, Y. (2020). Why do firms obey?: The state of regulatory compliance research in China. *Journal of Chinese Political Science*, 25(2), 339–352. DOI: 10.1007/s11366-020-09657-9

Zheng, Z., Xie, S., Dai, H. N., Chen, X., & Wang, H. (2018). Blockchain challenges and opportunities: A survey. *International Journal of Web and Grid Services*, 14(4), 352–375. DOI: 10.1504/IJWGS.2018.095647

Zhou, J. (2017). Exploring the factors affecting learners' continuance intention of MOOCs for online collaborative learning: An extended ECM perspective. *Australasian Journal of Educational Technology*, 33(5). Advance online publication. DOI: 10.14742/ajet.2914

Zhu, H., Zhao, J., & Li, H. (2022). Q-ROF-SIR methods and their applications to multiple attribute decision making. *International Journal of Machine Learning and Cybernetics*, 1–13. DOI: 10.1007/s13042-021-01330-8

Zhu, S., Song, M., Lim, M. K., Wang, J., & Zhao, J. (2020). The development of energy blockchain and its implications for China's energy sector. *Resources Policy*, 66, 101595. DOI: 10.1016/j.resourpol.2020.101595

Zhu, W., Zhou, G., Yen, I. L., & Bastani, F. (2015). A PT-SOA Model for CPS/IoT Services, In *Proceedings of the 2015 IEEE International Conference on Web Services*, New York, NY, USA, 27 June – 2 July 2015. DOI: 10.1109/ICWS.2015.91

Zhu, X., Zheng, Y., Zhang, Z., Li, J., & Yu, P. S. (2020). Deep learning for online advertising: A comprehensive review. *SIGKDD Explorations*, 22, 5–20.

Zohar, A. (2015). Bitcoin: Under the hood. *Communications of the ACM*, 58(9), 104–113. DOI: 10.1145/2701411

Zou, J., Han, Y., & So, S. S. (2009). Overview of artificial neural networks. *Artificial neural networks: methods and applications*, 14-22.

Zuzaku, A., & Abazi, B. (2022). Digital transformation in the western balkans as an opportunity for managing innovation in small and medium businesses-Challenges and opportunities. *IFAC-PapersOnLine*, 55(39), 60–65. DOI: 10.1016/j.ifacol.2022.12.011

About the Contributors

Mohammed Albakri is a senior fellow of higher education with over a decade of academic experience, serving institutions such as the University of Manchester, University of Bolton and currently the University of Salford. With a Ph.D. in information systems and a specialisation in digital transformation, he has left a significant mark on the academic landscape. Dr. Albakri's research interests span a wide range of multidisciplinary topics, and his extensive publication record reflects his contributions to the academic community. His dedication to leadership roles, and commitment to fostering innovation make him a respected figure in the world of academia.

***

Aryan is a dedicated scholar at Maharishi Markandeshwar Deemed to be University, building on his experience as a former Assistant Professor at APIIT SD Panipat. Alongside his academic pursuits, he's also a Sub-broker with Upstox, blending his passion for finance with his scholarly endeavors. Aryan's contributions extend beyond the classroom; he's published five research papers in both national and international journals, showcasing his commitment to academic excellence and intellectual curiosity.

Fadi Abdelfattah is an associate professor and department head at the Modern College of Business and Science in Muscat, Sultanate of Oman. Dr. Abdelfattah has been published in several indexed international journals. In addition, he has been appointed to the editorial boards and advisory boards of international journals. Dr. Abdelfattah also acquired multiple research grants, supervised many postgraduate students, and served as both an external and an internal examiner for postgraduate students. His research interests in Consumers Behavior; Leadership; Entrepreneurship and Innovation Technology Adoption. Throughout his teaching career, he has taught a variety of undergraduate and graduate courses. He has led numerous committees and initiatives in his current and past roles.

Cynthia Akiotu is a Data Scientist with an MSc in Financial Technology from the University of Salford and a BSc in Computer Science. She specialises in business analysis, data science, and digital transformation. Cynthia is passionate about simplifying complex concepts and sharing knowledge.

Muktar Bello is an expert in the field of Digital Forensics, Cybersecurity, Counter-Terrorism, Artificial Intelligence (AI) and Digital Transformation with a wealth of experience spanning over 20 years of experience in Law Enforcement, Academia, and Consultancy. Currently serving as a Researcher and Lecturer at the University of Salford, Manchester. He is a Cyber First Ambassador and Consultant for the National Cyber Security Centre UK, a part of the GCHQ. Dr. Bello holds a PhD in Cybersecurity, MSc in Forensics Computing and BSc in IT. He is a certified ISO/IEC 27001 Senior Lead Implementer, ISO 9001 Lead Auditor, and ISO/IEC 17025 Lead Assessor. He has conducted investigation as analyst and expert witness. Dr. Bello is also an Expert Forensics Consultant for the UNODC in the implementation of the EU-Nigeria-UNODC-CTED Partnership Project in assisting Nigeria to strengthen rule of law-based criminal justice responses to terrorism and violent extremism. He oversees a joint Military-Police-DSS workshop on the collection and preservation of electronic evidence in the field of war (Northeast Nigeria). He played a pivotal role in various initiatives such as implementing the UNODC IT component of the EU-funded project NGAS08, establishing the Nigerian National Computer Emergency Response Team (NG-CERT) centre, and setting up standards for digital and computer forensics in Nigeria in collaboration with organizations like NITDA.

Damla Cevik Aka is an Assistant Professor at the Faculty of Economics and Administrative Sciences at Kirklareli University. In recent years, I have been actively engaged in instructing undergraduate and postgraduate students, as well as overseeing and conducting research, and publishing academic papers. Author of 11 journal articles on operation management and sustainable supply chain management. To date, have contributed to 7 conferences by presenting research results and findings.

Pratichi Dash, MFC, M.Com is currently working as a Research Scholar in the School of Finance, Centurion University of Technology and Management, Bhubaneswar Campus, Odisha and pursuing her doctorate under Prof. Dr. Susanta Kumar Mishra. After completing her B.Com, she undertook MFC (Master of Finance and Control) under Utkal University and then IGNOU for PG Diploma in

International Business Operations and M.Com. She shifted her career as a Financial Planning Advisor to teaching in 2011. She has more than 13 years of teaching and research experience. Her area of teaching and research is financial management, behavioral finance, accounting and portfolio management, financial derivative, financial market, corporate restructuring, corporate law and tax. She has authored a book and published papers in peer reviewed journals. She is also a life member of Indian Commerce Association.

Ivana Domazet is a Principal Research Fellow at the Institute of Economic Sciences and Professor at the Faculty for Banking, Insurance and Finance, Union University. She teaches courses on Marketing Management, Market Research and Competitiveness Enhancement (postgraduate studies). Her scientific interest refers to: Improving Competitiveness, National Branding, Marketing Research and Strategy, CRM and Strategic Management. She published a numerous papers related to foregoing topics. She is President of Scientific Council at the Institute of Economic Sciences, Vice-president of Board member of the Institute of Economics Sciences, Board member of the Institute of Social Science, member of Serbian Scientific Association of Economists and Serbian Marketing Association.

Gurwinder Dua is an Assistant Professor at Post Graduate Government College - 11, Chandigarh.

Shaierah Gulabdin is a lecturer at Universiti Malaysia Sabah, where she specializes in entrepreneurship. With a keen interest in teaching and research, her focus areas include human resource management, entrepreneurship & innovation, and technology adoption & evolution .

Mohd Arif Hussain, is a research scholar, pursuing PhD from GITAM School of Business, GITAM University, Hyderabad, Telangana in subject area Marketing Management, focusing on AI role in Banking services and its effect on Customer Loyalty. Author is also an academician working as an Assistant Professor in MBA Department at Shadan College of Engineering and Technology, Hyderabad. In relation to AI technology and its impact in banking services author has published number of research papers in Scopus indexed good Quartile journals. Also he has presented papers in International and National Conferences on AI technology effects in banking industry that can assist banks in framing marketing strategies to enhance its services.

Vishal Jain is presently working as an Associate Professor at Department of Computer Science and Engineering, School of Engineering and Technology, Sharda University, Greater Noida, U. P. India. Before that, he has worked for several years as an Associate Professor at Bharati Vidyapeeth's Institute of Computer Applications and Management (BVICAM), New Delhi. He has more than 14 years of experience in the academics. He obtained Ph.D (CSE), M.Tech (CSE), MBA (HR), MCA, MCP and CCNA. He has authored more than 90 research papers in reputed conferences and journals, including Web of Science and Scopus. He has authored and edited more than 30 books with various reputed publishers, including Elsevier, Springer, Apple Academic Press, CRC, Taylor and Francis Group, Scrivener, Wiley, Emerald, NOVA Science and IGI-Global. His research areas include information retrieval, semantic web, ontology engineering, data mining, ad hoc networks, and sensor networks. He received a Young Active Member Award for the year 2012–13 from the Computer Society of India, Best Faculty Award for the year 2017 and Best Researcher Award for the year 2019 from BVICAM, New Delhi.

Suaad Jassem is an Assistant Professor of Accounting and Auditing at the College of Banking and Financial Studies in Muscat, Oman. She received her Ph.D. in Accountancy from the University of Malaya. She has over 17 years of teaching experience across multiple universities in Iraq, Malaysia, and Oman. Dr. Jassem has published extensively in high-impact journals on topics such as managerial accounting, sustainability practices, internal auditing, and enterprise risk management, making significant contributions to both academic understanding and practical applications in accounting and auditing. Her current research interests centre on the integration of artificial intelligence within accounting practices, particularly how AI can improve accuracy and efficiency in the field.

Sehrish Javaid, a young author with a foundation in Electronics and Communication Engineering and an MBA in HR and Marketing. With a PhD in Strategic Marketing from the Central University of Kashmir, Sehrish's writing blends her technical skills and strategic insights, helping readers understand the modern world of marketing with confidence. Through her work, she aims to inspire and inform, making complex ideas accessible and clear.

Darko Marjanović is Senior Research Associate at the Institute of Economic Sciences, Belgrade. He served as a financial director (CFO) in a large trading company BB Trade ad from 2015 to 2018. His current areas of professional interest are digitalization, competitiveness, FDI and public finance. He has published, as author or co-author, more than 70 scientific papers. He has participated in a few international projects, as well as several research and scientific projects, financed by the Ministry of Education, Science, and Technological Development of the Republic of Serbia and Provincial Secretariat for Science and Technological Development of the Autonomous Province of Vojvodina. He is a member of the Scientific Board at the Institute of Economic Sciences and associate member of the Scientific Society of Economists of Serbia. He was a Vice President of the Scientific Board at the Institute of Economic Sciences, head of the Center for Strategic Cooperation, coordinator of the Macroeconomics Department and editor-in-chief of the international publication SEE-6 Economic Outlook.

David Mark is a versatile and accomplished multidisciplinary researcher, teacher, and consultant with over a decade of experience. His expertise spans various fields, from digital transformation to infrastructure implementation. As an educator, he excels at making complex concepts accessible, inspiring a love for learning. David's lead consulting and implementer work provides valuable insights and innovative solutions to organisations seeking strategic guidance on various digital transformation solutions. His dedication to knowledge and innovation ensures a lasting and transformative impact in his areas of expertise.

Archan Mitra is an Assistant Professor at School of Media Studies (SOMS) at Presidency University, Bangalore. He is the author of two book "Cases for Classroom Media and Entertainment Business" and "Multiverse and Media", he also has other several edited books to his credit. He has done his doctorate from Visva-Bharati Santiniketan, West Bengal in the field of "environmental informatics and communication for sustainability". In addition to that he is a certified Science Communicator and Journalism from Indian Science Communication Society (ISCOS), certified Corporate Trainer with Amity Institute of Training and Development, Certified Social Media Network Analyst. He has a strong interest in environmental communication. He was awarded certificate of merit by PRSI, Kolkata Chapter and Medal of Honor by Journalistic Club of Kolkata. He was working as a research assistant with the World Bank's "Environmental Capacity Building in Southeast Asia" project at IIM Kashipur. He was instrumental in launching the World Bank's Green MBA MOOC, he has also assisted in the research project on Uttarakhand disaster mitigation by ICSSR, the leading research on Uttarakhand disaster.

Debbra Toria Nipo is currently a Senior Lecturer at Faculty of Business, Economics and Accountancy, Universiti Malaysia Sabah.

Oluwaseun Okegbola is a seasoned AML Compliance Specialist passionate about driving regulatory compliance using technology. He has a strong record in technical and non-technical roles, including compliance reviews and regulatory implementation. Oluwaseun has 12 years of experience working in Governance, Risk, Control and Compliance across three Financial Institutions in Nigeria. He currently works with a RegTech company in the UK (CleverChain Ltd) as a Senior AML Compliance Specialist.

Kamalendu Pal is with the Department of Computer Science, School of Mathematics, Computer Science and Engineering, City University London. Kamalendu received his BSc (Hons) degree in Physics from Calcutta University, India, Postgraduate Diploma in Computer Science from Pune, India; MSc degree in Software Systems Technology from Sheffield University, Postgraduate Diploma in Artificial Intelligence from Kingston University, MPhil degree in Computer Science from University College London, and MBA degree from University of Hull, United Kingdom. He has published dozens of research papers in international journals and conferences. His research interests include knowledge-based systems, decision support systems, computer integrated design, software engineering, and service oriented computing. He is a member of the British Computer Society, the Institution of Engineering and Technology, and the IEEE Computer Society.

Saizal Pinjaman is currently a Senior Lecturer at Faculty of Business, Economics and Accountancy, Universiti Malaysia Sabah. He is also a Research Fellow at the Centre for Economic Development and Policy, Universiti Malaysia Sabah.

Karima Sayari is an Associate Professor in the Department of Managerial and Financial Sciences at Al Zahra College for Women. She holds a bachelor's degree in international trade, a master's degree in economics and international finance, and a PhD in Finance and Economic Sciences. Dr. Sayari has over 10 years of teaching experience and has published extensively in reputable international journals indexed in Scopus and Web of Science. Her research focuses on economics, finance, banking, and digital finance. She is an active peer reviewer in various academic journals.

Wong Sing Yun is currently a Senior Lecturer at Faculty of Business, Economics and Accountancy, Universiti Malaysia Sabah. She is also a Research Fellow at the Centre for Economic Development and Policy, Universiti Malaysia Sabah.

Shreyanshu Singh is an Assistant Professor of Management at BBD University, Lucknow, India. He has completed his doctorate in Applied Economics from the University of Lucknow, where he held a position as both JRF & SRF. His area of specialization is Marketing, Business Statistics and Operations Research. He has qualified UGC-NET seven times and UGC-JRF thrice in Management and Commerce. He holds a Master's degree in Electronics, Business Administration and Commerce. He also holds a Post Graduate Diploma in International Business Operations. He has numerous publications in ABDC, Scopus, UGC, and peer-reviewed refereed journals. As the editor, He contributed to the academic community with the publications of two books focusing on digital transformation. He has reviewed many papers for Web of Science-indexed and peer-reviewed refereed journals. He has more than nine years of research and teaching experience in different institutes and universities. He also had more than two years of Industry Experience in the FMCG sector. He has presented 31 research papers at various national and international conferences and seminars. He is associated with Indira Gandhi National Open University (IGNOU) as an Academic Counselor. He is an Editorial Board Member at the international peer-reviewed e-journal Multidisciplinary Cosmopolitan Journal of Research (MUCOJOR) and Edwin Group of Journals. He is a registered Ph.D. Co-Guide at JJT University, Rajasthan. He is an active life member of the Indian Commerce Association (ICA) and Indian Accounting Association (IAA).

Karnika Srivastava is an Assistant Professor at Techno group of Institutions. Having a experience of 7 years. Done M.com in applied economics from University of Lucknow and PhD from Shri Ramswaroop Memorial University.

Zeeshan Syed is an experienced academic with over six years of experience as a lecturer, course leader, and program leader. He's the current MSc International Technology programme leader and is also an International Exchange Coordinator. He has led the development of new courses, modules, and degree programs. He is currently the program leader of the MSc. Fintech. As a lecturer and supervisor, he supervises master's and PhD students in Finance, Fintech, and AI. He teaches and researches in Corporate Finance, Python for Finance, Blockchain and Crypto Currency Economics, Fin-Tech, and Introductory Econometrics.

Mohammad Badruddoza Talukder is an Associate Professor, College of Tourism and Hospitality Management, IUBAT - International University of Business Agriculture and Technology, Dhaka-1230, Bangladesh. He holds PhD in Hotel Management from Lovely Professional University, India. He has been teaching various courses in the Department of Tourism and Hospitality at various universities in Bangladesh since 2008. His research areas include tourism management, hotel management, hospitality management, food & beverage management, and accommodation management, where he has published research papers in well-known journals in Bangladesh and abroad. Mr. Talukder is one of the executive members of the Tourism Educators Association of Bangladesh. He has led training and consulting for a wide range of hospitality organizations in Bangladesh. He just became an honorary facilitator at the Bangladesh Tourism Board's Bangabandhu international tourism and hospitality training institution.

Rinki Verma is a proficient academician in the field of management and has extensive research experience. She carries a wide experience of 15 years in academics and corporate. She shouldered responsibilities from IQAC and NAAC in her current and prior serving institutions. She served as the Project Director for an ICSSR-funded project. Currently, she is an Associate Professor at Babu Banarasi Das University, Lucknow. She holds a doctorate from an institute of national importance, MNNIT, Allahabad. She has qualified UGC NET in Management. She has many national and international research papers in her credit, which are published in ABDC, Scopus, UGC CARE, and reputed peer-reviewed journals. She made significant contributions to the academic field as the editor, publishing two books centered on the theme of digital transformation. She is passionate, purposeful, high-spirited and has a never-ending approach to learning. She has supervised many students for their PhD and Masters dissertations.

Index

www.ingramcontent.com/pod-product-compliance
Ingram Content Group UK Ltd.
Pitfield, Milton Keynes, MK11 3LW, UK
UKHW012330151224
452404UK00007B/34